Polynomial Sequences and Their Applications

Polynomial Sequences and Their Applications

Editors

Francesco Aldo Costabile
Maria I. Gualtieri
Anna Napoli

 Basel • Beijing • Wuhan • Barcelona • Belgrade • Novi Sad • Cluj • Manchester

Editors
Francesco Aldo Costabile
University of Calabria
Rende
Italy

Maria I. Gualtieri
University of Calabria
Rende
Italy

Anna Napoli
University of Calabria
Rende
Italy

Editorial Office
MDPI
St. Alban-Anlage 66
4052 Basel, Switzerland

This is a reprint of articles from the Special Issue published online in the open access journal *Mathematics* (ISSN 2227-7390) (available at: https://www.mdpi.com/journal/mathematics/special_issues/polynomial_sequences_applications).

For citation purposes, cite each article independently as indicated on the article page online and as indicated below:

Lastname, A.A.; Lastname, B.B. Article Title. *Journal Name* **Year**, *Volume Number*, Page Range.

ISBN 978-3-7258-0191-6 (Hbk)
ISBN 978-3-7258-0192-3 (PDF)
doi.org/10.3390/books978-3-7258-0192-3

© 2024 by the authors. Articles in this book are Open Access and distributed under the Creative Commons Attribution (CC BY) license. The book as a whole is distributed by MDPI under the terms and conditions of the Creative Commons Attribution (CC BY) license.

Contents

About the Editors vii

Francesco Aldo Costabile, Maria Italia Gualtieri and Anna Napoli
Polynomial Sequences and Their Applications
Reprinted from: *Mathematics* **2022**, *10*, 4804, doi:10.3390/math10244804 1

Ghulam Muhiuddin, Waseem Ahmad Khan and Ugur Duran
Two-Variable Type 2 Poly-Fubini Polynomials
Reprinted from: *Mathematics* **2021**, *9*, 281, doi:10.3390/math9030281 4

Dmitry Kruchinin, Vladimir Kruchinin and Yuriy Shablya
Method for Obtaining Coefficients of Powers of Bivariate Generating Functions
Reprinted from: *Mathematics* **2021**, *9*, 428, doi:10.3390/math9040428 17

Abey S. Kelil, Alta S. Jooste and Appanah R. Appadu
On Certain Properties and Applications of the Perturbed Meixner–Pollaczek Weight
Reprinted from: *Mathematics* **2021**, *9*, 955, doi:10.3390/math9090955 34

Francesco A. Costabile, Maria I. Gualtieri and Anna Napoli
General Bivariate Appell Polynomials via Matrix Calculus and Related Interpolation Hints
Reprinted from: *Mathematics* **2021**, *9*, 964, doi:10.3390/math9090964 62

Claude Brezinski, F. Alexander Norman and Michela Redivo-Zaglia
The Legacy of Peter Wynn
Reprinted from: *Mathematics* **2021**, *9*, 1240, doi:10.3390/math9111240 91

Waleed Mohamed Abd-Elhameed and Badah Mohamed Badah
New Approaches to the General Linearization Problem of Jacobi Polynomials Based on Moments and Connection Formulas
Reprinted from: *Mathematics* **2021**, *9*, 1573, doi:10.3390/math9131573 136

Sergey Goncharov and Andrey Nechesov
Polynomial Analogue of Gandy's Fixed Point Theorem
Reprinted from: *Mathematics* **2021**, *9*, 2102, doi:10.3390/math9172102 164

Masato Shinjo, Tan Wang, Masashi Iwasaki and Yoshimasa Nakamura
Roots of Characteristic Polynomial Sequences in Iterative Block Cyclic Reductions
Reprinted from: *Mathematics* **2021**, *9*, 3213, doi:10.3390/math9243213 175

Cuixia Niu, Huiqing Liao, Heping Ma and Hua Wu
Approximation Properties of Chebyshev Polynomials in the Legendre Norm
Reprinted from: *Mathematics* **2021**, *9*, 3271, doi:10.3390/math9243271 192

Sergey Goncharov and Andrey Nechesov
Solution of the Problem $P = L$
Reprinted from: *Mathematics* **2022**, *10*, 113, doi:10.3390/math10010113 202

Angelamaria Cardone, Dajana Conte, Raffaele D'ambrosio and Beatrice Paternoster
Multivalue Collocation Methods for Ordinary and Fractional Differential Equations
Reprinted from: *Mathematics* **2022**, *10*, 185, doi:10.3390/math10020185 210

Francesco Aldo Costabile, Maria Italia Gualtieri and Anna Napoli
General Odd and Even Central Factorial Polynomial Sequences
Reprinted from: *Mathematics* **2022**, *10*, 978, doi:10.3390/math10060978 227

Faruk Özger, Ekrem Aljimi and Merve Temizer Ersoy
Rate of Weighted Statistical Convergence for Generalized Blending-Type
Bernstein-Kantorovich Operators
Reprinted from: *Mathematics* **2022**, *10*, 2027, doi:10.3390/math10122027 249

Camilo Garcia-Tenorio and Alain Vande Wouwer
A Matlab Toolbox for Extended Dynamic Mode Decomposition Based on Orthogonal
Polynomials and p-q Quasi-Norm Order Reduction
Reprinted from: *Mathematics* **2022**, *10*, 3859, doi:10.3390/math10203859 270

Francesco Aldo Costabile, Maria Italia Gualtieri and Anna Napoli
Towards the Centenary of Sheffer Polynomial Sequences: Old and Recent Results
Reprinted from: *Mathematics* **2022**, *10*, 4435, doi:10.3390/math10234435 288

About the Editors

Francesco Aldo Costabile

Francesco Aldo Costabile currently retired, was a full professor at University of Calabria (Unical). He collaborates in the research activities of his former students, now Associate Professors at Unical. He has held numerous academic positions at Unical, including that of Dean of the Faculty of s.m.f.n. and Director of the Department of Mathematics. Previously he held academic positions at the Universities of Rome, Bari and Lecce. Research interests include: approximation theory, initial and boundary value problems, numerical quadrature, polynomial sequences and their applications, approximation with positive operators, asymptotic expansion and extrapolation.

Maria I. Gualtieri

Maria I. Gualtieri is an Associate Professor at the Department of Mathematics and Computer Science, University of Calabria, Italy. She graduated in Mathematics at University of Calabria in 1986. She has studied numerical solutions of ordinary differential equations with initial and boundary condition, approximation of continuous functions by positive operators and extrapolation processes, numerical solution of nonlinear equations. Her current research interests concern polynomial sequences and applications to approximation theory and numerical quadrature.

Anna Napoli

Anna Napoli is an Associate Professor at the Department of Mathematics and Computer Science, University of Calabria, Italy. She graduated in Mathematics at University of Calabria in 1992. Her research interests are mainly in the fields of polynomials and their applications in approximation theory, boundary and initial value problems, numerical quadrature.

Editorial

Polynomial Sequences and Their Applications †

Francesco Aldo Costabile, Maria Italia Gualtieri and Anna Napoli *

Department of Mathematics and Computer Science, University of Calabria, 87036 Rende, CS, Italy
* Correspondence: anna.napoli@unical.it
† This book is dedicated to Prof. Francesco Aldo Costabile on the occasion of his 75th birthday.

Citation: Costabile, F.A.; Gualtieri, M.I.; Napoli, A. Polynomial Sequences and Their Applications. *Mathematics* 2022, 10, 4804. https://doi.org/10.3390/math10244804

Received: 5 December 2022
Accepted: 7 December 2022
Published: 16 December 2022

Publisher's Note: MDPI stays neutral with regard to jurisdictional claims in published maps and institutional affiliations.

Copyright: © 2022 by the authors. Licensee MDPI, Basel, Switzerland. This article is an open access article distributed under the terms and conditions of the Creative Commons Attribution (CC BY) license (https://creativecommons.org/licenses/by/4.0/).

The purpose of this Special Issue is to present, albeit partially, the state of the art on the theory and application of polynomial sequences.

Polynomials are incredibly useful mathematical tools, as they are simply defined and can be calculated quickly on computer systems. They can be differentiated and integrated easily and can be pieced together to form spline curves.

Stemming from Weierstrass's well-known approximation theorem (1885) [1], sequences of polynomials perform an important role in several branches of science: mathematics, physics, engineering, etc. For example, polynomial sequences arise in physics and approximation theory as the solutions of certain ordinary differential equations. Among these sequences of polynomials, we highlight orthogonal polynomials. In statistics, Hermite polynomials are very important, and they are also orthogonal polynomials and Sheffer A-type zero polynomials [2]. In algebra and combinatorics, umbral polynomials are used, such as rising factorials, falling factorials and Abel, Bell, Bernoulli, Euler, Boile, ciclotomic, Dickson, Fibonacci, Lucas and Touchard polynomials. Finally, in computational and numerical mathematics, polynomial sequences are particularly important and frequently used.

This volume contains both theoretical works and practical applications in the field of polynomial sequences and their applications. In the following, a brief overview of the published papers is presented.

Contributions

In [3], Extended Dynamic Mode Decomposition (EDMD) is used for the approximation of the Koopman operator in the form of a truncated (finite dimensional) linear operator in a lifted space of nonlinear observable functions. Orthogonal polynomials are used for the expression of the observable functions, in conjunction with an order-reduction procedure called p-q quasi-norm reduction. The authors present a Matlab library to automate the computation of the EDMD. The performance of this library is illustrated with a few representative examples.

Motivated by the improvements of Bernstein polynomials in computational disciplines, Özger et al. [4] propose a new generalization of Bernstein–Kantorovich operators involving shape parameters λ, α and a positive integer as an original extension of Bernstein–Kantorovich operators. Some approximation and convergence results are presented. Finally, illustrative graphics that demonstrate the approximation behavior and consistency of the proposed operators are provided by a computer program.

In [5], odd and even polynomial sequences associated with the $\delta^2(\cdot)$ operator are determined, being $\delta(\cdot)$ the known central difference operator. Many aspects, including matrix and determinant forms, recurrence formulas, generating functions and an algorithm for effective calculation, are covered. New examples of odd and even central polynomial sequences are presented.

In [6], the authors address the problem associated with the construction of polynomial complexity computer programs. One of the new approaches to the problems is representing a class of polynomial algorithms as a certain class of special logical programs. One of the main contributions of this paper is the construction of a new logical programming language describing the class of polynomial algorithms. Particularly, the authors find p−iterative terms that simulate the work of the Turing machine. This language allows one to create fast and reliable programs and describes any algorithms of polynomial complexity. Its main limitation is that the implementation of algorithms of complexity is not higher than polynomial.

Niu et al. [7] give some important approximation results of Chebyshev polynomials in the Legendre norm. Particularly, interpolation operators at the Chebyshev–Gauss–Lobatto points are studied. The single-domain and multidomain cases for both one dimension and multi-dimensions are analyzed.

In [8], the authors focus on the coefficients of the block tridiagonal matrices in linear systems obtained from block iterative cyclic reductions. They examine the roots of characteristic polynomials by regarding each block cyclic reduction as a composition of two types of matrix transformations and then examining changes in the existence range of roots. The fact that the roots are not very scattered allows one to accurately solve linear systems in floating-point arithmetic.

A general method for proving whether a certain set is p−computable or not is proposed in [9]. The method is based on a polynomial analogue of the classical Gandy fixed-point theorem. Gandy's theorem deals with the extension of a predicate through a special operator and states that the smallest fixed point of this operator is a Σ-set. In this paper, a new type of operator is used which extends predicates so that the smallest fixed point remains a p−computable set. Polynomial algorithms for checking if a certain element belongs to a given data type or not are used.

Paper [10] deals with the general linearization problem of Jacobi polynomials. The authors provide two approaches for finding closed analytical forms of the linearization coefficients of these polynomials. An application of some of the derived linearization formulas to the solution of the non-linear Riccati differential equation based on the application of the spectral tau method is presented.

In paper [11], the authors analyze some manuscript documents of Peter Winn that came to their knowledge after his death. They concern continued fractions, rational (Padé) approximation, Thiele interpolation, orthogonal polynomials, moment problems, series, and abstract algebra. The authors think that these works are valuable additions to the literature on these topics and that they can lead to new research and results.

A matrix calculus-based approach to general bivariate Appell polynomials is proposed in [12]. This approach, which is new in the literature, generates a systematic, simple theory which is in perfect analogy with the theory in the univariate case. Known and new basic results are given, such as recurrence relations, the generating function, determinant forms and differential equations.

Paper [13] deals with monic orthogonal polynomials with respect to the perturbed Meixner–Pollaczek measure. By introducing a time variable to the Meixner–Pollaczek measure, the authors find some interesting properties such as some recursive relations, moments of finite order, concise hypergeometric formulae and orthogonality relations. Moreover, certain analytic properties of the zeros of the corresponding monic perturbed Meixner–Pollaczek polynomials are studied. Finally, some practical applications are considered.

Kruchinin et al. in [14] study methods for obtaining explicit formulas for the coefficients of generating functions. These methods are based on using the powers of generating functions. The concept of compositae is generalized to the case of generating functions in two variables. Basic operations on such compositae are defined, such as composition, addition, multiplication, reciprocation and compositional inversion. These operations allow obtaining explicit formulas for compositae and coefficients of bivariate generating functions. Some applications are presented.

In paper [15], an extension of the two-variable Fubini polynomials is introduced by means of the polyexponential function. Some new relations are derived, including the

Stirling numbers of the first and second kinds, the usual Fubini polynomials, and the higher-order Bernoulli polynomials. Two-variable unipoly-Fubini polynomials are introduced and some relationships between the two-variable unipoly-Fubini polynomials, the Stirling numbers and the Daehee polynomials are derived.

In [16], as the centenary of the publication of I.M. Sheffer's famous paper approaches [2], the authors want to honor his memory by recalling some old and recent results. In particular, the classification of polynomials by means of suitable linear differential operators and Sheffer's method for the study of A-type zero polynomials. Moreover, the theory of Rota and his collaborators, the isomorphism between the group of Sheffer polynomial sequences and the so-called Riordan matrices group are considered. The interesting problem of orthogonality in the context of Sheffer sequences is also reported, recalling the results of Sheffer, Meixner, Shohat, and the very recent ones of Galiffa et al. and Costabile et al.

Some classes of multivalue methods for the numerical solution of ordinary and fractional differential equations are considered in [17]. Particularly, the authors focus on two-step and mixed collocation methods, Nordsieck GLM collocation methods for ordinary differential equations, and on two-step spline collocation methods for fractional differential equations. The convergence and stability of the proposed methods are reported and some numerical experiments are carried out to show the efficiency of the methods.

Acknowledgments: The Guest Editors would like to thank all the authors of the papers for their quality contributions to this Special Issue and also all the reviewers for their valuable comments towards the improvement of the submitted works. Moreover, a thanks to mathematics editorial office for their technical and administrative support.

Conflicts of Interest: The authors declare no conflict of interest.

References

1. Weierstrass, K. Über die analytische Darstellbarkeit sogenannter willkürlicher Funktionen einer reellen Veränderlichen. *Sitzungsberichte der Königlich Preussischen Akademie der Wissenschaften zu Berlin* **1885**, *2*, 633–639.
2. Sheffer, I. Some properties of polynomial sets of type zero. *Duke Math. J.* **1939**, *5*, 590–622. [CrossRef]
3. Garcia-Tenorio, C.; Vande Wouwer, A. A Matlab Toolbox for Extended Dynamic Mode Decomposition Based on Orthogonal Polynomials and p-q Quasi-Norm Order Reduction. *Mathematics* **2022**, *10*, 3859. [CrossRef]
4. Özger, F.; Aljimi, E.; Temizer Ersoy, M. Rate of Weighted Statistical Convergence for Generalized Blending-Type Bernstein-Kantorovich Operators. *Mathematics* **2022**, *10*, 2027. [CrossRef]
5. Costabile, F.A.; Gualtieri, M.I.; Napoli, A. General Odd and Even Central Factorial Polynomial Sequences. *Mathematics* **2022**, *10*, 978. [CrossRef]
6. Goncharov, S.; Nechesov, A. Solution of the Problem P = L. *Mathematics* **2022**, *10*, 113. [CrossRef]
7. Niu, C.; Liao, H.; Ma, H.; Wu, H. Approximation Properties of Chebyshev Polynomials in the Legendre Norm. *Mathematics* **2021**, *9*, 3271. [CrossRef]
8. Shinjo, M.; Wang, T.; Iwasaki, M.; Nakamura, Y. Roots of Characteristic Polynomial Sequences in Iterative Block Cyclic Reductions. *Mathematics* **2021**, *9*, 3213. [CrossRef]
9. Goncharov, S.; Nechesov, A. Polynomial Analogue of Gandy's Fixed Point Theorem. *Mathematics* **2021**, *9*, 2102. [CrossRef]
10. Abd-Elhameed, W.M.; Badah, B.M. New Approaches to the General Linearization Problem of Jacobi Polynomials Based on Moments and Connection Formulas. *Mathematics* **2021**, *9*, 1573. [CrossRef]
11. Brezinski, C.; Norman, F.A.; Redivo-Zaglia, M. The Legacy of Peter Wynn. *Mathematics* **2021**, *9*, 1240. [CrossRef]
12. Costabile, F.A.; Gualtieri, M.I.; Napoli, A. General Bivariate Appell Polynomials via Matrix Calculus and Related Interpolation Hints. *Mathematics* **2021**, *9*, 964. [CrossRef]
13. Kelil, A.S.; Jooste, A.S.; Appadu, A.R. On Certain Properties and Applications of the Perturbed Meixner–Pollaczek Weight. *Mathematics* **2021**, *9*, 955. [CrossRef]
14. Kruchinin, D.; Kruchinin, V.; Shablya, Y. Method for Obtaining Coefficients of Powers of Bivariate Generating Functions. *Mathematics* **2021**, *9*, 428. [CrossRef]
15. Muhiuddin, G.; Khan, W.A.; Duran, U. Two-Variable Type 2 Poly-Fubini Polynomials. *Mathematics* **2021**, *9*, 281. [CrossRef]
16. Costabile, F.A.; Gualtieri, M.I.; Napoli, A. Towards the Centenary of Sheffer Polynomial Sequences: Old and Recent Results. *Mathematics* **2022**, *10*, 4435. [CrossRef]
17. Cardone, A.; Conte, D.; D'Ambrosio, R.; Paternoster, B. Multivalue Collocation Methods for Ordinary and Fractional Differential Equations. *Mathematics* **2022**, *10*, 185. [CrossRef]

Article

Two-Variable Type 2 Poly-Fubini Polynomials

Ghulam Muhiuddin [1], Waseem Ahmad Khan [2] and Ugur Duran [3,*]

[1] Department of Mathematics, University of Tabuk, Tabuk 71491, Saudi Arabia; chistygm@gmail.com or gmuhiuddin@ut.edu.sa
[2] Department of Mathematics and Natural Sciences, Prince Mohammad Bin Fahd University, P.O. Box 1664, Al Khobar 31952, Saudi Arabia; wkhan1@pmu.edu.sa
[3] Department of the Basic Concepts of Engineering, Faculty of Engineering and Natural Sciences, Iskenderun Technical University, Hatay TR-31200, Turkey
* Correspondence: mtdrnugur@gmail.com or ugur.duran@iste.edu.tr

Abstract: In the present work, a new extension of the two-variable Fubini polynomials is introduced by means of the polyexponential function, which is called the two-variable type 2 poly-Fubini polynomials. Then, some useful relations including the Stirling numbers of the second and the first kinds, the usual Fubini polynomials, and the higher-order Bernoulli polynomials are derived. Also, some summation formulas and an integral representation for type 2 poly-Fubini polynomials are investigated. Moreover, two-variable unipoly-Fubini polynomials are introduced utilizing the unipoly function, and diverse properties involving integral and derivative properties are attained. Furthermore, some relationships covering the two-variable unipoly-Fubini polynomials, the Stirling numbers of the second and the first kinds, and the Daehee polynomials are acquired.

Keywords: polyexponential function; Fubini polynomials; poly-Fubini polynomials; unipoly function; Stirling numbers

1. Introduction

Throughout the paper, we use $\mathbb{N} := \{1, 2, 3, \cdots\}$ and $\mathbb{N}_0 = \mathbb{N} \cup \{0\}$. Let $\mathbb{C}$ denote the set of complex numbers, $\mathbb{R}$ denote the set of real numbers, and $\mathbb{Z}$ denote the set of integers.

The usual Euler $E_n(x)$ and Bernoulli polynomials $B_n(x)$ are defined via the following exponential generating functions (cf. [1–6]):

$$\frac{2}{e^z+1}e^{xz} = \sum_{n=0}^{\infty} E_n(x)\frac{z^n}{n!} \ (|z| < \pi) \text{ and } \frac{z}{e^z-1}e^{xz} = \sum_{n=0}^{\infty} B_n(x)\frac{z^n}{n!} \ (|z| < 2\pi). \qquad (1)$$

The two-variable Fubini polynomials are defined as follows (cf. [1,2,4,7–10]):

$$\frac{e^{xz}}{1-y(e^z-1)} = \sum_{n=0}^{\infty} F_n(x,y)\frac{z^n}{n!}. \qquad (2)$$

Substituting $x = 0$ in (2), we have $F_n(0,y) := F_n(y)$ called the usual Fubini polynomials given by

$$\frac{1}{1-y(e^z-1)} = \sum_{n=0}^{\infty} F_n(y)\frac{z^n}{n!}. \qquad (3)$$

It is easy to see from (1) and (2) that

$$F_n\left(x, -\frac{1}{2}\right) = E_n(x).$$

Upon letting $y = 1$ in (3), we get the Fubini numbers as follows

$$\frac{1}{2 - e^z} = \sum_{n=0}^{\infty} F_n \frac{z^n}{n!}. \tag{4}$$

For more detailed information of the Fubini polynomials with applications, see [1,2,4,7–10].

The Bernoulli polynomials of the second kind are defined as follows (cf. [5,11,12]):

$$\frac{z}{\log(1 + z)} (1 + z)^x = \sum_{n=0}^{\infty} b_n(x) \frac{z^n}{n!} \tag{5}$$

The Bernoulli polynomials of order $\alpha \in \mathbb{N}$ are defined by (cf. [5,6,11–13])

$$\left(\frac{z}{e^z - 1}\right)^\alpha e^{xz} = \sum_{n=0}^{\infty} B_n^{(\alpha)}(x) \frac{z^n}{n!}. \tag{6}$$

By (5) and (6),

$$B_n^{(n)}(x + 1) := b_n(x). \tag{7}$$

The polyexponential function $\mathrm{Ei}_k(x)$ is introduced by Kim-Kim [12] as follows

$$\mathrm{Ei}_k(x) = \sum_{n=1}^{\infty} \frac{x^n}{(n-1)! n^k}, \quad (k \in \mathbb{Z}) \tag{8}$$

as inverse the polylogarithm function $Li_k(z)$ (cf. [6,13–15]) given by

$$Li_k(z) = \sum_{n=1}^{\infty} \frac{z^n}{n^k}, \quad |z| < 1. \tag{9}$$

Using the polyexponential function $\mathrm{Ei}_k(x)$, Kim-Kim [12] considered type 2 poly-Bernoulli polynomials, given by

$$\frac{\mathrm{Ei}_k(\log(1+z))}{e^z - 1} e^{xz} = \sum_{n=0}^{\infty} \beta_n^{(k)}(x) \frac{z^n}{n!}, \quad (k \in \mathbb{Z}) \tag{10}$$

and attained several properties and formulas for these polynomials. Upon setting $x = 0$ in (10), $\beta_n^{(k)}(0) := \beta_n^{(k)}$ are called type 2 poly-Bernoulli numbers.

We also notice that $\mathrm{Ei}_1(z) = e^z - 1$. Hence, when $k = 1$, the type 2 poly-Bernoulli $\beta_n^{(k)}(x)$ polynomials reduce to the Bernoulli polynomials $B_n(x)$ in (1).

Some mathematicians have considered and examined several extensions of special polynomials via polyexponential function, cf. [5,11,13,16,17] and see also the references cited therein. For example, Duran et al. [11] defined type 2 poly-Frobenius-Genocchi polynomials by the following Maclaurin series expansion (in a suitable neighborhood of $z = 0$):

$$\frac{\mathrm{Ei}_k(\log(1 + (1-u)z))}{e^z - u} e^{xz} = \sum_{n=0}^{\infty} G_n^{(F,k)}(x; u) \frac{z^n}{n!} \quad (k \in \mathbb{Z})$$

and Lee et al. [17] introduced type 2 poly-Euler polynomials given by

$$\frac{\mathrm{Ei}_k(\log(1 + 2z))}{z(e^z + 1)} e^{xz} = \sum_{n=0}^{\infty} \mathcal{E}_n^{(k)}(x) \frac{z^n}{n!}.$$

Kim-Kim [12] also introduced unipoly function $u_k(x|p)$ attached to p being any arithmetic map which is a complex or real-valued function defined on $\mathbb{N}$ as follows:

$$u_k(x|p) = \sum_{n=1}^{\infty} \frac{p(n)}{n^k} x^n, \quad (k \in \mathbb{Z}). \tag{11}$$

It is readily seen that

$$u_k(x|1) = \sum_{n=1}^{\infty} \frac{x^n}{n^k} = Li_k(x)$$

is the ordinary polylogarithm function in (9). By utilizing the unipoly function $u_k(x|p)$, Kim-Kim [12] defined unipoly-Bernoulli polynomials as follows:

$$\sum_{n=0}^{\infty} B_{n,p}^{(k)}(x) \frac{z^n}{n!} = \frac{u_k(1 - e^{-z}|p)}{1 - e^{-z}} e^{xz}. \tag{12}$$

They derived diverse formulas and relationships for these polynomials, see [12].

The Stirling numbers of the first kind $S_1(n,k)$ and the second kind $S_2(n,k)$ are given below:

$$\frac{(\log(1+z))^k}{k!} = \sum_{n=0}^{\infty} S_1(n,k) \frac{z^n}{n!} \text{ and } \frac{(e^z - 1)^k}{k!} = \sum_{n=0}^{\infty} S_2(n,k) \frac{z^n}{n!}. \tag{13}$$

From (13), for $n \geq 0$, we obtain

$$(x)_n = \sum_{k=0}^{n} S_1(n,k) x^k \text{ and } x^n = \sum_{k=0}^{n} S_1(n,k) (x)_k, \tag{14}$$

where $(x)_0 = 1$ and $(x)_n = x(x-1)(x-2) \cdots (x-n+1)$, cf. [1–4,6–9,12–15].

From (3) and (13), we get

$$F_n(y) = \sum_{k=0}^{n} S_2(n,k) k! y^k. \tag{15}$$

In the following sections, we introduce a new extension of the two-variable Fubini polynomials by means of the polyexponential function, which we call two-variable type 2 poly-Fubini polynomials. Then, we derive some useful relations including the Stirling numbers of the first and the second kinds, the usual Fubini polynomials, and the Bernoulli polynomials of higher-order. Also, we investigate some summation formulas and an integral representation for type 2 poly-Fubini polynomials. Moreover, we introduce two-variable unipoly-Fubini polynomials via unipoly function and acquire diverse properties including derivative and integral properties. Furthermore, we provide some relationships covering the Stirling numbers of the first and the second kinds, the two-variable unipoly-Fubini polynomials, and the Daehee polynomials.

2. Two-Variable Type 2 Poly-Fubini Polynomials and Numbers

Inspired and motivated by the definition of type 2 poly-Bernoulli polynomials in (10) given by Kim-Kim [12], here, we introduce two-variable type 2 poly-Fubini polynomials by Definition 1 as follows.

Definition 1. *For $k \in \mathbb{Z}$, we define two-variable type 2 poly-Fubini polynomials via the following exponential generating function (in a suitable neighborhood of $z = 0$) as given below:*

$$\frac{Ei_k(\log(1+z))}{z(1 - y(e^z - 1))} e^{xz} = \sum_{n=0}^{\infty} F_n^{(k)}(x;y) \frac{z^n}{n!}. \tag{16}$$

Upon setting $x = 0$ in (16), we have $F_n^{(k)}(0;y) := F_n^{(k)}(y)$ which we call type 2 poly-Fubini polynomials possessing the following generating function:

$$\frac{\mathrm{Ei}_k(\log(1+z))}{z(1-y(e^z-1))} = \sum_{n=0}^{\infty} F_n^{(k)}(y)\frac{z^n}{n!}. \qquad (17)$$

We note that, for $k = 1$, the two-variable type 2 poly-Fubini polynomials reduce to the usual two-variable Fubini polynomials in (2) because of $\mathrm{Ei}_1(z) = e^z - 1$.

Now, we develop some relationships and formulas for two-variable type 2 poly-Fubini polynomials as follows.

Theorem 1. *The following relationship*

$$F_n^{(k)}(x;y) = \sum_{l=0}^{n} \binom{n}{l} F_{n-l}^{(k)}(y)(u)x^l \qquad (18)$$

holds for $k \in \mathbb{Z}$ and $n \geq 0$.

Proof. By (16) and (17), we consider that

$$\sum_{n=0}^{\infty} F_n^{(k)}(x;y)\frac{z^n}{n!} = \frac{\mathrm{Ei}_k(\log(1+z))}{z(1-y(e^z-1))}e^{xz}$$

$$= \sum_{n=0}^{\infty} \frac{x^n z^n}{n!} \sum_{n=0}^{\infty} F_n^{(k)}(y)\frac{z^n}{n!}$$

$$= \sum_{n=0}^{\infty} \left(\sum_{l=0}^{n} \binom{n}{l} F_{n-l}^{(k)}(y)(u)x^l \right) \frac{z^n}{n!},$$

which gives the asserted result (18). □

A relationship involving Stirling numbers of the first kind, the two-variable Fubini polynomials, and two-variable type 2 poly-Fubini polynomials is stated by the following theorem.

Theorem 2. *For $k \in \mathbb{Z}$ and $n \geq 0$, we have*

$$F_n^{(k)}(x;y) = \sum_{l=0}^{n} \sum_{m=0}^{l} \binom{n}{l} \frac{S_1(l+1,m+1)}{(m+1)^{k-1}} \frac{F_{n-l}(x;y)}{l+1}. \qquad (19)$$

Proof. From (13) and (17), we observe that

$$\sum_{n=0}^{\infty} F_n^{(k)}(x;y)\frac{z^n}{n!} = \frac{e^{xz}}{z(1-y(e^z-1))} \sum_{m=1}^{\infty} \frac{(\log(1+z))^m}{(m-1)!m^k}$$

$$= \frac{e^{xz}}{z(1-y(e^z-1))} \sum_{m=0}^{\infty} \frac{(\log(1+z))^{m+1}}{(m+1)^k} \frac{1}{m!}$$

$$= \sum_{n=0}^{\infty} F_n(x;y)\frac{z^n}{n!} \sum_{n=0}^{\infty} \sum_{n=m}^{\infty} \frac{1}{n+1} \frac{S_1(n+1,m+1)}{(m+1)^{k-1}} \frac{z^n}{n!}$$

$$= \sum_{n=0}^{\infty} \left(\sum_{l=0}^{n} \sum_{m=0}^{l} \binom{n}{l} \frac{S_1(l+1,m+1)}{(m+1)^{k-1}} \frac{F_{n-l}(x;y)}{l+1} \right) \frac{z^n}{n!},$$

which means the desired result (19). □

Some special cases of Theorem 2 are examined below.

Corollary 1. *For $k \in \mathbb{Z}$ and $n \geq 0$, we get*

$$F_n^{(k)}(y) = \sum_{l=0}^{n} \sum_{m=0}^{l} \binom{n}{l} \frac{S_1(l+1, m+1)}{l+1} \frac{F_{n-l}(y)}{(m+1)^{k-1}}.$$

Corollary 2. *For $k = 1$ and $n \geq 0$, we acquire*

$$F_n(x;y) = \sum_{l=0}^{n} \sum_{m=0}^{l} \binom{n}{l} \frac{F_{n-l}(x;y)}{l+1} S_1(l+1, m+1).$$

The following differentiation property holds (cf. [12])

$$\frac{d}{dx} \text{Ei}_k(\log(1+x)) = \frac{1}{(1+x)\log(1+x)} \text{Ei}_{k-1}(\log(1+x)). \tag{20}$$

and also, the following integral representations are valid for $k > 1$:

$$\text{Ei}_k(\log(1+x)) = \int_0^x \frac{1}{(1+z)\log(1+z)}$$
$$\times \underbrace{\int_0^z \frac{1}{(1+z)\log(1+z)} \cdots \int_0^z \frac{z}{(1+z)\log(1+z)} dz dz \ldots dz}_{(k-2) \text{ times}}$$

$$= x \sum_{m=0}^{\infty} \sum_{m_1+\cdots+m_{k-1}=m} \binom{m}{m_1, \ldots, m_{k-1}}$$
$$\times \frac{B_{m_1}^{(m_1)}}{m_1+1} \frac{B_{m_2}^{(m_2)}}{m_1+m_2+1} \cdots \frac{B_{m_{k-1}}^{(m_{k-1})}}{m_1+\cdots+m_{k-1}+1} \frac{x^m}{m!}. \tag{21}$$

Theorem 3. *The following relationship*

$$F_n^{(k)}(y) = \sum_{m=0}^{n} \binom{n}{m} \sum_{m_1+\cdots+m_{k-1}=m} \binom{m}{m_1, \ldots, m_{k-1}}$$
$$\times \frac{B_{m_1}^{(m_1)}}{m_1+1} \frac{B_{m_2}^{(m_2)}}{m_1+m_2+1} \cdots \frac{B_{m_{k-1}}^{(m_{k-1})}}{m_1+\cdots+m_{k-1}+1} F_{n-m}(y)$$

holds for $n \in \mathbb{N}_0$ and $k > 1$.

Proof. From (17) and (21), for $k > 1$, we can write

$$\sum_{n=0}^{\infty} F_n^{(k)}(y) \frac{z^n}{n!} = \frac{\text{Ei}_k(\log(1+z))}{z(1-y(e^z-1))}$$
$$= \frac{z}{z(1-y(e^z-1))} \sum_{m=0}^{\infty} \sum_{m_1+\cdots+m_{k-1}=m} \binom{m}{m_1, \ldots, m_{k-1}}$$
$$\times \frac{B_{m_1}^{(m_1)}}{m_1+1} \frac{B_{m_2}^{(m_2)}}{m_1+m_2+1} \cdots \frac{B_{m_{k-1}}^{(m_{k-1})}}{m_1+\cdots+m_{k-1}+1} \frac{x^m}{m!},$$

□

Theorem 4. *The following relationship*

$$F_n^{(k)}(y) = \frac{1}{1+y} \left(y \sum_{m=0}^{n} \binom{n}{m} F_{n-m}^{(k)}(y) + \sum_{m=0}^{n} \frac{1}{(m+1)^{k-1}} \frac{S_1(n+1, m+1)}{n+1} \right) \tag{22}$$

holds for $n \geq 0$.

Proof. From (17), we attain

$$\frac{\mathrm{Ei}_k(\log(1+z))}{z} = \sum_{n=0}^{\infty} F_n^{(k)}(y) \frac{z^n}{n!} (1 - y(e^z - 1))$$

$$= \sum_{n=0}^{\infty} F_n^{(k)}(y) \frac{z^n}{n!} - y \sum_{n=0}^{\infty} \sum_{m=0}^{n} \binom{n}{m} F_{n-m}^{(k)}(y) \frac{z^n}{n!} + y \sum_{n=0}^{\infty} F_n^{(k)}(y) \frac{z^n}{n!}$$

$$= \sum_{n=0}^{\infty} \left((1+y) F_n^{(k)}(y) - y \sum_{m=0}^{n} \binom{n}{m} F_{n-m}^{(k)}(y) \right) \frac{z^n}{n!}$$

and, also, we have

$$\mathrm{Ei}_k(\log(1+z)) = \frac{1}{z} \sum_{m=1}^{\infty} \frac{(\log(1+z))^m}{m^k} \frac{1}{(m-1)!}$$

$$= \frac{1}{z} \sum_{m=0}^{\infty} \frac{(\log(1+z))^{m+1}}{(m+1)^k} \frac{1}{m!} = \frac{1}{z} \sum_{m=0}^{\infty} \frac{(\log(1+z))^{m+1}}{(m+1)^{k-1}} \frac{1}{(m+1)!}$$

$$= \frac{1}{z} \sum_{m=0}^{\infty} \sum_{n=m+1}^{\infty} \frac{S_1(n,m+1)}{(m+1)^{k-1}} \frac{z^n}{n!},$$

which implies the asserted result (22). □

For $s \in \mathbb{C}$ and $k \in \mathbb{Z}$ with $k \geq 1$, let

$$\eta_k(s) := \frac{1}{\Gamma(s)} \int_0^{\infty} \frac{z^{s-1}}{z(1-y(e^z-1))} \mathrm{Ei}_k(\log(1+z)) dz, \qquad (23)$$

where $\Gamma(s)$ is the classical gamma function given below:

$$\Gamma(s) = \int_0^{\infty} z^{s-1} e^z dz \quad (\Re(s) > 0).$$

From (23), we see that $\eta_k(s)$ is a holomorphic map for $\Re(s) > 0$, since $\mathrm{Ei}_k(\log(1+z)) \leq \mathrm{Ei}_1(\log(1+z))$ with $z \geq 0$. Thus, we have

$$\eta_k(s) = \frac{1}{\Gamma(s)} \int_0^1 \frac{z^{s-2}}{1-y(e^z-1)} \mathrm{Ei}_k(\log(1+z)) dz + \frac{1}{\Gamma(s)} \int_1^{\infty} \frac{z^{s-2}}{1-y(e^z-1)} \mathrm{Ei}_k(\log(1+z)) dz. \qquad (24)$$

We see that the second integral in (24) converges absolutely for any $s \in \mathbb{C}$ and hence, the second term on the right hand side vanishes at non-positive integers. Therefore, we obtain

$$\lim_{s \to -m} \left| \frac{1}{\Gamma(s)} \int_1^{\infty} \frac{z^{s-2}}{1-y(e^z-1)} \mathrm{Ei}_k(\log(1+z)) dz \right| \leq \frac{1}{\Gamma(-m)} M = 0,$$

since

$$\Gamma(s)\Gamma(1-s) = \frac{\pi}{\sin(\pi s)}. \qquad (25)$$

Also, for $\Re(s) > 0$, the first integral in (24) can be written as

$$\frac{1}{\Gamma(s)} \int_0^1 \frac{z^{s-1}}{z(1-y(e^z-1))} \mathrm{Ei}_k(\log(1+z)) dz = \frac{1}{\Gamma(s)} \sum_{n=0}^{\infty} \frac{F_n^{(k)}(y)}{n!} \int_0^1 z^{n+s-1} dz$$

$$= \frac{1}{\Gamma(s)} \sum_{n=0}^{\infty} \frac{F_n^{(k)}(y)}{n!} \frac{1}{n+s}, \qquad (26)$$

which defines an entire function of s. Therefore, we derive that $\eta_k(s)$ can be continued to an entire map of s.

Theorem 5. For $k \in \mathbb{N}$, the map $\eta_k(s)$ has an analytic continuation to a map of $s \in \mathbb{C}$, and the special values at non-positive integers are as follows

$$\eta_k(-m) = (-1)^m F_m^{(k)}(y), (m \in \mathbb{N}_0). \tag{27}$$

Proof. By means of (24)–(26), we acquire

$$\begin{aligned}
\eta_k(-m) &= \lim_{s \to -m} \frac{1}{\Gamma(s)} \int_0^1 \frac{z^{s-1}}{z(1 - y(e^z - 1))} \mathrm{Ei}_k(\log(1+z)) dz \\
&= \cdots + \cdots + 0 + \lim_{s \to -m} \frac{1}{\Gamma(s)} \frac{F_m^{(k)}}{m!(m+s)} + 0 + 0 + \cdots \\
&= \lim_{s \to -m} \frac{1}{m+s} \frac{\Gamma(1-s)\sin(\pi s)}{\pi} \frac{F_m^{(k)}(y)}{m!} \\
&= \frac{\Gamma(1+m)}{m!} \cos(\pi m) F_m^{(k)}(y) = (-1)^m F_m^{(k)}(y),
\end{aligned}$$

which is the desired relation in (27). □

Now, we state a summation formula for $F_n^{(k)}(x;y)$ as given below.

Theorem 6. The following formula

$$F_n^{(k)}(x_1 + x_2; y) = \sum_{m=0}^n \binom{n}{m} F_{n-m}^{(k)}(x_1; y) x_2^m. \tag{28}$$

holds for $k \in \mathbb{Z}$ and $n \geq 0$.

Proof. By (17), we observe that

$$\begin{aligned}
\sum_{n=0}^\infty F_n^{(k)}(x_1+x_2;y) \frac{z^n}{n!} &= \left(\frac{\mathrm{Ei}_k(\log(1+z))}{z(1-y(e^z-1))}\right) e^{(x_1+x_2)z} \\
&= \left(\sum_{n=0}^\infty F_n^{(k)}(x_1;y) \frac{z^n}{n!}\right) \left(\sum_{m=0}^\infty x_2^m \frac{z^m}{m!}\right) \\
&= \sum_{n=0}^\infty \left(\sum_{m=0}^n \binom{n}{m} F_{n-m}^{(k)}(x_1;y) x_2^m\right) \frac{z^n}{n!},
\end{aligned}$$

which means the claimed result (28). □

Theorem 7. The following formula

$$y F_n^{(k)}(x+1;y) = (1+y) F_n^{(k)}(x;y) - \sum_{l=0}^n \sum_{m=0}^l \binom{n}{l} \frac{1}{(m+1)^{k-1}} \frac{S_1(l+1, m+1)}{l+1} x^{n-l} \tag{29}$$

is valid for $k \in \mathbb{Z}$ and $n \geq 0$.

Proof. By (14) and (17), we consider that

$$\sum_{n=0}^{\infty} \left(F_n^{(k)}(x+1;y) - F_n^{(k)}(x;y) \right) \frac{z^n}{n!} = e^{xz}(e^z - 1) \frac{\text{Ei}_k(\log(1+z))}{z(1-y(e^z-1))}$$

$$= \left(\frac{e^{xz}}{1-y(e^z-1)} - e^{xz} \right) \frac{\text{Ei}_k(\log(1+z))}{yz}$$

$$= \frac{1}{y} \left(\sum_{n=0}^{\infty} F_n^{(k)}(x;y) - \sum_{l=0}^{n} \sum_{m=0}^{l} \binom{n}{l} \frac{x^{n-l}}{l+1} \frac{S_1(l+1,m+1)}{(m+1)^{k-1}} \right) \frac{z^n}{n!},$$

which means the desired result (29). □

Theorem 8. *The following formula*

$$\sum_{m=0}^{n} \binom{n}{m} F_{n-m}^{(k)}(x_1;y_1) F_m^{(k)}(x_2;y_2) = \frac{y_2 F_n^{(k)}(x_1+x_2;y_2) - y_1 F_n^{(k)}(x_1+x_2;y_1)}{y_2 - y_1} \quad (30)$$

holds for $k \in \mathbb{Z}$ and $n \geq 0$.

Proof. By means of (17), we acquire

$$Y = \sum_{n=0}^{\infty} F_n^{(k)}(x_1;y_1) \frac{z^n}{n!} \sum_{n=0}^{\infty} F_n^{(k)}(x_2;y_2) \frac{z^n}{n!} = \frac{\text{Ei}_k(\log(1+z))}{z(1-y_1(e^z-1))} e^{x_1 z} \frac{\text{Ei}_k(\log(1+z))}{z(1-y_2(e^z-1))} e^{x_2 z}$$

$$= \frac{\text{Ei}_k(\log(1+z))}{z} \left(\frac{e^{x_1 z}}{1-y_1(e^z-1)} \frac{e^{x_2 z}}{1-y_2(e^z-1)} \right)$$

$$= \frac{\text{Ei}_k(\log(1+z))}{z} \left(\frac{y_2}{y_2-y_1} \frac{e^{(x_1+x_2)z}}{1-y_2(e^z-1)} - \frac{y_1}{y_2-y_1} \frac{e^{(x_1+x_2)z}}{1-y_1(e^z-1)} \right)$$

$$= \sum_{n=0}^{\infty} \left(\frac{y_2 F_n^{(k)}(x_1+x_2;y_2) - y_1 F_n^{(k)}(x_1+x_2;y_1)}{y_2 - y_1} \right) \frac{z^n}{n!}$$

and

$$Y = \sum_{n=0}^{\infty} \left(\sum_{m=0}^{n} \binom{n}{m} F_{n-m}^{(k)}(x_1;y_1) F_m^{(k)}(x_2;y_2) \right) \frac{z^n}{n!},$$

which means the claimed result (30). □

Theorem 9. *The following relationship*

$$F_n^{(k)}(y) = \sum_{l=0}^{n} \sum_{m=0}^{n-l} \sum_{r=0}^{l} \binom{n}{l} \frac{S_1(n-l+1,m+1)S_2(l,r)}{n-l+1} \frac{y^r r!}{(m+1)^{k-1}} \quad (31)$$

holds for $k \in \mathbb{Z}$ and $n \geq 0$.

Proof. Using (18), we get

$$\sum_{n=0}^{\infty} F_n^{(k)}(y) \frac{z^n}{n!} = \frac{\text{Ei}_k(\log(1+z))}{z} \sum_{m=0}^{\infty} y^m \sum_{l=m}^{\infty} m! S_2(l,m) \frac{z^l}{l!}$$

$$= \left(\sum_{n=0}^{\infty} \sum_{m=0}^{n} \frac{S_1(n+1,m+1)}{(m+1)^{k-1}} \frac{z^n}{(n+1)!} \right) \left(\sum_{l=0}^{\infty} \sum_{r=0}^{l} y^r r! S_2(l,r) \frac{z^l}{l!} \right)$$

$$= \sum_{n=0}^{\infty} \left(\sum_{l=0}^{n} \sum_{m=0}^{n-l} \sum_{r=0}^{l} \binom{n}{l} S_2(l,r) \frac{S_1(n-l+1,m+1)}{n-l+1} \frac{y^r r!}{(m+1)^{k-1}} \right) \frac{z^n}{n!},$$

which means the desired result (31). □

Theorem 10. *The following correlation*

$$\sum_{m=0}^{n} F_m^{(k)}(y) S_2(n,m) = \sum_{q=0}^{n} \sum_{i=0}^{q} \sum_{p=0}^{i} \binom{q}{i}\binom{n}{q} F_p(y) S_2(i,p) B_{q-i} \frac{1}{(n-q+1)^k} \quad (32)$$

hold for $k \in \mathbb{Z}$ *and* $n \geq 0$.

Proof. Using (18), replacing z by $e^z - 1$, we acquire that

$$\sum_{n=0}^{\infty} F_n^{(k)}(y) \frac{(e^z-1)^n}{n!} = \frac{1}{1-y(e^{e^z-1}-1)} \frac{z}{e^z-1} \frac{\operatorname{Ei}_k(z)}{z}$$

$$= \sum_{p=0}^{\infty} F_p(y) \sum_{p=i}^{\infty} S_2(i,p) \frac{z^i}{i!} \sum_{q=0}^{\infty} B_q \frac{z^q}{q!} \sum_{n=0}^{\infty} \frac{z^n}{n!(n+1)^k}$$

$$= \sum_{i=0}^{\infty} \left(\sum_{p=0}^{i} F_p(y) S_2(i,p) \right) \frac{z^i}{i!} \sum_{q=0}^{\infty} B_q \frac{z^q}{q!} \sum_{n=0}^{\infty} \frac{z^n}{n!(n+1)^k}$$

$$= \sum_{n=0}^{\infty} \left(\sum_{q=0}^{n} \sum_{i=0}^{q} \sum_{p=0}^{i} \binom{n}{q}\binom{q}{i} F_p(y) S_2(i,p) B_{q-i} \frac{1}{(n-q+1)^k} \right) \frac{z^n}{n!}$$

and

$$\sum_{m=0}^{\infty} F_m^{(k)}(y) \frac{(e^z-1)^m}{m!} = \sum_{m=0}^{\infty} F_m^{(k)}(y) \sum_{n=m}^{\infty} S_2(n,m) \frac{z^n}{n!} = \sum_{n=0}^{\infty} \left(\sum_{m=0}^{n} F_m^{(k)}(y) S_2(n,m) \right) \frac{z^n}{n!},$$

which provides the asserted result (32). □

3. Two-Variable Unipoly-Fubini Polynomials

Using the unipoly function $u_k(z|p)$ in (11), we introduce two-variable unipoly-Fubini polynomials attached to p via the following generating function:

$$\frac{u_k(\log(1+z)|p)}{z(1-y(e^z-1))} e^{xz} = \sum_{n=0}^{\infty} F_{n,p}^{(k)}(x;y) \frac{z^n}{n!}. \quad (33)$$

Upon setting $x = 0$ in (33), we have $F_{n,p}^{(k)}(0;y) := F_{n,p}^{(k)}(y)$ which we call unipoly-Fubini polynomials attached to p as follows

$$\frac{u_k(\log(1+z)|p)}{z(1-y(e^z-1))} = \sum_{n=0}^{\infty} F_{n,p}^{(k)}(y) \frac{z^n}{n!}. \quad (34)$$

We now investigate some properties of two-variable unipoly-Fubini polynomials attached to p as follows.

Theorem 11. *The following relationship*

$$F_{n,p}^{(k)}(x;y) = \sum_{l=0}^{n} \binom{n}{l} F_{n-l,p}^{(k)}(y) x^l \quad (35)$$

holds for $k \in \mathbb{Z}$ *and* $n \geq 0$.

Proof. By (33) and (34), we consider that which gives the asserted result (35). □

Theorem 12. *The following derivative rule*

holds for $k \in \mathbb{Z}$ and $n \geq 1$.

Proof. From (33), we observe that

$$\sum_{n=1}^{\infty} \frac{d}{dx} F_{n,p}^{(k)}(x;y) \frac{z^n}{n!} = \frac{1}{z(1-y(e^z-1))} u_k(\log(1+z)|p) \frac{d}{dx} e^{xz} = \sum_{n=0}^{\infty} F_{n,p}^{(k)}(x;y) \frac{z^{n+1}}{n!},$$

which means the desired result (36). □

Theorem 13. *The following integral representation*

$$\int_\alpha^\beta F_{n,p}^{(k)}(x;y) dx = \frac{F_{n+1,p}^{(k)}(\beta;y) - F_{n+1,p}^{(k)}(\alpha;y)}{n+1} \tag{37}$$

holds for $n \geq 0$ and $k \in \mathbb{Z}$.

Proof. By Theorem 12, we derive that

$$\int_\alpha^\beta F_{n,p}^{(k)}(x;y) dx = \frac{1}{n+1} \int_\alpha^\beta \frac{d}{dx} F_{n+1,p}^{(k)}(x;y) dx = \frac{F_{n+1,p}^{(k)}(\alpha;y) - F_{n,p}^{(k)}(\beta;y)}{n+1},$$

which means the asserted result (37). □

Taking $p(n) = \frac{1}{\Gamma(n)}$ in (11) gives

$$u_k\left(\log(1+z)\Big|\frac{1}{\Gamma}\right) = \sum_{m=1}^{\infty} \frac{(\log(1+z))^m}{m^k(m-1)!},$$

by which we get

$$\sum_{n=0}^{\infty} F_{n,\frac{1}{\Gamma}}^{(k)}(x;y) \frac{z^n}{n!} = \frac{1}{z(1-y(e^z-1))} e^{xz} u_k\left(\log(1+z)\Big|\frac{1}{\Gamma}\right) \tag{38}$$

$$= \frac{e^{xz}}{z(1-y(e^z-1))} \sum_{m=1}^{\infty} \frac{(\log(1+z))^m}{m^k(m-1)!}.$$

Especially, for $k=1$ in (38), we obtain

$$\sum_{n=0}^{\infty} F_{n,\frac{1}{\Gamma}}^{(1)}(x;y) \frac{z^n}{n!} = \frac{e^{xz}}{z(1-y(e^z-1))} \sum_{m=1}^{\infty} \frac{(\log(1+z))^m}{m!} = \sum_{n=0}^{\infty} F_n(x;y) \frac{z^n}{n!},$$

which gives the following equality

$$F_{n,\frac{1}{\Gamma}}^{(1)}(x;y) = F_n(x;y). \tag{39}$$

Theorem 14. *The following correlation*

$$F_{n,p}^{(k)}(x;y) = \sum_{l=0}^{n} \sum_{m=0}^{l} \binom{n}{l} \frac{m! p(m+1)}{(m+1)^{k-1}} \frac{F_{n-l}(x;y)}{l+1} S_{1,\lambda}(l+1, m+1) \tag{40}$$

holds for $n \geq 0$ and $k \in \mathbb{Z}$. Moreover, for $p(n) = \frac{1}{\Gamma(n)}$,

$$F_{n,\frac{1}{\Gamma}}^{(k)}(x;y) = \sum_{l=0}^{n} \sum_{m=0}^{l} \binom{n}{l} \frac{S_1(l+1, m+1)}{l+1} \frac{F_{n-l}(x;y)}{(m+1)^{k-1}}. \tag{41}$$

Proof. From (33), we have

$$\sum_{n=0}^{\infty} F_{n,p}^{(k)}(x;y)\frac{z^n}{n!} = \frac{e^{xz}}{z(1-y(e^z-1))} \sum_{m=1}^{\infty} \frac{(\log(1+z))^m}{m^k} p(m)$$

$$= \frac{e^{xz}}{z(1-y(e^z-1))} \sum_{m=0}^{\infty} \frac{(\log(1+z))^{m+1}}{(m+1)^k} p(m+1)$$

$$= \frac{e^{xz}}{z(1-y(e^z-1))} \sum_{m=0}^{\infty} \frac{m!p(m+1)}{(m+1)^{k-1}} \sum_{l=m+1}^{\infty} S_1(l,m+1)\frac{z^l}{l!}$$

$$= \sum_{n=0}^{\infty} F_n(x;y)\frac{z^n}{n!} \sum_{m=0}^{\infty} \frac{p(m+1)(m+1)!}{(m+1)^k} \sum_{l=m}^{\infty} \frac{S_1(l+1,m+1)}{l+1}\frac{z^l}{l!}$$

$$= \sum_{n=0}^{\infty} \left(\sum_{l=0}^{n} \sum_{m=0}^{l} \binom{n}{l} \frac{m!p(m+1)}{(m+1)^{k-1}} \frac{F_{n-l}(x;y)}{l+1} S_1(l+1,m+1) \right) \frac{z^n}{n!},$$

which is the desired result (40). □

Theorem 15. *For $n \geq 0$ and $k \in \mathbb{Z}$, we have*

$$F_{n,p}^{(k)}(x;y) = \sum_{l=0}^{n} \sum_{m=0}^{l} \binom{n}{l} F_{n-l,p}^{(k)}(y) S_2(l,m)(x)_m. \tag{42}$$

Proof. By (33), we attain

$$\sum_{n=0}^{\infty} F_{n,p}^{(k)}(x;y)\frac{z^n}{n!} = (e^z-1+1)^x \frac{u_k(\log(1+z)|p)}{z(1-y(e^z-1))}$$

$$= \left(\sum_{m=0}^{\infty} (x)_m \frac{(e^z-1)^m}{m!} \right) \frac{u_k(\log(1+z)|p)}{z(1-y(e^z-1))}$$

$$= \left(\sum_{l=0}^{\infty} \sum_{m=0}^{l} (x)_m S_2(l,m)\frac{z^l}{l!} \right) \left(\sum_{n=0}^{\infty} F_{n,p}^{(k)}(y)\frac{z^n}{n!} \right)$$

$$= \sum_{n=0}^{\infty} \left(\sum_{l=0}^{n} \sum_{m=0}^{l} \binom{n}{l} F_{n-l,p}^{(k)}(y) S_2(l,m)(x)_m \right) \frac{z^n}{n!},$$

which provides the claimed result (42). □

Lastly, we state the following theorem.

Theorem 16. *Let $k \in \mathbb{Z}$ and $n \geq 0$. We have*

$$F_{n,p}^{(k)}(y) = \sum_{l=0}^{n} \sum_{r=0}^{n-l} \sum_{m=0}^{l} \binom{n}{l}\binom{n-l}{r} \frac{D_r F_{n-r-l}(y) S_1(l,m)}{(m+1)^k} p(m+1)m!, \tag{43}$$

where D_r is r-th Daehee number given by (cf. [18])

$$\frac{\log(1+z)}{z} = \sum_{r=0}^{\infty} D_r \frac{z^r}{r!}.$$

Proof. From (14), (17), and (34), we have

$$\sum_{n=0}^{\infty} F_{n,p}^{(k)}(y) \frac{z^n}{n!} = \frac{\sum_{m=1}^{\infty} \frac{p(m)}{m^k}(\log(1+z))^m}{z(1-y(e^z-1))}$$

$$= \frac{\log(1+z)}{z} \frac{1}{1-y(e^z-1)} \sum_{m=0}^{\infty} \frac{p(m+1)m!}{(m+1)^k} \sum_{l=m}^{\infty} S_1(l,m) \frac{z^l}{l!}$$

$$= \sum_{r=0}^{\infty} D_r \frac{z^r}{r!} \sum_{n=0}^{\infty} F_n(y) \frac{z^n}{n!} \sum_{l=0}^{\infty} \left(\sum_{m=0}^{l} \frac{p(m+1)m!}{(m+1)^k} S_1(l,m) 2^l \right) \frac{z^l}{l!}$$

$$= \sum_{n=0}^{\infty} \sum_{r=0}^{n} \sum_{l=0}^{r} \binom{n}{r} \binom{r}{l} D_r F_{n-r-l}(y) \sum_{m=0}^{l} \frac{p(m+1)m!}{(m+1)^k} S_1(l,m) \frac{z^n}{n!}.$$

Therefore, we obtain the claimed correlation (43). □

4. Conclusions

Inspired and motivated by the definition of the type 2 poly-Bernoulli given by Kim-Kim [12], in the present paper, we have introduced a new extension of the two-variable Fubini polynomials using the polyexponential function, which we call two-variable type 2 poly-Fubini polynomials. Then, we have acquired some useful relations including the Stirling numbers of the first and the second kinds, the Bernoulli polynomials of higher-order, and the usual Fubini polynomials. Also, we have developed some summation formulas and an integral representation for type 2 poly-Fubini polynomials. Moreover, we have considered two-variable unipoly-Fubini polynomials via unipoly function and have investigated diverse properties including derivative and integral properties. Furthermore, we have provided some relationships covering the two-variable unipoly-Fubini polynomials, the Stirling numbers of the first and the second kinds, and the Daehee polynomials.

Author Contributions: Writing—original draft, G.M., W.A.K. and U.D.; Writing—review & editing, G.M., W.A.K. and U.D. All authors have read and agreed to the published version of the manuscript.

Funding: This research received no external funding.

Institutional Review Board Statement: Not applicable.

Informed Consent Statement: Not applicable.

Data Availability Statement: Not applicable.

Conflicts of Interest: The authors declare no conflict of interest.

References

1. Duran, U.; Acikgoz, M. On degenerate truncated special polynomials. *Mathematics* **2020**, *8*, 144. [CrossRef]
2. Guohui, C.; Li, C. Some identities involving the Fubini polynomials and Euler polynomials. *Mathematics* **2018**, *6*, 300. [CrossRef]
3. Kargın, L. Exponential polynomials and its applications to the related polynomials and numbers. *arXiv* **2016**, arXiv:1503.05444v2.
4. Kilar, N.; Simsek, Y. A new family of Fubini type numbers and polynomials associated with Apostol-Bernoulli numbers and polynomials. *J. Korean Math. Soc.* **2017**, *54*, 1605–1621.
5. Kwon, J.; Jang, L.C. A note on the type 2 poly-Apostol-Bernoulli polynomials. *Proc. Jangjeon Math. Soc.* **2020**, *30*, 253–262.
6. Ma, Y.; Kim, D.S.; Lee, H.; Kim, T. Poly-Dedekind sums associated with poly-Bernoulli functions. *J. Inequal. Appl.* **2020**, *2020*, 248. [CrossRef]
7. Duran, U.; Acikgoz, M. Truncated Fubini polynomials. *Mathematics* **2019**, *7*, 431. [CrossRef]
8. Kim, D.S.; Kim, T.; Kwon, H.-I.; Park, J.-W. Two-variable higher-order Fubini polynomials. *J. Korean Math. Soc.* **2018**, *55*, 975–986. [CrossRef]
9. Sharma, S.K.; Khan, W.A.; Ryoo, C.S. A parametric kind of the degenerate Fubini numbers and polynomials. *Mathematics* **2020**, *8*, 405. [CrossRef]
10. Su, D.D.; He, Y. Some identities for the two-variable Fubini polynomials. *Mathematics* **2019**, *7*, 115. [CrossRef]
11. Duran, U.; Acikgoz, M.; Araci, S. Construction of the type 2 poly-Frobenius-Genocchi polynomials with their certain applications. *Adv. Differ. Equ.* **2020**, *2020*, 432. [CrossRef]

12. Kim, D.S.; Kim, T. A note on polyexponential and unipoly functions. *Russ. J. Math. Phys.* **2019**, *26*, 40–49. [CrossRef]
13. Kim, T.; Kim, D.S.; Lee, H.; Jang, L.-C. Identities on poly-Dedekind sums. *Adv. Differ. Equ.* **2020**, *2020*, 563. [CrossRef]
14. Eastham, M.S.P. On Polylogarithms. *Proc. Glasgow Math. Assoc.* **1964**, *6*, 169–171. [CrossRef]
15. Lewin, L. *Polylogarithms and Associated Functions*; With a Foreword by Vander Poorten, A.J.; North-Holland Publishing Co.: Amsterdam, NY, USA, 1981.
16. Dolgy, D.V.; Jang, L.C. A note on the polyexponential Genocchi polynomials and numbers. *Symmetry* **2020**, *12*, 1007. [CrossRef]
17. Lee, D.S.; Kim, H.K.; Jang, L.-C. Type 2 degenerate poly-Euler polynomials. *Symmetry* **2020**, *12*, 1011. [CrossRef]
18. Khan, W.A.; Nisar, K.S.; Duran, U.; Acikgoz, M.; Araci, S. Multifarious implicit summation formulae of Hermite-based poly-Daehee polynomials. *Appl. Math. Inf. Sci.* **2018**, *12*, 305–310. [CrossRef]

Article

Method for Obtaining Coefficients of Powers of Bivariate Generating Functions

Dmitry Kruchinin [1], Vladimir Kruchinin [2] and Yuriy Shablya [1,*]

[1] Department of Complex Information Security of Computer Systems, Tomsk State University of Control Systems and Radioelectronics, 634050 Tomsk, Russia; kdv@fb.tusur.ru
[2] Institute of Innovation, Tomsk State University of Control Systems and Radioelectronics, 634050 Tomsk, Russia; kru@2i.tusur.ru
* Correspondence: shablya-yv@mail.ru

Abstract: In this paper, we study methods for obtaining explicit formulas for the coefficients of generating functions. To solve this problem, we consider the methods that are based on using the powers of generating functions. We propose to generalize the concept of compositae to the case of generating functions in two variables and define basic operations on such compositae: composition, addition, multiplication, reciprocation and compositional inversion. These operations allow obtaining explicit formulas for compositae and coefficients of bivariate generating functions. In addition, we present several examples of applying the obtained results for getting explicit formulas for the coefficients of bivariate generating functions. The introduced mathematical apparatus can be used for solving different problems that are related to the theory of generating functions.

Keywords: formal power series; composition of generation functions; bivariate generating function; composita; explicit formula

MSC: 05A15; 40B05

1. Introduction

Generating functions are a widely used and powerful tool for solving problems in combinatorics, mathematical analysis, statistics, etc. For example, methods of the theory of generating functions are used for solving problems in combinatorics, since generating functions allow obtaining a compact representation of discrete structures and process them. For the first time, methods of generating functions were applied by de Moivre to solve recurrence equations. Next, Euler expanded the methods of generating functions for solving research problems related to partitions. In this case, a generating function through its coefficients shows the value for some special numbers that have combinatorial interpretations. Great contributions to the development of methods of generating functions and their application for solving mathematical problems in combinatorics were made by Riordan [1], Comtet [2], Flajolet and Sedgewick [3], Wilf [4], Stanley [5], Egorychev [6], Lando [7] and other scientists.

Moreover, generating functions are the main means of describing polynomials. Polynomials are one of the basic mathematical objects, and they are used in different areas of pure and applied mathematics. In this case, the coefficients of the generating function for a polynomial show the form of the polynomial for the fixed values of its parameters. Many studies present various properties of polynomials and their generating functions (e.g., those by Boas and Buck [8], Roman [9], Srivastava [10–12] and Simsek [13–15]).

The development of new methods for obtaining explicit formulas for the coefficients of generating functions is relevant research trend. The solution of this problem allows finding explicit formulas for special numbers and polynomials that are described by these generating functions. Different approaches for solving this problem can be found in papers by the following authors: Srivastava [16,17], Boyadzhiev [18], Cenkci [19] and other scientists.

Note that many research papers that are devoted to combinatorial problems and generating functions use the coefficients of the powers of generating functions. The coefficients of the powers of generating functions were first obtained by Euler when he obtained the coefficient function for $(1 + x + x^2 + \ldots + x^n + \ldots)^k$. The Binomial theorem, which is also the power of the generating function $(x + y)$, was known even before de Moivre and Euler's works were published. In addition, the coefficients of the powers of generating functions play an important role in performing the composition of the generating functions.

The following concepts are related to the coefficients of the powers of generating functions:

1. Potential polynomials introduced by Comtet [2]: The potential polynomial $P_n^{(k)}$ is the kth power of an exponential generating function (k is a complex number):

$$\left(1 + \sum_{n>0} g_n \frac{x^n}{n!}\right)^k = 1 + \sum_{n>0} P_n^{(k)} \frac{x^n}{n!}.$$

For the coefficients of potential polynomials, there is a relationship with the Bell polynomials, but operations on such polynomials are not defined.

2. Riordan arrays introduced by Shapiro et al. [20]: A Riordan array is a pair of generating functions $D = (F(x), G(x))$ where $F(x) = \sum_{n \geq 0} f(n) x^n$ and $G(x) = \sum_{n > 0} g(n) x^n$. It forms an infinite matrix $D = (d_{n,k})_{n,k \geq 0}$ where $d_{n,k} = [x^n] F(x) G(x)^k$. If we consider the associated subgroup of the Riordan group $D = (1, G(x))$, then we get $d_{n,k} = [x^n] G(x)^k$ or

$$G(x)^k = \sum_{n \geq k} d_{n,k} x^n.$$

However, there are no universal rules for obtaining explicit formulas for $d_{n,k}$.

3. Power matrices introduced by Knuth [21]: The power matrix of a given power series $V(x) = V_1 x + V_2 x^2 + \ldots$ is the infinite array of coefficients $v_{n,k} = \frac{n!}{k!}[x^n] V(x)^k$. Thus, the kth power of $V(x)$ can be presented in the form

$$V(x)^k = \sum_{n \geq k} \frac{k!}{n!} v_{n,k} x^n.$$

In addition, there are formulas for obtaining the coefficients $w_{n,k}$ for the composition of power series $W(z) = U(V(z))$ and for a power series of the form $W(x) = \alpha U(\beta x)$. However, the development of this mathematical apparatus is not presented.

4. Compositae introduced by Kruchinin [22,23]: The composita $F^\Delta(n,k)$ of a generating function $F(x) = \sum_{n>0} f(n,k) x^n$ is a coefficients function of its kth power:

$$F(x)^k = \sum_{n \geq k} F^\Delta(n,k) x^n.$$

For two generating functions $F(x)$ and $G(x)$ and their compositae $F^\Delta(n,k)$ and $G^\Delta(n,k)$, we can find the composita $A^\Delta(n,k)$ of the generating function $A(x)$ for the following cases:

- addition of generating functions: $A(x) = F(x) + G(x)$;
- multiplication of generating functions: $A(x) = F(x) \cdot G(x)$;
- composition of generating functions: $A(x) = G(F(x))$;
- reciprocation of generating functions: $A(x) \cdot F(x) = 1$;
- compositional inversion of generating functions: $F(A(x)) = x$.

In this way, it is possible to obtain an explicit formula for the composita for various

It is also worth noting the results derived by M. Drmota [24] and aimed at obtaining an asymptotic expansion of the coefficients of the powers of generating functions.

However, all these concepts mainly consider generating functions in one variable, while there are many problems associated with generating functions in several variables (multivariate generating functions). Attempts to systematize the process of finding the coefficients of multivariate generating functions were made by Pemantle et al. [25], but they also investigated asymptotic methods for solving this problem. More on asymptotics derived from multivariate generating functions can be found in [26].

To solve this problem explicitly, we propose to generalize the concept of compositae to the case of generating functions in two variables (bivariate generating functions). The effectiveness of applying compositae is shown in obtaining explicit formulas for the coefficients of many ordinary generating functions that are related to special numbers and polynomials [27–34]. This research aims to improve and extend the original method.

The organization of this paper is as follows. Section 2 is devoted to a brief description of the proposed generalization of the concept of compositae. In Section 3, we introduce basic operations on compositae of bivariate generating functions: composition, addition, multiplication, reciprocation and compositional inversion. To confirm the effectiveness of using the proposed generalization of the concept of compositae, we present several examples of finding explicit formulas for coefficients of bivariate generating functions. The obtained results are shown in Section 4.

2. Composita of a Multivariate Generating Function

A multivariate generating function is the following formal power series:

$$F(x,y,\ldots,z) = \sum_{n \geq 0} \sum_{m \geq 0} \cdots \sum_{l \geq 0} f(n,m,\ldots,k) x^n y^m \cdots z^l.$$

By $ord(F)$, we denote the order of a formal power series $F(x,y,\ldots,z)$, which is defined as follows [35]:

$$ord(F) = \begin{cases} \min\{r = n+m+\ldots+l : f(n,m,\ldots,l) \neq 0\}, & \text{if } F(x,y,\ldots,z) \neq 0; \\ +\infty, & \text{if } F(x,y,\ldots,z) = 0. \end{cases}$$

For two formal power series $F(x,y,\ldots,z)$ and $G(x,y,\ldots,z)$ with $ord(F) > 0$ and $ord(G) > 0$, the order of $F(x,y,\ldots,z) \cdot G(x,y,\ldots,z)$ is

$$ord(F \cdot G) = ord(F) + ord(G). \tag{1}$$

For a formal power series $F(x,y,\ldots,z)$ with $ord(F) > 0$, the order of $F(x,y,\ldots,z)^k$, $k \in \mathbb{N}$, satisfies the inequality

$$ord(F^k) \geq k. \tag{2}$$

Next, we consider the coefficients of the kth power of a multivariate generating function

$$F(x,y,\ldots,z)^k = \sum_{n \geq 0} \sum_{m \geq 0} \cdots \sum_{l \geq 0} f(n,m,\ldots,l,k) x^n y^m \cdots z^l,$$

where $k \in \mathbb{N}_0$.

In general, to calculate the coefficients $f(n,m,\ldots,l,k)$, we can use the method based on the following formula:

$$f(n,m,\ldots,l,k) = \sum_{\eta_1+\eta_2+\ldots+\eta_k=n} \left(\sum_{\mu_1+\mu_2+\ldots+\mu_k=m} \left(\cdots \left(\sum_{\lambda_1+\lambda_2+\ldots+\lambda_k=l} \left(\prod_{i=1}^{k} f(\eta_i,\mu_i,\ldots,\lambda_i) \right) \right) \cdots \right) \right),$$

where $\eta_i, \mu_i, \ldots, \lambda_i \in \mathbb{N}_0$.

Definition 1. *The composita* $F^\Delta(n, m, \ldots, l, k)$ *of a multivariate generating function*

$$F(x, y, \ldots, z) = \sum_{n \geq 0} \sum_{m \geq 0} \cdots \sum_{l \geq 0} f(n, m, \ldots, k) x^n y^m \cdots z^l, \quad ord(F) \geq 1,$$

is a coefficients function of the kth power of the generating function $F(x, y, \ldots, z)$:

$$F(x, y, \ldots, z)^k = \sum_{n \geq 0} \sum_{m \geq 0} \cdots \sum_{l \geq 0} F^\Delta(n, m, \ldots, l, k) x^n y^m \cdots z^l.$$

In addition, we set the following condition: $F(x, y, \ldots, z)^0 = 1$.
Hence, the composita $F^\Delta(n, m, \ldots, l, k)$ for $k = 0$ is defined as follows:

$$F^\Delta(n, m, \ldots, l, 0) = \begin{cases} 1, & \text{if } n = m = \ldots = l = 0; \\ 0, & \text{otherwise.} \end{cases}$$

We can also write a recurrence for calculating compositae for $k > 0$

$$F^\Delta(n, m, \ldots, l, k) = \begin{cases} f(n, m, \ldots, l), & \text{if } k = 1; \\ \sum_{i=0}^{n} \sum_{j=0}^{m} \cdots \sum_{s=0}^{l} f(i, j, \ldots, s) F^\Delta(n-i, m-j, \ldots, l-s, k-1), & \text{if } k > 1, \end{cases}$$

that is based on using the convolution operation for

$$F(x, y, \ldots, z)^k = F(x, y, \ldots, z) F(x, y, \ldots, z)^{k-1}, \quad F(x, y, \ldots, z)^0 = 1.$$

3. Operations on Compositae of Bivariate Generating Functions

A bivariate generating function is the following formal power series:

$$F(x, y) = \sum_{n \geq 0} \sum_{m \geq 0} f(n, m) x^n y^m.$$

Using the concept of compositae, the kth power of the bivariate generating function $F(x, y)$, with $ord(F) \geq 1$, can be presented as follows:

$$F(x, y)^k = \sum_{n \geq 0} \sum_{m \geq 0} F^\Delta(n, m, k) x^n y^m.$$

Next, we introduce basic operations on compositae of bivariate generating functions: composition, addition, multiplication, reciprocation and compositional inversion. These operations allow obtaining explicit formulas for compositae and coefficients of bivariate generating functions.

3.1. Composition of Bivariate Generating Functions
Theorem 1. *Suppose that:*

$$H(x, y) = \sum_{n \geq 0} \sum_{m \geq 0} h(n, m) x^n y^m,$$

$$A(x, y)^k = \sum_{n \geq 0} \sum_{m \geq 0} A^\Delta(n, m, k) x^n y^m, \quad ord(A) \geq 1,$$

$$B(x, y)^k = \sum_{n \geq 0} \sum_{m \geq 0} B^\Delta(n, m, k) x^n y^m, \quad ord(B) \geq 1.$$

Then, the coefficients $g(n,m)$ of the composition of the bivariate generating functions

$$G(x,y) = H(A(x,y), B(x,y)) = \sum_{n\geq 0}\sum_{m\geq 0} g(n,m) x^n y^m$$

are equal to

$$g(n,m) = \sum_{k_a=0}^{n+m}\sum_{k_b=0}^{n+m-k_a} h(k_a, k_b) \sum_{i=0}^{n}\sum_{j=0}^{m} A^{\Delta}(i,j,k_a) B^{\Delta}(n-i, m-j, k_b). \quad (3)$$

Proof. Consider the given composition of bivariate generating functions

$$G(x,y) = H(A(x,y), B(x,y)) = \sum_{n\geq 0}\sum_{m\geq 0} h(n,m) A(x,y)^n B(x,y)^m.$$

Next, we represent the end part of this generating function as follows:

$$C(x,y) = A(x,y)^{k_a} B(x,y)^{k_b} = \sum_{n\geq 0}\sum_{m\geq 0} c(n,m,k_a,k_b) x^n y^m.$$

To obtain an explicit formula for the coefficients $c(n, m, k_a, k_b)$, we apply the convolution operation and get

$$c(n,m,k_a,k_b) = \sum_{i=0}^{n}\sum_{j=0}^{m} A^{\Delta}(i,j,k_a) B^{\Delta}(n-i, m-j, k_b). \quad (4)$$

Using Equation (1) and Inequality (2), we also have

$$\mathrm{ord}(A(x,y)^n B(x,y)^m) \geq n+m.$$

Then, taking into account the restriction for the indices of summation

$$k_a + k_b \leq n+m,$$

we can construct the following two summation schemes for obtaining the coefficients $g(n,m)$:

$$g(n,m) = \sum_{k_a=0}^{n+m}\sum_{k_b=0}^{n+m-k_a} h(k_a, k_b) c(n,m,k_a,k_b)$$

or

$$g(n,m) = \sum_{k_b=0}^{n+m}\sum_{k_a=0}^{n+m-k_b} h(k_a, k_b) c(n,m,k_a,k_b).$$

Combining the formula for $g(n,m)$ with Equation (4), we obtain the desired result presented in Equation (3). □

Table 1 presents the obtained results for special cases of using the results of Theorem 1 for a bivariate generating function $G(x,y)$ that is presented as the composition of bivariate and ordinary generating functions.

Next, we consider the process of finding coefficients for the kth power of a bivariate generating function that is obtained using the composition of bivariate generating functions. This result can be derived by generalizing the bivariate generating function $H(x,y)$ from Theorem 1 to the case of its kth power. The obtained result is presented in Theorem 2.

Table 1. Special cases of using the results of Theorem 1.

Composition	Coefficient
$G(x,y) = H(A(x,y), B(x,y))$	$g(n,m) = \sum_{k_a=0}^{n+m} \sum_{k_b=0}^{n+m-k_a} h(k_a, k_b) \sum_{i=0}^{n} \sum_{j=0}^{m} A^\Delta(i,j,k_a) B^\Delta(n-i, m-j, k_b)$
$G(x,y) = H(A(x,y), B(y))$	$g(n,m) = \sum_{k_a=0}^{n+m} \sum_{k_b=0}^{n+m-k_a} h(k_a, k_b) \sum_{j=0}^{m} A^\Delta(n,j,k_a) B^\Delta(m-j, k_b)$
$G(x,y) = H(A(y), B(x,y))$	$g(n,m) = \sum_{k_a=0}^{n+m} \sum_{k_b=0}^{n+m-k_a} h(k_a, k_b) \sum_{j=0}^{m} A^\Delta(j,k_a) B^\Delta(n, m-j, k_b)$
$G(x,y) = H(A(x,y), B(x))$	$g(n,m) = \sum_{k_a=0}^{n+m} \sum_{k_b=0}^{n+m-k_a} h(k_a, k_b) \sum_{i=0}^{n} A^\Delta(i,m,k_a) B^\Delta(n-i, k_b)$
$G(x,y) = H(A(x), B(x,y))$	$g(n,m) = \sum_{k_a=0}^{n+m} \sum_{k_b=0}^{n+m-k_a} h(k_a, k_b) \sum_{i=0}^{n} A^\Delta(i,k_a) B^\Delta(n-i, m, k_b)$
$G(x,y) = H(A(x,y), y)$	$g(n,m) = \sum_{k_a=0}^{n+m} \sum_{k_b=0}^{n+m-k_a} h(k_a, k_b) A^\Delta(n, m-k_b, k_a)$
$G(x,y) = H(y, B(x,y))$	$g(n,m) = \sum_{k_a=0}^{n+m} \sum_{k_b=0}^{n+m-k_a} h(k_a, k_b) B^\Delta(n, m-k_a, k_b)$
$G(x,y) = H(A(x,y), x)$	$g(n,m) = \sum_{k_a=0}^{n+m} \sum_{k_b=0}^{n+m-k_a} h(k_a, k_b) A^\Delta(n-k_b, m, k_a)$
$G(x,y) = H(x, B(x,y))$	$g(n,m) = \sum_{k_a=0}^{n+m} \sum_{k_b=0}^{n+m-k_a} h(k_a, k_b) B^\Delta(n-k_a, m, k_b)$
$G(x,y) = H(A(x), B(y))$	$g(n,m) = \sum_{k_a=0}^{n} \sum_{k_b=0}^{m} h(k_a, k_b) A^\Delta(n, k_a) B^\Delta(m, k_b)$
$G(x,y) = H(A(x), y)$	$g(n,m) = \sum_{k=0}^{n} h(k,m) A^\Delta(n,k)$
$G(x,y) = H(x, B(y))$	$g(n,m) = \sum_{k=0}^{m} h(n,k) B^\Delta(m,k)$
$G(x,y) = H(A(x,y))$	$g(n,m) = \sum_{k=0}^{n+m} h(k) A^\Delta(n,m,k)$

Theorem 2. *Suppose that:*

$$H(x,y)^k = \sum_{n \geq 0} \sum_{m \geq 0} h(n,m,k) x^n y^m,$$

$$A(x,y)^k = \sum_{n \geq 0} \sum_{m \geq 0} A^\Delta(n,m,k) x^n y^m, \quad ord(A) \geq 1,$$

$$B(x,y)^k = \sum_{n \geq 0} \sum_{m \geq 0} B^\Delta(n,m,k) x^n y^m, \quad ord(B) \geq 1.$$

Then, the coefficients $g(n,m,k)$ of the kth power of the composition of the bivariate generating functions

$$G(x,y)^k = H(A(x,y), B(x,y))^k = \sum_{n \geq 0} \sum_{m \geq 0} g(n,m,k) x^n y^m$$

are equal to

$$g(n,m,k) = \sum_{k_a=0}^{n+m} \sum_{k_b=0}^{n+m-k_a} h(k_a, k_b, k) \sum_{i=0}^{n} \sum_{j=0}^{m} A^\Delta(i,j,k_a) B^\Delta(n-i, m-j, k_b). \tag{5}$$

Proof. The proof of Theorem 2 is similar to the proof of Theorem 1. □

Corollary 1. *Suppose that:*

$$H(x,y)^k = \sum_{n \geq 0} \sum_{m \geq 0} H^\Delta(n,m,k) x^n y^m, \quad ord(H) \geq 1,$$

$$A(x,y)^k = \sum_{n\geq 0}\sum_{m\geq 0} A^\Delta(n,m,k)x^n y^m, \quad ord(A) \geq 1,$$

$$B(x,y)^k = \sum_{n\geq 0}\sum_{m\geq 0} B^\Delta(n,m,k)x^n y^m, \quad ord(B) \geq 1.$$

Then, the composita $G^\Delta(n,m,k)$ of the composition of the bivariate generating functions

$$G(x,y) = H(A(x,y), B(x,y)) = \sum_{n\geq 0}\sum_{m\geq 0} g(n,m)x^n y^m$$

is equal to

$$G^\Delta(n,m,k) = \sum_{k_a=0}^{n+m}\sum_{k_b=0}^{n+m-k_a} H^\Delta(k_a, k_b, k) \sum_{i=0}^{n}\sum_{j=0}^{m} A^\Delta(i, j, k_a) B^\Delta(n-i, m-j, k_b). \quad (6)$$

Corollary 1 can be applied for calculating the composita of a given bivariate generating function based on its decomposition into simpler functions. For example, it can be used for addition or multiplication of bivariate generating functions.

3.2. Addition of Bivariate Generating Functions

Theorem 3. *Suppose that:*

$$A(x,y)^k = \sum_{n\geq 0}\sum_{m\geq 0} A^\Delta(n,m,k)x^n y^m, \quad ord(A) \geq 1,$$

$$B(x,y)^k = \sum_{n\geq 0}\sum_{m\geq 0} B^\Delta(n,m,k)x^n y^m, \quad ord(B) \geq 1.$$

Then, the composita $G^\Delta(n,m,k)$ of the addition of the bivariate generating functions

$$G(x,y) = A(x,y) + B(x,y) = \sum_{n\geq 0}\sum_{m\geq 0} g(n,m)x^n y^m$$

is equal to

$$G^\Delta(n,m,k) = \sum_{k_a=0}^{n+m}\binom{k}{k_a}\sum_{i=0}^{n}\sum_{j=0}^{m} A^\Delta(i,j,k_a) B^\Delta(n-i, m-j, k-k_a). \quad (7)$$

Proof. Consider a bivariate generating function

$$H(x,y) = x + y$$

and its kth power, that is based on the binomial theorem,

$$H(x,y)^k = (x+y)^k = \sum_{n\geq 0}\sum_{m\geq 0} H^\Delta(n,m,k)x^n y^m = \sum_{n\geq 0}\sum_{m\geq 0} \binom{k}{n}\delta(m, k-n)x^n y^m,$$

where $\delta(i,j)$ is the Kronecker delta function:

$$\delta(i,j) = \begin{cases} 0, & \text{if } i \neq j; \\ 1, & \text{if } i = j. \end{cases}$$

Applying Equation (6) for the composition of generating functions

$$G(x,y) = A(x,y) + B(x,y) = H(A(x,y), B(x,y)),$$

we obtain

$$G^\Delta(n,m,k) = \sum_{k_a=0}^{n+m}\sum_{k_b=0}^{n+m-k_a} \binom{k}{k_a}\delta(k_b, k-k_a)\sum_{i=0}^{n}\sum_{j=0}^{m} A^\Delta(i,j,k_a)B^\Delta(n-i,m-j,k_b).$$

Using the properties of the Kronecker delta function, we get $k_b = k - k_a$.
Simplifying the formula for $G^\Delta(n,m,k)$, we obtain the desired result presented in Equation (7). □

3.3. Multiplication of Bivariate Generating Functions

Theorem 4. *Suppose that:*

$$A(x,y)^k = \sum_{n\geq 0}\sum_{m\geq 0} A^\Delta(n,m,k)x^n y^m, \quad \text{ord}(A) \geq 1,$$

$$B(x,y)^k = \sum_{n\geq 0}\sum_{m\geq 0} B^\Delta(n,m,k)x^n y^m, \quad \text{ord}(B) \geq 1.$$

Then, the composita $G^\Delta(n,m,k)$ of the addition of the bivariate generating functions

$$G(x,y) = A(x,y) \cdot B(x,y) = \sum_{n\geq 0}\sum_{m\geq 0} g(n,m)x^n y^m$$

is equal to

$$G^\Delta(n,m,k) = \sum_{i=0}^{n}\sum_{j=0}^{m} A^\Delta(i,j,k)B^\Delta(n-i,m-j,k). \tag{8}$$

Proof. Consider a bivariate generating function

$$H(x,y) = xy$$

and its kth power

$$H(x,y)^k = (xy)^k = \sum_{n\geq 0}\sum_{m\geq 0} H^\Delta(n,m,k)x^n y^m = \sum_{n\geq 0}\sum_{m\geq 0} \delta(n,k)\delta(m,k)x^n y^m.$$

Applying Equation (6) for the composition of generating functions

$$G(x,y) = A(x,y) \cdot B(x,y) = H(A(x,y), B(x,y)),$$

we obtain

$$G^\Delta(n,m,k) = \sum_{k_a=0}^{n+m}\sum_{k_b=0}^{n+m-k_a} \delta(k_a,k)\delta(k_b,k)\sum_{i=0}^{n}\sum_{j=0}^{m} A^\Delta(i,j,k_a)B^\Delta(n-i,m-j,k_b).$$

Using the properties of the Kronecker delta function, we get $k_a = k$, $k_b = k$.
Simplifying the formula for $G^\Delta(n,m,k)$, we obtain the desired result presented in Equation (8). □

3.4. Reciprocation of Bivariate Generating Functions

A reciprocal generating function $G(x,y)$ of a bivariate generating function

$$F(x,y) = \sum_{n\geq 0}\sum_{m\geq 0} f(n,m)x^n y^m$$

is a formal power series such that satisfies the condition

$$F(x,y) \cdot G(x,y) = 1.$$

Theorem 5. *Suppose that:*

$$F(x,y) = \sum_{n \geq 0} \sum_{m \geq 0} f(n,m) x^n y^m, \quad f(0,0) \neq 0, \quad F(x,y)^k = \sum_{n \geq 0} \sum_{m \geq 0} f(n,m,k) x^n y^m,$$

$$G(x,y) = \sum_{n \geq 0} \sum_{m \geq 0} g(n,m) x^n y^m, \quad g(0,0) \neq 0, \quad G(x,y)^k = \sum_{n \geq 0} \sum_{m \geq 0} g(n,m,k) x^n y^m,$$

$$F(x,y) \cdot G(x,y) = 1.$$

Then, the coefficients $g(n,m,k)$ are equal to

$$g(n,m,k) = \sum_{i=0}^{n+m} \binom{n+m+k}{i+k} \binom{i+k-1}{i} \frac{(-1)^i}{f(0,0)^{i+k}} f(n,m,i). \tag{9}$$

Proof. Consider the kth power of the generating function $G(x,y)$ as the following composition of generating functions:

$$G(x,y)^k = \left(\frac{1}{F(x,y)}\right)^k = \frac{1}{f(0,0)^k} \left(\frac{1}{1 + \left(\frac{F(x,y)}{f(0,0)} - 1\right)}\right)^k = \frac{1}{f(0,0)^k} H(A(x,y))^k,$$

where

$$H(x) = \frac{1}{1+x}, \quad H(x)^k = \sum_{n \geq 0} h(n,k) x^n,$$

$$A(x,y) = \frac{F(x,y)}{f(0,0)} - 1, \quad A(x,y)^k = \sum_{n \geq 0} \sum_{m \geq 0} A^\Delta(n,m,k) x^n y^m.$$

The coefficients $h(n,k)$ can be calculating by

$$h(n,k) = (-1)^n \binom{n+k-1}{n}.$$

Using the binomial theorem, the composita $A^\Delta(n,m,k)$ is equal to

$$A^\Delta(n,m,k) = \sum_{i=0}^{k} \binom{k}{i} \frac{f(n,m,i)}{f(0,0)^i} (-1)^{k-i}.$$

Applying Equation (5) for $G(x,y)$, we obtain

$$g(n,m,k) = \frac{1}{f(0,0)^k} \sum_{k_a=0}^{n+m} h(k_a,k) A^\Delta(n,m,k_a) = \sum_{k_a=0}^{n+m} \sum_{i=0}^{k_a} \binom{k_a+k-1}{k_a} \binom{k_a}{i} \frac{f(n,m,i)}{f(0,0)^{i+k}} (-1)^i.$$

Then, we change the order of summation and get

$$g(n,m,k) = \sum_{i=0}^{n+m} \sum_{k_a=0}^{n+m-i} \binom{k_a+i+k-1}{k_a+i} \binom{k_a+i}{i} \frac{f(n,m,i)}{f(0,0)^{i+k}} (-1)^i.$$

To remove the coefficient k_a from the right binomial coefficient, we transform the binomial coefficient and obtain

$$g(n,m,k) = \sum_{i=0}^{n+m} \sum_{k_a=0}^{n+m-i} \binom{k_a+i+k-1}{k_a} \binom{i+k-1}{i} \frac{f(n,m,i)}{f(0,0)^{i+k}} (-1)^i.$$

Next, we can simplify this formula by using the following identity (Identity (1.49) in [36]):

$$\sum_{k_a=0}^{n+m-i} \binom{k_a+i+k-1}{k_a} = \binom{n+m+k}{n+m-i}.$$

Thus, we obtain the desired result presented in Equation (9). □

3.5. Compositional Inversion of Bivariate Generating Functions

A compositional inverse $\overline{F}(x,y)$ of a bivariate generating function

$$F(x,y) = \sum_{n\geq 0}\sum_{m\geq 0} f(n,m)x^n y^m$$

with respect to the variable x is a formal power series such that satisfies the condition

$$F(\overline{F}(x,y),y) = x.$$

Theorem 6. *Suppose that:*

$$F(x,y) = \sum_{n\geq 0}\sum_{m\geq 0} f(n,m)x^n y^m, \quad f(0,0) = 0, \quad F(x,y)^k = \sum_{n\geq 0}\sum_{m\geq 0} F^\Delta(n,m,k)x^n y^m,$$

$$\overline{F}(x,y) = \sum_{n\geq 0}\sum_{m\geq 0} \overline{f}(n,m)x^n y^m, \quad \overline{F}(0,0) = 0, \quad \overline{F}(x,y)^k = \sum_{n\geq 0}\sum_{m\geq 0} \overline{F}^\Delta(n,m,k)x^n y^m,$$

$$F(\overline{F}(x,y),y) = x.$$

Then, the composita $\overline{F}^\Delta(n,m,k)$ is equal to

$$\overline{F}^\Delta(n,m,k) = \frac{k}{n}\sum_{i=0}^{n+m}\binom{2n+m-k}{i+n}\binom{i+n-1}{i}\frac{(-1)^i}{f(1,0)^{i+n}}F^\Delta(i+n-k,m,i). \quad (10)$$

Proof. Using the Lagrange inversion theorem [37] for the functional equation

$$\overline{F}(x,y) = xG(\overline{F}(x,y),y),$$

where

$$G(x,y) = \sum_{n\geq 0}\sum_{m\geq 0} g(n,m)x^n y^m, \quad g(0,0) \neq 0, \quad G(x,y)^k = \sum_{n\geq 0}\sum_{m\geq 0} g(n,m,k)x^n y^m,$$

we obtain

$$\overline{F}^\Delta(n,m,k) = \frac{k}{n}g(n-k,m,n). \quad (11)$$

In addition, we can represent this functional equation as follows:

$$x = \frac{\overline{F}(x,y)}{G(\overline{F}(x,y),y)} = F(\overline{F}(x,y),y),$$

$$F(x,y) = \frac{x}{G(x,y)}.$$

Applying Equation (9) for $G(x,y)$, we get the coefficients of its kth power

$$g(n,m,k) = \sum_{i=0}^{n+m}\binom{n+m+k}{i+k}\binom{i+k-1}{i}\frac{(-1)^i}{f(1,0)^{i+k}}F^\Delta(i+n,m,i). \quad (12)$$

Combining Equation (11) with Equation (12), we obtain the desired result presented

4. Application of Compositae for Obtaining Coefficients of Bivariate Generating Functions

Next, we present several examples of applying the obtained results for getting explicit formulas for coefficients of bivariate generating functions.

Example 1. *First, let consider the following simple composition of generating functions:*

$$G(x,y) = \sum_{n\geq 0}\sum_{m\geq 0} g(n,m)x^n y^m = H(A(x,y)) = H(x+y).$$

The composita of the generating function $A(x,y) = x+y$ is

$$A^\Delta(n,m,k) = \binom{k}{n}\delta(m,k-n).$$

Applying Theorem 1, we can obtain the coefficients $g(n,m)$ of the generating function $G(x,y)$

$$g(n,m) = \sum_{k=0}^{n+m} h(k)A^\Delta(n,m,k) = \sum_{k=0}^{n+m} h(k)\binom{k}{n}\delta(m,k-n) = h(n+m)\binom{n+m}{n}.$$

If we have the generating function

$$H(x) = \sum_{n\geq 0} h(n)x^n = \sum_{n\geq 0} x^n = \frac{1}{1-x},$$

then we get

$$G(x,y) = H(x+y) = \frac{1}{1-x-y},$$

$$g(n,m) = h(n+m)\binom{n+m}{n} = \binom{n+m}{n}.$$

If we have the generating function

$$H(x) = \sum_{n\geq 0} h(n)x^n = \sum_{n\geq 0} \frac{1}{n!}x^n = e^x,$$

then we get

$$G(x,y) = H(x+y) = e^{x+y},$$

$$g(n,m) = h(n+m)\binom{n+m}{n} = \frac{1}{(n+m)!}\binom{n+m}{n} = \frac{1}{n!m!}.$$

If we have the generating function

$$H(x) = \sum_{n>0} h(n)x^n = \sum_{n>0} \frac{(-1)^{n-1}}{n}x^n = \log(1+x),$$

then we get

$$G(x,y) = H(x+y) = \log(1+x+y),$$

$$g(n,m) = h(n+m)\binom{n+m}{n} = \frac{(-1)^{n+m-1}}{n+m}\binom{n+m}{n}, \quad g(0,0) = 0.$$

If we have the generating function of the Catalan numbers (the sequence A000108 in OEIS [38])

$$H(x) = \sum_{n\geq 0} C_n x^n = \sum_{n\geq 0} \frac{1}{n+1}\binom{2n}{n}x^n = \frac{1-\sqrt{1-4x}}{2x},$$

then we get

$$G(x,y) = H(x+y) = \frac{1 - \sqrt{1 - 4(x+y)}}{2(x+y)},$$

$$g(n,m) = h(n+m)\binom{n+m}{n} = C_{n+m}\binom{n+m}{n} = \frac{1}{n+m+1}\binom{2n+2m}{n+m}\binom{n+m}{n}.$$

Example 2. Let consider the generating function of the Eulerian numbers (the sequence A173018 in OEIS [38])

$$E(x,y) = \sum_{n \geq 0} \sum_{m \geq 0} \frac{E_{n,m}}{n!} x^n y^m = \frac{y-1}{y - e^{x(y-1)}}.$$

Consider this generating function $E(x,y)$ as the following composition of generating functions:

$$E(x,y) = \frac{y-1}{y - e^{x(y-1)}} = \frac{x(y-1)}{x(y-1) - x(e^{x(y-1)} - 1)} = \frac{1}{1 - x\frac{e^{x(y-1)}-1}{x(y-1)}} = H(A(x,y)),$$

where

$$H(x) = \sum_{n \geq 0} h(n) x^n = \sum_{n \geq 0} x^n = \frac{1}{1-x},$$

$$A(x,y) = x\frac{e^{x(y-1)} - 1}{x(y-1)} = B(x, C(x,y)),$$

$$B(x,y) = \frac{x}{y}(e^y - 1),$$

$$C(x,y) = x(y-1).$$

Using the identity for the Stirling numbers of the second kind

$$(e^x - 1)^k = \sum_{n \geq k} \left\{ {n \atop k} \right\} \frac{k!}{n!} x^n,$$

we get the composita of the generating function $B(x,y)$

$$B^\Delta(n, m, k) = \left\{ {m+k \atop k} \right\} \frac{k!}{(m+k)!} \delta(n, k).$$

Using the binomial theorem for

$$(xy - x)^k = \sum_{m \geq 0} \binom{k}{m}(xy)^m(-x)^{k-m} = \sum_{m \geq 0} \binom{k}{m} x^k y^m (-1)^{k-m},$$

we get the composita of the generating function $C(x,y)$

$$C^\Delta(n, m, k) = \binom{k}{m}(-1)^{k-m}\delta(n, k).$$

Combining the obtained results and applying Theorem 1 for the composition $B(x, C(x,y))$, we obtain the composita of the generating function $A(x,y)$

$$A^\Delta(n, m, k) = \sum_{k_a=0}^{n+m} \sum_{k_b=0}^{n+m-k_a} B^\Delta(k_a, k_b, k) C^\Delta(n - k_a, m, k_b)$$

$$= \sum_{k_a=0}^{n+m} \sum_{k_b=0}^{n+m-k_a} \left\{ {k_b+k \atop k} \right\} \frac{k!}{(k_b+k)!} \delta(k_a, k) \binom{k_b}{m}(-1)^{k_b-m}\delta(n - k_a, k_b).$$

Simplifying the formula for $A^\Delta(n,m,k)$, we obtain

$$A^\Delta(n,m,k) = \left\{{n \atop k}\right\}\binom{n-k}{m}\frac{k!}{n!}(-1)^{n-k-m}.$$

Applying Theorem 1 for the composition $H(A(x,y))$, we can obtain the following well-known explicit formula for the Eulerian numbers ([39], Equation (6.40)):

$$E_{n,m} = n!\sum_{k=0}^{n+m} h(k)A^\Delta(n,m,k) = \sum_{k=0}^{n}\left\{{n \atop k}\right\}\binom{n-k}{m}(-1)^{n-k-m}k!.$$

Example 3. *Let consider the generating function of the Euler–Catalan numbers [40] (the sequence A316773 in OEIS [38])*

$$EC(x,y) = \sum_{n\geq 0}\sum_{m\geq 0}\frac{EC_{n,m}}{n!}x^n y^m = \frac{y-1}{y-e^{C(x)(y-1)}},$$

where

$$C(x) = \frac{1-\sqrt{1-4x}}{2}$$

is the generating function of the Catalan numbers.

Consider this generating function $EC(x,y)$ as the following composition of generating functions:

$$EC(x,y) = E(C(x),y),$$

where $E(x,y)$ is the generating function of the Eulerian numbers.
The composita of the generating function $C(x)$ is (cf. [22])

$$C^\Delta(n,k) = \frac{k}{n}\binom{2n-k-1}{n-1}.$$

Applying Theorem 1 for the composition $EC(C(x),y)$, we can obtain the following explicit formula for the Euler-Catalan numbers:

$$EC_{n,m} = n!\sum_{k=0}^{n} E(k,m)C^\Delta(n,k) = n!\sum_{k=0}^{n}\frac{E_{k,m}}{k!}\frac{k}{n}\binom{2n-k-1}{n-1} = \sum_{k=m+1}^{n} E_{k,m}\frac{(2n-k-1)!}{(k-1)!(n-k)!}.$$

Example 4. *Let consider the generating function of the number triangle that forms the sequence A064189 in OEIS [38]*

$$G(x,y) = \sum_{n\geq 0}\sum_{m\geq 0} g(n,m)x^n y^m = \frac{2}{1-x-2xy+\sqrt{1-2x-3x^2}} = \frac{M(x)}{1-xyM(x)},$$

where

$$M(x) = \frac{1-x-\sqrt{1-2x-3x^2}}{2x^2}$$

is the generating function of the Motzkin numbers (the sequence A001006 in OEIS [38]).
The elements $g(n,m)$ of this number triangle define the number of lattice paths from $(0,0)$ to (n,m), staying weakly above the x-axis and consisting of steps $(1,1)$, $(1,-1)$ and $(1,0)$.
Consider this generating function $G(x,y)$ as the following composition of generating functions:

$$G(x,y) = \frac{H(x,y)}{xy} = \frac{B(M_{xy}(x,y))}{xy},$$

where

$$H(x,y) = \sum_{n>0}\sum_{m>0} h(n,m)x^n y^m = \frac{xyM(x)}{1-xyM(x)} = \frac{M_{xy}(x,y)}{1-M_{xy}(x,y)} = B(M_{xy}(x,y)),$$

$$B(x) = \sum_{n>0} b(n)x^n = \sum_{n>0} x^n = \frac{x}{1-x},$$

$$M_{xy}(x,y) = xyM(x).$$

The generating function $M(x)$ satisfies the following functional equation:

$$M(x) = 1 + xM(x) + x^2 M(x).$$

This functional equation can be transformed into

$$M_x(x) = xA(M_x(x)), \qquad (13)$$

where

$$A(x) = 1 + x + x^2,$$
$$M_x(x) = xM(x).$$

Using the binomial theorem for

$$(1+x+x^2)^k = \sum_{j=0}^{k}\binom{k}{j}(x+x^2)^j = \sum_{j=0}^{k}\binom{k}{j}x^j \sum_{n=0}^{j}\binom{j}{n}x^n = \sum_{n\geq 0}\sum_{j=0}^{k}\binom{k}{j}\binom{j}{n-j}x^n,$$

we get the coefficients of the kth power of the generating function $A(x)$

$$a(n,k) = \sum_{j=0}^{k}\binom{k}{j}\binom{j}{n-j}.$$

Using the Lagrange inversion theorem for (13), we obtain the composita of the generating function $M_x(x)$

$$M_x^\Delta(n,k) = \frac{k}{n}a(n-k,n).$$

Hence, the composita of the generating function $M_{xy}(x,y)$ is

$$M_{xy}^\Delta(n,m,k) = M_x^\Delta(n,k)\delta(m,k).$$

Applying Theorem 1 for the composition $B(M_{xy}(x,y))$, we obtain the coefficients $h(n,m)$ of the generating function $H(x,y)$

$$h(n,m) = \sum_{k=0}^{n+m} b(k)M_{xy}^\Delta(n,m,k) = \sum_{k=1}^{n+m} M_x^\Delta(n,k)\delta(m,k) = M_x^\Delta(n,m).$$

Finally, we get the coefficients $g(n,m)$ of the generating function $G(x,y)$

$$g(n,m) = h(n+1,m+1) = \frac{m+1}{n+1}\sum_{j=0}^{n-m}\binom{n+1}{j}\binom{j}{n-m-j}.$$

Example 5. *Let consider the generating function of the number triangle that forms the sequence A336524 in OEIS [38]*

$$G(x,y) = \sum\sum g(n,m)x^n y^m = \frac{1-\sqrt{1-4x-4xy}}{2x}.$$

The elements $g(n,m)$ of this number triangle define the number of unlabeled binary trees with n internal nodes and exactly m distinguished external nodes.

Consider this generating function $G(x,y)$ as the following composition of generating functions:

$$G(x,y) = \frac{H(x,y)}{x} = \frac{C(A(x,y))}{x},$$

where

$$H(x,y) = \sum_{n>0}\sum_{m\geq 0} h(n,m)x^n y^m = \frac{1-\sqrt{1-4x-4xy}}{2} = C(A(x,y)),$$

$$C(x) = \sum_{n>0} c(n)x^n = \sum_{n>0} C_{n-1} x^n = \frac{1-\sqrt{1-4x}}{2},$$

$$A(x,y) = x + xy.$$

Using the binomial theorem for

$$(x+xy)^k = \sum_{m\geq 0} \binom{k}{m} x^{k-m}(xy)^m = \sum_{m\geq 0} \binom{k}{m} x^k y^m,$$

we get the composita of the generating function $A(x,y)$

$$A^{\Delta}(n,m,k) = \binom{k}{m}\delta(n,k).$$

Applying Theorem 1 for the composition $C(A(x,y))$, we obtain the coefficients $h(n,m)$ of the generating function $H(x,y)$

$$h(n,m) = \sum_{k=0}^{n+m} c(k) A^{\Delta}(n,m,k) = \sum_{k=1}^{n+m} C_{k-1}\binom{k}{m}\delta(n,k) = C_{n-1}\binom{n}{m}.$$

Finally, we get the coefficients $g(n,m)$ of the generating function $G(x,y)$

$$g(n,m) = h(n+1,m) = C_n \binom{n+1}{m} = \frac{1}{n+1}\binom{2n}{n}\binom{n+1}{m}.$$

5. Conclusions

This paper is devoted to the study of methods for obtaining explicit formulas for the coefficients of generating functions. To solve this problem, we consider the methods that are based on using the powers of generating functions. We propose to generalize the concept of compositae to the case of generating functions in two variables and define basic operations on such compositae: composition, addition, multiplication, reciprocation and compositional inversion. These operations allow obtaining explicit formulas for compositae and coefficients of bivariate generating functions. In addition, we present several examples of applying the obtained results for getting explicit formulas for coefficients of bivariate generating functions.

The introduced mathematical apparatus can be used for solving different problems that are related to the theory of generating functions. For example, it contributes to obtaining new explicit formulas for polynomials and special numbers. In addition, it can be applied for obtaining explicit formulas for the cardinality functions of combinatorial sets. This task is relevant in combinatorics, discrete mathematics and computer science when it is necessary to develop combinatorial generation algorithms [41].

Author Contributions: Investigation, D.K., V.K. and Y.S.; methodology, D.K.; writing—original draft preparation, V.K. and Y.S.; and writing—review and editing, D.K. All authors have read and agreed to the published version of the manuscript.

Funding: The reported study was funded by RFBR, project number 20-31-70037.

Institutional Review Board Statement: Not applicable.

Informed Consent Statement: Not applicable.

Data Availability Statement: Not applicable.

Acknowledgments: The authors would like to thank the referees for their helpful comments and suggestions.

Conflicts of Interest: The authors declare no conflict of interest.

References

1. Riordan, J. *An Introduction to Combinatorial Analysis*; Princeton University Press: Princeton, NJ, USA, 1980.
2. Comtet, L. *Advanced Combinatorics*; D. Reidel Publishing Company: Dordrecht, The Netherlands, 1974.
3. Flajolet, P.; Sedgewick, R. *Analytic Combinatorics*; Cambridge University Press: Cambridge, UK, 2009.
4. Wilf, H.S. *Generatingfunctionology*; Academic Press: Cambridge, MA, USA, 1994.
5. Stanley, R. *Enumerative Combinatorics*, 2nd ed.; Cambridge University Press: New York, NY, USA, 2012.
6. Egorychev, G.P.; Zima, E.V. Integral representation and algorithms for closed form summation. In *Handbook of Algebra*; Hazewinkel, M., Ed.; Elsevier: Amsterdam, The Netherlands, 2008; Volume 5, pp. 459–529.
7. Lando, S.K. *Lectures on Generating Functions*; American Mathematical Society: Providence, RI, USA, 2003.
8. Boas, R.P.J.; Buck, R.C. *Polynomial Expansions of Analytic Functions*; Springer: Berlin/Heidelberg, Germany, 1958.
9. Roman, S. *The Umbral Calculus*; Academic Press: Cambridge, MA, USA, 1984.
10. Srivastava, H.M.; Manocha, H.L. *A Treatise on Generating Functions (Mathematics and Its Applications)*; Ellis Horwood: Hemel Hempstead, UK, 1984.
11. Ozden, H.; Simsek, Y.; Srivastava, H.M. A unified presentation of the generating functions of the generalized Bernoulli, Euler and Genocchi polynomials. *Comput. Math. Appl.* **2010**, *60*, 2779–2787. [CrossRef]
12. Srivastava, H.M. Some generalizations and basic (or q-) extensions of the Bernoulli, Euler and Genocchi polynomials. *Appl. Math. Inf. Sci.* **2011**, *5*, 390–444.
13. Simsek, Y.; Acikgoz, M. A new generating function of (q-) Bernstein-type polynomials and their interpolation function. *Abstr. Appl. Anal.* **2010**, *2010*, 769095. [CrossRef]
14. Simsek, Y. Complete sum of products of (h, q)-extension of Euler polynomials and numbers. *J. Differ. Equ. Appl.* **2010**, *16*, 1331–1348. [CrossRef]
15. Dere, R.; Simsek, Y. Applications of umbral algebra to some special polynomials. *Adv. Stud. Contemp. Math.* **2012**, *22*, 433–438.
16. Srivastava, H.M.; Todorov, P.G. An explicit formula for the generalized Bernoulli polynomials. *J. Math. Anal. Appl.* **1988**, *130*, 509–513. [CrossRef]
17. Liu, G.D.; Srivastava, H.M. Explicit formulas for the Norlund polynomials $B_n^{(x)}$ and $b_n^{(x)}$. *Comput. Math. Appl.* **2006**, *51*, 1377–1384. [CrossRef]
18. Boyadzhiev, K.N. Derivative polynomials for tanh, tan, sech and sec in explicit form. *Fibonacci Quart.* **2007**, *45*, 291–303.
19. Cenkci, M. An explicit formula for generalized potential polynomials and its applications. *Discret. Math.* **2009**, *309*, 1498–1510. [CrossRef]
20. Shapiro, L.W.; Getu, S.; Woan, W.J.; Woodson, L.C. The Riordan group. *Discret. Appl. Math.* **1991**, *34*, 229–239. [CrossRef]
21. Knuth, D.E. *The Art of Computer Programming, Volume 2: Seminumerical Algorithms*, 3rd ed.; Addison-Wesley Professional: Boston, MA, USA, 1997.
22. Kruchinin, D.V.; Kruchinin, V.V. A method for obtaining generating functions for central coefficients of triangles. *J. Integer Seq.* **2012**, *15*, 12.9.3.
23. Kruchinin, D.V.; Kruchinin, V.V. Application of a composition of generating functions for obtaining explicit formulas of polynomials. *J. Math. Anal. Appl.* **2013**, *404*, 161–171. [CrossRef]
24. Drmota, M. A bivariate asymptotic expansion of coefficients of powers of generating functions. *Eur. J. Combin.* **1994**, *15*, 139–152. [CrossRef]
25. Asymptotics of Multivariate Sequences. Available online: www.cs.auckland.ac.nz/~mcw/Research/mvGF/asymultseq/ (accessed on 1 February 2021).
26. Pemantle, R.; Wilson, M.C. Twenty combinatorial examples of asymptotics derived from multivariate generating functions. *SIAM Rev.* **2008**, *50*, 199–272. [CrossRef]
27. Kruchinin, D.V.; Kruchinin, V.V. A method for obtaining expressions for polynomials based on a composition of generating functions. In Proceedings of the International Conference of Numerical Analysis and Applied Mathematics (ICNAAM 2012), Kos, Greece, 19–25 September 2012; Volume 1479, pp. 383–386. [CrossRef]
28. Kruchinin, D.V.; Kruchinin, V.V. Explicit formulas for some generalized polynomials. *Appl. Math. Inf. Sci.* **2013**, *7*, 2083–2088. [CrossRef]

30. Dewi, I.P.; Utama, S.; Aminah, S. Deriving the explicit formula of Chebyshev polynomials of the third kind and the fourth kind. *AIP Conf. Proc.* **2017**, *2023*, 020202. [CrossRef]
31. Kruchinin, D.V. Explicit formulas for Korobov polynomials. *Proc. Jangjeon Math. Soc.* **2017**, *20*, 43–50. [CrossRef]
32. Cambazard, H. Fixed-parameter algorithms for rectilinear Steiner tree and rectilinear traveling salesman problem in the plane. *Eur. J. Oper. Res.* **2018**, *270*, 419–429. [CrossRef]
33. Banderier, C.; Krattenthaler, C.; Krinik, A.; Kruchinin, D.; Kruchinin, V.; Nguyen, D.; Wallner, M. Explicit formulas for enumeration of lattice paths: Basketball and the kernel method. In *Lattice Path Combinatorics and Applications*; Springer: Berlin/Heidelberg, Germany, 2019; pp. 78–118.
34. Simsek, Y. Peters type polynomials and numbers and their generating functions: Approach with *p*-adic integral method. *Math. Methods Appl. Sci.* **2019**, *42*, 7030–7046. [CrossRef]
35. Gan, X.X.; Bugajewski, D. A note on formal power series. *Comment. Math. Univ. Carolin.* **2010**, *51*, 595–604.
36. Gould, H.W. *Combinatorial Identities: A standardized Set of Tables Listing 500 Binomial Coefficient Summations*, 3rd ed.; Morgantown Printing: Morgantown, WV, USA, 1972.
37. Gessel, I.M. A combinatorial proof of the multivariable Lagrange inversion formula. *Combin. Theory Ser. A* **1987**, *45*, 178–195. [CrossRef]
38. Sloane, N.J.A. The On-Line Encyclopedia of Integer Sequences. Available online: www.oeis.org (accessed on 1 February 2021).
39. Graham, R.L.; Knuth, D.E.; Patashnik, O. *Concrete Mathematics*, 2nd ed.; Addison-Wesley: Boston, MA, USA, 1994.
40. Shablya, Y.; Kruchinin, D. Euler–Catalan's number triangle and its application. *Symmetry* **2020**, *12*, 600. [CrossRef]
41. Shablya, Y.; Kruchinin, D.; Kruchinin, V. Method for developing combinatorial generation algorithms based on AND/OR trees and its application. *Mathematics* **2020**, *8*, 962. [CrossRef]

Article

On Certain Properties and Applications of the Perturbed Meixner–Pollaczek Weight

Abey S. Kelil [1,*], Alta S. Jooste [2] and Appanah R. Appadu [1]

[1] Department of Mathematics and Applied Mathematics, Nelson Mandela University, Port Elizabeth 6019, South Africa; Rao.Appadu@mandela.ac.za or Rao.Appadu31@gmail.com
[2] Department of Mathematics and Applied Mathematics, University of Pretoria, Hatfield 0028, South Africa; alta.jooste@up.ac.za
[*] Correspondence: abey@aims.ac.za or abeysh2001@gmail.com

Abstract: This paper deals with monic orthogonal polynomials orthogonal with a perturbation of classical Meixner–Pollaczek measure. These polynomials, called Perturbed Meixner–Pollaczek polynomials, are described by their weight function emanating from an exponential deformation of the classical Meixner–Pollaczek measure. In this contribution, we investigate certain properties such as moments of finite order, some new recursive relations, concise formulations, differential-recurrence relations, integral representation and some properties of the zeros (quasi-orthogonality, monotonicity and convexity of the extreme zeros) of the corresponding perturbed polynomials. Some auxiliary results for Meixner–Pollaczek polynomials are revisited. Some applications such as Fisher's information, Toda-type relations associated with these polynomials, Gauss–Meixner–Pollaczek quadrature as well as their role in quantum oscillators are also reproduced.

Keywords: orthogonal polynomials; Meixner; perturbed Meixner–Pollaczek; moments; recurrence coefficients; difference equations; differential equations; zeros

1. Introduction

First, let us define some terminologies, notations and conventions that we will use throughout this paper. The set of complex numbers will be denoted by $\mathbb{C}$ and i will stand for the imaginary number ($i^2 = -1$); the set of positive integers will be denoted by $\mathbb{N}$, and $\mathbb{N}_0$ will denote the set of non-negative integers. All polynomials considered will be real-valued in one real variable, and $\mathbb{P}$ will stand for the set of all such polynomials. For each $n \in \mathbb{N}_0$, the subset of $\mathbb{P}$ of all polynomials of degree not greater than n will be denoted by $\mathbb{P}_n$. By a system of monic polynomials, we will mean a sequence $\{\Phi_n\}_{n=0}^{\infty}$ of polynomials satisfying $\Phi_n^{(n)} = n!$ for each $n \in \mathbb{N}_0$.

A sequence of real polynomials $\{\Phi_n\}_{n=0}^{\infty}$, where Φ_n is of exact degree n, is orthogonal with respect to a (positive) measure μ supported on an interval $[a, b]$, if the scalar product

$$\langle \Phi_m, \Phi_n \rangle = \int_a^b \Phi_m(x) \, \Phi_n(x) \, d\mu(x) = 0, \quad m \neq n.$$

If $\mu(x)$ is absolutely continuous, then it can be represented by a real weight function $w(x) > 0$ so that $d\mu(x) = w(x) \, dx$. If $\mu(x)$ is discrete with support in $\mathbb{N}_0$, then it can be represented by a discrete weight $w(x) \geq 0$ ($x \in \mathbb{N}_0$), and the scalar product given by

$$\langle \Phi_m, \Phi_n \rangle = \sum_{x=0}^{\infty} \Phi_m(x) \, \Phi_n(x) \, w(x).$$

The orthogonal polynomial families under consideration in this paper are the follow-

- Meixner polynomials ([1], Section 9.10)

$$M_n(x;\beta,c) = {}_2F_1\left(\begin{array}{c}-n,-x\\ \beta\end{array}\Big|1-\frac{1}{c}\right), \qquad (1)$$

are orthogonal with respect to the discrete weight $\rho(x) = \frac{c^x(\beta)_x}{x!}$ on $(0,\infty)$, for $0 < c < 1$ and $\beta > 0$, with $\beta \neq -1, -2, \ldots, -n+1$. Here, ${}_2F_1$ is the hypergeometric function defined by

$${}_2F_1\left(\begin{array}{c}p,q\\ r\end{array}\Big|s\right) = \sum_{k=0}^{\infty}\frac{(p)_k(q)_k}{(r)_k}\frac{s^k}{k!}, \qquad (2)$$

where the Pochhammer symbol, or rising factorial, $(z)_n$, takes the form

$$(z)_n := (z)(z+1)\cdots(z+n-1) = \prod_{i=1}^{n}(z+i-1). \qquad (3)$$

- Monic Meixner polynomials ([1], Section 9.10) are given by

$$\mathcal{M}_n(x;\beta,c) = (\beta)_n\left(\frac{c}{c-1}\right)^n {}_2F_1\left(\begin{array}{c}-n,-x\\ \beta\end{array}\Big|1-\frac{1}{c}\right) = (\beta)_n\left(\frac{c}{c-1}\right)^n M_n(x;\beta,c). \qquad (4)$$

- Meixner–Pollaczek polynomials ([1], Section 9.7)

$$p_n^{(\lambda)}(x;\phi) = \frac{(2\lambda)_n}{n!}e^{in\phi}\left(\frac{e^{2i\phi}}{e^{2i\phi}-1}\right)^n {}_2F_1\left(\begin{array}{c}-n,\lambda+ix\\ 2\lambda\end{array}\Big|1-\frac{1}{e^{2i\phi}}\right), \qquad (5)$$

are orthogonal with respect to the continuous weight

$$w(x;\phi) = |\Gamma(\lambda+ix)|^2 e^{(2\phi-\pi)x}, \qquad (6)$$

on the interval $(-\infty,\infty)$, for $n \in \mathbb{N}$, $\lambda > 0$ and $0 < \phi < \pi$. Note that the complex Gamma function in Equation (6) takes the form [2]

$$\left|\Gamma(\lambda+ix)\right|^2 = \Gamma(\lambda+ix)\,\Gamma(\lambda-ix).$$

- Monic Meixner–Pollaczek polynomials ([1], Section 9.7) are given by

$$P_n^{(\lambda)}(x;\phi) = i^n(2\lambda)_n\left(\frac{e^{2i\phi}}{e^{2i\phi}-1}\right)^n {}_2F_1\left(\begin{array}{c}-n,\lambda+ix\\ 2\lambda\end{array}\Big|1-\frac{1}{e^{2i\phi}}\right) = \frac{n!\,i^n}{e^{in\phi}}p_n^{(\lambda)}(x;\phi). \qquad (7)$$

For some properties of Meixner–Pollaczek polynomials including asymptotics, we refer to [3–9].

We recall the following essential facts.

Definition 1 ([8]). *Let $\{\eta_n\}_{n=0}^{\infty}$ be a sequence of complex numbers and let $\mathcal{L}$ be a complex valued function on the linear space of all polynomials by*

$$\begin{cases}\mathcal{L}[x^n] = \eta_n, & n \in \mathbb{N}_0, \\ \mathcal{L}[\alpha f_1(x) + \beta f_2(x)] = \mathcal{L}[\alpha f_1(x)] + \mathcal{L}[\beta f_2(x)],\end{cases}$$

for $\alpha, \beta \in \mathbb{C}$ and $f_i(x)$ ($i = 1, 2$). Then $\mathscr{L}$ is said to be the moment functional determined by the moments η_n of order n.

Let $\mathcal{P}(x;t)$ denote $R(t)[x]$, the linear space of all polynomials with rational function (in t) coefficients in one variable x. We call such polynomials, parameterized polynomials. We extend the classical orthogonality results in [3,8,10] to parameterized polynomials. We denote the linear subspace of degree m parameterized polynomials by $\mathcal{P}_m[t]$. The following is an extension of ([8], Theorem 2.1).

Lemma 1. *Consider a moment functional $\mathscr{L}$ and a parameterized polynomial sequence $\{\Psi_n(x;t)\}_{n=0}^{\infty}$. Then the following are equivalent (cf. [8], Theorem 2.1):*

(i) $\{\Psi_n(x;t)\}_{n=0}^{\infty}$ *is an orthogonal polynomial sequence with respect to $\mathscr{L}$,*

(ii) $\mathscr{L}[\pi(x;t)\,\Psi_n(x;t)] = 0$ *for every polynomial $\pi(x;t)$ of degree $m < n$; while $\mathscr{L}[\pi(x;t)\,\Psi_n(x;t)] \neq 0$ if $m = n$,*

(iii) $\mathscr{L}[x^m\,\Psi_n(x;t)] = \zeta_n(t)\,\delta_{m,n}$ *where $\zeta_n(t) \neq 0$, for $0 \leq m \leq n$.*

In [11], Meixner–Pollaczek polynomials are used to explore thermodynamic susceptibilities in the thermodynamic relations of Hermitian Ensembles. One can apply an exponential modification of the measure μ and to investigate orthogonal polynomials for the measure $d\mu_t(x) = e^{-xt}\,d\mu(x)$, whenever all the moments of this modified measure exist, and this leads to a new class of semi-classical (non-classical) orthogonal polynomials with respect to the modified measure.

Definition 2. *Perturbed Meixner–Pollaczek polynomials $\{Q_n^{(\lambda,\varphi)}(x;t)\}_{n=0}^{\infty}$ are monic real polynomials which are orthogonal with respect to the weight function*

$$w^{(\lambda,\varphi)}(x;t) := \frac{1}{2\pi} e^{(2\varphi-\pi)x} |\Gamma(\lambda + ix)|^2 e^{-axt}, \quad x \in \mathbb{R}, \tag{8}$$

with parameters $\lambda > 0$, $a > 0$ and $0 \leq t < \frac{2\varphi}{a}$.

Chen and Ismail [11] also discussed Toda lattice equations in the context of Coulomb fluid relations. Perturbed Meixner–Pollaczek polynomials have some applications as shown in ([11], pp. 12–13). In the context of Physics literature, the parameter φ in Equation (8) is the phase of an oscillation, t is time and a can be perceived as a positive angular frequency (in Hertz) (angular velocity or angular speed) of a wave, an oscillation (in cycle per second or 2π rad per second) or a field (electromagnetic). For example, $a > 0$ in the mathematical model of (nonlinear) tornado system as the wave speed of frequency of tornadoes is so huge.

The objective of this paper is to unravel some properties of monic orthogonal polynomials with respect to the perturbed Meixner–Pollaczek measure (8) and to explore some of their practical applications.

The structure of the paper is as follows. In Section 1, certain properties and auxiliary results of Meixner–Pollaczek polynomials are given. This section also introduces perturbed Meixner–Pollaczek polynomials with some properties. Section 2 gives the relation between Meixner–Pollaczek and Perturbed Meixner–Pollaczek polynomials. In Section 3, we investigate some results of perturbed Meixner–Pollaczek polynomials with proofs. Certain properties of these polynomials such as orthogonality, concise formulation, new recursive relations and some properties of the zeros (convexity and monotonicity of the extreme zeros) are discussed. Section 4 provides some practical applications; in particular, the applicability of the monic perturbed Meixner-Pollaczek polynomials in the study of Toda lattices in Random Matrix theory, Fisher information, Gaussian quadrature using Meixner-Pollaczek weight and solution to a quantum oscillator in quantum physics [12]. Section 5 ends with

1.1. Some Auxiliary Results for the Meixner and Meixner–Pollaczek Weight

In this Subsection, we revisit some properties of Meixner and Meixner–Pollaczek polynomials. The following proposition gives some properties of Meixner polynomials.

Proposition 1. *For Meixner polynomials, we have*

(i) *Orthogonality:*

$$\langle M_m, M_n \rangle := \sum_{x=0}^{\infty} \frac{(\beta)_x}{x!} c^x M_m(x;\beta,c) M_n(x;\beta,c) = \frac{c^{-n} n!}{(\beta)_n (1-c)^\beta} \delta_{m,n}, \quad m,n \in \mathbb{N}_0;$$

(ii) *Forward shift operator identity:*

$$\Delta M_n(x;\beta,c) := M_n(x+1;\beta,c) - M_n(x;\beta,c) = \frac{n}{\beta} \frac{c-1}{c} M_{n-1}(x;\beta+1,c);$$

(iii) *Three-term recursion relation:*

$$(n+\beta) M_n(x;\beta+1,c) = \beta M_n(x;\beta,c) + n M_{n-1}(x;\beta+1,c);$$

(iv) *Expansion formula:*

$$M_n(x;\beta+1,c) = \frac{n!}{(\beta+1)_n} \sum_{k=0}^{n} \frac{(\beta)_k}{k!} M_k(x;\beta,c), \quad n \in \mathbb{N}_0. \tag{9}$$

Proof.
- For the proof of (i) and (ii), we refer to ([1], (1.9.2), (1.9.6)).
- Property (iii) follows, by considering $z = 1 - \frac{1}{c}$, from the formulae for $M_n(x;\beta+1,c)$ and $M_n(x;\beta,c)$:

$$M_n(x;\beta+1,c) = 1 + \sum_{k=1}^{n} \binom{n}{k} \frac{x(x-1)\cdots(x-k+1)}{(\beta+1)(\beta+2)\cdots(\beta+k)} z^k \tag{10}$$

$$M_n(x;\beta,c) = 1 + \sum_{k=1}^{n} \binom{n}{k} \frac{x(x-1)\cdots(x-k+1)}{\beta(\beta+1)\cdots(\beta+k-1)} z^k \tag{11}$$

If we take β multiplied by Equation (11) and then subtract it from Equation (10) multiplied by $n+\beta$, the required result immediately follows.

- For the proof of property (iv), we use mathematical induction on n. One can see easily that Equation (9) holds for $n = 0$. We assume it holds true for some $n \in \mathbb{N}_0$. By applying induction hypothesis and Equation (9), we have

$$M_{n+1}(x;\beta+1,c) = \frac{\beta}{n+1+\beta} M_{n+1}(x;\beta,c) + \frac{n+1}{n+1+\beta} M_n(x;\beta+1,c)$$

$$= \frac{\beta}{n+1+\beta} M_{n+1}(x;\beta,c) + \frac{(n+1)!}{(\beta+1)_{n+1}} \sum_{k=0}^{n} \frac{(\beta)_k}{k!} M_k(x;\beta,c)$$

$$= \frac{(n+1)!}{(\beta+1)_{n+1}} \sum_{k=0}^{n+1} \frac{(\beta)_k}{k!} M_k(x;\beta,c).$$

This completes the inductive result.
□

We note from Equation (4) that

$$P_n^{(\lambda)}(x;\phi) = i^n M_n(-\lambda - ix; 2\lambda, e^{2i\phi}), \tag{12}$$

and Meixner polynomials and Meixner–Pollaczek polynomials are the same polynomials, with a discrete variable in the first case and a continuous variable in the second (cf. [13]). Monic Meixner polynomials satisfy the three-term recurrence relation

$$\mathcal{M}_n(x;\beta,c) = \left(x + \frac{c(\beta+n-1)+n-1}{c-1}\right)\mathcal{M}_{n-1}(x;\beta,c) - \frac{c(n-1)(\beta+n-2)}{(c-1)^2}\mathcal{M}_{n-2}(x;\beta,c)$$

and when we substitute x with $-\lambda - ix$, β with 2λ and c with $e^{2i\phi}$, multiply by i^n and apply Equation (12), we obtain the three-term recurrence relation for the Meixner–Pollaczek polynomials

$$P_n^{(\lambda)}(x;\phi) = \left(x + \alpha_n^{(\lambda,\phi)}\right) P_{n-1}^{(\lambda)}(x;\phi) - C_n P_{n-2}^{(\lambda)}(x;\phi). \tag{13}$$

where

$$\alpha_n^{(\lambda,\phi)} := \frac{\lambda+n-1}{\tan\phi}; \quad C_n := C_n^{(\lambda,\phi)} = \frac{(n-1)(2\lambda+n-2)}{4\sin^2\phi}, \tag{14}$$

with $P_{-1}^\lambda(x) = 0$, $P_0^{(\lambda)}(x) = 1$ and $\alpha_n^{(\lambda,\frac{\pi}{2})} = \lim_{\phi\to\frac{\pi}{2}} \alpha_n^{(\lambda,\phi)} = 0$. We note that the coefficient of $P_{n-2}^{(\lambda)}(x;\phi)$, behaves like $O(n^2)$ as $n \to \infty$ and using Carleman's condition [8], the uniqueness of the orthogonality measure holds ([1], Section 9.7).

Let's recall the following result [14] (see also [6]).

Proposition 2 ([14]). *For $\lambda > 0$, the moments for Meixner–Pollaczek measure are finite; i.e.,*

$$\int_\mathbb{R} x^n\, e^{(2\phi-\pi)x} |\Gamma(\lambda+ix)|^2 dx < \infty.$$

Proof. The finiteness of the moments follow from [14]

$$\int_{-\infty}^\infty e^{(2\phi-\pi)x} |\Gamma(\lambda+ix)|^2 dx = \frac{\pi\Gamma(2\lambda)}{(2\sin\phi)^{2\lambda}}, \tag{15}$$

and by differentiating Equation (15) n-times with respect to ϕ ([15], Lemma 1); i.e.,

$$\int_\mathbb{R} x^n\, e^{(2\phi-\pi)x} |\Gamma(\lambda+ix)|^2 dx = 2^{-n}\, \pi\, \Gamma(2\lambda)\, \frac{d^n}{d\phi^n}(2\sin\phi)^{-2\lambda}.$$

□

We now consider some results on quasi-orthogonality and interlacing of the zeros of the Meixner–Pollaczek polynomials.

Definition 3. *A polynomial Φ_n of exact degree $n \geq r$, is quasi-orthogonal of order r on $[a,b]$ with respect to a weight function $w(x) > 0$, if (cf. ([16], p. 159))*

$$\int_a^b x^j \Phi_n(x) w(x) dx \begin{cases} = 0, & \text{for } j = 0, 1, \ldots, n-r-1, \\ \neq 0, & \text{for } j = n-r. \end{cases}$$

For a more general definition of quasi-orthogonality, we refer to [8].

Since the Meixner-Pollaczek polynomials are orthogonal on the real line, zeros departing from the interval of orthogonality will do so in complex conjugate pairs. (This fact is later checked with numerical experiments of the zeros of these polynomials). The quasi-orthogonality of the monic Meixner-Pollaczek polynomials is therefore of even order, as detailed in the next result ([17], Theorem 3.3).

Theorem 1. *Let $n \in \mathbb{N}$, $k \in \{1, 2, \ldots, \lfloor\frac{n}{2}\rfloor\}$ and $0 < \phi < \pi$. For $0 < \lambda < 1$, the sequence*

$e^{(2\phi-\pi)x}|\Gamma(\lambda+ix)|^2$ on $(-\infty,\infty)$ and the polynomials have at least $n-2k$ real zeros on the real line.

By a change in the variable λ, the result in Theorem 1 can be rephrased by stating that $P_n^{(\lambda)}(x;\phi)$, with $-k<\lambda<-k+1$, is quasi-orthogonal of order $2k$ with respect to $e^{(2\phi-\pi)x}|\Gamma(\lambda+k+ix)|^2$ on the interval $(-\infty,\infty)$.

We can say the following about the interlacing of the zeros of polynomials $P_n^{(\lambda-1)}$ and $P_{n-1}^{(\lambda)}$, $\lambda>0$.

Lemma 2. Let $n \in \mathbb{N}$, $\lambda > 0$ and $0 < \phi < \pi$.

(a) If $\lambda > 1$, the n zeros of $P_n^{(\lambda-1)}(x;\phi)$ interlace with the $(n-1)$ zeros of $P_{n-1}^{(\lambda)}(x;\phi)$.

(b) If $0 < \lambda < 1$, then $(n-2)$ zeros of the order two quasi-orthogonal polynomial $P_n^{(\lambda-1)}(x;\phi)$ interlace with the $(n-1)$ zeros of $P_{n-1}^{(\lambda)}(x;\phi)$.

Proof. The polynomial $P_n^{(\lambda-1)}(x;\phi)$ can be expressed as follows ([17], Equation (2).2):

$$P_n^{(\lambda-1)}(x;\phi) = P_n^{(\lambda)}(x;\phi) - \frac{n}{\tan\phi} P_{n-1}^{(\lambda)}(x;\phi) + b_n P_{n-2}^{(\lambda)}(x;\phi) \tag{16}$$

with $b_n = \frac{n(n-1)}{4\sin^2\phi}$.

(a) Let $\lambda > 1$. Then the polynomial $P_n^{(\lambda-1)}(x;\phi)$ is part of an orthogonal sequence and all its zeros are real. Furthermore, $b_n < C_n$, where C_n, given in (14), is obtained from the three-term recurrence relation satisfied by the Meixner–Pollaczek polynomials and the result follows from (16) and ([18], Theorem 15 (i)).

(b) Let $0 < \lambda < 1$. From Theorem 1 we see that at least $(n-2)$ zeros of $P_n^{(\lambda-1)}(x;\phi)$ are real. Furthermore, $b_n > C_n$ when $0 < \lambda < 1$, and the result follows from (16) and ([18], Theorem 15 (i)).

□

For a detailed discussion on the quasi-orthogonality and location of the zeros of the Meixner polynomials, we refer the reader to [19].

1.1.1. Some Numerical Experiment on the Zeros of $P_n^{(\lambda)}(x;\delta)$, $\delta \in \mathbb{R}$

We now validate the above results related to the zeros of Meixner–Pollaczek polynomials by considering pictorial representations of the first few polynomials. Let $\delta = \cot\phi \in \mathbb{R}$ and $\phi \in (0,\pi)$, the first few polynomials $P_n^{(\lambda)}(x;\delta)$ are obtained from Equation (13) using symbolic packages (Maple) as follows.

$P_0^{(\lambda)}(x;\delta) = 1;$

$P_1^{(\lambda)}(x;\delta) = x + \delta\lambda;$

$P_2^{(\lambda)}(x;\delta) = x^2 + (\delta\lambda + \lambda + 1)x - 2\delta^2\lambda + \delta\lambda^2 + \delta\lambda - 2\lambda;$

$P_3^{(\lambda)}(x;\delta) = x^3 + (\delta\lambda + 2\lambda + 3)x^2 + \left(-6\delta^2\lambda + 2\delta\lambda^2 - 2\delta^2 + 3\delta\lambda + \lambda^2 - 3\lambda\right)x$
$\qquad - 4\delta^3\lambda^2 - 2\delta^3\lambda - 2\delta^2\lambda^2 + \delta\lambda^3 - 4\delta^2\lambda - \delta\lambda^2 - 2\lambda^2 - 4\lambda.$

Let's consider the following cases:

Case I: When $\phi = \frac{\pi}{6}$, ($\delta = \cot(\frac{\pi}{6}) = \sqrt{3} \approx 1.73$) and $\lambda = 0.55$.

The first few Meixner–Pollaczek polynomials in this case are given by

$P_1^{(0.55)}(x;\sqrt{3}) = x + 0.95262,$

$P_2^{(0.55)}(x;\sqrt{3}) = x^2 + 2.502627944\,x - 2.923426687,$

$P_3^{(0.55)}(x;\sqrt{3}) = x^3 + 5.052627944\,x^2 - 13.34172543\,x,$

$P_4^{(0.55)}(x;\sqrt{3}) = x^4 + 8.602627944\,x^3 - 32.60489624\,x^2 - 163.9197723\,x + 25.47242210,$

$P_5^{(0.55)}(x;\sqrt{3}) = x^5 + 13.15262794\,x^4 - 59.06293911\,x^3 - 643.7244434\,x^2 + 154.8546466\,x + 1654.802543,$

and their corresponding real zeros are tabulated as follows.

Table 1 and Figure 1 show that the zeros of $\{P_n^{(0.55)}(x;\sqrt{3})\}_{n=1}^{5}$ are real and simple, which confirms the classical result for $\phi \in (0, \pi)$ and $\lambda > 0$ [6].

Table 1. Real zeros for $P_n^{(\lambda)}(x;\delta)$ for $\lambda = 0.55$ and $\delta = \sqrt{3}$.

$P_n^{(0.55)}(x;\sqrt{3})$	Corresponding (Real) Zeros
$P_1^{(0.55)}(x;\sqrt{3})$	-0.95262
$P_2^{(0.55)}(x;\sqrt{3})$	$[-3.370090351,\ 0.8674624068]$
$P_3^{(0.55)}(x;\sqrt{3})$	$[-6.5436518550,\ -1.2893767698,\ 2.7804006808]$
$P_4^{(0.55)}(x;\sqrt{3})$	$[-10.1996365410,\ -3.40704030,\ 0.1510418707,\ 4.853007027]$
$P_5^{(0.55)}(x;\sqrt{3})$	$[-14.088331505,\ -6.1197704981,\ -1.6483271898,\ 1.650996725,\ 7.052804527]$

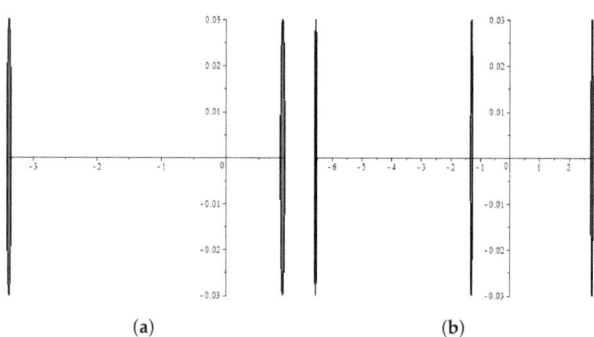

(a)   (b)

Figure 1. Plots for the real zeros of $P_n^{(\lambda)}(x;\delta)$ (with $\lambda = 0.55$, and $\delta = \sqrt{3}$) for $n = 2, 3$. (a) Plots for the (real) zeros of $P_2^{(0.55)}(x;\sqrt{3})$. (b) Plots for the (real) zeros of $P_3^{(0.55)}(x;\sqrt{3})$.

Case II: When $\phi = \frac{\pi}{8} \in [0, \frac{\pi}{4}]$, ($\delta = \cot(\frac{\pi}{8}) = 1 + \sqrt{2} \approx 2.41$) and $\lambda = -2.75$.

For $\lambda < 0$ and $\delta > 0$, we see that real orthogonality fails as complex zeros appear in conjugate pairs for the first few polynomials. For extended orthogonality, see [20] for more details. The first few monic polynomials for case II are given by

$P_1^{(0.55)}(x;2.41) = x - 6.6275,$

$P_2^{(-2.75)}(x;2.41) = x^2 - 8.389087296\,x + 49.17475195,$

$P_3^{(-2.75)}(x;2.41) = x^3 - 9.139087296\,x^2 + 116.9224115\,x,$

and their corresponding zeros with plots in the complex plane are given as follows.

Figure 2 demonstrates the pictorial representation of the complex zeros of $P_n^{(-2.75)}(x;2.41)$ for $n = 2, 3$, whereas Table 2 shows that the zeros of the polynomials $\{P_n^{(-2.75)}(x;2.41)\}_{n=1}^{4}$ exhibit one real and remaining complex zeros in conjugate pairs except $P_1^{(-2.75)}(x;2.41)$. This may likely suggest that for $\lambda < 0$ and $\delta > 0$, complex zeros appear in conjugate pairs for $n > 1$.

Table 2. The zeros for $P_n^{(\lambda)}(x;\delta)$ when $\lambda = -2.75$ and $\delta = 2.41$.

$P_n^{(-2.75)}(x;2.41)$	Corresponding (Real/Complex) Zeros
$P_1^{(-2.75)}(x;2.41)$	6.6275
$P_2^{(-2.75)}(x;2.41)$	[4.194543648 − 5.6196579551, 4.194543648 + 5.6196579551]
$P_3^{(-2.75)}(x;2.41)$	[2.253498955 − 9.5376798421, 2.2534989556 + 9.5376798424I, 4.6320893848]
$P_4^{(-2.75)}(x;2.41)$	[1.188253595 − 12.0969643912I, 1.1882535946 + 12.0969643911, 3.2562900534 − 3.5365254217I, 3.25629005341 + 3.5365254217I]

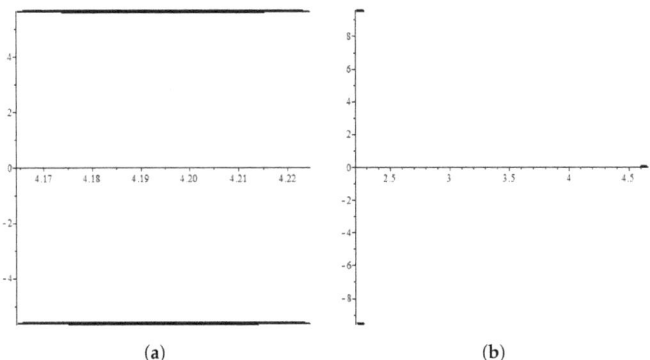

Figure 2. Plots for the complex zeros of $P_n^{(\lambda)}(x;\delta)$ (with $\lambda = -2.75$ and $\delta \approx 2.41$) for $n = 2, 3$. (a) Plots for the complex zeros of $P_2^{(-2.75)}(x;2.41)$. (b) Plots for the complex zeros of $P_3^{(-2.75)}(x;2.41)$.

Case III: When $\phi = -\frac{\pi}{3} \in [-\frac{\pi}{2}, 0]$, $(\delta = \cot(-\frac{\pi}{3}) = 0.577)$, $\lambda = -3.67$.

The first few polynomials in this case are

$P_1^{(-3.67)}(x; -0.577) = x + 3.8412,$

$P_2^{(-3.67)}(x; -0.577) = x^2 - 0.551124512\, x + 4.129269119,$

$P_3^{(-3.67)}(x; -0.577) = x^3 - 2.221124512\, x^2 + 21.95631373\, x + 28.92724218,$

$P_4^{(-3.67)}(x; -0.577) = x^4 - 2.891124512\, x^3 + 44.80446716\, x^2 + 2.44449240\, x + 68.81993616,$

and their corresponding zeros are given as follows.

Table 3 shows that all the zeros of $\{P_n^{(-3.67)}(x; -0.577)\}_{n=1}^{4}$ are complex in conjugate pairs, and plots for the complex zeros of $P_n^{(-3.67)}(x; -0.577)$ for $n = 2, 3$ are given below in Figure 3.

Table 3. Complex zeros for $P_n^{(\lambda)}(x;\delta)$ for $\lambda = -3.67$ and $\delta = -0.577$.

$P_n^{(-3.67)}(x;-0.577)$	Corresponding Zeros
$P_2^{(-3.67)}(x;-0.577)$	[4.194543648 − 5.6196579551, 4.194543648 + 5.6196579551]
$P_3^{(-3.67)}(x;-0.577)$	[2.25349895559073 − 9.537679842360431, 2.25349895559073 + 9.537679842360431, 4.63208938481853]
$P_4^{(-3.67)}(x;-0.577)$	[1.188253590 − 12.096964401, 1.1882536 + 12.0969644I, 3.256290053 − 3.536525421, 3.25629005 + 3.5365254I]

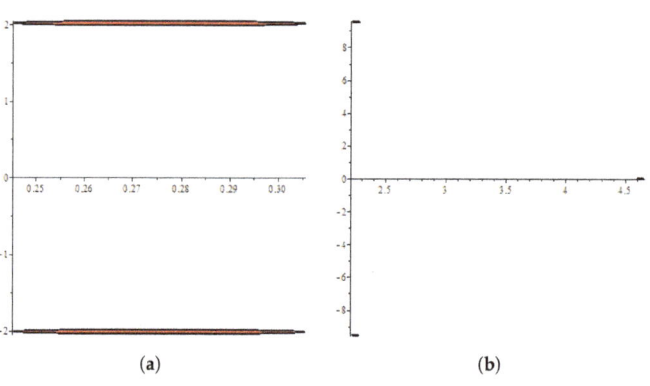

(a) (b)

Figure 3. Plots for complex zeros of $P_n^{(\lambda)}(x;\delta)$ (with $\lambda = -3.67$ and $\delta \approx -0.577$) for $n = 2, 3$. (a) Plots for the complex zeros of $P_2^{(-3.67)}(x;-0.577)$. (b) Plots for the complex zeros of $P_3^{(-3.67)}(x;-0.577)$.

Remark 1. *The above numerical experiments elaborate how the restriction of parameter values influence real orthogonality and these numerical findings also likely verify the results given in Lemma 1 and Theorem 1.*

2. Relation between the Monic Polynomials $P_n^{(\lambda)}$ and $\mathcal{Q}_n^{(\lambda,\varphi)}$

It is known that classical orthogonal polynomials, namely the polynomials of Jacobi, Laguerre, and Hermite, obey numerous well-known properties corresponding to their several explicit relations [3]; nevertheless, when the conditions on such relations are less restricted, semi-classical (non-classical) orthogonal polynomials [21] are obtained. For mathematical completeness and applications of polynomials in numerous fields, one requires polynomials that are orthogonal with respect to shifting of the weight function in transcendental forms. For semi-classical measure modification from classical weights, we refer to some works [21–24].

It is known that the classical polynomial $P_n^{(\lambda)}$ is orthogonal with respect to the weight [1,3]

$$w(x;\lambda,\phi) = \frac{1}{2\pi} e^{(2\phi-\pi)x} |\Gamma(\lambda + ix)|^2, \quad x \in \mathbb{R}, \ \lambda > 0, \ \varphi \in (0,\pi). \quad (17)$$

However, the polynomial $\mathcal{Q}_n^{(\lambda,\varphi)}$ is orthogonal with the weight in Equation (17) perturbed by e^{-axt}. This perturbation leads to the phase shift from phase φ to $(\varphi - \frac{at}{2})$, which likely turns out to guarantee certain shared properties such as orthogonality, three-term recurrence relation, generating functions, etc. In this sense, $P_n^{(\lambda)}$ and $\mathcal{Q}_n^{(\lambda,\varphi)}$ behave like the same polynomials with different parameters involved in their respective weight function polynomials; for e.g., certain properties of the zeros (such as monotonicity, convexity, quasi-orthogonality, etc.), concise formulation of the recurrence coefficients, etc are some that may deviate as shown in literature [22,25–27]. This work also signifies the need for time-dependent orthogonal polynomials, mainly in terms of their practical applications. We believe that there are few works in related literature that treated certain properties and applications of perturbed classical weights and we hope this work would then contribute to filling this gap.

3. Main Results of the Perturbed Meixner–Pollaczek Weight
3.1. Finite Moments

It is shown in Proposition 2 that the moments of the Meixner–Pollaczek measure are finite. We now present a result proving the finiteness of moments of the perturbed Meixner–Pollaczek measure.

Theorem 2. *Suppose $a > 0$, $t > 0$, $\varphi \in (0, \pi)$ and $x \in \mathbb{R}$. The moments $\eta_j(t; \varphi)$ associated with the weight Equation (8) are finite of all orders.*

Proof. For the weight given in Equation (8), the moments $\eta_j(t; \varphi)$ take the form

$$\eta_k\left(w^{(\lambda,\varphi)}\right) = \frac{1}{2\pi} \int_{-\infty}^{\infty} x^k e^{(2\varphi - \pi)x} |\Gamma(\lambda + ix)|^2 e^{-axt} dx, \quad k \in \mathbb{N}_0. \tag{18}$$

Now, using the fact that $\int_{-\infty}^{\infty} f(x)\, dx = \int_0^{\infty} [f(x) + f(-x)] dx$, Equation (18) gives

$$\eta_k\left(w^{(\lambda,\varphi)}\right) = \frac{1}{2\pi} \int_0^{\infty} x^k |\Gamma(\lambda + ix)|^2 \left(e^{(2\varphi - \pi - at)x} + (-1)^k e^{-(2\varphi - \pi - at)x}\right) dx, \quad k \in \mathbb{N}_0. \tag{19}$$

From Stirling's approximation (cf. [28]) for the complex Gamma function, we have

$$\Gamma(z) \approx \sqrt{\frac{2\pi}{z}} \left(\frac{z}{e}\right)^z,$$

and from the fact that $\Gamma(z)$ is a holomorphic function for $\Re(z) > 0$, $\Gamma(\bar{z}) = \overline{\Gamma(z)}$, we obtain

$$|\Gamma(z)|^2 = \Gamma(z)\Gamma(\bar{z}) \approx \frac{2\pi}{\sqrt{z\bar{z}}} \left(\frac{z}{e}\right)^z \left(\frac{\bar{z}}{e}\right)^{\bar{z}} = \frac{2\pi}{|z|} \left(\frac{z}{e}\right)^z \left(\frac{\bar{z}}{e}\right)^{\bar{z}}.$$

By employing $z = re^{i\theta} = \lambda + ix$, we have

$$|\Gamma(z)|^2 \approx \frac{2\pi}{r} (re^{-1+i\theta})^z (re^{-1-i\theta})^{\bar{z}} = 2\pi r^{z+\bar{z}-1} \exp(z(-1+i\theta) - \bar{z}(1+i\theta)).$$

Using $z + \bar{z} = 2\lambda$, $z - \bar{z} = 2ix$ and $r^2 = \lambda^2 + x^2$, we obtain

$$|\Gamma(z)|^2 \approx 2\pi \left(\lambda^2 + x^2\right)^{\frac{(2\lambda - 1)}{2}} \exp(-2\lambda - 2x\theta).$$

By assuming that $x \gg \lambda$ & $x \gg 1$, we have $\lambda^2 + x^2 \approx x^2$ and using $\theta \approx \frac{\pi}{2}$ gives

$$|\Gamma(z)|^2 = |\Gamma(\lambda + ix)|^2 \approx 2\pi x^{2\lambda - 1} \exp(-\pi x),$$

in which the term 2λ in the argument of the exponential vanishes since 2λ is negligible compared to πx. Since $2\cosh x = e^x + e^{-x} \approx e^x$ for large x, we finally attain that

$$|\Gamma(\lambda + ix)|^2 \approx \frac{\pi x^{2\lambda - 1}}{\cosh(\pi x)}. \tag{20}$$

Substituting Equation (20) into Equation (19) yields

$$\eta_k\left(w^{(\lambda,\varphi)}\right) \approx \frac{1}{2\pi}\int_0^\infty x^k \frac{\pi x^{2\lambda-1}}{\cosh(\pi x)}\left(e^{(2\varphi-\pi-at)x} + (-1)^k e^{-(2\varphi-\pi-at)x}\right)dx \approx \frac{1}{2}\int_0^\infty \frac{x^{k+2\lambda-1}}{\cosh(\pi x)}\left(e^{Mx} + (-1)^k e^{-Mx}\right)dx, \quad (21)$$

where $M := 2\varphi - \pi - at$, with $M < 0$ for the weight to be defined.

By using Equation (21), the even and odd moments are given as follows.

(i) The even moments (η_{2n}):

$$\eta_{2n}\left(w^{(\lambda,\varphi)}\right) \approx \frac{1}{2}\int_0^\infty \frac{x^{2n+2\lambda-1}}{\cosh(\pi x)}\left(e^{Mx} + e^{-Mx}\right)dx \approx \frac{1}{2}\int_0^\infty x^{2n+2\lambda-1}\frac{2\cosh(Mx)}{\cosh(\pi x)}dx, \quad (22)$$

By employing the following cosh inequality: $\frac{e^x - e^{-x}}{2} = \cosh x \leq e^{\frac{x^2}{2}}, \forall x \in \mathbb{R}$, we write

$$\frac{\cosh(Mx)}{\cosh(\pi x)} \leq \frac{e^{M^2x^2/2}}{e^{\pi^2 x^2/2}} = e^{(M^2-\pi^2)x^2/2},$$

so that Equation (22) reduces to

$$\eta_{2n}\left(w^{(\lambda,\varphi)}\right) \approx \frac{1}{2}\int_0^\infty x^{2n+2\lambda-1}\frac{2\cosh(Mx)}{\cosh(\pi x)}dx \leq \int_0^\infty x^{2n+2\lambda-1}e^{(M^2-\pi^2)x^2}dx = \frac{1}{(M^2-\pi^2)^{(n+\lambda)}}\Gamma(n+\lambda) < \infty. \quad (23)$$

(ii) Similarly, for the odd moments (η_{2n+1}), we use the following sinh inequality:

$$\sinh(x) = \frac{e^x - e^{-x}}{2} \leq \frac{e^x}{2}, \quad \text{as} \quad e^{-x} > 0, \forall x \in \mathbb{R},$$

to obtain

$$\eta_{2n+1}\left(w^{(\lambda,\varphi)}\right) \approx \frac{1}{2}\int_0^\infty \frac{x^{2n+2\lambda}}{\cosh(\pi x)}\left(e^{Mx} - e^{-Mx}\right)dx = \int_0^\infty x^{2n+2\lambda}\frac{\sinh(Mx)}{\cosh(\pi x)}dx,$$

$$\leq \frac{1}{2}\int_0^\infty x^{2n+2\lambda}e^{Mx - \frac{\pi^2 x^2}{2}}dx = \frac{1}{2}\int_0^\infty x^{2n+2\lambda} e^{-\frac{\pi^2}{2}\left(-\frac{M}{\pi^4} + (x-\frac{M}{\pi^2})^2\right)}dx < \infty. \quad (24)$$

Thus, from Equations (22)–(24), we see that the moments associated with the weight in Equation (8) are finite of all orders. □

3.2. Orthogonality and Generating Function

We now present some result related to orthogonality of the perturbed Meixner–Pollaczek weight given in (8).

Proposition 3. *Let $\lambda > 0$, $t > 0$ and $\varphi > 0$. The orthogonality relation of the monic perturbed Meixner–Pollaczek polynomials is given by*

$$\mathcal{L}[x^m Q_n^{(\lambda,\varphi)}(x;t)] = \int_{-\infty}^\infty Q_n^{(\lambda,\varphi)}(x;t)\, x^m\, w^{(\lambda,\varphi)}(x;t)\, dx = \zeta_n^{(\lambda,\varphi)}(t)\, \delta_{n,m}, \quad n, m \in \mathbb{N}_0, \quad (25)$$

where the weight $w^{(\lambda,\varphi)}(x;t)$ is as given in Equation (6) with

$$\zeta_n^{(\lambda,\varphi)}(t) = \mathcal{L}\left[x^n Q_n^{(\lambda,\varphi)}(x;t)\right] \neq 0, \quad n \geq 0. \quad (26)$$

Proof. The result immediately follows from Lemma 1 together with fact that the parameter t, which likely leads to shifting the phase φ to $\varphi - \frac{at}{2}$. Equation (26) also follows from the positivity condition of the coefficient $\beta_n^{(\lambda,\varphi)}(t) > 0$ of the recurrence relation for orthogonality to occur [3]. The constant $\zeta_n^{(\lambda,\varphi)}(t)$, $n \geq m \geq 0$, takes the form

$$\zeta_n^{(\lambda,\varphi)}(t) = \int_{-\infty}^\infty \left(Q_n^{(\lambda,\varphi)}(x;t)\right)^2 w^{(\lambda,\varphi)}(x;t)\, dx = \zeta_m^{(\lambda,\varphi)}(t)\prod_{j=m+1}^n \beta_j(t) = \zeta_0^{(\lambda,\varphi)}(t)\prod_{j=1}^n \beta_j(t), \quad (27)$$

where $\zeta_0^{(\lambda,\varphi)} > 0$; in particular, $\zeta_0^{(\lambda,\varphi)} = 1$. We see, for $\lambda > 0$, that

$$\zeta_n^{(\lambda,\varphi)}(t) = \prod_{j=1}^n \beta_j(t) = \prod_{j=1}^n \frac{1}{4} j(j+2\lambda-1)\csc^2\left(\varphi - \frac{at}{2}\right) = (n!)\left(\frac{1}{2}\csc\left(\varphi - \frac{at}{2}\right)\right)^{2n} \prod_{j=1}^n (j+k) > 0,$$

with $k = 2\lambda - 1$, and using the fact that $\prod_{j=1}^n j = n!$ and $\prod_{j=1}^n j^2 = (n!)^2$ and hence the result holds. □

It now follows that the sequence of monic polynomials $\{\mathcal{Q}_n^{(\lambda,\varphi)}(x;t)\}_{n=0}^\infty$ obey the three-term recurrence relation

$$x\mathcal{Q}_n^{(\lambda,\varphi)}(x;t) = \mathcal{Q}_{n+1}^{(\lambda,\varphi)}(x;t) + \alpha_n^{(\lambda,\varphi)}(t)\,\mathcal{Q}_n^{(\lambda,\varphi)}(x;t) + \beta_n^{(\lambda,\varphi)}(t)\,\mathcal{Q}_{n-1}^{(\lambda,\varphi)}(x;t), \quad n \geq 1, \quad (28)$$

with initial conditions $\mathcal{Q}_{-1}^{(\lambda,\varphi)} = 0;\ \mathcal{Q}_0^{(\lambda,\varphi)} = 1$, where the recurrence coefficients are given by

$$\begin{cases} \alpha_n(t) := \alpha_n^{(\lambda,\varphi)}(t) = -(\lambda+n)\cot(\varphi - \frac{at}{2}), \\ \beta_n(t) := \beta_n^{(\lambda,\varphi)}(t) = \frac{1}{4}n(n+2\lambda-1)\csc^2(\varphi - \frac{at}{2}). \end{cases} \quad (29)$$

Lemma 3. *Let $\lambda > 0$, $a > 0$, $0 \leq t < \frac{2\varphi}{a}$, fixed. The following holds for the monic perturbed Meixner-Pollaczek polynomials $\mathcal{Q}_n^{(\lambda,\varphi)}(x;t)$:*

(i) *The generating function*

$$\sum_{n=0}^\infty \mathcal{Q}_n^{(\lambda,\varphi)}(x;t)\, s^n = (1 - e^{i(\varphi - \frac{at}{2})}s)^{-\lambda+ix}(1 - e^{-i(\varphi - \frac{at}{2})}s)^{-\lambda-ix}, \quad |e^{\pm i(\varphi - \frac{at}{2})}s| < 1, \quad (30)$$

(ii) *The hypergeometric representation*

$$\mathcal{Q}_n^{(\lambda,\varphi)}(x;t) = \frac{e^{in(\varphi - \frac{at}{2})}(2\lambda)_n}{n!}\,{}_2F_1\left(\begin{array}{c} -n, \lambda+ix \\ 2\lambda \end{array}\bigg|\, 1 - e^{-2i(\varphi - \frac{at}{2})}\right). \quad (31)$$

Proof. (i) This result follows from the modification of the weight

$$W^{(\lambda,\varphi)}(x) := e^{(2\varphi - \pi)x}|\Gamma(\lambda + ix)|^2 \longrightarrow W^{(\lambda,\varphi)}(x)e^{-axt} := w^{(\lambda,\varphi)}(x;t),$$

which leads to the modification $P_n^{(\lambda)}(x;\varphi) \to P_n^{(\lambda)}(x;\varphi - \frac{at}{2}) := \mathcal{Q}_n^{(\lambda,\varphi)}(x;t)$, and hence Equation (30) is immediate from the hypergeometric formulation of Meixner–Pollaczek polynomials ([1], Section 9.7).

(ii) In order to prove the result in Equation (31), we employ the generating function (30) together with the identity ([29], p. 82)

$$(1-u)^{a-b}(1-u+uz)^{-a} = \sum_{n=0}^\infty \frac{(b)_n}{n!}\,{}_2F_1\left(\begin{array}{c} -n, a \\ b \end{array}\bigg|\, z\right) u^n,$$

with $u = se^{i(\varphi - \frac{at}{2})}$, $a = \lambda + ix$, $b = 2\lambda$, $z = 1 - e^{-2i(\varphi - \frac{at}{2})}$ to obtain

$$\left(1 - e^{i(\varphi - \frac{at}{2})}s\right)^{-\lambda+ix}\left(1 - e^{-i(\varphi - \frac{at}{2})}s\right)^{-\lambda-ix} = \sum_{n=0}^\infty \frac{e^{i(n+1)(\varphi - \frac{at}{2})}(2\lambda)_n}{n!}\,{}_2F_1\left(\begin{array}{c} -n, \lambda+ix \\ 2\lambda \end{array}\bigg|\, 1 - e^{-2i(\varphi - \frac{at}{2})}\right) s^n,$$

and later comparing the coefficients of the power series of both sides to arrive at the desired result.
□

3.3. Concise Formulation

In the sequel, we use Lemma 3 to obtain concise formulations of the perturbed Meixner–Pollaczek polynomials.

Theorem 3. *Let $\lambda > 0$, $a > 0$, $0 \leq t < \frac{2\varphi}{a}$, fixed. The following formulations hold for the monic perturbed Meixner–Pollaczek polynomials $Q_n^{(\lambda,\varphi)}(x;t)$:*

(i) $Q_n^{(\lambda,\varphi)}(x;t) = (-1)^n e^{in(\varphi - \frac{at}{2})} \sum_{k=0}^{n} \binom{-\lambda + ix}{n-k} \binom{-\lambda - ix}{k} e^{-2ik(\varphi - \frac{at}{2})}$

$\qquad = \sum_{k=0}^{n} \binom{n}{k} \frac{(\lambda - ix)_{n-k} \, (\lambda + ix)_k}{n!} e^{i(n-2k)(\varphi - \frac{at}{2})},$

(ii) $Q_n^{(\lambda,\varphi)}(x;t) = \sum_{\ell=0}^{n} \frac{1}{n!} \binom{n}{\ell} (\lambda + ix)_{n-\ell} \, (2\lambda + n - \ell)_\ell \, e^{i(n-\ell)\varphi} e^{-\frac{i(n-\ell)at}{2}} \left[e^{-2i(\varphi - \frac{at}{2})} - 1 \right]^{n-\ell} e^{i(\varphi - \frac{at}{2})\ell}.$

Proof. (i) The proof for (i) uses generalized binomial Theorem

$$(1 + x)^\alpha = \sum_{n=0}^{\infty} \binom{\alpha}{n} x^n$$

on the generating function in Equation (30) and applying Cauchy's product of the series by using the identity

$$\binom{-a}{n} = \frac{(-1)^n \, (a)_n}{n!}, \quad a \in \mathbb{C},$$

where $(a)_n$ is the Pochhammer symbol given in Equation (3).

(ii) By considering ([1], Equation (1.7.11)) and upon some rearrangement as in ([10], p. 172), the generating function takes the form

$$\sum_{n=0}^{\infty} P_n^{(\lambda)}(x;\varphi) \, s^n = \sum_{n=0}^{\infty} \frac{(\lambda + ix)_k}{k!} e^{ik\varphi} \left(e^{-2i\varphi} - 1 \right)^k \left(1 - se^{i\varphi} \right)^{-2\lambda - k} s^k, \quad (32)$$

where $P_n^{(\lambda)}(x;\varphi)$ is the Meixner–Pollaczek polynomial. Since $Q_n^{(\lambda,\varphi)}(x;t) := P_n^{(\lambda)}(x, \varphi - \frac{at}{2})$, it follows that

$$\sum_{n=0}^{\infty} Q_n^{(\lambda,\varphi)}(x;t) \, s^n = \sum_{n=0}^{\infty} \frac{(\lambda + ix)_k}{k!} e^{ik(\varphi - \frac{at}{2})} \left(e^{-2i(\varphi - \frac{at}{2})} - 1 \right)^k \left(1 - se^{i(\varphi - \frac{at}{2})} \right)^{-2\lambda - k} s^k$$

$$= \sum_{n=0}^{\infty} \frac{(\lambda + ix)_k}{k!} e^{ik\varphi} e^{-\frac{ikat}{2}} \left(e^{-2i(\varphi - \frac{at}{2})} - 1 \right)^k \left(1 - se^{i(\varphi - \frac{at}{2})} \right)^{-2\lambda - k} s^k. \quad (33)$$

Expanding $\left(1 - se^{i(\varphi - \frac{at}{2})} \right)^{-2\lambda - k}$ using Pochhammer's identity $(-\lambda)_k = (-1)^k \frac{(\lambda)_k}{k!}$ gives

$$\left(1 - se^{i(\varphi - \frac{at}{2})} \right)^{-2\lambda - k} = \sum_{\ell=0}^{\infty} \binom{-2\lambda - k}{\ell} \left(-se^{i(\varphi - \frac{at}{2})} \right)^\ell$$

$$= \sum_{\ell=0}^{\infty} \frac{(-1)^\ell (2\lambda + k)_\ell}{\ell!} (-1)^\ell e^{i(\varphi - \frac{at}{2})\ell} s^\ell = \sum_{\ell=0}^{\infty} \frac{(2\lambda + k)_\ell}{\ell!} e^{i\varphi\ell} e^{-\frac{iat\ell}{2}} s^\ell. \quad (34)$$

By substituting Equations (34) into (33) and using the summation identity

$$\sum_{n=0}^{\infty} \sum_{k=0}^{\infty} f(k,n) = \sum_{n=0}^{\infty} \sum_{k=0}^{n} f(k, n - k),$$

we obtain

$$\sum_{n=0}^{\infty} \mathcal{Q}_n^{(\lambda,\varphi)}(x;t) s^n = \sum_{k=0}^{\infty} \sum_{\ell=0}^{\infty} \frac{(\lambda+ix)_k}{k!} \frac{(2\lambda+k)_\ell}{\ell!} e^{ik\varphi} e^{-\frac{ikat}{2}} \left[e^{-2i(\varphi-\frac{at}{2})}-1\right]^k e^{i\varphi\ell} e^{-\frac{iat\ell}{2}} s^\ell s^k$$

$$= \sum_{k=0}^{\infty} \sum_{\ell=0}^{k} \frac{(\lambda+ix)_{k-\ell}}{(k-\ell)!} \frac{(2\lambda+k-\ell)_\ell}{\ell!} e^{i(k-\ell)\varphi} e^{-\frac{i(k-\ell)at}{2}} \left[e^{-2i(\varphi-\frac{at}{2})}-1\right]^{(k-\ell)} e^{i\varphi\ell} e^{-\frac{iat\ell}{2}} s^k. \quad (35)$$

By writing n instead of k in Equation (35), we may write

$$\sum_{n=0}^{\infty} \mathcal{Q}_n^{(\lambda,\varphi)}(x;t) s^n = \sum_{n=0}^{\infty} \sum_{\ell=0}^{n} \frac{(\lambda+ix)_{n-\ell}}{(n-\ell)!} \frac{(2\lambda+n-\ell)_\ell}{\ell!} e^{i(n-\ell)\varphi} e^{-\frac{i(n-\ell)at}{2}} \left[e^{-2i(\varphi-\frac{at}{2})}-1\right]^{n-\ell} e^{i\varphi\ell} e^{-\frac{iat\ell}{2}} s^n$$

$$= \sum_{n=0}^{\infty} \left(\sum_{\ell=0}^{n} \frac{1}{n!} \binom{n}{\ell} (\lambda+ix)_{n-\ell} (2\lambda+n-\ell)_\ell \, e^{i(n-\ell)\varphi} e^{-\frac{i(n-\ell)at}{2}} \left[e^{-2i(\varphi-\frac{at}{2})}-1\right]^{n-\ell} e^{i(\varphi-\frac{at}{2})\ell}\right) s^n. \quad (36)$$

Thus, the required result follows by comparing the coefficients of s on both sides of the last equality. □

3.4. Some New Recursive Relations

In this Subsection, let's now denote, for notational convenience, the perturbed Meixner–Pollaczek polynomials by $\mathcal{Q}_n^{(\lambda,a)}(x;\varphi,t)$ in order to show the role of the parameters in Equation (8). We may also sometimes omit some parameters for simplicity. We can now state one of our main results giving new recursive relations fulfilled by the perturbed polynomials using hypergeometric identities.

Theorem 4. *Let $a > 0$, $\varphi > 0$ and $t > 0$. Then the following recursive relations hold for monic perturbed Meixner–Pollaczek polynomials $\mathcal{Q}_n^{(\lambda,a)}(x;\varphi,t)$:*

(i)

$$2i(\lambda+ix)\sin\varphi \, \mathcal{Q}_n^{(\lambda+\frac{1}{2},a)}\left(x-\frac{1}{2}i;\varphi,t\right) = e^{i\varphi}(n+2\lambda) \, \mathcal{Q}_n^{(\lambda,a)}(x;\varphi,t) - 2\sin\varphi \, \mathcal{Q}_{n+1}^{(\lambda,a)}(x;\varphi,t), \quad (37)$$

(ii)

$$e^{i\varphi} \, \mathcal{Q}_n^{(\lambda+\frac{1}{2},a)}\left(x-\frac{1}{2}i;\varphi,t\right) - e^{i\varphi} \mathcal{Q}_n^{(\lambda,a)}(x;\varphi,t) = \frac{n}{2\sin\varphi} \mathcal{Q}_{n-1}^{(\lambda+\frac{1}{2},a)}\left(x-\frac{1}{2}i;\varphi,t\right). \quad (38)$$

Proof. (i) In order to prove the result in (37), let's rewrite the monic perturbed Meixner–Pollaczek polynomials

$$\mathcal{Q}_n^{(\lambda,a)}(x;\varphi,t) = \frac{n!}{(2\sin\varphi)^n} P_n^{(\lambda)}\left(x;\varphi-\frac{at}{2}\right) = \frac{(2\lambda)_n}{(2\sin\varphi)^n} e^{in\varphi} \, {}_2F_1\left(\begin{array}{c}-n,\lambda+ix\\2\lambda\end{array}\Big|\, 1-e^{-2i\varphi}\right). \quad (39)$$

Now, by using the $_2F_1$-hypergeometric formulation given in Equation (39), we rewrite Equation (37) as

$$2i(\lambda+ix)\sin\varphi \left\{\frac{(2\lambda+1)_n}{(2\sin\varphi)^n} e^{in\varphi} \, {}_2F_1\left(\begin{array}{c}-n,\lambda+ix+1\\2\lambda+1\end{array}\Big|\, 1-e^{-2i\varphi}\right)\right\}$$

$$= e^{i\varphi}(n+2\lambda) \left\{\frac{(2\lambda)_n}{(2\sin\varphi)^n} e^{in\varphi} \, {}_2F_1\left(\begin{array}{c}-n,\lambda+ix\\2\lambda\end{array}\Big|\, 1-e^{-2i\varphi}\right)\right\}$$

$$-2\sin\varphi \left\{\frac{(2\lambda)_{n+1}}{(2\sin\varphi)^{n+1}} e^{in\varphi} e^{i\varphi} \, {}_2F_1\left(\begin{array}{c}-n,\lambda+ix\\2\lambda\end{array}\Big|\, 1-e^{-2i\varphi}\right)\right\}. \quad (40)$$

Simplifying Equation (40) and using the identities in ([30], Theorem 9.2)

$$\left.\begin{array}{r}(2\lambda+1)_n = \frac{n+2\lambda}{2\lambda}(2\lambda)_n,\\ (2\lambda)_n = \frac{(2\lambda)_{n+1}}{n+2\lambda},\\ \sin\varphi = \frac{1}{2i}(e^{i\varphi}-e^{-i\varphi}),\end{array}\right\} \qquad (41)$$

we obtain the following relations:

$$(\lambda+ix)(1-e^{-2i\varphi})(2\lambda+1)_n\,{}_2F_1\left(\begin{array}{c}-n,\lambda+ix+1\\ 2\lambda+1\end{array}\bigg|1-e^{-2i\varphi}\right)$$

$$= (n+2\lambda)(2\lambda)_n\,{}_2F_1\left(\begin{array}{c}-n,\lambda+ix\\ 2\lambda\end{array}\bigg|1-e^{-2i\varphi}\right) - (2\lambda)_{n+1}\,{}_2F_1\left(\begin{array}{c}-n-1,\lambda+ix\\ 2\lambda\end{array}\bigg|1-e^{-2i\varphi}\right). \quad (42)$$

Thus, the result in Equation (37) immediately follows from Equation (42) together with the $_2F_1$-contagious hypergeometric identity (cf. [31], Equation (2.11))

$${}_2F_1\left(\begin{array}{c}a,b\\ c\end{array}\bigg|z\right) = {}_2F_1\left(\begin{array}{c}a-1,b\\ c\end{array}\bigg|z\right) + \frac{bz}{c}\,{}_2F_1\left(\begin{array}{c}a,b+1\\ c+1\end{array}\bigg|z\right), \qquad (43)$$

where $a = -n$, $b = \lambda+ix$, and $c = 2\lambda$.

(ii) To prove the second, we rewrite the left hand side of Equation (38), using Equation (39), to obtain

$$e^{i\varphi}\mathcal{Q}_n^{(\lambda+\frac{1}{2},a)}\left(x-\frac{1}{2}i;\varphi,t\right) - e^{i\varphi}\mathcal{Q}_n^{(\lambda,a)}(x;\varphi,t)$$

$$= \frac{e^{i(n+1)\varphi}}{(2\sin\varphi)^n}\left\{(2\lambda+1)_n\,{}_2F_1\left(\begin{array}{c}-n,\lambda+ix+1\\ 2\lambda+1\end{array}\bigg|1-e^{-2i\varphi}\right) - (2\lambda)_{n+1}\,{}_2F_1\left(\begin{array}{c}-n,\lambda+ix\\ 2\lambda\end{array}\bigg|1-e^{-2i\varphi}\right)\right\}. \quad (44)$$

Besides, the right hand side of Equation (38) also takes the form

$$\frac{n}{2\sin\varphi}\mathcal{Q}_{n-1}^{(\lambda+\frac{1}{2},a)}\left(x-\frac{1}{2}i;\varphi,t\right) = \frac{n}{2\sin\varphi}\left\{\frac{(2\lambda+1)_{n-1}}{(2\sin\varphi)^{n-1}}e^{i(n-1)\varphi}\,{}_2F_1\left(\begin{array}{c}-n,\lambda+ix+1\\ 2\lambda+1\end{array}\bigg|1-e^{-2i\varphi}\right)\right\}$$

$$= \frac{n}{(2\sin\varphi)^n}(2\lambda+1)_{n-1}e^{i(n-1)\varphi}\,{}_2F_1\left(\begin{array}{c}-n,\lambda+ix+1\\ 2\lambda+1\end{array}\bigg|1-e^{-2i\varphi}\right). \qquad (45)$$

We now see that the result in Equation (38) follows by combining Equations (44) and (45) together with the $_2F_1$ hypergoemetric contagious identity (cf. ([31], Equation (2.6))

$$(a-c+1)\,{}_2F_1\left(\begin{array}{c}a,b\\ c\end{array}\bigg|z\right) + (c-1)\,{}_2F_1\left(\begin{array}{c}a,b-1\\ c-1\end{array}\bigg|z\right) - a(1-z)\,{}_2F_1\left(\begin{array}{c}a+1,b\\ c\end{array}\bigg|z\right) = 0, \qquad (46)$$

where $a = -n$, $b = \lambda+ix+1$, $c = 2\lambda+1$ and $z = 1-e^{-2i\varphi}$.
□

Our next proposition gives some properties of the perturbed Meixner–Pollaczek polynomials.

3.5. Addition Formulation and Integral Representation

Proposition 4. Let $\lambda > 0$, $a > 0$ and $0 \leq t < \frac{2\varphi}{a}$. The following properties hold for $\mathcal{Q}_n^{(\lambda,\varphi)}(x;t)$:

(i) Addition formulation

$$\mathcal{Q}_n^{(\alpha+\beta,\varphi)}(x+y;t) = \sum_{k=0}^{n} \mathcal{Q}_{n-k}^{(\alpha,\varphi)}(x;t)\, \mathcal{Q}_k^{(\beta,\varphi)}(y;t). \tag{47}$$

(ii) Integral representation

$$\mathcal{Q}_n^{(\lambda,\varphi)}(x;t) = \frac{1}{n!} \frac{e^{in(\varphi-\frac{\pi}{2})}}{|\Gamma(\lambda+ix)|^2} \int_0^\infty \int_0^\infty e^{-(s+r)} (sr)^{\lambda-1} \left(s + e^{-2i(\varphi-\frac{\pi}{2})} r\right)^n \left(\frac{r}{s}\right)^{ix} ds\, dr. \tag{48}$$

Proof. (i) By replacing $\lambda \to \alpha + \beta$, $(\alpha > 0,\, \beta > 0)$ and $x \to x+y$ in Equation (30) and then applying Cauchy's product, we obtain

$$\sum_{n=0}^{\infty} \mathcal{Q}_n^{(\alpha+\beta,\varphi)}(x+y;t)\, s^n = \left[1 - e^{i(\varphi-\frac{\pi}{2})} s\right]^{-(\alpha+\beta-ix-iy)} \left[1 - e^{-i(\varphi-\frac{\pi}{2})} s\right]^{-(\alpha+\beta+ix+iy)}$$

$$= \left(\sum_{n=0}^{\infty} \mathcal{Q}_n^{(\alpha,\varphi)}(x;t)\, s^n\right)\left(\sum_{n=0}^{\infty} \mathcal{Q}_n^{(\beta,\varphi)}(y;t)\, s^n\right)$$

$$= \sum_{n=0}^{\infty}\sum_{k=0}^{\infty} \mathcal{Q}_n^{(\alpha,\varphi)}(x;t)\, \mathcal{Q}_k^{(\beta,\varphi)}(y;t)\, s^{k+n}$$

$$= \sum_{n=0}^{\infty}\sum_{k=0}^{n} \mathcal{Q}_{n-k}^{(\alpha,\varphi)}(x;t)\, \mathcal{Q}_k^{(\beta,\varphi)}(y;t)\, s^n. \tag{49}$$

Thus, Equation (47) follows by comparing the coefficients of s on both sides of the last equality.

(ii) In order to prove (48), we use the generating function in ([1], Equation (9.7.13)) (by setting $\gamma = 2\lambda$) and by applying the definition of Gamma function

$$\Gamma(z)\, b^{-z} = \int_0^\infty e^{-bt} t^{z-1} dt, \quad [\Re(z) > 0],$$

to obtain

$$\sum_{n=0}^{\infty} e^{-in(\varphi-\frac{\pi}{2})} \mathcal{Q}_n^{(\lambda,\varphi)}(x;t)\, u^n = (1-u)^{-(\lambda-ix)} \left(1 - ue^{-2i(\varphi-\frac{\pi}{2})}\right)^{-(\lambda+ix)}$$

$$= \frac{1}{\Gamma(\lambda-ix)}\frac{1}{\Gamma(\lambda+ix)} \int_0^\infty \int_0^\infty e^{-(1-u)s} s^{\lambda-1-ix} ds\, e^{-(1-ue^{-2i(\varphi-\frac{\pi}{2})})r} r^{\lambda-1+ix} dr$$

$$= \frac{1}{|\Gamma(\lambda+ix)|^2} \int_0^\infty \int_0^\infty e^{-(s+r)} (sr)^{\lambda-1} e^{u(s+e^{-2i(\varphi-\frac{\pi}{2})}r)} (sr)^{\lambda-1} \left(\frac{r}{s}\right)^{ix} ds\, dr$$

$$= \sum_{n=0}^{\infty} \frac{1}{n!} \left[\frac{1}{|\Gamma(\lambda+ix)|^2} \int_0^\infty \int_0^\infty e^{-(s+r)} (sr)^{\lambda-1} \left(s + e^{-2i(\varphi-\frac{\pi}{2})} r\right)^n \left(\frac{r}{s}\right)^{ix} ds\, dr\right] u^n. \tag{50}$$

Thus, (48) follows by comparing the coefficients of u^n on both sides of Equation (50). □

3.6. Some Properties of the Zeros Associated with the Perturbed Weight in (8)

For $\varphi \in (0, \pi)$ and $\lambda > 0$, the zeros of the Meixner–Pollaczek polynomials, $\{P_n^{(\lambda)}(x;\varphi)\}_{n=0}^{\infty}$, are simple and real, and consequently, the zeros interlace [3]. The monotonicity properties of all the zeros with respect to a parameter of orthogonal polynomials associated with an even weight function, specifically, the symmetric Meixner–Pollaczek case, are given in [26] (see also [32]). In what follows, we state some fresh results related to certain properties of the zeros of the perturbed Meixner–Pollaczek polynomials.

3.6.1. Monotonicity of the Zeros

Proposition 5. Let $\lambda > 0$, $a > 0$ and $x \in \mathbb{R}$. The zeros $\left\{x_{nk}^{(\lambda,\varphi)}(t)\right\}_{k=1}^{n}$ of the monic perturbed Meixner–Pollaczek polynomials $\mathcal{Q}_n^{(\lambda,a)}(x;\varphi,t)$ are

(i) monotone decreasing functions of t on the interval $2\varphi - 2\pi < at < 2\varphi$, $t > 0$.

(ii) monotone increasing functions of φ for $0 < \varphi - \frac{at}{2} < \pi$ and fixed $t > 0$.

Proof. (i) By applying Markov's monotonicity Theorem (cf. [10], Theorem 7.1.1), it is easy to check that for the weight in Equation (8), we have

$$\ln w^{(\lambda,\varphi)}(x;t) = (2\varphi - \pi)x + \ln\left(|\Gamma(\lambda + ix)|^2\right) - axt, \quad a > 0, \; x \in \mathbb{R}. \quad (51)$$

Differentiating Equation (51) with respect to t gives $G(x;t) = \dfrac{\partial \ln w^{(\lambda,\varphi)}(x;t)}{\partial t} = -ax$, and hence $G(x;t)$ is decreasing function of x for $x \in \mathbb{R}$ since $\dfrac{\partial G}{\partial x} = -a < 0$ for $a > 0$ and $x \in \mathbb{R}$. We can easily infer from (cf. [10], Theorem 7.1.1) that the zeros of $Q_n^{(\lambda,a)}(x;\varphi,t)$ decrease as a function of t, for $t \in (\frac{2\varphi - 2\pi}{a}, \frac{2\varphi}{a})$.

(ii) It is easy to check that for the perturbed weight in Equation (8), we have

$$\ln w^{(\lambda,\varphi)}(x;t) = (2\varphi - \pi)x + \ln\left(|\Gamma(\lambda + ix)|^2\right) - axt, \quad a > 0, \; x \in \mathbb{R}. \quad (52)$$

Differentiating Equation (52) with respect to t gives $H(x;t) = \dfrac{\partial \ln w^{(\lambda,\varphi)}(x;t)}{\partial \varphi} = 2x$.

Since $H(x;t)$ is monotone increasing of x for $x \in \mathbb{R}$, as $\dfrac{\partial H}{\partial x} > 0$ for $a > 0$ and $x \in \mathbb{R}$, it is easy to deduce from ([10], Theorem 7.1.1) that the zeros of $Q_n^{(\lambda,a)}(x;\varphi,t)$ increase as a function of φ, for $\varphi \in (\frac{at}{2}, \pi + \frac{at}{2})$, $a > 0$, with $t \in (\frac{2\varphi - 2\pi}{a}, \frac{2\varphi}{a})$. □

Our next result gives the connection between Hellmann–Feynman Theorem [33] and the monotonicity of the zeros associated with the perturbed weight given in Equation (8).

Theorem 5. Let $\lambda > \frac{1}{2}$, $\{x_{n,k}(\varphi,t)\}_{k=1}^n$ be the zeros of $Q_n^{(\lambda,a)}(x;\varphi,t)$ in such a way that

$$x_{n,1}(\varphi,t) > x_{n,2}(\varphi,t) > \cdots > x_{n,n}(\varphi,t).$$

The following monotone properties of the zeros hold true for $t \in [0, \frac{2\varphi}{a})$:

(i) $\dfrac{\partial x_{n,1}(\varphi,t)}{\partial \varphi} > 0$ for $\frac{\pi}{2} < \varphi - \frac{at}{2} < \pi$, $a > 0$.

(ii) $\dfrac{\partial x_{n,n}(\varphi,t)}{\partial \varphi} > 0$ for $0 < \varphi - \frac{at}{2} < \frac{\pi}{2}$, $a > 0$.

(iii) $\dfrac{\partial x_{n,1}(\varphi,t)}{\partial t} < 0$ for $\frac{\pi}{2} < \varphi - \frac{at}{2} < \pi$, $a > 0$.

(iv) $\dfrac{\partial x_{n,n}(\varphi,t)}{\partial t} < 0$ for $\varphi - \frac{at}{2} \in (0, \frac{\pi}{2})$, $a > 0$.

Proof. To apply Hellmann–Feynman's Theorem in terms of the three-term recurrence relation (cf. [34], Theorem 1.1), we have to consider recurrence coefficients of the monic perturbed Meixner–Pollaczek polynomials in Equation (28),

$$\alpha_n^{(\lambda,\varphi)}(t) = -(\lambda + n)\cot\left(\varphi - \frac{at}{2}\right); \quad \beta_n^{(\lambda,\varphi)}(t) = \frac{n(n + 2\lambda - 1)}{4}\csc^2\left(\varphi - \frac{at}{2}\right).$$

(i) We now first consider the derivative of the coefficient $\alpha_n(\lambda, \varphi)$; i.e., $\alpha_n'(\lambda, \varphi)$ as

$$\alpha_n'(\varphi) := \frac{\partial \alpha_n^{(\lambda,\varphi)}(t)}{\partial \varphi} = -(\lambda + n)\csc^2\left(\varphi - \frac{at}{2}\right), \quad n \geq 0, \quad (53)$$

and we see from (53) that $\alpha_n'(\varphi) < 0$ for $\varphi - \frac{at}{2} \in (k\pi, \pi + k\pi)$, $k \in \mathbb{Z}$. Hence the

Next, we examine the derivative of $\beta'_n(\lambda, \varphi)$. For $n \geq 1$,

$$\beta'_n(\varphi) := \frac{\partial \beta_n^{(\lambda,\varphi)}(t)}{\partial \varphi} = -\frac{1}{2}(n)(\lambda + n - 1) \csc\left(\varphi - \frac{at}{2}\right) \cot\left(\varphi - \frac{at}{2}\right). \tag{54}$$

From Equation (54), we see that $\beta'_n(\varphi) < 0$ for $\varphi - \frac{at}{2} \in (k\pi, \frac{\pi}{2} + k\pi)$, $k \in \mathbb{Z}$ with fixed parameter $t > 0$; and $\beta'_n(\varphi) > 0$ for $\varphi - \frac{at}{2} \in (\frac{\pi}{2} + k\pi, k\pi)$, $k \in \mathbb{Z}$. In particular, for $k = 0$, we see that $\beta'_n(\varphi) < 0$ if $\varphi - \frac{at}{2} \in (0, \frac{\pi}{2})$ and $\beta'_n(\varphi) > 0$ if $\varphi - \frac{at}{2} \in (\frac{\pi}{2}, \pi)$ for fixed positive t. Thus, the coefficient $\beta_n(\lambda, \varphi)$, $n \geq 0$ is a monotone decreasing function of the parameter φ in the interval $\varphi \in (at, \frac{\pi}{2} + at)$ for $k \in \mathbb{Z}$ and for fixed positive t; and $\beta_n(\lambda, \varphi)$, $n \geq 0$ is a monotone increasing function of φ in the interval $\varphi \in (\frac{\pi}{2} + at, \pi + at)$, $k \in \mathbb{Z}$ and fixed $t > 0$. Thus, the assumptions of Hellman–Feynman Theorem are fulfilled, and so is Theorem 5.

(ii) The proofs for $(ii), (iii)$ and (iv) share similar approach. □

3.6.2. Convexity of the Extreme Zeros

In the following, we shall now prove the convexity of zeros related to the perturbed Meixner–Pollaczek weight (8).

Theorem 6. Let $\lambda > \frac{1}{2}$, $\{x_{n,k}(\varphi, t)\}_{k=1}^n$ be the zeros of $Q_n^{(\lambda, a)}(x; \varphi, t)$ in such a way that $x_{n,1}(\varphi, t) > x_{n,2}(\varphi, t) > \cdots > x_{n,n}(\varphi, t)$. The following convexity results of the extreme zeros hold true:

(i) $\frac{\partial^2 x_{n,1}(\varphi,t)}{\partial \varphi^2} > 0$ and $\frac{\partial^2 x_{n,1}(\varphi,t)}{\partial t^2} > 0$ for $\varphi - \frac{at}{2} \in (\frac{\pi}{2}, \pi)$, $a, t > 0$.

(ii) $\frac{\partial^2 x_{n,1}(\varphi,t)}{\partial \varphi^2} < 0$ and $\frac{\partial^2 x_{n,1}(\varphi,t)}{\partial t^2} < 0$ for $\varphi - \frac{at}{2} \in (0, \frac{\pi}{2})$, $a, t > 0$.

Proof. (i) By following the idea of Dimitrov (cf. [35], Lemma 1), the convexity of the extreme zeros follows from the derivatives

$$\frac{d^2 \alpha_n^{(\lambda,\varphi)}}{dt^2} = -(n+\lambda)\frac{d^2}{d\varphi^2}\left(\cot\left(\varphi - \frac{at}{2}\right)\right)$$

$$= -2(n+\lambda)a^2 \csc^2\left(\varphi - \frac{at}{2}\right)\cot\left(\varphi - \frac{at}{2}\right)$$

$$= \begin{cases} < 0, & \text{if } 0 < \varphi - \frac{at}{2} < \frac{\pi}{2}, \\ > 0, & \text{if } \frac{\pi}{2} < \varphi - \frac{at}{2} < \pi, \end{cases} \tag{55}$$

and

$$\frac{d^2 \beta_n^{(\lambda,\varphi)}}{d\varphi^2} = \frac{d^2}{d\varphi^2}\left(\csc^2\left(\varphi - \frac{at}{2}\right)\right)$$

$$= \frac{n(n+2\lambda-1)a^2}{4}\left[4\csc^2\left(\varphi - \frac{at}{2}\right)\cot^2\left(\varphi - \frac{at}{2}\right) + 2\csc^4\left(\varphi - \frac{at}{2}\right)\right]$$

$$= n(n+2\lambda-1)a^2\left[\csc^2\left(\varphi - \frac{at}{2}\right)\cot^2\left(\varphi - \frac{at}{2}\right) + \frac{1}{2}\csc^4\left(\varphi - \frac{at}{2}\right)\right] > 0, \tag{56}$$

for all values of $\varphi - \frac{at}{2}$, and in particular, $0 < \varphi - \frac{at}{2} \in \pi$ for fixed $t > 0$ and $a > 0$. By combining Equations (55) and (56) and applying ([35], Lemma 1), the above convexity result of the largest zero of the perturbed Meixner–Pollaczek polynomials follows immediately.

(ii) The concavity of the smallest zero of the perturbed Meixner–Pollaczek polynomials also follows from Equations (55) and (56), in a similar manner, by applying ([35], Lemma 1). □

Remark 2. *A similar numerical experimentation of the zeros of the perturbed Meixner–Pollaczek polynomials can be done to give analog results to the ones in Section 1.1.1 with careful restriction of involved parameters.*

4. Some Applications of the Polynomial $\mathcal{Q}_n^{(\lambda,a)}(x;\varphi,t)$

In this Section, certain applications of the perturbed Meixner-Pollaczek polynomials are explored. These polynomials have wider applicability in the Random matrix theory of level statistics using partition functions (via Toda molecule equation) [11], wave functions in Quantum Mechanics, the Fisher information theory and in the study of Gaussian quadrature (cf. [36]), to mention a few.

4.1. Exposition of Toda-Type Lattice/Molecule Equation

Toda lattice is a system of particles on the line with exponential interaction of nearest neighbours [37]. Toda was the first to study such a system for infinitely many particles on the line [38]. The Toda lattice equations are investigated from the Newtonian equations of motion (see, for example, [37])

$$\ddot{x}_n = e^{x_{n-1}-x_n} - e^{x_n-x_{n+1}}, \quad n \geq 1,$$

when one takes $\alpha_n = \dot{x}_n$ and $\beta_n = e^{x_{n-1}-x_n}$ for $n \in \mathbb{N}$. (Note that α_n and β_n are the recurrence coefficients for corresponding monic orthogonal polynomials on the real line [3,8]).

The fact that perturbed Meixner–Pollaczek polynomials are time-dependent orthogonal polynomials, allows us to study the time-evolution equation related to Toda lattices. The Perturbed Meixner–Pollaczek weight in (8) is obtained from deformation of classical Meixner–Pollaczek weight by $\exp(-axt)$. For similar measure deformation, we refer to [21,23,27] (See also [39]). We now mention in the following result of the perturbed Meixner–Pollaczek polynomials satisfying a similar scaled Toda lattice/molecule equation.

Proposition 6. *The recurrence coefficients $\alpha_n(t)$ and $\beta_n(t)$ in (29) associated with the monic perturbed Meixner–Pollaczek polynomials $\mathcal{Q}_n^{(\lambda,\varphi)}(x;t)$ for $\varphi \in \left(\frac{at}{2}, \pi + \frac{at}{2}\right)$, obey a scaled Toda molecule equation*

$$\begin{cases} \dfrac{\partial \alpha_n}{\partial t} = a(\beta_n - \beta_{n+1}), \\ \dfrac{\partial \beta_n}{\partial t} = a\beta_n(\alpha_{n-1} - \alpha_n), \quad a > 0. \end{cases} \tag{57}$$

Proof. This result immediately follows from orthogonality and iterated recurrences, see [21,39]. □

The proof of this result is given in Appendix A.1 of Appendix A just for the reader's convenience.

Remark 3. *We now see that Equation (29) solves the differential-recurrence (Toda) equation in Equation (57) associated with the monic perturbed Meixner–Pollaczek polynomials.*

4.2. Fisher Information of the Monic Polynomial $\mathcal{Q}_n^{(\lambda,a)}(x;\varphi,t)$

Following the approach given in [36], the Fisher information of the Meixner–Pollaczek polynomials is computed using the concept introduced for general orthogonal polynomials by Sanchéz-Ruiz and Dehesa in [40]. They considered a sequence of real polynomials orthogonal with respect to the weight function $\rho(x)$ on the interval $[a,b]$

$$\int_a^b P_n(x)\, P_m(x)\, \rho(x)\, dx = \zeta_n\, \delta_{n,m}, \quad n,m = 0,1,\ldots,$$

with $\deg(P_n) = n$. Introducing the normalized density functions

$$\rho_n(x) = \frac{[P_n(x)]^2 \rho(x)}{\zeta_n}, \tag{58}$$

they in fact defined the Fisher information corresponding to the densities in Equation (58)

$$\mathcal{I}(n) = \int_a^b \frac{[\rho_n'(x)]^2}{\rho_n(x)} dx. \tag{59}$$

Applying the formula in Equation (59) to the classical hypergeometric polynomials, the authors in [41] evaluated $\mathcal{I}(n)$ for Jacobi, Laguerre and Hermite polynomials. We quote the following result by Dominici from [36]:

Theorem 7 ([36]). *The Fisher information of the Meixner–Pollaczek polynomials is given by*

$$I_\varphi\left(P_n^{(\lambda)}\right) = \int_{-\infty}^{\infty} \left[\frac{\partial}{\partial \varphi} \rho_n(x)\right]^2 \frac{1}{\rho_n(x)} dx = \frac{2[n^2 + (2n+1)\lambda]}{\sin^2(\varphi)}, \quad n \in \mathbb{N}_0,$$

where the normalized function $\rho_n(x)$ is as defined in Equation (58).

Based on the above discussion, we shall now reproduce the following application of the monic perturbed Meixner–Pollaczek polynomials.

Theorem 8. *The Fisher information of the monic perturbed Meixner–Pollaczek polynomials with respect to the parameter φ is given, in terms of the recurrence coefficients, by*

$$I_\varphi\left(\mathcal{Q}_n^{(\lambda,\varphi)}(x;t)\right) = \int_{-\infty}^{\infty} \left[\frac{\partial}{\partial \varphi} \rho_n(x;t)\right]^2 \frac{1}{\rho_n(x;t)} dx = 4\left(\beta_n^{(\lambda,\varphi)} + \beta_n^{(\lambda,\varphi)} + [\alpha_n^{(\lambda,\varphi)}]^2\right)$$

$$+ 4(2n + 2\lambda - 1)\alpha_n^{(\lambda,\varphi)} + (2n + 2\lambda - 1)^2 \left(\cot\left(\varphi - \frac{at}{2}\right)\right)^2, \tag{60}$$

where the normalized function $\rho_n(x;t)$ is as given in Equation (58).

Proof. By employing the three-term recurrence relation in Equation (28) associated with the weight in (8) and using the orthogonality relation in Equation (25) with its (monic) normalization constant, we have normalized function

$$\rho_n(x;t) = \frac{\left[\mathcal{Q}_n^{(\lambda,\varphi)}(x;t)\right]^2 w^{(\lambda,\varphi)}(x;t)}{\zeta_n^{(\lambda,\varphi)}} = \frac{e^{(2\varphi-\pi)x}|\Gamma(\lambda+ix)|^2 e^{-axt}[2\sin(\varphi - \frac{at}{2})]^{2n+2\lambda}\left[\mathcal{Q}_n^{(\lambda,\varphi)}(x;t)\right]^2}{2\pi\Gamma(n+2\lambda)\Gamma(n+1)} \tag{61}$$

and we note that $\int_\mathbb{R} \rho_n(x;t) = 1$ for $n \in \mathbb{N}_0$.

By taking the derivatives of ρ_n with respect to φ and using the perturbed weight (8)

$$\frac{\partial w^{(\lambda,\varphi)}}{\partial \varphi} = (2x) w^{(\lambda,\varphi)}, \tag{62}$$

together with the result in ([36], Equation (12)) gives

$$\frac{\partial \mathcal{Q}_n^{(\lambda,\varphi)}(x;t)}{\partial \varphi} = \frac{\partial}{\partial \varphi}\left(\frac{n!}{(2\sin\varphi)^n} P_n^{(\lambda)}\left(x; \varphi - \frac{at}{2}\right)\right) = \frac{-n(n + 2\lambda - 1)}{2\sin^2(\varphi - \frac{at}{2})} \mathcal{Q}_{n-1}^{(\lambda,\varphi)}(x;t). \tag{63}$$

Using Equation (61), it follows that

$$\frac{\partial \rho_n(x;t)}{\partial \varphi} = \frac{Q_n^{(\lambda,\varphi)}(x;t) w^{(\lambda,\varphi)}(x;t)}{\zeta_n^{(\lambda,\varphi)}} \left\{ \frac{-n(n+2\lambda-1)}{\sin^2\left(\varphi - \frac{at}{2}\right)} Q_{n-1}^{(\lambda,\varphi)}(x;t) + 2x Q_n^{(\lambda,\varphi)}(x;t) - \left(\frac{1}{\zeta_n^{(\lambda,\varphi)}} \frac{\partial \zeta_n^{(\lambda,\varphi)}}{\partial \varphi}\right) Q_n^{(\lambda,\varphi)}(x;t) \right\} \quad (64)$$

From the orthogonality of Meixner-Pollaczek polynomials [1], we note here that

$$\zeta_n^{(\lambda,\varphi)}(t) = \frac{2\pi(n!)\Gamma(n+2\lambda)}{[2\sin(\varphi - \frac{at}{2})]^{2n+2\lambda}} = \frac{2\pi\Gamma(n+1)\Gamma(n+2\lambda)}{[2\sin(\varphi - \frac{at}{2})]^{2n+2\lambda}}, \quad (65)$$

for the perturbed Meixner-Pollaczek polynomials. It then follows from Equation (65) that

$$\frac{1}{\zeta_n^{(\lambda,\varphi)}} \frac{\partial \zeta_n^{(\lambda,\varphi)}}{\partial \varphi} = \frac{(-2\pi)(2n+2\lambda-1)\Gamma(n+1)\Gamma(n+2\lambda)(\frac{1}{2})^{2n+2\lambda}[2\csc(\varphi-\frac{at}{2})]^{2n+2\lambda}\cot(\varphi-\frac{at}{2})}{\Gamma(n+1)\Gamma(n+2\lambda)(\frac{1}{2})^{2n+2\lambda}[2\csc(\varphi-\frac{at}{2})]^{2n+2\lambda}}$$

$$= -(2n+2\lambda-1)\cot\left(\varphi - \frac{at}{2}\right). \quad (66)$$

By using Equations (66) and (61), Equation (64) becomes

$$\frac{\partial \rho_n(x;t)}{\partial \varphi} = \frac{1}{\zeta_n^{(\lambda,\varphi)}} Q_n^{(\lambda,\varphi)}(x;t) w^{(\lambda,\varphi)}(x;t) \left\{ \frac{-n(n+2\lambda-1)}{\sin^2\left(\varphi-\frac{at}{2}\right)} Q_{n-1}^{(\lambda,\varphi)}(x;t) + 2x Q_n^{(\lambda,\varphi)}(x;t) - \left(\frac{1}{\zeta_n^{(\lambda,\varphi)}} \frac{\partial \zeta_n^{(\lambda,\varphi)}}{\partial \varphi}\right) Q_n^{(\lambda,\varphi)}(x;t) \right\}$$

$$= \frac{\rho_n(x;t)}{Q_n^{(\lambda,\varphi)}(x;t)} \left\{ \frac{-n(n+2\lambda-1)}{\sin^2\left(\varphi-\frac{at}{2}\right)} Q_{n-1}^{(\lambda,\varphi)}(x;t) + 2x Q_n^{(\lambda,\varphi)}(x;t) + (2n+2\lambda-1)\cot\left(\varphi-\frac{at}{2}\right) Q_n^{(\lambda,\varphi)}(x;t) \right\}$$

$$= \frac{\rho_n(x;t)}{Q_n^{(\lambda,\varphi)}(x;t)} \left\{ \left[2x + (2n+2\lambda-1)\cot\left(\varphi-\frac{at}{2}\right)\right] Q_n^{(\lambda,\varphi)}(x;t) - 4\beta_n^{(\lambda,\varphi)} Q_{n-1}^{(\lambda,\varphi)}(x;t) \right\}. \quad (67)$$

Thus, using Equation (67), we attain that

$$\left(\frac{\partial \rho_n}{\partial \varphi}\right)^2 \frac{1}{\rho_n} = \frac{\rho_n(x;t)}{[Q_n^{(\lambda,\varphi)}(x;t)]^2} \left\{ \left[2x + (2n+2\lambda-1)\cot\left(\varphi-\frac{at}{2}\right)\right]^2 \left[Q_n^{(\lambda,\varphi)}(x;t)\right]^2 \right.$$

$$\left. - 8\beta_n^{(\lambda,\varphi)}[2x+(2n+2\lambda-1)\cot\left(\varphi-\frac{at}{2}\right)] Q_{n-1}^{(\lambda,\varphi)}(x;t) Q_n^{(\lambda,\varphi)}(x;t) + 16\left[\beta_n^{(\lambda,\varphi)}\right]^2 \left[Q_{n-1}^{(\lambda,\varphi)}(x;t)\right]^2 \right\}$$

$$= \frac{w^{(\lambda,\varphi)}(x;t)}{\zeta_n^{(\lambda,\varphi)}} \left\{ \left[4x^2 + 4(2n+2\lambda-1)\cot\left(\varphi-\frac{at}{2}\right)x + (2n+2\lambda-1)^2\left(\cot\left(\varphi-\frac{at}{2}\right)\right)^2\right] \left[Q_n^{(\lambda,\varphi)}(x;t)\right]^2 \right.$$

$$\left. - 16\beta_n^{(\lambda,\varphi)} x Q_{n-1}^{(\lambda,\varphi)}(x;t) Q_n^{(\lambda,\varphi)}(x;t) - 8\beta_n^{(\lambda,\varphi)}(2n+2\lambda-1)\cot\left(\varphi-\frac{at}{2}\right) Q_{n-1}^{(\lambda,\varphi)}(x;t) Q_n^{(\lambda,\varphi)}(x;t) \right.$$

$$\left. + 16\left[\beta_n^{(\lambda,\varphi)}\right]^2 \left[Q_{n-1}^{(\lambda,\varphi)}(x;t)\right]^2 \right\}. \quad (68)$$

By integrating Equation (68) and using the orthogonality relation in Equation (25) and iterating the recurrence (28)

$$x Q_n^{(\lambda,\varphi)}(x;t) = Q_{n+1}^{(\lambda,\varphi)}(x;t) + \alpha_n(t) Q_n^{(\lambda,\varphi)}(x;t) + \beta_n(t) Q_{n-1}^{(\lambda,\varphi)}(x;t),$$

$$x^2 Q_n^{(\lambda,\varphi)}(x;t) = Q_{n+2}^{(\lambda,\varphi)}(x;t)(\alpha_n + \alpha_{n+1}) Q_{n+1}^{(\lambda,\varphi)}(x;t) + \left(\beta_{n+1} + \beta_n + \alpha_n^2\right) Q_n^{(\lambda,\varphi)}(x;t)$$

$$+ \beta_n \alpha_{n-1} Q_{n-1}^{(\lambda,\varphi)}(x;t) + \beta_n \beta_{n-1} Q_{n-2}^{(\lambda,\varphi)}(x;t), \quad (69)$$

we obtain

$$\left(\frac{\partial \rho_n}{\partial \varphi}\right)^2 \frac{1}{\rho_n} = \frac{1}{\zeta_n^{(\lambda,\varphi)}} \int 4x^2 \left[Q_n^{(\lambda,\varphi)}(x;t)\right]^2 w^{(\lambda,\varphi)}(x;t) \, dx$$

$$+ \frac{1}{\zeta_n^{(\lambda,\varphi)}} \int 4(2n+2\lambda-1)\cot\left(\varphi-\frac{at}{2}\right) x \left[Q_n^{(\lambda,\varphi)}(x;t)\right]^2 w^{(\lambda,\varphi)}(x;t) \, dx$$

$$+ \frac{1}{\zeta_n^{(\lambda,\varphi)}} \int (2n+2\lambda-1)^2 \left(\cot\left(\varphi-\frac{at}{2}\right)\right)^2 \left[Q_n^{(\lambda,\varphi)}(x;t)\right]^2 w^{(\lambda,\varphi)}(x;t) \, dx$$

$$- 16\beta_n^{(\lambda,\varphi)} \frac{1}{\zeta_n^{(\lambda,\varphi)}} \int x Q_{n-1}^{(\lambda,\varphi)}(x;t) Q_n^{(\lambda,\varphi)}(x;t) w^{(\lambda,\varphi)}(x;t) \, dx + 16\left[\beta_n^{(\lambda,\varphi)}\right]^2 \frac{1}{\zeta_n^{(\lambda,\varphi)}} \int \left[Q_{n-1}^{(\lambda,\varphi)}(x;t)\right]^2 w^{(\lambda,\varphi)}(x;t) \, dx$$

$$\quad (70)$$

and this completes the proof. □

Remark 4. *The Fisher information of the classical orthogonal polynomials with respect to a parameter is given in [41]. In our case, the Fisher information of the perturbed Meixner-Pollaczek polynomials with respect to the parameter $a > 0$ can also be obtained in a similar procedure, using the fact that*

$$\frac{\partial w^{(\lambda,\varphi)}}{\partial a} = (-tx)\, w^{(\lambda,\varphi)}.$$

4.3. Guass–Meixner–Pollaczek Quadrature

Let's first recall a quadrature rule,

$$\int_{\mathbb{R}} f(x)d\mu(x) \approx \sum_{\nu=1}^{n} \omega_j\, f(x_j),$$

where the integral of a function f relative to some (in general positive) measure $d\mu$ is approximated by a finite sum involving n values of f at suitably selected distinct nodes x_j, where these nodes are obtained from the zeros of orthogonal polynomials $\Phi_n(x;w)$ and the quadrature weights ω_j, $j = 1,2,\ldots,n$ can also be given by [42]

$$\omega_j = \frac{\langle \Phi_{n-1}, \Phi_{n-1}\rangle_w}{\Phi_{n-1}(x_j)\, \Phi'_n(x_j)}. \tag{71}$$

where the prime denotes differentiation with respect to x.

Just for simplicity, this Subsection emphasizes to explore Gaussian quadrature rule related to symmetric monic Meixner-Pollaczek polynomials, which are special cases of the perturbed Meixner-Pollaczek polynomials $Q_n^{(\lambda,\varphi)}(x;t)$ when $t = 0$ and $\varphi = \frac{\pi}{2}$. As given in ([1], Section 9.7), symmetric monic Meixner-Pollaczek polynomials, are defined by

$$S_n^{(\lambda)}(x) := P_n^{(\lambda)}\left(x;\frac{\pi}{2}\right) = \frac{(2\lambda)_n}{n!}\, {}_2F_1\left(\begin{array}{c}-n,\lambda+ix\\2\lambda\end{array}\bigg|\, 2\right), \tag{72}$$

and are orthogonal on $\mathbb{R}$ for $\lambda > 0$ with respect to the continuous weight

$$W(x;\lambda) = \frac{1}{2\pi}|\Gamma(\lambda+ix)|^2,\quad \lambda > 0,\ x \in \mathbb{R}. \tag{73}$$

Since the sequence of monic polynomials $\{S_n^{(\lambda)}\}_{n=0}^{\infty}$ defined in Equation (72) are symmetric with respect to the origin, it follows from orthogonality that they obey symmetric recurrence relation [6]

$$\begin{cases} xS_n^{(\lambda)}(x) = S_{n+1}^{(\lambda)}(x) + \beta_n(\lambda)\, S_{n-1}^{(\lambda)}(x),\quad n \in \mathbb{N},\\ S_0^{(\lambda)}(x) \equiv 1,\ S_{-1}^{(\lambda)}(x) \equiv 0, \end{cases} \tag{74}$$

where the coefficient $\beta_n(\lambda)$ from Equation (74) is given by [6]

$$\beta_n(\lambda) = \frac{(n)(2\lambda+n-1)}{4\sin^2(\frac{\pi}{2})} = \frac{(n)(n+2\lambda-1)}{4},\quad n \geq 1. \tag{75}$$

It now follows from [1] that the normalization constant associated with the weight in (73) is given by

$$\zeta_n^{(\lambda)} = \frac{2\pi\,\Gamma(n+1)\,\Gamma(n+2\lambda)}{2^{2n+2\lambda}}. \tag{76}$$

We note that, for $\lambda = \frac{1}{2}$, taking into account of Euler's duplication formula ([2], Equation (5.5.5)), we have from (73)

$$W\left(x;\frac{1}{2}\right) = \frac{1}{2\pi}\left|\Gamma\left(\frac{1}{2}+ix\right)\right|^2 = \frac{1}{2\pi}\left(\frac{\pi}{\cosh(\pi x)}\right) = \frac{1}{2\cosh(\pi x)}.$$

Similarly, if we take $\lambda = 1$, again using Euler's duplication formula [2], we obtain

$$W(x;1) = \frac{1}{2\pi}\left|\Gamma(1+ix)\right|^2 = \frac{1}{2\pi}\Gamma(1+ix)\,\Gamma(1-ix) = \frac{1}{2\pi}\left(\frac{\pi x}{\sin(\pi x)}\right) = \frac{x}{2\sin(\pi x)}.$$

We now establish the following result, which is an application of Gaussian quadrature formula based on (symmetric) Meixner-Pollaczek weight (74).

Proposition 7. *The Gauss quadrature rule for a continuous function $f(x)$ associated with symmetric Meixner-Pollaczek weight in (73) is given by*

$$\int_{-\infty}^{\infty} f(x)\,W(x;\lambda)\,dx \approx \sum_{k=1}^{j} w_{j,k}^{(\lambda)}\,f(x_{j,k}^{(\lambda)}), \tag{77}$$

where $f(x)$ can be a polynomial, and the quadrature weights are given by

$$w_{j,n}^{(\lambda)} = \int_{\mathbb{R}} \left|\Gamma(\lambda+ix)\right|^2 \left[\prod_{\substack{n\neq k \\ k=1}}^{j}\left(\frac{x-x_{j,k}^{(\lambda)}}{(x_{j,n}^{(\lambda)}-x_{j,k}^{(\lambda)})}\right)\right]dx,$$

for $n = 1, 2, 3, \ldots, j$ and $\left\{x_{j,1}^{(\lambda)}, x_{j,2}^{(\lambda)}, \ldots, x_{j,j}^{(\lambda)}\right\}$ are the zeros of Meixner-Pollaczek polynomials $S_j^{(\lambda)}$.

Proof. Suppose $f \in \mathbb{P}_{2j-1}$. Then, by using division algorithm, we have

$$f = S_j^{(\lambda)}(x)\,V(x) + R_j(x), \tag{78}$$

where the degree of $R_j(x)$ is $(j-1)$ and $S_j^{(\lambda)}(x)$ is orthogonal to any polynomials of degree $<j$, and $V(x)$ is of degree $(j-1)$ and then we have $\langle S_j^{(\lambda)}, V(x)\rangle = 0$. Now, by using orthogonality property and Equation (78), we have

$$\int_{\mathbb{R}} f(x)\,W(x;\lambda)\,dx = \int_{\mathbb{R}} W(x;\lambda)\left[S_j^{(\lambda)}(x)\,V(x) + R_j(x)\right]dx$$

$$= \int_{\mathbb{R}} W(x;\lambda)\,S_j^{(\lambda)}(x)\,V(x)\,dx + \int_{\mathbb{R}} W(x;\lambda)\,R_j(x)\,dx$$

$$= \int_{\mathbb{R}} W(x;\lambda)\,R_j(x)\,dx.$$

However, by orthogonality, and since $R_j(x)$, a polynomial of degree $(j-1)$, is approximated by using Lagrange interpolating polynomial, $L_j(x)$, and it is given as,

$$R_j(x) \approx L_j(x) = \sum_{k=1}^{j} \ell_{j,k}(x)\,R_j(x), \quad \text{where} \quad \ell_{j,k}(x) = \prod_{\substack{\ell=1 \\ k\neq \ell}}^{j}\left(\frac{x-x_{j,\ell}^{(\lambda)}}{x_{j,k}^{(\lambda)}-x_{j,\ell}^{(\lambda)}}\right).$$

Now,

$$\int_{\mathbb{R}} W(x;\lambda) f(x) \, dx = \int_{\mathbb{R}} W(x;\lambda) R_j(x) \, dx = \int_{\mathbb{R}} W(x;\lambda) \left[\sum_{k=1}^{j} \ell_{j,k}(x) R_j(x_k) \right] dx$$

$$= \sum_{k=1}^{j} \int_{\mathbb{R}} W(x;\lambda) \ell_{j,k}(x) R_j(x_k) \, dx = \sum_{k=1}^{j} R_j(x_k) \int_{\mathbb{R}} W(x;\lambda) \ell_{j,k}(x) \, dx$$

$$= \sum_{k=1}^{j} R_j(x_k) \, \omega_{j,k}^{(\lambda)} \qquad \left(\text{where } \omega_{j,k}^{(\lambda)} = \int_{\mathbb{R}} W(x;\lambda) \ell_{j,k}(x) \, dx \right)$$

$$= \sum_{k=1}^{j} \omega_{j,k}^{(\lambda)} f(x_{j,k}^{(\lambda)}) \qquad \left(\text{since } f(x_{j,k}^{(\lambda)}) = R_j(x_k) \right).$$

Therefore, $\int_{\mathbb{R}} f(x) W(x;\lambda) \, dx = \sum_{k=1}^{j} \omega_{j,k}^{(\lambda)} f(x_{j,k}^{(\lambda)})$ where $\omega_{j,k}^{(\lambda)} = \int_{\mathbb{R}} \ell_{j,k}(x) W(x;\lambda) \, dx$. □

In order to implement Proposition 7, the first few monic polynomials $\mathcal{S}_n^{(\lambda)}(x)$, for some values of λ, are shown in the following Table 4.

Table 4. $\mathcal{S}_n^{(\lambda)}(x)$ for $0 \leq n \leq 4$ and $\lambda = 1, \frac{1}{2}, \frac{1}{4}$.

	$\lambda = 1$	$\lambda = \frac{1}{2}$	$\lambda = \frac{1}{4}$
$n = 0$	1	1	1
$n = 1$	x	x	x
$n = 2$	$x^2 - \frac{1}{2}$	$x^2 - \frac{1}{4}$	$x^2 - \frac{1}{8}$
$n = 3$	$x^3 - 2x$	$x^3 - \frac{5}{4}x$	$x^3 - \frac{7}{8}x$
$n = 4$	$x^4 - 5x^2 + \frac{3}{2}$	$x^4 - \frac{7}{2}x^2 + \frac{9}{16}$	$x^4 - \frac{11}{4}x^2 + \frac{15}{64}$
$n = 5$	$x^5 - 10x^3 + \frac{23}{2}x$	$x^5 - \frac{15}{2}x^3 + \frac{89x}{16}$	$x^5 - \frac{25x^3}{4} + \frac{211x}{64}$

The following example elaborates the applicability of Proposition 7.

Example 1. *Construct a two-point Gauss quadrature rule for the symmetric Meixner-Pollaczek weight $W(x;\lambda) = \left|\Gamma(1+ix)\right|^2$ with parameters ($\lambda = \frac{1}{2}$ and $\lambda = 1$) and also compute the specific zeros $x_{j,k}^{(\lambda)}$ and the quadrature weights $\omega_{j,k}^{(\lambda)}$ of this quadrature rule.*

Solution: By considering the zeros of symmetric Meixner-Pollaczek polynomials, $\mathcal{S}_n^{(\lambda)}(x)$ with parameter ($\lambda = \frac{1}{2}$ and $\lambda = 1$) and by recalling that $f \in \mathbb{P}_{2j-1}$, we compute the Gauss quadrature rule, as given in (77), as follows.

The case when $\lambda = 1$:
The zeros of $\mathcal{S}_2^{(1)}(x) = x^2 - \frac{1}{2}$ are $x_{2,1}^{(1)} = \frac{1}{\sqrt{2}}$ and $x_{2,2}^{(1)} = -\frac{1}{\sqrt{2}}$ and the corresponding quadrature weights are given by

$$\omega_{2,1}^{(1)} = \int_{\mathbb{R}} |\Gamma(1+ix)|^2 \left[\prod_{\substack{n \neq k \\ k=1}}^{2} \left(\frac{x - x_{2,k}^{(1)}}{x_{2,1}^{(1)} - x_{2,k}^{(1)}} \right) \right] dx = \int_{-\infty}^{\infty} \frac{\pi x}{\sin \pi x} \left(\frac{x - x_{2,2}^{(1)}}{x_{2,1}^{(1)} - x_{2,2}^{(1)}} \right) dx = \int_{-\infty}^{\infty} \frac{\pi x}{\sin \pi x} \left(\frac{x + \frac{1}{\sqrt{2}}}{\sqrt{2}} \right) dx, \qquad (79)$$

and

$$\omega_{2,2}^{(1)} = \int_{\mathbb{R}} |\Gamma(1+ix)|^2 \left[\prod_{\substack{n \neq k \\ k=1}}^{2} \left(\frac{x - x_{2,k}^{(1)}}{x_{2,2}^{(1)} - x_{2,k}^{(1)}} \right) \right] dx = \int_{-\infty}^{\infty} \frac{\pi x}{\sin \pi x} \left(\frac{x - x_{2,1}^{(1)}}{x_{2,2}^{(1)} - x_{2,1}^{(1)}} \right) dx = \int_{-\infty}^{\infty} \frac{\pi x}{\sin \pi x} \left(\frac{x - \frac{1}{\sqrt{2}}}{-\sqrt{2}} \right) dx. \qquad (80)$$

In order to determine the quadrature weights in Equations (79) and (80), we use Equations (71) and (76) and Table 4 together with orthogonality, to obtain

$$\begin{cases} \omega_{2,1}^{(1)} = \dfrac{\langle P_1, P_1 \rangle_W}{2\left(\frac{1}{\sqrt{2}}\right)^2} = \dfrac{2\pi\,\Gamma(n+1)\,\Gamma(n+2\lambda)}{2^{2n+2\lambda}}, \\[2ex] \omega_{2,2}^{(1)} = \dfrac{\langle P_1, P_1 \rangle_W}{2\left(-\frac{1}{\sqrt{2}}\right)^2} = \dfrac{2\pi\,\Gamma(n+1)\,\Gamma(n+2\lambda)}{2^{2n+2\lambda}}. \end{cases} \quad (81)$$

Hence,

$$\int_\mathbb{R} f(x)\, W(x;\lambda)\, dx = \left(\frac{2\pi\,\Gamma(n+1)\,\Gamma(n+2\lambda)}{2^{2n+2\lambda}}\right) f(x_{2,1}^{(1)}) + f(x_{2,2}^{(1)}) \left(\frac{2\pi\,\Gamma(n+1)\,\Gamma(n+2\lambda)}{2^{2n+2\lambda}}\right).$$

The case when $\lambda = \frac{1}{2}$: The computation of Gaussian nodes and weights can be done in a similar manner.

Remark 5. *For numerical computation of Gauss weights and nodes for an arbitrary weight function using Matlab, see [43] and also [42].*

4.4. Meixner-Pollaczek Polynomials as Solution for Cauchy Problem

It is shown in [12] that the Cauchy problem for the n-dimensional Schrödinger equation for a free particle

$$i\psi_t + \Delta\psi = 0$$

with

$$i\frac{\partial \psi}{\partial t} = \mathcal{H}\psi, \qquad \mathcal{H} = -\Delta = \frac{1}{2}\sum_{s=1}^{n}\left(a_s + a_s^\dagger\right)^2, \quad (82)$$

and the Hamiltonian $\mathcal{H}$ takes the form

$$\mathcal{H}\psi = \left[\frac{1}{2}\sum_{s=1}^{n}\left(-(1+\cos 2t)\frac{\partial^2}{\partial x_s^2} + (1-\cos 2t)\,x_s^2\right) - \frac{i}{2}\sin 2t\sum_{s=1}^{n}\left(2x_s\frac{\partial}{\partial x_s} + 1\right)\right]\psi,$$

the particular solution for Equation (82) is explained in terms of Meixner-Pollaczek polynomials, which satisfies conditions in quantum mechanics (orthogonality and normalizability). The result in [12] generalizes time-dependent simple harmonic motion oscillator and angular momentum problem oscillator of quantum mechanics in a Cartesian and spherical coordinate system.

5. Conclusions

By introducing a time variable to the Meixner–Pollaczek measure, we have found certain interesting properties such as some recursive relations, moments of finite order, concise hypergeometric formulae and orthogonality relation, certain analytic properties of the zeros of the corresponding monic perturbed Meixner–Pollaczek polynomials. As practical applications, we have reproduced the scaled Toda molecule equation in Random matrix theory, Fisher's information with respect to some new parameter, and Gaussian-type quadrature related to the perturbed Meixner–Pollaczek polynomials and also their role as a solution to quantum oscillators.

Author Contributions: Conceptualization, A.S.K., A.S.J. and A.R.A.; methodology, A.S.K., A.S.J. and A.R.A.; software, A.S.K.; validation, A.S.J. and A.R.A.; formal analysis, A.S.K., A.S.J. and A.R.A.; investigation, A.S.K., A.S.J. and A.R.A.; resources, A.S.J. and A.R.A.; data curation, A.S.K.; writing-original draft preparation, A.S.K., A.S.J. and A.R.A.; visualization, A.S.K., A.S.J. and A.R.A.; supervision, A.R.A.; project administration, A.S.J. and A.R.A.; funding acquisition, A.S.J. and A.R.A.

Funding: A. S. Kelil would like to acknowledge the NMU Council postdoctoral fellowship (March 2020 to April 2021), during this period, this work was completed.

Institutional Review Board Statement: Not applicable.

Informed Consent Statement: Not applicable.

Data Availability Statement: Not applicable.

Acknowledgments: A. S. Kelil wants to thank T. K. Araaya for sharing resources and directions on this work, and he also sincerely thanks K. H. Jordaan for the kind support and teachings in his previous studies. The authors would like to thank the three reviewers who provided feedback which allowed them to significantly improve the manuscript.

Conflicts of Interest: The authors declare no conflict of interest.

Appendix A

In this appendix, we provide the proof to Proposition 6 to aid the reader.

Appendix A.1. Proof for Proposition 6

Proof. The proof follows from orthogonality and the corresponding recurrence coefficients for monic polynomials that are orthogonal with respect to the weight $w^{(\lambda,\varphi)}(x;t)$ given in (8). Now, by considering the three-term recurrence relation in (29) and taking derivatives of the coefficients in Equation (29) with respect to t, we have that

$$x \frac{d\mathcal{Q}_n^{(\lambda,\varphi)}(x;t)}{dt} = \frac{d\mathcal{Q}_{n+1}^{(\lambda,\varphi)}(x;t)}{dt} + \alpha_n^{(\lambda,\varphi)}(t) \frac{d\mathcal{Q}_n^{(\lambda,\varphi)}(x;t)}{dt} + \frac{d\alpha_n}{dt} \mathcal{Q}_n^{(\lambda,\varphi)}(x;t) + \frac{d\beta_n}{dt} \mathcal{Q}_{n-1}^{(\lambda,\varphi)} + \beta_n^{(\lambda,\varphi)} \frac{d\mathcal{Q}_{n-1}^{(\lambda,\varphi)}(x;t)}{dt}. \quad (A1)$$

Multiplying Equation (A1) by $\mathcal{Q}_n^{(\lambda,\varphi)}(x;t)$ and integrating with respect to the measure $w^{(\lambda,\varphi)}(x;t)$ yields

$$\frac{d\alpha_n^{(\lambda,\varphi)}}{dt} \zeta_n^{(\lambda,\varphi)} = \int \frac{d\mathcal{Q}_n^{(\lambda,\varphi)}(x;t)}{dt} (x\mathcal{Q}_n(x)) w^{(\lambda,\varphi)}(x;t)\,dx - \int \mathcal{Q}_n^{(\lambda,\varphi)}(x;t) \frac{d\mathcal{Q}_{n+1}^{(\lambda,\varphi)}(x;t)}{dt} w^{(\lambda,\varphi)}(x;t)dx$$
$$- \alpha_n^{(\lambda,\varphi)} \int \mathcal{Q}_n^{(\lambda,\varphi)}(x;t) \frac{d\mathcal{Q}_n^{(\lambda,\varphi)}(x;t)}{dt} w^{(\lambda,\varphi)}(x;t)\,dx - \beta_n^{(\lambda,\varphi)} \int \mathcal{Q}_n^{(\lambda,\varphi)}(x;t) \frac{d\mathcal{Q}_{n-1}^{(\lambda,\varphi)}(x;t)}{dt} w^{(\lambda,\varphi)}(x;t)dx, \quad (A2)$$

where we have used the orthogonality of $\frac{d\mathcal{Q}_{n-1}^{(\lambda,\varphi)}}{dt}$ and $\mathcal{Q}_n^{(\lambda,\varphi)}$.

Again, employing the recurrence relation (29) and the orthogonality relation, (A2) is equivalently given as

$$\frac{d\alpha_n}{dt} \zeta_n^{(\lambda,\varphi)} = \int \frac{d\mathcal{Q}_n^{(\lambda,\varphi)}(x;t)}{dt} \left(\mathcal{Q}_{n+1}^{(\lambda,\varphi)} + \alpha_n^{(\lambda,\varphi)} \mathcal{Q}_n^{(\lambda,\varphi)} + \beta_n^{(\lambda,\varphi)} \mathcal{Q}_{n-1}^{(\lambda,\varphi)} \right) w^{(\lambda,\varphi)}(x;t)\,dx$$
$$- \int \mathcal{Q}_n^{(\lambda,\varphi)}(x;t) \frac{d\mathcal{Q}_{n+1}^{(\lambda,\varphi)}(x;t)}{dt} w^{(\lambda,\varphi)}(x;t)dx - \alpha_n^{(\lambda,\varphi)} \int \mathcal{Q}_n^{(\lambda,\varphi)}(x;t) \frac{d\mathcal{Q}_n^{(\lambda,\varphi)}(x;t)}{dt} w^{(\lambda,\varphi)}(x;t)\,dx$$
$$= \beta_n^{(\lambda,\varphi)} \int \mathcal{Q}_{n-1}^{(\lambda,\varphi)}(x;t) \frac{d\mathcal{Q}_n^{(\lambda,\varphi)}(x;t)}{dt} w^{(\lambda,\varphi)}(x;t)dx - \int \mathcal{Q}_n^{(\lambda,\varphi)}(x;t) \frac{d\mathcal{Q}_{n+1}^{(\lambda,\varphi)}(x;t)}{dt} w^{(\lambda,\varphi)}(x;t)\,dx. \quad (A3)$$

Now, if we consider the weight given in Equation (8) and if we differentiate the orthogonality condition

$$\int \mathcal{Q}_n^{(\lambda,\varphi)}(x;t) \mathcal{Q}_{n\pm 1}^{(\lambda,\varphi)}(x;t) w^{(\lambda,\varphi)}(x;t)\,dx = 0$$

with respect to t, we obtain the following relations respectively:

$$\int \mathcal{Q}_{n-1}^{(\lambda,\varphi)}(x;t) \frac{d\mathcal{Q}_n^{(\lambda,\varphi)}(x;t)}{dt} w^{(\lambda,\varphi)}(x;t)dx + \int \mathcal{Q}_n^{(\lambda,\varphi)}(x;t) \frac{d\mathcal{Q}_{n-1}^{(\lambda,\varphi)}(x;t)}{dt} w^{(\lambda,\varphi)}(x;t)dx - \int x\mathcal{Q}_n^{(\lambda,\varphi)}(x;t) \mathcal{Q}_{n-1}^{(\lambda,\varphi)}(x;t) w^{(\lambda,\varphi)}(x;t)dx = 0, \quad (A4)$$

$$\int \mathcal{Q}_{n+1}^{(\lambda,\varphi)}(x;t) \frac{d\mathcal{Q}_n^{(\lambda,\varphi)}(x;t)}{dt} w^{(\lambda,\varphi)}(x;t)dx + \int \mathcal{Q}_n^{(\lambda,\varphi)}(x;t) \frac{d\mathcal{Q}_{n+1}^{(\lambda,\varphi)}(x;t)}{dt} w^{(\lambda,\varphi)}(x;t)dx - \int x\mathcal{Q}_{n+1}^{(\lambda,\varphi)}(x;t) \mathcal{Q}_n^{(\lambda,\varphi)}(x;t) w^{(\lambda,\varphi)}(x;t)dx = 0. \quad (A5)$$

Now using iterated three-term recurrences, Equations (A4) and (A5) lead to

$$\int \mathcal{Q}_{n-1}^{(\lambda,\varphi)}(x;t) \frac{d\mathcal{Q}_n^{(\lambda,\varphi)}(x;t)}{dt} w^{(\lambda,\varphi)}(x;t) dx = \int x\, \mathcal{Q}_{n-1}^{(\lambda,\varphi)}(x;t) \mathcal{Q}_n^{(\lambda,\varphi)}(x;t) w^{(\lambda,\varphi)}(x;t)\, dx = \beta_n^{(\lambda,\varphi)} \zeta_{n-1}^{(\lambda,\varphi)}. \qquad (A6)$$

and

$$\int \mathcal{Q}_n^{(\lambda,\varphi)}(x;t) \frac{d\mathcal{Q}_{n+1}^{(\lambda,\varphi)}(x;t)}{dt} w^{(\lambda,\varphi)}(x;t) dx = \int x \mathcal{Q}_n^{(\lambda,\varphi)}(x;t)\, \mathcal{Q}_{n+1}^{(\lambda,\varphi)}(x;t)\, w^{(\lambda,\varphi)}(x;t)\, dx$$
$$= \beta_{n+1}^{(\lambda,\varphi)} \zeta_n^{(\lambda,\varphi)}. \qquad (A7)$$

Thus, using orthogonality, (A6) and (A7) into Equation (A3), we obtain the first equation in (57).

Similarly, if we differentiate the normalization constant
$\zeta_n^{(\lambda,\varphi)} = \int \mathcal{Q}_n^{(\lambda,\varphi)}(x;t)\, w^{(\lambda,\varphi)}(x;t)\, dx$, where

$$(w^{(\lambda,\varphi)}(x;t))' = -xw^{(\lambda,\varphi)}(x;t)$$

with the prime denoting differentiation with respect to x and if we use the orthogonality relation and the recurrence relation, we find that

$$\frac{d\zeta_n^{(\lambda,\varphi)}}{dt} = \alpha_n^{(\lambda,\varphi)} \zeta_n^{(\lambda,\varphi)}. \qquad (A8)$$

Now using (A8) and considering the derivative of $\beta_n^{(\lambda,\varphi)}(t)$ with respect to t, we have that

$$\frac{d\beta_n^{(\lambda,\varphi)}}{dt} = \frac{d}{dt}\left(\frac{\zeta_n^{(\lambda,\varphi)}}{\zeta_{n-1}^{(\lambda,\varphi)}}\right) = \frac{1}{\zeta_{n-1}^{2\,(\lambda,\varphi)}} \left(\zeta_{n-1}^{(\lambda,\varphi)} \frac{d\zeta_n^{(\lambda,\varphi)}}{dt} - \zeta_n^{(\lambda,\varphi)} \frac{d\zeta_{n-1}^{(\lambda,\varphi)}}{dt}\right)$$
$$= \frac{1}{\zeta_{n-1}^{2\,(\lambda,\varphi)}} \left(\zeta_{n-1}^{(\lambda,\varphi)} \alpha_n^{(\lambda,\varphi)} \zeta_n^{(\lambda,\varphi)} - \zeta_n^{(\lambda,\varphi)} \alpha_{n-1}^{(\lambda,\varphi)} \zeta_{n-1}^{(\lambda,\varphi)}\right) = \alpha_n^{(\lambda,\varphi)} \beta_n^{(\lambda,\varphi)} - \alpha_{n-1}^{(\lambda,\varphi)} \beta_n^{(\lambda,\varphi)},$$

which yields the second equation in Equation (57) and this completes the proof. □

References

1. Koekoek, R.; Lesky, P.A.; Swarttouw, R.F. *Hypergeometric Orthogonal Polynomials and Their q-Analogues*; Springer: Berlin/Heidelberg, Germany, 2010.
2. Olver, F.W.J.; Lozier, D.W.; Boisvert, R.F.; Clark, C.W. (Eds.) *DLMF Handbook of Mathematical Functions*; Cambridge University Press: Cambridge, UK, 2010.
3. Szegő, G. *Orthogonal Polynomials*, 4th ed.; Amer. Math. Soc: Providence, RI, USA, 1975; Volume 23.
4. Araaya, T.K. Linearization and connection problems for the symmetric Meixner-Pollaczek polynomials. *Int. J. Pure Appl. Math.* **2004**, *17*, 409–422.
5. Araaya, T.K. The Meixner-Pollaczek polynomials and a system of orthogonal polynomials in a strip. *J. Comput. Appl. Math.* **2004**, *170*, 241–254. [CrossRef]
6. Araaya, T.K. The symmetric Meixner-Pollaczek polynomials with real parameter. *J. Math. Anal. Appl.* **2005**, *305*, 411–423. [CrossRef]
7. Chen, Y.; Ismail, M.E.H. Asymptotics of extreme zeros of the Meixner-Pollaczek polynomials. *J. Comput. Appl. Math.* **1997**, *82*, 59–78. [CrossRef]
8. Chihara, T.S. *An Introduction to Orthogonal Polynomials*, Gordon and Breach; Dover Publications: New York, NY, USA, 1978; Reprinted in 2011.
9. Li, X.; Wong, R. On the asymptotics of the Meixner-Pollaczek polynomials and their zeros. *Constr. Approx.* **2001**, *17*, 59–90. [CrossRef]
10. Ismail, M.E.H. *Classical and Quantum Orthogonal Polynomials in One Variable*; Cambridge University Press: Cambridge, UK, 2005; Volume 98.
11. Chen, Y.; Ismail, M.E.H. Thermodynamic relations of the Hermitian matrix ensembles. *J. Phys. A* **1997**, *30*, 6633. [CrossRef]
12. Meiler, M.R.; Soto, C.; Suslov, S.K. Solution of the Cauchy problem for a time-dependent Schrödinger equation. *J. Math Phys.*

13. Atakishiyev, N.M.; Suslov, S.K. The Hahn and Meixner polynomials of an imaginary argument and some of their applications. *J. Phys. A.* **1985**, *18*, 1583. [CrossRef]
14. Pollaczek, F. Sur une famille de polynomes orthogonaux qui contient les polynomes d'Hermite et de Laguerre comme cas limites. *Comptes Rendus Hebd. Des Seances De L Acad. Des Sci.* **1950**, *230*, 1563–1566.
15. Zeng, J. Weighted derangements and the linearization coefficients of orthogonal Sheffer polynomials. *Proc. Lond. Math. Soc.* **1992**, *3*, 1–22. [CrossRef]
16. Brezinski, C.; Driver, K.A.; Redivo-Zaglia, M. Quasi-orthogonality with applications to some families of classical orthogonal polynomials. *Appl. Numer. Math.* **2004**, *48*, 157–168. [CrossRef]
17. Johnston, S.J.; Jooste, A.; Jordaan, K. Quasi-orthogonality of some hypergeometric polynomials. *Integral Transform. Spec. Funct.* **2016**, *27*, 111–125. [CrossRef]
18. Joulak, H. A contribution to quasi-orthogonal polynomials and associated polynomials. *Appl. Numer. Math.* **2005**, *54*, 65–78. [CrossRef]
19. Jooste A.; Jordaan K.; Toókos F. On the zeros of Meixner polynomials. *Numer. Math.* **2013**, *124*, 57–71.
20. Moreno, S.G.; Garciá-Caballero, E.M. Orthogonality of the Meixner-Pollaczek polynomials beyond Favard's theorem. *Bull. Belg. Soc. Simon Stevin* **2013**, *20*, 133–143. [CrossRef]
21. Van Assche, W. *Orthogonal Polynomials and Painlevé Equations*; Cambridge University Press: Cambridge, UK, 2017; Volume 27.
22. Clarkson, P.A.; Jordaan, K. The relationship between semiclassical Laguerre polynomials and the fourth Painlevé equation. *Constr. Approx.* **2014**, *39*, 223–254. [CrossRef]
23. Clarkson, P.A.; Jordaan, K.; Kelil, A. A generalized Freud weight. *Stud. Appl. Math.* **2016**, *136*, 288–320. [CrossRef]
24. Nevai, P. Orthogonal polynomials associated with $\exp(-x^4)$. *Proc. Canad. Math. Soc.* **1983**, *3*, 263–285.
25. Driver, K.; Jordaan, K. Zeros of quasi-orthogonal Jacobi polynomials, Sigma Symmetry Integr. *Geom. Methods Appl.* **2016**, *12*, 42.
26. Jordaan, K.; Wang, H.; Zhou, J. Monotonicity of zeros of polynomials orthogonal with respect to an even weight function. *Integral Transform. Spec. Funct.* **2014**, *25*, 721–729. [CrossRef]
27. Kelil, A.S.; Appadu, A.R. Semi-Class. Orthogonal Polynomials Assoc. A Modif. Sextic Freud-Type Weight. *Mathematics* **2020**, *8*, 1250. [CrossRef]
28. Abramowitz, M.; Stegun, I.A. *Handbook of Mathematical Functions*; National Bureau of Standards: Gaithersburg, MD, USA, 1964.
29. Erdélyi, A. *Higher Transcendental Functions*; Bateman Manuscript Project McGraw-Hill Book Company: New York, NY, USA, 1953; Volume I.
30. Andrews, L.C. *Special Functions of Mathematics for Engineers*; McGraw-Hill: New York, NY, USA, 1992; p. 407.
31. Rakha, M.A.; Rathie, A.K.; Chopra, P. On some new contiguous relations for the Gauss hypergeometric function with applications. *Comput. Math. Appl.* **2011**, *61*, 620–629. [CrossRef]
32. Dimitrov, D.K.; Ranga, A.S. Zeros of a family of hypergeometric para-orthogonal polynomials on the unit circle. *Math. Nachrichten* **2013**, *286*, 1778–1791. [CrossRef]
33. Ismail, M.E. The variation of zeros of certain orthogonal polynomials. *Adv. Appl. Math.* **1987**, *8*, 111–118. [CrossRef]
34. Erb, W.; Toókos, F. Applications of the monotonicity of extremal zeros of orthogonal polynomials in interlacing and optimization problems. *Appl. Math. Comput.* **2011**, *217*, 4771–4780. [CrossRef]
35. Dimitrov, D.K. Convexity of The extreme zeros of classical orthogonal polynomials. *Monograph* **2000**, 1–8. Available online: https://www.researchgate.net/publication/2382036_Convexity_Of_The_Extreme_Zeros_Of_Classical_Orthogonal_Polynomials (accessed on 24 February 2021).
36. Dominici, D. Fisher information of orthogonal polynomials I. *J. Comput. Appl. Math.* **2010**, *233*, 1511–1518. [CrossRef]
37. Suris, Y.B. *The Problem of Integrable Discretization: Hamiltonian Approach, Progress in Mathematics*; Birkhäuser: Basel, Switzerland, 2003; Volume 219.
38. Toda, M. Vibration of a chain with nonlinear interaction. *J. Phys. Soc. Jpn.* **1967**, *22*, 431–436. [CrossRef]
39. Peherstorfer, F. On Toda lattices and orthogonal polynomials. *J. Comput. Appl. Math.* **2001**, *133*, 519–534. [CrossRef]
40. Sanchez-Ruiz, J.; Dehesa, J.S. Fisher information for orthogonal hypergeometric polynomials. *J. Comput. Appl. Math.* **2005**, *182*, 150–164. [CrossRef]
41. Dehesa, J.S.; Olmos, B.; Yáñez, R.J. Parameter-based Fisher's information of orthogonal polynomials. *J. Comput. Appl. Math.* **2008**, *214*, 136–147. [CrossRef]
42. De Villiers, J.M. *Mathematics of Approximation*; Springer Science & Business Media: Berlin/Heidelberg, Germany, 2012; Volume 1.
43. Gautschi, W. *Orthogonal Polynomials: Computation and Approximation*; Oxford University Press: Oxford, UK, 2004.

Article

General Bivariate Appell Polynomials via Matrix Calculus and Related Interpolation Hints

Francesco Aldo Costabile, Maria Italia Gualtieri and Anna Napoli *

Department of Mathematics and Computer Science, University of Calabria, 87036 Rende (CS), Italy; francesco.costabile@unical.it (F.A.C.); mariaitalia.gualtieri@unical.it (M.I.G.)
* Correspondence: anna.napoli@unical.it

Abstract: An approach to general bivariate Appell polynomials based on matrix calculus is proposed. Known and new basic results are given, such as recurrence relations, determinant forms, differential equations and other properties. Some applications to linear functional and linear interpolation are sketched. New and known examples of bivariate Appell polynomial sequences are given.

Keywords: Polynomial sequences; Appell polynomials; bivariate Appell sequence

1. Introduction

Appell polynomials have many applications in various disciplines: probability theory [1–5], number theory [6], linear recurrence [7], general linear interpolation [8–12], operators approximation theory [13–17]. In [18], P. Appell introduced a class of polynomials by the following equivalent conditions: $\{A_n\}_{n\in\mathbb{N}}$ is an Appell sequence (A_n being a polynomial of degree n) if either

$$\begin{cases} \dfrac{d\, A_n(x)}{dx} = n A_{n-1}(x), & n \geq 1, \\ A_n(0) = \alpha_n, & \alpha_0 \neq 0, \quad \alpha_n \in \mathbb{R}, \quad n \geq 0, \\ A_0(x) = 1, \end{cases}$$

or

$$A(t)e^{xt} = \sum_{n=0}^{\infty} A_n(x)\frac{t^n}{n!},$$

where $A(t) = \sum_{k=0}^{\infty} \alpha_k \dfrac{t^k}{k!}$, $\alpha_0 \neq 0$, $\alpha_k \in \mathbb{R}$, $k \geq 0$.

Subsequentely, many other equivalent characterizations have been formulated. For example, in [19] [p. 87], there are seven equivalences.

Properties of Appell sequences are naturally handled within the framework of modern classic umbral calculus (see [19,20] and references therein).

Special polynomials in two variables are useful from the point of view of applications, particularly in probability [21], in physics, expansion of functions [22], etc. These polynomials allow the derivation of a number of useful identities in a fairly straightforward way and help in introducing new families of polynomials. For example, in [23] the authors introduced general classes of two variables Appell polynomials by using properties of an iterated isomorphism related to the Laguerre-type exponentials. In [24], the two-variable general polynomial (2VgP) family $p_n(x,y)$ has been considered, whose members are defined by the generating function

$$e^{xt}\phi(y,t) = \sum_{n=0}^{\infty} p_n(x,y)\frac{t^n}{n!},$$

where $\phi(y,t) = \sum_{k=0}^{\infty} \phi_k(y) \frac{t^k}{k!}$.

Later, the authors considered the two-variable general Appell polynomials (2VgAP) denoted by $_p A_n(x,y)$ based on the sequence $\{p_n\}_{n \in \mathbb{N}}^b$, that is

$$A(t) e^{xt} \phi(y,t) = \sum_{n=0}^{\infty} {}_p A_n(x,y) \frac{t^n}{n!},$$

where $A(t) = \sum_{k=0}^{\infty} \alpha_k \frac{t^k}{k!}$, $\alpha_0 \neq 0$, $\alpha_k \in \mathbb{R}$, $k \geq 0$.

These polynomials are framed within the context of monomiality principle [24–27].

Generalizations of Appell polynomials can be also found in [22,28–31] (see also the references therein).

In this paper, we will reconsider the 2VgAP, but with a systematic and alternative theory, that is matrix calculus-based. To the best of authors knowledge, a systematic approach to general bivariate Appell sequences does not appear in the literature. New properties are given and a general linear interpolation problem is hinted. Some applications of the previous theory are given and new families of bivariate polynomials are presented. Moreover a biorthogonal system of linear functionals and polynomials is constructed.

In particular, the paper is organized as follows: in Section 2 we give the definition and the first characterizations of general bivariate Appell polynomial sequences; in Sections 3–5 we derive, respectively, matrix form, recurrence relations and determinant forms for the elements of a general bivariate Appell polynomial sequence. These sequences satisfy some interesting differential equations (Section 6) and properties (Section 7). In Section 8 we consider the relations with linear functional of linear interpolation. Section 9 introduces new and known examples of polynomial sequences. Finally, Section 10 contains some concluding remarks.

We point out that the first recurrence formula and the determinant forms, as well as the relationship with linear functionals and linear interpolation, to the best of authors' knowledge, do not appear in the literature.

We will adopt the following notation for the derivatives of a polynomial f

$$f^{(i,j)} = \frac{\partial^{i+j} f}{\partial x^i \partial y^j}, \quad f^{(0,0)} = f(x,y), \quad f^{(i,j)}(\alpha, \beta) = f^{(i,j)}(x,y) \big|_{(x,y) \equiv (\alpha,\beta)}.$$

A set of polynomials is denoted, for example, by $\{p_0, \ldots, p_n \mid n \in \mathbb{N}\}$, where the subscripts $0, \ldots, n$ represent the (total) degree of each polynomial. Moreover, for polynomial sequences, we will use the notation $\{a_n\}_{n \in \mathbb{N}}$ for univariate sequence and $\{r_n\}_{n \in \mathbb{N}}^b$ in the bivariate case. Uppercase letters will be used for particular and well-known sequences.

2. Definition and First Characterizations

Let $A(t)$ be the power series

$$A(t) = \sum_{k=0}^{\infty} \alpha_k \frac{t^k}{k!}, \quad \alpha_0 \neq 0, \ \alpha_k \in \mathbb{R}, \ k \geq 0, \tag{1}$$

(usually $\alpha_0 = 1$) and let $\phi(y,t)$ be the two-variable real function defined as

$$\phi(y,t) = \sum_{k=0}^{\infty} \varphi_k(y) \frac{t^k}{k!}, \tag{2}$$

where $\varphi_k(y)$ are real polynomials in the variable y, with $\varphi_0(y) = 1$.

It is known ([19], p. 78) that the power series $A(t)$ generates the univariate Appell polynomial sequence $\{A_n\}_{n \in \mathbb{N}}$ such that

$$A_0(x) = 1, \qquad A_n(x) = \sum_{k=0}^{n} \binom{n}{k} \alpha_{n-k} x^k, \quad n \geq 1. \tag{3}$$

Now we consider the bivariate polynomials r_n with real variables. We denote by $\mathcal{A}(\phi, A)$, or simply $\mathcal{A}$ where there is no possibility of misunderstanding, the set of bivariate polynomial sequences $\{r_n\}_{n \in \mathbb{N}}^b$ such that

$$\begin{cases} r_0(x, y) = 1 & (4a) \\ r_n^{(1,0)}(x, y) = n\, r_{n-1}(x, y), \quad n \geq 1 & (4b) \\ r_n(0, y) = \sum_{k=0}^{n} \binom{n}{k} \alpha_{n-k} \varphi_k(y). & (4c) \end{cases}$$

In the following, unless otherwise specified, the previous hypotheses and notations will always be used.

Remark 1. *We observe that in [21,32] a polynomial sequence $\{P_i\}_{n \in \mathbb{N}}^b$ is said to satisfy the Appell condition if*

$$\frac{\partial}{\partial t} P_i(t, x) = P_{i-1}(t, x), \qquad P_0(t, x) = 1.$$

This sequence in [32] is used to obtain an expansion of bivariate, real functions with integral remainder (generalization of Sard formula [33]. Nothing is said about the theory of this kind of sequences.

Proposition 1. *A bivariate polynomial sequence $\{r_n\}_{n \in \mathbb{N}}^b$ is an element of $\mathcal{A}$ if and only if*

$$r_n(x, y) = \sum_{k=0}^{n} \binom{n}{k} A_{n-k}(x) \varphi_k(y), \quad n \geq 1. \tag{5}$$

Proof. If $\{r_n\}_{n \in \mathbb{N}}^b \in \mathcal{A}$, relations (4a) hold. Then, by induction and partial integration with respect to the variable x ([19] p. 93), we get relation (5), according to (3). Vice versa, from (5), we easily get (4a). □

Proposition 2. *A bivariate polynomial sequence $\{r_n\}_{n \in \mathbb{N}}^b$ is an element of $\mathcal{A}$ if and only if*

$$A(t) e^{xt} \phi(y, t) = \sum_{n=0}^{\infty} r_n(x, y) \frac{t^n}{n!}. \tag{6}$$

Proof. If $\{r_n\}_{n \in \mathbb{N}}^b \in \mathcal{A}$, from Proposition 1 the identity (5) holds. Then

$$\sum_{n=0}^{\infty} r_n(x, y) \frac{t^n}{n!} = \sum_{n=0}^{\infty} \left(\sum_{k=0}^{n} \binom{n}{k} A_{n-k}(x) \varphi_k(y) \right) \frac{t^n}{n!}.$$

From the Cauchy product of series, according to (1) and (2), we get (6). Vice-versa, from (6) we obtain (5). Therefore relations (4a) hold. □

We call the function $F(x, y; t) = A(t) e^{xt} \phi(y, t)$ exponential generating function of the bivariate polynomial sequence $\{r_n\}_{n \in \mathbb{N}}^b$.

Remark 2. *From Propositions 1 and 2 we note explicitly that relations (4a) are equivalent to the identity (6).*

Example 1. Let $\phi(y,t) = 1$, that is $\varphi_0(y) = 1$, $\varphi_k(y) \equiv 0$, $k > 0$. Then $\{r_n\}_{n\in\mathbb{N}}^b$, constructed as in Proposition 1, or, equivalently, Proposition 2, is a polynomial sequence in one variable, with elements
$$r_n(x,y) \equiv r_n(x) = A_n(x).$$
Therefore $\{r_n\}_{n\in\mathbb{N}}^b$ is a univariate Appell polynomial sequence [18,19].

Example 1 suggests us the following definition.

Definition 1. *A bivariate polynomial sequence* $\{r_n\}_{n\in\mathbb{N}}^b \in \mathcal{A}$, *that is a polynomial sequence satisfying relations (4a) or relation (6), is called* **general bivariate Appell polynomial sequence**.

Remark 3. (Elementary general bivariate Appell polynomial sequences) *Assuming* $A(t) = 1$, *that is* $\alpha_0 = 1$, $\alpha_i = 0$, $i \geq 1$, *relations (4a) become*

$$\begin{cases} r_0(x,y) = 1 & (7a) \\ r_n^{(1,0)}(x,y) = n\, r_{n-1}(x,y), \quad n > 1 & (7b) \\ r_n(0,y) = \varphi_n(y). & (7c) \end{cases}$$

Moreover, the univariate Appell sequence is $A_n(x) = x^n$, $n \geq 0$. *Hence, from (5),*

$$r_n(x,y) = \sum_{k=0}^{n} \binom{n}{k} x^{n-k} \varphi_k(y), \quad n \geq 1. \tag{8}$$

Relation (6) becomes

$$e^{xt}\phi(y,t) = \sum_{n=0}^{\infty} r_n(x,y) \frac{t^n}{n!}. \tag{9}$$

In this case, we call the polynomial sequence $\{r_n\}_{n\in\mathbb{N}}^b$ **elementary bivariate Appell sequence**. We will denote it by $\{p_n\}_{n\in\mathbb{N}}^b$, that is

$$p_n(x,y) = \sum_{k=0}^{n} \binom{n}{k} x^{n-k} \varphi_k(y), \quad \forall n \in \mathbb{N}. \tag{10}$$

The set of elementary bivariate Appell sequences will be denoted by $\mathcal{A}(\phi, 1)$, or $\mathcal{A}^e$. Of course, $\mathcal{A}^e \subset \mathcal{A}$. We observe that the set $\mathcal{A}^e$ coincides with the set of $2VgP$ considered in [24].
We note that $\{p_0, \ldots, p_n | n \in \mathbb{N}\}$ is a set of $n+1$ linearly independent polynomials in $\mathcal{A}^e$.

Proposition 3. *Let* $\{r_n\}_{n\in\mathbb{N}}^b \in \mathcal{A}(\phi, A)$ *and* $\{p_n\}_{n\in\mathbb{N}}^b \in \mathcal{A}(\phi, 1)$. *Then, the following identities hold*

$$\sum_{k=0}^{n} \binom{n}{k} A_{n-k}(x) \varphi_k(y) = r_n(x,y) = \sum_{k=0}^{n} \binom{n}{k} \alpha_{n-k} p_k(x,y). \tag{11}$$

Proof. From (9), $e^{xt}\phi(y,t) = \sum_{n=0}^{\infty} p_n(x,y) \frac{t^n}{n!}$. Hence the result follows from (1), (6) and the Cauchy product of series. □

It is known that ([19] p. 11) the power series $A(t)$ is invertible and it results

$$\frac{1}{A(t)} \equiv A^{-1}(t) = \sum_{k=0}^{\infty} \beta_k \frac{t^k}{k!},$$

with $\beta_k, k \geq 0$, defined by

$$\sum_{k=0}^{n} \binom{n}{k} \alpha_{n-k} \beta_k = \delta_{n0}. \tag{12}$$

The identity (9) (with $r_n = p_n$) yelds

$$A^{-1}(t)e^{xt}\phi(y,t) = \sum_{n=0}^{\infty} \hat{p}_n(x,y)\frac{t^n}{n!},$$

with

$$\hat{p}_n(x,y) = \sum_{k=0}^{n} \binom{n}{k}\beta_{n-k}p_k(x,y). \tag{13}$$

The polynomial sequence $\{\hat{p}_n\}_{n\in\mathbb{N}}^b$ is called *conjugate bivariate Appell polynomial sequence* of $\{r_n\}_{n\in\mathbb{N}}^b$.

Observe that the bivariate polynomial sequence $\{\hat{p}_n\}_{n\in\mathbb{N}}^b$ is an element of the set $\mathcal{A}$.

3. Matrix Form

We denote by $A = (a_{i,j})_{i,j\in\mathbb{N}}$ the infinite lower triangular matrix [19,34] with

$$a_{i,j} = \binom{i}{j}\alpha_{i-j}, \quad i,j = 0,\ldots, j \leq i, \quad \alpha_0 \neq 0,\ \alpha_k \in \mathbb{R},\ k \geq 0,$$

and let $B = (b_{i,j})_{i,j\in\mathbb{N}}$ be the inverse matrix. It is known ([19] p. 11) that

$$b_{i,j} = \binom{i}{j}\beta_{i-j}, \quad i,j = 0,\ldots, j \leq i,$$

where β_k are defined as in (12).

Observe that the matrices A and B can be factorized ([19] p. 11) as

$$A = D_1 T^\alpha D_1^{-1}, \quad B = D_1 T^\beta D_1^{-1},$$

where $D_1 = diag(i!)_{i\geq 0}$ is a factorial diagonal matrix and T^α, T^β are lower triangualar Toeplitz matrices with entries, respectively, $t_{i,j}^\alpha = \dfrac{\alpha_{i-j}}{(i-j)!}$ and $t_{i,j}^\beta = \dfrac{\beta_{i-j}}{(i-j)!}, i \geq j$.

We denote by A_n and B_n the principal submatrices of order n of A and B, respectively.

Let P and R be the infinite vectors

$$P = [p_0(x,y),\ldots,p_n(x,y),\cdots]^T \quad \text{and} \quad R = [r_0(x,y),\ldots,r_n(x,y),\cdots]^T.$$

Moreover, for every $n \in \mathbb{N}$, let

$$P_n = [p_0(x,y),\ldots,p_n(x,y)]^T \quad \text{and} \quad R_n = [r_0(x,y),\ldots,r_n(x,y)]^T. \tag{14}$$

Proposition 4. *The following matrix identities hold:*

$$R = AP, \quad \text{and } \forall n \in \mathbb{N} \quad R_n = A_n P_n; \tag{15a}$$

$$P = BR, \quad \text{and } \forall n \in \mathbb{N} \quad P_n = B_n R_n. \tag{15b}$$

Proof. Identities (15a) follow directly from (11). The relations (15b) follow from (15a). □

The identities (15a) are called *matrix forms* of the bivariate general Appell sequence and we call A the related associated matrix.

Now, we consider the vectors

$$\hat{R} = [\hat{p}_0(x,y),\ldots,\hat{p}_n(x,y),\cdots]^T, \quad \text{and, } \forall n \in \mathbb{N}, \quad \hat{R}_n = [\hat{p}_0(x,y),\ldots,\hat{p}_n(x,y)]^T.$$

From (13) we get

$$\hat{R}_n = B_n P_n, \tag{16a}$$

$$P_n = A_n \hat{R}_n. \tag{16b}$$

By combining (16a) and the second in (15a) we obtain

$$\hat{R}_n = B_n^2 R_n \quad \text{and} \quad R_n = \left(B_n^2\right)^{-1} \hat{R}_n = A_n^2 \hat{R}_n.$$

If $B_n^2 = \left(b_{i,j}^2\right)_{i,j \in \mathbb{N}}$ and $A_n^2 = \left(a_{i,j}^2\right)_{i,j \in \mathbb{N}}$, we get the inverse formulas

$$r_n(x,y) = \sum_{j=0}^{n} a_{n,j}^2 \hat{r}_j(x,y), \qquad \hat{r}_n(x,y) = \sum_{j=0}^{n} b_{n,j}^2 r_j(x,y).$$

Remark 4. *For the elementary Appell sequence* $\{p_n\}_{n \in \mathbb{N}}^b$ *with* p_n *given in (10), we observe that the associated matrix is*

$$A^* = \left(a_{i,j}^*\right)_{i,j \in \mathbb{N}} \quad \text{with} \quad a_{i,j}^* = \binom{i}{j},$$

that is the known Pascal matrix [12]. Hence the inverse matrix is

$$B^* = \left(b_{i,j}^*\right)_{i,j \in \mathbb{N}} \quad \text{with} \quad b_{i,j}^* = \binom{i}{j}(-1)^{i-j}.$$

Then we can obtain the conjugate sequence, $\{\hat{p}_n\}_{n \in \mathbb{N}}^b$. Therefore, from (16a) and (16b), we get

$$\hat{p}_n(x,y) = \sum_{k=0}^{n} \binom{n}{k}(-1)^{n-k} p_k(x,y), \tag{17a}$$

$$p_n(x,y) = \sum_{k=0}^{n} \binom{n}{k} \hat{p}_k(x,y). \tag{17b}$$

If we introduce the vectors

$$\hat{P} = [\hat{p}_0(x,y), \ldots, \hat{p}_i(x,y), \cdots]^T, \quad \text{and} \quad \forall n \in \mathbb{N}, \ \hat{P}_n = [\hat{p}_0(x,y), \ldots, \hat{p}_n(x,y)]^T,$$

we get the matrix identities

$$P = A^* \hat{P}, \quad \text{and} \quad \forall n \in \mathbb{N}, \ P_n = A_n^* \hat{P}_n,$$
$$\hat{P} = B^* P, \quad \text{and} \quad \forall n \in \mathbb{N}, \ \hat{P}_n = B_n^* P_n. \tag{18}$$

Combining this with (15a) we get

$$R_n = (A_n A_n^*) \hat{P}_n = C_n \hat{P}_n, \quad \text{with} \quad C_n = A_n A_n^*, \tag{19}$$

From (19) we have

$$\forall n \in \mathbb{N}, \quad r_n(x,y) = \sum_{j=0}^{n} c_{n,j} \hat{p}_j(x,y) \tag{20}$$

with $c_{n,j} = \sum_{k=j}^{n} \binom{n}{k}\binom{k}{j} \alpha_{n-k}.$

Since the matrix C_n is invertible, we get from (10)

$$\hat{P}_n = C_n^{-1} R_n \qquad (21)$$

that is,

$$\forall n \in \mathbb{N}, \qquad \hat{p}_n(x,y) = \sum_{j=0}^{n} \hat{c}_{n,j} r_j(x,y), \qquad (22)$$

with

$$\hat{c}_{n,j} = \sum_{k=j}^{n} \binom{n}{k}\binom{k}{j}(-1)^{n-k} \beta_{k-j}, \qquad (23a)$$

$$\hat{c}_{n,j} = \binom{n}{j} \hat{c}_{n-j,0} = \binom{n}{j} \hat{c}_{n-j}, \quad \text{with} \quad \hat{c}_{n-j} \equiv \hat{c}_{n-j,0}. \qquad (23b)$$

Formulas (20) and (22) are the inverse each other.
In order to determine the generating function of the sequence $\{\hat{p}_n\}_{n \in \mathbb{N}}^b$ we observe that

$$\frac{1}{A(t)} = \sum_{k=0}^{\infty} \beta_k \frac{t^k}{k!}, \quad \text{and hence} \quad \beta_k = (-1)^k.$$

Consequently, the generating function of $\{\hat{p}_n\}_{n \in \mathbb{N}}^b$ is

$$G(x,y;t) = e^{-t} e^{xt} \phi(y,t). \qquad (24)$$

that is $\{\hat{p}_n\}_{n \in \mathbb{N}}^b$ is an element of $\mathcal{A}(\phi, A)$.

Proposition 5. *For the conjugate sequence $\{\hat{p}_n\}_{n \in \mathbb{N}}^b$ the following identity holds*

$$\forall n \in \mathbb{N}, \qquad \hat{p}_n(x,y) = \sum_{k=0}^{n} \binom{n}{k}(x-1)^k \phi_{n-k}(y). \qquad (25)$$

Proof. From (24) and (17a) we get

$$e^{-t} e^{xt} \phi(y,t) = \sum_{n=0}^{\infty} \left(\sum_{k=0}^{n} \binom{n}{k}(-1)^k p_{n-k}(x,y) \right) \frac{t^n}{n!}. \qquad (26)$$

By applying the Cauchy product of series to the left-hand term in (26), and substituting (17a) in the right-hand term, we obtain (25). □

Corollary 1.

$$\forall n \in \mathbb{N}, \qquad \sum_{k=0}^{n} \binom{n}{k}(-1)^k p_{n-k}(x,y) = \sum_{k=0}^{n} \binom{n}{k}(x-1)^k \phi_{n-k}(y). \qquad (27)$$

4. Recurrence Relations

In [35] has been noted that recurrence relations are a very interesting tool for the study of the polynomial sequences.

Theorem 1 (Recurrence relations). *Under the previous hypothesis and notations for the elements of $\{r_n\}_{n \in \mathbb{N}}^b \in \mathcal{A}(\phi, A)$ the following recurrence relations hold:*

$$r_n(x,y) = n r_n(x,y) - \sum_{i=1}^{n-1} \binom{n}{i} \beta_{n-i} r_i(x,y), \quad n \geq 1; \qquad (28)$$

$$r_0(x,y) = 1, \qquad r_n(x,y) = \hat{p}_n(x,y) - \sum_{j=0}^{n-1} \binom{n}{j} \hat{c}_{n-j} r_j(x,y), \quad n \geq 1, \qquad (29)$$

with β_k defined as in (12) and $\hat{c}_k$ given as in (23b).

Proof. The proof follows easily by identities (15a) and (21). □

We call relations (28) and (29), first and second recurrence relations, respectively.

The third recurrence relations can be obtained from the generating function.

Theorem 2 (Third recurrence relation). *For the elements of $\{r_n\}_{n\in\mathbb{N}}^b \in \mathcal{A}(\phi, A)$ the following identity holds: $\forall n \geq 0$*

$$r_{n+1}(x,y) = [x + b_0 + c_0(y)] r_n(x,y) + \sum_{k=0}^{n-1} \binom{n}{k} [b_{n-k} + c_{n-k}(y)] r_k(x,y), \qquad (30)$$

where b_k and c_k are such that

$$\frac{A'(t)}{A(t)} = \sum_{k=0}^{\infty} b_k \frac{t^k}{k!}, \qquad \frac{\phi^{(0,1)}(y,t)}{\phi(y,t)} = \sum_{k=0}^{\infty} c_k(y) \frac{t^k}{k!}. \qquad (31)$$

Proof. Partial differentiation with respect to the variable t in (6) gives

$$\left[x + \frac{A'(t)}{A(t)} + \frac{\phi^{(0,1)}(y,t)}{\phi(y,t)} \right] A(t) e^{xt} \phi(y,t) = \sum_{n=1}^{\infty} n\, r_n(x,y) \frac{t^{n-1}}{n!} = \sum_{n=0}^{\infty} r_{n+1}(x,y) \frac{t^n}{n!} \qquad (32)$$

Hence we get

$$\sum_{n=0}^{\infty} \left(\sum_{k=0}^{n} \binom{n}{k} [b_{n-k} + c_{n-k}(y)] r_k(x,y) + x r_n(x,y) \right) \frac{t^n}{n!} = \sum_{n=0}^{\infty} r_{n+1}(x,y) \frac{t^n}{n!},$$

and from this, relation (30) follows. □

The same techniques used previously can be used to derive recurrence relations for the conjugate sequence. Particularly, the third recurrence relation is similar to (30) by exchanging b_k with d_k, $k = 0, \ldots, n$, being d_k such that

$$\frac{\left(A^{-1}(t)\right)'}{A^{-1}(t)} = \sum_{k=0}^{\infty} d_k \frac{t^k}{k!}. \qquad (33)$$

Remark 5. *Observe that if $\sum_{k=0}^{n-2} \binom{n}{k} [b_{n-k} + c_{n-k}(y)] r_k(x,y) = 0$, the recurrence relation (30) becomes a three-terms relation.*

5. Determinant Forms

The previous recurrence relations provide determinant forms [36,37], which can be useful for both numerical calculations and new combinatorial identities.

Theorem 3 (Determinant forms). *For the elements of $\{r_n\}_{n\in\mathbb{N}}^b \in \mathcal{A}(\phi, A)$ the following identities hold:*

$$r_0(x,y) = 1, \quad r_n(x,y) = (-1)^n \begin{vmatrix} p_0(x,y) & p_1(x,y) & p_2(x,y) & \cdots & p_n(x,y) \\ \beta_0 & \beta_1 & \beta_2 & \cdots & \beta_n \\ 0 & \beta_0 & \binom{2}{1}\beta_1 & \cdots & \binom{n}{1}\beta_{n-1} \\ \vdots & & \ddots & \ddots & \vdots \\ \vdots & & & \ddots & \ddots \\ 0 & \cdots & 0 & \beta_0 & \binom{n}{n-1}\beta_1 \end{vmatrix}, \quad n > 0. \tag{34}$$

$$r_0(x,y) = 1, \quad r_n(x,y) = (-1)^n \begin{vmatrix} \hat{p}_0(x,y) & \hat{p}_1(x,y) & \hat{p}_2(x,y) & \cdots & \hat{p}_n(x,y) \\ \hat{c}_0 & \hat{c}_1 & \hat{c}_2 & \cdots & \hat{c}_n \\ 0 & \hat{c}_0 & \binom{2}{1}\hat{c}_1 & \cdots & \binom{n}{1}\hat{c}_{n-1} \\ \vdots & & \ddots & \ddots & \vdots \\ \vdots & & & \ddots & \ddots \\ 0 & \cdots & 0 & \hat{c}_0 & \binom{n}{n-1}\hat{c}_1 \end{vmatrix}, \quad n > 0. \tag{35}$$

Proof. For $n > 1$ relation (28) can be regarded as an infinite lower triangular system in the unknowns $r_0(x,y), \ldots, r_n(x,y), \ldots$. By solving the first $n+1$ equations by Cramer's rule, after elementary determinant operations we get (34). Relation (35) follows from (29) by the same technique. □

We note that the determinant forms are Hessenberg determinants. It is known ([19] p. 28) that Gauss elimination for the calculation of an Hessenberg determinant is stable.

Theorem 4 (Third determinant form). *For the elements of $\{r_n\}_{n \in \mathbb{N}}^b \in \mathcal{A}(\phi, A)$ the following determinant form holds:*

$$r_0(x,y) = 1,$$
$$r_{n+1}(x,y) = \begin{vmatrix} x + b_0 + c_0(y) & -1 & 0 & \cdots & 0 \\ b_1 + c_1(y) & x + b_0 + c_0(y) & -1 & \cdots & 0 \\ \vdots & & \ddots & \ddots & \vdots \\ \vdots & & & \ddots & -1 \\ b_n + c_n(y) & \binom{n}{1}[b_{n-1} + c_{n-1}(y)] & \cdots & \binom{n}{n-1}[b_1 + c_1(y)] & x + b_0 + c_0(y) \end{vmatrix}, \quad n \geq 0. \tag{36}$$

Proof. The result follows from (30) with the same technique used in the previous Theorem. □

We point out that the first and second recurrence relations and the determinant forms (34)–(36) do not appear in the literature. They will be fundamental in the relationship with linear interpolation.

Remark 6. *For the elements of $\{\hat{r}_n\}_{n \in \mathbb{N}}^b \in \mathcal{A}(\phi, A)$ an expression similar to (36) is obtained by exchanging b_k with d_k, $k = 0, \ldots, n$, d_k being defined as in (33).*

Remark 7. *For the elements of $\{p_n\}_{n \in \mathbb{N}}^b \in \mathcal{A}(\phi, 1)$, from (17a), we get the recurrence relation*

$$p_n(x,y) = \hat{p}_n(x,y) - \sum_{k=0}^{n-1} \binom{n}{k}(-1)^{n-k} p_k(x,y). \tag{37}$$

By the same technique used in the proof of Theorem 3 we obtain the following determinant form

$$p_0(x,y) = 1, \quad p_n(x,y) = (-1)^n \begin{vmatrix} \hat{p}_0(x,y) & \hat{p}_1(x,y) & \hat{p}_2(x,y) & \hat{p}_3(x,y) & \cdots & \hat{p}_n(x,y) \\ 1 & -1 & 1 & -1 & \cdots & (-1)^n \\ 0 & 1 & -2 & 3 & \cdots & \binom{n}{1}(-1)^{n-1} \\ \vdots & & \ddots & \ddots & \ddots & \vdots \\ \vdots & & & \ddots & \ddots & \vdots \\ 0 & \cdots & \cdots & 0 & 1 & -\binom{n}{n-1} \end{vmatrix}, \quad n > 0. \qquad (38)$$

From (30) we obtain

$$p_{n+1}(x,y) = x\, p_n(x,y) + \sum_{k=0}^{n} \binom{n}{k} c_{n-k}(y) p_k(x,y),$$

where c_k are defined as in (31). The related determinant form is

$$p_0(x,y) = 1,$$

$$p_{n+1}(x,y) = \begin{vmatrix} x + c_0(y) & -1 & 0 & \cdots & 0 \\ c_1(y) & x + c_0(y) & -1 & \cdots & 0 \\ \vdots & & \ddots & \ddots & \vdots \\ \vdots & & & \ddots & -1 \\ c_n(y) & \binom{n}{1} c_{n-1}(y) & \cdots & \binom{n}{n-1} c_1(y) & x + c_0(y) \end{vmatrix}, \quad n \geq 0.$$

6. Differential Operators and Equations

The elements of a general bivariate Appell sequence satisfy some interesting differential equations.

Proposition 6. *For the elements of $\{r_n\}_{n \in \mathbb{N}}^b \in \mathcal{A}(\phi, A)$ the following identity holds*

$$\forall n, k \in \mathbb{N}, \ k < n, \quad r_{n-k}(x,y) = \frac{1}{n(n-1)\cdots(n-k+1)} r_n^{(k,0)}(x,y). \qquad (39)$$

Proof. The proof follows easily after k partial differentiation of (7b) with respect to x. □

Theorem 5 (Differential equations). *The elements of $\{r_n\}_{n \in \mathbb{N}}^b \in \mathcal{A}(\phi, A)$ satisfy the following differential equations*

$$\frac{\beta_n}{n!} \frac{\partial^n}{\partial x^n} f(x,y) + \frac{\beta_{n-1}}{(n-1)!} \frac{\partial^{n-1}}{\partial x^{n-1}} f(x,y) + \ldots + f(x,y) = \sum_{i=0}^{n} \binom{n}{i} x^i \varphi_{n-i}(y);$$

$$\hat{c}_n \frac{\partial^n}{\partial x^n} f(x,y) + \frac{n\, \hat{c}_{n-1}}{(n-1)!} \frac{\partial^{n-1}}{\partial x^{n-1}} f(x,y) + \frac{n(n-1)\hat{c}_{n-2}}{2(n-2)!} \frac{\partial^{n-2}}{\partial x^{n-2}} f(x,y) + \ldots + f(x,y) = \sum_{i=0}^{n} \binom{n}{i} (x-1)^i \varphi_{n-i}(y).$$

Proof. The results follow by replacing relation (39) in the first recurrence relation (28) and in the second recurrence relation (29), respectively. □

Theorem 6. *The elements of $\{p_n\}_{n \in \mathbb{N}}^b \in \mathcal{A}(\phi, 1)$ satisfy the following differential equation*

$$\frac{(-1)^n}{n!} \frac{\partial^n}{\partial x^n} f(x,y) + \frac{(-1)^{n-1}}{(n-1)!} \frac{\partial^{n-1}}{\partial x^{n-1}} f(x,y) + \ldots + f(x,y) = \sum_{i=0}^{n} \binom{n}{i} (x-1)^i \varphi_{n-i}(y).$$

Proof. The result follows by replacing relation (39) in (27). □

We observe that the results in Theorems 5 and 6 are new in the literature.

In order to make the paper as autonomous as possible, we remind that a polynomial sequence $\{q_n\}_{n\in\mathbb{N}}$ is said to be quasi-monomial if two operators $\tilde{M}$ and $\tilde{P}$, called multiplicative and derivative operators respectively, can be defined in such a way that

$$\tilde{P}\{q_n(x)\} = nq_{n-1}(x), \tag{40a}$$

$$\tilde{M}\{q_n(x)\} = q_{n+1}(x). \tag{40b}$$

If these operators have a differential realization, some important consequences follow:
- differential equation: $\tilde{M}\tilde{P}\{q_n(x)\} = nq_n(x)$;
- it $q_0(x) = 1$, then $q_n(x) = \tilde{M}^n\{1\}$, and this yields the series definition for $q_n(x)$;
- the exponential generating function of $q_n(x)$ is $e^{t\tilde{M}\{1\}} = \sum_{n=0}^{\infty} q_n(x)\dfrac{t^n}{n!}$.

For the general bivariate Appell sequence $\{r_n\}_{n\in\mathbb{N}}^b$ we also have multiplicative and derivative operators.

Theorem 7 (Multiplicative and derivative operators [24]). *For $\{r_n\}_{n\in\mathbb{N}}^b \in \mathcal{A}(\phi, A)$ multiplicative and derivative operators are respectively*

$$\tilde{M}_r = x + \frac{A'(D_x)}{A(D_x)} + \frac{\phi'(y, D_x)}{\phi(y, D_x)}, \tag{41a}$$

$$\tilde{P}_r = D_x. \tag{41b}$$

where $\phi'(y, t) = \phi^{(0,1)}(y, t)$ and $D_x = \dfrac{\partial}{\partial x}$.
Thus the set $\{r_n\}_{n\in\mathbb{N}}^b$ is quasi-monomial under the action of the operators $\tilde{M}_r$ and $\tilde{P}_r$.

Proof. Relations (41a) and (41b) follow from (32) and (4b), respectively [24,38]. □

Theorem 8 (Differential identity). *The elements of a general bivariate Appell sequence $\{r_n\}_{n\in\mathbb{N}}^b$ satisfy the following differential identity*

$$\sum_{k=0}^{n}\frac{b_k + c_k(y)}{k!}r_n^{(k,0)}(x,y) + xr_n(x,y) \equiv \tilde{M}_r\{r_n(x,y)\} = r_{n+1}(x,y).$$

Proof. From (41a) we get the first identity. The second equality follows by (40b), according to Theorem 7. □

Remark 8. *The operators (41a) and (41b) satisfy the commutation relation [24] $\tilde{P}_r\tilde{M}_r - \tilde{M}_r\tilde{P}_r = I$, and this shows the structure of a Weyl group.*

Remark 9. *From Theorem 7 and Remark 8 we get $\tilde{M}_r\tilde{P}_r\{r_n(x,y)\} = n\,r_n(x,y)$ that can be interpreted as a differential equation.*

7. General Properties

The general bivariate Appell polynomial sequences satisfy some properties.

Proposition 7 (Binomial identity). *Let $\{r_n\}_{n\in\mathbb{N}}^b \in \mathcal{A}(\phi, A)$. The following identity holds*

$$\forall n \in \mathbb{N}, \qquad r_n(x_1 + x_2, y) = \sum_{k=0}^{n}\binom{n}{k}r_k(x_1, y)x_2^{n-k}. \tag{42}$$

Proof. From the generating function

$$A(t)e^{(x_1+x_2)t}\phi(y,t) = A(t)e^{x_1 t}\phi(y,t)e^{x_2 t} = \sum_{n=0}^{\infty}\left[\sum_{k=0}^{n}\binom{n}{k}r_k(x_1,y)x_2^{n-k}\right]\frac{t^n}{n!}.$$

Thus the result follows. □

Corollary 2. *For $n \in \mathbb{N}$ we get*

$$\sum_{k=0}^{n}\binom{n}{k}r_k(x,y)(-x)^{n-k} = \sum_{k=0}^{n}\binom{n}{k}\alpha_{n-k}\varphi_k(y).$$

Proof. The proof follows from Proposition 7 for $x_2 = -x_1$ and $x_1 = x$ and from (4c). □

Corollary 3 (Forward difference). *For $n \in \mathbb{N}$ we get*

$$\Delta_x r_n(x,y) \equiv r_n(x+1,y) - r_n(x,y) = \sum_{k=0}^{n-1}\binom{n}{k}r_k(x,y).$$

Remark 10. *Proposition 7 suggests us to consider general Appell polynomial sequences with three variables. In fact, setting in (42) $x_1 = x$, $x_2 = z$ and*

$$v_n(x,y,z) = \sum_{k=0}^{n}\binom{n}{k}r_k(x,y)z^{n-k},$$

the sequence $\{v_n\}_n$ can be consider a general Appell polynomial sequence in three variables. Analogously, we can consider Appell polynomial sequences in d variables with $d \geq 3$.

Proposition 8 (Integration with respect to the variable x). *For $n \in \mathbb{N}$ we get*

$$\int_0^x r_n(t,y)dt = \frac{1}{n+1}[r_{n+1}(x,y) - r_{n+1}(0,y)] \tag{43}$$

$$\int_0^1 p_n(x,y)dx = \frac{1}{n+1}\sum_{k=0}^{n}\binom{n+1}{k}\varphi_k(y). \tag{44}$$

Proof. Relation (43) follows from (4b). The (44) is obtained from (7c), (7b) and Proposition 7 for $x_1 = 0$, $x_2 = 1$. □

Proposition 9 (Partial matrix differentiation with respect to the variable x). *Let R_n be the vector defined in (14). Then*

$$R_n^{(1,0)} = D\, R_n,$$

where D is the matrix with entries

$$d_{i,j} = \begin{cases} i & i = j+1 \\ 0 & \text{otherwise} \end{cases} \qquad i,j = 0,\ldots,n.$$

Proof. The proof follows from (4b). □

In order to give an algebraic structure to the set $\mathcal{A}$, we consider two elements $\{r_n\}_{n\in\mathbb{N}}^b$ and $\{s_n\}_{n\in\mathbb{N}}^b$. From (11) we get, $\forall n \in \mathbb{N}$,

$$r_n(x,y) = \sum_{k=0}^{n}\binom{n}{k}\alpha_{n-k}p_k(x,y), \qquad s_n(x,y) = \sum_{k=0}^{n}\binom{n}{k}\bar{\alpha}_{n-k}p_k(x,y).$$

That is, $A_n = (a_{i,j})_{i,j \leq n}$ with $a_{i,j} = \binom{i}{j} \alpha_{i-j}$ is the associated matrix to $\{r_n\}_{n\in\mathbb{N}}^b$, and
$\overline{A}_n = (\overline{a}_{i,j})_{i,j \leq n}$ with $\overline{a}_{i,j} = \binom{i}{j} \overline{\alpha}_{i-j}$ is the associated matrix to $\{s_n\}_{n\in\mathbb{N}}^b$.
Then we define

$$(r_n \circ s_n)(x,y) = r_n(s_n(x,y)) := \sum_{k=0}^{n} \binom{n}{k} \alpha_{n-k} s_k(x,y)$$

and we set

$$z_n^{r,s}(x,y) = (r_n \circ s_n)(x,y). \tag{45}$$

Proposition 10 (Umbral composition). *The polynomial sequence $\{z_n^{r,s}\}_{n\in\mathbb{N}}^b$, with $z_n^{r,s}$ defined as in (45), is a general bivariate Appell sequence and we call it umbral composition of $\{r_n\}_{n\in\mathbb{N}}^b \in \mathcal{A}(\phi, A)$ and $\{s_n\}_{n\in\mathbb{N}}^b \in \mathcal{A}(\phi, A)$.*

Proof. It's easy to verify that the matrix associated to the sequence $\{z_n^{r,s}\}_{n\in\mathbb{N}}^b$ is $V = A\overline{A}$. In fact

$$z_n^{r,s}(x,y) = \sum_{k=0}^{n} \binom{n}{k} \alpha_{n-k} \sum_{i=0}^{k} \binom{k}{i} \overline{\alpha}_{k-i} p_i(x,y) = \sum_{k=0}^{n} \binom{n}{k} v_{n,k} p_k(x,y)$$

with $v_{n,k} = \sum_{i=0}^{n-k} \binom{n-k}{i} \alpha_{n-i-k} \overline{\alpha}_i$.

Moreover V is an Appell-type matrix [19]. In fact

$$V = D_1 T^\alpha D_1^{-1} D_1 T^{\overline{\alpha}} D_1^{-1} = D_1 T^\alpha T^{\overline{\alpha}} D_1^{-1}.$$

□

The set $\mathcal{A}(\phi, A)$ with the umbral composition operation is an algebraic structure $(\mathcal{A}(\phi, A), \circ)$.

Let $(\mathcal{L}, \cdot)$ be the group of infinite, lower triangular matrix with the usual product operation.

Proposition 11 (Algebraic structure). *The algebraic structure $(\mathcal{A}(\phi, A), \circ)$ is a group isomorphic to $(\mathcal{L}, \cdot)$.*

Proof. We have observed that $\mathcal{A}(\phi, A)$ is an algebraic structure. Then we have
(i) the elementary Appell sequence $\{p_n\}_{n\in\mathbb{N}}^b$ is the identity in $(\mathcal{A}(\phi, A), \circ)$.
(ii) for every $\{r_n\}_{n\in\mathbb{N}}^b \in \mathcal{A}(\phi, A)$ the conjugate sequence $\{\hat{r}_n\}_{n\in\mathbb{N}}^b$ is its inverse.
□

Remark 11. *Given $\lambda, \mu \in \mathbb{R}$, with $(\lambda, \mu) \neq (0,0)$, if $\{r_n\}_{n\in\mathbb{N}}^b$ and $\{s_n\}_{n\in\mathbb{N}}^b$ are two elements of $\mathcal{A}(\phi, A)$, the sequence $\{\lambda r_n + \mu s_n\}_{n\in\mathbb{N}}^b$ is also an element of $\mathcal{A}(\phi, A)$. Hence the algebraic structure $(\mathcal{A}(\phi, A), \circ, +, \cdot)$ is an algebra on $\mathbb{K}(\mathbb{R} \text{ or } \mathbb{C})$.*

8. Relations with Linear Functional and Linear Interpolation

Let $\{p_n\}_{n\in\mathbb{N}}^b \in \mathcal{A}(\phi, 1)$. We consider the set of polynomials

$$\mathcal{S}_n = \text{span}\{p_0, \ldots, p_n \mid n \in \mathbb{N}\}.$$

where p_i, $i = 0, \ldots, n$, are defined as in (10). Let L be a linear functional on $\mathcal{S}_n^*$. If we set

we can consider the general bivariate Appell polynomial sequence in $\mathcal{A}(\phi, A)$ as in (34) and we call it the *polynomial sequence related to the functional L*. We denote it by $\{r_n^{L,p}\}_{n\in\mathbb{N}}^b$.

Now we define the $n+1$ linear functionals L_i, $i = 0, \ldots, n$, in $\mathcal{S}_n^*$ as

$$L_0(p_k) = L(p_k) = \beta_k, \quad L_i(p_k) = L\left(p_k^{(i,0)}\right) = i!\binom{k}{i}\beta_{k-i}, \quad i = 1, \ldots, k, \ k = 0, \ldots, n,$$

where in the second relation we have applied (7b).

Theorem 9. *For the elements of the bivariate general Appell sequence* $\{r_n^{L,p}\}_{n\in\mathbb{N}}^b$ *the following identity holds*

$$L_i\left(r_n^{L,p}\right) = n!\delta_{ni}, \quad i = 0, \ldots, n,$$

where δ_{ni} is the known Kronecker symbol.

Proof. The proof follows from the first determinant form (Theorem 3). □

Corollary 4. *The bivariate general Appell polynomial sequence* $\{r_n^{L,p}\}_{n\in\mathbb{N}}^b$ *is the solution of the following general linear interpolation problem on $\mathcal{S}_n$*

$$L_i(z_n) = n!\delta_{ni}, \quad i = 0, \ldots, n, \ z_n \in \mathcal{S}_n.$$

Proof. The proof follows from Theorem 9 and the known theorems on general linear interpolation problem [39] since L_i, $i = 0, \ldots, n$, are linearly independent functionals. □

Theorem 10 (Representation theorem). *For every $z_n \in \mathcal{S}_n$ the following relation holds*

$$z_n(x,y) = \sum_{k=0}^{n} L\left(z_n^{(k,0)}\right) \frac{r_k^{L,p}(x,y)}{k!}.$$

Proof. The proof follows from Theorem 9 and the previous definitions. □

9. Some Bivariate Appell Sequences

In order to illustrate the previous results, we construct some two variables Appell sequences. As we have shown, to do this, for each sequence we need two power series $A(t)$ and $\phi(y,t)$, where y is considered as a parameter.

Example 2. *Let $\phi(y,t) = e^{yt}$. There are several choices for $A(t)$.*
(1) $A(t) = 1$.
   In this case, the elementary bivariate Appell sequence is the classical bivariate monomials. These polynomials are known in the literature also as Hermite polynomials in two variables and denoted by $H_n^{(1)}(x,y)$ [40,41]:

$$H_n^{(1)}(x,y) = (x+y)^n.$$

Figure 1 provides the graphs of the first four polynomials.

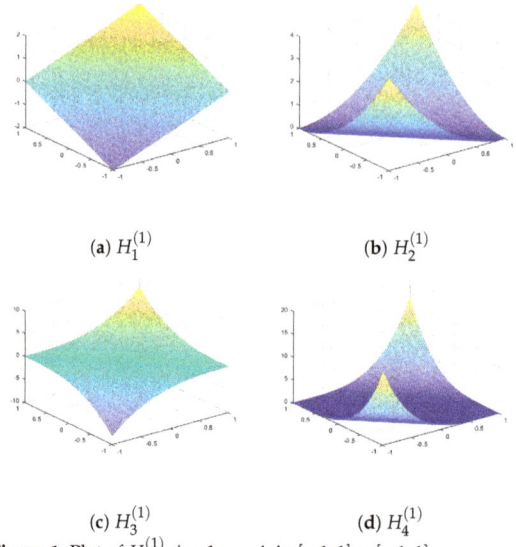

(a) $H_1^{(1)}$ (b) $H_2^{(1)}$

(c) $H_3^{(1)}$ (d) $H_4^{(1)}$

Figure 1. Plot of $H_i^{(1)}$, $i = 1, \ldots, 4$, in $[-1,1] \times [-1,1]$.

The matrix form is obtained by using the known Pascal matrix [34]. From (25) we get the conjugate sequence

$$\hat{H}_n^{(1)}(x,y) = \sum_{k=0}^{n} \binom{n}{k}(x-1)^{n-k}y^k = [(x-1)+y]^n,$$

hence, from (17a) and (17b), the inverse relations are

$$(x+y)^n = \sum_{k=0}^{n} \binom{n}{k}[(x-1)+y]^k \qquad (46a)$$

$$[(x-1)+y]^n = \sum_{k=0}^{n} \binom{n}{k}(-1)^{n-k}(x+y)^k. \qquad (46b)$$

Note that from (46a) and (46b) we obtain the basic relations for binomial coefficients ([42] p. 3). From (46b) we get the second recurrence relation

$$(x+y)^n = (x+y-1)^n - \sum_{j=0}^{n-1} \binom{n}{j}(-1)^{n-j}(x+y)^j, \qquad n \geq 1.$$

and the related determinant form for $n > 0$

$$(x+y)^n = (-1)^n \begin{vmatrix} 1 & x+y-1 & (x+y-1)^2 & \cdots & (x+y-1)^n \\ 1 & -1 & 1 & \cdots & (-1)^n \\ 0 & 1 & -2 & \cdots & (-1)^{n-1}n \\ \vdots & & \ddots & \ddots & \vdots \\ \vdots & & & \ddots & \vdots \\ 0 & \cdots & 0 & 1 & -n \end{vmatrix}.$$

From this we can derive many identities. For example, for $n > 0$,

$$1 = (-1)^n \begin{vmatrix} -1 & 1 & -1 & \cdots & (-1)^n \\ 1 & -2 & \cdots & & (-1)^{n-1}n \\ \vdots & \ddots & \ddots & \ddots & \vdots \\ \vdots & & \ddots & \ddots & \vdots \\ 0 & \cdots & 0 & 1 & -n \end{vmatrix},$$

and

$$x^n = (-1)^n \begin{vmatrix} 1 & x-1 & (x-1)^2 & \cdots & (x-1)^n \\ 1 & -1 & 1 & \cdots & (-1)^n \\ 0 & 1 & -2 & \cdots & (-1)^{n-1}n \\ \vdots & & \ddots & \ddots & \vdots \\ \vdots & & & \ddots & \vdots \\ 0 & \cdots & 0 & 1 & -n \end{vmatrix}.$$

(2) $A(t) = \dfrac{t}{e^t - 1}$.

It is known ([19] p. 107) that this power series generates the univariate Bernoulli polynomials. Hence, directly from (11) we obtain a general bivariate Appell sequence which we call natural bivariate Bernoulli polynomials and denote it by $\{\mathcal{B}_n\}^b_{n \in \mathbb{N}}$, where

$$\mathcal{B}_n(x,y) = \sum_{k=0}^{n} \binom{n}{k} B_{n-k}(x) y^k = \sum_{k=0}^{n} \binom{n}{k} (x+y)^k B_{n-k}. \tag{47}$$

$B_j(x)$ and B_j are, respectively, the Bernoulli polynomial of degree j and the j-th Bernoulli number ([19] p. 109).

We note that

$$\mathcal{B}_n(x,0) = B_n(x), \qquad \mathcal{B}_n(0,0) = B_n, \qquad n \geq 1.$$

From the second equality in (47) and the known properties of Bernoulli polynomials ([19] p. 109) we have

$$\mathcal{B}_n(x,y) = B_n(x+y), \qquad n \geq 1.$$

The first natural bivariate Bernoulli polynomials are

$$\mathcal{B}_0(x,y) = 1, \qquad \mathcal{B}_1(x,y) = x+y-\frac{1}{2}, \qquad \mathcal{B}_2(x,y) = (x+y)^2 - (x+y) + \frac{1}{6},$$

$$\mathcal{B}_3(x,y) = (x+y)^3 - \frac{3}{2}(x+y)^2 + \frac{1}{2}(x+y),$$

$$\mathcal{B}_4(x,y) = (x+y)^4 - 2(x+y)^3 + (x+y)^2 - \frac{1}{30}.$$

Figure 2 shows the graphs of the first four polynomials $\mathcal{B}_i$, $i = 1, \ldots, 4$.

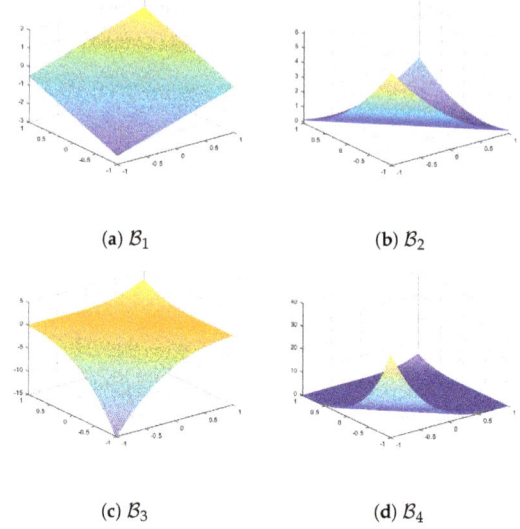

(a) $\mathcal{B}_1$ (b) $\mathcal{B}_2$

(c) $\mathcal{B}_3$ (d) $\mathcal{B}_4$

Figure 2. Plot of $\mathcal{B}_i$, $i = 1,\ldots,4$, in $[-1,1] \times [-1,1]$.

From (11), (12) and (47) we get $\alpha_k = B_k$ and $\beta_k = \dfrac{1}{k+1}$, $k = 0, 1, \ldots$
Therefore the first recurrence relation is

$$\mathcal{B}_0(x,y) = 1, \qquad \mathcal{B}_n(x,y) = (x+y)^n - \sum_{j=0}^{n-1} \binom{n}{j} \frac{\mathcal{B}_j(x,y)}{n-j+1}, \qquad n \geq 1.$$

The related determinant form for $n > 0$ is

$$\mathcal{B}_n(x,y) = (-1)^n \begin{vmatrix} 1 & x+y & (x+y)^2 & (x+y)^3 & \cdots & (x+y)^n \\ 1 & \frac{1}{2} & \frac{1}{3} & \frac{1}{4} & \cdots & \frac{1}{n+1} \\ 0 & 1 & 1 & 1 & \cdots & 1 \\ 0 & 0 & 1 & \frac{3}{2} & & \binom{n}{2}\frac{1}{n-1} \\ \vdots & & \ddots & & \ddots & \vdots \\ \vdots & & & \ddots & \ddots & \vdots \\ 0 & \cdots & & 0 & 1 & \frac{n}{2} \end{vmatrix}. \qquad (48)$$

For the coefficients of $\dfrac{A'(t)}{A(t)} = \sum_{k=0}^{\infty} b_k \dfrac{t^k}{k!}$ we find $b_0 = B_1$, $b_k = -\dfrac{B_{k+1}}{k+1}$, $k \geq 1$. Moreover, $c_0(y) = y$, $c_k(y) = 0$, $k \geq 1$. Hence the third recurrence relation is

$$\mathcal{B}_{n+1}(x,y) = \left(x + y - \frac{1}{2}\right)\mathcal{B}_n(x,y) - \sum_{k=1}^{n-1} \binom{n}{k} \frac{B_{k+1}}{k+1} \mathcal{B}_{n-k}(x,y).$$

The related determinant form for $n > 0$ is

$$\mathcal{B}_{n+1}(x,y) = \begin{vmatrix} x - \frac{1}{2} + y & -1 & 0 & \cdots & \cdots & 0 \\ -\frac{1}{2} & x - \frac{1}{2} + y & -1 & \cdots & \cdots & 0 \\ -\frac{B_3}{3} & & \ddots & \ddots & \ddots & \vdots \\ \vdots & & & \ddots & \ddots & \vdots \\ \vdots & & & & \ddots & -1 \\ -\frac{B_{n+1}}{n+1} & -\binom{n}{1}\frac{B_n}{n} & \cdots & \cdots & -\binom{n}{n-1}\frac{1}{2} & x - \frac{1}{2} + y \end{vmatrix}.$$

(3) $A(t) = \dfrac{2}{e^t + 1}$.

This power series generates the univariate Euler polynomials ([19] p. 123). Hence, directly from (11) we obtain a general bivariate Appell sequence which we call natural bivariate Euler polynomials and denote it by $\{\mathcal{E}_n\}_{n \in \mathbb{N}}^b$, where

$$\mathcal{E}_n(x,y) = \sum_{k=0}^{n} \binom{n}{k} E_{n-k}(x) y^k = \sum_{k=0}^{n} \binom{n}{k} (x+y)^k E_{n-k}(0). \tag{49}$$

$E_j(x)$ is the Euler polynomial of degree j ([19] p. 124).
We note that

$$\mathcal{E}_n(x,0) = E_n(x), \quad n \geq 1,$$

and

$$\mathcal{E}_n(x,y) = E_n(x+y), \quad n \geq 1.$$

The first natural bivariate Euler polynomials are

$$\mathcal{E}_0(x,y) = 1, \quad \mathcal{E}_1(x,y) = x + y - \frac{1}{2}, \quad \mathcal{E}_2(x,y) = (x+y)^2 - (x+y),$$

$$\mathcal{E}_3(x,y) = (x+y)^3 - \frac{3}{2}(x+y)^2 + \frac{1}{4}, \quad \mathcal{E}_4(x,y) = (x+y)^4 - 2(x+y)^3 + x + y.$$

Figure 3 shows the graphs of the first four polynomials $\mathcal{E}_i$, $i = 1,\ldots,4$.

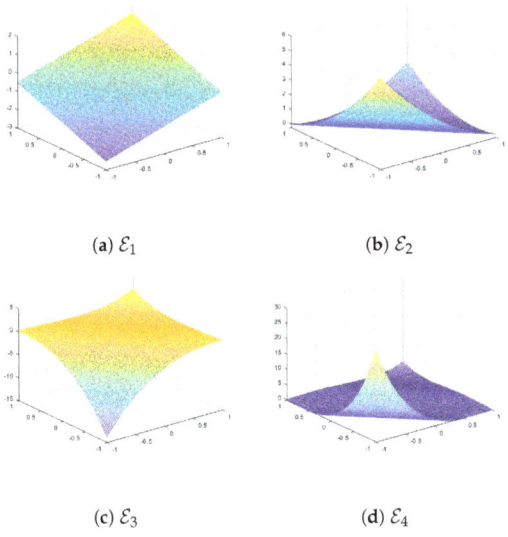

(a) $\mathcal{E}_1$ (b) $\mathcal{E}_2$

(c) $\mathcal{E}_3$ (d) $\mathcal{E}_4$

Figure 3. Plot of $\mathcal{E}_i$, $i = 1,\ldots,4$, in $[-1,1] \times [-1,1]$.

From (11), (12) and (49) we get $\alpha_k = E_k(0)$, hence ([19] p. 124) $\beta_0 = 1$ and $\beta_k = \dfrac{1}{2}$, $k \geq 1$. Therefore the first recurrence relation is

$$\mathcal{E}_0(x,y) = 1, \qquad \mathcal{E}_n(x,y) = (x+y)^n - \frac{1}{2}\sum_{j=0}^{n-1}\binom{n}{j}\mathcal{E}_j(x,y), \qquad n \geq 1.$$

The related determinant form for $n > 0$ is

$$\mathcal{E}_n(x,y) = (-1)^n \begin{vmatrix} 1 & x+y & (x+y)^2 & \cdots & (x+y)^n \\ 1 & \frac{1}{2} & \frac{1}{2} & \cdots & \frac{1}{2} \\ 0 & 1 & \frac{1}{2}\binom{2}{1} & \cdots & \frac{1}{2}\binom{n}{1} \\ \vdots & & \ddots & \ddots & \vdots \\ \vdots & & & \ddots & \vdots \\ 0 & \cdots & 0 & 1 & \frac{1}{2}\binom{n}{n-1} \end{vmatrix}.$$

For the coefficients of the power series $\dfrac{A'(t)}{A(t)} = \sum_{k=0}^{\infty} b_k \dfrac{t^k}{k!}$ we find $b_0 = -\dfrac{1}{2}$, $b_k = -\dfrac{E_k(0)}{2}$, $k \geq 1$. Hence the third recurrence relation becomes

$$\mathcal{E}_{n+1}(x,y) = \left(x+y-\frac{1}{2}\right)\mathcal{E}_n(x,y) + \frac{1}{2}\sum_{k=1}^{n-1}\binom{n}{k}E_{n-k}(0)\mathcal{E}_k(x,y).$$

The related determinant form for $n > 0$ is

$$\mathcal{E}_{n+1}(x,y) = \begin{vmatrix} x-\frac{1}{2}+y & -1 & 0 & \cdots & 0 \\ -\frac{E_1(0)}{2} & x-\frac{1}{2}+y & -1 & \cdots & 0 \\ \vdots & & \ddots & \ddots & \vdots \\ \vdots & & & \ddots & -1 \\ -\frac{E_n(0)}{2} & -\binom{n}{1}\frac{E_{n-1}(0)}{2} & \cdots & -\binom{n}{n-1}\frac{E_1(0)}{2} & x-\frac{1}{2}+y \end{vmatrix}.$$

For other choices of $A(t)$ we proceed in a similar way.

Example 3. Let $\phi(y,t) = e^{yt^2}$. We can consider the power series $A(t)$ as in the previous example.
(1) $A(t) = 1$.
In this case we obtain the Hermite-Kampé de Fériet polynomials. They are denoted by $H_n^{(2)}(x,y)$, $n \geq 0$ [23,28,40]. From (9) we get

$$H_n^{(2)}(x,y) = n!\sum_{k=0}^{\lfloor \frac{n}{2} \rfloor} \frac{x^{n-2k}y^k}{k!(n-2k)!}.$$

The first polynomials are:

$$H_0^{(2)}(x,y) = 1, \qquad H_1^{(2)}(x,y) = x, \qquad H_2^{(2)}(x,y) = x^2 + 2y,$$
$$H_3^{(2)}(x,y) = x^3 + 6xy, \qquad H_4^{(2)}(x,y) = x^4 + 12x^2y + 12y^2.$$

Their graphs are displayed in Figure 4.

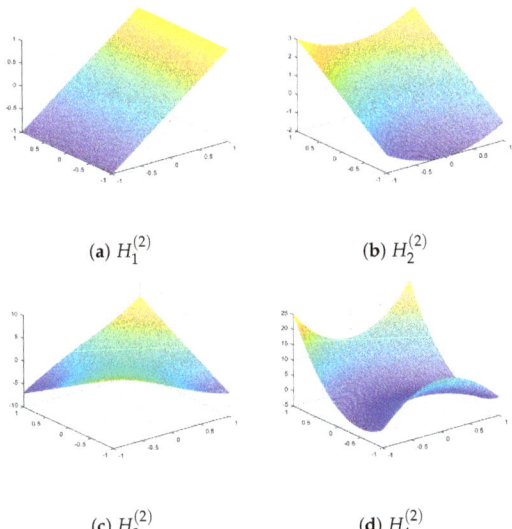

(a) $H_1^{(2)}$
(b) $H_2^{(2)}$
(c) $H_3^{(2)}$
(d) $H_4^{(2)}$

Figure 4. Plot of $H_i^{(2)}$, $i = 1, \ldots, 4$, in $[-1, 1] \times [-1, 1]$.

Particular cases are

(a) $H_n^{(2)}\left(x, -\dfrac{1}{2}\right) = H_n^e(x)$, known as probabilistic Hermite univariate polynomials [19] (p. 134);

(b) $H_n^{(2)}(2x, -1) = H_n(x)$, known as physicist Hermite or simply Hermite polynomials [19] (p. 134);

(c) $H_n^{(2)}(x, 0) = x^n$;

(d) $H_n^{(2)}(0, y) = s_n(y) = \begin{cases} \dfrac{n!}{\left(\frac{n}{2}\right)!} y^{\frac{n}{2}} & n \text{ even} \\ 0 & n \text{ odd}. \end{cases}$

From (13) we obtain the conjugate sequence

$$\hat{H}_n^{(2)}(x, y) = n! \sum_{k=0}^{\lfloor \frac{n}{2} \rfloor} \frac{(x-1)^{n-2k} y^k}{k!(n-2k)!},$$

and the second recurrence relation:

$$H_n^{(2)}(x, y) = \hat{H}_n^{(2)}(x, y) - \sum_{j=0}^{n-1} \binom{n}{j} (-1)^{n-j} H_j^{(2)}(x, y), \quad n \geq 1.$$

The related determinant form for $n > 0$ is

$$H_n^{(2)}(x, y) = (-1)^n \begin{vmatrix} \hat{H}_0^{(2)}(x,y) & \hat{H}_1^{(2)}(x,y) & \hat{H}_2^{(2)}(x,y) & \cdots & \hat{H}_n^{(2)}(x,y) \\ 1 & -\binom{1}{0} & \binom{2}{0}(-1)^2 & \cdots & \binom{n}{0}(-1)^n \\ 0 & 1 & -\binom{2}{1} & \cdots & \binom{n}{1}(-1)^{n-1} \\ \vdots & & \ddots & \ddots & \vdots \\ \vdots & & & \ddots & \vdots \\ 0 & \cdots & 0 & 1 & -\binom{n}{n-1} \end{vmatrix}. \quad (50)$$

From (50) for $x = 1$ and $n > 0$ we have

$$n! \sum_{k=0}^{\lfloor \frac{n}{2} \rfloor} \frac{y^k}{k!(n-2k)!} = (-1)^n \begin{vmatrix} 1 & s_1(y) & s_2(y) & \cdots & s_n(y) \\ 1 & -\binom{1}{0} & \binom{2}{0}(-1)^2 & \cdots & \binom{n}{0}(-1)^n \\ 0 & 1 & -\binom{2}{1} & \cdots & \binom{n}{1}(-1)^{n-1} \\ \vdots & & \ddots & \ddots & \vdots \\ \vdots & & & \ddots & \vdots \\ 0 & \cdots & 0 & 1 & -\binom{n}{n-1} \end{vmatrix}. \quad (51)$$

Observe that $\dfrac{\phi^{(0,1)}(y,t)}{\phi(y,t)} = 2yt$. Therefore the third recurrence relation becomes

$$H_{n+1}^{(2)}(x,y) = x H_n^{(2)}(x,y) + 2ny H_{n-1}^{(2)}(x,y).$$

The related determinant form for $n > 0$ is

$$H_n^{(2)}(x,y) = \begin{vmatrix} x & -1 & 0 & \cdots & 0 \\ 2y & x & -1 & \cdots & 0 \\ & & \ddots & \ddots & \vdots \\ & & & \ddots & -1 \\ \cdots & & & 2y\binom{n}{n-1} & x \end{vmatrix}.$$

To the best of authors knowledge the first recurrence relation, the first determinant form and the last determinant form are new.
For $x = 1$ and $n > 0$ we get the identity

$$n! \sum_{k=0}^{\lfloor \frac{n}{2} \rfloor} \frac{y^k}{k!(n-2k)!} = (-1)^n \begin{vmatrix} 1 & -1 & 0 & \cdots & 0 \\ 2y & 1 & -1 & \cdots & 0 \\ & & \ddots & \ddots & \vdots \\ & & & \ddots & -1 \\ \cdots & & & 2y\binom{n}{n-1} & 1 \end{vmatrix}.$$

From the comparison with (51) the following identity is obtained:

$$\begin{vmatrix} 1 & s_1(y) & s_2(y) & \cdots & s_n(y) \\ 1 & -\binom{1}{0} & \binom{2}{0}(-1)^2 & \cdots & \binom{n}{0}(-1)^n \\ 0 & 1 & -\binom{2}{1} & \cdots & \binom{n}{1}(-1)^{n-1} \\ \vdots & & \ddots & \ddots & \vdots \\ \vdots & & & \ddots & \vdots \\ 0 & \cdots & 0 & 1 & -\binom{n}{n-1} \end{vmatrix} = \begin{vmatrix} 1 & -1 & 0 & \cdots & 0 \\ 2y & 1 & -1 & \cdots & 0 \\ & & \ddots & \ddots & \vdots \\ & & & \ddots & -1 \\ \cdots & & & 2y\binom{n}{n-1} & 1 \end{vmatrix}.$$

The Hermite-Kampé de Fériet polynomials $H_n^{(2)}(x,y)$ satisfy the following differential equations

1. $\dfrac{(-1)^n}{n!} \dfrac{\partial^n}{\partial x^n} f(x,y) + \cdots + f(x,y) = \sum_{k=0}^{\lfloor \frac{n}{2} \rfloor} \dfrac{n!(x-1)^{n-2k} y^k}{k!(n-2k)!};$

2. $\dfrac{\partial}{\partial y} H_n^{(2)}(x,y) = \dfrac{\partial^2}{\partial x^2} H_n^{(2)}(x,y)$ (heat equation);

3. $\left(2y \dfrac{\partial^2}{\partial x^2} + x \dfrac{\partial}{\partial x} - n\right) H_n^{(2)}(x,y) = 0.$

In this case we get the bivariate Appell sequence whose elements can be called Bernoulli–Hermite–Kampé de Fériet polynomials and denoted by $\mathcal{K}_n^B$.
From (6) and (11) we obtain

$$\mathcal{K}_n^B(x,y) = \sum_{k=0}^n \binom{n}{k} B_{n-k}(x)\varphi_k(y) = \sum_{k=0}^n \binom{n}{k} H_k^{(2)}(x,y) B_{n-k},$$

with

$$\varphi_k(y) = \frac{w_k k!}{\lfloor \frac{k}{2} \rfloor!} y^{\lfloor \frac{k}{2} \rfloor}, \quad \text{being } w_k = \begin{cases} 1 & \text{even } k \\ 0 & \text{odd } k. \end{cases} \tag{52}$$

The first bivariate Bernoulli–Hermite–Kampé de Fériet polynomials are

$$\mathcal{K}_0^B(x,y) = 1, \quad \mathcal{K}_1^B(x,y) = x - \frac{1}{2}, \quad \mathcal{K}_2^B(x,y) = x^2 - x + 2y + \frac{1}{6},$$

$$\mathcal{K}_3^B(x,y) = x^3 - \frac{3}{2}x^2 + \frac{1}{2}x - 3y + 6xy,$$

$$\mathcal{K}_4^B(x,y) = x^4 - 2x^3 + x^2 + 2y - 12xy + 12x^2y + 12y^2 - \frac{1}{30}.$$

Their graphs are in Figure 5.

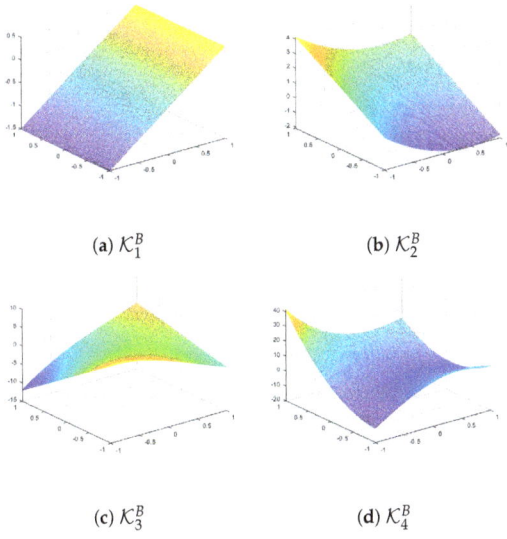

(a) $\mathcal{K}_1^B$ (b) $\mathcal{K}_2^B$

(c) $\mathcal{K}_3^B$ (d) $\mathcal{K}_4^B$

Figure 5. Plot of $\mathcal{K}_i^B$, $i = 1,\ldots,4$, in $[-1,1]\times[-1,1]$.

In this case we observe that $\mathcal{K}_n^B(x,0) = B_n(x)$.
The first recurrence relation is

$$\mathcal{K}_0^B(x,y) = 1, \quad \mathcal{K}_n^B(x,y) = H_n(x,y) - \sum_{j=0}^{n-1}\binom{n}{j}\frac{\mathcal{K}_j^B(x,y)}{n-j+1}, \quad n \geq 1.$$

The related determinant form is obtained from (48) by replacing $(x+y)^k$ by $H_k^{(2)}(x,y)$, $k = 0,\ldots,n$.

As we observed, for $\phi(y,t) = e^{yt^2}$, $c_0(y) = 0$, $c_1(y) = 2y$, $c_k(y) = 0$, $k \geq 2$. Moreover, as in the Example 2, case 2), $b_0 = B_1$, $b_k = -\dfrac{B_{k+1}}{k+1}$, $k \geq 1$. Hence the third recurrence relation is

$$\mathcal{K}_{n+1}^B(x,y) = \left(x - \frac{1}{2}\right)\mathcal{K}_n^B(x,y) + n\left(2y - \frac{1}{12}\right)\mathcal{K}_{n-1}^B(x,y) - \sum_{k=1}^{n-2}\binom{n}{k}\frac{B_{n-k+1}}{n-k+1}\mathcal{K}_k^B(x,y).$$

The related determinant form for $n > 0$ is

$$\mathcal{K}_{n+1}^B(x,y) = \begin{vmatrix} x - \frac{1}{2} & -1 & 0 & \cdots & & 0 \\ 2y - \frac{1}{2} & x - \frac{1}{2} & -1 & \cdots & & 0 \\ -\frac{B_3}{3} & \ddots & \ddots & \ddots & & \vdots \\ \vdots & & \ddots & \ddots & & \vdots \\ & & & & \ddots & -1 \\ -\frac{B_{n+1}}{n+1} & -\binom{n}{1}\frac{B_n}{n} & \cdots & \cdots & \binom{n}{n-1}\left(2y - \frac{1}{2}\right) & x - \frac{1}{2} \end{vmatrix}.$$

(3) $A(t) = \dfrac{2}{e^t + 1}$.

In this case we get the bivariate Appell sequence whose elements can be called Euler–Hermite–Kampé de Fériet polynomials and denoted by $\mathcal{K}_n^E$.

$$\mathcal{K}_n^E(x,y) = \sum_{k=0}^n \binom{n}{k} E_{n-k}(x)\varphi_k(y) = \sum_{k=0}^n \binom{n}{k} H_k^{(2)}(x,y) E_{n-k}(0).$$

with $\varphi_k(y)$ as in (52).

The first polynomials of the sequence $\{\mathcal{K}_n^E\}_{n \in \mathbb{N}}^b$ are

$\mathcal{K}_0^E(x,y) = 1$, $\quad \mathcal{K}_1^E(x,y) = x - \dfrac{1}{2}$, $\quad \mathcal{K}_2^E(x,y) = x^2 - x + 2y$,

$\mathcal{K}_3^E(x,y) = x^3 - \dfrac{3}{2}x^2 - 3y + 6xy + \dfrac{1}{4}$, $\quad \mathcal{K}_4^E(x,y) = x^4 - 2x^3 + 12x^2 y - 12xy + 12y^2 + x$.

Their graphs are in Figure 6.

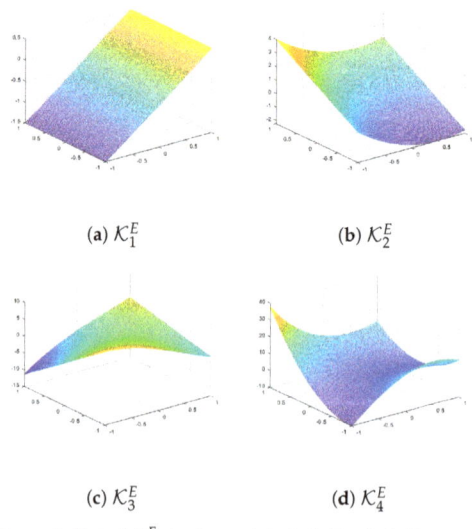

(a) $\mathcal{K}_1^E$ (b) $\mathcal{K}_2^E$

(c) $\mathcal{K}_3^E$ (d) $\mathcal{K}_4^E$

Figure 6. Plot of $\mathcal{K}_i^E$, $i = 1,\ldots,4$, in $[-1,1] \times [-1,1]$.

Since $\alpha_k = E_k(0)$, $k = 0, \ldots, n$, from (12) we get $\beta_0 = 1$, $\beta_k = \frac{1}{2}$, $k = 1, \ldots, n$. Therefore, the first recurrence relation is

$$\mathcal{K}_0^E(x,y) = 1, \qquad \mathcal{K}_n^E(x,y) = H_n^{(2)}(x,y) - \frac{1}{2}\sum_{j=1}^{n-1}\binom{n}{j}\mathcal{K}_j^E(x,y), \qquad n \geq 1.$$

Since in this case $b_0 = -\frac{1}{2}$, $b_k = \frac{E_k(0)}{2}$, $k \geq 1$, the third recurrence relation is

$$\mathcal{K}_{n+1}^E(x,y) = \left(x - \frac{1}{2}\right)\mathcal{K}_n^E(x,y) + n\left(2y - \frac{1}{4}\right)\mathcal{K}_{n-1}^E(x,y) + \frac{1}{2}\sum_{k=0}^{n-2}\binom{n}{k}E_{n-k}(0)\mathcal{K}_k^E(x,y).$$

The related determinant form for $n > 0$ is

$$\mathcal{K}_{n+1}^E(x,y) = \begin{vmatrix} x+y-\frac{1}{2} & -1 & 0 & \cdots & 0 \\ \frac{E_1(0)}{2} & x+y-\frac{1}{2} & -1 & \cdots & 0 \\ \vdots & \ddots & \ddots & \ddots & \vdots \\ \vdots & & \ddots & \ddots & -1 \\ \frac{E_n(0)}{2} & \binom{n}{1}\frac{E_{n-1}(0)}{2} & \cdots & \binom{n}{n-1}\frac{E_1(0)}{2} & x+y-\frac{1}{2} \end{vmatrix}.$$

Example 4. Let $\phi(y,t) = \dfrac{1}{1-yt}$.

(1) $A(t) = 1$.

Being $\phi(y,t) = \sum_{k=0}^{\infty} k! y^k \dfrac{t^k}{k!}$, from (10) we get the elementary bivariate Appell sequence

$$p_n(x,y) = \sum_{k=0}^{n} \frac{n!}{k!} x^k y^{n-k},$$

and from (25) the conjugate sequence

$$\hat{p}_n(x,y) = \sum_{k=0}^{n} \frac{n!}{k!}(x-1)^k y^{n-k}.$$

The first polynomials of the sequence $\{p_n\}_{n\in\mathbb{N}}^b$ are

$p_0(x,y) = 1$, $\quad p_1(x,y) = x+y$, $\quad p_2(x,y) = x^2 + 2xy + 2y^2$,

$p_3(x,y) = x^3 + 3x^2y + 6xy^2 + 6y^3$, $\quad p_4(x,y) = x^4 + 4x^3y + 12x^2y^2 + 24xy^3 + 24y^4$.

Their graphs are in Figure 7.

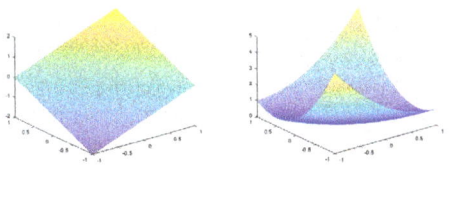

(a) p_1 (b) p_2

Figure 7. *Cont.*

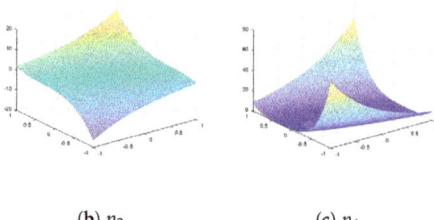

(b) p_3 (c) p_4

Figure 7. Plot of polynomials p_i, $i = 1, \ldots, 4$, in $[-1, 1] \times [-1, 1]$.

For $p_n(x, y)$ relations (37) and (38) hold. Furthermore, since $\dfrac{\phi^{(0,1)}(y,t)}{\phi(y,t)} = \dfrac{y}{1-yt}$, then $c_k(y) = k! \, y^{k+1}$, $k \geq 0$. Hence, from Remark (7), for $n > 0$

$$p_{n+1}(x,y) = x\, p_n(x,y) + n! \sum_{k=0}^{n} \frac{y^{k+1}}{(n-k)!} p_{n-k}(x,y),$$

and

$$p_{n+1}(x,y) = \begin{vmatrix} x+y & -1 & 0 & \cdots & 0 \\ y^2 & x+y & -1 & \cdots & 0 \\ \vdots & & \ddots & \ddots & \vdots \\ & & & \ddots & -1 \\ n!y^{n+1} & \binom{n}{1}(n-1)!y^n & \cdots & \binom{n}{n-1}y^2 & x+y \end{vmatrix}.$$

(2) $A(t) = \dfrac{t}{e^t - 1}$.

In this case we obtain

$$r_n^B(x,y) = \sum_{k=0}^{n} \frac{n!}{k!} B_k(x) y^{n-k}.$$

We note that

$$r_n^B(x,0) = B_n(x), \qquad r_n^B(0,0) = B_n, \qquad n \geq 1,$$

Moreover, $\alpha_k = B_k$ and from (12) $\beta_k = \dfrac{1}{k+1}$, $k = 0, 1, \ldots$

Hence the first recurrence relation is

$$r_0^B(x,y) = 1, \qquad r_n^B(x,y) = p_n(x,y) - \sum_{j=0}^{n-1} \binom{n}{j} \frac{r_j^B(x,y)}{n-j+1}, \qquad n \geq 1,$$

and the conjugate sequence is

$$\hat{r}_n^B(x,y) = \sum_{k=0}^{n} \frac{n!}{k!(n-k+1)!} p_k(x,y).$$

The first polynomials of the sequence $\{r_n^B\}_{n \in \mathbb{N}}$ are

$$r_0^B(x,y) = 1, \quad r_1^B(x,y) = -\frac{1}{2} + x + y, \quad r_2^B(x,y) = \frac{1}{6} - x + x^2 - y + 2xy + 2y^2,$$

$$r_3^B(x,y) = \frac{x}{2} - \frac{3}{2}x^2 + x^3 + \frac{y}{2} - 3xy + 3x^2y - 3y^2 + 6xy^2 + 6y^3,$$

$$+ 12x^a y^a - 12y^d + 24xy^a + 24y^a.$$

Their graphs are in Figure 8.

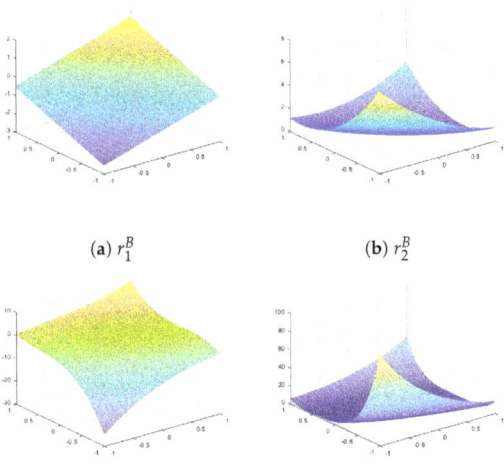

(a) r_1^B (b) r_2^B

(c) r_3^B (d) r_4^B

Figure 8. Plot of r_i^B, $i = 1, \ldots, 4$, in $[-1,1] \times [-1,1]$.

As in the case (2) of the previous Examples, $b_0 = B_1$, $b_k = -\dfrac{B_{k+1}}{k+1}$, $k \geq 1$. Hence the third recurrence relation is

$$r_{n+1}^B(x,y) = \left(x + y - \frac{1}{2}\right) r_n^B(x,y) + n! \sum_{k=0}^{n-1} \left(y^{n-k+1} - \frac{B_{n-k+1}}{(n-k+1)!} \right) \frac{r_k^B(x,y)}{k!}.$$

The related determinant form for $n > 0$ is

$$r_{n+1}^B(x,y) = \begin{vmatrix} x+y-\frac{1}{2} & -1 & 0 & \cdots & 0 \\ b_1 + y^2 & x+y-\frac{1}{2} & -1 & \cdots & 0 \\ \vdots & \ddots & \ddots & \ddots & \vdots \\ \vdots & \ddots & \ddots & \ddots & -1 \\ b_n + n! y^{n+1} & \binom{n}{1}(b_{n-1} + (n-1)! y^n) & \cdots & \binom{n}{n-1}(b_1 + y^2) & x+y-\frac{1}{2} \end{vmatrix}.$$

(3) $A(t) = \dfrac{2}{e^t + 1}$. In this case we obtain

$$r_n^E(x,y) = \sum_{k=0}^n \frac{n!}{k!} E_k(x) y^{n-k}.$$

The first polynomials of the sequence $\{r_n^E\}_{n \in \mathbb{N}}^b$ are

$r_0^E(x,y) = 1$, $r_1^E(x,y) = -\dfrac{1}{2} + x + y$, $r_2^E(x,y) = -x + x^2 - y + 2xy + 2y^2$,

$r_3^E(x,y) = \dfrac{1}{4} - \dfrac{3}{2}x^2 + x^3 - 3xy + 3x^2 y - 3y^2 + 6xy^2 + 6y^3$,

$r_4^E(x,y) = x - 2x^3 + x^4 + y - 6x^2 y + 4x^3 y - 12xy^2 + 12x^2 y^2 - 12y^3 + 24xy^3 + 24y^4$.

Their graphs are in Figure 9.

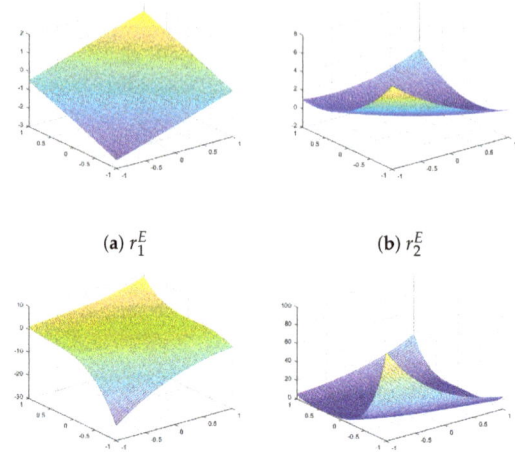

(a) r_1^E (b) r_2^E

(c) r_3^E (d) r_4^E

Figure 9. Plot of r_i^E, $i = 1, \ldots, 4$, in $[-1,1] \times [-1,1]$.

Moreover, since $\beta_0 = 1$, $\beta_k = \dfrac{1}{2}$, $k = 1, \ldots, n$, the first recurrence relation is

$$r_0^E(x,y) = 1, \qquad r_n^E(x,y) = \sum_{j=0}^{n} \frac{n!}{j!} x^j y^{n-j} - \frac{1}{2} \sum_{j=0}^{n-1} \binom{n}{j} r_j^E(x,y), \qquad n \geq 1,$$

and the conjugate sequence is

$$\hat{r}_n^E(x,y) = \frac{1}{2} \sum_{k=0}^{n} \binom{n}{k} p_k(x,y).$$

As in the case (3) of the previous Examples, $b_0 = -\dfrac{1}{2}$, $b_k = \dfrac{E_k(0)}{2}$, $k \geq 1$. Hence the third recurrence relation is

$$r_{n+1}^E(x,y) = \left(x + y - \frac{1}{2}\right) r_n^E(x,y) + \sum_{k=0}^{n-1} \binom{n}{k}\left((n-k)! y^{n-k+1} + \frac{E_{n-k}(0)}{2}\right) r_k^E(x,y).$$

The related determinant form for $n > 0$ is

$$r_{n+1}^E(x,y) = \begin{vmatrix} x+y-\frac{1}{2} & -1 & 0 & \cdots & 0 \\ y^2 + \frac{E_1(0)}{2} & x+y-\frac{1}{2} & -1 & \cdots & 0 \\ \vdots & \ddots & \ddots & \ddots & \vdots \\ \vdots & & \ddots & \ddots & -1 \\ n!y^{n+1} + \frac{E_n(0)}{2} & \binom{n}{1}\left((n-1)!y^n + \frac{E_{n-1}(0)}{2}\right) & \cdots & \binom{n}{n-1}\left(y^2 + \frac{E_1(0)}{2}\right) & x+y-\frac{1}{2} \end{vmatrix}.$$

Remark 12. *In [29,30] the authors introduced the functions $\phi(y,t) = \cos yt$, $\phi(y,t) = \sin yt$. They studied the related elementary sequences and respectively the Bernoulli and Genocchi sequences but matricial and determinant forms are not considered. Most of their results are a consequence of our general theory.*

10. Concluding Remarks

In this work, an approach to general bivariate Appell polynomial sequences based on elementary matrix calculus has been proposed.

This approach, which is new in the literature [3,22,24,27,28], generated a systematic, simple theory. It is in perfect analogy with the theory in the univariate case (see [19] and the references therein). Moreover, our approach provided new results such as recurrence formulas and related differential equations and determinant forms. The latter are useful both for numerical calculations and for theoretical results, such as combinatorial identities and biorthogonal systems of linear functionals and polynomials. In particular, after some definitions, the generating function for a general bivariate Appell sequence is given. Then matricial forms are considered, based on the so called elementary bivariate Appell polynomial sequences. These forms provide three recurrence relations and the related determinant forms. Differential definitions and recurrence relations generate differential equations. For completeness of discussion the multiplicative and derivatives differential operators are hinted. A linear functional on $\mathcal{S}_n = \text{span}\{p_0, \ldots, p_n \mid n \in \mathbb{N}\}$ is considered. It generates a general bivariate Appell sequence. Hence, an interesting theorem on representation for any polynomial belonging to $\mathcal{S}_n$ is established. Finally, some examples of general bivariate Appell sequences are given.

Further developments are possible. In particular, the extension of the considered linear functional to a suitable class of bivariate real functions and the related Appell interpolant polynomial. These interpolant polynomials can be applied not only as an approximant of a function, but also to generate new cubature and summation formulas. It would also be interesting to consider the bivariate generating functions for polynomials.

Author Contributions: Conceptualization, F.A.C., M.I.G. and A.N.; methodology, F.A.C., M.I.G. and A.N.; software, M.I.G. and A.N. All authors have read and agreed to the published version of the manuscript.

Funding: This research received no external funding.

Institutional Review Board Statement: Not applicable.

Informed Consent Statement: Not applicable.

Data Availability Statement: Not applicable.

Acknowledgments: One of the authors wish to thank the support of INdAM—GNCS Project 2020.

Conflicts of Interest: The authors declare no conflict of interest.

References

1. Craciun, M.; Di Bucchianico, A. Sheffer Sequences, Probability Distributions and Approximation Operators. Available online: https://www.win.tue.nl/math/bs/spor/2005-04.pdf (accessed on 10 December 2019).
2. Di Bucchianico, A. *Probabilistic and Analytical Aspects of the Umbral Calculus*; CW/TRACT: Amsterdam, The Netherlands, 1996.
3. Di Nardo, E.; Senato, D. An umbral setting for cumulants and factorial moments. *Eur. J. Comb.* **2006**, *27*, 394–413. [CrossRef]
4. Rota, G.; Shen, J. On the combinatorics of cumulants. *J. Comb. Theory Ser. A* **2000**, *91*, 283–304. [CrossRef]
5. Shixue, C. Characterization for binomial sequences among renewal sequences. *Appl. Math. J. Chin. Univ.* **1992**, *7*, 114–128.
6. Dong Quan, N. The classical umbral calculus and the flow of a Drinfeld module. *Trans. Am. Math. Soc.* **2017**, *369*, 1265–1289. [CrossRef]
7. Niederhausen, H. *Finite Operator Calculus with Applications to Linear Recursions*; Florida Atlantic University: Boca Roton, FL, USA, 2010.
8. Costabile, F.; Longo, E. The Appell interpolation problem. *J. Comput. Appl. Math.* **2011**, *236*, 1024–1032. [CrossRef]
9. Costabile, F.; Longo, E. Algebraic theory of Appell polynomials with application to general linear interpolation problem. *Linear Algebra-Theorems and Applications*; InTech: Split, Croatia, 2012; pp. 21–46.
10. Costabile, F.; Longo, E. Umbral interpolation. *Publ. Inst. Math.* **2016**, *99*, 165–175. [CrossRef]
11. Lidstone, G. Notes on the Extension of Aitken's Theorem (for Polynomial Interpolation) to the Everett Types. *Proc. Edinb. Math. Soc.* **1930**, *2*, 16–19. [CrossRef]
12. Verde-Star, L. Polynomial sequences of interpolatory type. *Stud. Appl. Math* **1993**, *53*, 153–171. [CrossRef]
13. Agratini, O. *Binomial Polynomials and Their Applications in Approximation Theory*; Aracne: Rome, Italy, 2001.

14. Jakimovski, A.; Leviatan, D. Generalized Szász operators for the approximation in the infinite interval. *Mathematica* **1969**, *11*, 97–103.
15. Popa, E. Sheffer polynomials and approximation operators. *Tamkang J. Math.* **2003**, *34*, 117–128. [CrossRef]
16. Sucu, S.; Büyükyazici, I. Integral operators containing Sheffer polynomials. *Bull. Math. Anal. Appl.* **2012**, *4*, 56–66.
17. Sucu, S.; Ibikli, E. Rate of convergence of Szász type operators including Sheffer polynomials. *Stud. Univ. Babes-Bolyai Math.* **2013**, *1*, 55–63.
18. Appell, P. Sur une classe de polynômes. In *Annales Scientifiques de l'École Normale Supérieure*; Société mathématique de France: Paris, France, 1880; Volume 9, pp. 119–144.
19. Costabile, F. *Modern Umbral Calculus. An Elementary Introduction with Applications to Linear Interpolation and Operator Approximation Theory*; Walter de Gruyter GmbH & Co KG: Berlin, Germany, 2019; Volume 72.
20. Roman, S. Theory of the Umbral Calculus II. *J. Math. Anal. Appl.* **1982**, *89*, 290–314. [CrossRef]
21. Anshelevich, M. Appell polynomials and their relatives. *Int. Math. Res. Not.* **2004**, *2004*, 3469–3531. [CrossRef]
22. Qi, F.; Luo, Q.; Guo, B. Darboux's formula with integral remainder of functions with two independent variables. *Appl. Math. Comput.* **2008**, *199*, 691–703. [CrossRef]
23. Bretti, G.; Cesarano, C.; Ricci, P. Laguerre-type exponentials and generalized Appell polynomials. *Comput. Math. Appl.* **2004**, *48*, 833–839. [CrossRef]
24. Khan, S.; Raza, N. General-Appell polynomials within the context of monomiality principle. *Int. J. Anal.* **2013**, *2013*, 328032. [CrossRef]
25. Dattoli, G. Hermite-Bessel, Laguerre-Bessel functions: A by-product of the monomiality principle. In Proceedings of the Melfi School on Advanced Topics in Mathematics and Physics, Melfi, Italy, 9–12 May 1999; pp. 147–164.
26. Dattoli, G.; Migliorati, M.; Srivastava, H. Sheffer polynomials, monomiality principle, algebraic methods and the theory of classical polynomials. *Math. Comput. Model.* **2007**, *45*, 1033–1041. [CrossRef]
27. Steffensen, J. The poweroid, an extension of the mathematical notion of power. *Acta Math.* **1941**, *73*, 333–366. [CrossRef]
28. Bretti, G.; Natalini, P.; Ricci, P. Generalizations of the Bernoulli and Appell polynomials. *Abstr. Appl. Anal.* **2004**, *2004*, 613–623. [CrossRef]
29. Jamei, M.; Beyki, M.; Koepf, W. On a bivariate kind of Bernoulli polynomials. *Bull. Sci. Math.* **2019**, *156*, 1–22.
30. Masjed-Jamei, M.; Beyki, M.; Omey, E. On a parametric kind of Genocchi polynomials. *J. Inequal. Spec. Funct.* **2018**, *9*, 68–81.
31. Ryoo, C.; Khan, W. On two bivariate kinds of poly-Bernoulli and poly-Genocchi polynomials. *Mathematics* **2020**, *8*, 417. [CrossRef]
32. Dragomir, S.; Qi, F.; Hanna, G.; Cerone, P. New Taylor-like expansions for functions of two variables and estimates of their remainders. *J. Korean Soc. Ind. Appl. Math.* **2005**, *9*, 1–15.
33. Sard, A. *Linear Approximation*; American Mathematical Soc.: Providence, Rhode Island, 1963.
34. Verde-Star, L. Infinite triangular matrices, q-Pascal matrices, and determinantal representations. *Linear Algebra Appl.* **2011**, *434*, 307–318. [CrossRef]
35. Costabile, F.; Gualtieri, M.; Napoli, A. Polynomial sequences: Elementary basic methods and application hints. A survey. *RACSAM* **2019**, *113*, 3829–3862. [CrossRef]
36. Costabile, F.; Longo, E. A determinantal approach to Appell polynomials. *J. Comput. Appl. Math.* **2010**, *234*, 1528–1542. [CrossRef]
37. Yang, Y.; Youn, H. Appell polynomial sequences: A linear algebra approach. *JP J. Algebr. Number Theory Appl.* **2009**, *13*, 65–98.
38. Yasmin, G. Some properties of Legendre–Gould Hopper polynomials and operational methods. *J. Math. Anal. Appl.* **2014**, *413*, 84–99. [CrossRef]
39. Davis, P. *Interpolation and Approximation*; Dover Publications: New York, NY, USA, 1975.
40. Cesarano, C. A note on generalized Hermite polynomials. *Int. J. Appl. Math. Inform.* **2014**, *8*, 1–6.
41. Ricci, P.; Tavkhelidze, I. An introduction to operational techniques and special polynomials. *J. Math. Sci.* **2009**, *157*. [CrossRef]
42. Riordan, J. *Combinatorial Identities*; Wiley: Hoboken, NJ, USA, 1968.

Article

The Legacy of Peter Wynn

Claude Brezinski [1], F. Alexander Norman [2] and Michela Redivo-Zaglia [3,*]

[1] Laboratoire Paul Painlevé, Université de Lille, CNRS, UMR 8524, F-59000 Lille, France; claude.brezinski@univ-lille.fr
[2] Department of Mathematics, University of Texas at San Antonio, One UTSA Circle, San Antonio, TX 78249, USA; sandy.norman@utsa.edu
[3] Department of Mathematics "Tullio Levi-Civita", University of Padua, Via Trieste 63, 35121 Padua, Italy
* Correspondence: michela.redivozaglia@unipd.it

Abstract: After the death of Peter Wynn in December 2017, manuscript documents he left came to our knowledge. They concern continued fractions, rational (Padé) approximation, Thiele interpolation, orthogonal polynomials, moment problems, series, and abstract algebra. The purpose of this paper is to analyze them and to make them available to the mathematical community. Some of them are in quite good shape, almost finished, and ready to be published by anyone willing to check and complete them. Others are rough notes, and need to be reworked. Anyway, we think that these works are valuable additions to the literature on these topics and that they cannot be left unknown since they contain ideas that were never exploited. They can lead to new research and results. Two unpublished papers are also mentioned here for the first time.

Keywords: orthogonal polynomials; extrapolation methods; Padé approximation; continued fractions; rational interpolation; complex analysis; software; abstract algebra

---

Contents

Introduction	2
The Discovery	4
Mathematical Background	7
The Shanks Transformation and the ε-Algorithms	7
Padé Approximation	9
Continued Fractions	9
Rational Interpolation	11
The Legacy	11
Main Documents	11
Complex Analysis and Continued Fractions	11
Interpolation	17
The ε-Algorithm	25
Project for a Book	32
Algebra	33
Software	35
Unpublished Typewritten Documents	36
Other Documents	36
Drafts on Analysis	36
Drafts on Algebra	37
Personal Documents	38
References	40
References	40

Citation: Brezinski, C.; Norman, F.A.; Redivo-Zaglia, M. The Legacy of Peter Wynn. *Mathematics* **2021**, *9*, 1240. https://doi.org/10.3390/math9111240

Academic Editor: Francesco Aldo Costabile

Received: 30 March 2021
Accepted: 27 April 2021
Published: 28 May 2021

Publisher's Note: MDPI stays neutral with regard to jurisdictional claims in published maps and institutional affiliations.

Copyright: © 2021 by the authors. Licensee MDPI, Basel, Switzerland. This article is an open access article distributed under the terms and conditions of the Creative Commons Attribution (CC BY) license (https://creativecommons.org/licenses/by/4.0/).

References 44

References 44

1. Introduction

Peter Wynn (1931–2017) was a mathematician, a numerical analyst, and a computer scientist (see in Figure 1 a photo of him taken in 1975). In his scientific life he produced 109 publications (see References [1–109]), and he translated two books from Russian [110,111]. He is mostly known for his discovery of the ε-algorithm [3], a recursive method for the implementation of the Shanks transformation for scalar sequences [112], for its extensions to the vector, matrix, and confluent cases [12,13,23,24], and for his numerous reports and papers on Padé approximants and continued fractions. His works influenced a generation of pure and numerical analysts, with an important impact on the creation of new methods for the acceleration of scalar, vector, matrix, and tensor sequences, on the approximation of functions, and on iterative procedures for the solution of fixed point problems. Volume 80, No. 1 of the journal *Numerical Algorithms* was dedicated to him with his full biography. More recently, a complete analysis of all his works was provided in Reference [113], together with those of other scientists who worked and are still working on these domains.

Figure 1. Peter Wynn in 1975. © C. Brezinski.

Thus, one can wonder why it was necessary to publish an additional paper on Wynn's work. During the last years of his life, Peter Wynn was living in Zacatecas, Mexico. Each year, he had to come back to the United States for some administrative reasons. On one occasion, he was visiting friends in San Antonio and left them boxes containing mathematical documents he did not want, for some unknown reason, to keep with him in Mexico. In January 2020, C.B. was contacted by F.A.N., a colleague of these friends, who informed him of the existence of these documents. This is how Wynn's legacy came to light. Then, the authors of this paper decided to analyze these unpublished works.

As everyone can understand, it was a quite difficult task. Only a part of the documents have been extracted from the boxes and studied. The handwritten lists made by Wynn for indicating the contents of the boxes show that he put together several kinds of documents. What he named *"rough notes"* are very difficult to read and understand. In these lists, he often indicated what he called *"notes"* and, in this case, they are usually well written

sometimes wrote new notes on the back of another document! In addition, he also made Xerox copies of documents, and inserted them into the boxes. However, his lists help us to try to identify the kind of document we were considering. But, sometimes, this was quite impossible. Moreover, most of the documents we found have no date and, often, pages are not numbered. When unnumbered sheets of paper are stacked on top of each other, without any separation, it has sometimes been difficult to know where a document begins and where it ends. It is also possible that Wynn himself mixed up some texts. For these reasons, certain groupings of pages may be questionable. Thus, we apologize in advance for all possible mistakes contained in this paper.

Let us motivate the potential reader by giving an idea of the main themes covered by Wynn. The most important documents left by Wynn, which are almost complete and in a good shape are the following. One of them concerns Bürmann series over a field; they generalize Taylor series and are used in the reversion of series. Another one (187 pages) is on stability and F-functions that play a role in the solution of the differential equation $y'(t) = Ay(t)$, variation diminishing functions, interpolating rational functions, exponential fitting forms. The Hamburger-Pick-Nevanlinna problem is treated in a document of 179 pages. There is a document on continued fraction transformations of the Euler-Mclaurin series that has 202 pages; it contains applications to various series. The convergence of associated continued fractions, and truncation error bounds for Thiele's continued fractions are the topics of another document. Then, we analyze various documents on interpolation. The first one is about functional interpolation, in which a recursive algorithm, which seems to be new, is given for constructing interpolating rational functions. Interpolation by the use of rational functions is studied in another document. Wynn gave two recursive algorithms for their computation. They also seem to be new. A document extends a report of Wynn on the abstract theory of the ε-algorithm [69]. The ε-algorithm is applied to sequences of elements of a ring. An interesting pedagogical document is on iterated complex number spirals. We present some numerical experiments illustrating Wynn's ideas. There is a document that looks like a book project on extrapolation, Padé approximation, continued fractions, and orthogonal polynomials. It can certainly serve as a basis for lectures on continued fractions, Padé approximation, and the ε-algorithm. Other documents are on algebra. One of them (266 pages) is on S-rings. It is quite theoretical, without any application nor reference to the literature. A second one treats factorisations of a triangular matrix. There are also unfinished manuscripts on various topics, which can be of interest. Two unpublished papers of Wynn are also mentioned here for the first time. The documents left by Wynn show the intellectual process leading to the elaboration of new results until their publication. They are also a testimony on the human side of research by describing the friendship and the collaboration between researchers, and their mutual influence.

The purpose of this paper is to make this legacy available to the international mathematical community. It contains a description of the unpublished manuscripts of Wynn. They offer many new results and developments. Despite the fact that not all documents have been sorted yet, we decided to propose them immediately since we think that the research must go on. We hope to encourage some readers to resume the work of Wynn and bring it to an end. We are sure that several of his ideas are worth pursuing.

All the documents extracted up to now from the boxes left by Wynn have been digitized, and they can be downloaded from the following URL (Legacy Archive: Peter Wynn). The main material is mentioned in this paper. The unusable or incomplete documents we found are not listed here, but they are also inserted in the same website together with a small description. Other information on Peter Wynn can also be found in the site *Mathematics Research* of the Department of Mathematics at the University of Texas at San Antonio (UTSA) https://mathresearch.utsa.edu/Legacy/Peter-Wynn/ (accessed on 30 April 2021).

The history of the discovery of these documents is told in Section 2 with the testimony of F.A.N. and of the friends of Wynn who inherited them. For readers who are not familiar with the topics touched upon by Wynn, a short mathematical introduction is provided in Section 3. More details can easily be found in the literature, particularly in Reference [113].

Some of the documents left by Wynn in San Antonio are analyzed and commented in Section 4. Some others will be analyzed in a second paper if they are of interest.

All quotations from Wynn are in *italics*. Inside a quotation, our own comments (when necessary) are in roman characters into square brackets. When Wynn mentions a reference given at the end of his text, we replaced it by that of our own bibliography numbered in arabic figures between square brackets [·]. The documents of Wynn are numbered in bold italics arabic figures. For referring to them in the text, these numbers are placed between curly brackets {·} to distinguish them from the bibliographical references. Concerning the references of Wynn, we were able to update them, by inserting new DOI, MR (Mathematical Reviews) and Zbl (Zentralblatt reviews) numbers, and by adding newly discovered papers. Let us also mention that in 1960, the journal *Mathematical Tables and Other Aids to Computation* (known in short as MTAC) changed its name and became *Mathematics of Computation*, and that from its Volume 5, the journal *Revue française de traitement de l'information, Chiffres* became simply *Chiffres*. Several papers and communications of Wynn, when he was at the *Stichting Mathematisch Centrum* (now *Centrum Wiskunde & Informatica*) in Amsterdam, from 1960 to 1964, can also be found at the CWI's Institutional Repository at the address https://ir.cwi.nl/ (accessed on 30 April 2021).

2. The Discovery

On 14 January 2020, C.B. received the following message from F.A.N.:

I have just now read your recent remembrance of Peter Wynn appearing in Numerical Algorithms. I was charmed—thank you for that. But I am also very much interested because, serendipitously, I have just today "inherited" from a retired colleague several rather heavy boxes of Wynn's papers which had been left with my colleague for safekeeping (or convenience) some years earlier.

I have not yet opened the boxes, but I will begin examining the contents soon. The reason I am writing you is to ask if you would be willing to answer a couple of questions, which I pose below.

As I begin looking at the material, I could find (1) drafts of papers that might be of interest to mathematicians, (2) personal items that might be of interest to family or friends, (3) miscellany that would be of little interest to anyone, or (4) items for which I am at a loss to know whether to keep or discard [...]

Here are my questions to you:

In case I find material that looks as if it might have some mathematical import, would you be willing to take look at it, or could you suggest someone who would be?

The colleague he was speaking about is Manuel Philip Berriozábal. He was born in 1931. He was awarded the Bachelor of Science degree in mathematics from Rockhurst College in 1952, a Master of Science degree in mathematics from the University of Notre Dame in 1956, and a Ph.D. in mathematics from the University of California at Los Angeles (UCLA) in 1961. After serving for one year as a lecturer at UCLA, he joined the faculty at Tulane University as an Assistant Professor. Four years later, he moved to the University of New Orleans as an Associate Professor. He was promoted to Professor six years later. In 1975, Manuel Berriozábal married Maria Antonietta Rodriguez (see Figure 2). He joined the faculty at the University of Texas at San Antonio (UTSA) in 1976, and in 1979, he started the now nationally recognized Prefreshman Engineering Program (PREP) at UTSA. San Antonio PREP received a Presidential Award for Excellence in Science, Mathematics and Engineering Mentoring and a La Promesa Program Award from the National Latino Children's Institute. Several years ago, TexPREP (Texas Prefreshman Engineering Program) received a special commendation from the Texas Senate. These accomplishments caught the attention of the Washington, DC-based Quality Education for Minorities Network and resulted in Berriozábal being named one of the six Giants in Science at a conference held in February 1998. In May 1998, he was a recipient of the San Antonio "I Have a Dream" Foundation Endeavors Award. PREP has also been replicated on eight college campuses in eight states outside of Texas. It was during his professorship at the Louisiana State

Figure 2. Maria Antonietta and Manuel Philip Berriozábal. ©M.A. and M.P. Berriozábal.

Of course, C.B. and M.R.-Z. were very much interested in the contents of these boxes since they were in the final preparation of their book which contains, among others, an analysis of all the publications of Peter Wynn [113]. F.A.N. began to look at them, to scan a lot of their material, and to send it to us. The correspondence with him was completely taken up by M.R.-Z., since the same day C.B. received F.A.N.'s first message, he had to enter a hospital for a health problem.

On 15 January, F.A.N. wrote to C.B. and M.R.-Z.:

I have opened two of the four boxes, looking thoroughly through the contents of one of them.
<u>FIRST BOX</u>
The first box was a smaller one containing several hundreds of pages of handwritten notes and a few other random items. In this and the next message, I have attached several of the smaller items that might be indicative of material to come. Nothing is dated so I have no idea whether this material simply anticipates papers that have been completed and published or represents new work. In addition, not much is paginated, so I generally presume that the order in which pages appear is the order in which they were completed and assembled. Some of this material was left with Dr. Berriozábal here in San Antonio after Peter had visited Mexico and there are some suggestions (e.g., written accounts of receipts) that suggest that some of the material was produced while he was living in Mexico. Whether this was after his last publication in 1981, I do not know.

To Do List: *The first document above appears to be a list of various topics he wished to address, mainly through the construction of relevant notes.*

Projects: *This document lists a number of projects that he had planned and may well have completed. Whether these "projects" have found their way into the literature as published papers, I do not know. I've copied a snapshot from the document and you will note that some of the items have been denoted with a "D__". Perhaps this is Peter's shorthand for "Done" or fait accompli. I didn't see in his publications any that specifically included, for example, "stratified commutative ring" or "Bürmann series", so perhaps this represents some work that hasn't yet been published, but will appear somewhere in his collection of notes. I did find the beginnings of what looks to be a monograph on Interpolation Theory–the first in his list of projects and one that doesn't seem to have been completed at that time.*

Duplicate List: *This may reflect a list of some of the items that Peter included in his boxes of documents.*

The next messages will include 2 larger documents, one a bibliography and the other a more extensive list of documents.

Other items in this first box include the aforementioned piece of a monograph on Interpolation Theory, as well as a couple of hundred pages of paginated notes of another document. In that case, I see pages 70–300+ so I can't be sure of the initial title. There is another paginated treatment of a topic (I don't recall exactly what at the moment), a book review, and some hundreds of other pages of notes that do not appear to fit together well.

SECOND BOX

I'll mention here that the second box, one that originally held a dozen reams of office paper, now holds about 20 kg of handwritten notes. I have not yet examined these notes in detail, and when I do, I want to be careful not to disturb the assembly of any documents.

Bibliography: This is likely not anything that you would use. I imagine Peter kept this bibliography simply for reference purposes.

List of documents: This seems to be a list of documents and/or things he felt he needed to do, such as copy this or Xerox that. I don't know if it has any intrinsic value, but it might reflect documents included among his papers.

In a message to F.A.N., 17 January 2020, Maria Antonietta Berriozábal wrote:

We liked his visits. Each time he came it was without much notice and we would just go out to eat. For me I was so very busy for so many years and so was Manny [her husband Manuel] that a surprise visit took creativity to get the three of us together, but we did it for Peter. He liked nice places. And I loved hearing he and Manny talk old times. He would also talk about living in Mexico which he loved.

He was such a mystery to me because he was pretty much alone and he liked it that way.

I do not recall meeting Peter when we were in New Orleans which was August 1975 to June 1976 [...]

What I do recall is that after we married I was sorting and clearing papers for Manny from our apartment which he had lived in for many years and I came across a letter from Peter written around the time Manny and I met. In that letter I gathered Peter was a bachelor friend of Manny who was not the marrying kind and he was commenting that Manny had met "the one". He was happy for Manny but it seemed to me Peter was happy being alone. Now that I think of it I don't think I ever got to know who Peter was. He had a wonderful smile. He liked to laugh and joke and was very very blond.

C.B. and M.R.-Z. wrote to Maria Berriozábal and sent her the photo of Wynn inserted above (also see References [113,114]). She answered on 21 January 2020:

[...] The photos are valuable. I met Peter when he was a much older man but still had that incredibly beautiful smile and lots and lots of hair!

Each time he came to the US for many years, he would call Manny and we would go to dinner. If I recall correctly, it was mostly on Peter's nickel and as I stated to Sandy [F.A.N.] we went to nice restaurants, although Manny may have won some times and we would go to our famous Luby's Cafeteria—always the frugal Manny.

I do not recall Peter in New Orleans when I lived there with Manny the first nine months of our marriage. I left San Antonio to join him as he was waiting and hoping to join UTSA. The New Orleans scholars community from the four universities and colleges there met socially and regularly at people's homes but I do not recall Peter in any of that circle. It could have been that he was no longer in New Orleans. This was August 1975 to June 1976.

This morning when I read your note the words that rang in my head is how youth is wasted on the young. I wish I had paid more attention and had retained the conversations with Peter, but at that time my life was incredibly full and so was Manny's. There were times when I had to make major changes in my schedule to join Manny and Peter and I always did and looked forward to those dinners. My questions to Peter were always about Mexico and his life there. That is what I wish I could recall more. I just know that he was very happy there. I do not recall what his conversations with Manny were all about and now Manny is forgetting a lot of things.

On one of these trips which had to occur every six months, I believe, because that is how he kept his US citizenship active he said he had some boxes with him and asked if we could store them for him for safekeeping. I recall his taking them out of his car. When I looked at them again seriously in recent years I saw how big the boxes were and soon learned how heavy they were. Yet, I seem to recall Peter carrying them by himself. Maybe a Dolly helped. I just know he trusted us with them.

One of my last year's resolutions was to clean the garage and I did. It took some weeks but

we did not hear from him anymore. He quit coming. Manny and I would comment from time to time that we still had those boxes and that we needed to do something about them.

A year ago when the boxes were the last unsettled things in the garage I told our gardener who was helping me with the project the story of the boxes. He said what if it is money. Since it had been so long that Peter had left the boxes with us I gave myself permission to open them. Hilario, my helper, even wondered if they were full of money! I only opened two boxes and all I saw were reams of papers with math problems. Pages and pages and pages. When Sandy [F.A.N.] helped us with Manny's papers after he retired I decided to ask him to go over the papers and determine what they were. Manny looked at them but had no idea what the material was. When Sandy [F.A.N.] took the boxes out I saw how at least one of them had folders of some kind so the papers were not only sheets of math problems. I hope someone who has Peter's interest and his career uppermost in their mind will continue to review it and possibly record it for posterity.

To close, thank you again for honoring Peter's work.

3. Mathematical Background

Some documents written by Wynn are pure algebra or complex analysis. They require, at least for some of them, quite a good knowledge of these fields. However, it is impossible to give herein a full account of the definitions and notions necessary for their complete understanding. We will restrict ourselves to the most specialized topics addressed by Wynn in the domain of numerical analysis, namely the Shanks transformation and the ε-algorithms, Padé approximation, continued fractions, and rational interpolation. In this section, we only present the definitions and the main algebraic properties that are sufficient for understanding most of the documents analyzed. The fundamental question of convergence is not addressed. We refer to References [113,115–119] for more details.

3.1. The Shanks Transformation and the ε-Algorithms

When a sequence (S_n) of numbers is slowly converging to its limit S, and when one has no access to the process building it, it can be transformed into a new sequence (or a set of new sequences), which, under some assumptions, converge(s) faster to the same limit. Many such *sequence transformations* exist and have been studied; see References [115,117–119]. Among them, one of the most well known, studied, and used is due to Shanks [112]. It consists in transforming (S_n) into a set of sequences denoted $\{e_k(S_n)\}$, indexed by k and n, and defined by

$$e_k(S_n) = \frac{\begin{vmatrix} S_n & S_{n+1} & \cdots & S_{n+k} \\ \Delta S_n & \Delta S_{n+1} & \cdots & \Delta S_{n+k} \\ \vdots & \vdots & & \vdots \\ \Delta S_{n+k-1} & \Delta S_{n+k} & \cdots & \Delta S_{n+2k-1} \end{vmatrix}}{\begin{vmatrix} 1 & 1 & \cdots & 1 \\ \Delta S_n & \Delta S_{n+1} & \cdots & \Delta S_{n+k} \\ \vdots & \vdots & & \vdots \\ \Delta S_{n+k-1} & \Delta S_{n+k} & \cdots & \Delta S_{n+2k-1} \end{vmatrix}}, \quad k, n = 0, 1, \ldots. \tag{1}$$

These numbers can be recursively computed by the *scalar ε-algorithm* of Wynn [3], whose rule is

$$\varepsilon_{k+1}^{(n)} = \varepsilon_{k-1}^{(n+1)} + (\varepsilon_k^{(n+1)} - \varepsilon_k^{(n)})^{-1}, \quad k, n = 0, 1, \ldots, \tag{2}$$

with $\forall n, \varepsilon_{-1}^{(n)} = 0$ and $\varepsilon_0^{(n)} = S_n$, and it holds $\varepsilon_{2k}^{(n)} = e_k(S_n), k, n = 0, 1, \ldots$ The $\varepsilon_{2k+1}^{(n)}$ are only intermediate results with no interest for our purpose. In fact, quantities with a different parity can be eliminated from (2), thus leading to the *cross-rule* of Wynn [48] which only links those of the same parity

$$(\varepsilon_{k+2}^{(n)} - \varepsilon_k^{(n+1)})^{-1} + (\varepsilon_{k-2}^{(n+2)} - \varepsilon_k^{(n+1)})^{-1} = (\varepsilon_k^{(n+2)} - \varepsilon_k^{(n+1)})^{-1} + (\varepsilon_k^{(n)} - \varepsilon_k^{(n+1)})^{-1},$$

with the initial conditions $\varepsilon_{-2}^{(n)} = \infty, \varepsilon_{-1}^{(n)} = 0$, and $\varepsilon_0^{(n)} = S_n$ for $n = 0, 1, \ldots$

It can be proved that $\forall n, \varepsilon_{2k}^{(n)} = S$ if and only if the sequence (S_n) satisfies a linear difference equation of order k

$$a_0(S_n - S) + a_1(S_{n+1} - S) + \cdots + a_k(S_{n+k} - S) = 0, \quad n = 0, 1, \ldots,$$

where the coefficients a_i are such that $a_0 a_k \neq 0$ and $a_0 + \cdots + a_k \neq 0$. In other words, if and only if S_n has the form

$$S_n = S + \sum_{i=1}^{p} A_i(n) r_i^n + \sum_{i=p+1}^{q} [B_i(n) \cos(b_i n) + C_i(n) \sin(b_i n)] e^{w_i n} + \sum_{i=0}^{m} c_i \delta_{in},$$

where A_i, B_i and C_i are polynomials in n such that, if d_i is the degree of A_i plus 1 for $i = 1, \ldots, p$, and the maximum of the degrees of B_i and C_i plus 1 for $i = p+1, \ldots, q$, one has

$$m + 1 + \sum_{i=1}^{p} d_i + 2 \sum_{i=p+1}^{q} d_i = k,$$

with the conventions that the second sum vanishes if there are no complex zeros, and $m = -1$ if there is no term in δ_{in} (Kronecker's symbol). The set of such sequences is named the *kernel* of the transformation. Since many sequences produced by iterative methods have this form or are close to it, it explains the success of this algorithm.

In Reference [24], Wynn extended his algorithm to the case where the S_n are vectors or square matrices. In the matrix case, the significance of the power -1 in (2) is clear. For vectors, the inverse y^{-1} of a vector y is defined as $y^{-1} = y/(y, y)$, thus leading to the *vector ε-algorithm*.

Similarly, when a function $f(t)$ is slowly converging to its limit S when t tends to infinity, it can be transformed into a set of functions converging faster to S under certain assumptions. For that purpose, Wynn extended his algorithm to that case by proposing the *first confluent form of the ε-algorithm* whose rule is, for all t,

$$\varepsilon_{k+1}(t) = \varepsilon_{k-1}(t) + (\varepsilon_k'(t))^{-1}, \quad k = 0, 1, \ldots,$$

with $\varepsilon_{-1}(t) = 0$ and $\varepsilon_0(t) = f(t)$. Again the $\varepsilon_{2k+1}(t)$ are intermediate computation. It can be proved that, for all t, $\varepsilon_{2k}(t) = S$ if and only if f satisfies the differential equation of order k

$$a_0(f(t) - S) + a_1 f'(t) + \cdots + a_k f^{(k)}(t) = 0,$$

with $a_0 a_k \neq 0$, that is, in other words,

$$f(t) = S + \sum_{i=1}^{p} A_i(t) e^{r_i t} + \sum_{i=p+1}^{q} [B_i(t) \cos(b_i t) + C_i(t) \sin(b_i t)] e^{w_i t},$$

where A_i, B_i and C_i are polynomials in t such that, if d_i is the degree of A_i plus 1 for $i = 1, \ldots, p$, and the maximum of the degrees of B_i and C_i plus 1 for $i = p+1, \ldots, q$, one has

$$\sum_{i=1}^{p} d_i + 2 \sum_{i=p+1}^{q} d_i = k.$$

Moreover, the $\varepsilon_{2k}(t)$ can be expressed by a ratio of determinants quite similar to (1), but in which the derivatives of f are replacing the powers of the difference operator Δ (see, for example, Reference [113] (p. 24) or Reference [115] (p. 257)).

3.2. Padé Approximation

Let f be a formal power series

$$f(t) = \sum_{i=0}^{\infty} c_i t^i,$$

in which the coefficients c_i and the variable t can be complex. A Padé approximant of f is a rational function with a numerator of degree p at most and a denominator of degree q at most such that its power series expansion agrees with f as far as possible, that is up to the degree $p + q$ inclusively. Such an approximant is denoted $[p/q]_f$ and, by construction, it holds

$$[p/q]_f(t) - f(t) = \mathcal{O}(t^{p+q+1}), \quad (t \to 0).$$

Let us set $[p/q]_f(t) = N_p(t)/D_q(t)$ with

$$N_p(t) = a_0 + a_1 t + \cdots + a_p t^p \quad \text{and} \quad D_q(t) = b_0 + b_1 t + \cdots + b_q t^q.$$

Then, linearizing the conditions of the definition as $f(t)D_q(t) - N_p(t) = \mathcal{O}(t^{p+q+1})$ leads to the relations

$$\begin{aligned}
a_0 &= c_0 b_0 \\
a_1 &= c_1 b_0 + c_0 b_1 \\
&\vdots \\
a_p &= c_p b_0 + c_{p-1} b_1 + \cdots + c_{p-q} b_q \\
0 &= c_{p+1} b_0 + c_p b_1 + \cdots + c_{p-q+1} b_q \\
&\vdots \\
0 &= c_{p+q} b_0 + c_{p+q-1} b_1 + \cdots + c_p b_q
\end{aligned}$$

with the convention that $c_i = 0$ for $i < 0$ which allows to treat simultaneously the cases $p \leq q$ and $p \geq q$.

Setting $b_0 = 1$ allows to solve the system formed by the preceding last q equations for the coefficients $b_1, \ldots, b_q$. Knowing the b_i's, the first $p + 1$ equations directly provide the a_i's. It holds

$$[p/q]_f(t) = \begin{vmatrix} t^q f_{p-q}(t) & t^{q-1} f_{p-q+1}(t) & \cdots & f_p(t) \\ c_{p-q+1} & c_{p-q+2} & \cdots & c_{p+1} \\ \vdots & \vdots & & \vdots \\ c_p & c_{p+1} & \cdots & c_{p+q} \end{vmatrix} \Bigg/ \begin{vmatrix} t^q & t^{q-1} & \cdots & 1 \\ c_{p-q+1} & c_{p-q+2} & \cdots & c_{p+1} \\ \vdots & \vdots & & \vdots \\ c_p & c_{p+1} & \cdots & c_{p+q} \end{vmatrix},$$

where f_m denotes the partial sum of f up to the term of degree m inclusively.

It is easy to see from (1) that, applying the ε-algorithm to $S_n = \sum_{i=0}^{n} c_i t^i$ leads to $\varepsilon_{2k}^{(n)} = [n + k/k]_f(t)$. Let g be the reciprocal series of f defined by $f(t)g(t) = 1$ (it exists if and only if $c_0 \neq 0$). If the ε-algorithm is applied to the sequence of the partial sums of g, then $\varepsilon_{2k}^{(n)} = [n + k/k]_g(t) = 1/[k/n + k]_f(t)$.

3.3. Continued Fractions

A *continued fraction* is an expression of the form

$$C = b_0 + \cfrac{a_1}{b_1 + \cfrac{a_2}{b_2 + \cfrac{a_3}{b_3 + \cfrac{a_4}{\ddots}}}}.$$

For evident typographical reasons, it is written as

$$C = b_0 + \frac{a_1}{\mid b_1} + \frac{a_2}{\mid b_2} + \frac{a_3}{\mid b_3} + \cdots$$

The numbers a_k and b_k are called the kth *partial numerator* and *partial denominator*, respectively, a_k/b_k is the kth *partial quotient*, and

$$C_n = b_0 + \frac{a_1}{\mid b_1} + \cdots + \frac{a_{n-1}}{\mid b_{n-1}} + \frac{a_n}{\mid b_n}$$

is called the nth *convergent* of the continued fraction C (even if the sequence (C_n) does not converge). A continued fraction is said to converge if the sequence (C_n) converges when n tends to infinity.

After reducing to the same denominator, C_n can be written as $C_n = A_n/B_n$. It can be computed by the recurrence relationships

$$\begin{aligned} A_k &= b_k A_{k-1} + a_k A_{k-2} \\ B_k &= b_k B_{k-1} + a_k B_{k-2}, \quad k = 1, 2, \ldots \end{aligned}$$

with

$$\begin{aligned} A_0 &= b_0, \quad A_{-1} = 1 \\ B_0 &= 1, \quad B_{-1} = 0. \end{aligned}$$

Let (C_n) be the sequence of convergents of the continued fraction C and let (C_{p_n}) be a subsequence. The continued fraction

$$C' = b'_0 + \frac{a'_1}{\mid b'_1} + \frac{a'_2}{\mid b'_2} + \frac{a'_3}{\mid b'_3} + \cdots$$

whose convergents satisfy $C'_n = C_{p_n}$ is given by

$$a'_n = \frac{C_{p_{n-1}} - C_{p_n}}{C_{p_{n-1}} - C_{p_{n-2}}}, \quad b'_n = \frac{C_{p_n} - C_{p_{n-2}}}{C_{p_{n-1}} - C_{p_{n-2}}},$$

with $b'_0 = C_{p_0}$, $b'_1 = 1$ and $a'_1 = C_{p_1} - C_{p_0}$. This operation is called a *contraction* of the continued fraction. Usually, $p_n = 2n$.

The analytic theory of continued fractions is concerned with continued fractions whose partial numerators and/or denominators are functions of the complex variable z. Let us consider the continued fraction

$$C = b_0 + \frac{a_1 z}{\mid 1} + \frac{a_2 z}{\mid 1} + \frac{a_3 z}{\mid 1} + \cdots$$

From the recurrence relations, we see that A_{2k-1}, A_{2k} and B_{2k} are polynomials of degree k in z and that B_{2k-1} is a polynomial of degree $k-1$. The expansions of C_k and C_{k-1} in ascending powers of z agree up to the term of degree $k-1$ inclusively. It is possible to choose $b_0, a_1, a_2, \ldots$ so that the expansion of C_k agrees with that of a given series $f(z) = c_0 + c_1 z + c_2 z^2 + \cdots$ up to the term of degree k. This continued fraction is called the continued fraction *corresponding* to the series f. By a contraction of this continued fraction, with $p_k = 2k$ as explained above, we obtain a continued fraction whose convergent C'_k agrees with that of f up to the term of degree $2k$. This is the continued fraction *associated* to the series f. Thus, by the uniqueness property of Padé approximants, we have $C_{2k} = [k/k]_f(z)$ and $C_{2k+1} = [k+1/k]_f(z)$.

3.4. Rational Interpolation

Consider the continued fraction

$$C^{(n)}(x) = \alpha_0^{(n)} + \dfrac{x-x_n}{\alpha_1^{(n)}} + \dfrac{x-x_{n+1}}{\alpha_2^{(n)}} + \cdots,$$

with $\alpha_k^{(n)} = \varrho_k^{(n)} - \varrho_{k-2}^{(n)}$ for $k = 1, 2, \ldots$, and $\alpha_0^{(n)} = \varrho_0^{(n)} = f(x_n)$, and where the scalars $\varrho_k^{(n)}$ are recursively computed by

$$\varrho_{k+1}^{(n)} = \varrho_{k-1}^{(n+1)} + \dfrac{x_{n+k+1} - x_n}{\varrho_k^{(n+1)} - \varrho_k^{(n)}} \quad (3)$$

with $\varrho_{-1}^{(n)} = 0$ and $\varrho_0^{(n)} = f(x_n)$. The quantities $\varrho_{2k}^{(n)}$ can be expressed as a ratio of two determinants.

The kth convergent $C_k^{(n)}$ of this continued fraction satisfies the interpolation conditions $C_k^{(n)}(x_i) = f(x_i)$ for $i = n, \ldots, n+k$. The quantities $\varrho_{k+1}^{(n)}$ are the *reciprocal differences* of f. They formed the ϱ-algorithm used by Wynn for rational extrapolation at infinity [2].

Let us now consider the confluent reciprocal differences of a function f defined by

$$\varrho_{k+1}(t) = \varrho_{k-1}(t) + \dfrac{k+1}{\varrho_k'(t)}$$

with $\varrho_{-1}(t) = 0$ and $\varrho_0(t) = f(t)$. This formula will be used as an extrapolation method for functions by Wynn, and named the *confluent form of the ϱ-algorithm* [12].

Thiele's expansion of a function f consists in the continued fraction

$$f(t+h) = f(t) + \dfrac{h}{\alpha_1(t)} + \dfrac{h}{\alpha_2(t)} + \cdots,$$

with $\alpha_k(t) = \varrho_k(t) - \varrho_{k-2}(t)$ for $k = 1, 2, \ldots$ Replacing t by 0 and h by x, we get

$$f(x) = f(0) + \dfrac{x}{\alpha_1(0)} + \dfrac{x}{\alpha_2(0)} + \cdots$$

The successive convergents $C_k(x) = A_k(x)/B_k(x)$ of this continued fraction are such that $f(x) - C_k(x) = \mathcal{O}(x^{k+1})$. Since Padé approximants are uniquely defined, it holds

$$C_{2k}(x) = [k/k]_f(x), \quad C_{2k+1}(x) = [k+1/k]_f(x).$$

4. The Legacy

Let us now describe the various documents contained in the boxes left by Wynn at his friends' house in San Antonio. All, except two, are handwritten.

4.1. Main Documents

We tried to sort the documents by themes. However, our classification is only an attempt since there are many connections between the topics, the documents are not dated, and, maybe, some of them contain pages coming out from various sources since they are not numbered and, maybe, inserted by Wynn in disorder into the boxes.

4.1.1. Complex Analysis and Continued Fractions

1   Bürmann series over a field
    These titled notes (52 pages) are devoted to Bürmann series. They are mentioned in documents {26–28}, and were probably written at the same time as {14}, since both titles are listed together.

The Bürmann series of a function f is a generalized form of a Taylor series in which, instead of a series in powers of $z - z_0$, we have a series in powers of the analytic function $\phi(z) - \phi(z_0)$. It is used in the reversion of series which consists, starting from $z = f(w)$, in expressing w as $w = g(z)$. The problem was considered by Joseph Louis Lagrange (1736–1813) in 1770 [120] and generalized by Hans Heinrich Bürmann (?–1817). A report on Bürmann's theorem by Joseph-Louis Lagrange and Adrien-Marie Legendre (1752–1833) appeared in *Rapport sur deux mémoires d'analyse du professeur Bürmann*, Mémoires de l'Institut National des Sciences et Arts: Sciences Mathématiques et Physiques, vol. 2, pages 13–17 (1799). An exhaustive treatment of this topics is given in Reference [121] (pp. 55 ff.). The Lagrange-Bürmann series, as it is often called, also allows for two functions f and g, both holomorphic in the neighborhood of a point, to be expanded in a power series of the other one in two overlapping regions. Series reversion related to Hankel determinants, continued fractions, and combinatorics as explained in Section 6.10.4 of Reference [113] about combinatorics; also see Reference [122]. Wynn wrote:

> *This paper is directed towards the transformation of series expansions* [...]
> *The general results derived are illustrated by application to a problem concerning the transformation of asymptotic relationships.*
> Notation. Let $n > 0$ be fixed finite integer.
> (1) With w a fixed point in $\mathbb{C}$, the finite part of the complex plane, $\Omega(w)$ an open set of points in $\mathbb{C}\setminus\{w\}$ with limit point at w, $\bar{\Omega}(w) \equiv \{w\} \cup \Omega(w)$, and p, q mappings of $\bar{\Omega}(w)$ into $\mathbb{C}$,
> $$p(z) \simeq_{(w,\Omega)} q(z)$$
> means that $p(z) - q(z) = o\{(z-w)^n\}$ as z tends through $\Omega(w)$ to w.
> (2) Let M be a nonvoid set of points in $\mathbb{C}$. For each $w \in M$, let $\Omega(w), \bar{\Omega}(w)$ be as in (1) and $p(w, \cdot), q(w, \cdot) : \bar{\Omega}(w) \to \mathbb{C}$.
> $$p(w,z) \simeq_{[M,\Omega]} q(w,z)$$
> means that for each $w \in M$, $p(w,z) \simeq_{(w,\Omega)} q(w,z)$. [We have] $\bar{\Omega} = \bigcup_{w \in M} \bar{\Omega}(w)$ and $\Omega' = \bigcup_{w \in M} \Omega'(w)$ where $\{\Omega'(w) : z - w \text{ for all } z \in \bar{\Omega}(w)\}$.
> The main problem considered has a simple form as follows: let $a_j, f_j \in \mathbb{C}$ $(j : n)$ [This notation means that j runs from 1 to n. The notation $(j : 0, n)$ means that j goes from 0 to n] with $a_1 \neq 0$ and, with $w \in \mathbb{C}$ fixed, let $a, f : \bar{\Omega}(w) \to \mathbb{C}$ be such that
> $$a(z) \simeq_{(w,\Omega)} a(w) + \sum_{j=1}^{n} a_j(z-w)^j$$
> $$f(z) \simeq_{(w,\Omega)} f(w) + \sum_{j=1}^{n} f_j(z-w)^j.$$
>
> *Determine $g_i \in \mathbb{C}$ for which*
> $$f(z) \simeq_{(w,\Omega)} f(w) + \sum_{i=1}^{n} g_i\{a(z)-a(w)\}^i.$$
>
> In the general form of the problem $a_j, f_j : M \to \mathbb{C}$ $(j : n)$ are mappings with $a_1(w) \neq 0$ for all $w \in M$; for each $w \in M$, $a(w, \cdot) : \bar{\Omega}(w) \to \mathbb{C}$ is such that
> $$a(w,z) \simeq_{[M,\Omega]} a(w,w) + \sum_{j=1}^{n} a_j(w)(z-w)^j$$
>
> *the mapping $f : \bar{\Omega} \to \mathbb{C}$ satisfies the relationship*
> $$f(z) \simeq_{[M,\Omega]} f(w) + \sum_{j=1}^{n} f_j(w)(z-w)^j$$

and $g_i : M \to \mathbb{C}$ for which

$$f(z) \simeq_{[M,\Omega]} f(w) + \sum_{i=1}^{n} g_i(w)\{a(w,z) - a(w,w)\}^i$$

are to be determined.

Then, Wynn described three variants of the problem corresponding to various properties of the function a. The particular case of polynomials is treated. The text ends by:

> The function $c(z) = \ln(1+z)$ is inverse to $a(z) = e^z - 1$. $c(e^{i\theta}) = \ln\{2(1+\cos\theta)\} + i\theta/2$ maps the segment $-\pi \leq \theta \leq \pi$ onto a curve $\mathcal{C}$, symmetric about the real axis, enclosing its nonpositive part, containing the real point $\ln(z)$, the imaginary points $\pm i\pi/3$, and having as asymptotes the lines $z = \pm i\pi/2$, $\mathcal{D}$ being the open domain bounded by $\mathcal{C}$, a maps $\mathcal{D}$ bijectively onto the unit open disc.

2 On Stability Functions

The handwritten paper *On stability functions* (mentioned in {26} as "Paper, latest version") contains 187 pages with a bibliography at the end. Its first section is an introduction and a presentation of the notations:

> This paper is concerned with functions of the form
>
> $$(1) \quad f(z) = 1 + \frac{az}{1 - az/2 + z^2 s(z)}$$
>
> where $0 < a < \infty$, and
>
> $$(2) \quad s(z) = \int_0^\infty \frac{d\psi(t)}{1 + z^2 t}$$
>
> where $\psi(t)$ is a nondecreasing function of bounded variation for $0 \leq t \leq \infty$ such that all moments
>
> $$(3) \quad c_\nu = \int_0^\infty t^\nu \, d\psi(t)$$
>
> for $\nu = 0, 1, \ldots$ exist.
> A function f of this form will be called an F-function. If the context permits, the notation $f \in F$ or, where convenience dictates, $f(z) \in F$, will be used. The function s in the representation (1) plays a significant role in the theory of the function f. A function of the form (2) with ψ as described will be called an S-function; again the notations $s \in S$ or $s(z) \in S$ will be used.
> The mapping properties of F- and S-functions, in particular, will be investigated.

Then, Wynn stated that an F-function f is real for finite negative values of z with $f(z) > 0$ for all sufficiently small negative values of z, is asymptotically represented as z tends to zero over an open set in the sector $\pi/2, 3\pi/2$ with the limit point 0, and that the function f can be asymptotically represented by a series of the form $f(z) = \sum_{\nu=0}^{\infty} c_\nu z^\nu$ (formula scratched) which generates an associated continued fraction whose even convergents map the closed infinite left half-plane $\mathbb{L}$ into the closed unit disc $\mathbb{D}$ if and only if f is an F-function. The proof is given with a reference to his paper (Reference [98]) for details. An example of an F-function is e^z, and Wynn added:

> The study of F-functions was motivated by the following consideration: With A a bounded linear operator, the solution of the differential equation
>
> $$(9) \quad \frac{dy(t)}{dt} = Ay(t)$$
>
> with $y(0)$ prescribed, satisfies the relationship
>
> $$(10) \quad y(nh + h) = \exp(Ah) y(nh)$$
>
> for $n = 0, 1, \ldots$ If $0 < h < \infty$ and the eigenvalues of A lie in $\mathbb{L}$, those of $\exp(Ah)$ lie in $\mathbb{D}$. $\|y(nh)\|$ remains bounded and, indeed, decreases to zero as n increases indefinitely. An

approximation $y^*(t)$ to the solution of Equation (9) may be obtained by use of a Taylor series method based upon use of an approximate identity

$$(11) \quad \sum_{i=0}^{m} a_i \frac{d^i y^*(t+h)}{dt^i} = \sum_{i=0}^{n} b_i \frac{d^i y^*(t)}{dt^i}.$$

Setting $m = n = r$ and taking the a_i and b_i to be the denominator and numerator coefficients of powers of z in $C_{2r}(hz)$, where $C_{2r}(z)$, with $r \geq 1$ fixed, is a convergent of the continued fraction associated with the exponential series, and setting $t = nh$, the special form of the approximate identity (11) applied to Equation (10) yields the relationship

$$(12) \quad y^*(nh+h) = C_{2r}(Ah)y^*(nh)$$

for $n = 0, 1, \ldots$ As a consequence of the mapping properties of $C_{2r}(t)$ described above, the eigenvalues of $C_{2r}(Ah)$ lie in $\mathbb{D}$, and the remarks concerning the behaviour of $\|y(nh)\|$ apply with equal force to $\|y^*(nh)\|$: the exact and approximate solutions of Equation (9) behave in the same way. The practical details of the way in which relation (12) is implemented are not of immediate concern; any method for the approximate solution of Equation (9) based upon use of recursion (12) is stable.

Let us remember that the convergent C_{2r} of the associated continued fraction to a series is its $[r/r]$ Padé approximant. Since the computation of Padé approximants to the exponential function are highly numerically unstable (see References [123,124]) one can doubt the practical usefulness of the procedure mentioned.

Other examples of F-functions are given. Wynn claimed that they open up the possibility of constructing stable schemes for the approximate solution of certain nonlinear differential equations. A characterisation of F-functions which is independent of the continued fraction theory is given. Based on the proof of this result, Wynn asserted that it is possible to demonstrate the existence of functions with mapping properties less specific than those of F-functions. Indeed, a number of F-functions can be derived from a given F-function. This remark reminds the way some totally monotone sequences can be derived from a totally monotone one as explained in Reference [125]. Then, Wynn proved that F-functions are closed with respect to multiplication. Meromorphic F-functions are then considered.

The next part of the work deals with variation diminishing functions. Let (x_i) be a sequence of real numbers. The transformation $(x_i) \longmapsto (y_j)$ given by $y_j = \sum_{i=0}^{n} a_{n-i} x_i$, $j = 0, 1, \ldots$ (it seems that n should be replaced by j), is said to be variation diminishing if the number of changes of sign of the y_j is less than or equal to the number of changes of sign of the x_j. Wynn wrote: *Transformations of this type underly the theory of many smoothing operations, and also occur in the numerical solution of certain partial differential equations by iterative methods*, and he referred to Reference [126]. Several results are proved.

The next section of this manuscript is devoted to interpolation. Wynn wrote:

> It is possible to construct a rational F-function whose derivative values agree with those of a generating F-function up to prescribed orders not only at the origin but at a prescribed sequence of points in $\mathbb{L}$; furthermore this rational function may be derived by the use of purely algebraic methods of rational function interpolation.

A theorem is proved and recurrences for the coefficients occurring in the interpolating rational F-function are given. A long discussion, where orthogonal polynomials play a role, follows. The algebraic problem of determining a rational function with denominator and numerator of degrees equal to m and $m-1$ respectively, which satisfies the interpolation conditions may be solved by a recursive process which is described and justified in his *Appendix 3 Extremal solutions of the Pick-Nevanlinna problem*. It could be of interest to code and test this algorithm, and to compare it with the other existing ones.

$dy(x)/dx = f(y(x))$. Linearizing it yields $dy(x)/dx = f(0) + Jy(x)$ where J is the Jacobian matrix of f. Assuming its nonsingularity, we have

$$y(x+h) = e^{Jh}[y(x) + J^{-1}f(0)] - J^{-1}f(0).$$

Assuming that the eigenvalues λ_j of J are distinct, and ... what follows is not clearly stated and it seems that one page of the manuscript is missing. Anyway, Wynn constructed a rational function such that its derivatives of prescribed orders agree with those of e^{Jh} at the points $\lambda_j h$, and he wrote:

> It is eminently desirable that a method for the construction of general rational functions mapping $\mathbb{L}$ into $\mathbb{D}$ and having prescribed orders of contact with the exponential function at the origin and other specified points in $\mathbb{L}$ should be made available. This is precisely the service offered by Section [not identified] of this paper. In Theorem 4 [not identified], the F-function producing the interpolation data is taken to be the exponential function; the results of that theorem then show that the required function is obtained simply by means of rational function interpolation.

A section on meromorphic F-functions follows in which the properties of the corresponding continued fractions they generate are studied. The even and odd convergents are examined.

The first Appendix has the title *The asymptotic expansion of positive real functions*. Appendix two is on *The construction of functions belonging to certain classes*. It deals with a general theory of the derivation of functions of the form

$$F(\lambda) = \int_{-\infty}^{\infty} (\lambda - t)^{-1} \, d\sigma(t)$$

from others of the same form. In a previous Appendix (without a number) Wynn already treated the same problem for S-functions. The third Appendix, already mentioned above, considers the Pick-Nevanlinna problem in a wider setting. Let us remember that this problem consists in finding a holomorphic function φ that interpolates the data $\lambda_1, \ldots, \lambda_n \in \mathbb{D}$ subject to the constraint $|\varphi(\lambda)| < 1$ for all $\lambda \in \mathbb{D}$; see Reference [127]. Wynn wrote:

> It is clear from the above conspectus of results from the Pick-Nevanlinna theory, that the solution of the problem of determining a rational function which satisfies the mapping and interpolation conditions described above differs from that of constructing a rational function which satisfies interpolation conditions alone in at least two respects: in the solution of the first problem a combination of function-theoretic and algebraic methods is involved, while in that of the second, algebraic methods are exclusively deployed; furthermore, each stage of the solution of the first problem results, not in the construction of a single interpolating function as is the case for the second problem, but in that of a family of functions with the required properties.

Developments and theoretical results follow. A bibliography of 26 items ends the paper. One can wonder why Wynn never published it.

3 The Hamburger-Pick-Nevanlinna problem

This manuscript contains 179 pages but with many portions scratched (it probably contains a mixing of a draft of a paper, notes and rough notes all cited in {26,28}).

Let p, q, r be finite positive integers, let a_ν ($\nu : 0, 2p-2$) be finite real numbers, let x_k ($k : q$) be distinct real argument values, $T(1,k)$ ($k : q$) be the corresponding finite positive integers, and $b_{k,\nu}$ ($k : q \mid \nu : 0, 2T(1,k) - 1$) sets of finite real valued coefficients, let λ_k ($k : r$) be distinct argument values in $\mathbb{L}$, $T(2,k)$ ($k : r$) be the corresponding finite positive integers, and $c_{k,\tau}$ ($k : r \mid \tau : 0, T(2,k) - 1$) sets of finite complex valued coefficients. The problem is to determine a function G which satisfies the asymptotic relationship

$$\lambda^{2p-1}\left\{G(\lambda) - \sum_{\nu=0}^{2p-2} a_\nu \lambda^{-\nu-1}\right\} = \mathcal{O}(1)$$

as λ tends to infinity in a sector of the form $\pi < \gamma \leq \arg(\lambda) \leq \delta < 2\pi$, and satisfies also the asymptotic relationship for $k : q$

$$(\lambda - x_k)^{-2T(1,k)}\left\{G(\lambda) - \sum_{\nu=0}^{2T(1,k)-1} b_{k,\nu}(\lambda - x_k)^\nu\right\} = \mathcal{O}(1)$$

as λ tends to x_k over an open set contained in $\mathbb{L}$ with limit point at x_k, for $k : r$, and moreover satisfies the interpolation conditions $\lambda^\tau G(\lambda_k)/\tau! = c_{k,\tau}$ for $\tau : 0, T(2,k)-1$, and finally maps $\mathbb{L}$ into $\mathbb{D}$ (or $\mathbb{U}$?). According to Wynn *The proof of the principal theorem of this section is largely based upon results, due to M. Riesz, in the theory of linear functionals.* Since this part is a draft in quite bad shape, we will not pursue its analysis. The document contains another interesting section

> *Matrix criteria*
> *In this section Akhiezer's treatment of the simple Pick-Nevanlinna problem is extended to the diminished Hamburger-Pick-Nevanlinna problem; conditions that are necessary and sufficient for the solubility of the latter problem are established and, assuming this problem to be nondegenerate, inclusion discs for its solutions are located.*

As a preliminary, a Hermitian matrix is constructed from the data which leads to an extension of a theorem on the existence of inclusion discs for the values of all solutions to the Hamburger problem and the simple Pick-Nevanlinna problem.
Wynn concluded:

> *The results of the above theorem are exclusively concerned with the diminished version of the Hamburger-Pick-Nevanlinna problem. It is possible to extend the method of proof to the treatment of the Hamburger-Pick-Nevanlinna problem itself, to examine the structure of the rational function solutions to this problem and its diminished form, and to describe the relative positions of the inclusion discs deriving from a sequence of subordinate problems. These matters are, however, more conveniently dealt with methods described in the following section, in which explicit expressions for the general solutions to the interpolation problems concerned are described.*

Unfortunately, this *following section* of the manuscript is not under a form which allows to give a clear account of it.

4 **Continued fraction transformations of the Euler-Mclaurin series**

The document is 202 pages long. It dates from December 1976. The first part of the document is in a quite good shape (probably a draft of the paper mentioned in {26}, with an abstract and a bibliography) with some corrections done with a pencil. Not all pages have been written with the same pen. Some of them are missing or not in the right order since all of them are not numbered (they could be some additional notes on integral transform and analytic continuation). Moreover, references to some formulas are missing, and some authors quoted in the text are not listed into the bibliography given at the end. An in-depth study of this document is needed to fully understand it if possible to exploit it.
It begins by a long abstract from which we extract the main points.

> *Results concerning the convergence of forward diagonal sequences of quotients in the Padé table are given. In particular, it is shown that, if (*) $f_\nu = \int_0^\infty t^\nu \, d\sigma(t)$ ($\nu = 0, 1, \ldots$), σ being a bounded nondecreasing real valued function such that all moments (*) exist, and (**) $f_\nu = \mathcal{O}\{(\chi \nu)! \xi^\nu\}$ ($0 < \chi \leq 2, 0 < \xi < \infty$) then all forward diagonal sequences of Padé quotients derived from the series $\sum_{\nu=0}^\infty f_\nu z^\nu$ converge uniformly over any bounded region in the z-plane not containing any point of the nonnegative real axis to (* * *)*

This result extends results given by various authors, and it can also be extended to the case where the lower limit in (∗) and (∗ ∗ ∗) is replaced by −∞. These results are applied to the delayed Euler-Mclaurin series

$$\sum_{\nu=0}^{\infty} b_{j+\nu} \mathcal{D}^{2j+\nu+1} \Psi(\mu) k^{2\nu},$$

($j \geq 0$, and $\mathcal{D}$ being $d/d\mu$) regarded as a series expansion in ascending powers of k^2. Convergence results for the Padé approximants of this series are derived, and also for the same series in which single zeros are inserted between its successive terms. Applications to Stirling's asymptotic expansion of the logarithm of the gamma function, and to the asymptotic expansion of the generalised Riemann zeta-function are presented.

5   **Convergence and truncation error bounds for associated continued fractions**
This is a short document (13 pages), probably only the notes mentioned in {26}.
In this work, he proposes to give a convergence theorem for the functions $\varrho_{2r}\{\psi(\mu)\}$, where, presumably, ϱ_{2r} is the $2r$th convergent of Thiele's continued fraction. He begins to prove other results (not reproduced herein since they contain too many erasures) upon which the proof of the theorem is based. It is:

> **Theorem 3.** Let $[\alpha, \beta]$ be a fixed interval of the finite real axis, and $\xi(s)$ be a bounded nondecreasing real valued function for $\alpha \leq s \leq \beta$, and not a step function with a finite number of salti. Let $\mu \in (-\infty, \infty) \times [\alpha, \beta]$ be fixed and
>
> $$\psi(\mu) = \int_{\alpha}^{\beta} (\mu - s)^{-2} \, d\xi(s)$$
>
> $$\varrho\{\psi(\mu)\} = \int_{\alpha}^{\beta} (\mu - s)^{-1} \, d\xi(s).$$
>
> Then $\lim_{r=\infty} \varrho_{2r}\{\psi(\mu)\} = \varrho\{\psi(\mu)\}$, and
>
> $$|\varrho\{\psi(\mu)\} - \varrho_{2r}\{\psi(\mu)\}| \leq (\beta - \alpha)|\psi(\mu)|p(\mu;\alpha,\beta)^{2r-1}, \quad r = 1, 2, \ldots$$
>
> where $p(\mu; \alpha, \beta) = \left||\mu - \alpha|^{1/2} - |\mu - \beta|^{1/2}\right| / \left||\mu - \alpha|^{1/2} + |\mu - \beta|^{1/2}\right|$.

According to what precedes, it seems that the sign that looks like × in $\mu \in (-\infty, \infty) \times [\alpha, \beta]$ has to be replaced by $\notin [\alpha, \beta]$. We do not know if this result had been later rediscovered by other researchers. Thus, it was interesting to reproduce it here.

4.1.2. Interpolation

6   **Functional Interpolation**
This very well handwritten manuscript has 52 pages and seems to be the paper mentioned several times in all the list of documents, projects and activities, with a bibliography with a last reference dating from 1984. The first section is *Interpolation and extrapolation* with a subsection 1.1–*Procrustean technique*. This word was already used by Wynn in the title of the published paper of Reference [2] where he introduced a particular form of the ϱ-algorithm for extrapolation at infinity by a rational function in n (see Reference [113]). It describes situations where different properties are fitted to an arbitrary standard. In the Greek myth, Procrustes was a son of Poseidon. He compelled travelers to lie on a bed, he cut off their legs that were longer than bed, and stretched the feet of those who were too small. The manuscript begins by:

> Most general theories arise from investigations of particular problems, and in this respect the theory to be described is not exceptional. By way of motivation, the problem of deriving an extrapolation method from an interpolatory formula and its converse are considered. It is first supposed that an interpolatory function of complex variables
>
> (1) $\quad F_r^{(m)}(d \mid y; \lambda) = F_r^{(m)}(d_m, \ldots, d_{m+r} \mid y_m, \ldots, y_{m+r}; \lambda)$

is available for which (a) $F_r^{(m)}(d \mid y; y_\nu) = d_\nu$ ($\nu \in I_{m,m+r}$; throughout the paper $I_{i,j}$ is the sequence $i, i+1, \ldots, i+j$; I_i is the sequence $i, i+1, \ldots$; I is I_0) and (b) for certain distributions of the d_ν and y_ν

$$G_r^{(m)}(d \mid y) = \lim F_r^{(m)}(d \mid y; \lambda) \qquad (\lambda \to \infty)$$

exists. The function $F_r^{(m)}$ serves as the basis of an extrapolation method: given the sequence $S_\nu (\nu \in I)$ the number $G_r^{(m)}(d \mid y)$ obtained by setting $d_\nu = S_\nu (\nu \in I_{m,m+r})$ in $G_r^{(m)}(d \mid y)$ is an estimate of $\lim S_\nu (\nu \to \infty)$. (The numbers y_ν used are suggested by the process producing the sequence $\{S_\nu\}$: the choice $y_\nu = \nu (\nu \in I)$ is natural; the choice $y_\nu = 2^\nu$ arises, for example, in Romberg's method of integration [2 references] in which the number of integration subranges is doubled at each stage, $F_r^{(m)}$ being a polynomial in λ^{-1}.)

Then, Wynn illustrates the method by taking $F_{2i}^{(m)}$ as the quotient of two polynomials of degree i in λ. Subject to certain existence conditions, the coefficient of λ^i in the denominator is 1, and that in the numerator is $\varrho_{2i}^{(m)}(d \mid y)$ which can be expressed as the quotient of two determinants involving $d_\tau, y_\tau, \tau \in I_{m,m+2i}$. In this case $G_{2i}^{(m)} = \varrho_{2i}^{(m)}(d \mid y)$. Replacing d_τ by S_τ, the determinantal formula for $\varrho_{2i}^{(m)}(d \mid y)$ gives the extrapolated limit. These numbers can be recursively computed by Thiele's reciprocal difference algorithm (see (3) in Section 3.4), and they can be displayed in a two dimensional array for which Wynn does not use the usual notation but a new one, and he writes:

> [The process] involves numbers $\varepsilon_{i,j}$ which may be set at the intersections of the full rows and columns and of the half rows and columns of a chipped triangular array in which the row index i ranges over $\bar{I}_{-1/2}$ ($\bar{I}_k$ is the sequence $k, k+1/2, k+1, \ldots$; $\bar{I}$ is $\bar{I}_0$) and the column index j over the range I_i, the number $\varepsilon_{-1/2,-1/2}$ being missing. The numbers $\varepsilon_{i,j}$ are constructed from the initial vales $\varepsilon_{0,j} = S_j$ ($j \in I$), $\varepsilon'_{0,j} = 0$ ($j \in I$) (the dash is used to indicate a displacement operation acting upon numbers with two suffixes, whose effect is illustrated by the relationships $\varepsilon'_{0,j} = \varepsilon_{-1/2, j+1/2}$ and $\varepsilon'_{i,j} = \varepsilon_{i-1/2, j+1/2}$) by use of the relationship
>
> $$(3) \qquad (\Delta_j \varepsilon_{i,j})(\Delta_i \varepsilon'_{i,j}) = w_{i,j}$$
>
> for $i \in \bar{I}; j \in I_i$ where Δ_j is the difference operator $\Delta_j \varepsilon_{i,j} = \varepsilon_{i,j+1} - \varepsilon_{i,j}$ and Δ_i is similarly defined. With
>
> $$w_{i,j} = (y_{i+j+1} - y_{j-i})^{-1} \qquad (i \in \bar{I}, j \in I_i)$$
>
> [it holds]
>
> $$\varrho_{2i}^{(m)}(S \mid y) = \varepsilon_{i,i+m} \qquad (i, m \in I).$$

And he concludes with his personal sense of humor:

> We have called an extrapolation method of the above type a Procrustean technique [2], although in fitting function values to a sequence, i.e. the bed to the victim, we are a little kinder than Procrustes is reputed to have been.

He continues:

> If in formula (1) λ is fixed and one of the y_ν is very large, e_ν [not defined] is approximately equal to $\lim F_r^{(m)}(\lambda)$ ($\lambda \to \infty$): if λ is fixed and the $y_\tau \neq y_\nu$ are fixed and finite, $\lim F_r^{(m)}(\lambda) = e_\nu$ ($\lambda \to \infty$). This observation may be made in terms of the behaviour of $G_r^{(m)}(d \mid y)$ as y_ν tends to infinity, the other y_τ remaining finite; expressed in terms of the S_τ it is that, under suitable conditions, $\lim G_r^{(m)}(S \mid y) = S_\nu$ ($y_\nu \to \infty$).

There should be an error in what Wynn wrote. Since he states that λ is fixed, $\lambda \to \infty$ should be replaced by $y_\nu \to \infty$ (remark of one of the reviewers). Wynn concludes that this property is, for example, satisfied by the ratio of determinants expressing

The second subsection is named *1.2–Interpolatory functions*. He claims that *The steps taken in the above derivation of an extrapolation method from an interpolatory formula may be reversed*. Then, he shows how to reverse the recursive rule given in the preceding subsection.

[...] set $d_\nu = d(y_\nu), e_\nu(z) = e(y_\nu, z)$ and $f_\nu(z) = f(y_\nu, z)$ ($\nu \in I$). Suppose that a function of complex variables

$$G_r^{(m)}(S \mid y) = G_r^{(m)}(S_m, \ldots, S_{m+r} \mid y_m, \ldots, y_{m+r})$$

for which $\lim G_r^{(m)}(S \mid y) = S_\nu$ as $y_\nu \to \infty$ ($\nu \in I_{m,m+r}$), obtained either from an interpolatory or from an extrapolation method or in some other way is available. Set

$$H_r^{(m)}(e, f \mid z) = G_r^{(m)}(e_m(z), \ldots, e_{m+r}(z) \mid f_m(z)^{-1}, \ldots, f_{m+r}(z)^{-1}).$$

[...] Thus in view of the property attributed to $G_r^{(m)}(S \mid y)$ just described, $\lim H_r^{(m)}(e, f \mid z) = d_\nu$ as $z \to y_\nu$ over Z ($\nu \in I_{m,m+r}$): [Z is an open set of points in $\mathbb{C}$] $H_r^{(m)}(e, f \mid z)$ is an interpolatory function. If the $G_r^{(m)}(S \mid y)$ ($r, m \in I$) may be computed by means of a recursive process, appropriate modification yields a process for computing numerical values of the $H_r^{(m)}(e, f \mid z)$ ($r, m \in I$).

Then, Wynn develops the particular case of the extrapolation estimate $\varrho_{2i}(S \mid y)$, and he obtains a set of rational functions $r_{i,j}^{(m)}(z)$. He proves that $\lim r_{i,j}^{(m)}(z) = d_\nu$ as $z \to y_\nu$ ($\nu \in I_{m,m+i+j}$). Imposing the further condition

$$e_\nu(z) - d_\nu = \mathcal{O}\{f_\nu(z)\} \quad (z \to y_\nu; \nu \in I)$$

it follows that

(7) $\quad r_{i,j}^{(m)}(z) - d_\nu = \mathcal{O}\{f_\nu(z)\} \quad (z \to y_\nu; \nu \in I_{m,m+i+j}; m, i, j \in I).$

The interpolatory function derived from the extrapolation estimate $\varrho_{2i}^{(m)}(d \mid y)$ is $r_{i,i}^{(m)}(z)$. He proves that $\lim r_{i,j}^{(m)}(z) = d_\nu$ as $z \to y_\nu$ ($\nu \in I_{m,m+i+j}$). Then

Setting now $\varepsilon'_{0,j} = 0, \varepsilon_{0,j} = e_j(z)$ ($j \in I$) and $w_{i,j} = \{f_{j-i}(z)^{-1} - f_{i+j+1}(z)^{-1}\}$ ($i \in \bar{I}, j \in I_1$), $r_{i,i}^{(m)}(z) = \varepsilon_{i,i+m}(z)$ ($i, m \in I$).
In this result, the conditions of the simple case in which

(8) $\quad e(y, z) = d(y), \quad f(y, z) = z - y$

may be imposed upon e and f. Now $e_\nu(z) = d_\nu$ is a constant, independent of z ($\nu \in I$) and $f_\nu(z)$ is the difference $z - y_\nu$ ($\nu \in I$). In this case, $r_{i,i}^{(m)}$ is the quotient of two ith degree polynomials in z, the rational function from which the extrapolation limit $\varrho_{2i}^{(m)}(S \mid y)$ was derived. The above process now reduces to an algorithm for rational function interpolation due to Brezinski [128] of which a generalisation has been proposed by Cordellier [129].
The discussion of interpolatory formulæ and extrapolation methods is terminated by the remark that under appropriate conditions cyclic derivation of extrapolation methods from interpolatory formulæ and conversely may be repeated indefinitely.

Section 2 of this document is entitled *Approximants of general order*. In the simple case (8), $r_{i,j}^{(m)}$ is a ratio of two polynomials of degree i. In this Section, he proposes to study the more general system of approximants $r_{i,j}^{(m)}$. The first subsection is *Nonuniform approximation*. Under the condition (8), the relationship (7) reduces to $r_{i,j}^{(m)}(z) - d_\nu = \mathcal{O}(z - y_\nu)$: approximation is uniform, the form of the function $z - y_\nu$ being the same for all relevant y_ν. Wynn notices that a suitable choice of the functions f_ν in the non simplified case, non uniform approximation is possible.
The next subsection is *Remainder term formulæ*. Wynn explains that

In certain circumstances an interpolation property of the form (7) holding at points induces on the function possessing it a corresponding property of approximation over a set containing the points. By imposing severe restrictions upon the functions e and f it is possible in a few lines to exhibit the $r_{i,j}^{(m)}$ as approximations to a function defined over Z, and to provide associated remainder terms.

He imposes the conditions

$$e(y,z) = d(y), \quad f(y,z) = \phi(z) - \phi(y)$$

with $\phi'(y) \neq 0$ for all y in Z. By a straightforward (as he writes) adaptation of an argument of Nörlund [130] (Ch. 15, §3), Wynn obtains the expression of the error. The following subsection is on *Algorithms for approximation evaluation* in which Wynn gives formulæ for the recursive computation of the approximant values $r_{i,j}^{(m)}(z)$ for a fixed $z \in Z$. After quite long developments involving Lagrange forms and divided differences, Wynn shows that his relationship (3) can be applied with $w_{i,j} = f_{m+i+j+1}(z)^{-1}$ to yield $r_{i,j}^{(m)}(z) = \varepsilon_{i,j}$ $(i,j \in I)$ starting from two different sets of initializations. However, in (3), the $\varepsilon'_{i,j}$ are intermediate computations which can be eliminated, and he arrives at the rule

$$(23) \qquad \Delta_j \{w_{i,j} (\Delta_j \varepsilon_{i,j})^{-1}\} = \Delta_i \{w'_{i,j} (\Delta_i \varepsilon_{i-1,j+1})^{-1}\},$$

where $\varepsilon_{i,-1} = 0$ $(i \in I)$, $\varepsilon_{-1,j} = \infty$ $(j \in I)$. The initializations are $\varepsilon_{0,j} = L_j^{(m)}(z)$ in the row by row order $i \in I$, $j \in I_{-1}$ or $\varepsilon_{i,0} = M_i^{(m)}(z)$ $(i \in I)$ in the column order $j \in I_{-1}, i \in I$ with

$$L_j^{(m)}(z) = \sum_{\nu=0}^{j} e_{m+\nu}(z) \prod_{\substack{\tau=0 \\ \tau \neq \nu}}^{j} \frac{f_{m+\tau}(z)}{f_{m+\tau}(z) - f_{m+\nu}(z)} \qquad (m, j \in I)$$

and

$$M_i^{(m)}(z) = \left\{ \sum_{\nu=0}^{i} e_{m+\nu}(z)^{-1} \prod_{\substack{\tau=0 \\ \tau \neq \nu}}^{i} \frac{f_{m+\tau}(z)}{f_{m+\tau}(z) - f_{m+\nu}(z)} \right\}^{-1} \qquad (m, j \in I).$$

Recursive relations for the $L_j^{(m)}$'s and the $M_i^{(m)}(z)$'s are also given. Using divided differences, they are also expressed in Newton form. Determinantal formulæ are related to the recursive rules given.

It is showed that particular cases for the e_ν and the f_ν give back the usual Lagrange interpolation formula, the Neville-Aitken scheme, and Newton series. The work of Stoer on interpolation by rational functions [131] and the variant of the ε-algorithm due to Claessens [132] are also recovered as special cases.

The next subsection is named *Termination*. When $e(y,z)$ is a polynomial or rational function of $f(y,z)$, termination of the algorithms previously given is proved.

The following subsection treats *Confluence* that is when some argument values coincide. Wynn examines what happens to the previous formulæ and recursions. In that case, for $n \in I_2$,

$$(31) \qquad f(y,z) - \sum_{\nu=1}^{n-1} c_\nu(y,z) x(y,z)^\nu = \mathcal{O}\{x(y,z)^n\}$$

$$(32) \qquad e(y,z) - d(y) - \sum_{\nu=1}^{n-1} b_\nu(y,z) x(y,z)^\nu = \mathcal{O}\{x(y,z)^n\},$$

and formulæ for the computation of the coefficients c_ν and d_ν are given. They implement a truncated composition of polynomials. The d_ν's are the coefficients of the Newton series representations of the corresponding Lagrange forms, which are confluent forms of the functional divided differences. They are related to the b_ν, but all details are too complex to be given herein.

Then, comes a subsection on *Zero finding algorithms*. Under suitable conditions, the above algorithm for the truncated composition of polynomials can be used for the inversion of formal power series. Moreover

> In so doing it serves as the basis of a number of algorithms for determining the zeros of a function and motivates the use of the approximants $r_{i,j}^{(m)}(z)$ for the same purpose. Setting $e(y,z) = z - y$ and $f(y,z) = \phi(z) - \phi(y)$, ϕ being the function under treatment, relationships of the form (31,32) hold with $x(y,z) = z - y$, $c_\nu(y,z) = \phi^{(\nu)}(y)/\nu!$ ($\nu \in I_1$) are Taylor series coefficients, $d(y) = 0$, $b_1(y,z) = 1$ and $b_\nu(y,z) = 0$ ($\nu \in I_2$).
> [...] Taking the points y_0, y_1 and y_2 to be confluent, the Lagrange forms [...] are
>
> $$\begin{aligned} L_0^{(0)} &= z - y_0 \\ L_1^{(0)} &= L_0^{(0)} - (\phi_0')^{-1}\{\phi(z) - \phi_0\} \\ L_2^{(0)} &= L_1^{(0)} - (\phi_0')^{-3}\phi_0''\{\phi(z) - \phi_0\}^2/2 \end{aligned}$$
>
> where $\phi_0 = \phi(y_0), \ldots, \phi_0'' = \phi''(y_0)$. Newton's process $z = y_0 - \phi_0/\phi_0'$ is obtained from $L_1^{(0)}(z)$ by equating the latter to zero after setting $\phi(z) = 0$. The third order process $z = y_0 - \{\phi_0/\phi_0'\} - \{\frac{1}{2}\phi_0^2\phi_0''/\phi_0'^3\}$ is obtained from $L_2^{(0)}$ in the same way. Applying relationship (3) to the initial values $\varepsilon_{0,j} = L_j^{(0)}(z)$ ($j \in I_{0,2}$ with $w_{0,0} = w_{1,1} = w_{1/2,1/2} = \{\phi(z) - \phi_0\}^{-1}$ (since $y_1 = y_2 = y_0$) and using $\varepsilon_{1,1} = r_{1,1}^{(0)}(z)$ as just described, the further third order process $z = y_0 - \phi_0\phi_0'/\{\phi'^2 - \frac{1}{2}\phi_0\phi_0''\}$ is obtained.
> The artifice described above is capable of further application.

For example, if $y_1 \neq y_2$, $L_1^{(1)}(z)$ leads to the method regula falsi $z = (y_2\phi_1 - y_1\phi_2)/(\phi_1 - \phi_2)$. If $y_0 = y_1$, then Wynn obtains two combinations of Newton's method and regula falsi

$$\begin{aligned} z &= y - (\phi_0/\phi_0') - \{\phi_0^2(\phi_2 - \phi_0 - (y_2 - y_0)\phi_0')/\{(\phi_2 - \phi_0)^2\phi_0'\} \\ z &= y_0 + \phi_0/\{[\phi_0/(y_2 - y_0)] - [\phi_0'\phi_2/(\phi_2 - \phi_0)]\}. \end{aligned}$$

In the same way, an nth order single point iteration process can be obtained. The subsection ends by

> The more general theory yields multipoint processes (for a further application of the ε-algorithm to the problem of finding the zeros of a function, see [133,134]).

The last subsection of this document is entitled *Extensions of the Lagrange-Bürmann expansion*. Wynn claims that *The above treatment of the confluent case offers an interpretation of the theory of this paper*. He first gives the Lagrange-Bürmann expansion of $d(z)$ in powers of $\phi(z) - \phi(y_\mu)$ where y_μ belongs to a close contour in the complex plane. Then, he obtains an algorithm for determining the coefficients in the Lagrange-Bürmann expansion and in an asymptotic version of it from the Taylor series coefficients of $d(z) - d(y)$ and $\phi(z) - \phi(y)$ at the point $y = y_\mu$. The case of confluence is also treated. In addition, in this case, we do not know why Wynn never published this work since it was ready to be submitted.

7. Interpolation by the use of rational functions

This handwritten complete paper of 90 pages with a bibliography of 27 items, the last one dated 1979, is present in the projects and in the Lists of documents, and it was never published. It seems to be related to the previous manuscript {6}.

In the Section 1 of this document, titled *The Thiele-Nörlund interpolation theory*, Wynn reminds how to construct rational interpolating functions $C_{2s}^{(m)}$ in which the numerator and the denominator have degree s, and $C_{2s+1}^{(m)}$ with a numerator of degree $s+1$ and a denominator of degree s and such that $C_r^{(m)}(x_i) = f_i$ for $i = m, \ldots, m+r$, where the x_i and the f_i are assumed to be complex numbers. After having constructed the reciprocal differences $\varrho_r^{(m)}$ by Thiele process (this is the ϱ-algorithm (3), where now r and m are arbitrary indexes)

$$\varrho_{r+1}^{(m)} = \varrho_{r-1}^{(m+1)} + (x_{m+r+1} - x_m)(\varrho_r^{(m+1)} - \varrho_r^{(m)})^{-1}$$

for $r, m = 0, 1, \ldots$ with $\varrho_{-1}^{(m)} = 0$ $(m = 1, 2, \ldots)$ and $\varrho_0^{(m)} = f_m$ $(m = 0, 1, \ldots)$, it holds

$$C_r^{(m)}(\lambda) = \frac{N_r^{(m)}(\lambda)}{D_r^{(m)}(\lambda)} = \left[\frac{\lambda - x_m}{\varrho_1^{(m)} - \varrho_{-1}^{(m)}}\right] + \left[\frac{\lambda - x_{m+1}}{\varrho_2^{(m)} - \varrho_0^{(m)}}\right] + \cdots + \left[\frac{\lambda - x_{m+r-1}}{\varrho_r^{(m)} - \varrho_{r-2}^{(m)}}\right].$$

The successive numerators and denominators are recursively computed by

$$N_r^{(m)}(\lambda) = (\varrho_r^{(m)} - \varrho_{r-2}^{(m)})N_{r-1}^{(m)}(\lambda) + (\lambda - x_{m+r-1})N_{r-2}^{(m)}(\lambda)$$
$$D_r^{(m)}(\lambda) = (\varrho_r^{(m)} - \varrho_{r-2}^{(m)})D_{r-1}^{(m)}(\lambda) + (\lambda - x_{m+r-1})D_{r-2}^{(m)}(\lambda)$$

with

$$N_{-1}^{(m)}(\lambda) = 1, \quad N_0^{(m)}(\lambda) = f_m, \quad D_{-1}^{(m)}(\lambda) = 0, \quad D_0^{(m)}(\lambda) = 1.$$

Wynn asserts that conditions to ensure that all rational functions $C_r^{(m)}$ can be constructed by the above scheme and that they have the required interpolation properties can be formulated in terms of determinants, and that determinantal formulæ can also be given for the numbers and the functions involved, and he claims that *Such formulae are made more concise by the use of a special notation*. It takes 6 pages to establish these notations. After quoting a remark in German by Nörlund [130] (Ch. 15, p. 420) that Wynn finds *perhaps a little exuberant*, he writes that:

> It is the principal purpose of this paper to point out that, using another very simple relationship (namely, in particular, that, if x_i is replaced by $(\lambda - x_i)^{-1}$, $\varrho_{2r}^{(m)}$ becomes $C_{2r}^{(m)}(\lambda)$) many results suggested by the behaviour of reciprocal differences may be obtained for convergents.

These procedures are described in Section 2 of this document, titled *The σ- and μ-algorithms*. After explaining how to obtain them, Wynn writes

> Theorem 1. Let λ be a fixed finite complex number unequal to x_i $(i = 0, 1, \ldots)$. Set $z_i = (\lambda - x_i)^{-1}$ for $i = 0, 1, \ldots$ […] Numbers $\sigma_r^{(m)}(\lambda)$ $(r, m = 0, 1, \ldots)$ can be constructed from the initial values $\sigma_{-1}^{(m)}(\lambda) = 0$ $(m = 1, 2, \ldots)$, $\sigma_0^{(m)}(\lambda) = f_m$ $(m = 0, 1, \ldots)$ by use of the relationship
>
> (16) $\sigma_{r+1}^{(m)}(\lambda) = \sigma_{r-1}^{(m+1)}(\lambda) + \{z_{m+r+1}(\lambda) - z_m(\lambda)\}\{\sigma_r^{(m+1)}(\lambda) - \sigma_r^{(m)}(\lambda)\}^{-1}$
>
> with $r, m = 0, 1, \ldots$ and, in particular,
>
> $$\sigma_{2s}^{(m)}(\lambda) = C_{2s}^{(m)}(\lambda)$$
>
> for $s, m = 0, 1, \ldots$

Then, the document becomes unclear. It seems that replacing in the above recurrence, z_i by $z_i f_i$ (this is the unclear point), and renaming $\mu_r^{(m)}$'s the $\sigma_r^{(m)}$'s, Wynn obtains $\mu_{2s+1}^{(m)}(\lambda) = C_{2s+1}^{(m)}(\lambda)^{-1}$. A proof of this result is given.

112

The simple observation that, if the argument values x_i are replaced by functions $(\lambda - x_i)^{-1}$ the reciprocal differences $\varrho_{2s}^{(m)}$ become interpolating functions $C_{2s}^{(m)}(\lambda)$ has already produced the σ-algorithm of relationship (16), the simplest and most economical method, subject to the stated conditions, for evaluating these functions; the observation also leads directly, as will be shown below, to new interpolatory theory. Once made, the observation is trivial, and its implications are not difficult to work out; perhaps its most interesting feature is that it has not been made before. The simple relationship between reciprocal differences and rational interpolating functions was not so much discovered as forced upon the author's attention while working out the consequences of principles underlying the process of interpolation and the transformation of divergent series. These two subjects have recently became increasingly important in computational mathematics; new theory in what once might have been considered dead subjects is constantly being developed (mention may be made of recent generalisations of polynomial interpolation described in [135–138]); it is highly probable that the principles concerned will find further applications, and for this reason they are now outlined.

It is difficult to summarize what follows without quoting large parts of the document. Moreover, some notations and their inferences are not clear enough. Basically, Wynn comes back to the link between interpolation and extrapolation already discussed in the document {6}, that he named *Functional Interpolation*. In particular, he considered the following extended ε-algorithm (which contains the ϱ-algorithm and some other extensions [128])

$$(25) \quad \varepsilon_{r+1}^{(m)} = \varepsilon_{r-1}^{(m+1)} + \gamma_r^{(m)} (\varepsilon_r^{(m+1)} - \varepsilon_r^{(m)})^{-1},$$

with $\gamma_r^{(m)} = \psi(m+r+1) - \psi(m)$. He considers the particular case $\gamma_r^{(m)} = 1$, which corresponds to the ε-algorithm. He reminds that, when applied to the partial sums of a formal power series, this algorithm furnishes the Padé approximants belonging to the lower half, diagonal included, of the Padé table, and that he derived (no reference) various determinantal formulæ from a more general form of approximating fractions given by Jacobi [139]. He also mentions that, in its special form, the problem was also studied by Frobenius [140] and Padé [141], and he adds the following remark in which he explains how he obtained his ε-algorithm

> While idly investigating the formulæ resulting from the choice $\gamma_r^{(m)} = 1$ in the relationship (25) [...] the author noted that expressions obtained for the numbers $\varepsilon_{2r}^{(m)}$ were equivalent to extrapolatory determinantal expressions, simplified versions of those due to Jacobi and used by Frobenius, previously published by Schmidt [142] and republished by Shanks [112]. In this way the ε-algorithm was discovered.

Then, Wynn notices that (25) has been used by Claessens with $\gamma_r^{(m)} = (\lambda - x_{m+r+1})^{-1}$, and applied to the partial sums of the Newton interpolation series, for obtaining rational interpolating functions [132], and he explains the theoretical basis of this algorithm

> Claessens was led to the discovery of the extended ε-algorithm by the consideration of interpolatory continued fractions not of Thiele form, but of a form introduced by Kronecker [143] in connection with a process initiated by Rosenhain [144] and Borchardt [145] for constructing the resolvent of two polynomials from systems of their numerical values.

If all the x_i tend to a common value x, the interpolation fractions tend to the Padé approximants and the extended ε-algorithm (25) tends to the usual one. When $\gamma_r^{(m)} = m + r + 1$, (25) gives back the ϱ-algorithm studied by Wynn in Reference [2].

The following Section is on *Lozenge algorithms*, which are algorithms relating quantities located at the four corners of a lozenge in a table where the lower index indicates a columns and the upper index a descending diagonal. The ε-algorithm and its generalizations [146], the ϱ-algorithm, and the algorithms numbered by Wynn (23) (see the manuscript {6}), (16) and (25) (see above in this manuscript) enter into this class. They share some algebraic properties when, instead of applying them to a sequence (S_n), they are applied to $(aS_n + b)$, when $\gamma_r^{(m)}$ in (25) is multiplied by a constant, and when a fractional linear transformation is applied to the elements with an even lower index (property named *homographic invariance*). In these algorithms, the quantities with an odd lower index are only intermediate results with no interest for their purpose. They can be eliminated and a new rule relating five quantities disposed at the center and at the extremities of a cross are obtained. The first algorithm to have been treated in that way is the ε-algorithm for which Wynn obtained this *cross rule* [48]. Concerning this rule, he writes in the document under consideration *Despite the author's pianissimo protests, this relationship and others of its kind have been referred to by various writers as Wynn identities*. This extended cross rule and the homographic invariance property were independently presented by Cordellier in his Doctoral Thesis [147]. They were also published by the same author in Reference [129] without, of course, knowing this unpublished document by Wynn. On the contrary, Wynn was knowing Cordellier's results through his correspondence with C.B., and he indeed refers to Reference [129] for the extension of his cross rule. The homographic invariance for the σ's and the μ's presented above is treated. In the same document, Wynn also discusses the possible breakdown of these relations when a denominator becomes zero. Singular rules for continuing the computations in the case of only one isolated singularity are given. They extend the singular rules he gave in References [20,36] for the usual ε-algorithm. All these results are gathered into Theorem 2 in which Wynn also gives the cross rule for formulæ (16) and (25). If the relationship $\gamma_{2s}^{(m)} + \gamma_{2s}^{(m+1)} = \gamma_{2s-1}^{(m+1)} + \gamma_{2s+1}^{(m)}$ is satisfied between the γ, then the cross rule also holds as described with the five ε's replaced by $(\alpha\varepsilon + \beta)(\gamma\varepsilon + \delta)^{-1}$. Then, if an extended cross rule holds between five numbers as explained above, Wynn looks at which conditions a recurrence relationship of the form (25) holds between them.

The following Section deals with *Invariance properties*. Denoting by $\varrho_r^{(m)}(x,f)$ the reciprocal differences obtained by Thiele's formula (that is the ϱ-algorithm given by (3)) from the argument and functions values $x_i, f_i, i = 0, 1, \ldots$, and setting $y_i = Ax_i + B$ and $g_i = (\alpha f_i + \beta)/(\gamma f_i + \delta)$ with $\alpha\delta - \beta\gamma \neq 0$, Wynn proves that

$$\varrho_{2s}^{(m)}(y,g) = \frac{\alpha\varrho_{2s}^{(m)}(x,f) + \beta}{\gamma\varrho_{2s}^{(m)}(x,f) + \delta}.$$

If $\gamma = 0$, a property for $\varrho_{2s}^{(m)}(y,g)$ is also given. These invariance properties have their counterparts for the convergents $C_s^{(m)}$.

Section 4 is on *Confluent algorithms*. Up to now, all the x_i have been assumed to be distinct. Now Wynn sets $x_i = x + ih$ and allows h to tend to zero. The functions $C_r^{(m)}(\lambda)$ evolve, in particular, to a confluent form $C_r(\lambda, x)$ and become the successive convergents of the continued fraction corresponding to the Taylor series $\sum_{i=0}^{\infty} f^{(i)}(x)(\lambda - x)^i/i!$. The coefficients of this continued fraction may be expressed in terms of Thiele's reciprocal derivatives. He refers to Reference [130] (Ch. 15) for the corresponding theory, and explains that the confluent forms of the algorithms of formulæ (16) are

$$\sigma_{r+1}(\lambda, x) = \sigma_{r-1}(\lambda, x) + (r+1)(\lambda - x)^{-2}\{d\sigma_r(\lambda, x)/dx\}^{-1},$$

with $\sigma_{-1}(\lambda, x) = 0$ and $\sigma_0(\lambda, x) = f(x)$. Determinantal formulæ for these σ's are given. The functions μ are treated similarly. Complete proofs are given.

4.1.3. The ε-Algorithm

8 Sequel to the abstract theory of the ε-algorithm

In February 1971, when he was working at the *Centre de Recherches Mathématiques* of the *Université de Montréal*, Wynn published a report on the abstract theory of the ε-algorithm [69]. In the boxes he left with his friends, we found a document with the title *Notes on sequel to the abstract theory of the ε-algorithm*. All topics treated are in the noncommutative case. It probably corresponds to the rough notes indicated in {26}. It consists of 153 pages including numerous corrections and additions as well as strikethrough passages, and pages from Reference [69] intercalated. In the lists, a corresponding paper is also mentioned, but, unfortunately, we have not found it yet. The document begins with a discussion about the application of Euclid's algorithm to rational functions in a ring with a zero and a unit element. Another one on noncommutative continued fractions follows. Recurrence relations for the numerators and the denominators of their successive convergents are given. They are the same as the usual ones. Wynn claims that:

> the theory of continued fractions may be used to recover the original rational function from the sequence of polynomials $\{B_r(z)\}$ produced by means of Euclids' algorithm. [...] The above theorem offers a method for determining the rational function of the form $\tilde{N}(z)\tilde{D}(z)^{-1}$ equivalent to a given function $D(z)^{-1}N(z)$.

Then, he discusses Euclid's algorithm for formal power series with coefficients over a ring. Wynn proves that they have two sided reciprocal series. It is difficult to extract some results from this part without much work. Then, he considers systems of continued fractions derived from a single power series. Notions on $\mathbb{C}$-regularity and semi-normality are introduced. Applying a recursive algorithm whose rule is that of the vector ε-algorithm, that is $E_{r+1}^{(m)} = E_{r-1}^{(m+1)} + (E_r^{(m+1)} - E_r^{(m)})^{-1}$, but without giving the definition of the inverse, to the partial sums of a semi-normal series he proves that $E_{2r}^{(m)} = D(z)^{-1}N(z)$ for a certain value of r. Other theoretical results are given, but they are difficult to exploit. Then, pages 93–96 of Reference [69] are reproduced which leads to think that what precedes is a complement to that report. Wynn then shows that both halves of the Padé table can be constructed via this algorithm under certain assumptions. A cross-rule is given for each half.

Pages on vector continued fractions follow. Arithmetic operations upon vectors and formal power series with vector coefficients are first explained. But the pages, the concepts (vector valued rational functions, McLeod isomorphism [148], ...), and the results are so entangled that it seems difficult to extract something coherent. There are pages on Euclid's algorithm for formal power series with vector valued coefficients, a vector qd-algorithm, and the vector ε-algorithm. However, an interesting result is given but it needs to be verified. Let us give it after a simplification of the notations. Summations are over ν:

> **Theorem.** *If the finite dimensional vectors of the sequence $\{f_\nu\}$ satisfy a system of relationships of the form*
>
> $$\sum_0^{r'} d_{r'-\nu} f_{m+\nu} = 0, \quad m = 0, 1, \ldots,$$
>
> *where the $\{d_\nu\}$ are real numbers, then the series $\sum f_\nu z^\nu$ is generated by a vector values rational function $f(z)$. If vector value rational functions $\varepsilon_r^{(m)}$ ($r = 1, \ldots, 2r'; m = 0, 1, \ldots$) can be constructed from the initial values*
>
> $$\varepsilon_{-1}^{(m)} = 0 \qquad \varepsilon_0^{(m)} = \sum_0^{m-1} f_\nu z^\nu \ (m = 1, 2, \ldots)$$
>
> *by means of the recursion*
>
> $$\varepsilon_{r+1}^{(m)} = \varepsilon_{r-1}^{(m+1)} + \{\varepsilon_r^{(m+1)} - \varepsilon_r^{(m)}\}^{-1}$$

for $r = 0, \ldots, 2r' - 1, m = 0, 1, \ldots$, then $\varepsilon_{2r'}^{(m)} = f(z), m = 0, 1, \ldots$

Looking at the proof, which is not complete, one can understand that the words *the series $\sum f_\nu z^\nu$ is generated by the rational function $f(z)$* means that

$$f(z) = (\sum_0^{r'} d_\nu z^\nu)^{-1} \sum_0^{r'-1} \eta_\nu z^\nu,$$

where $\sum_0^r d_\nu f_{r-\nu} = \eta_r$ $(r = 0, \ldots, r' - 1)$.

The vector valued Padé table is presented. Then, Wynn gives *some elementary results in the theory of ε-algorithm as applied to sequences of elements of a ring*. In particular, a cross rule is obtained. Rational functions with coefficients over a ring are discussed.

Then, Wynn studies the application of the ε-algorithm to a sequence of numbers satisfying an inhomogeneous linear difference equation. He proves the following result (notations slightly changed)

> Theorem. *Let the numbers S_ν satisfy the recursion $\sum_0^r d_\nu S_{m+\nu} = H, m = 0, 1, \ldots$ and no recursion of a similar form with r replaced by a smaller integer; set $\sum_0^r d_\nu = D$. It is not possible that both D and H are both factors of zero.*

It is then proved that, for such a sequence, $\varepsilon_{2r}^{(m)} = D^{-1}H$ for all m. Other results of a lower interest are given. Then, Wynn looks at the properties of the hierarchies of ε-arrays, as defined in Reference [79], that are obtained for such sequences. Since pages 23–28 of his report from the *Université de Montréal* corresponding to the paper of Reference [79] are inserted here between the pages of the manuscript, and preceded by *If* followed by a difference equation, what precedes can be considered as an addition to them. Using the vector-matrix isomorphism of McLeod [148], Wynn writes that, for recursions involving vectors, *it is a relatively simple matter to derive results analogous to those of the preceding section*. Further notes end the document.

9 **How to find the centre of a spiral**

This handwritten document contains 49 pages that correspond to the slides for a talk. There are parts in the text separated by numbers in bold from 1 to 30 in large square boxes (see {28}). Its title could be *How to find the centre of a spiral*, and it was delivered by Wynn after 1987 since a book dating 1987 is quoted. After there are 30 pages where the same content is detailed and illustrated very carefully, probably some notes to copy and distribute.

The document gives an interesting new interpretation of extrapolation by the ε-algorithm.

> We start with a fixed complex number λ. If the modulus of λ is less than 1, λ lies inside the unit circle. If the modulus of λ is greater than 1, λ lies outside the unit circle.
>
> Next, we form the successive powers $\lambda^0, \lambda^1, \lambda^2, \ldots$ of λ. They lie on a spiral in the complex plane. The argument of λ^2 is twice $\arg(\lambda)$, the argument of λ^3 is three times $\arg(\lambda)$ and so on. If the modulus of λ is less than 1, the powers of $|\lambda|$ tend to zero and the spiral contracts to the origin. If the modulus of λ is greater than 1, the spiral expands away from the origin. Then, we multiply each of the points $\lambda^0, \lambda^1, \lambda^2, \ldots$ by a constant complex number b. This does no more than rotate the spiral through $\arg(b)$ and magnify or diminish it by a factor of $|b|$. But a contracting spiral remains contracting and an expanding spiral remains expanding. Lastly we add a constant C to each of the transformed points and produce members
>
> $$s_i = C + b\lambda^i \quad (i = 0, 1, \ldots)$$
>
> of a first order spiral sequence. In the case in which $|\lambda| < 1$, the sequence converges to C and the spiral upon which its members lie contracts toward C. In the case in which $|\lambda| > 1$, the spiral expands away from C. If $\lim_{i \to \infty} s_i$ is finite, $\lim_{i \to \infty} s_i = C$.
>
> Already we may pose a problem in connection with first order spiral sequences. It is known that three successive members S_k, S_{k+1} and S_{k+2} of a sequence have the form

but the values of C, b, λ and k are unknown. Find the value of C alone. If we can solve this problem then what we are able to do is fit a first order spiral sequence to the subsequence S_k, S_{k+1} and S_{k+2} and find its centre.

Then, Wynn shows that the problem can be solved by computing $\varepsilon_2^{(k)}$ by a rule which is that of the ε-algorithm (without mentioning its name). He gave the formulæ for $\varepsilon_1^{(k)}$ and $\varepsilon_1^{(k+1)}$. Then, he computes $\varepsilon_2^{(k)}$, and shows that it holds $\varepsilon_2^{(k)} = C$. Thus, the spiral has been fitted without the determination of the values of b and λ. Then, he considers three other members S_{k+1}, S_{k+2} and S_{k+3} having the form

$$S_{k+1} = C' + b'\lambda'^{k+1}, \quad S_{k+2} = C' + b'\lambda'^{k+2}, \quad S_{k+3} = C' + b'\lambda'^{k+3}.$$

Another spiral can be fitted through these three numbers, and a similar computation leads to $\varepsilon_2^{(k+1)} = C'$. He mentions that $\varepsilon_1^{(k+1)}$ is identical to the one computed before. The same process can be continued with S_{k+2}, S_{k+3} and S_{k+4}, and so on. For each value of the upper index, the center of the spiral can be computed by the rule

$$\varepsilon_{r+1}^{(m)} = \varepsilon_{r-1}^{(m+1)} + \frac{1}{\varepsilon_r^{(m+1)} - \varepsilon_r^{(m)}}$$

from $\varepsilon_{-1}^{(m)} = 0$, and $\varepsilon_0^{(m)} = S_m, m = 0, 1, \ldots$ This is the ε-algorithm [3]. Wynn mentions that, if $S_0, S_1, S_2, \ldots$ are successive members of the same first order spiral sequence, that is $S_i = C + b\lambda^i$ for $i = 0, 1, \ldots$, then $\varepsilon_2^{(i)} = C$ for all i. This set of sequences is the kernel of the sequence transformation $(S_m) \longmapsto (\varepsilon_2^{(m)})$ which is, in fact, Aitken's Δ^2 process. Then, Wynn considers a second spiral entangled into the first one.

The members of a second order spiral sequence have the representation

$$s_i = C + \sum_{j=1}^{h} \lambda_j^i \left\{ \sum_{v=0}^{\tau(j)} b_{j,v} i^v \right\}; \quad \sum_{j=1}^{h} \{\tau(j) + 1\} = 2$$

$(i = 0, 1, \ldots)$. This sequence has two forms: either
(a) only one geometric term accompanied by a linear function of i is present and

$$s_i = C + \lambda_1^i (b_{1,0} + b_{1,1} i)$$

or
(b) two geometric terms accompanied by constant coefficients are present and

$$s_i = C + b_{1,0}\lambda_1^i + b_{2,0}\lambda_2^i$$

In the latter case a second order spiral sequence may be regarded as a first order spiral sequence whose members are represented by $b_{2,0}\lambda_2^i$ whose center moves on a further first order spiral upon which the points $C + b_{1,0}\lambda_1^i$ lie.

In these forms, the kernel of the transformation $(S_m) \longmapsto (\varepsilon_4^{(m)})$ is recognized. Then, Wynn considers nth order spirals with the s_i satisfying the same formula but now with the condition $\sum_{j=1}^{h}\{\tau(j)+1\} = n$, and he discusses their various special forms. The center C of such spirals can be obtained via the ε-algorithm which, starting from $S_k, \ldots, S_{k+2n}$, delivers $\varepsilon_{2n}^{(k)} = C$. Since he writes that: *There is no time to give a proof of this result* this confirms that these notes were written for lectures. The same process is repeated with $S_{k+1}, \ldots, S_{k+2n+1}$, and it gives $\varepsilon_{2n}^{(k+1)} = C'$. As before, the two schemes have some ε in common, and, if $S_0, S_1, \ldots$ are successive members of the same nth order spiral, then, for all m, $\varepsilon_{2n}^{(m)} = C$. This is a known property of the ε-algorithm since the sequence (S_n) belongs to the kernel of the transformation $(S_m) \longmapsto (\varepsilon_{2n}^{(m)})$.

If the parameters C, b and λ in the equation of the first order spiral are real, the $s_i = C + b\lambda^i, i = 0, 1, \ldots$, still lie on a spiral in the complex plane, but the numbers s_i themselves lie on the real axis. In that case, the ε are also real.

Then, Wynn explains how *the process for finding the centres of spirals which we have described serve as the basis of a method for obtaining estimates of the limit of a sequence*. Starting from S_0, S_1 and S_2, the center $\varepsilon_2^{(0)}$ of the corresponding first order spiral is an estimate of the limit. Then, from S_1, S_2 and S_3, a second estimate $\varepsilon_2^{(1)}$ is obtained, and so on. Now, from $S_0, \ldots, S_4$, the center $\varepsilon_4^{(0)}$ of the second order spiral passing through these numbers furnishes another estimate of the limit. The process can be repeated by increasing the number of terms of the sequence (S_m) used in the construction of the successive spirals. And Wynn writes *This method of estimating the limit of a sequence is known as the ε-algorithm* [...]*A question now arises: does this method work?* Wynn gives two numerical examples: partial sums of the series $1 - 1/2 + 1/3 - 1/4 + \cdots$ which converge to $\ln 2$, and those of the series $\sum_i C^i_{-1/2} 1/(i+1)$ ($C^i_{-1/2}$ represents the binomial coefficient) which tends to $2(2^{1/2} - 1)$. He tentatively explains the success of the process:

> *Perhaps a happier interpretation is to suggest that a great deal of information lies lurking in the first few members of a sequence: we have only to think of a way of getting it out. This interpretation serves us a little better when we come to consider the transformation of divergent sequences.*

In saying that, Wynn is too much optimistic. Indeed, the behavior of a sequence can completely change after a certain number of terms, and change again later. As proved in Reference [149], an algorithm to accelerate the convergence of all sequences cannot exist. It is the same even for restricted classes of sequences [150]. Then, Wynn gives examples of divergent series and explains that the reasons why the ε-algorithm works in these examples are found in the classical theory of continued fractions.

After that, he describes the use of the algorithm in the solution of the fixed point problem $x = f(x)$. He explains graphically the convergence of the Picard iterates, and what the notion of order of convergence of a sequence is. Since Newton's and higher order methods require the use of the derivatives of f, he explains how this drawback can be avoided. He starts from an initial estimate $C^{(0)}$ of the fixed point, sets $S_0 = C^{(0)}$, performs the iterations $S_{i+1} = f(S_i)$ for $i = 0, \ldots, 2r - 1$, and finds the center $C^{(1)} = \varepsilon_{2r}^{(0)}$ of the spiral constructed from these iterates, and restarts the Picard iterates from $S_0 = C^{(1)}$. When $r = 1$, this is exactly Steffensen's method which has order 2. Wynn claims that under suitable conditions $C^{(k+1)} - x = \mathcal{O}((C^{(k)} - x)^r)$. Let us mention that this claim has never been proved.

Then, Wynn explains that the ε-algorithm can be applied to sequences of functions, of vectors, of a field or of *any mathematical system over which addition, subtraction and the formation of an inverse are defined*, and that the theory of continued fractions has been developed for such cases.

The continuous case of the preceding method is considered. It is aimed at the estimation of $\lim_{t\to\infty} S(t)$. In what precedes, i is replaced by t and λ_j^i by $e^{-\alpha_j t}$, and he names an rth order spiral function, the expression

$$S(t) = C + \sum_{j=1}^{h} e^{-\alpha_j t} \left\{ \sum_{v=0}^{\tau(j)} b_{j,v} t^v \right\}; \quad \sum_{j=1}^{h} \{\tau(j) + 1\} = r.$$

Wynn proposes to estimate $\lim_{t\to\infty} S(t)$ by fitting a spiral function $s(t)$ to $S(t)$ at one value x of t, and to take its center as this estimate. For that purpose, he assumes that

finding the center C of the nth order spiral function, Wynn gives the following lozenge algorithm (defined in Reference [88,89]):

$$\omega_{2r+1}^{(m)} = \omega_{2r-1}^{(m+1)} + \frac{\omega_{2r}^{(m)}}{\omega_{2r}^{(m+1)}}, \quad \omega_{2r+2}^{(m)} = \omega_{2r}^{(m+1)}(\omega_{2r+1}^{(m)} - \omega_{2r+1}^{(m+1)}),$$

with $\omega_{-1}^{(m)} = 0$ and $\omega_0^{(m)} = S^{(m)}$, he obtains $\omega_{2n}^{(0)} = C$, and writes *This method of estimating the limit of a function is known as the ω-algorithm.* He adds:

> This method has application in estimating the end-point of the trajectory of an aerodynamic vehicle, given its position, velocity components, etc. [...]
> Since Texas is an oil-producing state the last problem we consider is that of the owner of a well producing oil with cast price c per barrel who wishes to determine
> (a) the price P par barrel which maximizes his profit
> and
> (b) his profit at the optimal price P.
> We now describe a solution and hasten to say that the economic part of the argument is taken directly from the mid nineteenth century French economist Cournot who considered the problem of the owner of a spring producing mineral water at zero cost per bottle.

After giving the solution of this problem, Wynn proposes some references for those who are interesting in studying the matter further. Among them, the book of Antoine Augustin Cournot (1801–1877) [151]. As said before, at the end, there are 30 particularly nicely written pages with figures about spirals (see Figure 3), implementation schemes for the ε and the ω algorithms, an illustration of Picard iterates, numerical results, illustrations for the order of convergence, details about the problem of oil pricing policy, and references. It seems that these pages were ready to be copied for distribution to participants. Since the application was about an oil problem in Texas, this document could have been prepared for a seminar at the University of Texas at San Antonio.

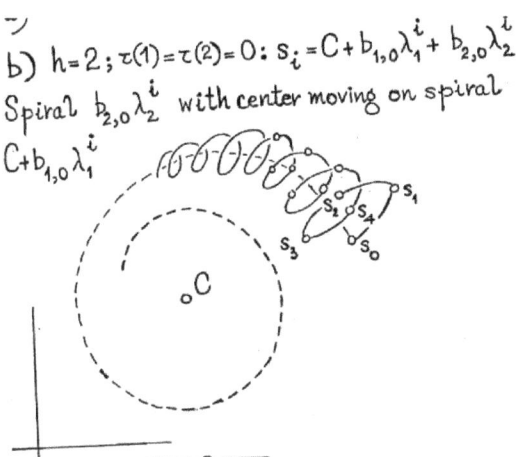

Figure 3. Second order spiral of form (b) drawn by Wynn.

Let us mention that the interpretation of the scalar and vector Aitken's process and ε-algorithm by means of spirals was independently rediscovered in 2014 by Berlinet [152], together with other interesting geometrical analyses of them.
We did some numerical experiments with the spirals introduced by Wynn, and, in particular, we wanted to test his drawing reproduced in Figure 3. Remember that, according to Wynn's nomenclature, a *first order spiral* has the form (our notation) $S_n = C + a_1 \lambda_1^n$,

and that a *second order spiral* can have two forms (a) $S_n = C + \lambda_1^n(a_1 + b_1 n)$ or (b) $S_n = C + a_1\lambda_1^n + a_2\lambda_2^n$. If the ε-algorithm is applied to a first order spiral, then, $\forall n, \varepsilon_2^{(n)} = C$, which is Aitken's Δ^2 process. Applied to a second order spiral of form (a) or (b), this algorithm gives $\forall n, \varepsilon_4^{(n)} = C$, while the iterated Δ^2 process (that is the Δ^2 process applied to the sequence $(\varepsilon_2^{(n)})$) does not possess this property.

Wynn's drawing of Figure 3 corresponds to the case (b). He wanted to illustrate the fact that $S_n = C + a_1\lambda_1^n + a_2\lambda_2^n$ can be written as $S_n = C_n + a_2\lambda_2^n$, with $C_n = C + a_1\lambda_1^n$, which he described as the *spiral $a_2\lambda_2^n$ with center moving on spiral $C + a_1\lambda_1^n$*.

In our numerical experiments, we always took $C = 1.5 + i$. In Figure 4, we show two first order spirals with $a_1 = 1 - i$: the one on the left is obtained with $\lambda_1 = 0.8 - 0.5i$, and it converges to C, the one on the right is with $\lambda_1 = -0.8 + 0.6i$ and does not converge or diverge since $|\lambda_1| = 1$.

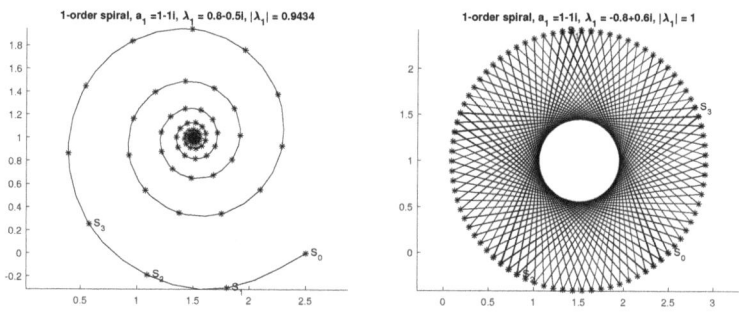

Figure 4. First order spirals with $\lambda_1 = 0.8 - 0.5i$ (**left**) and $\lambda_1 = -0.8 + 0.6i$ (**right**).

Now, we consider second order spirals of forms (a) and (b). We took, for the form (a), $a_1 = 2 - 4i, b_1 = 2.3 - 0.3i, \lambda_1 = 0.92 + 0.2i$, and, for the form (b), $a_1 = 1 - i, \lambda_1 = 0.8 + 0.5i, a_2 = 1.2 + 2i, \lambda_2 = 0.7 + 0.65i$. All spirals are converging to C since $|\lambda_1| < 1$ and $|\lambda_2| < 1$. Figure 5 shows the corresponding second order spirals: (a) on the left and (b) on the right.

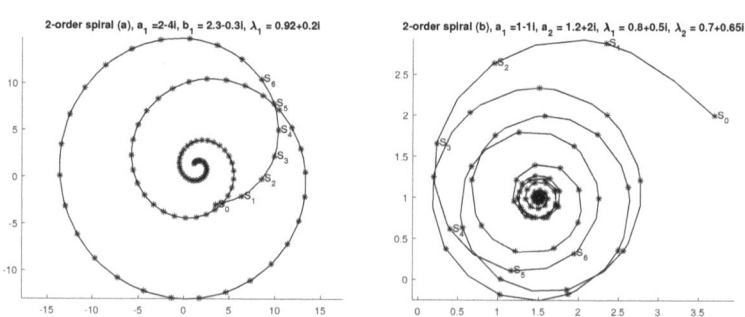

Figure 5. Second order spirals: (a) on the **left** and (b) on the **right**.

spirals: (a) on the left and (b) on the right. Comparing these curves with those of Figure 5 shows that, in fact, Aitken's process acts as if it was suppressing one of the spirals of the curve (which contains two of them) since the sequence $(\varepsilon_2^{(n)})$ still looks like another spiral, and is not reduced to a single point as in the case where only one spiral was present.

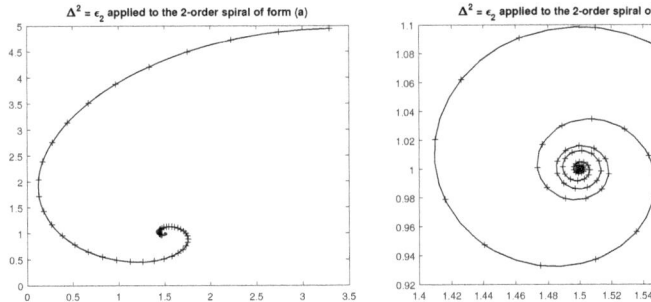

Figure 6. Δ^2 process applied to second order spirals: (a) on the **left** and (b) on the **right**.

Indeed, if (S_n) has the form (b) with $|\lambda_2| > |\lambda_1|$, we have $S_n - C = \mathcal{O}(\lambda_2^n)$. It is easy to see that

$$\varepsilon_2^{(n)} = C + \frac{a_1 a_2 \lambda_1^n \lambda_2^n (\lambda_2 - \lambda_1)^2}{a_1 \lambda_1^n (\lambda_1 - 1)^2 + a_2 \lambda_2^n (\lambda_2 - 1)^2}$$

$$= C + \frac{a_1 a_2 \lambda_1^n (\lambda_2 - \lambda_1)^2}{a_1 (\lambda_1/\lambda_2)^n (\lambda_1 - 1)^2 + a_2 (\lambda_2 - 1)^2} = \mathcal{O}(\lambda_1^n),$$

which shows the gain brought by Aitken's process by almost suppressing the role played by λ_2, the most important one.

If (S_n) has the form (a), that is $S_n = C + (a_1 + b_1 n)\lambda^n$, then $S_n - C = \mathcal{O}(n\lambda^n)$. Aitken's process leads to

$$\varepsilon_2^{(n)} = C - \frac{b_1^2 \lambda^{n+2}}{(\lambda - 1)((a_1 + b_1 n)(\lambda - 1) + 2b_1 \lambda)} = \mathcal{O}(\lambda^n),$$

which shows the acceleration brought by suppressing the leading error term.

In Figure 7, we see the results obtained by the iterated Δ^2 process applied twice to second order spirals: (a) on the left and (b) on the right. Thus, the iterated Δ^2 process does not gives the exact value of C, which should be a single point and not a curve although $(\varepsilon_2^{(n)})$ is a spiral (see Figure 6), while $(\varepsilon_4^{(n)})$, in exact arithmetic, gives exactly C. However, the iterated Δ^2 process has a faster convergence, and it also has the form of a spiral.

Spirals with different values of the parameters can have various shapes. It is sufficient, for instance, to change one sign in λ_1 or λ_2. We intend to deepen this subject in a forthcoming paper.

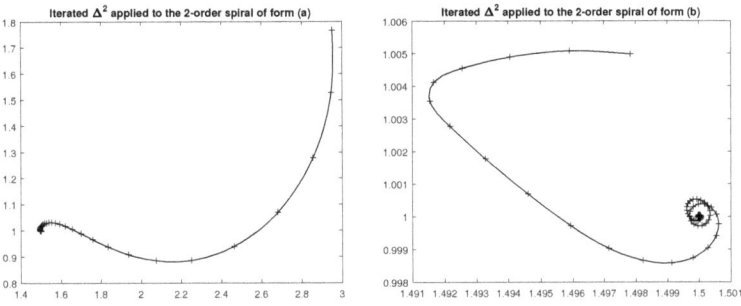

Figure 7. Iterated Δ^2 process applied to second order spirals: (a) on the **left** and (b) on the **right**.

4.1.4. Project for a Book

We separated this document from the others since it treats a large range of topics and seems to be an advanced skeleton for a book.

10 Book on ε-algorithm

This 120 pages document is clearly a preparatory work for a book. Looking at its contents, it is probably the *Resumé of book* on the ε-algorithm, mentioned by Wynn in {26}, and also at the end of his document {28}, with an O (ongoing) in front of the name. In this manuscript, he stated in detail what he intended to treat. It contains an incredible succession of theorems whose proofs are not given, and comments and explanations between them are missing. It is divided into chapters.

Chapter 1: Theorem concerning determinants. It contains identities for compound determinants, Schweins' lemmata, simple and extended Hankel determinants.

Chapter 2: Prediction based upon a linear model. Its sections are on exponential extrapolation (that is, the Aitken Δ^2 process), and extrapolation using a linear recursion (that is the Shanks transformation).

Chapter 3: The epsilon algorithm. The sections are on the auxiliary numbers $\varepsilon_{2r+1}^{(m)}$, the fundamental formulæ, and the algebraic theory of the epsilon algorithm (invariance properties and the cross rule).

Chapter 4: The Padé table. Sections are on the Padé quotients and the Padé table.

Chapter 5: The epsilon algorithm and the Padé table. The first section is on the even order epsilon numbers and the Padé table. The second section studies the epsilon array associated with a rational function. The next one is on the extended epsilon array, that is the second half of the Padé table. Recursions for primitive Padé quotients are then given.

Chapter 6: Continued fractions. The chapter begins by the general theory (definitions, recurrences, equivalence transformation, contraction and extension, the Euler-Minding formulæ). The second section is about continued fractions derived from power series (corresponding and associated continued fractions). Then, the connection between continued fractions and the Padé table is studied. The continued fractions of the even order epsilon array are then discussed, and again those derived from power series. Transformations of corresponding continued fractions are presented, and a method of deriving an associated continued fraction is explained.

Chapter 7: The epsilon algorithm and orthogonal polynomials. Definition, determinantal formula, associated polynomials, recurrence relationships in the case of formal orthogonality are first given. The *qd*-algorithm and Bauer's bridge are presented.

Chapter 8: The convergence behaviour of the row and column sequences of the Padé table. There is a section on Hadamard's theory of the Taylor series, and two sections on the convergence of the rows and columns of the Padé table. Another section deals with the construction and convergence of the even order epsilon-array.

Chapter 9: The convergence of the sequence $\{\varepsilon_2^{(n)}\}$. It presents Samuel Lubkin's lemmata, and consequences.

Chapter 10: Some analysis. The chapter gives classical results on functions of a real variable, definition and properties of the Stieltjes integral, theorems of choice, orthogonal polynomials derived from a positive distribution, the problem of moments, the Hausdorff moment problem, completely monotonic functions, complex variable theory.

Chapter 11: Integral transforms. The first section is on the Riesz-Herglotz theorem, followed by one on Hamburger-Nevanlinna functions. Then, Wynn gives results on the Laplace transform, the Stieltjes inversion formula, the Riesz-Herglotz-Wall functions.

Chapter 12: Power series. The chapter begins by the series generated by Hamburger-Nevanlinna and Stieltjes functions. Then, asymptotic series are discussed. The next section is on the transformation of divergent power series (Borel integrals and Watson-Nevanlinna lemma).

Nevanlinna functions. It is followed by a study of nested circular value regions. Convergence criteria expressed in terms of the coefficients of the continued fraction and of those of the series are then given. The next section is on what Wynn names theorems of access (logarithmic derivatives and Laplace transforms). The equivalence between the method of Borel and the use of continued fractions is then discussed. A characterisation of Stieltjes fractions is proposed.

Chapter 14: The diagonal sequences of the Padé table and the even order ε-array. Wynn begins by the structure of the Padé table associated with a Hamburger-Nevanlinna and a Stieltjes function. The convergence of the diagonals of the Padé table for such functions is discussed, and, then, the construction and the convergence of the diagonal sequences of the even order epsilon array. There is a section on the Padé table derived from a Stieltjes series. A comparison between the epsilon algorithm and the generalised Euler transformation is proposed. Then, Wynn considers the epsilon algorithm and the transformation of trigonometric series, and that of operational formulæ in numerical analysis.

Chapter 15: The operator epsilon algorithm. The chapter treats noncommutative continued fractions and orthogonal polynomials, the operator qd-algorithm, the noncommutative version of Bauer's bridge. Wynn gives a fundamental theorem concerning operator valued orthogonal polynomials.

Chapter 16: The vector epsilon algorithm. McLeod's isomorphism and Clifford algebra are explained. Then, come the vector valued and the functional Padé tables.

Chapter 17: The first confluent form of the epsilon algorithm: the rational function limit and the continued fraction limit. This chapter has two sections where these topics are treated.

Chapter 18: The second confluent form of the epsilon algorithm: the definition of an integral as the limit of a continued fraction. After defining this second confluent form, Wynn explains the connection between both forms. Then, he treats the rational function and the continued fractions integrals. Euler integration ends the chapter.

Chapter 19: The rational function integral. The degenerate theory in treated in the first section, and the general theory in the second one. A special convergence result is then given.

Chapter 20: The continued fraction integral. The chapter begins by the degenerate theory before coming to a remarkable equivalence.

Chapter 21: The third and fourth confluent forms of the epsilon algorithm. The fourth one is given but not the third one.

Chapter 22: A partial differential equation associated with the epsilon algorithm. The first section is about a so-called ϕ-array. Then, partial differential equations are derived for it. The cases of the epsilon algorithm and that of the Padé surface are then treated. The following section is about self conjugate systems of partial differential equations for symmetric algorithms. Adjoint partial differential equations are discussed, and special solutions of the partial differential equation of the Padé surface are given.

Chapter 23: Error analyses of the epsilon algorithm. The chapter begins by a perturbation analysis. Then, the convergence and stability of the epsilon algorithm are studied. The singular rule for the algorithm is given.

This preparatory work for a book is in an advanced form since the results are well positioned in it. It only remains to link them by explanations and to give the proofs of the theoretical results (or the corresponding references to the literature).

4.1.5. Algebra

11 *Theory of stratified commutative field*

This document presents a total of 266 pages. These notes, mentioned in many of the lists of Wynn, seem in a final form because they contain no erasures.

After defining his notations for the ranges of the indexes, Wynn writes (all indexes are in $\mathbb{Z}$):

> Definition. A stratified commutative ring, or S-ring, is a system S of numbers arranged into strata $S\{j\}$ such that
> (i) the members of $S\{j\}$ form an additive Abelian group;
> (ii) commutative and associative multiplication is defined between elements of the various $S\{j\}$: with $a \in S\{j\}, b \in S\{k\}$, $ab = ba \in S\{j+k\}$ and $(ab)c = a(bc)$ for such products;
> (iii) multiplication is distributive with respect to addition within appropriate strata: with $a, b \in S\{j\}, c \in S\{k\}$, $(a+b)c = ac + bc$, addition on the left being within $S\{j\}$, that on the right within $S\{j+k\}$.
> A number belonging to the above system is an S-number and the $S\{j\}$ to which it belongs is its stratum.
> $\mathbb{S}$ is the class of S-rings.
> It is not assumed in the above definition that addition and subtraction between disparate strata should be possible, although in special cases this may be so. It is so, for example, when all $S\{j\}$ are the same additive Abelian group; S is then simply a commutative ring. More generally, it is also possible between congruent strata if $S\{j\} \equiv S\{k\}$ when $j = k \mod m$, m being a prescribed integer.

Two special S-rings are described, and then:

> The above examples serve to draw attention to a salient feature of theory to follow. It will be shown that the end results of certain computations involving S-numbers are members of fixed strata–for example that certain bilinear forms with S-number coefficients are expressible as linear sums of squares with coefficients that are S-numbers.

The rest of the document cannot be summarized without going into detail. It is a purely theoretical work. No practical application is given, and there are no references to the literature.

12 **Stratified field, determinantal identities and LU decomposition in such field**

This document of 105 pages probably follows the preceding document {11}. It contains theoretical notes about determinantal identities and LU decomposition over stratified commutative ring. He defines the so-called P-numbers that, in fact, have the same definition of the S-number of the document {11}. He defines the P-array and the P-matrices that are different in their definition. Several result were proved, concerning, for instance Jacobi's theorem on the adjugate, product of determinants, Sylvester's and Schweins' determinantal identities, and so on. A LU decomposition is also proposed. This document, purely theoretical, is in almost good shape, and it seems to be complete since the numbered pages correspond to what Wynn indicates in {26}.

13 **Equations in field extensions**

This theoretical document, without title, contains 37 pages numbered from 1 to 37. Probably it is also intended to follow the work {11}, since inside there are references to that theory. It is perhaps what Wynn called *Last notes* (see {26}).

14 **Factorisations of a triangular matrix**

This document contains 43 pages of well written notes with this title. This work is mentioned in {26–28}, together with the notes {1} on Bürmann series.

As usual in many of his works, Wynn begins by introducing a plethora of notations which makes the results more difficult to apprehend. However, we need to give some of them.

> [...] (2a) $(i : j; k)$ indicates that the integer i should take the values $i = j, \ldots, k$. (b) If the lower limit j is unity, it and the subsequent semi-colon are omitted, thus $(i : k)$ is an abbreviation for $i = 1, \ldots, k$. Conjoint descriptions are separated by a vertical bar, thus $(i : n \mid j : i)$ is an abbreviation for $i = 1, \ldots, n; j = 1, \ldots, i$. [...]
> For $(i : n \mid j : n - i + 1)$, $a(i, j)$ is the jth order determinant formed from the array whose τth row contains the elements $a_{i+\tau-1,\nu}$ $(\nu : j)$ for $(\tau : j)$; when $j < 1$, $a(i, j) = 1$ $(i : n)$.

A bunch of results are then presented but without any explanation on their purpose.

Notation. A being a lower triangular $n \times n$ matrix with elements $a_{i,j} \in \mathbb{K}$, $a(i, k; j)$ is, for $(i, k : n \mid j : \min(n - i + 1, n - k + 1)$, the jth order determinant formed from the array whose τth row $(\tau : j)$ contains the elements $a_{i+\tau-1, k+\nu-1}$ $(\nu : j)$. Also, $a(i, k; 0) = 1$ $(i : n \mid k : i)$ [...]

Theorem. Let $a_{i,j}$ $(i : n \mid j : i)$ be the elements of a nonsingular lower triangular matrix, and $c_{i,j}$ $(i : n \mid j : i)$ those of its inverse. Then

$$c(i,k;j) = \frac{(-1)^{i+k} a(j+k, k; i-k)}{\prod_{\tau=k}^{i+j-1} a_{\tau,\tau}} \quad (i : n \mid k : i \mid j : \min(n-i+1, n-k+1)).$$

Proof. The formula

$$c_{i,k} = c(i, k; 1) = \frac{(-1)^{i+k} a(k+1, k; i-k)}{\prod_{\tau=k}^{i} a_{\tau,\tau}}$$

is obtained from the system of equations

$$a_{k,k} c_{k,k} = 1, \quad \sum_{\nu=k}^{\mu} a_{\mu,\nu} c_{\nu,k} = 0 \quad (\mu : k+1; i).$$

The result is correct when $j = 1$. A short inductive proof based upon the use of the formula, suffices to show that the result is true as stated.

The last page of the document is a list of possible applications, not all of them being intelligible. But Wynn also mentions: Examine band matrix decomposition for $a_{i,j}$ deriving from differential equation; Partial sum transformation $\sum_{\tau=0}^{i} f_\tau x^\tau \longmapsto \sum_{\tau=0}^{i} g_\tau a(x)$. Convergence acceleration; Integral transform of transformation as in motivation of γ-algorithm; Band matrix decomposition of $C\{a\}$ and Newton series extension; Extension of Bernoulli polynomials $\{a(xy) + 1\}\beta(x)^j = \sum \beta_\nu^{(j)}(y) x^\nu$, etc.

4.1.6. Software

15 Numal in FORTRAN

Numal was a library of numerical algorithms written in Algol 60 and developed by members of the Mathematical Center in Amsterdam. Remember that Wynn belonged to this Center from 1960 to 1964. During his stay in München, he privately participated actively to the development of Algol 60 and used it for his programmes (see, i.e., References [33,44,55]). When he was in North America, he supervised a translation of the library into a FORTRAN version suitable for mini-computers and wrote a detailed documentation. As he wrote [...] *the translation it self was carried out almost single-handedly by H.T. Lau.* It is interesting to remark that Hang T. Lau made the same for C-language and Java, and published two books on that, respectively in 1994 and in 2003. According to the Wynn explanation, this is a translation into Fortran of a Numerical Algorithms Library written in Algol 60. Its table of contents shows that it covers the main domains of numerical analysis: computer arithmetic, linear algebra, polynomials, series, numerical solution of differential equations, numerical integration, Fourier series, zero finding algorithms, minimisation, parameter estimation and special functions. The document found, submitted on 11 February 1981 has 29 pages and a preface, and it is the first part of this work and it is entitled *0. Introduction and Summary*. The titles and contents of the other parts are given. This part begins by a comparison of the respective merits of Algol and FORTRAN. Then, Wynn describes the modifications he did and the improvements he brought. He also explains how the translation was performed and that the FORTRAN versions of the Algol procedures are far longer because *the petty restrictions with which FORTRAN is afflicted cannot directly be overcome.* Finally, he describes the machine and compiler dependent features which had to be taken into consideration.

4.2. Unpublished Typewritten Documents

We found two typewritten documents which seem to be ready for publication. They are reproduced in the website.

16 Commuting Cayley numbers

This is a one page note but complete with abstract and references. It can be downloaded from our website. A *necessary and sufficient conditions are given for α and β, belonging to a division algebra of generalized Cayley numbers, to satisfy the relationship* $\alpha\beta = \beta\alpha$. References and the AMS subject classifications are given. Cayley numbers, also known as octonions, are elements of the 8-dimensional normed division algebra over the field of real numbers. It is the only 8-dimensional real alternative algebra without zero divisors. The Cayley algebra is an algebra with unique division and with an identity; it is alternative, non-associative and non-commutative.

Octonions were discovered by John Thomas Graves (1806–1870) in December 1843, two months after the discovery of quaternions by Hamilton. Graves communicated his discovery to Hamilton in a letter dated 4 January 1844 but it was only published in 1848 after having been rediscovered by Arthur Cayley (1821–1895) in 1845. Since then they have been called Cayley numbers; see Reference [153]. Wynn already discussed them in several of his publications [65,66,69,99].

17 On rational approximations to the exponential function

This is a 8 pages paper that can be downloaded from our website. In the personal document {25}, this paper is mentioned as *to appear* in 1981 or after. It seems that it was never published. It is on the precise locations for the roots with large modulus of the equation $[\nu/\mu]_{e^z} = e^z$. Notice that the approximants $[\nu/\mu]_{e^z}$ were given in closed form by Padé [141].

4.3. Other Documents

4.3.1. Drafts on Analysis

18 Connections between various classes of functions of a complex variable

The first page of this document of 18 pages only contains the title. It seems to be a copy of Wynn's original notes, and unfortunately it is incomplete since it contains only pages 8–14, 21–25, 28–32. Only the first two theorems are exploitable:

Th 1. $f(z)$ maps $Re(z) < 0$ into $|f(z)| < 1$ iff

$$f(z) = e^{i\phi}\left\{1 + \frac{2z}{A + (ic' - 1)z + iz \int_{-\infty}^{\infty} \frac{z-it}{zt+i} d\sigma'(t)}\right\}$$

where $-\infty < \phi < 0, 0 \leq A < \infty, -\infty < c' < \infty$, σ' bounded nondecreasing over $(-\infty, \infty)$.

Th 2. $f(z)$ maps $Re(z) < 0$ into $|f(z)| < 1$ and $f(z) \sim \sum t_\nu z^\nu$ as $z \to 0$ in $\pi/2 + \delta < \arg(z) < 3\pi/2 - \delta$ (for $\delta < (0, \pi/2)$ fixed) iff

$$f(z) = e^{i\phi}\left\{1 + \frac{2z}{A + (ic - 1)z + z^2 \int_{-\infty}^{\infty} \frac{d\sigma(t)}{1-itz}}\right\}$$

where $-\infty < \phi < 0, 0 \leq A < \infty, -\infty < c < \infty$, σ bounded nondecreasing over $(-\infty, \infty)$ such that all moments $\int_{-\infty}^{\infty} t^\nu d\sigma(t)$ exist.

The following pages are not in a sufficiently good shape to be analyzed.

19 Generalization of the β- and γ-algorithm integration processes

Unfortunately these notes (may be a copy of the original) start from the page numbered 8 and, thus, it is difficult to analyze them. Perhaps the other pages have not yet been found in the boxes left by Wynn. As the title explains, they contain an attempt to generalize the β- and γ-algorithm integration processes. This generalization consists

constant (slowly varying), and $-\psi(\mu) = f'(\mu)J(\mu) + f(\mu)J'(\mu)$, and he assumes that the sequence (e_ν) such that $\psi(\mu)/f'(\mu) = \sum e_\nu (f(\mu))^\nu$ is known. Then, he introduces many notations and conditions upon them, but after 20 pages, no clear conclusion follows from this work.

In the same document, there is the original review of 11 pages written by Wynn himself of his paper in Reference [106]. It appeared, shortened, in Zentralblatt MATH, as Zbl 0531.40002. Wynn almost surely put these pages together since they both concern the computation of integrals of the form $\int_\mu^\infty \psi(\mu') \, d\mu'$.

20 **Extraction of totally monotone sequences from convergents of a continued fraction**

This document is a partial copy (pages 31–35) of original notes. There are some pages on an attempt to extract a totally oscillating sequence from the successive convergents of a continued fraction

$$C_i = \frac{a_1}{\vert b_1} + \cdots + \frac{a_i}{\vert b_i}.$$

If $\forall i, a_i = \varrho(\varrho - 1)$ with $\varrho \in (1, \infty)$, then C_i tends to $\varrho - 1$, and the sequence $(C_{2i+1} - C_{2i+3})$ is totally monotone. No other interesting result can be extracted from this partial document.

Then, there are 2 pages of rough notes on *"Auxiliary sequence transformation before application of the ε-algorithm"*, which could be related to what precedes, and 3 pages on *"Transformation of monotonic sequences by means of the ε-algorithm"*, which seem to be independent of the topic.

4.3.2. Drafts on Algebra

21 **Interpolation Theory**

This is an unfinished document of 60 pages, not numbered but in a good shape, entitled *Interpolation theory*. It is probably a part of a monograph (an important project) referenced in several documents (see {26,28}).

Wynn wrote:

> The following notes concern interpolation in a field by the use of polynomials and rational functions, the interpolatory argument values being assumed to be discrete. The notes serve both as a basis for subsequent more general theory concerning interpolation in the presence of confluent arguments and as a framework for the theory of the transformation of Schweins' series.
>
> I. Notations, definitions and classes of matrices and mappings
> II. Formulae from the calculus of finite differences
> III. Matrix formulations of finite difference formulae
> IV. Interpolation by the use of polynomials and rational functions

Only the part I. has been found. It is a list of notations and it is too vague to be of interest. A Schweins' series is related to minor identities for quasi-determinants of noncommutative matrices; see, for example, Reference [154]. Schweins obtained it in 1825 for the quotient of two n-rowed determinants which differ only in one column [155].

22 **Linear equations in a commutative ring**

This untitled document of 38 pages (numbered from the 9th one) begins by a first list of 7 topics he wanted to treat. Then, 8 pages that look like two tables of contents with several topics covered follow. After that, these items are detailed and, hopefully, Wynn also inserted in front of them the number of the pages where each subitem can be found. In the first page, Wynn inserted also a sketch of the following notes {23}. The first section begins by

> 1. Linear equations in a commutative ring.
> It is proposed to study the systems of solutions of equations of the form
>
> $$bx = a \quad \mod I$$

where, W being a prescribed commutative ring, $a, b, x \in W$, and I being a system of numbers in W, the above equation is to be interpreted in the sense that $u \in I$ exists for which $bx - a = u$.

The other main sections are:

2. Systems of numbers
3. Divisibility
4. Numerator systems
5. Solution systems
6. Square free ideals
7. The ideal reduction

A complete analysis of this first section, also if it looks quite complete, seems to be difficult.

23 **Mapping**

This only theoretical handwritten draft of 81 pages (there is a page 18 followed by page 18′) and is about what Wynn named *Aggregates*. A sketch of these notes can be found in {22}. It is quite difficult to understand what it is about since the manuscript is not entirely well written, and seems not to have been finished.

Let $R, S \subseteq W$. A nonvoid aggregate σ in (R, S) is composed of a nonvoid set $I(\sigma) \subseteq R$ and a system of nonvoid sets $M(\sigma, a) \subseteq S$ defined for each $a \in I(\sigma)$. Then, other definitions and properties follow. Parts of the document are on mappings and classes of aggregates. There is no indication of the purpose of this work, and, searching on internet, nothing similar or related was found.

24 **Factor relationships of the form** $c = Ed$

This is a long theoretical text of 115 pages, entitled *Factor relationships of the form $c = Ed$*, where c, E, and d are mapping systems. At the beginning, there is a sketch of the topics that are developed in the sequel.

After introducing a lot of notations, Wynn treated the existence of domains of constancy and intersection mapping systems. Then, there is a section on invariance of spaces with respect to sequence rearrangement, one on the properties of domains of constancy, another one on properties of prequotient spaces with respect to domains of constancy and intersection systems, a section giving complete factorisation results, and one on spaces of ordered pairs of mapping systems.

4.3.3. Personal Documents

25 **Curriculum vitæ of Peter Wynn**

This document is a typewritten curriculum vitæ by Wynn himself (born 1 September 1931; Hoddesdon, Herts (U.K.)). Then, he reports his education, his professional experience from 1952 to 1980 (thus, it does not contain his positions after that). In this curriculum, we can see that he occupied several positions in different countries in the World. Moreover, we were able to confirm his date and place of birth with certainty. This curriculum contains a bibliography with publications from 1956 to 1981. In this bibliography, Wynn mentioned two references that we did not know: a paper *On rational approximations to the exponential function*, 1981, to appear, which was found in the boxes and is reproduced at the end of this paper, and a monograph, *Numal in Fortran. 0*, Comunicaciones Técnicas, Universidad Nacional Autónoma de México, Instituto de Investigaciones en Matemáticas Aplicadas y en Sistemas (IIMAS), México. The number of the reports written by Wynn were 48.0–48.11. Certainly it is a completed project (he mentioned it in {28}, with an O) and, looking into the web, we found that the report 48.0 was published in *Serie azul, monografías–Instituto de Investigaciones en Matemáticas Aplicadas y en Sistemas. UNAM, México, 1981*, Pag. 1–93. On the URL https://biblat.unam.mx/en/buscar/wynn-p/ (accessed on 30 April 2021) the part 48.0 is cited (93 pages). We found the number 48.0 in one of the boxes (see {15}).

26 ***Lists of documents***

In each of the two opened boxes, we found a list of documents (one of them with the title *Duplicate list*. They are probably the lists of documents (xerox copies, handwritten notes and papers, reviews, and so on) that Wynn holds, and that he inserted into the boxes, since we also found a (sometime) partial correspondence mixed with the documents found and analyzed in this paper. There are plenty of what Wynn named *"rough notes"*. Among these rough notes, we find the ones showed in Figure 8, that lead us to think he was looking for a determinantal expression for the even vectors obtained by the vector ε-algorithm.

Since the text could be difficult to read, we reproduce below what Wynn wrote:

> *Rough notes on extensions of determinantal relationships, algorithmic recursions, etc. to noncommutative, possibly nonassociative elements, by use of linear algebraic equations.*
> *Rough notes of derivation of expressions representing ε-algorithm vectors by differentiation of scalar expressions involving inner product.*
> *Rough notes on expression in closed form of vectors produced by vector ε-algorithm & other forms.*

Thus, one can wonder if Wynn was trying to express the vectors computed by his vector ε-algorithm as ratios of some kind of (generalized) determinants. Such a result would be of great interest for the understanding of this algorithm, but, unfortunately, it has not been obtained yet. In any case, these rough notes are difficult to read and understand!

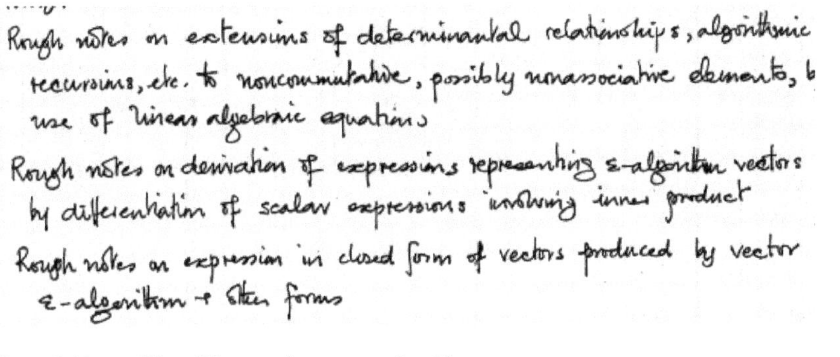
Rough notes on extensions of determinantal relationships, algorithmic recursions, etc. to noncommutative, possibly nonassociative elements, b
use of linear algebraic equations
Rough notes on derivation of expressions representing ε-algorithm vectors
by differentiation of scalar expressions involving inner product
Rough notes on expression in closed form of vectors produced by vector
ε-algorithm & other forms

Figure 8. Notes of Peter Wynn on the vector ε-algorithm.

27 ***List of activities***

This is a list of activities that have to be accomplished: construct notes and Resumé on different topics. The activities are structured in subitems of an itemized list (from (A) to (J)). Are they separated subjects or the skeleton of a book or for other papers? It is difficult to say. The itemized main topics are: Preparatory algebraic theory; Polynomials and rational functions; Interpolation theory; Moment problem and stability functions; Anti-derivative theory; An array of functions; Functions defined by an integral transform; the Euler-Maclaurin and Boole series; Sequence transformations (a subtopic is about auxiliary transformation before application of the ε-algorithm, a problem addressed in Reference [156]). The item *(J) Low priority* seems to contains activities having another scope (documentation for Algol programmes, preparation of talks, and another Resumé).

This document was probably written after 1981 since Reference [109] is mentioned.

28 ***List of projects***

There are 3 pages containing a list of projects. Some of them were probably realized (those preceded by a D) and some of them, with an O, perhaps meaning Ongoing. But we are not sure that some other remained in the state of projects, although some of them are preceded by a D. Among this list, we find: theory of stratified commutative ring, functional interpolation, variants of the remainder terms in the Euler Maclaurin and

Boole series, auxiliary sequence transformation before application of the ε-algorithm (such a pre-processing or preconditioning as already evoked in References [56,72]), extension of determinantal identities and algorithmic recursions to noncommutative and nonassociative forms by use of linear algebraic equations, numerical experiments in nonassociative algebras, numerical experiments in optimisation, vector ε-algorithm, etc., the analytic continuation of functions defined by an integral transform. And, finally, there is a mention of a book on the ε-algorithm.

29 **Bibliography of various authors**

It is a list of references by various authors, probably a list of Xerox copied papers.

30 **Reviews of Wynn for zbMATH**

This document contains two papers published in the journal Ukrainskii Matematicheskii Zhurnal (Ukrainian Mathematical Journal) in Russian. The first one is authored by R. I. Mikhal'chuk & M. S. Syavavko and its title (in English) is *A continual analog of continued fraction* (Vol. 34, No. 5, pp. 559–564, September–October (1982), doi: 10.1007/BF01093130 for English translation). The second one is the paper by Y.R. Batyuk & M.S. Syavavko entitled *Integral continued fractions*, Dokl. Akad. Nauk Ukrain. SSR Ser.A7, 6–8 (1984), also in Russian. This is not strange since Wynn knew Russian (and also German, Duch, Spanish, and some French) and translated two books in this language [110,111]. There are also four handwritten reviews written for zbMATH. The first two are related to the papers (Zbl 0579.40001, Zbl 0571.40003) on continued fractions previously indicated, and the last one (Zbl 0554.65003) to a paper by Naoyuki Tokuda (*A new application of Lagrange-Bürmann expansions. I. General principle*, Z. Angew. Math. Phys. 34, 697–727 (1983)). Wynn, during his stay in Mexico, was a very active mathematical reviewer for zbMATH (145 reviews) by analyzing papers and books published from 1971 to 2011, some of them in Russian. The last one, very detailed, contains a review of a paper on rational function interpolation and the ε-algorithm, but it is not present in zbMATH.

The first three handwritten reviews have been shortened when published in zbMATH.

Author Contributions: All authors contributed equally to this work. All authors have read and agreed to the published version of the manuscript.

Funding: C.B. acknowledges support from the Labex CEMPI (ANR-11-LABX-0007-01). The work of M.R.-Z. was partially supported by the University of Padua, Project No. DOR2007788/20 Numerical Linear Algebra and Extrapolation methods with applications. M.R.-Z. is a member of the INdAM (Istituto Nazionale di Alta Matematica "Francesco Severi") Research group GNCS.

Acknowledgments: We would like to thank Manuel Berriozábal and Maria Antonietta Berriozábal, Manuel's wife, whose friendship with Peter Wynn and safekeeping of his works were invaluable. Special thanks are due to Maria, who was kind enough to share with us her memories of Peter. They made this paper still more alive, and a personal human testimony. We thank Andrea Rosolen who helps us to develop the website as part of his B.S. thesis at Padua University (IT). We are grateful to Juan B. Gutiérrez, Chair of Mathematics at the University of Texas at San Antonio (USA) who agreed to host the web site at his department. Finally, we thank the reviewers for their very careful reading and the constructive comments they made.

Conflicts of Interest: The authors declare no conflict of interest.

References

The first part of the bibliography concerns the works of Wynn, numbered in chronological order from [1–109], and his two translations [110,111], while the second one contains the general bibliography.

References of Peter Wynn

1. Wynn, P. A note on Salzer's method for summing certain convergent series. *J. Math. Phys.* **1956**, *35*, 318–320. MR0086910, Zbl 0075.12802, Submitted 19 July 1955. [CrossRef]
2. Wynn, P. On a procrustean technique for the numerical transformation of slowly convergent sequences and series. *Math. Proc. Camb. Philos. Soc.* **1956**, *52*, 663–671. MR0081979, Zbl 0072.33802, Submitted 31 October 1955. [CrossRef]

3. Wynn, P. On a device for computing the $e_m(S_n)$ transformation. *Math. Tables Aids Comput.* **1956**, *10*, 91–96. MR0084056, Zbl 0074.04601. [CrossRef]
4. Wynn, P. On a cubically convergent process for determining the zeros of certain functions. *Math. Tables Aids Comput.* **1956**, *10*, 97–100. MR0081547, Zbl 0073.10703. [CrossRef]
5. Wynn, P. Central difference and other forms of the Euler transformation. *Quart. J. Mech. Appl. Math.* **1956**, *9*, 249–256. MR0080782, Zbl 0074.29004, Submitted 28 July 1955. [CrossRef]
6. Wynn, P. On the propagation of error in certain non-linear algorithms. *Numer. Math.* **1959**, *1*, 142–149. MR0107988, Zbl 0087.32502, Submitted 26 February 1959. [CrossRef]
7. Wynn, P. A sufficient condition for the instability of the q-d algorithm. *Numer. Math.* **1959**, *1*, 203–207. MR0109426, Zbl 0096.09501, Submitted 25 March 1959. [CrossRef]
8. Wynn, P. Converging factors for continued fractions, I. *Numer. Math.* **1959**, *1*, 272–307. MR0116158, Zbl 0092.05101, Submitted 25 March 1959. [CrossRef]
9. Wynn, P. Converging factors for continued fractions, II. *Numer. Math.* **1959**, *1*, 308–320, MR0116158, Zbl 0092.05101, Submitted 25 March 1959. [CrossRef]
10. Wynn, P. Über einen Interpolations-algorithmus und gewisse andere Formeln, die in der Theorie der Interpolation durch rationale Funktionen bestehen. *Numer. Math.* **1960**, *2*, 151–182. MR0128597, Zbl 0222.65007, Submitted 31 July 1959. [CrossRef]
11. Wynn, P. The rational approximation of functions which are formally defined by a power series expansion. *Math. Comp.* **1960**, *14*, 147–186. MR0116457, Zbl 0173.18803, Submitted 5 November 1959. [CrossRef]
12. Wynn, P. Confluent forms of certain non-linear algorithms. *Arch. Math.* **1960**, *11*, 223–236. MR0128068, Zbl 0096.09502, Submitted 5 October 1959. [CrossRef]
13. Wynn, P. A note on a confluent form of the ε-algorithm. *Arch. Math.* **1960**, *11*, 237–240. MR0128069, Zbl 0096.09601, Submitted 27 March 1959. [CrossRef]
14. Wynn, P. On the tabulation of indefinite integrals. *BIT* **1961**, *1*, 286–290, Zbl 0114.07003. [CrossRef]
15. Wynn, P. L'ε-algoritmo e la tavola di Padé. *Rend. Mat. Roma* **1961**, *20*, 403–408. MR0158206, Zbl 0104.34205.
16. Wynn, P. The epsilon algorithm and operational formulas of numerical analysis. *Math. Comp.* **1961**, *15*, 151–158. MR0158513, Zbl 0102.33205. [CrossRef]
17. Wynn, P. On repeated application of the epsilon algorithm. *Rev. Fr. Trait. Inf. Chiffres* **1961**, *4*, 19–22. MR0149145, Zbl 0102.33301.
18. Wynn, P. A comparison between the numerical performances of the Euler transformation and the ε-algorithm. *Rev. Fr. Trait. Inf. Chiffres* **1961**, *4*, 23–29. Zbl 0102.33302.
19. Wynn, P. The numerical transformation of slowly convergent series by methods of comparison, Part I. *Rev. Fr. Trait. Inf. Chiffres* **1961**, *4*, 177–210. MR0162350, Zbl 0113.04601.
20. Wynn, P. A sufficient condition for the instability of the ε-algorithm. *Nieuw Arch. Wiskd.* **1961**, *9*, 117–119. MR0139252, Zbl 0154.40305.
21. Wynn, P. *Upon the Expression of an Integral as the Limit of a Continued Fraction*; Report DR 24/61; Sticht. Math. Centrum. Rekenafd.: Amsterdam, The Netherlands, 1961. Available online: https://ir.cwi.nl/pub/9537 (accessed on 30 April 2021).
22. Wynn, P. A note on a method of Bradshaw for transforming slowly convergent series and continued fractions. *Am. Math. Mon.* **1962**, *69*, 883–889. [CrossRef]
23. Wynn, P. Upon a second confluent form the ε-algorithm. *Proc. Glasgow Math. Assoc.* **1962**, *5*, 160–165. MR0139253, Zbl 0118.32502, Submitted 21 July 1961. [CrossRef]
24. Wynn, P. Acceleration techniques for iterated vector and matrix problems. *Math. Comp.* **1962**, *16*, 301–322. MR0145647, Zbl 0105.10302. [CrossRef]
25. Wynn, P. A comparison technique for the numerical transformation of slowly convergent series based on the use of rational functions. *Numer. Math.* **1962**, *4*, 8–14. MR0136500, Zbl 0138.09901, Submitted 17 July 1961. [CrossRef]
26. Wynn, P. Numerical efficiency profile functions. *Koninkl. Nederl. Akad. Wet.* **1962**, *65A*, 118–126. MR0139257, Zbl 0105.10002, Submitted 30 September 1961. [CrossRef]
27. Wynn, P. The numerical efficiency of certain continued fraction expansions, IA. *Koninkl. Nederl. Akad. Wet.* **1962**, *65A*, 127–137. MR0139254, Zbl 0105.10003, Submitted 30 September 1961. [CrossRef]
28. Wynn, P. The numerical efficiency of certain continued fraction expansions, IB. *Koninkl. Nederl. Akad. Wet.* **1962**, *65A*, 138–148. MR0139255, Zbl 0105.10003, Submitted 30 September 1961. [CrossRef]
29. Wynn, P. On a connection between two techniques for the numerical transformation of slowly convergent series. *Koninkl. Nederl. Akad. Weten.* **1962**, *65A*, 149–154. MR0139256, Zbl 0138.09902, Submitted 30 September 1961. [CrossRef]
30. Wynn, P. Una nota su un analogo infinitesimale del q-d algoritmo. *Rend. Mat. Roma* **1962**, *21*, 77–85. MR0144127, Zbl 0107.28203, Submitted 11 September 1961.
31. Wynn, P. A note on fitting certain types of experimental data. *Stat. Neerl.* **1962**, *16*, 145–150. MR0150517. [CrossRef]
32. Wynn, P. Note on the solution of a certain boundary-value problem. *BIT* **1962**, *2*, 61–64. MR0155445, Zbl 0105.32103. [CrossRef]
33. Wynn, P. An arsenal of Algol procedures for complex arithmetic. *BIT* **1962**, *2*, 232–255. MR0166945, Zbl 0113.11605. [CrossRef]
34. Wynn, P. The numerical transformation of slowly convergent series by methods of comparison. Part II. *Rev. Fr. Trait. Inf. Chiffres* **1962**, *5*, 65–88. MR0149146, Zbl 0221.65007.

35. Wynn, P. Acceleration technique in numerical analysis with particular reference to problems in one independent variable. In *Information Processing 1962, Proceedings of the IFIP Congress 62, Munich, Germany, 27 August–1 September 1962*; Popplewell, C.M., Ed.; North-Holland: Amsterdam, The Netherlands, 1963; pp. 149–156. Zbl 0146.14201.
36. Wynn, P. Singular rules for certain non-linear algorithms. *BIT* **1963**, *3*, 175–195. MR0166946, Zbl 0123.11101. [CrossRef]
37. Wynn, P. Note on a converging factor for a certain continued fraction. *Numer. Math.* **1963**, *5*, 332–352. MR0166902, Zbl 0117.10802, Submitted 5 February 1963. [CrossRef]
38. Wynn, P. On a connection between the first and the second confluent forms of the ε-algorithm. *Niew. Arch. Wisk.* **1963**, *11*, 19–21. MR0149147, Zbl 0116.33101, Submitted 29 October 1962.
39. Wynn, P. Continued fractions whose coefficients obey a non-commutative law of multiplication. *Arch. Rat. Mech. Anal.* **1963**, *12*, 273–312. MR0145231, Zbl 0122.30604, Submitted 13 August 1962. [CrossRef]
40. Wynn, P. A numerical study of a result of Stieltjes. *Rev. Fr. Trait. Inf. Chiffres* **1963**, *6*, 175–196. MR0157470, Zbl 0116.09202.
41. Wynn, P. Converging factors for the Weber parabolic cylinder function of complex argument, IA. *Proc. Kon. Nederl. Akad. Weten.* **1963**, *66*, 721–736. MR0158514, Zbl 0235.65015, Submitted 29 June 1963. [CrossRef]
42. Wynn, P. Converging factors for the Weber parabolic cylinder function of complex argument, IB. *Proc. Kon. Nederl. Akad. Weten.* **1963**, *66*, 737–754. MR0158515, Zbl 0235.65015, Submitted 29 June 1963. [CrossRef]
43. Wynn, P. Partial differential equations associated with certain non-linear algorithms. *Z. Angew. Math. Phys.* **1964**, *15*, 273–289. MR0166944, Zbl 0252.65096, Submitted 1 September 1963. [CrossRef]
44. Wynn, P. General purpose vector epsilon-algorithm Algol procedures. *Numer. Math.* **1964**, *6*, 22–36. MR0166947, Zbl 0113.32609, Submitted 12 July 1963. [CrossRef]
45. Wynn, P. On some recent developments in the theory and application of continued fractions. *SIAM J. Numer. Anal. Ser. B* **1964**, *1*, 177–197. MR0178269, Zbl 0143.17804, Submitted 4 November 1963. [CrossRef]
46. Wynn, P. Four lectures on the numerical application of continued fractions. In *Alcune Questioni di Analisi Numerica*; Ghizzetti, A., Ed.; Series: C.I.M.E. Summer Schools; Springer: Heidelberg, Germany, 1965; Volume 35, pp. 111–251. Zbl 0202.43904. [CrossRef]
47. Wynn, P. A note on programming repeated application of the epsilon-algorithm. *Rev. Fr. Trait. Inf. Chiffres* **1965**, *8*, 23–62; Errata, 156, MR0181081, Zbl 0132.36903.
48. Wynn, P. Upon systems of recursions which obtain among the quotients of the Padé table. *Numer. Math.* **1966**, *8*, 264–269. MR0215499, Zbl 0163.39502, Submitted 5 May 1965. [CrossRef]
49. Wynn, P. On the convergence and stability of the epsilon algorithm. *SIAM J. Numer. Anal.* **1966**, *3*, 91–122. MR0207180, Zbl 0299.65003, Submitted 16 September 1965. [CrossRef]
50. Wynn, P. *Upon a Conjecture Concerning a Method for Solving Linear Equations, and Certain Other Matters*; MRC Technical Summary Report 626; University of Wisconsin: Madison, WI, USA, 1966.
51. Wynn, P. *Complex Numbers and Other Extensions to the Clifford Algebra with an Application to the Theory of Continued Fractions*; MRC Technical Summary Report 646; University of Wisconsin: Madison, WI, USA, 1966.
52. Wynn, P. *Upon the Diagonal Sequences of the Padé Table*; MRC Technical Summary Report 660; University of Wisconsin: Madison, WI, USA, 1966.
53. Wynn, P. *Upon an Invariant Associated with the Epsilon Algorithm*; MRC Technical Summary Report 675; University of Wisconsin: Madison, WI, USA, 1966.
54. Wynn, P. On the computation of certain functions of large argument and parameter. *BIT* **1966**, *6*, 228–259. MR0203912, Zbl 0196.48301. [CrossRef]
55. Wynn, P. An arsenal of Algol procedures for the evaluation of continued fractions and for effecting the epsilon algorithm. *Rev. Fr. Trait. Inf. Chiffres* **1966**, *9*, 327–362. MR0203963.
56. Wynn, P. *Accelerating the Convergence of a Monotonic Sequence by a Method of Intercalation*; MRC Technical Summary Report 674; University of Wisconsin: Madison, WI, USA, 1967.
57. Wynn, P. A general system of orthogonal polynomials. *Quart. J. Math. Oxf.* **1967**, *18*, 81–96. MR0210963, Zbl 0185.30001, Submitted 8 September 1966. [CrossRef]
58. Wynn, P. Transformations to accelerate the convergence of Fourier series. In *Gertrude Blanch Anniversary Volume*; Wright Patterson Air Force Base, 1967; pp. 339–379; MRC Technical Summary Report 673; Mond, B., Blanch, G., Eds.; University of Wisconsin: Madison, WI, USA, 1966; MR0215553, Zbl 0242.65004.
MRC Technical Summary Report 673; University of Wisconsin: Madison, WI, USA, 1966; MR0215553, Zbl 0242.65004.
59. Wynn, P. *A Note on the Convergence of Certain Noncommutative Continued Fractions*; MRC Technical Summary Report 750; University of Wisconsin: Madison, WI, USA, 1967.
60. Wynn, P. Upon the Padé table derived from a Stieltjes series. *SIAM J. Numer. Anal.* **1968**, *5*, 805–834. MR0239734, Zbl 0175.36102, Submitted 22 March 1968, Revised 5 July 1968. [CrossRef]
61. Wynn, P. Vector continued fractions. *Linear Algebra Appl.* **1968**, *1*, 357–395. MR0231848, Zbl 0164.18503, Submitted 5 March 1968. [CrossRef]
62. Wynn, P. Upon the definition of an integral as the limit of a continued fraction. *Arch. Rat. Mech. Anal.* **1968**, *28*, 83–148. MR0221152, Zbl 0162.37202, Submitted 24 May 1967. [CrossRef]

63. Wynn, P. Zur Theorie der mit gewissen speziellen Funktionen verknüpften Padéschen Tafeln. *Math. Z.* **1969**, *109*, 66–70. MR0243242, Zbl 0175.36103, Submitted 17 April 1968. [CrossRef]
64. Wynn, P. *Five Lectures on the Numerical Application of Continued Fractions*; Orientation Lecture Series 5; Mathematical Research Center, University of Wisconsin: Madison, WI, USA, 1970; 183p.
65. Wynn, P. *Upon a Recursive System of Flexible Rings Permitting Involution*; Report CRM-50; Centre de Recherches Mathématiques, Université de Montréal: Montréal, QC, Canada, 1970.
66. Wynn, P. *Upon the Inverse of Formal Power Series over Certain Algebra*; Report CRM-53; Centre de Recherches Mathématiques, Université de Montréal: Montréal, QC, Canada, 1970.
67. Wynn, P. *Upon a Hierarchy of Epsilon Arrays*; Technical Report 46; Louisiana State University: New Orleans, LA, USA, 1970.
68. Wynn, P. A note on the generalised Euler transformation. *Comput. J.* **1971**, *14*, 437–441.; Erratum in **1972**, *15*, 175; MR0321266, Zbl 0227.65002. [CrossRef]
69. Wynn, P. *The Abstract Theory of the Epsilon Algorithm*; Report CRM-74; Centre de Recherches Mathématiques, Université de Montréal: Montréal, QC, Canada, 1971.
70. Wynn, P. *Upon a Class of Functions Connected with the Approximate Solution of Operator Equations*; Report CRM-103; Centre de Recherches Mathématiques, Université de Montréal: Montréal, QC, Canada, 1971.
71. Wynn, P. *A note Upon Totally Monotone Sequences*; Report CRM-139; Centre de Recherches Mathématiques, Université de Montréal: Montréal, QC, Canada, 1971.
72. Wynn, P. A transformation of series. *Calcolo* **1971**, *8*, 255–272. MR0303675, Zbl 0236.65006, Submitted 1 September 1971. [CrossRef]
73. Wynn, P. Difference-differential recursions for Padé quotients. *Proc. Lond. Math. Soc.* **1971**, *3*, 283–300. MR0313682, Zbl 0221.40005, Submitted 4 May 1970. [CrossRef]
74. Wynn, P. Upon the generalized inverse of a formal power series with vector valued coefficients. *Compos. Math.* **1971**, *23*, 453–460. MR306224, Zbl 0239.15003, Submitted 13 January 1971. Available online: www.numdam.org/item/CM_1971__23_4_453_0 (accessed on 30 April 2021).
75. Wynn, P. Über orthonormale Polynome und ein assoziiertes Momentproblem. *Math. Scand.* **1971**, *29*, 104–112. MR0308406, Zbl 0231.30037, Submitted 27 April 1971. [CrossRef]
76. Wynn, P. On an extension of a result due to Pólya. *J. Reine Angew. Math.* **1971**, *248*, 127–132. MR0289771, Zbl 0219.30002, Submitted 22 November 1969. [CrossRef]
77. Wynn, P. Convergence acceleration by a method of intercalation. *Computing* **1972**, *9*, 267–273. MR0315861, Zbl 0248.65003, Submitted 6 August 1971. [CrossRef]
78. Wynn, P. Invariants associated with the epsilon algorithm and its first confluent form. *Rend. Circ. Mat. Palermo* **1972**, *21*, 31–41. MR0346367, Zbl 0268.65076, Submitted January 1972. [CrossRef]
79. Wynn, P. Hierarchies of arrays and function sequences associated with the epsilon algorithm and its first confluent form. *Rend. Mat. Roma Ser. VI* **1972**, *5*, 819–852. MR0355405, Zbl 0278.65002, Submitted 15 May 1972.
80. Wynn, P. *A Note on a Partial Differential Equation*; Report CRM-22; Centre de Recherches Mathématiques, Université de Montréal: Montréal, QC, Canada, 1972.
81. Wynn, P. Sur les suites totalement monotones. *CR Acad. Sci. Paris* **1972**, *275A*, 1065–1068. MR0310480, Zbl 0251.40001, Accepted 6 November 1972.
82. Wynn, P. Transformation de séries à l'aide de l'ε-algorithm. *CR Acad. Sci. Paris* **1972**, *275A*, 1351–1353. MR0311068, Zbl 0257.65005, Accepted 18 December 1972.
83. Wynn, P. Upon a convergence result in the theory of the Padé table. *Trans. Am. Math. Soc.* **1972**, *165*, 239–249. MR0293106, Zbl 0236.30013, Received 26 October 1970, Revised 21 May 1971. [CrossRef]
84. Wynn, P. *A Convergence Theory of Some Methods of Integration*; Report CRM-193; Centre de Recherches Mathématiques, Université de Montréal: Montréal, QC, Canada, 1972.
85. Wynn, P. *The Partial Differential Equation of the Padé surface*; Report CRM-197; Centre de Recherches Mathématiques, Université de Montréal: Montréal, QC, Canada, 1972.
86. Wynn, P. *The Algebra of Certain Formal Power Series*; Report CRM-216; Centre de Recherches Mathématiques, Université de Montréal: Montréal, QC, Canada, 1972.
87. Wynn, P. *On Some Extensions of Euclid's Algorithm, and Some Consequences Thereof*; Report CRM; Centre de Recherches Mathématiques, Université de Montréal: Montréal, QC, Canada, 1972.
88. Wynn, P. Upon some continuous prediction algorithms. I. *Calcolo* **1973**, *9*, 197–234. MR0362820, Zbl 0248.65007, Submitted 20 June 1972. [CrossRef]
89. Wynn, P. Upon some continuous prediction algorithms. II. *Calcolo* **1973**, *9*, 235–278. MR0362821, Zbl 0281.65001, Submitted 20 June 1972. [CrossRef]
90. Wynn, P. On the zeros of certain confluent hypergeometric functions. *Proc. Am. Math. Soc.* **1973**, *40*, 173–183. MR0318529, Zbl 0268.33004, Submitted 7 July 1972, Revised 26 October 1972. [CrossRef]
91. Wynn, P. Accélération de la convergence de séries d'opérateurs en analyse numérique. *CR Acad. Sci. Paris* **1973**, *276A*, 803–806. MR0317519, Zbl 0268.65001, Accepted 12 March 1973.
92. Wynn, P. On the intersection of two classes of functions. *Rev. Roum. Math. Pures Appl.* **1974**, *19*, 949–959. MR0390195, Zbl 0302.30011.

93. Wynn, P. Extremal properties of Padé quotients. *Acta Math. Hung.* **1974**, *25*, 291–298. MR0352431, Zbl 0323.30043, Submitted 14 July 1972. [CrossRef]
94. Wynn, P. Sur l'équation aux dérivées partielles de la surface de Padé. *CR Acad. Sci. Paris* **1974**, *278A*, 847–850. MR0341910, Zbl 0276.35015.
95. Wynn, P. *A Numerical Method for Estimating Parameters in Mathematical Models*; Report CRM-443; Centre de Recherches Mathématiques, Université de Montréal: Montréal, QC, Canada, 1974.
96. Wynn, P. Some recent developments in the theories of continued fractions and the Padé table. *Rocky Mt. J. Math.* **1974**, *4*, 297–324. MR0340880, Zbl 0302.65005, Submitted 8 February 1973. [CrossRef]
97. Wynn, P. How to integrate without integrating. In Proceedings of the Euromech 58 Conference on Padé Method and Its Applicatons in Mechanics, Toulon, France, 12–14 May 1975; Unpublished.
98. Wynn, P. Upon a class of functions connected with the approximate solution of operator equations. *Ann. Mat. Pura Appl.* **1975**, *104*, 1–29. MR0387553, Zbl 0315.65015, Submitted 10 October 1972. [CrossRef]
99. Wynn, P. Distributive rings permitting involution. *Math. Balk.* **1975**, *5*, 299–318; Report CRM-281; Centre de Recherches Mathématiques, Université de Montréal: Montréal, QC, Canada, 1973; MR0506478, Zbl 0381.17001.
100. Wynn, P. The algebra of certain formal power series. *Riv. Mat. Univ. Parma* **1976**, *2*, 155–176. MR0447220, Zbl 0369.16002, Submitted 28 August 1974. Available online: www.rivmat.unipr.it/fulltext/1976-2/1976-2-155.pdf (accessed on 30 April 2021).
101. Wynn, P. *An Array of Functions*; Report; School of Computer Science, McGill University: Montreal, QC, Canada, 1976.
102. Wynn, P. *A Continued Fraction Transformation of the Euler-MacLaurin Series*; Report; School of Computer Science, McGill University: Montreal, QC, Canada, 1976.
103. Wynn, P. A convergence theory of some methods of integration. *J. Reine Angew. Math.* **1976**, *285*, 181–208. MR0415119, Zbl 0326.40005, Submitted 22 March 1974. [CrossRef]
104. Wynn, P. The calculus of finite differences over certain systems of numbers. *Calcolo* **1977**, *14*, 303–341. MR0503568, Zbl 0379.65005, Submitted 30 August 1976. [CrossRef]
105. Wynn, P. The transformation of series by the use of Padé quotients and more general approximants. In *Padé and Rational Approximation. Theory and Applications*; Saff, E.B., Varga, R.S., Eds.; Academic Press: New York, NY, USA, 1977; pp. 121–144. MR0473660, Zbl 0368.41014. [CrossRef]
106. Wynn, P. The evaluation of singular and highly oscillatory integrals by use of the anti-derivative. *Calcolo* **1978**, *15*, 1–123; Report; School of Computer Science, McGill University: Montreal, QC, Canada, 1976; Zbl 0531.40002, Submitted 17 July 1977.
107. Wynn, P. The work of E.B. Christoffel on the theory of continued fractions. In *E.B. Christoffel: The Influence of His Work on Mathematics and the Physical Sciences*; Butzer, P.L., Fehér, F., Eds.; Birkhäuser Verlag: Basel, Switzerland, 1981; pp. 190–202. MR0661065, Zbl 0476.30004, Submitted 9 October 1979. [CrossRef]
108. Wynn, P. Remark upon developments in the theories of the moment problem and of quadrature, subsequent to the work of Christoffel. In *E.B. Christoffel: The Influence of His Work on Mathematics and the Physical Sciences*; Butzer, P.L., Fehér, F., Eds.; Birkhäuser Verlag: Basel, Switzerland, 1981; pp. 731–734. MR0661114, Zbl 0484.41040, Submitted 28 April 1980. [CrossRef]
109. Wynn, P. The convergence of approximating fractions. *Bol. Soc. Mat. Mex.* **1981**, *26*, 57–71. MR0742016, Zbl 0479.40004.

Translations by Peter Wynn

110. Khintchine, A.Y. *Continued Fractions*; Translated from Russian by Peter Wynn; P. Noordhoff N.V.: Groningen, The Netherlands, 1963.
111. Khovanskii, A.N. *The Application of Continued Fractions and their Generalizations to Problems in Approximation Theory*; Translated from Russian by Peter Wynn; P. Noordhoff N.V.: Groningen, The Netherlands, 1963.

General Bibliography

112. Shanks, D. Non-linear transformations of divergent and slowly convergent sequences. *J. Math. Phys.* **1955**, *34*, 1–42. [CrossRef]
113. Brezinski, C.; Redivo-Zaglia, M. *Extrapolation and Rational Approximation. The Works of the Main Contributors*; Springer Nature: Cham, Switzerland, 2020.
114. Brezinski, C.; Redivo-Zaglia, M. The genesis and early developments of Aitken's process, Shanks' transformation, the ε-algorithm, and related fixed point methods. *Numer. Algorithms* **2019**, *80*, 11–133. [CrossRef]
115. Brezinski, C.; Redivo-Zaglia, M. *Extrapolation Methods. Theory and Practice*; North-Holland: Amsterdam, The Netherlands, 1991.
116. Lorentzen, L.; Waadeland, H. *Continued Fractions with Applications*; North-Holland: Amsterdam, The Netherlands, 1992.
117. Sidi, A. *Practical Extrapolation Methods. Theory and Applications*; Cambridge University Press: Cambridge, UK, 2003.
118. Weniger, E.J. Nonlinear sequence transformations for the acceleration of convergence and the summation of divergent series. *Comput. Phys. Rep.* **1989**, *10*, 189–371. [CrossRef]
119. Wimp, J. *Sequence Transformations and Their Applications*; Academic Press: New York, NY, USA, 1981.
120. Lagrange, J.L. Nouvelle méthode pour résoudre les équations littérales par le moyen des séries. *Mém. Acad. R. Sci. Berl.* **1770**, *24*, 251–326.
121. Henrici, P. *Applied and Computational Complex Analysis*; Wiley: New York, NY, USA, 1974; Volume 1.
122. Bacher, R.; Lass, B. Développements limités et réversion des séries. *Enseign. Math.* **2006**, *52*, 267–293.
123. Moler, C.; van Loan, C. Nineteen dubious ways to compute the exponential of a matrix. *SIAM Rev.* **1978**, *20*, 801–836. [CrossRef]
124. Moler, C.; van Loan, C. Nineteen dubious ways to compute the exponential of a matrix, twenty-five years later. *SIAM Rev.* **2003**,

125. Brezinski, C. Génération de suites totalement monotones et oscillantes. *CR Acad. Sci. Paris* **1975**, *280A*, 729–731.
126. Schoenberg, I.J. On smoothing operations and their generating functions. *Bull. Am. Math. Soc.* **1953**, *59*, 199–230. [CrossRef]
127. Donoghue, W.F. *Monotone Matrix Functions and Analytic Continuation*; Springer: New York, NY, USA; Berlin/Heidelberg, Germany, 1974.
128. Brezinski, C. Généralisation des extrapolations polynomiales et rationnelles. *RAIRO* **1972**, *R1*, 61–66.
129. Cordellier, F. Utilisation de l'invariance homographique dans les algorithmes de losange. In *Padé Approximation and Its Applications Bad Honnef 1983*; Werner, H., Bünger, H.J., Eds.; Lecture Notes in Mathematiques; Springer: Berlin, Germany, 1984; Volume 1071, pp. 62–94.
130. Nörlund, N.E. *Vorlesung über Differenzenrechnung*; Springer: Berlin/Heidelberg, Germany, 1937.
131. Stoer, J. Über zwei Algorithmen zur Interpolation mit rationalen Funktionen. *Numer. Math.* **1961**, *3*, 285–304. [CrossRef]
132. Claessens, G. A useful identity for the rational Hermite interpolation table. *Numer. Math.* **1978**, *29*, 227–231. [CrossRef]
133. Brezinski, C. Sur un algorithme de résolution des systèmes non linéaires. *CR Acad. Sci. Paris* **1971**, *272 A*, 145–148.
134. Gekeler, E. Über den ε-Algorithmus von Wynn. *ZAMM* **1971**, *51*, 53–54.
135. Håvie, T. Generalized Neville type extrapolation schemes. *BIT* **1979**, *19*, 204–213. [CrossRef]
136. Lyche, T. A Newton form for trigonometric Hermite interpolation. *Nord. Tids. Inf. Beh. (BIT)* **1979**, *19*, 229–235. [CrossRef]
137. Mühlbach, G. The general Neville-Aitken algorithm and some application. *Numer. Math.* **1978**, *31*, 97–110. [CrossRef]
138. Mühlbach, G. The general recurrence relation for divided differences and the general Newton interpolation algorithm with application to trigonometric interpolation. *Numer. Math.* **1979**, *32*, 393–408. [CrossRef]
139. Jacobi, C.G.J. Über die Darstellung einer Reihe gegebener Werthe durch einer gebrochnen rationale Funktion. *J. Reine Angew. Math.* **1845**, *30*, 127–156.
140. Frobenius, G. Ueber Relationen zwischen den Näherungsbruchen von Potenzreihen. *J. Reine Angew. Math.* **1881**, *90*, 1–17.
141. Padé, H. Sur la représentation approchée d'une fonction par des fractions rationnelles. *Ann. Sci. L'École Norm. Supérieure* **1892**, *9*, 3–93. [CrossRef]
142. Schmidt, R.J. On the numerical solution of linear simultaneous equations by an iterative method. *Lond. Edinb. Dublin Philos. Mag. J. Sci.* **1941**, *7*, 369–383. [CrossRef]
143. Kronecker, L. Zur Theorie der Elimination einer Variablen aus zwei Algebraischen Gleichungen. *Monat. Kön. Preuss. Akad. Wiss. Berl.* **1881**, 535–600.
144. Rosenhain, G. Neue Darstellung der Resultante der Elimination von z aus zwei algebraischen Gleichungen $f(z) = 0$ und $\phi(z) = 0$ vermittelst der Werthe welche fie Funktionen $f(z)$ und $\phi(z)$ für gegebne Werthe von z annehmen. *J. Reine Angew. Math.* **1846**, *30*, 157–165.
145. Borchardt, C.W. Ueber eine Interpolation entsprechende Darstellung der Eliminations-Resultante. *J. Reine Angew. Math.* **1860**, *57*, 111–121.
146. Brezinski, C. Review of methods to accelerate the convergence of sequences. *Rend. Mat. Roma.* **1974**, *7*, 303–316.
147. Cordellier, F. Interpolation Rationnelle et autres Questions: Aspects Algorithmiques et Numériques. Thèse de Doctorat d'État ès Sciences Mathématiques, Université des Sciences et Techniques de Lille, Lille, France, 1989.
148. McLeod, J.B. A note on the ε-algorithm. *Computing* **1971**, *7*, 17–24. [CrossRef]
149. Delahaye, J.P.; Germain-Bonne, B. Résultats négatifs en accélération de la convergence. *Numer. Math.* **1980**, *35*, 443–457. [CrossRef]
150. Delahaye, J.P. *Sequence Transformations*; Springer: Berlin, Germany, 1988.
151. Cournot, A.A. *Recherches sur les Principes Mathématiques de la Théorie des Richesses*; L. Hachette: Paris, France, 1838. Available online: https://gallica.bnf.fr/ark:/12148/bpt6k6117257c.texteImage (accessed on 30 April 2021).
152. Berlinet, A.F. Geometric approach to the parallel sum of vectors and application to the vector ε-algorithm. *Numer. Algorithms* **2014**, *65*, 783–807. [CrossRef]
153. Koecher, M.; Remmert, R. Cayley numbers or alternative division algebras. In *Numbers*; Ewing, J.H., Ed.; Springer: New York, NY, USA, 1991.
154. Krob, D.; Leclerc, D. Minor identities for quasi-determinants and quantum determinants. *Commun. Math. Phys.* **1995**, *169*, 1–23. [CrossRef]
155. Schweins, F. *Theorie der Differenzen und Differentiale, der Gedoppelten Verbindungen, der Producte mit Versetzungen, der Reihen, der Wiederholenden Functionen, der Allgemeinsten Facultäten und der Fortlaufenden Brüche*; Verlag der Universitäts—Buchhandlung von C.F. Winter: Heidelberg, Germany 1825. Available online: https://babel.hathitrust.org/cgi/pt?id=mdp.39015068512063 (accessed on 30 April 2021).
156. Brezinski, C.; Delahaye, J.P.; Germain-Bonne, B. Convergence acceleration by extraction of linear subsequences. *SIAM J. Numer. Anal.* **1983**, *20*, 1099–1105. [CrossRef]

Article

New Approaches to the General Linearization Problem of Jacobi Polynomials Based on Moments and Connection Formulas

Waleed Mohamed Abd-Elhameed [1,2,*] and Badah Mohamed Badah [2]

1. Department of Mathematics, Faculty of Science, Cairo University, Giza 12613, Egypt
2. Department of Mathematics, College of Science, University of Jeddah, Jeddah 23218, Saudi Arabia; BALDOSARI0001.stu@uj.edu.sa
* Correspondence: waleed@sci.cu.edu.eg

Abstract: This article deals with the general linearization problem of Jacobi polynomials. We provide two approaches for finding closed analytical forms of the linearization coefficients of these polynomials. The first approach is built on establishing a new formula in which the moments of the shifted Jacobi polynomials are expressed in terms of other shifted Jacobi polynomials. The derived moments formula involves a hypergeometric function of the type $_4F_3(1)$, which cannot be summed in general, but for special choices of the involved parameters, it can be summed. The reduced moments formulas lead to establishing new linearization formulas of certain parameters of Jacobi polynomials. Another approach for obtaining other linearization formulas of some Jacobi polynomials depends on making use of the connection formulas between two different Jacobi polynomials. In the two suggested approaches, we utilize some standard reduction formulas for certain hypergeometric functions of the unit argument such as Watson's and Chu-Vandermonde identities. Furthermore, some symbolic algebraic computations such as the algorithms of Zeilberger, Petkovsek and van Hoeij may be utilized for the same purpose. As an application of some of the derived linearization formulas, we propose a numerical algorithm to solve the non-linear Riccati differential equation based on the application of the spectral tau method.

Keywords: Jacobi polynomials; generalized hypergeometric functions; Chebyshev polynomials; linearization coefficients; connection formulas; moments formulas; symbolic computation; Riccati differential equation; tau method

1. Introduction

Special functions are crucial in several disciplines such as mathematical physics and numerical analysis. A large number of researchers are interested in investigating different special functions from numerical and practical points of view; see, for example, [1–3].

Jacobi polynomials are of basic importance in mathematical analysis from both theoretical and practical points of view. There are six important particular classes of Jacobi polynomials. In fact, ultraspherical, Legendre, and Chebyshev polynomials of the first- and second- kinds are symmetric Jacobi polynomials, while the two classes of Chebyshev polynomials of third- and fourth- kinds are non-symmetric Jacobi polynomials (see, for example, [4–6]). The linearization and connection problems of different orthogonal polynomials are of fundamental importance. They play a role in the computation of physical and chemical properties of quantum-mechanical systems [7]. The standard linearization formula is applied in the calculation of the position and momentum information entropies of quantum systems (see Dehesa et al. [8]). Furthermore, they are useful in treating some kinds of differential equations. For example, Abd-Elhameed [9] has employed some linearization formulas to solve a non-linear Riccati differential equation. Recently, Abd-Elhameed in [10]

Citation: Abd-Elhameed, W.M.; Badah, B.M. New Approaches to the General Linearization Problem of Jacobi Polynomials Based on Moments and Connection Formulas. *Mathematics* 2021, 9, 1573. https://doi.org/10.3390/math9131573

Academic Editors: Francesco Aldo Costabile, Maria I. Gualtieri and Anna Napoli

Received: 10 June 2021
Accepted: 30 June 2021
Published: 4 July 2021

Publisher's Note: MDPI stays neutral with regard to jurisdictional claims in published maps and institutional affiliations.

Copyright: © 2021 by the authors. Licensee MDPI, Basel, Switzerland. This article is an open access article distributed under the terms and conditions of the Creative Commons Attribution (CC BY) license (https://creativecommons.org/licenses/by/

along with some other formulas to develop a spectral solution to the one-dimensional non-linear Burgers' equation. Due to the importance of the linearization formulas, intensive studies regarding these problems have been performed. Linearization and connection problems for a variety of classical continuous and discrete orthogonal polynomials have been established by many methods (see, for instance, [11–20]).

If we assume three families of polynomials $\{\phi_i(x)\}_{i\geq 0}$ $\{\psi_j(x)\}_{j\geq 0}$ and $\{\theta_k(x)\}_{k\geq 0}$, then to solve the general linearization problem

$$\phi_i(x)\,\psi_j(x) = \sum_{k=0}^{i+j} A_{k,i,j}\,\theta_k(x),$$

we have to find the linearization coefficients $A_{k,i,j}$.

It is worth mentioning here that among the important problems that are related to the linearization problems are the problems concerned with summing the finite products of several special functions. In this direction, the authors of [21], developed some results for the sums of finite products of the second, third, and fourth kinds Chebyshev polynomials. In [22], the authors studied the connection problem for sums of finite products of Chebyshev polynomials of the third and fourth kinds. Expressions for sums of finite products of Legendre and Laguerre polynomials can be found in [23]. In [24], the authors established representations by several orthogonal polynomials for sums of finite products of Chebyshev polynomials of the first kind and Lucas polynomials. Fourier series expansions for functions related to sums of finite products of Chebyshev polynomials of the first kind, and those of Lucas polynomials are derived in [25]. In [26], the authors represented by orthogonal polynomials the sums of finite products of Fubini polynomials. Some new formulas that express the sums of finite products of balancing polynomials can be found in [27]. In the series of papers [28–31], the authors developed specific linearization formulas of Jacobi polynomials of certain parameters. The linearization coefficients were often expressed in terms of certain terminating hypergeometric functions of unit argument that can be reduced for some particular cases. In [28], the authors derived new linearization formulas of Chebyshev polynomials of the third and fourth kinds. The authors in [32,33] established some formulas of the squares of certain Jacobi polynomials. In addition, in [30], the author derived a product formula of two certain Jacobi polynomials in terms of the squares of ultraspherical polynomials. The coefficients are expressed in terms of a certain terminating $_6F_5(1)$. This product formula led to some simplified linearization formulas for certain choices of the involved parameters. In [34], the authors established some specific and general linearization formulas of some classes of Jacobi polynomials based on the reduction of certain hypergeometric functions of unit arguments. For some other articles concerned with linearization problem, one can refer to [35–39]. The principal aim of the current paper is to derive new expressions for the linearization coefficients $B_{p,i,j}$ in the problem

$$R_i^{(\alpha,\beta)}(x)\,R_j^{(\lambda,\mu)}(x) = \sum_{p=0}^{i+j} B_{p,i,j}\,R_{i+j-p}^{(\gamma,\delta)}(x), \qquad (1)$$

where $R_i^{(\alpha,\beta)}(x)$ is the normalized Jacobi polynomial defined in [15] for certain choices of the involved parameters.

We point out here that the main difference between our study in the current paper and the study in the recent paper [34] is that the authors in [34] investigated the linearization formula

$$R_i^{(\alpha,\beta)}(x)\,R_j^{(\lambda,\mu)}(x) = \sum_{p=0}^{i+j} B_{p,i,j}\,R_{i+j-p}^{(\alpha+\lambda,\beta+\mu)}(x). \qquad (2)$$

It is clear that the linearization formula in (2) is a special case of the linearization Formula (1).

The linearization coefficients of problem (2) were found in terms of a product of two terminating hypergeometric functions of the type $_3F_2(1)$ (see [17]). In [34], the authors found closed forms for one or two of the appearing $_3F_2(1)$ for some specific choices of the involved parameters, and therefore, some new reduced linearization formulas were developed. In the current paper, we follow two different approaches to develop some linearization formulas in the form of (1). In fact, we follow the following two approaches:

- An approach based on deriving a new formula of the moments of the shifted normalized Jacobi polynomials in terms of their original shifted Jacobi polynomials but with different parameters;
- An approach based on making use of the connection formulas between two different normalized Jacobi polynomials.

We comment here that the main advantages of our two presented methods to establish the linearization formulas in this paper compared with some of the previously published papers can be listed as follows:

- In the articles [28,31,34], the linearization formulas were established by reducing some exiting ones in the literature with the aid of some celebrated reduction formulas or via some symbolic algorithms; however, in the current article, we establish two new approaches for deriving some linearization formulas, and after that reduce these linearization formulas by symbolic computation.
- The articles [9,29,30] deal with some special linearization formulas. In fact, the approaches followed were based on expressing products of hypergeometric functions in terms of a single generalized hypergeometric function using some suitable transformation formulas; however, the current article deals with some general linearization formulas.
- We do believe that the approach based on the moments formulas can be followed to establish linearization formulas of different orthogonal polynomials and not restricted to Jacobi polynomials.

The rest of the paper is as follows. Section 2 presents some properties of Jacobi polynomials and their shifted ones. Section 3 is interested in establishing a new unified formula for the moments of the four kinds of Chebyshev polynomials. Furthermore, in this section, a general moments formula of the shifted normalized Jacobi polynomials of general parameters is given explicitly in terms of a certain terminating $_4F_3(1)$. Section 4 is devoted to presenting new linearization formulas based on employing the moments formulas derived in Section 3. Another approach based on making use of the connection formulas between two different Jacobi polynomials is followed in Section 5. To show the importance and applicability of the presented formulas, we propose a numerical algorithm in Section 6 to solve the non-linear Riccati differential equation based on the application of the spectral tau method. Finally, the conclusion is given in Section 7.

2. Some Elementary Properties of the Classical Jacobi Polynomials and Their Shifted Ones

In this section, we display some properties of the classical Jacobi polynomials and their shifted ones, which are useful in the following. The sequence of orthogonal polynomials $P_j^{(\gamma,\delta)}(x)$, $x \in [-1,1]$, $j \geq 0$, and $\gamma > -1$, $\delta > -1$, (see Olver et al. [40], Andrews et al. [41] and Rainville [42]), may be constructed by means of the following Rodrigues' formula:

$$P_j^{(\gamma,\delta)}(x) = \frac{(-1)^j}{2^j j!}(1-x)^{-\gamma}(1+x)^{-\delta} D^j \left[(1-x)^{\gamma+j}(1+x)^{\delta+j}\right],$$

where $D \equiv \frac{d}{dx}$.

They also may be represented by means of the following hypergeometric form:

It is useful to use the normalized Jacobi polynomials, which were introduced in [15] and used in [43]. They are given by the following formula:

$$R_j^{(\gamma,\delta)}(x) = {}_2F_1\left(\begin{array}{c}-j, j+\gamma+\delta+1 \\ \gamma+1\end{array}\bigg|\frac{1-x}{2}\right). \quad (3)$$

The definition in (3) has the advantage that

$$R_j^{(\gamma,\delta)}(1) = 1, \quad j = 0, 1, 2, \ldots.$$

All relations and formulas of $P_j^{(\gamma,\delta)}(x)$ can be easily transformed to give their counterparts for $R_j^{(\gamma,\delta)}(x)$. The polynomials $R_j^{(\gamma,\delta)}(x)$ satisfy the following orthogonality relation:

$$\int_{-1}^{1}(1-x)^{\gamma}(1+x)^{\delta}R_j^{(\gamma,\delta)}(x)R_k^{(\gamma,\delta)}(x)\,dx = \begin{cases}0, & k\neq j, \\ h_j^{\gamma,\delta}, & k = j,\end{cases} \quad (4)$$

where

$$h_j^{\gamma,\delta} = \frac{2^{\gamma+\delta+1}\,j!\,\Gamma(j+\delta+1)\,(\Gamma(\gamma+1))^2}{(2j+\gamma+\delta+1)\,\Gamma(j+\gamma+\delta+1)\,\Gamma(j+\gamma+1)}. \quad (5)$$

It is worth mentioning that the six special families of polynomials of the normalized Jacobi polynomials $R_j^{(\gamma,\delta)}(x)$ are given by the following relations:

$$T_j(x) = R_j^{(-\frac{1}{2},-\frac{1}{2})}(x), \qquad U_j(x) = (j+1)R_j^{(\frac{1}{2},\frac{1}{2})}(x),$$

$$V_j(x) = R_j^{(-\frac{1}{2},\frac{1}{2})}(x), \qquad W_j(x) = (2j+1)R_j^{(\frac{1}{2},-\frac{1}{2})}(x),$$

$$C_j^{(\alpha)}(x) = R_j^{(\alpha-\frac{1}{2},\alpha-\frac{1}{2})}(x), \qquad L_j(x) = R_j^{(0,0)}(x),$$

where $T_j(x)$, $U_j(x)$, $V_j(x)$, $W_j(x)$ represent, respectively, the first, second, third, and fourth kinds Chebyshev polynomials, while $C_j^{(\alpha)}(x)$ and $L_j(x)$ denote, respectively, the ultraspherical and Legendre polynomials.

Regarding the four kinds of Chebyshev polynomials, they have the following trigonometric representations (see, [44]):

$$T_j(x) = \cos(j\theta), \qquad U_j(x) = \frac{\sin((j+1)\theta)}{\sin\theta},$$

$$V_j(x) = \frac{\cos\left(\left(j+\frac{1}{2}\right)\theta\right)}{\cos\left(\frac{\theta}{2}\right)}, \qquad W_j(x) = \frac{\sin\left(\left(j+\frac{1}{2}\right)\theta\right)}{\sin\left(\frac{\theta}{2}\right)},$$

where $\theta = \cos^{-1}(x)$.

It can be noted that the polynomials $W_j(x)$ are linked with the polynomials $V_j(x)$ by the relation:

$$W_j(x) = (-1)^j V_j(-x),$$

and therefore any relation of $V_j(x)$ has a corresponding one of $W_j(x)$.

In what follows, we will denote by $\phi_j(x)$ any Chebyshev polynomial of degree j of the well-known four kinds, and let $\phi_j^*(x)$ denote the shifted Chebyshev polynomial on $[0,1]$, defined as

$$\phi_j^*(x) = \phi_j(2x-1).$$

One of the important properties of Chebyshev polynomials is that they can be constructed by a unified recurrence relation but with different initials. In fact, the polynomials $\phi_j(x)$ satisfies the following recurrence relation:

$$\phi_j(x) = 2x\,\phi_{j-1}(x) - \phi_{j-2}(x), \quad j \geq 2, \tag{6}$$

but with the following different initial values:

$$T_0(x) = 1,\ T_1(x) = x,\quad U_0(x) = 1,\ U_1(x) = 2x,$$

$$V_0(x) = 1,\ V_1(x) = 2x - 1,\quad W_0(x) = 1,\ W_1(x) = 2x + 1.$$

Furthermore, note that the polynomials $\phi_{-j}(x)$, $j \geq 0$ can be defined in terms of $\phi_j(x)$. In fact, we have the following explicit relations

$$T_{-j}(x) = T_j(x),\quad U_{-j}(x) = -U_{j-2}(x),$$

$$V_{-j}(x) = V_{j-1}(x),\quad W_{-j}(x) = -W_{j-1}(x).$$

The shifted normalized Jacobi polynomials $\tilde{R}_j^{(\gamma,\delta)}(x)$ on $[0,1]$ are defined by:

$$\tilde{R}_j^{(\gamma,\delta)}(x) = R_j^{(\gamma,\delta)}(2x - 1).$$

All relations of the normalized Jacobi polynomials $R_j^{(\gamma,\delta)}(x)$ can be transformed to give their counterparts of their shifted ones. The orthogonality relation of $\tilde{R}_j^{(\gamma,\delta)}(x)$ is given by

$$\int_0^1 (1-x)^\gamma\, x^\delta\, \tilde{R}_j^{(\gamma,\delta)}(x)\, \tilde{R}_k^{(\gamma,\delta)}(x)\, dx = \begin{cases} 0, & k \neq j, \\ \tilde{h}_j^{\gamma,\delta}, & k = j, \end{cases} \tag{7}$$

where

$$\tilde{h}_j^{\gamma,\delta} = \frac{k!\,\Gamma(\gamma+1)^2\,\Gamma(k+\delta+1)}{(2k+\gamma+\delta+1)\,\Gamma(k+\gamma+1)\,\Gamma(k+\gamma+\delta+1)}. \tag{8}$$

In addition, among the most important properties of the shifted normalized Jacobi polynomials $\tilde{R}_j^{(\gamma,\delta)}(x)$ are their power form and inversion formulas ([41]). The power from representation is

$$\tilde{R}_j^{(\gamma,\delta)}(x) = \sum_{r=0}^{j} \frac{(-1)^r\, j!\,\Gamma(\gamma+1)\,(\delta+1)_j\,(\gamma+\delta+1)_{2j-r}}{r!\,(j-r)!\,\Gamma(j+\gamma+1)\,(\gamma+\delta+1)_j\,(\delta+1)_{j-r}}\, x^{j-r}, \tag{9}$$

while the inversion formula is

$$x^j = \sum_{r=0}^{j} \frac{\binom{j}{r}(\gamma+1)_{j-r}(j-r+\delta+1)_r}{(2j-2r+\gamma+\delta+2)_r(j-r+\gamma+\delta+1)_{j-r}}\, \tilde{R}_{j-r}^{(\gamma,\delta)}(x). \tag{10}$$

Furthermore, the Rodrigues' formula of $\tilde{R}_j^{(\gamma,\delta)}(x)$ is given by

$$\tilde{R}_j^{(\gamma,\delta)}(x) = \frac{(-1)^j\,\Gamma(\gamma+1)}{\Gamma(j+\gamma+1)}\,(1-x)^{-\gamma}\,x^{-\delta}\,D^j\!\left[(1-x)^{\gamma+j}\,x^{\delta+j}\right]. \tag{11}$$

For more properties of Jacobi polynomials in general and their special polynomials in particular, one can be referred to the useful books of Andrews et al. [41] and Mason and Handscomb [44].

3. New Moments Formulas of the Shifted Normalized Jacobi Polynomials

In this section, we develop a unified formula for computing the moments of any one of the four kinds of the shifted Chebyshev polynomials in terms of their original shifted polynomials. In addition, we establish a new formula that expresses the moments of the shifted normalized Jacobi polynomials of any degree in terms of their original shifted polynomials but with other parameters. We show that the moments coefficients involve a hypergeometric function of the type $_4F_3(1)$, which can be summed in closed analytical formulas for special choices of the involved parameters. In this regard, we state and prove the following two main theorems.

Theorem 1. *Let $\phi_n^*(x)$ be any kind of the four kinds of shifted Chebyshev polynomials. For every non-negative integers r and n, one has*

$$x^r \phi_n^*(x) = \frac{1}{2^{2r}} \sum_{\ell=0}^{2r} \binom{2r}{\ell} \phi_{n+r-\ell}^*(x). \tag{12}$$

Proof. We will proceed by induction on r. For $r = 1$, if x is replaced by $(2x-1)$ in the recurrence relation (6), then it is easy to see that

$$x \phi_n^*(x) = \frac{1}{4}\{\phi_{n+1}^*(x) + 2\phi_n^*(x) + \phi_{n-1}^*(x)\}, \tag{13}$$

and therefore, the result is true for $r = 1$. Now assume the validity of relation (12); hence, to complete the proof of Theorem 1, we have to prove the following formula:

$$x^{r+1} \phi_n^*(x) = \frac{1}{2^{2r+2}} \sum_{\ell=0}^{2r+2} \binom{2r+2}{\ell} \phi_{n+r+1-\ell}^*(x).$$

If we make use of the valid relation (12) along with relation (13), then we get

$$x^{r+1} \phi_n^*(x) = \frac{1}{2^{2r}} \sum_{\ell=0}^{2r} \binom{2r}{\ell} x \phi_{n+r-\ell}^*(x)$$

$$= \frac{1}{2^{2r+2}} \sum_{\ell=0}^{2r} \binom{2r}{\ell} \{\phi_{n+r-\ell+1}^*(x) + 2\phi_{n+r-\ell}^*(x) + \phi_{n+r-\ell-1}^*(x)\}$$

$$= \frac{1}{2^{2r+2}} \left(\sum_{\ell=0}^{2r} \binom{2r}{\ell} \phi_{n+r-\ell+1}^*(x) + 2 \sum_{\ell=1}^{2r+1} \binom{2r}{\ell-1} \phi_{n+r-\ell+1}^*(x) + \sum_{\ell=2}^{2r+2} \binom{2r}{\ell-2} \phi_{n+r-\ell+1}^*(x) \right)$$

$$= \frac{1}{2^{2r+2}} \left(\sum_{\ell=2}^{2r} \left\{ \binom{2r}{\ell} + 2\binom{2r}{\ell-1} + \binom{2r}{\ell-2} \right\} \phi_{n+r-\ell+1}^*(x) + (2r+2)\phi_{n+r}^*(x) \right.$$

$$\left. + (2r+2)\phi_{n-r}^*(x) + \phi_{n+r+1}^*(x) + \phi_{n-r-1}^*(x) \right).$$

With the aid of the simple combinatorial identity:

$$\binom{2r}{\ell} + 2\binom{2r}{\ell-1} + \binom{2r}{\ell-2} = \binom{2r+2}{\ell}, \quad \ell \geq 2,$$

it is easy to see that

$$x^{r+1} \phi_n^*(x) = \frac{1}{2^{2r+2}} \sum_{\ell=0}^{2r+2} \binom{2r+2}{\ell} \phi_{n+r+1-\ell}^*(x).$$

Theorem 1 is now proved. □

Now, we shall state and prove a new important theorem in which the moments of the shifted normalized Jacobi polynomials $\tilde{R}_i^{(\alpha,\beta)}(x)$ are expressed in terms of $\tilde{R}_i^{(\gamma,\delta)}(x)$.

Theorem 2. *For all non-negative integers r and i, one has the following moments relation:*

$$x^r \tilde{R}_i^{(\alpha,\beta)}(x) = \frac{(i+r)!\, \Gamma(\alpha+1)\, \Gamma(2i+\alpha+\beta+1)\, \Gamma(i+r+\delta+1)}{\Gamma(\gamma+1)\, \Gamma(i+\alpha+1)\, \Gamma(i+\alpha+\beta+1)}$$
$$\times \sum_{m=0}^{i+r} \frac{(\gamma+\delta+2i-2m+2r+1)\, \Gamma(i-m+r+\gamma+1)\, \Gamma(i-m+r+\gamma+\delta+1)}{m!\,(i-m+r)!\, \Gamma(i-m+r+\delta+1)\, \Gamma(2i-m+2r+\gamma+\delta+2)} \tag{14}$$
$$\times\ {}_4F_3\!\left(\begin{array}{c} -m,\, -i,\, -\beta-i,\, -\gamma-\delta-2i+m-2r-1 \\ -i-r,\, -\alpha-\beta-2i,\, -\delta-i-r \end{array}\bigg|\, 1\right) \tilde{R}_{i+r-m}^{(\gamma,\delta)}(x).$$

Proof. First, since $x^r \tilde{R}_i^{(\alpha,\beta)}(x)$ is a polynomial of degree $(i+r)$, we can assume the formula

$$x^r \tilde{R}_i^{(\alpha,\beta)}(x) = \sum_{m=0}^{i+r} A_{m,i,r}\, \tilde{R}_{i+r-m}^{(\gamma,\delta)}(x),$$

where $A_{m,i,r}$ are the moments coefficients to be determined. The orthogonality relation of $\tilde{R}_i^{(\gamma,\delta)}(x)$ over $[0,1]$ enables one to express $A_{m,i,r}$ in the following integral form:

$$A_{m,i,r} = \frac{1}{h_{i-m+r}^{\gamma,\delta}} \int_0^1 (1-x)^\gamma\, x^\delta\, \tilde{R}_{i+r-m}^{(\gamma,\delta)}(x)\left(x^r \tilde{R}_i^{(\alpha,\beta)}(x)\right) dx,$$

and with the aid of Rodrigues' formula of the shifted normalized Jacobi polynomials (11), the last integral form turns into

$$A_{m,i,r} = \frac{(-1)^{i-m+r}\, \Gamma(\gamma+1)}{h_{i-m+r}^{\gamma,\delta}\, \Gamma(i-m+r+\gamma+1)} \int_0^1 D^{i-m+r}\!\left\{(1-x)^{\gamma+i-m+r} x^{\delta+i-m+r}\right\}\left(x^r \tilde{R}_i^{(\alpha,\beta)}(x)\right) dx, \tag{15}$$

where $h_k^{\gamma,\delta}$ is given by (5).

If we integrate the right-hand side of (15) by parts $(i+r-m)$ times, then we get

$$A_{m,i,r} = \frac{(\gamma+\delta+2i-2m+2r+1)\, \Gamma(i-m+r+\gamma+\delta+1)}{\Gamma(\gamma+1)\,(i-m+r)!\, \Gamma(i-m+r+\delta+1)}$$
$$\times \int_0^1 (1-x)^{\gamma+i-m+r} x^{\delta+i-m+r} D^{i-m+r}\!\left(x^r \tilde{R}_i^{(\alpha,\beta)}(x)\right) dx.$$

The power form representation of $\tilde{R}_i^{(\alpha,\beta)}(x)$ in (9), together with the simple identity

$$D^s x^\ell = (\ell-s+1)_s\, x^{\ell-s},$$

leads to the following formula for $A_{m,i,r}$

$$A_{m,i,r} = \frac{i!\, \Gamma(\alpha+1)\, (\gamma+\delta+2i-2m+2r+1)\, \Gamma(i-m+r+\gamma+\delta+1)\, (\beta+1)_i}{(i-m+r)!\, \Gamma(\gamma+1)\, \Gamma(i+\alpha+1)\, \Gamma(i-m+r+\delta+1)\, (\alpha+\beta+1)_i}$$
$$\times \sum_{\ell=0}^i \frac{(-1)^\ell\, (-\ell+m+1)_{i-m+r}\, (\alpha+\beta+1)_{2i-\ell}}{\ell!\,(i-\ell)!\,(\beta+1)_{i-\ell}} \int_0^1 (1-x)^{\gamma+i-m+r} x^{\delta+i+r-\ell}\, dx.$$

It is easy to show the validity of the following identity:

$$\int_0^1 (1-x)^{\gamma+i-m+r} x^{\delta+i-m+r-\ell} dx = B(\gamma+i-m+r+1, \delta+i-\ell+r+1)$$

$$= \frac{\Gamma(\gamma+i-m+r+1)\Gamma(\delta+i-\ell+r+1)}{\Gamma(\gamma+\delta+2i-\ell-m+2r+2)},$$

and therefore, the coefficients $A_{m,i,r}$ are given by

$$A_{m,i,r} = \frac{i!\,\Gamma(\alpha+1)\,(\beta+1)_i\,(\gamma+\delta+2i-2m+2r+1)\,\Gamma(i-m+r+\gamma+\delta+1)}{(i-m+r)!\,\Gamma(\gamma+1)\,\Gamma(i+\alpha+1)\,\Gamma(i-m+r+\delta+1)\,(\alpha+\beta+1)_i}$$

$$\times \sum_{\ell=0}^{m} \frac{(-1)^\ell\,(-\ell+m+1)_{i-m+r}\,(\alpha+\beta+1)_{2i-\ell}\,\Gamma(i-\ell+r+\delta+1)\,\Gamma(i-m+r+\gamma+1)}{\ell!\,(i-\ell)!\,(\beta+1)_{i-\ell}\,\Gamma(2i-\ell-m+2r+\gamma+\delta+2)}. \quad (16)$$

The sum that appears in the right-hand side of (16) can be written in the following hypergeometric representation

$$\sum_{\ell=0}^{m} \frac{(-1)^\ell\,(-\ell+m+1)_{i-m+r}\,(\alpha+\beta+1)_{2i-\ell}\,\Gamma(i-\ell+r+\delta+1)\,\Gamma(i-m+r+\gamma+1)}{\ell!\,(i-\ell)!\,(\beta+1)_{i-\ell}\,\Gamma(2i-\ell-m+2r+\gamma+\delta+2)} =$$

$$\frac{(i+r)!\,\Gamma(\beta+1)\,\Gamma(2i+\alpha+\beta+1)\,\Gamma(i+r+\delta+1)\,\Gamma(i-m+r+\gamma+1)}{i!\,m!\,\Gamma(\alpha+\beta+1)\,\Gamma(i+\beta+1)\,\Gamma(2i-m+2r+\gamma+\delta+2)}$$

$$\times {}_4F_3\left(\begin{matrix} -m, -i, -\beta-i, -\gamma-\delta-2i+m-2r-1 \\ -i-r, -\alpha-\beta-2i, -\delta-i-r \end{matrix}\bigg|\, 1\right),$$

and this leads to the desired moments relation (14). □

Corollary 1. *For all non-negative integers r and i, the following moments relation of the normalized Jacobi polynomials is obtained:*

$$x^r \tilde{R}_i^{(\alpha,\beta)}(x) = \frac{(i+r)!\,\Gamma(\alpha+1)\,\Gamma(2i+\alpha+\beta+1)\,\Gamma(i+r+\delta+1)}{\Gamma(\gamma+1)\,\Gamma(i+\alpha+1)\,\Gamma(i+\alpha+\beta+1)}$$

$$\times \sum_{m=0}^{i+r} \frac{(\gamma+\delta+2i-2m+2r+1)\,\Gamma(i-m+r+\gamma+1)\,\Gamma(i-m+r+\gamma+\delta+1)}{m!\,(i-m+r)!\,\Gamma(i-m+r+\delta+1)\,\Gamma(2i-m+2r+\gamma+\delta+2)} \quad (17)$$

$$\times {}_4F_3\left(\begin{matrix} -m, -i, -\beta-i, -\gamma-\delta-2i+m-2r-1 \\ -i-r, -\alpha-\beta-2i, -\delta-i-r \end{matrix}\bigg|\, 1\right) \tilde{R}_{i+r-m}^{(\alpha,\beta)}(x).$$

Proof. If we set $\gamma = \alpha$, $\delta = \beta$ in Formula (14), then Formula (17) can be obtained. □

Remark 1. *For some particular choices of $\alpha, \beta, \gamma, \delta$, the hypergeometric series that appears in (14) can be summed, and hence some moments relations can be obtained in reduced forms. In the following, we give some of these cases.*

Corollary 2. *For all non-negative integers i and r, one has*

$$x^r T_i^*(x) = \frac{(2r+1)!}{2^{2r+1}} \sum_{m=0}^{2r+1} \frac{1}{m!\,(-m+2r+1)!} V_{i+r-m}^*(x). \quad (18)$$

Proof. The substitution by $\alpha = \beta = \gamma = -\frac{1}{2}$, and $\delta = \frac{1}{2}$, into relation (14) yields

$$x^r T_i^*(x) = \frac{(2i+2r+1)!}{2^{2r+1}} \sum_{m=0}^{i+r} \frac{1}{m!\,(2i-m+2r+1)!}$$

$$\times {}_4F_3\left(\begin{array}{c}-m, -i, \frac{1}{2}-i, -2i+m-2r-1 \\ 1-2i, -i-r-\frac{1}{2}, -i-r\end{array}\bigg|\, 1\right) V_{i+r-m}^*(x). \tag{19}$$

We note that the terminating ${}_4F_3(1)$ that appears in (19) involves the two non-negative integers i and m in the numerator parameters. In order to reduce it, we set

$$S_{m,i,r} = {}_4F_3\left(\begin{array}{c}-m, -i, \frac{1}{2}-i, -2i+m-2r-1 \\ 1-2i, -i-r-\frac{1}{2}, -i-r\end{array}\bigg|\, 1\right),$$

and we consider the following two cases:

(i) If $m \leq i$, and then the ue Zeilberger's algorithm [45], it can be shown that $S_{m,i,r}$ satisfies the following recurrence relation

$$(1+m)(-1+m-2r)S_{m,i,r} + (1+i(2+4m-4r) - 2m(1+m-2r) + 6r)\,S_{m+1,i,r}$$
$$+ (-2+2i-m)(2i-m+2r)\,S_{m+2,i,r} = 0, \quad S_{0,i,r} = 1,\ S_{1,i,r} = \frac{2r+1}{2r+3},$$

which can be solved exactly to give

$$S_{m,i,r} = {}_4F_3\left(\begin{array}{c}-m, -i, \frac{1}{2}-i, -2i+m-2r-1 \\ 1-2i, -i-r-\frac{1}{2}, -i-r\end{array}\bigg|\, 1\right) = \frac{(2r+1)!\,(2i-m+2r+1)!}{(2i+2r+1)!\,(2r-m+1)!}. \tag{20}$$

(ii) If $m > i$, then it can be shown that $S_{m,i,r}$ satisfies the following recurrence relation:

$$(-4+2i-m)(-3+2i-m)(-1+4i-2m+2r)(-2+2i-m+2r)(-1+2i-m+2r)S_{m,i-2,r}$$
$$- 4(-1+i+r)(-1+2i+2r)(-3+4i-2m+2r)$$
$$\times \left(2-6i+4i^2+3m-4im+m^2-r+4ir-2mr+2r^2\right)S_{m,i-1,r}$$
$$+ 4(-1+i+r)(i+r)(-1+2i+2r)(1+2i+2r)(-5+4i-2m+2r)S_{m,i,r} = 0,$$
$$S_{m,0,r} = 1,\ S_{m,1,r} = \frac{m^2 - 2mr - 3m + 2r^2 + 5r + 3}{(r+1)(2r+3)}.$$

which can be exactly solved to give

$$S_{m,i,r} = \frac{(2r+1)!\left(\frac{m!}{(m-2i)!} + \frac{(2i-m+2r+1)!}{(2r-m+1)!}\right)}{(2i+2r+1)!}.$$

Now, if we take into consideration the reduction of $S_{m,i,r}$ for the two cases (i) and (ii), then we can write the following two formulas

$$x^r T_i^*(x) = \sum_{\ell=0}^{r+i} B_{\ell,r,i} V_\ell^*(x), \quad r \geq i,$$

and

$$x^r T_i^*(x) = \sum_{\ell=0}^{r+i} \tilde{B}_{\ell,r,i} V_\ell^*(x), \quad r < i,$$

where the coefficients $B_{\ell,r,i}$ and $\tilde{B}_{\ell,r,i}$ are given by

$$B_{\ell,r,i} = \frac{(2r+1)!}{2^{2r+1}}$$

$$\times \begin{cases} \frac{1}{(i-\ell+r)!(\ell+r-i+1)!} + \frac{1}{(-i-\ell+r)!(\ell+r+i+1)!}, & 0 \leq \ell \leq r-i, \\ \frac{1}{(i-\ell+r)!(1-i+\ell+r)!}, & r-i+1 \leq \ell \leq r+i, \end{cases} \quad (21)$$

and

$$\tilde{B}_{\ell,r,i} = \frac{(2r+1)!}{2^{2r+1}(i-\ell+r)!(1-i+\ell+r)!}, \quad 0 \leq \ell \leq r+i. \quad (22)$$

For the case corresponding to $r \geq i$. Based on (21), relation (19) turns into

$$x^r T_i^*(x) = \frac{(2r+1)!}{2^{2r+1}} \sum_{\ell=0}^{r-i} \left(\frac{1}{(i-\ell+r)!(1-i+\ell+r)!} + \frac{1}{(-i-\ell+r)!(1+i+\ell+r)!} \right) V_\ell^*(x)$$

$$+ \frac{(2r+1)!}{2^{2r+1}} \sum_{\ell=r-i+1}^{r+i} \frac{1}{(i-\ell+r)!(1-i+\ell+r)!} V_\ell^*(x)$$

$$= \frac{(2r+1)!}{2^{2r+1}} \left(\sum_{\ell=0}^{i+r} \frac{1}{(i-\ell+r)!(1-i+\ell+r)!} V_\ell^*(x) + \sum_{\ell=0}^{r-i} \frac{1}{(-i-\ell+r)!(1+i+\ell+r)!} V_\ell^*(x) \right)$$

$$= \frac{(2r+1)!}{2^{2r+1}} \left(\sum_{m=0}^{i+r} \frac{1}{m!(2r-m+1)!} V_{i+r-m}^*(x) + \sum_{m=i+r+1}^{2r+1} \frac{1}{m!(2r-m+1)!} V_{m-i-r-1}^*(x) \right).$$

Based on the well-known identity:

$$V_p(x) = V_{-p-1}(x), \; p \geq 0,$$

we can write

$$x^r T_i^*(x) = \frac{(2r+1)!}{2^{2r+1}} \left(\sum_{m=0}^{i+r} \frac{1}{m!(2r-m+1)!} V_{i+r-m}^*(x) + \sum_{m=i+r+1}^{2r+1} \frac{1}{m!(2r-m+1)!} V_{i+r+m}^*(x) \right).$$

$$= \frac{(2r+1)!}{2^{2r+1}} \sum_{m=0}^{2r+1} \frac{1}{m!(-m+2r+1)!} V_{i+r-m}^*(x).$$

In addition, for the case that corresponds to $i > r$, we can see that

$$x^r T_i^*(x) = \frac{(2r+1)!}{2^{2r+1}} \sum_{m=0}^{2r+1} \frac{1}{m!(-m+2r+1)!} V_{i+r-m}^*(x).$$

Therefore, the unified moments relation (18) is proved for all i and r. □

Corollary 3. *For all non-negative integers i and r, one has*

$$x^r T_i^*(x) = \frac{(2r+1)!}{2^{2r}} \sum_{m=0}^{2r+2} \frac{(-m+r+1)}{m!(-m+2r+2)!} U_{i+r-m}^*(x). \quad (23)$$

Corollary 4. *For all non-negative integers i and r, one has*

$$x^r V_i^*(x) = \frac{(2r)!}{2^{2r}} \sum_{m=0}^{2r+1} \frac{2r-2m+1}{m!(-m+2r+1)!} U_{i+r-m}^*(x). \quad (24)$$

Proof. Proofs of Corollaries 3 and 4 are similar to the proof of Corollary 2. □

Remark 2. *When employing Zeilberger's algorithm for the reduction of certain hypergeometric functions of the unit argument, a recurrence relation is obtained. The exact solution of this recurrence relation can be found by a suitable computer algebra algorithm. Petkovsek's and van Hoeij algorithms may be useful for obtaining the desired solutions (see, [45,46]).*

4. A New Approach for Solving Jacobi Linearization Problem via Moments Formulas

This section is confined to developing new linearization formulas of the normalized Jacobi polynomials of different parameters based on utilizing the new moments formulas derived in Section 3.

Theorem 3. *Let i and j be any two non-negative integers, and let $\phi_k(x)$ be any polynomial of the four kinds of Chebyshev polynomials. The following linearization formula is valid*

$$R_i^{(\alpha,\beta)}(x)\,\phi_j(x) = \frac{(2i)!\,\Gamma(\alpha+1)\,\Gamma(2i+\alpha+\beta+1)}{2^{2i}\,\Gamma(i+\alpha+1)\,\Gamma(i+\alpha+\beta+1)} \\ \times \sum_{p=0}^{2i} \frac{1}{p!\,(2i-p)!}\,{}_3F_2\!\left(\begin{array}{c}-p,\,p-2i,\,-\beta-i\\ \frac{1}{2}-i,\,-\alpha-\beta-2i\end{array}\bigg|1\right)\phi_{i+j-p}(x). \quad (25)$$

Proof. The power form representation of $\tilde{R}_i^{(\alpha,\beta)}(x)$ (9) together with the result of Theorem 1 yield

$$\tilde{R}_i^{(\alpha,\beta)}(x)\,\phi_j^*(x) = \frac{i!\,\Gamma(\alpha+1)\,(\beta+1)_i}{\Gamma(i+\alpha+1)\,(\alpha+\beta+1)_i} \sum_{r=0}^{i} \frac{(-1)^r\,4^{r-i}\,(\alpha+\beta+1)_{2i-r}}{r!\,(i-r)!\,(\beta+1)_{i-r}} \sum_{s=0}^{2i-2r} \binom{2i-2r}{s}\phi_{j+i-r-s}^*(x).$$

Expanding the right-hand side of the last relation and performing some algebraic calculations lead to the following relation:

$$\tilde{R}_i^{(\alpha,\beta)}(x)\,\phi_j^*(x) = \frac{i!\,\Gamma(\alpha+1)\,(\beta+1)_i}{\Gamma(i+\alpha+1)\,(\alpha+\beta+1)_i} \sum_{p=0}^{2i}\sum_{r=0}^{p} \frac{(-1)^r\,4^{r-i}\,\binom{2i-2r}{p-r}\,(\alpha+\beta+1)_{2i-r}}{r!\,(i-r)!\,(\beta+1)_{i-r}}\phi_{j+i-p}^*(x),$$

but it can be shown that

$$\sum_{r=0}^{p} \frac{(-1)^r\,4^{r-i}\,\binom{2i-2r}{p-r}\,(\alpha+\beta+1)_{2i-r}}{r!\,(i-r)!\,(\beta+1)_{i-r}} = \frac{(2i)!\,\Gamma(\beta+1)\,\Gamma(2i+\alpha+\beta+1)}{2^{2i}\,p!\,(2i-p)!\,\Gamma(\alpha+\beta+1)\,\Gamma(i+\beta+1)} \\ \times {}_3F_2\!\left(\begin{array}{c}-p,\,p-2i,\,-\beta-i\\ \frac{1}{2}-i,\,-\alpha-\beta-2i\end{array}\bigg|1\right),$$

and therefore, the following linearization formula is obtained:

$$\tilde{R}_i^{(\alpha,\beta)}(x)\,\phi_j^*(x) = \frac{(2i)!\,\Gamma(\alpha+1)\,\Gamma(2i+\alpha+\beta+1)}{2^{2i}\,\Gamma(i+\alpha+1)\,\Gamma(i+\alpha+\beta+1)} \\ \times \sum_{p=0}^{2i} \frac{1}{p!\,(2i-p)!}\,{}_3F_2\!\left(\begin{array}{c}-p,\,p-2i,\,-\beta-i\\ \frac{1}{2}-i,\,-\alpha-\beta-2i\end{array}\bigg|1\right)\phi_{i+j-p}^*(x).$$

In the last formula, if x is replaced by $\frac{1+x}{2}$, then the linearization Formula (25) is obtained. □

Corollary 5. For all non-negative integers i and j, the following linearization formula holds

$$C_i^{(\alpha)}(x)\phi_j(x) = \frac{i!\,2^{2\alpha-1}\Gamma\left(\alpha+\frac{1}{2}\right)}{\sqrt{\pi}\,\Gamma(\alpha)\Gamma(i+2\alpha)}\sum_{p=0}^{i}\frac{\Gamma(p+\alpha)\Gamma(i-p+\alpha)}{p!\,(i-p)!}\phi_{j+i-2p}(x). \tag{26}$$

Proof. If we set $\beta = \alpha$ in (25), and each of them is replaced by $\left(\alpha-\frac{1}{2}\right)$, then we get

$$C_i^{(\alpha)}(x)\phi_j(x) = \frac{2^{2\alpha-1}(2i-1)!\,\Gamma\left(\alpha+\frac{1}{2}\right)\Gamma(i+\alpha)}{\sqrt{\pi}\,\Gamma(i+2\alpha)}\sum_{p=0}^{2i}\frac{1}{p!\,(2i-p)!} \tag{27}$$

$$\times {}_3F_2\left(\begin{array}{c}-p, p-2i, -\alpha-i+\frac{1}{2}\\ \frac{1}{2}-i, -2\alpha-2i+1\end{array}\bigg|1\right)\phi_{j+i-p}(x).$$

The ${}_3F_2(1)$ in (27) can be summed with the aid of Watson's identity to give

$${}_3F_2\left(\begin{array}{c}-p, p-2i, -\alpha-i+\frac{1}{2}\\ \frac{1}{2}-i, -2\alpha-2i+1\end{array}\bigg|1\right) = \begin{cases}\dfrac{\Gamma\left(\frac{p+1}{2}\right)(\alpha)_{\frac{p}{2}}}{\sqrt{\pi}\left(i-\frac{p}{2}+\frac{1}{2}\right)_{\frac{p}{2}}\left(i-\frac{p}{2}+\alpha\right)_{\frac{p}{2}}}, & p\text{ even,}\\ 0, & p\text{ odd,}\end{cases}$$

and accordingly, relation (26) can be obtained. □

Corollary 6. For all non-negative integers i and j, the following linearization formulas hold

$$L_i(x)\phi_j(x) = \frac{1}{\pi}\sum_{p=0}^{i}\frac{\Gamma\left(p+\frac{1}{2}\right)\Gamma\left(i-p+\frac{1}{2}\right)}{p!\,(i-p)!}\phi_{j+i-2p}(x), \tag{28}$$

$$U_i(x)\phi_j(x) = \sum_{p=0}^{i}\phi_{j+i-2p}(x), \tag{29}$$

$$T_i(x)\phi_j(x) = \frac{1}{2}\left(\phi_{j+i}(x)+\phi_{j-i}(x)\right). \tag{30}$$

Proof. The above three formulas can be easily obtained if we substitute by $\alpha = \frac{1}{2}, 1, 0$, respectively, in Formula (26). □

Corollary 7. For all non-negative integers i and j, the following linearization formula holds

$$J_i^{(\alpha,-\frac{1}{2})}(x)\phi_j(x) = \frac{(2i)!\,\Gamma(\alpha+1)\Gamma\left(2i+\alpha+\frac{1}{2}\right)}{2^{2i}\,\Gamma\left(i+\alpha+\frac{1}{2}\right)\Gamma(i+\alpha+1)}\sum_{p=0}^{2i}\frac{\left(-p-\alpha+\frac{1}{2}\right)_p}{p!\,(2i-p)!\left(-2i-\alpha+\frac{1}{2}\right)_p}\phi_{j+i-p}(x). \tag{31}$$

Proof. Setting $\beta = -\frac{1}{2}$ in (25) yields

$$\tilde{R}_i^{(\alpha,-\frac{1}{2})}(x)\phi_j(x) = \frac{(2i)!\,\Gamma(\alpha+1)\Gamma\left(2i+\alpha+\frac{1}{2}\right)}{2^{2i}\,\Gamma\left(i+\alpha+\frac{1}{2}\right)\Gamma(i+\alpha+1)}\sum_{p=0}^{2i}\frac{{}_2F_1\left(\begin{array}{c}-p, p-2i\\ -2i-\alpha+\frac{1}{2}\end{array}\bigg|1\right)}{p!\,(2i-p)!}\phi_{j+i-p}(x).$$

The last ${}_2F_1(1)$ can be summed with the aid of Chu-Vandermonde identity, and consequently, formula (31) can be obtained. □

Corollary 8. For all non-negative integers i and j, the following linearization formula holds

$$J_i^{(\alpha,\alpha+1)}(x)\phi_j(x) = \frac{(2i)!\,\Gamma(\alpha+1)\,\Gamma(2i+2\alpha+2)}{\sqrt{\pi}\,2^{2i}\,\Gamma(i+\alpha+1)\,\Gamma(i+2\alpha+2)}$$

$$\times \sum_{p=0}^{i} \frac{\Gamma\left(p+\frac{1}{2}\right)\left(\alpha+\frac{3}{2}\right)_p}{(2p)!\,(2i-2p)!\,\left(i-p+\frac{1}{2}\right)_p \left(i-p+\alpha+\frac{3}{2}\right)_p} \left\{ \phi_{i+j-2p}(x) - \frac{2(i-p)}{2\alpha+2i-2p+1}\phi_{i+j-2p-1}(x) \right\}. \quad (32)$$

Proof. Substitution by $\beta = \alpha + 1$ into the linearization Formula (25) yields

$$\tilde{R}_i^{(\alpha,\alpha+1)}(x)\phi_j(x) = \frac{(2i)!\,\Gamma(\alpha+1)\,\Gamma(2i+2\alpha+2)}{2^{2i}\,\Gamma(i+\alpha+1)\,\Gamma(i+2\alpha+2)}$$

$$\times \sum_{p=0}^{2i} \frac{1}{p!\,(2i-p)!}\, {}_3F_2\left(\begin{array}{c} -p, p-2i, -\alpha-i-1 \\ \frac{1}{2}-i, -2\alpha-2i-1 \end{array} \Big| 1 \right) \phi_{j+i-p}(x).$$

Regarding the $_3F_2(1)$ that appears in the last formula, and to the best of our knowledge, no standard formula exists in the literature to sum it. Therefore, we resort to Zeilberger's algorithm for summing it, so we set

$$A_{p,i} = {}_3F_2\left(\begin{array}{c} -p, p-2i, -\alpha-i-1 \\ \frac{1}{2}-i, -2\alpha-2i-1 \end{array} \Big| 1 \right),$$

it can be shown that $A_{p,i}$ satisfies the following recurrence relation of order two:

$$(2i-p-1)(2\alpha+2i-p)G_{p+2,i} + 2(i-p-1)G_{p+1,i} - (p+1)(2\alpha+p+2)G_{p,i} = 0,$$

with the initial values:

$$G_{0,i} = 1, \quad G_{1,i} = \frac{-1}{2i+2\alpha+1},$$

whose exact solution is given by

$$A_{p,i} = {}_3F_2\left(\begin{array}{c} -p, p-2i, -\alpha-i-1 \\ \frac{1}{2}-i, -2\alpha-2i-1 \end{array} \Big| 1 \right) = \begin{cases} \dfrac{\Gamma\left(\frac{p+1}{2}\right)\left(\alpha+\frac{3}{2}\right)_{\frac{p}{2}}}{\sqrt{\pi}\left(i-\frac{p}{2}+\frac{1}{2}\right)_{\frac{p}{2}}\left(i-\frac{p}{2}+\alpha+\frac{3}{2}\right)_{\frac{p}{2}}}, & p \text{ even,} \\[2ex] \dfrac{-\Gamma\left(\frac{p}{2}+1\right)\Gamma\left(i-\frac{p}{2}+1\right)\left(\alpha+\frac{3}{2}\right)_{\frac{p-1}{2}}}{\sqrt{\pi}\,\Gamma\left(i+\frac{1}{2}\right)\left(i-\frac{p}{2}+\alpha+1\right)_{\frac{p+1}{2}}}, & p \text{ odd.} \end{cases}$$

Making use of the above reduction and performing some calculations yield the following linearization formula

$$\tilde{R}_i^{(\alpha,\alpha+1)}(x)\phi_j^*(x) = \frac{(2i)!\,\Gamma(\alpha+1)\,\Gamma(2(i+\alpha+1))}{\sqrt{\pi}\,2^{2i}\,\Gamma(i+\alpha+1)\,\Gamma(i+2\alpha+2)}$$

$$\times \sum_{p=0}^{i} \frac{\Gamma\left(p+\frac{1}{2}\right)\left(\alpha+\frac{3}{2}\right)_p}{(2p)!\,(2i-2p)!\,\left(i-p+\frac{1}{2}\right)_p \left(i-p+\alpha+\frac{3}{2}\right)_p} \left\{ \phi_{i+j-2p}^*(x) - \frac{2(i-p)}{2\alpha+2i-2p+1}\phi_{i+j-2p-1}^*(x) \right\}.$$

In the last formula, if x is replaced by $\frac{1+x}{2}$, then Formula (32) is obtained. The proof of Corollary 8 is now complete. □

Now, and based on the general formula of the moments of the shifted normalized Jacobi polynomials, we will state and prove a theorem in which a general linearization formula of Jacobi polynomials is given.

Theorem 4. *For all non-negative integers i and j, the following linearization formula holds*

$$R_i^{(\alpha,\beta)}(x) R_j^{(\lambda,\mu)}(x) = \frac{i!\,\Gamma(\alpha+1)\,\Gamma(\lambda+1)\,\Gamma(2j+\lambda+\mu+1)\,(\beta+1)_i}{\Gamma(\gamma+1) \times \Gamma(i+\alpha+1)\,\Gamma(j+\lambda+1)\,\Gamma(j+\lambda+\mu+1)\,(\alpha+\beta+1)_i}$$
$$\times \sum_{p=0}^{i+j} \frac{(\gamma+\delta+2i+2j-2p+1)\,\Gamma(i+j-p+\gamma+1)\,\Gamma(i+j-p+\gamma+\delta+1)}{(i+j-p)!\,\Gamma(i+j-p+\delta+1)}$$
$$\times \sum_{m=0}^{p} \frac{(-1)^{p+m}\,(i+j+m-p)!\,\Gamma(i+j+m-p+\delta+1)\,(\alpha+\beta+1)_{2i+m-p}}{m!\,(p-m)!\,(i+m-p)!\,(\beta+1)_{i+m-p}\,\Gamma(2i+2j+m-2p+\gamma+\delta+2)}$$
$$\times {}_4F_3\left(\begin{array}{c}-j,-m,-\gamma-\delta-2i-2j-m+2p-1,-j-\mu\\-i-j-m+p,-\delta-i-j-m+p,-2j-\lambda-\mu\end{array}\bigg|1\right) R_{i+j-p}^{(\gamma,\delta)}(x). \quad (33)$$

Proof. Starting with the power form representation of the shifted normalized Jacobi polynomials (9) enables one to write

$$\tilde{R}_i^{(\alpha,\beta)}(x)\,\tilde{R}_j^{(\lambda,\mu)}(x) = \sum_{r=0}^{i} A_{r,i}\,x^{i-r}\,\tilde{R}_j^{(\lambda,\mu)}(x), \quad (34)$$

where

$$A_{r,i} = \frac{(-1)^r\,i!\,\Gamma(\alpha+1)\,(\beta+1)_i\,(\alpha+\beta+1)_{2i-r}}{r!\,(i-r)!\,\Gamma(i+\alpha+1)\,(\alpha+\beta+1)_i\,(\beta+1)_{i-r}}.$$

Theorem 2 enables one to convert (34) into the following formula

$$\tilde{R}_i^{(\alpha,\beta)}(x)\,\tilde{R}_j^{(\lambda,\mu)}(x) = \sum_{r=0}^{i}\sum_{m=0}^{j+i-r} A_{r,i}\,B_{m,i,r,j}\,\tilde{R}_{j+i-r-m}^{(\gamma,\delta)}(x), \quad (35)$$

and

$$B_{m,i,r,j} = \frac{(i+j-r)!\,\Gamma(\lambda+1)\,\Gamma(2j+\lambda+\mu+1)(\gamma+\delta+2i+2j-2m-2r+1)}{m!\,(i+j-m-r)!\,\Gamma(\gamma+1)\,\Gamma(j+\lambda+1)}$$
$$\times \frac{\Gamma(i+j-r+\delta+1)\Gamma(i+j-m-r+\gamma+1)\Gamma(i+j-m-r+\gamma+\delta+1)}{\Gamma(j+\lambda+\mu+1)\Gamma(i+j-m-r+\delta+1)\Gamma(2i+2j-m-2r+\gamma+\delta+2)} \quad (36)$$
$$\times {}_4F_3\left(\begin{array}{c}-j,-m,-\gamma-\delta-2i-2j+m+2r-1,-j-\mu\\-i-j+r,-\delta-i-j+r,-2j-\lambda-\mu\end{array}\bigg|1\right).$$

Performing some lengthy manipulations on the right-hand side of (35) enables one to rewrite Equation (35) as

$$\tilde{R}_i^{(\alpha,\beta)}(x)\,\tilde{R}_j^{(\lambda,\mu)}(x) = \sum_{p=0}^{j+i}\left(\sum_{m=0}^{p} A_{m,i}\,B_{p-m,i,m,j}\right)\tilde{R}_{j+i-p}^{(\gamma,\delta)}(x).$$

The last relation leads to Formula (33), replacing x by $\frac{1+x}{2}$. □

The following corollary gives the general linearization formula of ultraspherical polynomials of different parameters. This relation of course generalizes the well-known formula of Dougall [41].

Corollary 9. *For all non-negative integers i and j, the following linearization formula holds*

$$C_i^{(\alpha)}(x) C_j^{(\lambda)}(x) = \frac{4^{j+\lambda} i! \Gamma\left(\alpha + \frac{1}{2}\right) \Gamma\left(\lambda + \frac{1}{2}\right) \Gamma(j+\lambda)}{\sqrt{\pi} \Gamma\left(\gamma + \frac{1}{2}\right) \Gamma(i+2\alpha) \Gamma(j+2\lambda)} \sum_{p=0}^{i+j} \frac{(\gamma + i + j - p) \Gamma(i+j-p+2\gamma)}{(i+j-p)!}$$

$$\times \sum_{m=0}^{p} \frac{(-1)^{p-m} (i+j+m-p)! \Gamma(2i+m-p+2\alpha) \Gamma\left(i+j+m-p+\gamma+\frac{1}{2}\right)}{m! (p-m)! (i+m-p)! \Gamma\left(i+m-p+\alpha+\frac{1}{2}\right) \Gamma(2i+2j+m-2p+2\gamma+1)}$$

$$\times {}_4F_3\left(\begin{array}{c} -j, -m, -2\gamma - 2i - 2j - m + 2p, -j - \lambda + \frac{1}{2} \\ -i - j - m + p, -\gamma - i - j - m + p + \frac{1}{2}, -2j - 2\lambda + 1 \end{array} \Big| 1\right) C_{i+j-p}^{(\gamma)}(x). \quad (37)$$

Now, we shall give some new linearization formulas based on the general formula in Theorem 4.

Theorem 5. *For all non-negative integers i and j, the following linearization formula holds:*

$$R_i^{(\alpha,\beta)}(x) T_j(x) = \frac{(2i+1)! \Gamma(1+\alpha) \Gamma(1+2i+\alpha+\beta)}{2^{2i} \Gamma(1+i+\alpha) \Gamma(1+i+\alpha+\beta)}$$

$$\times \sum_{p=0}^{2i+2} \frac{i-p+1}{p! (2i-p+2)!} {}_3F_2\left(\begin{array}{c} -p, -2i+p-2, -\beta - i \\ -i - \frac{1}{2}, -\alpha - \beta - 2i \end{array} \Big| 1\right) U_{i+j-p}(x). \quad (38)$$

Proof. The result of Theorem 5 is a special result of Theorem 4 for the case that corresponds to the values: $\lambda = \mu = -\frac{1}{2}, \gamma = \delta = \frac{1}{2}$. □

Corollary 10. *For all non-negative integers i and j, the following linearization formula holds:*

$$C_i^{(\alpha)}(x) T_j(x) = \frac{2^{2\alpha-2} i! \Gamma\left(\frac{1}{2} + \alpha\right)}{\sqrt{\pi} \Gamma(i+2\alpha)} \sum_{p=0}^{i+1} \frac{(1+i-2p) \Gamma(i-p+\alpha)(\alpha-1)_p}{p! (i-p+1)!} U_{j+i-2p}(x). \quad (39)$$

Proof. Setting $\beta = \alpha$ in (38) and replacing each with $\left(\alpha - \frac{1}{2}\right)$ yields the following relation:

$$C_i^{(\alpha)}(x) T_j(x) = \frac{2^{2\alpha-1} (2i+1)! \Gamma\left(\alpha + \frac{1}{2}\right) \Gamma(i+\alpha)}{\sqrt{\pi} \Gamma(i+2\alpha)} \sum_{p=0}^{2i+2} \frac{(i-p+1)}{p! (2i-p+2)!}$$

$$\times {}_3F_2\left(\begin{array}{c} -p, -2i+p-2, -\alpha - i + \frac{1}{2} \\ -i - \frac{1}{2}, -2\alpha - 2i + 1 \end{array} \Big| 1\right) U_{j+i-p}(x).$$

It can be shown with the aid of Watson's identity that

$${}_3F_2\left(\begin{array}{c} -p, -2i+p-2, -\alpha - i + \frac{1}{2} \\ -i - \frac{1}{2}, -2\alpha - 2i + 1 \end{array} \Big| 1\right) = \begin{cases} \frac{\Gamma\left(\frac{p+1}{2}\right) (\alpha - 1)_{\frac{p}{2}} \Gamma\left(i - \frac{p}{2} + \alpha\right)}{\sqrt{\pi} \Gamma(i+\alpha) \left(i - \frac{p}{2} + \frac{3}{2}\right)_{\frac{p}{2}}}, & p \text{ even,} \\ 0, & p \text{ odd,} \end{cases}$$

and hence Formula (39) can be obtained. □

Corollary 11. For all non-negative integers i and j, the following linearization formulas hold:

$$L_i(x) T_j(x) = \frac{1}{4\pi} \sum_{p=0}^{i+1} \frac{(-i+2p-1)\Gamma\left(p-\frac{1}{2}\right)\Gamma\left(i-p+\frac{1}{2}\right)}{p!(i-p+1)!} U_{i+j-2p}(x), \quad (40)$$

$$U_i(x) T_j(x) = \frac{1}{2}\left(U_{j+i}(x) - U_{j-i-2}(x)\right), \quad (41)$$

$$T_i(x) T_j(x) = \frac{1}{4}\left(U_{j+i}(x) + U_{j-i}(x)\right) - \frac{1}{4}\left(U_{j+i-2}(x) + U_{j-i-2}(x)\right). \quad (42)$$

Proof. Formulas (40), (41), and (42) can be obtained as direct special cases of Formula (39) by setting $\alpha = \frac{1}{2}, 1, 0$, respectively. □

Theorem 6. For all non-negative integers i and j, the following linearization formula holds:

$$R_i^{(\alpha,\beta)}(x) V_j(x) = \frac{(2i)!\,\Gamma(\alpha+1)\,\Gamma(2i+\alpha+\beta+1)}{2^{2i}\,\Gamma(i+\alpha+1)\,\Gamma(i+\alpha+\beta+1)}$$

$$\times \sum_{p=0}^{2i+1} \frac{2i-2p+1}{p!\,(2i-p+1)!} \,{}_3F_2\left(\begin{array}{c} -p,\, -2i+p-1,\, -\beta-i \\ \frac{1}{2}-i,\, -\alpha-\beta-2i \end{array} \Big| 1\right) U_{i+j-p}(x). \quad (43)$$

Proof. The result of Theorem 6 is a special result of Theorem 4 for the case that corresponds to the values $\lambda = -\frac{1}{2}, \mu = \gamma = \delta = \frac{1}{2}$. □

Corollary 12. For all non-negative integers i and j, the following linearization formula holds

$$C_i^{(\alpha)}(x) V_j(x) = \frac{2^{2\alpha-1}\, i!\, \Gamma\left(\alpha+\frac{1}{2}\right)}{\sqrt{\pi}\,\Gamma(\alpha)\,\Gamma(i+2\alpha)} \sum_{p=0}^{i} \frac{\Gamma(p+\alpha)\,\Gamma(i-p+\alpha)}{p!\,(i-p)!} \quad (44)$$

$$\times \left(U_{j+i-2p}(x) + U_{j+i-2p-1}(x)\right).$$

Proof. From (43), we get the following relation:

$$C_i^{(\alpha)}(x) V_j(x) = \frac{2^{2\alpha-1}\,(2i)!\,\Gamma\left(\alpha+\frac{1}{2}\right)\Gamma(i+\alpha)}{\sqrt{\pi}\,\Gamma(i+2\alpha)}$$

$$\times \sum_{p=0}^{i+j} \frac{2i-2p+1}{p!\,(2i-p+1)!} \,{}_3F_2\left(\begin{array}{c} -p,\, -2i+p-1,\, -\alpha-i+\frac{1}{2} \\ \frac{1}{2}-i,\, -2\alpha-2i+1 \end{array} \Big| 1\right) U_{i+j-p}(x). \quad (45)$$

It can be shown with the aid of Zeilberger's algorithm that

$${}_3F_2\left(\begin{array}{c} -p,\, -2i+p-1,\, -\alpha-i+\frac{1}{2} \\ \frac{1}{2}-i,\, -2\alpha-2i+1 \end{array} \Big| 1\right) = \frac{2}{\sqrt{\pi}(2i-2p+1)\Gamma\left(i+\frac{1}{2}\right)\Gamma(i+\alpha)}$$

$$\times \begin{cases} \Gamma\left(\frac{p+1}{2}\right)\Gamma\left(i-\frac{p}{2}+\frac{3}{2}\right)\Gamma\left(i-\frac{p}{2}+\alpha\right)(\alpha)_{\frac{p}{2}}, & p \text{ even,} \\ \dfrac{-\Gamma\left(\frac{p}{2}+1\right)\Gamma\left(i-\frac{p}{2}+1\right)\Gamma\left(\frac{p-1}{2}+\alpha\right)\Gamma\left(i-\frac{p}{2}+\alpha+\frac{1}{2}\right)}{\Gamma(\alpha)}, & p \text{ odd.} \end{cases}$$

Finally, some calculations lead to (44). □

Corollary 13. *For all non-negative integers i and j, the following linearization formulas hold:*

$$L_i(x) V_j(x) = \frac{1}{\pi} \sum_{p=0}^{i} \frac{\Gamma\left(\frac{1}{2}+i-p\right)\Gamma\left(\frac{1}{2}+p\right)}{p!\,(i-p)!} \left(U_{j+i-2p}(x) - U_{j+i-2p-1}(x)\right), \qquad (46)$$

$$U_i(x) V_j(x) = \sum_{p=0}^{i} \left(U_{j+i-2p}(x) - U_{j+i-2p-1}(x)\right), \qquad (47)$$

$$T_i(x) V_j(x) = \frac{1}{2}\left(U_{j-i}(x) - U_{j-i-1}(x) + U_{j+i}(x) - U_{j+i-1}(x)\right). \qquad (48)$$

Proof. Formulas (46), (47), and (48) can be obtained as direct special cases of the Formula (44) by setting $\alpha = \frac{1}{2}, 1, 0$, respectively. □

Theorem 7. *For all non-negative integers i and j, the following linearization formula holds:*

$$R_i^{(\alpha,\beta)}(x)\, T_j(x) = \frac{i!\,\Gamma(\alpha+1)\,\Gamma\left(i+\frac{3}{2}\right)\Gamma(2i+\alpha+\beta+1)}{\sqrt{\pi}\,\Gamma(i+\alpha+1)\,\Gamma(i+\alpha+\beta+1)}$$

$$\times \sum_{p=0}^{2i+1} \frac{1}{p!\,(2i-p+1)!}\; {}_3F_2\!\left(\begin{array}{c}-p,\,-1-2i+p,\,-i-\beta\\ -\frac{1}{2}-i,\,-2i-\alpha-\beta\end{array}\bigg|\,1\right) V_{i+j-p}(x).$$

Proof. The result of Theorem 7 is a special result of Theorem 4 for the case that corresponds to the values $\lambda = \mu = \gamma = -\frac{1}{2}, \delta = \frac{1}{2}$. □

Corollary 14. *For all non-negative integers i and j, the following linearization formula holds*

$$C_i^{(\alpha)}(x)\, T_j(x) = \frac{2^{2\alpha-2}(2i+1)!\,\Gamma\left(\alpha+\frac{1}{2}\right)}{\pi\,\Gamma(\alpha)\,\Gamma\left(i+\frac{3}{2}\right)\Gamma(i+2\alpha)} \sum_{p=0}^{i} \frac{\Gamma\left(p+\frac{1}{2}\right)\Gamma(i-p+\alpha)\,\Gamma(\alpha+p)\,\Gamma\left(\frac{3}{2}+i-p\right)}{(2p)!\,(2i-2p+1)!} \qquad (49)$$

$$\times \left(V_{j+i-2p}(x) + V_{j+i-2p-1}(x)\right).$$

Proof. Directly from Theorem 7. □

Corollary 15. *For all non-negative integers i and j, the following linearization formulas hold:*

$$L_i(x)\, T_j(x) = \frac{1}{2\pi} \sum_{p=0}^{i} \frac{\Gamma\left(\frac{1}{2}+i-p\right)\Gamma\left(\frac{1}{2}+p\right)}{p!\,(i-p)!}\left(V_{j+i-2p}(x) - V_{j+i-2p-1}(x)\right), \qquad (50)$$

$$U_i(x)\, T_j(x) = \frac{1}{2}\sum_{p=0}^{2i+1} V_{j-i+p-1}(x), \qquad (51)$$

$$T_i(x)\, T_j(x) = \frac{1}{4}\left(V_{j-i}(x) + V_{j-i-1}(x) + V_{j+i}(x) + V_{j+i-1}(x)\right). \qquad (52)$$

Proof. Direct from Corollary 14, taking into consideration the three well-known special classes of $C_i^{(\alpha)}(x)$. □

Remark 3. Many linearization formulas developed in this section can be translated into their trigonometric representations. For example, the linearization Formulas (47) and (51) are, respectively, identical to the following trigonometric identities:

$$\sum_{p=0}^{i}\left\{\sin(j+i-2p+1)\theta - \sin(j+i-2p)\theta\right\} = \frac{\sin((i+1)\theta)\cos\left(\left(j+\tfrac{1}{2}\right)\theta\right)}{\cos\left(\tfrac{\theta}{2}\right)},$$

$$\sum_{p=0}^{2i+1}\cos\left(j-i+p-\tfrac{1}{2}\right)\theta = \frac{2\sin((i+1)\theta)\cos\left(\tfrac{\theta}{2}\right)\cos(j\theta)}{\sin\theta}.$$

5. Some New Linearization Formulas of Chebyshev Polynomials Using the Connection Coefficients Approach

In this section, we give other new linearization formulas of the products of Chebyshev polynomials based on some connection formulas. First, the following theorem and corollary serve in deriving the desired linearization formulas.

Theorem 8. For every non-negative integer j, the following connection formula holds

$$R_j^{(\alpha,\beta)}(x) = \frac{j!\,\Gamma(\alpha+1)\,\Gamma(j+\delta+1)\,\Gamma(2j+\alpha+\beta+1)}{\Gamma(\gamma+1)\,\Gamma(j+\alpha+1)\,\Gamma(j+\alpha+\beta+1)}$$

$$\times \sum_{p=0}^{j} \frac{(\gamma+\delta+2j-2p+1)\,\Gamma(j-p+\gamma+1)\,\Gamma(j-p+\gamma+\delta+1)}{p!\,(j-p)!\,\Gamma(j-p+\delta+1)\,\Gamma(2j-p+\gamma+\delta+2)} \tag{53}$$

$$\times\; {}_3F_2\!\left(\begin{array}{c}-p,\,-\beta-j,\,-\gamma-\delta-2j+p-1\\-\alpha-\beta-2j,\,-\delta-j\end{array}\bigg|\,1\right) R_{j-p}^{(\gamma,\delta)}(x).$$

Corollary 16. For every non-negative integer j, the following connection formula holds

$$C_j^{(\lambda)}(x) = \frac{j!\,4^{\lambda-\mu}\,\Gamma\!\left(\lambda+\tfrac{1}{2}\right)\Gamma(j+\lambda)}{\Gamma\!\left(\mu+\tfrac{1}{2}\right)\Gamma(j+2\lambda)}$$

$$\times \sum_{p=0}^{\lfloor\tfrac{j}{2}\rfloor} \frac{(j+\mu-2p)\,\Gamma(j-2p+2\mu)\,(\lambda-\mu)_p}{p!\,(j-2p)!\,\Gamma(j-p+\mu+1)(j-p+\lambda)_p}\,C_{j-2p}^{(\mu)}(x). \tag{54}$$

Proof. For the proof of Theorem 8 and Corollary 16, one can refer to [41]. □

Theorem 9. For all non-negative integers i and j, and $j \geq i$, the following linearization formula holds:

$$T_i(x)\,U_j(x) = \sum_{r=0}^{j+i} F_{r,j,i}\,R_{j+i-r}^{(\gamma,\delta)}(x) + \sum_{r=0}^{j-i} G_{r,j,i}\,R_{j-i-r}^{(\gamma,\delta)}(x), \tag{55}$$

where

$$F_{r,i,j} = \frac{2^{2i+2j-1}\,(i+j)!\,\Gamma(i+j+\delta+1)\,(\gamma+\delta+2(i+j)-2r+1)}{\Gamma(\gamma+1)\,r!\,(i+j-r)!}$$

$$\times \frac{\Gamma(i+j-r+\gamma+1)\,\Gamma(i+j-r+\gamma+\delta+1)}{\Gamma(i+j-r+\delta+1)\,\Gamma(2(i+j)-r+\gamma+\delta+2)}$$

$$\times\; {}_3F_2\!\left(\begin{array}{c}-r,\,-i-j-\tfrac{1}{2},\,-\gamma-\delta-2i-2j+r-1\\-2i-2j-1,\,-\delta-i-j\end{array}\bigg|\,1\right),$$

and

$$G_{r,i,j} = \frac{2^{-2i+2j-1}(j-i)!\,\Gamma(-i+j+\delta+1)\,(\gamma+\delta-2i+2j-2r+1)}{r!\,\Gamma(\gamma+1)\,(-i+j-r)!}$$
$$\times \frac{\Gamma(-i+j-r+\gamma+1)\,\Gamma(-i+j-r+\gamma+\delta+1)}{\Gamma(-i+j-r+\delta+1)\,\Gamma(-2i+2j-r+\gamma+\delta+2)}$$
$$\times {}_3F_2\left(\begin{array}{c}-r, i-j-\tfrac{1}{2}, -\gamma-\delta+2i-2j+r-1 \\ 2i-2j-1, -\delta+i-j\end{array}\bigg|\,1\right).$$

Proof. Relation (55) can be followed with the aid of linearization Formula (29) along with Theorem 8. □

Theorem 10. *For all non-negative integers i and j, and $j \geq i$, the following linearization formula holds:*

$$T_i(x)\,U_j(x) = \frac{\sqrt{\pi}}{2^{2\mu}\Gamma\left(\mu+\tfrac{1}{2}\right)} \times$$
$$\left(\sum_{r=0}^{\lfloor\frac{i+j}{2}\rfloor} \frac{(-1)^r\,(i+j-r)!\,(\mu-r)_r\,(i+j+\mu-2r)\,\Gamma(i+j-2r+2\mu)}{r!\,(i+j-2r)!\,\Gamma(i+j-r+\mu+1)}\,C^{(\mu)}_{j+i-2r}(x)\right.$$
$$\left.+\sum_{r=0}^{\lfloor\frac{j-i}{2}\rfloor} \frac{(-1)^r\,(-i+j-r)!\,(\mu-r)_r\,(-i+j+\mu-2r)\,\Gamma(-i+j-2r+2\mu)}{r!\,(-i+j-2r)!\,\Gamma(-i+j-r+\mu+1)}\,C^{(\mu)}_{j-i-2r}(x)\right). \tag{56}$$

Proof. Relation (56) can be followed with the aid of linearization Formula (29) along with Corollary 16. □

Corollary 17. *For all non-negative integers i and j with $j \geq i$, the following linearization formula holds*

$$T_i(x)\,U_j(x) = \theta_{i,j} + 2\sum_{k=0}^{\lfloor\frac{j-i}{2}\rfloor} T_{j-i-2k}(x) + \sum_{k=0}^{i-1} T_{j+i-2k}(x),$$

and

$$\theta_{i,j} = \begin{cases} -1, & (i+j) \text{ even,} \\ 0, & (i+j) \text{ odd.} \end{cases}$$

Proof. The last formula can be obtained as a direct special case of the linearization Formula (56) for the special case corresponding to $\mu = 0$. □

Remark 4. *Some other linearization formulas can be derived using Formula (29) together with the two connection Formulas (53) and (54).*

Theorem 11. *For all non-negative integers i and j with $j \geq i$, one has*

$$T_i(x)\,T_j(x) = \sum_{p=0}^{j+i} \xi_{p,i,j}\,R^{(\alpha,\beta)}_{j+i-p}(x) + \sum_{p=0}^{j-i} \eta_{p,i,j}\,R^{(\alpha,\beta)}_{j-i-p}(x), \tag{57}$$

where

$$\xi_{p,i,j} = \frac{4^{-1+i+j}\,(i+j)!\,(1+2i+2j-2p+\alpha+\beta)\,\Gamma(1+i+j-p+\alpha)\,\Gamma(1+i+j+\beta)}{p!\,(i+j-p)!\,\Gamma(1+\alpha)\,\Gamma(1+i+j-p+\beta)}$$

$$\times \frac{\Gamma(1+i+j-p+\alpha+\beta)}{\Gamma(2+2i+2j-p+\alpha+\beta)}\,{}_3F_2\!\left(\begin{array}{c}-p,\tfrac{1}{2}-i-j,-1-2i-2j+p-\alpha-\beta\\ 1-2i-2j,-i-j-\beta\end{array}\Big|\,1\right), \quad (58)$$

and

$$\eta_{p,i,j} = \frac{4^{-1-i+j}\,(1-2i+2j-2p+\alpha+\beta)\,(j-i)!\,\Gamma(1-i+j-p+\alpha)\,\Gamma(1-i+j+\beta)}{p!\,(j-i-p)!\,\Gamma(\alpha+1)\,\Gamma(1-i+j-p+\beta)}$$

$$\times \frac{\Gamma(1-i+j-p+\alpha+\beta)}{\Gamma(2-2i+2j-p+\alpha+\beta)}\,{}_3F_2\!\left(\begin{array}{c}-p,\tfrac{1}{2}+i-j,-1+2i-2j+p-\alpha-\beta\\ 1+2i-2j,i-j-\beta\end{array}\Big|\,1\right). \quad (59)$$

Proof. In view of the well-known linearization formula

$$T_i(x)\,T_j(x) = \frac{1}{2}\bigl(T_{j-i}(x)+T_{j+i}(x)\bigr),$$

together with the connection formula in (53), the linearization Formula (57) can be obtained. □

Remark 5. *The two hypergeometric functions appearing in the coefficients (58) and (59) can be summed by Watson's identity, and hence a reduced linearization formula of Chebyshev polynomials of the first kind in terms of ultraspherical polynomials can be deduced. The following corollary exhibits this result.*

Corollary 18. *For all non-negative integers i and j with $j \geq i$, one has*

$$T_i(x)\,T_j(x) =$$

$$\frac{2^{-1-2\alpha}\,(i+j)\,\sqrt{\pi}\,\Gamma(1+\alpha)}{\Gamma\!\left(\tfrac{1}{2}+\alpha\right)}\sum_{p=0}^{\frac{j+i}{2}}\frac{(-1)^p\,(i+j-2p+\alpha)\,(1+i+j-2p)_{-1+2\alpha}}{p!\,\Gamma(1-p+\alpha)\,(i+j-p)_{1+\alpha}}\,C^{(\alpha)}_{j+i-2p}(x)$$

$$+\frac{2^{-1-2\alpha}\,(i-j)\,\sqrt{\pi}\,\Gamma(1+\alpha)}{\Gamma\!\left(\tfrac{1}{2}+\alpha\right)}\sum_{p=0}^{\frac{j-i}{2}}\frac{(-1)^p\,(i-j+2p-\alpha)\,(1-i+j-2p)_{-1+2\alpha}}{p!\,\Gamma(1-p+\alpha)\,(-i+j-p)_{1+\alpha}}\,C^{(\alpha)}_{j-i-2p}(x). \quad (60)$$

Proof. If we set $\beta = \alpha$ in (57) and each is replaced by $(\alpha - \tfrac{1}{2})$, then the following formula is obtained

$$T_i(x)\,T_j(x) = \frac{2^{-1+2i+2j}\,(i+j)!\,\Gamma\!\left(\tfrac{1}{2}+i+j+\alpha\right)}{\Gamma\!\left(\tfrac{1}{2}+\alpha\right)}\sum_{p=0}^{\frac{j+i}{2}}\frac{(i+j-p+\alpha)\,\Gamma(i+j-p+2\alpha)}{p!\,(i+j-p)!\,\Gamma(1+2i+2j-p+2\alpha)}$$

$$\times\,{}_3F_2\!\left(\begin{array}{c}-p,\tfrac{1}{2}-i-j,-2i-2j+p-2\alpha\\ 1-2i-2j,\tfrac{1}{2}-i-j-\alpha\end{array}\Big|\,1\right)C^{(\alpha)}_{j+i-p}(x)$$

$$+\frac{2^{-1-2i+2j}(j-i)!\,\Gamma\!\left(\tfrac{1}{2}-i+j+\alpha\right)}{\Gamma\!\left(\tfrac{1}{2}+\alpha\right)}\sum_{p=0}^{\frac{j-i}{2}}\frac{(-i+j-p+\alpha)\,\Gamma(-i+j-p+2\alpha)}{p!\,(-i+j-p)!\,\Gamma(1-2i+2j-p+2\alpha)}$$

$$\times\,{}_3F_2\!\left(\begin{array}{c}-p,\tfrac{1}{2}+i-j,2i-2j+p-2\alpha\\ 1+2i-2j,\tfrac{1}{2}+i-j-\alpha\end{array}\Big|\,1\right)C^{(\alpha)}_{j-i-p}(x). \quad (61)$$

Based on Watson's formula, it can be shown that

$$_3F_2\left(\begin{array}{c}-p,\frac{1}{2}-i-j,-2i-2j+p-2\alpha\\1-2i-2j,\frac{1}{2}-i-j-\alpha\end{array}\Big|1\right)=$$

$$\begin{cases}\dfrac{(-1)^{\frac{p}{2}}\left(i+j-\frac{p}{2}-1\right)!\,\Gamma\left(\frac{1+p}{2}\right)\left(1-\frac{p}{2}+\alpha\right)_{\frac{p}{2}}}{\sqrt{\pi}\,(i+j-1)!\,\left(\frac{1}{2}+i+j-\frac{p}{2}+\alpha\right)_{\frac{p}{2}}},&p\text{ even,}\\0,&p\text{ odd,}\end{cases}$$

and

$$_3F_2\left(\begin{array}{c}-p,\frac{1}{2}-i+j,2i-2j+p-2\alpha\\1+2i-2j,\frac{1}{2}i-j-\alpha\end{array}\Big|1\right)=$$

$$\begin{cases}\dfrac{(-1)^{\frac{p}{2}}\left(-i+j-\frac{p}{2}-1\right)!\,\Gamma\left(\frac{1+p}{2}\right)\left(1-\frac{p}{2}+\alpha\right)_{\frac{p}{2}}}{\sqrt{\pi}\,(-i+j-1)!\,\left(\frac{1}{2}-i+j-\frac{p}{2}+\alpha\right)_{\frac{p}{2}}},&p\text{ even,}\\0,&p\text{ odd,}\end{cases}$$

and therefore, Formula (60) can be obtained. □

Corollary 19. *For all non-negative integers i and j with $j \geq i$, the following two linearization formulas are valid*

$$T_i(x)\,T_j(x) = \frac{(i+j)\pi}{16}\sum_{p=0}^{\frac{j+i}{2}}\frac{(-1)^p(1+2i+2j-4p)(i+j-p-1)!}{\Gamma(\frac{3}{2}-p)\Gamma(\frac{3}{2}+i+j-p)p!}L_{j+i-2p}(x) \quad (62)$$

$$+ \frac{(i-j)\pi}{16}\sum_{p=0}^{\frac{j-i}{2}}\frac{(-1)^p(-1+2i-2j+4p)(-i+j-p-1)!}{\Gamma(\frac{3}{2}-p)\Gamma(\frac{3}{2}-i+j-p)p!}L_{j-i-2p}(x),$$

and

$$T_i(x)\,T_j(x) = \frac{1}{4}\left(U_{j+i}(x) - U_{j+i-2}(x) + U_{j-i}(x) - U_{j-i-2}(x)\right). \quad (63)$$

Proof. Setting $\alpha = \frac{1}{2}, 1$, respectively, in Formula (60) yields the two special linearization Formulas (62) and (63). □

6. Numerical Application on the Non-Linear Riccati Equation

In this section, and aiming to illustrate the importance and applicability of the linearization formulas presented in this paper, we shall present a numerical application to a certain non-linear differential equation. More precisely, we will apply the tau spectral method to solve the non-linear Riccai differential equation using some linearization formulas that are established in this paper.

6.1. Tau Algorithm for the Non-Linear Riccati Differential Equation

Here, we are interested in proposing a spectral tau solution for the following non-linear Riccati differential equation:

$$\zeta'(x) = b_1 + b_2\,\zeta(x) + b_3\,(\zeta(x))^2, \quad x \in [0,1], \quad (64)$$

subject to the initial condition:

$$\zeta(0) = \zeta_0, \quad (65)$$

where b_1, b_2 and b_3 are known real constants.

We suggest the following approximate solution to $\xi(x)$

$$\xi(x) \approx \xi_N(x) = \sum_{k=0}^{N} a_k \tilde{C}_k^{(\alpha)}(x); \qquad \tilde{C}_k^{(\alpha)}(x) = C_k^{(\alpha)}(2x-1).$$

In order to proceed in our proposed tau method for solving (64)–(65), the following two lemmas that are concerned with the shifted ultraspherical polynomials are required.

Lemma 1. *For every $k \geq 1$, the following derivative formula holds [47]:*

$$D\tilde{C}_k^{(\alpha)}(x) = \sum_{\ell=0}^{k-1} d_{\ell,k,\alpha} \tilde{C}_\ell^{(\alpha)}(x), \qquad (66)$$

where

$$d_{\ell,k,\alpha} = \frac{4\,\theta_{\ell,k}\,(\ell+\alpha)\,(1+\ell)_{2\alpha-1}}{(1+k)_{2\alpha-1}}, \qquad (67)$$

and

$$\theta_{\ell,k} = \begin{cases} 1, & (\ell+k)\ odd, \\ 0, & (\ell+k)\ even. \end{cases}$$

Lemma 2. *For all non-negative integers i and j, the following linearization formula holds*

$$\tilde{C}_i^{(\alpha)}(x)\,\tilde{C}_j^{(\alpha)}(x) = \sum_{p=0}^{i+j}\sum_{m=0}^{p} L_{p,i,j,\alpha,m}\,\tilde{C}_{i+j-p}^{(\alpha+\frac{1}{2})}(x), \qquad (68)$$

where the coefficients $L_{p,i,j,\alpha,m}$ are given by

$$L_{p,i,j,\alpha,m} = \frac{(-1)^{-m+p}\,2^{2(j+\alpha)}\left(\frac{1}{2}+i+j-p+\alpha\right)i!\,(i+j+m-p)!\left(\Gamma\left(\frac{1}{2}+\alpha\right)\right)^2 \Gamma(j+\alpha)}{\sqrt{\pi}\,m!\,(i+j-p)!\,(i+m-p)!\,(-m+p)!\,\Gamma(i+2\alpha)\,\Gamma(j+2\alpha)}$$

$$\times \frac{\Gamma(1+i+j+m-p+\alpha)\,\Gamma(1+i+j-p+2\alpha)\,\Gamma(2i+m-p+2\alpha)}{\Gamma(1+\alpha)\,\Gamma\left(\frac{1}{2}+i+m-p+\alpha\right)\,\Gamma(2+2i+2j+m-2p+2\alpha)} \qquad (69)$$

$$\times\;{}_4F_3\!\left(\begin{array}{c}-j,\,-m,\,-1-2i-2j-m+2p-2\alpha,\,\frac{1}{2}-j-\alpha\\ -i-j-m+p,\,1-2j-2\alpha,\,-i-j-m+p-\alpha\end{array}\Big|\,1\right).$$

Proof. From Corollary 9, if x is replaced by $(2x-1)$, and if we set $\lambda=\alpha$ and $\gamma=\alpha+\frac{1}{2}$, then Formula (68) can be obtained. □

Now, our strategy to solve (64) governed by (65) is to apply the spectral tau method. Therefore, first, we have to compute the residual of Equation (64). Based on the two expressions in (66) and (68), the residual $R(x)$ can be written in the following form:

$$R(x) = \xi'_N(x) - b_3\,(\xi_N(x))^2 - b_2\,\xi_N(x) - b_1$$

$$= \sum_{k=1}^{N}\sum_{\ell=0}^{k-1} a_k\,d_{\ell,k,\alpha}\,\tilde{C}_\ell^{(\alpha)}(x) - b_3 \sum_{i=0}^{N}\sum_{j=0}^{N}\sum_{p=0}^{i+j}\sum_{m=0}^{p} a_i\,a_j\,L_{p,i,j,\alpha,m}\,\tilde{C}_{i+j-p}^{(\alpha+\frac{1}{2})}(x) - b_2 \sum_{k=0}^{N} a_k\,\tilde{C}_k^{(\alpha)}(x) - b_1, \qquad (70)$$

where $d_{\ell,k,\alpha}$ and $L_{p,i,j,\alpha,m}$ are as given, respectively, in (67) and (69).

Now, by replacing x by $(2x-1)$ in Formula (39), the following linearization formula can be obtained

$$\tilde{C}_m^{(\alpha)}(x)\,T_s^*(x) = \sum_{r=0}^{m+1} \chi_{r,m,s,\alpha}\,U_{m+s-2r}^*(x), \qquad (71)$$

where

$$X_{r,m,s,\alpha} = \frac{4^{-1+\alpha}(1+m-2r)\,m!\,\Gamma\left(\frac{1}{2}+\alpha\right)\Gamma(m-r+\alpha)\Gamma(-1+r+\alpha)}{\sqrt{\pi}\,(1+m-r)!\,r!\,\Gamma(-1+\alpha)\,\Gamma(m+2\alpha)}.$$

Now, Formula (71), along with (70), enables one to get the following formula:

$$R(x)\,T_s^*(x) = \sum_{k=1}^{N}\sum_{\ell=0}^{k-1}\sum_{r=0}^{\ell+1} a_k\, d_{\ell,k,\alpha}\, X_{r,m,s,\alpha}\, U_{\ell+s-2r}^*(x)$$

$$-b_3 \sum_{i=0}^{N}\sum_{j=0}^{N}\sum_{p=0}^{i+j}\sum_{m=0}^{p}\sum_{r=0}^{i+j-p+1} a_i\, a_j\, L_{p,i,j,\alpha,m}\, X_{r,i+j-p,s,\alpha+\frac{1}{2}}\, U_{i+j+s-p-2r}^*(x) \qquad (72)$$

$$-b_2 \sum_{k=0}^{N}\sum_{r=0}^{k+1} a_k\, X_{r,k,s,\alpha}\, U_{k+s-2r}^*(x) - b_1\, T_s^*(x), \quad s \geq 0.$$

If we make use of the connection formula: ([44]):

$$T_s^*(x) = \frac{1}{2}\left(U_s^*(x) - U_{s-2}^*(x)\right), \quad s \geq 0,$$

then Equation (72) can be written alternatively as

$$R(x)\,\tilde{T}_s(x) = \sum_{k=1}^{N}\sum_{\ell=0}^{k-1}\sum_{r=0}^{\ell+1} a_k\, d_{\ell,k,\alpha}\, X_{r,m,s,\alpha}\, U_{\ell+s-2r}^*(x)$$

$$-b_3 \sum_{i=0}^{N}\sum_{j=0}^{N}\sum_{p=0}^{i+j}\sum_{m=0}^{p}\sum_{r=0}^{i+j-p+1} a_i\, a_j\, L_{p,i,j,\alpha,m}\, X_{r,i+j-p,s,\alpha+\frac{1}{2}}\, U_{i+j+s-p-2r}^*(x)$$

$$-b_2 \sum_{k=0}^{N}\sum_{r=0}^{k+1} a_k\, X_{r,k,s,\alpha}\, U_{k+s-2r}^*(x) - \frac{b_1}{2}\left(U_s^*(x) - U_{s-2}^*(x)\right).$$

Based on the application of the spectral tau method, we can assume that

$$\int_0^1 R(x)\,T_s^*(x)\,w(x)\,dx = 0, \quad s = 0,1,\cdots,N-1; \quad w(x) = \sqrt{x-x^2},$$

and accordingly, the orthogonality relation of $U_n^*(x)$ yields the following non-linear system of equations:

$$\sum_{k=1}^{N}\sum_{\ell=0}^{k-1}\sum_{r=0}^{\ell+1} a_k\, d_{\ell,k,\alpha}\, X_{r,m,s,\alpha}\, \delta_{\ell+s-2r,0} - b_3 \sum_{i=0}^{N}\sum_{j=0}^{N}\sum_{p=0}^{i+j}\sum_{m=0}^{p}\sum_{r=0}^{i+j-p+1} a_i\, a_j\, L_{p,i,j,\alpha,m}\, X_{r,i+j-p,s,\alpha+\frac{1}{2}}\, \delta_{i+j+s-p-2r,0}$$

$$-b_2 \sum_{k=0}^{N}\sum_{r=0}^{k+1} a_k\, X_{r,k,s,\alpha}\, \delta_{k+s-2r,0} - \frac{b_1}{2}\left(\delta_{s,0} - \delta_{s-2,0}\right) = 0, \quad s = 0,1,\cdots,N-1, \qquad (73)$$

where $\delta_{k,j}$ denotes the well-known Kronecker delta function.
Furthermore, the initial condition (65) yields

$$\sum_{k=0}^{N}(-1)^k a_k = \zeta_0. \qquad (74)$$

Equation (73), together with Equation (74), yields a non-linear system of equations of dimension N. This system can be solved numerically through a suitable technique such as ... and hence the numerical solution $\zeta_N(x)$ can be obtained.

6.2. Numerical Tests

Now, we give two numerical examples accompanied by some comparisons to show the effectiveness and applicability of the proposed ultraspherical tau method (UTM).

Example 1. *Consider the non-linear Riccati differential Equation ([9,48–51]):*

$$\xi'(x) = 1 + 2\xi(x) - \xi(x)^2, \quad x \in [0,1], \quad \xi(0) = 0, \tag{75}$$

with the following exact solution:

$$\xi(x) = \sqrt{2} \tanh\left(\sqrt{2}x - \tanh^{-1}\left(\frac{1}{\sqrt{2}}\right)\right) + 1.$$

In Table 1, the maximum absolute error E is listed for various values of N and for $\alpha = \frac{1}{2}$. Furthermore, Table 2 illustrates a comparison between the errors resulting from the application of our algorithm for the case corresponding to $N = 16$ and $\alpha = \frac{1}{2}$ with the best errors obtained by the application of the following four methods:

- Optimal homotopy asymptotic method (OHAM) [48],
- Modified homotopy perturbation method (MHPM) [49],
- Variational iteration method (VIM) [50],
- Iterative reproducing kernel Hilbert space method (IRKHSM) [51],
- The method in [9].

The errors are calculated at $x_i = 0.1\,i$, $0 \leq i \leq 10$. The findings of Table 2 demonstrate that our method is extremely accurate when compared to the above-mentioned methods. The generated numerical solutions are in good agreement with the precise one when just a few of the retained modes are used. In addition, different errors of Example 1 for different values of α are displayed in Figure 1.

Table 1. Maximum absolute error E for Example 1 ($\alpha = \frac{1}{2}$).

N	6	8	10	12	14	16
E	$2.358 \cdot 10^{-6}$	$3.264 \cdot 10^{-7}$	$6.382 \cdot 10^{-10}$	$5.943 \cdot 10^{-13}$	$2.975 \cdot 10^{-15}$	$6.241 \cdot 10^{-16}$

Table 2. Comparison between different methods for Example 1.

x	OHAM [48]	MHPM [49]	VIM [50]	IRKHSM [51]	The Method in [9]	UTM ($N = 16$, $\alpha = \frac{1}{2}$)
0	0	0	0	0	0	0
0.1	3.20×10^{-5}	1.00×10^{-6}	1.98×10^{-8}	3.58×10^{-5}	1.52×10^{-15}	1.27×10^{-17}
0.2	2.90×10^{-4}	1.20×10^{-5}	1.03×10^{-6}	7.58×10^{-5}	1.27×10^{-15}	2.23×10^{-17}
0.3	1.10×10^{-3}	1.00×10^{-6}	8.85×10^{-6}	1.20×10^{-4}	2.57×10^{-15}	1.34×10^{-16}
0.4	2.50×10^{-3}	3.03×10^{-4}	3.33×10^{-5}	1.66×10^{-4}	3.27×10^{-15}	2.31×10^{-16}
0.5	4.40×10^{-3}	1.55×10^{-3}	7.26×10^{-5}	2.12×10^{-4}	3.57×10^{-15}	3.68×10^{-16}
0.6	5.50×10^{-3}	4.69×10^{-3}	9.98×10^{-5}	2.52×10^{-4}	4.15×10^{-15}	4.32×10^{-16}
0.7	5.50×10^{-3}	1.05×10^{-2}	8.84×10^{-5}	2.87×10^{-4}	4.21×10^{-15}	4.95×10^{-16}
0.8	3.80×10^{-3}	1.88×10^{-2}	1.54×10^{-5}	3.40×10^{-4}	4.31×10^{-15}	5.62×10^{-16}
0.9	3.20×10^{-3}	2.80×10^{-2}	4.99×10^{-4}	4.90×10^{-4}	4.35×10^{-15}	5.94×10^{-16}
1.0	3.40×10^{-3}	3.43×10^{-2}	3.47×10^{-3}	9.22×10^{-4}	4.42×10^{-15}	6.24×10^{-16}

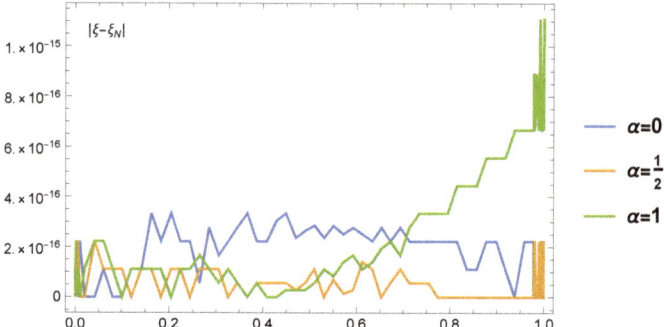

Figure 1. Different errors of Example 1 for different values of α.

Example 2. *Consider the non-linear Riccati differential Equation [52]:*

$$\xi'(x) = \frac{1}{4} + \frac{x^2}{64} - \frac{1}{4}(\xi(x))^2, \quad x \in [0,1], \quad \xi(0) = 1. \tag{76}$$

The exact solution of (76) is $\xi(x) = \frac{x}{4} + \dfrac{4e^{-\frac{x^2}{16}}}{4 + \int_0^x e^{-\frac{t^2}{16}} dt}$.

Table 3 displays the maximum absolute errors resulting from the application of the UTM for $\alpha = 0, \frac{1}{2}, 1$ and for different values of N. Furthermore, different errors for the cases corresponding to $N = 16$ and $\alpha = 0, \frac{1}{2}, 1$ are shown in Figure 2.

Table 3. Maximum absolute error for Example 2.

N	8	10	12	14	16
$\alpha = 0$	3.51×10^{-8}	2.45×10^{-9}	2.39×10^{-11}	5.94×10^{-13}	5.37×10^{-16}
$\alpha = \frac{1}{2}$	1.38×10^{-8}	3.27×10^{-10}	8.36×10^{-12}	4.62×10^{-12}	3.74×10^{-16}
$\alpha = 1$	4.58×10^{-8}	3.19×10^{-9}	4.94×10^{-11}	6.84×10^{-13}	2.22×10^{-16}

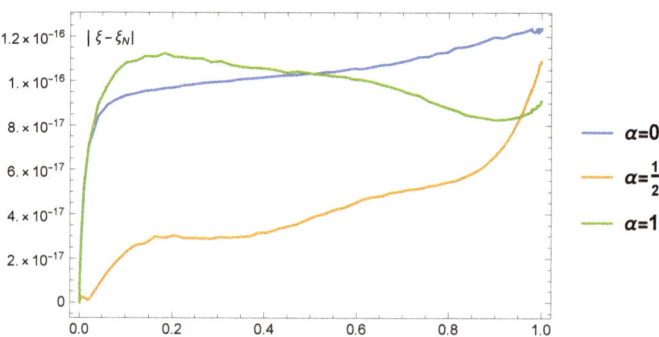

Figure 2. Different errors of Example 2 for different values of α.

Remark 6. *We report here that, the best error obtained by Lakestani and Dehghan is $\mathbf{O}(10^{-9})$, from the results depicted in Figure 2, we have a major superiority with few number of retained modes.*

7. Conclusions

In this paper, we have considered two different approaches for solving the linearization problems of Jacobi polynomials. The first approach is based on making use of the general linearization formulas of some Jacobi polynomials in terms of certain terminating hypergeometric functions of a unit argument. Symbolic algebra serves to simplify the linearization formulas of Jacobi polynomials for certain choices of the involved parameters. We also followed another approach to establish some linearization formulas. This approach depends on employing the connection formula between two different Jacobi polynomials. Again, the presented formulas were expressed in different terminating hypergeometric functions of unit argument. In many cases, and using some well-known reduction formulas or some symbolic computation, the appearing hypergeometric functions can be summed in closed analytical forms. The main advantage of using the moments formulas in establishing the linearization formulas is that this approach can be employed to derive the linearization formulas of different polynomials and not restricted to the Jacobi polynomials. To the best of our knowledge, most of the theoretical results of this paper are new and are very useful. To ensure the importance of the presented formulas, a numerical application is analyzed in detail to solve the non-linear Riccati differential equation with the aid of employing the spectral tau method. The presented numerical results and comparisons showed the high accuracy and applicability to the proposed numerical algorithm. We believe that other types of differential equations can be treated based on utilizing the presented linearization formulas.

Author Contributions: W.M.A.-E. presented the idea and algorithms as a supervisor. W.M.A.-E. and B.M.B. contributed to the preparation of the paper. All authors have read and agreed to the published version of the manuscript.

Funding: This research received no external funding.

Institutional Review Board Statement: Not applicable.

Informed Consent Statement: Not applicable.

Data Availability Statement: Not applicable.

Acknowledgments: The authors would like to thank the editor for their cooperation and the anonymous reviewers for their valuable comments, which have improved the paper in its present form.

Conflicts of Interest: The authors declare no conflict of interest.

References

1. Quintana, Y.; Ramírez, W.; Urieles, A. On an operational matrix method based on generalized Bernoulli polynomials of level m. *Calcolo* **2018**, *55*, 1–29. [CrossRef]
2. Fitri, S.; Thomas, D.K.; Wibowo, R.B.E. Coefficient inequalities for a subclass of Bazilevič functions. *Demonstratio Math.* **2020**, *53*, 27–37. [CrossRef]
3. Urieles, A.; Ortega, M.J.; Ramírez, W.; Vega, S. New results on the q-generalized Bernoulli polynomials of level m. *Demonstratio Math.* **2019**, *52*, 511–522. [CrossRef]
4. Doha, E.H.; Abd-Elhameed, W.M.; Bassuony, M.A. On the coefficients of differentiated expansions and derivatives of Chebyshev polynomials of the third and fourth kinds. *Acta Math. Sci.* **2015**, *35*, 326–338. [CrossRef]
5. Doha, E.H.; Abd-Elhameed, W.M. On the coefficients of integrated expansions and integrals of Chebyshev polynomials of third and fourth kinds. *Bull. Malays. Math. Sci. Soc.* **2014**, *37*, 383–398.
6. Abd-Elhameed, W.M.; Alkenedri, A.M. Spectral solutions of linear and nonlinear BVPs using certain Jacobi polynomials generalizing third-and fourth-kinds of Chebyshev polynomials. *CMES Comput. Model. Eng. Sci.* **2021**, *126*, 955–989.
7. Sánchez-Ruiz, J. Logarithmic potential of Hermite polynomials and information entropies of the harmonic oscillator eigenstates. *J. Math. Phys.* **1997**, *38*, 5031–5043. [CrossRef]
8. Dehesa, J.S.; Finkelshtdein, A.M.; Sánchez-Ruiz, J. Quantum information entropies and orthogonal polynomials. *J. Comput. Appl. Math.* **2001**, *133*, 23–46. [CrossRef]
9. Abd-Elhameed, W.M. New formulae between Jacobi polynomials and some fractional Jacobi functions generalizing some connection formulae. *Anal. Math. Phys.* **2019**, *9*, 73–98. [CrossRef]
10. Abd-Elhameed, W.M. Novel expressions for the derivatives of sixth-kind Chebyshev polynomials: Spectral solution of the non-linear one-dimensional Burgers' equation. *Fractal Fract.* **2021**, *5*, 74. [CrossRef]
11. Askey, R.; Gasper, G. Linearization of the product of Jacobi polynomials. III. *Canad. J. Math.* **1971**, *23*, 332–338. [CrossRef]
12. Gasper, G. Linearization of the product of Jacobi polynomials. I. *Canad. J. Math.* **1970**, *22*, 171–175. [CrossRef]
13. Gasper, G. Linearization of the product of Jacobi polynomials. II. *Canad. J. Math.* **1970**, *22*, 582–593. [CrossRef]

14. Hylleraas, E.A. Linearization of products of Jacobi polynomials. *Math. Scan.* **1962**, *10*, 189–200. [CrossRef]
15. Rahman, M. A non-negative representation of the linearization coefficients of the product of Jacobi polynomials. *Canad. J. Math.* **1981**, *33*, 915–928. [CrossRef]
16. Sánchez-Ruiz, J.; Dehesa, J.S. Some connection and linearization problems for polynomials in and beyond the Askey scheme. *J. Comput. Appl. Math.* **2001**, *133*, 579–591. [CrossRef]
17. Chaggara, H.; Koepf, W. On linearization coefficients of Jacobi polynomials. *Appl. Math. Lett.* **2010**, *23*, 609–614. [CrossRef]
18. Srivastava, H.M. A unified theory of polynomial expansions and their applications involving Clebsch-Gordan type linearization relations and Neumann series. *Astrophys. Space Sci.* **1988**, *150*, 251–266. [CrossRef]
19. Srivastava, H.M.; Niukkanen, A.W. Some Clebsch-Gordan type linearization relations and associated families of Dirichlet integrals. *Math. Comput. Model.* **2003**, *37*, 245–250. [CrossRef]
20. Niukkanen, A.W. Clebsch-Gordan-type linearisation relations for the products of Laguerre polynomials and hydrogen-like functions. *J. Phy. A Math. Gen.* **1985**, *18*, 1399. [CrossRef]
21. Kim, T.; Kim, D.S.; Lee, H.; Kwon, J. Studies in sums of finite products of the second, third, and fourth kind Chebyshev polynomials. *Mathematics* **2020**, *8*, 210. [CrossRef]
22. Dolgy, D.V.; Kim, D.S.; Kim, T.; Kwon, J. Connection problem for sums of finite products of Chebyshev polynomials of the third and fourth kinds. *Symmetry* **2018**, *10*, 617. [CrossRef]
23. Kim, T.; Kim, D.S.; Dolgy, D.V.; Park, J.W. Sums of finite products of Legendre and Laguerre polynomials. *Adv. Differ. Equ.* **2018**, *2018*, 277. [CrossRef]
24. Kim, T.; Kim, D.S.; Jang, L.C.; Dolgy, D.V. Representing by several orthogonal polynomials for sums of finite products of Chebyshev polynomials of the first kind and Lucas polynomials. *Adv. Difference Equ.* **2019**, *2019*, 162. [CrossRef]
25. Kim, T.; Kim, D.S.; Jang, L.C.; Jang, G.W. Fourier series for functions related to Chebyshev polynomials of the first kind and Lucas polynomials. *Mathematics* **2018**, *6*, 276. [CrossRef]
26. Kim, D.S.; Dolgy, D.V.; Kim, D.; Kim, T. Representing by orthogonal polynomials for sums of finite products of Fubini polynomials. *Mathematics* **2019**, *7*, 319. [CrossRef]
27. Kim, D.S.; Kim, T. On sums of finite products of balancing polynomials. *J. Comput. Appl. Math.* **2020**, *377*, 112913. [CrossRef]
28. Doha, E.H.; Abd-Elhameed, W.M. New linearization formulae for the products of Chebyshev polynomials of third and fourth kinds. *Rocky Mountain J. Math.* **2016**, *46*, 443–460. [CrossRef]
29. Abd-Elhameed, W.M.; Doha, E.H.; Ahmed, H.M. Linearization formulae for certain Jacobi polynomials. *Ramanujan J.* **2016**, *39*, 155–168. [CrossRef]
30. Abd-Elhameed, W.M. New product and linearization formulae of Jacobi polynomials of certain parameters. *Integral Transforms Spec. Funct.* **2015**, *26*, 586–599. [CrossRef]
31. Abd-Elhameed, W.M. New formulas for the linearization coefficients of some nonsymmetric Jacobi polynomials. *Adv. Differ. Equ.* **2015**, *2015*, 168. [CrossRef]
32. Sánchez-Ruiz, J. Linearization and connection formulae involving squares of Gegenbauer polynomials. *Appl. Math. Lett.* **2001**, *14*, 261–267. [CrossRef]
33. Abd-Elhameed, W.M. New formulae of squares of some Jacobi polynomials via hypergeometric functions. *Hacet. J. Math. Stat.* **2017**, *46*, 165–176. [CrossRef]
34. Abd-Elhameed, W.M.; Badah, B.M. New specific and general linearization formulas of some classes of Jacobi polynomials. *Mathematics* **2021**, *9*, 74. [CrossRef]
35. Srivastava, H.M. Some Clebsch-Gordan type linearisation relations and other polynomial expansions associated with a class of generalised multiple hypergeometric series arising in physical and quantum chemical applications. *J. Phys. A Math. Gen.* **1988**, *21*, 4463. [CrossRef]
36. Ahmed, H.M. Computing expansions coefficients for Laguerre polynomials. *Integral Transform Spec. Funct.* **2020**. [CrossRef]
37. Abd-Elhameed, W.M.; Youssri, Y.H. Neoteric formulas of the monic orthogonal Chebyshev polynomials of the sixth-kind involving moments and linearization formulas. *Adv. Difference Equ.* **2021**, *2021*. 84. [CrossRef]
38. Markett, C. Linearization of the product of symmetric orthogonal polynomials. *Constr. Approx.* **1994**, *10*, 317–338. [CrossRef]
39. Popov, B.S.; Srivastava, H.M. Linearization of a product of two polynomials of different orthogonal systems. *Facta Univ. Ser. Math. Inform* **2003**, *18*, 1–8.
40. Olver, F.W.; Lozier, D.W.; Boisvert, R.F.; Clark, C.W. *NIST Handbook of Mathematical Functions Hardback and CD-ROM*; Cambridge University Press: Cambridge, UK, 2010.
41. Andrews, G.E.; Askey, R.; Roy, R. *Special Functions*; Cambridge University Press: Cambridge, UK, 1999.
42. Rainville, E.D. *Special Functions*; The Maximalan Company: New York, NY, USA, 1960.
43. Doha, E.H.; Abd-Elhameed, W.M.; Ahmed, H.M. The coefficients of differentiated expansions of double and triple Jacobi polynomials. *Bull. Iranian Math. Soc.* **2012**, *38*, 739–765.
44. Mason, J.C.; Handscomb, D.C. *Chebyshev Polynomials*; Chapman and Hall: New York, NY, USA; CRC: Boca Raton, FL, USA, 2003.
45. Koepf, W. *Hypergeometric Summation: An Algorithmic Approach to Summation and Special Function Identities*, 2nd ed.; Springer Universitext; Springer: London, UK, 2014.
46. Van Hoeij, M. Finite singularities and hypergeometric solutions of linear recurrence equations. *J. Pure Appl. Algebra* **1999**,

47. Doha, E.H.; Abd-Elhameed, W.M. Efficient spectral-Galerkin algorithms for direct solution of second-order equations using ultraspherical polynomials. *SIAM J. Sci. Comput.* **2002**, *24*, 548–571. [CrossRef]
48. Mabood, F.; Ismail, A.; Hashim, I. Application of optimal homotopy asymptotic method for the approximate solution of Riccati equation. *Sains Malays.* **2013**, *42*, 863–867.
49. Odibat, Z.; Momani, S. Modified homotopy perturbation method: Application to quadratic Riccati differential equation of fractional order. *Chaos Solitons Fractals* **2008**, *36*, 167–174. [CrossRef]
50. Batiha, B.; Noorani, M.S.M.; Hashim, I. Application of variational iteration method to a general Riccati equation. *Int. Math. Forum* **2007**, *2*, 2759–2770. [CrossRef]
51. Sakar, M. Iterative reproducing kernel Hilbert spaces method for Riccati differential equations. *J. Comput. Appl. Math.* **2017**, *309*, 163–174. [CrossRef]
52. Lakestani, M.; Dehghan, M. Numerical solution of Riccati equation using the cubic B-spline scaling functions and Chebyshev cardinal functions. *Comput. Phys. Commun.* **2010**, *181*, 957–966. [CrossRef]

Article

Polynomial Analogue of Gandy's Fixed Point Theorem

Sergey Goncharov *,† and Andrey Nechesov *,†

Sobolev Institute of Mathematics, Academician Koptyug Ave., 4, 630090 Novosibirsk, Russia
* Correspondence: s.s.goncharov@math.nsc.ru (S.G.); nechesov@math.nsc.ru (A.N.)
† These authors contributed equally to this work.

Abstract: The paper suggests a general method for proving the fact whether a certain set is p-computable or not. The method is based on a polynomial analogue of the classical Gandy's fixed point theorem. Classical Gandy's theorem deals with the extension of a predicate through a special operator $\Gamma^{\Omega^*}_{\Phi(x)}$ and states that the smallest fixed point of this operator is a Σ-set. Our work uses a new type of operator which extends predicates so that the smallest fixed point remains a p-computable set. Moreover, if in the classical Gandy's fixed point theorem, the special Σ-formula $\Phi(\overline{x})$ is used in the construction of the operator, then a new operator uses special generating families of formulas instead of a single formula. This work opens up broad prospects for the application of the polynomial analogue of Gandy's theorem in the construction of new types of terms and formulas, in the construction of new data types and programs of polynomial computational complexity in Turing complete languages.

Keywords: polynomial computability; p-computability; Gandy's fixed point theorem; semantic programming; polynomial operators; Δ_0^p-operators; computer science

1. Introduction

In both mathematics and programming, we are increasingly confronted with inductively given constructs. These constructs can be, for example, new types of terms and formulas in logic or programs and new data types in high-level programming languages that are inductively defined using basic tools. All these inductively generated sets can be viewed as the smallest fixed points of a suitable operator. Classical Gandy's theorem [1,2] allows us to inductively define some abstract set through the special operator $\Gamma^{\Omega^*}_{\Phi(x)}$ [1] where the smallest fixed point will be a Σ-set. The Σ-set is most often not a computable set and, moreover, not a p-computable set. Therefore, the question arises of how to modify Gandy's theorem so that the smallest fixed point be a computable or a p-computable set. In this paper, we just talk about the construction of a Δ_0^p-operator with the smallest fixed point being a p-computable set, which allows us to consider many inductive formulas definable constructions as some polynomially computable set.

2. P-Computability

Let Σ be a finite alphabet and $A, B \subseteq \Sigma^*$ where Σ^* is the set of finite words over the alphabet Σ. We say that a function $f : A \to B$ is p-computable [3–5] if there exists a one-tape/multi-tapes deterministic Turing machine T over the alphabet Σ and numbers $C, p \in N$ such that for all a from A the value of the function $f(a)$ is computed on T in at most $C \cdot |a|^p$ steps, where $|a| \geq 1$. The set A is called p-computable if its characteristic function $\chi_A : \Sigma^* \to \{0,1\}$ is p-computable. The class P of problems which can be solved in polynomial time will often be denoted by Δ_0^p (accepted notation for the polynomial hierarchy). Therefore, the notation Δ_0^p-function for a p-computable function and Δ_0^p-set for a p-computable set will also be used. A partial function $f : A \to B$ is called a partial p-computable function, if there exists a set $D \subseteq A$ such that $f : D \to B$ is a p-computable

q_0) and $f(a)$ is undefined (notation $f(a) \uparrow^p$ or simple $\uparrow^p$) if $a \in A \backslash D$, while the Turing machine on the element $a \in A \backslash D$ stops at the final state q_1 and number of steps does not exceed $C * |a|^p$ steps. As we can see, the partial p-computable function is a p-computable function, but sometimes it is convenient to assume that the value of a p-computable function is undefined. We will also denote partial p-computable functions as Δ_0^p-functions.

3. Word Splitting

Now let Σ_0 be some finite alphabet and $\Sigma = \Sigma_0 \cup \{<,>\} \cup \{,\}$ is a new alphabet obtained by adding new symbols (brackets and comma) to Σ_0. Word splitting is the following partial function $R : \Sigma^* \to (\Sigma \cup \{\#\})^*$ such that:

$$R(w) = \begin{cases} w_1\#...\#w_n, \text{ where } w =< w_1,...,w_n > \text{ and every } w_i \in \Sigma^* \text{ satisfies (1) or (2)} \\ \uparrow, \text{ otherwise} \end{cases}$$

(1) $w_i \in \Sigma_0^*$
(2) w_i starts with a left bracket and the number of left brackets in the word is equal to the number of right brackets, while for any initial subword α_i such that $w_i = \alpha_i \beta_i$ it is not implemented, where the word w_i can be represented as some concatenation of the words $\alpha_i, \beta_i \in \Sigma^*$ and $|\alpha_i| \geq 1$.

Proposition 1. *The word splitting is unique.*

Proof. Prove by contradiction. Let there be two different splittings $R(w) = w_1\#...\#w_n$ and $R(w) = l_1\#...\#l_k$ such that $w =< w_1,...,w_n >$ and $w =< l_1,...,l_k >$. Then, by definition, either $w_1, l_1 \in \Sigma_0^*$, or w_1 and l_1 start with a left bracket and the number of right and left brackets for each word is the same. In the first case, w_1 and l_1 are the same. In the second case, w_1 is the subword of l_1 or l_1 is the subword of w_1. Then, by definition, no proper subword starting with a left bracket can have an equal number of right and left brackets. Equality of words was also obtained. Further, in a similar way, we show that the remaining $w_i = l_i$ and at the same time $n = k$. □

Proposition 2. $R(w)$ is Δ_0^p-function.

Proof. Consider a Turing machine T with two semi-tapes (hereafter called tapes) over the alphabet $\Sigma \cup \{1, B, \#\}$ where B is an empty symbol:
(1) The 1st tape: we will store the word w.
(2) The 2nd tape: we will store the difference between the number of left and right brackets of the word w.
Algorithm of the multi-tapes machine:
(1) If the first symbol on the first tape is not a left bracket, then T stops the work in the final state q_1. Otherwise, T replaces it on B symbol and goes on to the next steps.
(2) If the second symbol in the word w is from Σ_0, then T reads the word w until it meets a symbol, not from Σ_0. If it is not a comma or a right bracket then T stops the work in state q_1.
(3) If the second symbol is not from Σ_0 and is not a left bracket, then T stops the work in the state q_1.
(4) When T reads the left bracket of the word w, then T adds 1 on the second tape and shifts the head of the second tape to the right and when T reads the right bracket of the word w, then T replaces symbol 1 with B of the second tape and shifts the head of the second tape to the left.
(5) If there are no more symbols 1 on the second tape when T reads the right bracket from the first tape, then the machine replaces the right bracket with B on the first tape. If there are no other symbols from Σ after this right bracket, then the machine stops work in the final state q_0, otherwise, in the final state q_1.
(6) If T meets a comma on the first tape and there are no symbols 1 on the second tape, then T replaces this comma with $\#$ symbol.

Computational complexity $R(w)$:
(1) T reads the word w on the first tape periodically replacing the comma or brackets with symbol #. The number of such steps does not exceed $|w|$.
(2) On the second tape T writes or erases symbols 1. The number of such additions and removals does not exceed $|w|$.
(3) Steps from (1) and (2) taken simultaneously. It turns out that the computational complexity $t(R(w)) \leq |w|$. □

Inductively define the notion rank of element $r(w)$ for $w \in \Sigma^*$:

$$r(w) = \begin{cases} 0, & \text{if } R(w) \uparrow^p \\ sup\{r(w_1), \ldots, r(w_k)\} + 1, & \text{if } R(w) = w_1 \# \ldots \# w_k \end{cases}$$

4. Generating Formulas and Families. False Element

Let $\mathfrak{M}$ be a model of signature $\sigma = \{c_1, \ldots, c_r, f_1^{(m_1)}, \ldots, f_s^{(m_s)}, R_1^{(p_1)}, \ldots, R_t^{(p_t)}, P_1^{(1)}, \ldots, P_n^{(1)}\}$ with the basic set $M \subseteq \Sigma_0^*$, where c_l is constant symbols ($l \in [1, \ldots, r]$), f_i is functional symbols ($i \in [1, \ldots, s]$), R_j is predicate symbols ($j \in [1, \ldots, t]$), P_k is unary predicate symbols, $k \in [1, \ldots, n]$. $P(\Sigma^*)$ is the set of all subsets of the set Σ^*. $F_{P_1^+}, \ldots, F_{P_n^+}$ is families(generating families) positive quantifier-free formulas (hereafter called generating formulas) of signature σ which can include unary predicates $P_1, \ldots, P_n$ with inputs of the form $P_j(x_i)$. Moreover, we require that for any free variable x_i in the formula $\varphi_m \in F_{P_k^+}$ there should be no occurrences of the form $P_j(x_i)$ and $P_h(x_i)$ for each x_i, where $j \neq h$. This property will be called predicate separability.

The idea is to generate new elements in the form of lists $< a_1, \ldots, a_{n_m} >$ obtained from $a_1, \ldots, a_{n_m} \in M$ such that $\mathfrak{M} \models \varphi_m(a_1, \ldots, a_{n_m})$ and then add this set of elements Q_i to the main set of the model where:

$$Q_i = \cup_{\varphi_m(x_1, \ldots, x_{n_m}) \in F_{P_i^+}} \{< a_1, \ldots, a_{n_m} > \mid \mathfrak{M} \models \varphi_m(a_1, \ldots, a_{n_m})\}$$

If we are to extend the main set of elements M of the model $\mathfrak{M}$ to this new set of elements Q_i, then we need to redefine the functions on these new elements and redefine the truth of the predicates. It is clear that the functions on new elements will not be defined, so we will expand the basic set of elements M of the $\mathfrak{M}$ model of signature σ with a special $false$-element to $M \cup \{false\}$. Next, we define the semantic meaning of terms and formulas in the $\mathfrak{M}_{false}$ model for all elements from $\Sigma^* \cup \{false\}$ and not only for $M \cup \{false\}$.

Since everywhere below only positive quantifier-free formulas with a positive occurrence in the form of $P_i(x_j)$ for some P_i and x_j appear, then for these formulas on the model $\mathfrak{M}_{false}$ we inductively define the values of functions and the truth of predicates as well as the truth of positive quantifier-free formulas $\varphi_i, i \in I$:
(1) $\mathfrak{M} \models \varphi_i(a_1, \ldots, a_k)$ if and only if $\mathfrak{M}_{false} \models \varphi_i(a_1, \ldots, a_k)$ where $a_1, \ldots, a_k \in M$.
(2) the function value $f_j(a_1, \ldots, a_{n_j})$ equal $false$, if at least one $a_i \in \Sigma^* \cup \{false\} \setminus M$, $j \in [1, \ldots, s]$
(3) the function value $f_j(t_1(\bar{a}), \ldots, t_n(\bar{a}))$ equal $false$ if at least the value of one of the terms $t_j(\bar{a})$ equals $false$.
(4) the formulas of the form $false = t(a_1, \ldots, a_n)$ including $false = false$ will be considered false.
(5) the formulas of the form $a = a$ will be considered true for $a \in M$ and false otherwise.
(6) the formulas of the form $R_i(t_1(\bar{a}), \ldots, t_{n_i}(\bar{a}))$ will be considered false if at least one of the terms $t_j(\bar{a})$ has value $false$.
(7) $\mathfrak{M} \models P(a)$ if and only if $\mathfrak{M}_{false} \models P(a)$ where $a \in M$.
(8) $\Phi\&\Psi, \Phi \vee \Psi$ retain their standard definitions of truth.
Let us denote enrichment of the model $\mathfrak{M}_{false}$ by $< \mathfrak{M}_{false}, Q >$ such that:
(1) $M \cup \{false\} \cup Q$ is a new main set.

from M and are $false$ otherwise.

(3) All predicates $P_j(a)$ remain unchanged if $a \in M$ and $P_j(a)$ are *false* otherwise.
(4) All functions $f_i(a_1,\ldots,a_n)$ remain unchanged for $a_1,\ldots,a_n \in M$ and have a *false* value otherwise.

Denote the expression $< \mathfrak{M}_{false}, Q, P_i >$ it is $< \mathfrak{M}_{false}, Q >$ enrichment at which the truth set of the predicate P_i is extended to $P_i^{\mathfrak{M}_{false}} \cup Q$.

5. Fixed Points of Monotone Locally Finite Operators

Let $\mathfrak{M}_{false}$ be a model of signature σ and $Q = (Q_1,\ldots,Q_n)$, $Q_i \subseteq \Sigma^*$, $i \in [1,\ldots,n]$. Then we introduce the notation: $\mathfrak{M}_{false}^{(Q_1,\ldots,Q_n)} = <<\cdots < \mathfrak{M}_{false}, Q_1, P_1 > \cdots >, Q_n, P_n >$.

Construct an operator:

$$\Gamma^{\mathfrak{M}}_{F_{P_1^+},\ldots,F_{P_n^+}} : P(\Sigma^*) \times \cdots \times P(\Sigma^*) \to P(\Sigma^*) \times \ldots \times P(\Sigma^*), \tag{1}$$

which transfers n-th sets $(Q_1,\ldots,Q_n)$ to n-th sets $(Q'_1,\ldots,Q'_n)$ according to the following rule: $Q'_i = Q_i \cup \bigcup_{\varphi_m(x_1,\ldots,x_{k_m}) \in F_{P_i^+}} \{<a_1,\ldots,a_{k_m}> \mid \mathfrak{M}_{false}^{(i-1)} \models \varphi_m(a_1,\ldots,a_{k_m})\}$.

where $\varphi_m \in F_{P_i^+}$, $a_1,\ldots,a_{k_m} \in M^{(i-1)}$ and $\mathfrak{M}_{false}^{(i-1)}$ is built on the model $\mathfrak{M}_{false}$ of signature σ in the following way:

$$\mathfrak{M}_{false}^{(0)} = \mathfrak{M}_{false},\ldots, \mathfrak{M}_{false}^{(i)} = <\mathfrak{M}_{false}^{(i-1)}, Q'_i, P_i>, \text{where } i \in [1,\ldots,n].$$

We fix a partial order $\leq_n$: $(Q_1,\ldots,Q_n) \leq_n (R_1,\ldots,R_n)$, if $Q_i \subseteq R_i$ for all $i \in [1,\ldots,n]$

Remark 1. *Operator* $\Gamma^{\mathfrak{M}}_{F_{P_1^+},\ldots,F_{P_n^+}}$ *is monotone with respect to the order $\leq_n$, i.e.,*

$$(Q_1,\ldots,Q_n) \leq_n (R_1,\ldots,R_n) \Rightarrow \Gamma^{\mathfrak{M}}_{F_{P_1^+},\ldots,F_{P_n^+}}(Q_1,\ldots,Q_n) \leq_n \Gamma^{\mathfrak{M}}_{F_{P_1^+},\ldots,F_{P_n^+}}(R_1,\ldots,R_n).$$

Remark 2. *Operator* $\Gamma^{\mathfrak{M}}_{F_{P_1^+},\ldots,F_{P_n^+}}$ *possesses the property of a fixed point, i.e.:*

$$(Q_1,\ldots,Q_n) \leq_n \Gamma^{\mathfrak{M}}_{F_{P_1^+},\ldots,F_{P_n^+}}(Q_1,\ldots,Q_n).$$

Associate the operator $\Gamma^{\mathfrak{M}}_{F_{P_1^+},\ldots,F_{P_n^+}}$ with the sequence: $\Gamma_0, \Gamma_1,\ldots,\Gamma_t,\ldots$:

$$\Gamma_0 = \{\emptyset,\ldots,\emptyset\} \leq_n \cdots \leq_n \Gamma_{t+1} = \Gamma^{\mathfrak{M}}_{F_{P_1^+},\ldots,F_{P_n^+}}(\Gamma_t) \leq_n \cdots \leq_n \Gamma_w = \bigcup_{k<w} \Gamma_k. \tag{2}$$

Let us denote projection onto the j-th coordinate by $I_j(\Gamma_k) = Q_j$.

We will say that operator $\Gamma : P(\Sigma^*) \times \ldots \times P(\Sigma^*) \to P(\Sigma^*) \times \ldots \times P(\Sigma^*)$ is locally finite if for any $X_1,\ldots,X_n \subseteq \Sigma^*$ and any $j \in [1,\ldots,n]$ is done:

$$I_j(\Gamma(X_1,\ldots,X_n)) = \bigcup_{X'_1 \subseteq X_1} \cdots \bigcup_{X'_n \subseteq X_n} I_j(\Gamma(X'_1,\ldots,X'_n)), \tag{3}$$

where $X'_1,\ldots,X'_n$ are finite sets.

Proposition 3. *Operator* $\Gamma^{\mathfrak{M}}_{F_{P_1^+},\ldots,F_{P_n^+}}$ *is locally finite.*

Proof. Let $X_1,\ldots,X_n \subseteq \Sigma^*$, where X'_i are finite sets.
$\Leftarrow$ Inclusion in equality (3) for operator $\Gamma^{\mathfrak{M}}_{F_{P_1^+},\ldots,F_{P_n^+}}$ in one way is fulfilled by construction of our operator $\Gamma^{\mathfrak{M}}_{F_{P_1^+},\ldots,F_{P_n^+}}$.

$\Rightarrow$ Let w be from $I_j(\Gamma^{\mathfrak{M}}_{F_{P_1^+},\ldots,F_{P_n^+}}(X_1,\ldots,X_n))$. We get that w is a finite list made up of a finite number of elements from $M \cup X_1 \cup \cdots \cup X_n$. Mark all the elements involved in constructing w from X_j as C_j for all $j \in [1,\ldots,n]$. Note that all sets C_j are finite and $C_j \subseteq X_j$. Therefore, narrowing our sets X_i to C_i we get $w \in I_j(\Gamma^{\mathfrak{M}}_{F_{P_1^+},\ldots,F_{P_n^+}}(C_1,\ldots,C_n))$. □

Proposition 4. *The smallest fixed point of the operator* $\Gamma^{\mathfrak{M}}_{F_{P_1^+},\ldots,F_{P_n^+}}$ *is reached in w steps.*

Proof. Claim that the fixed point of the operator $\Gamma^{\mathfrak{M}}_{F_{P_1^+},\ldots,F_{P_n^+}}$ is reached in w steps following automatically from the fact that the operator $\Gamma^{\mathfrak{M}}_{F_{P_1^+},\ldots,F_{P_n^+}}$ is monotone, has the fixed point property and is locally finite. □

6. Formulas Families $F^*_{P_i^+}$

Further, we will consider generating families of formulas of the form $F_{P_i^+} = \{\varphi_m(\underline{x_1},\ldots,\underline{x_{n_m}})\}|m \in N\}$ where $\underline{x_i}$ is encoding the variable x_i with a string of v symbols length i. Let ϵ be a string of symbols above the alphabet $\{0,1\}$ length n_m. Then the formula $\varphi^\epsilon_m(\underline{x_1},\ldots,\underline{x_{n_m}})$ is obtained from $\varphi_m(\underline{x_1},\ldots,\underline{x_{n_m}})$ replacing all occurrences of the form $P_j(\underline{x_i})$ on i-th symbol in word ϵ. The number of free variables in this formula may be less, nevertheless we leave their number in the notation for φ^ϵ_m as before.

$$F^*_{P_i^+} = \{\varphi^\epsilon_m(\underline{x_1},\ldots,\underline{x_{n_m}})|\; \varphi_m(\underline{x_1},\ldots,\underline{x_{n_m}}) \in F_{P_i^+}, \epsilon \in \{0,1\}^* \text{ and } |\epsilon| = n_m\}$$

The formula $\varphi^\epsilon_m(l_1,\ldots,l_{n_m})$ is obtained from $\varphi^\epsilon_m(\underline{x_1},\ldots,\underline{x_{n_m}})$ substituting free variables $\underline{x_i}$ by the corresponding values l_i for all $i \in [1,\ldots,n_m]$. Due to the predicate separability of the formula φ_m the maximum number of such occurrences in φ^ϵ_m may not be more than n_m.

Define $\Omega = \Sigma \cup \sigma \cup \{0,1\} \cup \{v\} \cup \{\#\} \cup \{\vee,\&\} \cup \{(,)\}$ as a set of symbols such that any formula of the form $\varphi_m(\underline{x_1},\ldots,\underline{x_{n_m}})$, $\varphi_m(l_1,\ldots,l_{n_m})$, $\varphi^\epsilon_m(\underline{x_1},\ldots,\underline{x_{n_m}})$, $\varphi^\epsilon_m(l_1,\ldots,l_{n_m})$ $\in \Omega^*$, where $l_1,\ldots,l_{n_m} \in \Sigma^*$, $\varphi_m \in F_{P_j^+}$ for some $j \in [1,\ldots,n]$.

Define a potentially generating formula as a formula $\varphi_m(\underline{x_1},\ldots,\underline{x_k})$ potentially generating an element $l \in \Sigma^*$ such that $R(l) = l_1\#\ldots\#l_k$ and the following holds:

$$\mathfrak{M}_{false} \models \varphi^\epsilon_m(l_1,\ldots,l_k)$$

for some signification ϵ. If for any $l \in \Sigma^*$ there is only one potentially generating formula in the family, then we can define a partial function $\gamma_i : \Sigma^* \to \Omega^*$ that constructs from an element $l \in \Sigma^*$ its potentially generating formula $\varphi_m(\underline{x_1},\ldots,\underline{x_k})$ if such a formula exists and is undefined otherwise $\gamma_i(l) \uparrow$. In the next chapter we will require for functions γ_i to be p-computable.

7. Δ^p_0-Models and Δ^p_0-Operators

Model $\mathfrak{M}$ of the finite signature σ will be called a p-computable model (Δ^p_0-model) [4–7] if all functions are p-computable functions, all predicates and the main set are Δ^p_0-sets. If we want to mark the degree of the polynomial n and the constant C, we will write C-n-Δ^p_0-model instead of writing Δ^p_0-model. Sometimes, there will be records of the form C-p-Δ^p_0. In the first case, p is the degree of the polynomial and in the second, Δ^p_0 is the designation for the first level of the polynomial hierarchy. Designation of C-p-Δ^p_0-function will be also applied for functions and C-p-Δ^p_0-set will be also applied for sets. Note that $\mathfrak{M}_{false}$ will be a C-p-Δ^p_0-model if such is the model $\mathfrak{M}$.

Let us call Δ^p_0-operator the operator $\Gamma^{\mathfrak{M}}_{F_{P_1^+},\ldots,F_{P_n^+}}$ from (1) if for some $C, p \in N$ the fol-

(1) p-computable model: $\mathfrak{M}$ is a C-p-Δ^p_0-model.

(2) predicate separability, quantifier-free and positivity: each family $F_{P_1^+}, \ldots, F_{P_n^+}$ is either a finite or countable family of formulas, all formulas $\varphi_j \in F_{P_i^+}$ are positive, quantifier-free, predicate-separable.

(3) uniqueness of the generating formula: for any two formulas $\varphi_1(x_1, \ldots, x_k)$, $\varphi_2(x_1, \ldots, x_k)$ $\in F_{P_i^+}$ with the same number of free variables and for any signification $\mathfrak{E} : P_j(x_i) \to \{0,1\}$, $i \in [1, \ldots, k]$, $j \in [1, \ldots, n]$ it is not true that there exists such significations as ϵ_1 and ϵ_2 consistent with $\mathfrak{E}$ such that:

there exists $l_1, \ldots, l_k$ from M such that $\mathfrak{M}_{false} \models \varphi_1^{\epsilon_1}(l_1, \ldots, l_k) \& \varphi_2^{\epsilon_2}(l_1, \ldots, l_k)$

(4) p-computability of element: we also require that all functions γ_i should be C-(p-1)-Δ_0^p-functions and families $F_{P_i^+}^*$ - C-p-Δ_0^p-families (time for checking $t(\mathfrak{M}_{false} \models \varphi_m^\epsilon(l_1, \ldots, l_k)) \leq C \cdot |l|^p$, for all $\varphi_m \in F_{P_i^+}$ and $l_i \in \Sigma^* \cup \{false\}$), $i \in [1, \ldots, k]$.

Note that the Δ_0^p-operator thus defined retains all the original properties: it is monotone, has a fixed point property and is locally finite, and therefore the smallest fixed point of the operator is reached in w steps.

We say that the smallest fixed point $\Gamma_w = (P_1, \ldots, P_n)$ will be Δ_0^p-set if any P_i is a Δ_0^p-set, where $i \in [1, \ldots, n]$. Let γ_i be the C-(p-1)-Δ_0^p-function for Δ_0^p-operator $\Gamma_{F_{P_1^+}, \ldots, F_{P_n^+}}^\mathfrak{M}$ and $\varphi_m(\underline{x_1}, \ldots, \underline{x_k}) \in F_{P_i^+}$ - potential generating formula for l, where $R(l) = l_1 \# \ldots \# l_k$ and all $l_1, \ldots, l_k \in \Sigma^*$. Then the following lemma is true for any signification $\varphi_m^\epsilon(\underline{x_1}, \ldots, \underline{x_k})$:

Lemma 1. $\varphi_m^\epsilon(\underline{x_1}, \ldots, \underline{x_k})$ *is built according to the formula* $\varphi_m(\underline{x_1}, \ldots, \underline{x_k})$ *and by signification* ϵ *for the time not exceeding* $12 \cdot C \cdot |l|^{p-1}$.

Proof. Consider the Turing machine T over Ω alphabet consisting of five semi-tapes (hereafter called tapes):
(1) the 1st tape: the formula $\varphi_m(\underline{x_1}, \ldots, \underline{x_k})$ is written out.
(2) the 2nd tape: the word ϵ of length k is written out.
(3) the 3rd tape: for variables.
(4) the 4th tape: remembers the last position of the first tape.
(5) the 5th tape: builds a new formula $\varphi_m^\epsilon(\underline{x_1}, \ldots, \underline{x_k})$.

Let the formula $\varphi_m(\underline{x_1}, \ldots, \underline{x_k})$ be written out on the first tape and the second tape should contain the word ϵ. The machine T starts to work in the extreme left position and reads the formula from the first tape. As soon as T reaches the word of the form $P_j(x_i)$, T begins to read this word and writes out in parallel symbol 1 on the fourth tape for each symbol of $P_j(x_i)$ and symbol 1 for each symbol v of $P_j(x_i)$ on the third tape, moving in parallel, the machine head on the second tape containing the word ϵ with a single delay. When all the symbols $v \ldots v$ (x_i) are read, the head on the second tape will observe symbol ϵ_{i_1} which must be substituted for the word $P_j(x_i)$. Since the head position of the first tape is recorded on the fourth tape, T starts to overwrite on the first tape the word $P_j(x_i)$ on symbols # and reduce in parallel the number of symbols 1 on the fourth tape. One as soon as there are no one-symbols left on the fourth tape, then T write the symbol ϵ_{i_1} to the first tape. Then T returns the heads of second, third and fourth tapes to the extreme left position and continue to sequentially find and replace the remaining occurrences of the form $P_j(x_r)$ on the first tape and replace them with symbols # and ϵ_r. After all the replacements T must return the head of the first tape to the extreme left position and starts copying the formula of the first tape to the fifth tape while skipping the symbols #.

Calculate the total operating time of such a machine T:
(1) The machine T works with the formula $\varphi_m(\underline{x_1}, \ldots, \underline{x_{n_m}})$ on the first tape which includes words such as $P_j(x_i)$. The length of this formula does not exceed $C \cdot |l|^{p-1}$. In total, the number of steps does not exceed three lengths of $\varphi_m(\underline{x_1}, \ldots, \underline{x_{n_m}})$.
(2) On the second tape, the machine does not change the word ϵ, simply reads it in parallel

with the symbols v from the first tape and periodically returns the head to the extreme left position. The total number of shifts to the right of the machine head of the second tape does not exceed the length of the word on the first tape. The same goes for the number of the machine head shifts to the left. Therefore, on this tape, there will be no more than $2 \cdot C \cdot |l|^{p-1}$ steps.

(3) On the third tape, the last monitored variable is written out. The number of the machine head shifts to the right and to the left does not exceed $2 \cdot C \cdot |l|^{p-1}$ on this tape.

(4) For the fourth tape it is also does not exceed $2 \cdot C \cdot |l|^{p-1}$.

(5) To copy the final word from the first tape to the fifth and taking into account the preliminary setting of the head of the first tape to the extreme left position, it will also take no more than $2 \cdot C \cdot |l|^{p-1}$. □

Let $\varphi_m(\underline{x_1}, \ldots, \underline{x_k}) \in F_{p_i^+}$ be potentially generative formula for an element l.

Lemma 2. $\varphi_m^{\varepsilon}(l_1, \ldots, l_k)$ *is built by word l and the formula $\varphi_m^{\varepsilon}(\underline{x_1}, \ldots, \underline{x_k})$ for the time not exceeding* $4 \cdot C \cdot |l|^p$.

Proof. Consider a Turing machine T over alphabet Ω that also consists of three semi-tapes (hereafter called tapes):

(1) the 1st tape: the formula $\varphi_m^{\varepsilon}(\underline{x_1}, \ldots, \underline{x_k})$ is written out, where the length of the formula does not exceed $C \cdot |l|^{p-1}$.

(2) the second tape: the word $w_2 = \#R(l) = \#l_1\# \ldots \#l_k$ written out, where the length of the word does not exceeding $|l|$.

(3) the third tape: builds a new formula $\varphi_m^{\varepsilon}(l_1, \ldots, l_k)$.

The machine starts to work with the formula of the first tape, if necessary simultaneously copying the result to the third tape. If the machine T on the first tape reads a symbol that is not v, then T copies it to the third tape. If T reads the symbol v on the first tape, then T starts the process of finding the corresponding l_i for replacement. When the machine T reads the i-th symbol v successively from the first tape, T transfers the machine head of second tape to the i-th symbol # that comes before the corresponding l_i. When T reads all symbols v successively from first tape, then the machine will write the corresponding l_s from second tape to the third tape. By repeating this algorithm on the third tape the word $\varphi_m^{\varepsilon}(l_1, \ldots, l_k)$ will eventually be written.

Calculate the total operating time of such a machine T:

(1) the machine T reads a word from the first tape or just stands and waits for further reading. The number of movements to the right does not exceed $C \cdot |l|^{p-1}$

(2) on the second tape, the machine head moves both to the right and to the left, but again only reading. Therefore, the number of steps does not exceed $C \cdot |l|^{p-1} \times 2 \cdot |l| \leq 2 \cdot C \cdot |l|^p$.

(3) the third tape: the number of steps does not exceed $C \cdot |l|^{p-1}$. □

8. A Polynomial Analogue of Gandy's Theorem

Let Γ_w from equality (2) be the smallest fixed point of Δ_0^p-operator $\Gamma_{F_{p_1^+}, \ldots, F_{p_n^+}}$, then the next theorem is true:

Theorem 1 (polynomial analogue of Gandy's theorem). *The smallest fixed point Γ_w of Δ_0^p-operator $\Gamma_{F_{p_1^+}, \ldots, F_{p_n^+}}$ is a Δ_0^p-set.*

Proof. The main idea of the proof is to show that the time for checking the truth of the formula $P_i(l)$ on $\mathfrak{M}_{false}^{\Gamma_w}$ does not exceed the time $k \cdot C \cdot r(l) \cdot |l|^p$, where k and C are fixed constants and $r(l)$ is the rank of the element l and $r(l) \geq 1$, $i \in [1, \ldots, n]$. Since the rank $r(l) < |l|$, we get that for any l the complexity does not exceed $k \cdot C \cdot |l|^{p+1}$.

Without loss of generality, we show this for $P_1(l)$, assuming in the induction step that constant C is the maximum for all constants that participate in the splitting function $R(l)$, in functions γ_i and in the algorithm for checking the truth of the formula $\varphi_m^\epsilon(l_1, \ldots, l_{n_m})$.

Induction base $r(l) = 1$:

Case 1: $\gamma_i(l) \uparrow^p$, then the formula $P_1(l)$ is false.

Case 2: $\gamma_i(l) = \varphi_m(x_1, \ldots, x_k)$, then $R(l) = l_1 \# \ldots \# l_k$ and all elements of l_i (where $i \in [1, \ldots, k]$) are either elements of the base set M or elements from Σ^* for which $R(l_i) \uparrow^p$. Given all $P_i(l_j)$ are false on $\mathfrak{M}_{false}^{\Gamma_w}$, we can create $\varphi_m^\epsilon(x_1, \ldots, x_k)$ from the potentially generating formula $\varphi_m(x_1, \ldots, x_k)$ for element l, where $\epsilon = 0 \ldots 0$ and $|\epsilon| = k$. We get:

$$\mathfrak{M}_{false}^{\Gamma_w} \models P_1(l) \text{ if and only if } \mathfrak{M}_{false}^{\Gamma_w} \models \varphi_m(l_1, \ldots, l_k) \text{ if and only if } \mathfrak{M}_{false}^{\Gamma_w} \models \varphi_m^\epsilon(l_1, \ldots, l_k)$$
$$\text{if and only if } \mathfrak{M}_{false} \models \varphi_m^\epsilon(l_1, \ldots, l_k)$$

The time required to construct a potentially generating formula $\varphi_m(x_1, \ldots, x_k)$ using l does not exceed $C \cdot |l|^{p-1}$. Next, we build $\varphi_m^\epsilon(x_1, \ldots, x_k)$ and $\varphi_m^\epsilon(l_1, \ldots, l_k)$. The time required for this does not exceed $12 * C * |l|^{p-1}$ and $4 * C * |l|^p$ (Lemmas 1 and 2). Verifying the truth of the last formula for $\mathfrak{M}_{false}$ does not exceed $C * |l|^p$. Summing everything up, we get that the verification time does not exceed $25 * C * r(l) * |l|^p$.

The induction step: let our assumption be true for $r(l) = s$. We will show this for $s + 1$:

Case 1: $\gamma_i(l) \uparrow^p$, then the formula $P_1(l)$ is false. We get it in time:

$$t(P_1(l)) \leq C \cdot |l|^{p-1} \leq 25 \cdot C \cdot r(l) \cdot |l|^p$$

Case 2: $\gamma_i(l) = \varphi_m(x_1, \ldots, x_k)$

$$\mathfrak{M}_{false}^{\Gamma_w} \models P_1(l) \text{ if and only if } \mathfrak{M}_{false}^{\Gamma_w} \models \varphi_m(l_1, \ldots, l_k) \text{ if and only if } \mathfrak{M}_{false}^{\Gamma_w} \models \varphi_m^\epsilon(l_1, \ldots, l_k)$$
$$\text{if and only if } \mathfrak{M}_{false} \models \varphi_m^\epsilon(l_1, \ldots, l_k)$$

where ϵ string of symbols ϵ_i such that $\epsilon_i = 1$ if formula $P_j(l_i)$ is true on $\mathfrak{M}_{false}^{\Gamma_w}$ and 0 otherwise.

Let's calculate the time spent on all transitions:

(1) constructing a potentially generating formula $\varphi_m(x_1, \ldots, x_k)$ using l in time $C \cdot |l|^{p-1}$

(2) determining the truth of all predicates $P_{i_1}(l_1), \ldots, P_{i_k}(l_k)$ which are included in the formula. By the induction hypothesis, we obtain:

$$\sum_{j=1}^{k} t(P_{i_j}(l_j)) \leq \sum_{j=1}^{k} 25 \cdot C \cdot r(l_j) \cdot |l_j|^p \leq 25 \cdot C \cdot (r(l) - 1) \cdot |l|^p.$$

(3) further, we fix the signification $\epsilon : P_{i_j}(x_i) \to \{0, 1\}$ considering whether the predicate $P_{i_j}(l_i)$ is true or false, if the formula does not include any of the predicates P_{j_i} for the variable x_i, then we determine the truth for $P_1(x_i)$ by default.

(4) By the formula $\varphi_m(x_1, \ldots, x_k)$ and by the signification ϵ we construct $\varphi_m^\epsilon(x_1, \ldots, x_k)$. The time required for this does not exceed $12 \cdot |l|^{p-1} \leq 12 \cdot |l|^p$.

(5) By the formula $\varphi_m^\epsilon(x_1, \ldots, x_k)$ and l we construct $\varphi_m^\epsilon(l_1, \ldots, l_k)$. The time required for this does not exceed $4 \cdot C \cdot |l|^p$.

If we sum up all the time of calculations, then we get the following:

$$t(P_1(l)) \leq \sum_{i=1}^{k}(25 \cdot C \cdot r(l_i) \cdot |l_i|^p) + 25 \cdot C \cdot |l|^p \leq$$
$$\leq 25 \cdot C \cdot (r(l) - 1) \cdot |l|^p + 25 \cdot C \cdot |l|^p \leq 25 \cdot C \cdot r(l) \cdot |l|^p$$

We have shown that for any element l of rank $r(l)$ in time $25 \cdot C \cdot r(l) \cdot |l|^p$ we determine the fact whether it belongs to the predicate P_1. Since $r(l)$ is always less than $|l|$, we can write the following:

$$t(P_1(l)) \leq 25 \cdot C \cdot r(l) \cdot |l|^p \leq 25 \cdot C \cdot |l|^{p+1}.$$

□

9. Corollaries and Applications

For the Δ_0^p-model $\mathfrak{M}$ as an application of the polynomial analogue of Gandy's theorem, we present several corollaries. Some of these corollaries have already been proven earlier by other authors using other methods, some are presented for the first time.

Let the model $\mathfrak{M}$ have a one-place predicate U that selects the elements of the main set M and a distinguished one-place predicate $List = \emptyset$ (a predicate that will select list elements), then we will show how easy it is to prove the following statement on hereditarily finite lists $HW(M)$ which was already proven earlier in [8] but using a different technique:

Corollary 1. *If $\mathfrak{M}$ is a Δ_0^p-model, then $HW(M)$ is a Δ_0^p-set.*

Proof. A countable generating family of formulas F_{List^+} is as follows:

$$\varphi_n : \&_{i=1}^n (U(x_n) \vee List(x_n)), \; n \in \mathbb{N}$$

This family of formulas is predicate-separable, all formulas are positive quantifier-free, and the predicate $List$ is included in formulas positively. We can easily see that the operator $\Gamma_{F_{List^+}}^{\mathfrak{M}}$ is a Δ_0^p-operator. □

Let the signature σ have the form: $\sigma = \{c_0, \ldots, c_k, f_1^{(m_1)}, \ldots, f_s^{(m_s)}, R_1^{(p_1)}, \ldots, R_t^{(p_t)}\}$. Consider the model $\mathfrak{N}$ with the basic set of elements N and signatures $\sigma = \{\underline{1}, s^{(1)}\}$. The interpretation of the constant $\underline{1}$ will be 1 and s-the standard successor function. Further, an entry of the form $\underline{n+1}$ will mean a term of the form n-fold application of the function s to $\underline{1}$.

Corollary 2. *The set of quantifier-free formulas of signature σ is a Δ_0^p-set.*

Proof. The process of constructing auxiliary Δ_0^p-sets using generating families for the corresponding predicates in the Δ_0^p-model $\mathfrak{N}$ is as follows:
(1) Constants: F_{Cons^+}: $\varphi_i : (x_1 = \underline{1}) \& (x_2 = \underline{i}), i \in [1, \ldots, k]$
(2) Variables: F_{Var^+}: $\varphi_i : (x_1 = \underline{2}) \& (x_2 = \underline{i}), i \in \mathbb{N}$
(3) Function symbols: F_{Func^+}: $\varphi_i : (x_1 = \underline{3}) \& (x_2 = \underline{i}), i \in [1, \ldots, s]$
(4) Predicate symbols: F_{R^+}: $\varphi_i : (x_1 = \underline{4}) \& (x_2 = \underline{i}), i \in [1, \ldots, t]$.
(5) Terms that are not constants and variables:

$$F_{Term_1^+} : \varphi_i : (x_1 = \underline{5}) \& Func(x_2) \&_{i=3}^{p_i+2} (Term_1(x_i) \vee Cons(x_i) \vee Var(x_i))$$

(6) The set of standard terms: $F_{Term^+} : F_{Term_1^+} \cup F_{Cons^+} \cup F_{Var^+}$

Generating family for quantifier-free formulas F_{Free^+}:
(1) $\varphi_1(R_i) : (x_1 = \underline{8}) \& R(x_2) \&_{i=3}^{p_i+2} Term(x_i)$
(2) $\varphi_2(P_i) : (x_1 = \underline{9}) \& P(x_2) \& Term(x_i)$
(3) $\varphi_3(=) : (x_1 = \underline{10}) \& Term(x_2) \& Term(x_3)$
(4) $\varphi_4(\&) : (x_1 = \underline{11}) \& Free(x_2) \& Free(x_3)$
(5) $\varphi_5(\vee) : (x_1 = \underline{12}) \& Free(x_2) \& Free(x_3)$
(6) $\varphi_6(\rightarrow) : (x_1 = \underline{13}) \& Free(x_2) \& Free(x_3)$
(7) $\varphi_7(\neg) : (x_1 = \underline{14}) \& Free(x_2) \& Free(x_3)$ □

Define the signature $\sigma' = \sigma \cup \{Cons, Var, Func, Term, Free\} \cup \{\in^{(2)}, \subseteq^{(2)}\}$.

Corollary 3. *The set of Δ_0-formulas [9] signature σ' is a Δ_0^p-set.*

Proof. Define a family of Δ_0-formulas F_{D0^+}. Just as in Corollary 2, we write out generating formulas for terms and formulas, with the only difference that we also add formulas for the above predicates:
(8) $\varphi_8(\in) : (x_1 = \underline{15}) \& Term(x_2) \& Term(x_3)$
(9) $\varphi_9(\subseteq) : (x_1 = \underline{16}) \& Term(x_2) \& Term(x_3)$

We also write out generating formulas for $(\exists x_k \in t)\varphi(\bar{x})$, $(\forall x_m \in t)\varphi(\bar{x})$, $(\exists x_t \subseteq t)\varphi(\bar{x})$, $(\forall x_t \subseteq t)\varphi(\bar{x})$:

(10) $\varphi_{10}(\exists x_k \in t(\bar{x})) : (x_1 = \underline{17}) \& Var(x_2) \& Term(x_3) \& D0(x_4)$
(11) $\varphi_{11}(\forall x_m \in t(\bar{x})) : (x_1 = \underline{18}) \& Var(x_2) \& Term(x_3) \& D0(x_4)$
(12) $\varphi_{12}(\exists x_t \subseteq t(\bar{x})) : (x_1 = \underline{19}) \& Var(x_2) \& Term(x_3) \& D0(x_4)$
(13) $\varphi_{13}(\forall x_t \subseteq t(\bar{x})) : (x_1 = \underline{20}) \& Var(x_2) \& Term(x_3) \& D0(x_4)$ □

Corollary 4. *The set of conditional terms of signature σ' and Δ_0^*-formulas is a Δ_0^p-sets [9].*

Proof. This is where the approach gets more interesting. We need to simultaneously generate both conditional terms and formulas containing these conditional terms. Therefore, we construct two generating families: F_{TCond^+}, F_{FCond^+}. In addition to generating formulas for standard terms in F_{TCond^+}, we add countably many generating formulas for conditional terms:

(8) $\varphi_{k+8}: (x_1 = \underline{21}) \&_{i=1}^{k}(TCond(x_{2i}) \& FCond(x_{2i+1})) \& TCond(x_{2k+2}), k \in N$.

The family F_{FCond^+} is defined by the same generating formulas as the family F_{D0^+}, with the only difference that the predicates *Term* must be replaced with *TCond* everywhere. □

10. Conclusions

This work is a starting point for building a methodology for developing fast and reliable software. In this work, we study sufficient conditions for the Δ_0^p-operator under which the smallest fixed point remains a Δ_0^p-set. This allows us to create new elements and data types. Moreover, there are polynomial algorithms for checking the fact whether a certain element belongs to a given data type or not. The question of programming methodology is also of interest: which constructs can be used and which not for creating programs, if we want our programs to be polynomially computable. With the help of the main theorem of our paper and the theorems from the works [8–14] it is already possible to develop logical programming languages, with programs being of polynomial computational complexity.

Author Contributions: Conceptualization, S.G. and A.N.; methodology, S.G. and A.N.; formal analysis, S.G.; validation, S.G.; investigation, S.G. and A.N.; writing—original draft preparation, A.N.; writing—review and editing, A.N.; supervision, S.G.; project administration, S.G.; software, A.N. All authors have read and agreed to the published version of the manuscript.

Funding: This research received no external funding.

Institutional Review Board Statement: Not applicable.

Informed Consent Statement: Not applicable.

Data Availability Statement: Not applicable.

Conflicts of Interest: The authors declare no conflict of interest.

References

1. Barwise, J. *Admissible Sets and Structures*; Springer: New York, NY, USA, 1975.
2. Ershov, Y.L. *Definability and Computability*; Springer: New York, NY, USA, 1996.
3. Lewis, H.; Papadimitriou, C. *Elements of the Theory of Computation*; Prentice-Hall: Upper Saddle River, NJ, USA, 1998.
4. Alaev, P.E. Structures Computable in Polynomial Time. *Algebra Log.* **2017**, *55*, 421–435. [CrossRef]
5. Alaev, P.E. Existence and Uniqueness of Structures Computable in Polynomial Time. *Algebra Log.* **2016**, *55*, 72–76. [CrossRef]
6. Alaev, P.E.; Selivanov, V.L. Polynomial computability of fields of algebraic numbers. *Dokl. Math.* **2018**, *98*, 341–343. [CrossRef]
7. Cenzer, D.; Remmel, J. Polynomial-time versus recursive models. *Ann. Pure Appl. Log.* **1991**, *54*, 17–58. [CrossRef]
8. Ospichev, S.S.; Ponomaryov, D.K. On the complexity of formulas in semantic programming. *Sib. Electron. Math. Rep.* **2018**, *15*, 987–995.
9. Goncharov, S.S. Conditional Terms in Semantic Programming. *Sib. Math. J.* **2017**, *58*, 794–800. [CrossRef]
10. Ershov, Y.L.; Goncharov, S.S.; Sviridenko, D.I. Semantic programming. In Proceedings of the Information Processing 86: IFIP 10th World Computer Congress, Dublin, Ireland, 1–5 September 1986; Volume 10, pp. 1113–1120

11. Goncharov, S.S.; Sviridenko, D.I. Logical language of description of polynomial computing. *Dokl. Math.* **2019**, *99*, 121–124. [CrossRef]
12. Goncharov, S.S.; Sviridenko, D.I. Recursive terms in semantic programming. *Sib. Math. J.* **2018**, *59*, 1014–1023. [CrossRef]
13. Goncharov, S.S.; Ospichev, S.S.; Ponomaryov, D.K.; Sviridenko, D.I. The expressiveness of looping terms in the semantic programming. *Sib. Electron. Math. Rep.* **2020**, *17*, 380–394. [CrossRef]
14. Goncharov, S.S.; Sviridenko, D.I. Σ-programming. *Transl. II. Ser. Am. Math. Soc.* **1989**, *142*, 101–121.

Article

Roots of Characteristic Polynomial Sequences in Iterative Block Cyclic Reductions

Masato Shinjo [1,*], Tan Wang [2], Masashi Iwasaki [3] and Yoshimasa Nakamura [4]

[1] Faculty of Science and Engineering, Doshisha University, Kyotanabe 610-0394, Japan
[2] Digital Technology & Innovation, Siemens Healthineers Digital Technology (Shanghai) Co., Ltd., Shanghai 201318, China; lgodture@163.com
[3] Faculty of Life and Environmental Science, Kyoto Prefectural University, Kyoto 606-8522, Japan; imasa@kpu.ac.jp
[4] Department of Informatics and Mathematical Science, Osaka Seikei University, Osaka 533-0007, Japan; nakamura-yo@osaka-seikei.ac.jp
* Correspondence: mshinjo@mail.doshisha.ac.jp; Tel.: +81-0774-65-6239

Abstract: The block cyclic reduction method is a finite-step direct method used for solving linear systems with block tridiagonal coefficient matrices. It iteratively uses transformations to reduce the number of non-zero blocks in coefficient matrices. With repeated block cyclic reductions, non-zero off-diagonal blocks in coefficient matrices incrementally leave the diagonal blocks and eventually vanish after a finite number of block cyclic reductions. In this paper, we focus on the roots of characteristic polynomials of coefficient matrices that are repeatedly transformed by block cyclic reductions. We regard each block cyclic reduction as a composition of two types of matrix transformations, and then attempt to examine changes in the existence range of roots. This is a block extension of the idea presented in our previous papers on simple cyclic reductions. The property that the roots are not very scattered is a key to accurately solve linear systems in floating-point arithmetic. We clarify that block cyclic reductions do not disperse roots, but rather narrow their distribution, if the original coefficient matrix is symmetric positive or negative definite.

Keywords: block cyclic reduction; block tridiagonal matrix; characteristic polynomial; linear system

Citation: Shinjo, M.; Wang, T.; Iwasaki, M.; Nakamura, Y. Roots of Characteristic Polynomial Sequences in Iterative Block Cyclic Reductions. *Mathematics* **2021**, *9*, 3213. https://doi.org/10.3390/math9243213

Academic Editors: Francesco Aldo Costabile, Maria I. Gualtieri and Anna Napoli

Received: 16 November 2021
Accepted: 9 December 2021
Published: 12 December 2021

Publisher's Note: MDPI stays neutral with regard to jurisdictional claims in published maps and institutional affiliations.

Copyright: © 2021 by the authors. Licensee MDPI, Basel, Switzerland. This article is an open access article distributed under the terms and conditions of the Creative Commons Attribution (CC BY) license (https://creativecommons.org/licenses/by/4.0/).

1. Introduction

Solving systems of linear equations is one of the most important subjects in numerical linear algebra. In particular, applied mathematics and engineering often require the solution of linear systems with tridiagonal coefficient matrices. Solving tridiagonal linear systems generally involves finding N-dimensional vectors x, such that $Ax = b$ for given N-by-N tridiagonal matrices A and N-dimensional vectors b. The cyclic reduction method is a finite-step direct method for computing solutions x [1,2]. The cyclic reduction method first transforms tridiagonal coefficient matrices A to pentadiagonal matrices with all subdiagonal (and superdiagonal) entries equal to 0. The right vectors b are, of course, simultaneously changed. Two non-zero off-diagonals of the coefficient matrices gradually leave the diagonals in the iterative cyclic reductions, with the coefficient matrices eventually being reduced to diagonal matrices. Error analysis of the cyclic reduction method has been reported in [3], and a variant of the cyclic reduction method has been also presented, for example, in [4]. The stride reduction method is a generalization of the cyclic reduction method that can solve problems where A are M-tridiagonal matrices, M is the bandwidth, and there are two non-zero off-diagonals consisting of $(1, M+1), (2, M+2), \ldots, (N-M-1, N)$ and the $(M+1, 1), (M+2, 2), \ldots, (N, N-M-1)$ entries [5]. Each stride reduction, including cyclic reduction, narrows the distribution of the roots of characteristic polynomials associated with the coefficient matrices if A are symmetric positive definite [6,7]. This is a desirable property that does not increase the difficulty of solving systems of linear systems.

Here, we consider positive integers $N_1, N_2, \ldots, N_m$ satisfying $N = N_1 + N_2 + \cdots + N_m$. The cyclic reduction method is extended to solve a problem where coefficient matrices $A \in \mathbb{R}^{N \times N}$ are block tridiagonal matrices [2,8] expressed using m square matrices $D_1 \in \mathbb{R}^{N_1 \times N_1}$, $D_2 \in \mathbb{R}^{N_2 \times N_2}$, $\ldots$, $D_m \in \mathbb{R}^{N_m \times N_m}$ and $2m - 2$ rectangular matrices $E_1 \in \mathbb{R}^{N_1 \times N_2}$, $E_2 \in \mathbb{R}^{N_2 \times N_3}$, $\ldots$, $E_{m-1} \in \mathbb{R}^{N_{m-1} \times N_m}$ and $F_1 \in \mathbb{R}^{N_2 \times N_1}$, $F_2 \in \mathbb{R}^{N_3 \times N_2}$, $\ldots$, $F_{m-1} \in \mathbb{R}^{N_m \times N_{m-1}}$ as:

$$A := \begin{pmatrix} D_1 & E_1 & & \\ F_1 & D_2 & \ddots & \\ & \ddots & \ddots & E_{m-1} \\ & & F_{m-1} & D_m \end{pmatrix}. \tag{1}$$

A block tridiagonal matrix can be regarded as a block matrix obtained by replacing the diagonal entries in a tridiagonal matrix with square matrices and the subdiagonal entries with rectangular matrices. This extended method is called the block cyclic reduction method. The forward stability of iterative block cyclic reductions has been discussed in [9], but changes in roots of characteristic polynomials of coefficient matrices have not been studied. Block cyclic reductions do not work well in floating point arithmetic if they greatly disperse the roots. Thus, the main purpose of this paper is to clarify whether block cyclic reductions narrow the root distribution like stride reductions.

The remainder of this paper is organized as follows. Section 2 briefly explains the block cyclic reduction method used for solving block tridiagonal linear systems. Section 3 shows that block M-tridiagonal matrices can be transformed to block tridiagonal (1-tridiagonal) matrices without changing the eigenvalues. Then, we interpret the transformation from M-tridiagonal matrices to $2M$-tridiagonal matrices in the block cyclic reduction as a composite transformation of the block tridiagonalization, its inverse, and the transformation from block tridiagonal to block 2-tridiagonal matrices. In Section 4, we find the relationship between the inverses of block tridiagonal matrices and those of block 2-tridiagonal matrices. Section 5 looks at the roots of characteristic polynomials of coefficient matrices transformed by block cyclic reductions compared with those of original coefficient matrices A in cases where A are block tridiagonal and symmetric positive definite or negative definite. Section 6 gives two numerical examples for observing coefficient matrices and the roots of their characteristic polynomials appearing in iterative block cyclic reductions. Section 7 concludes the paper.

2. Block Cyclic Reduction

In this section, we briefly explain the block cyclic reduction method used for solving linear systems with block tridiagonal coefficient matrices.

We consider the following N-by-N block-band matrix given using m square matrices $D_1^{(M)} \in \mathbb{R}^{N_1 \times N_1}$, $D_2^{(M)} \in \mathbb{R}^{N_2 \times N_2}, \ldots, D_m^{(M)} \in \mathbb{R}^{N_m \times N_m}$ and $2(m - M)$ rectangular matrices $E_1^{(M)} \in \mathbb{R}^{N_1 \times N_{1+M}}$, $E_2^{(M)} \in \mathbb{R}^{N_2 \times N_{2+M}}, \ldots, E_{m-M}^{(M)} \in \mathbb{R}^{N_{m-M} \times N_m}$ and $F_1^{(M)} \in \mathbb{R}^{N_{1+M} \times N_1}$, $F_2^{(M)} \in \mathbb{R}^{N_{2+M} \times N_2}, \ldots, F_{m-M}^{(M)} \in \mathbb{R}^{N_m \times N_{m-M}}$ as:

$$A^{(M)} := \begin{pmatrix} D_1^{(M)} & & E_1^{(M)} & & & & \\ & \ddots & & \ddots & & & \\ F_1^{(M)} & & D_{1+M}^{(M)} & & \ddots & & \\ & \ddots & & \ddots & & \ddots & \\ & & \ddots & & D_{m-M}^{(M)} & & E_{m-M}^{(M)} \\ & & & \ddots & & \ddots & \\ & & & & F^{(M)} & & D^{(M)} \end{pmatrix}, \tag{2}$$

where the superscript in parentheses appearing in $A^{(M)}$ specifies the position of non-zero off-diagonal bands $E_i^{(M)}$ and $F_i^{(M)}$. If $D_i^{(M)}$, $E_i^{(M)}$, and $F_i^{(M)}$ are all 1-by-1 matrices for every i, then $A^{(M)}$ is the M-tridiagonal matrix [6] and $D_i^{(M)}$, $E_i^{(M)}$, and $F_i^{(M)}$ are the (i,i), $(i,i+M)$, and $(i+M,i)$ entries of $A^{(M)}$, respectively. Thus, we hereinafter refer to $A^{(M)}$ as the block M-tridiagonal matrix and $D_i^{(M)}$, $E_i^{(M)}$, and $F_i^{(M)}$ as the (i,i), $(i,i+M)$, and $(i+M,i)$ blocks of $A^{(M)}$, respectively. Note that block 1-tridiagonal matrices are the usual block tridiagonal matrices. In the case where $D_i^{(M)}$, $E_i^{(M)}$, and $F_i^{(M)}$ are not 1-by-1 matrices, we must pay attention to the number of rows and columns of $D_i^{(M)}$, $E_i^{(M)}$, and $F_i^{(M)}$. For example, we can compute the matrix product $D_1^{(M)} E_1^{(M)}$ but cannot define $E_1^{(M)} D_1^{(M)}$ if $N_1 \neq N_{1+M}$, unlike in the case where $D_i^{(M)}$, $E_i^{(M)}$, and $F_i^{(M)}$ are all 1-by-1 matrices.

We hereinafter consider the case where $D_i^{(M)}$ are all nonsingular. Here, we prepare an N-by-N block M-tridiagonal matrix involving non-zero blocks $D_i^{(M)}$, $E_i^{(M)}$, and $F_i^{(M)}$:

$$T^{(M)} := \begin{pmatrix} I_1 & & -E_1^{(M)}(D_{1+M}^{(M)})^{-1} & & & \\ & \ddots & & \ddots & & \\ -F_1^{(M)}(D_1^{(M)})^{-1} & & I_{1+M} & & \ddots & \\ & \ddots & & \ddots & & \ddots \\ & & \ddots & & I_{m-M} & & -E_{m-M}^{(M)}(D_m^{(M)})^{-1} \\ & & & \ddots & & \ddots & \\ & & & & -F_{m-M}^{(M)}(D_{m-M}^{(M)})^{-1} & & I_m \end{pmatrix}, \quad (3)$$

where I_i are the N_i-by-N_i identity matrices. The number of rows and columns of I_i, $-E_i^{(M)}(D_{i+M}^{(M)})^{-1}$, and $-F_i^{(M)}(D_i^{(M)})^{-1}$ coincide with those of $D_i^{(M)}$, $E_i^{(M)}$, and $F_i^{(M)}$, respectively. In other words, $T^{(M)}$ has the same block structure as $A^{(M)}$. Then, we can easily observe that the $(i,i+M)$ and $(i+M,i)$ blocks are all zero and the $(i,i+2M)$ and $(i+2M,i)$ blocks of $T^{(M)}A^{(M)}$ are all non-zero, meaning that $T^{(M)}A^{(M)}$ becomes an N-by-N block $2M$-tridiagonal matrix $A^{(2M)}$. The non-zero blocks $D_i^{(2M)}$, $E_i^{(2M)}$, and $F_i^{(2M)}$ appearing in the (i,i), $(i,i+2M)$, and $(i+2M,i)$ blocks are also expressed using $D_i^{(M)}$, $E_i^{(M)}$, and $F_i^{(M)}$ as:

$$\begin{cases} D_i^{(2M)} := D_i^{(M)} - E_i^{(M)}(D_{i+M}^{(M)})^{-1} F_i^{(M)}, & i = 1, 2, \ldots, M, \\ D_i^{(2M)} := D_i^{(M)} - F_{i-M}^{(M)}(D_{i-M}^{(M)})^{-1} E_{i-M}^{(M)} - E_i^{(M)}(D_{i+M}^{(M)})^{-1} F_i^{(M)}, & i = M+1, \ldots, m-M, \\ D_i^{(2M)} := D_i^{(M)} - F_{i-M}^{(M)}(D_{i-M}^{(M)})^{-1} E_{i-M}^{(M)}, & i = m-M+1, m-M+2, \ldots, m, \\ E_i^{(2M)} := -E_i^{(M)}(D_{i+M}^{(M)})^{-1} E_{i+M}^{(M)}, & i = 1, 2, \ldots, m-2M, \\ F_i^{(2M)} := -F_{i+M}^{(M)}(D_{i+M}^{(M)})^{-1} F_i^{(M)}, & i = 1, 2, \ldots, m-2M. \end{cases} \quad (4)$$

Thus, by multiplying the block M-tridiagonal linear system $A^{(M)}x = b^{(M)}$ by $T^{(M)}$ from the left on both sides, we transform it to the block $2M$-tridiagonal linear system $A^{(2M)}x = b^{(2M)}$, where $b^{(2M)} := T^{(M)}b^{(M)}$. This transformation is the block cyclic reduction [2]. We can again apply the block cyclic reduction to the block $2M$-tridiagonal linear system $A^{(2M)}x = b^{(2M)}$ if the diagonal blocks $D_i^{(2M)}$ in the block $2M$-tridiagonal matrix $A^{(2M)}$ are all nonsingular. The iterative block cyclic reductions therefore cause non-zero off-diagonal blocks to gradually leave the diagonal blocks, eventually generating linear systems with block diagonal matrices.

3. Composite Transformation

In this section, we first show that block M-tridiagonal matrices can be transformed into block tridiagonal (1-tridiagonal) matrices while preserving the eigenvalues. Next, we consider the transformation from the block M-tridiagonal matrix $A^{(M)}$ to the block $2M$-tridiagonal matrix $A^{(2M)}$ in terms of the transformation from the block tridiagonal (1-tridiagonal) matrix to the block 2-tridiagonal matrix with two similarity transformations.

We consider N-by-N_i matrices:

$$P_i := \begin{pmatrix} O \\ \vdots \\ O \\ I_i \\ O \\ \vdots \\ O \end{pmatrix} \begin{matrix} \text{1st block} \\ \\ (i-1)\text{th block} \\ i\text{th block} \\ (i+1)\text{th block} \\ \\ m\text{th block} \end{matrix}, \quad i = 1, 2, \ldots, m, \tag{5}$$

where O denotes the zero matrix, whose entries are all 0, and the number of rows in the 1st, 2nd, ..., mth blocks are equal to those in $D_1^{(M)}, D_2^{(M)}, \ldots, D_m^{(M)}$, respectively. Then, it is obvious that $A^{(M)}P_1 \in \mathbb{R}^{N \times N_1}, A^{(M)}P_2 \in \mathbb{R}^{N \times N_2}, \ldots, A^{(M)}P_m \in \mathbb{R}^{N \times N_m}$ become the 1st, 2nd, ..., mth block-columns of $A^{(M)}$, respectively. Furthermore, for $i = 1, 2, \ldots, m$, it is observed that $P_1^\top(A^{(M)}P_i) \in \mathbb{R}^{N_1 \times N_i}, P_2^\top(A^{(M)}P_i) \in \mathbb{R}^{N_2 \times N_i}, \ldots, P_m^\top(A^{(M)}P_i) \in \mathbb{R}^{N_m \times N_i}$ coincide with the 1st, 2nd, ..., mth block-rows of $A^{(M)}P_i$, respectively. Thus, we see that $P_j^\top A^{(M)} P_i$ are the (j, i) blocks of $A^{(M)}$ for $i, j = 1, 2, \ldots, m$—namely:

$$P_j^\top A^{(M)} P_i = \begin{cases} E_i^{(M)}, & j = i - M, \\ D_i^{(M)}, & j = i, \\ F_i^{(M)}, & j = i + M, \\ O, & \text{otherwise}. \end{cases}$$

Here, we introduce $N \times (N_i + N_{i+M} + \cdots + N_{i+qM})$ matrices $\mathcal{P}_i := (P_i, P_{i+M}, \ldots, P_{i+qM})$ for $i = 1, 2, \ldots, r$, where q and r are the quotient and the remainder after the division of m by M, respectively. Then, it follows that:

$$\mathcal{P}_i^\top A^{(M)} P_i = \begin{pmatrix} D_i^{(M)} \\ F_i^{(M)} \\ O \\ \vdots \\ O \end{pmatrix} \in \mathbb{R}^{(N_i + N_{i+M} + \cdots + N_{i+qM}) \times N_i}, \quad i = 1, 2, \ldots, r.$$

$$\mathcal{P}_i^\top A^{(M)} P_{i+kM} = \begin{pmatrix} O \\ \vdots \\ O \\ E_{i+(k-1)M}^{(M)} \\ D_{i+kM}^{(M)} \\ F_{i+kM}^{(M)} \\ O \\ \vdots \\ O \end{pmatrix} \in \mathbb{R}^{(N_i + N_{i+M} + \cdots + N_{i+qM}) \times N_{i+kM}},$$

$$\mathcal{P}_i^\top A^{(M)} \mathcal{P}_{i+qM} = \begin{pmatrix} O \\ \vdots \\ O \\ E_{i+(q-1)M}^{(M)} \\ D_{i+qM}^{(M)} \end{pmatrix} \in \mathbb{R}^{(N_i + N_{i+M} + \cdots + N_{i+qM}) \times N_{i+qM}}, \quad i = 1, 2, \ldots, r.$$

Thus, by gathering these, we can derive:

$$\mathcal{P}_i^\top A^{(M)} \mathcal{P}_i = \begin{pmatrix} D_i^{(M)} & E_i^{(M)} & & \\ F_i^{(M)} & D_{i+M}^{(M)} & \ddots & \\ & \ddots & \ddots & E_{i+(q-1)M}^{(M)} \\ & & F_{i+(q-1)M}^{(M)} & D_{i+qM}^{(M)} \end{pmatrix}$$

$$\in \mathbb{R}^{(N_i + N_{i+M} + \cdots + N_{i+qM}) \times (N_i + N_{i+M} + \cdots + N_{i+qM})}, \quad i = 1, 2, \ldots, r. \quad (6)$$

Similarly, by letting $\mathcal{P}_i := (P_i, P_{i+M}, \ldots, P_{i+(q-1)M}) \in \mathbb{R}^{N \times (N_i + N_{i+M} + \cdots + N_{i+(q-1)M})}$ for $i = r+1, r+2, \ldots, M$, we obtain:

$$\mathcal{P}_i^\top A^{(M)} \mathcal{P}_i = \begin{pmatrix} D_i^{(M)} & E_i^{(M)} & & \\ F_i^{(M)} & D_{i+M}^{(M)} & \ddots & \\ & \ddots & \ddots & E_{i+(q-2)M}^{(M)} \\ & & F_{i+(q-2)M}^{(M)} & D_{i+(q-1)M}^{(M)} \end{pmatrix}$$

$$\in \mathbb{R}^{(N_i + N_{i+M} + \cdots + N_{i+(q-1)M}) \times (N_i + N_{i+M} + \cdots + N_{i+(q-1)M})},$$

$$i = r+1, r+2, \ldots, M. \quad (7)$$

See, also, Figure 1 for an auxiliary example of gathering a block tridiagonal part, as shown in (6) and (7). Therefore, using the permutation matrix $\mathcal{P} := (\ \mathcal{P}_1\ \mathcal{P}_2\ \cdots\ \mathcal{P}_M\ )$, we can complete a block tridiagonalization of $A^{(M)}$ as:

$$\mathcal{P}^\top A^{(M)} \mathcal{P} = \mathrm{diag}(\tilde{A}_1^{(1)}, \tilde{A}_2^{(1)}, \ldots, \tilde{A}_M^{(1)}), \quad (8)$$

where $\tilde{A}_i^{(1)} := \mathcal{P}_i^\top A^{(M)} \mathcal{P}_i$. Here, we may regard $\mathrm{diag}(\tilde{A}_1^{(1)}, \tilde{A}_2^{(1)}, \ldots, \tilde{A}_M^{(1)})$ as a block diagonal matrix in terms of $\tilde{A}_1^{(1)}, \tilde{A}_2^{(1)}, \ldots, \tilde{A}_M^{(1)}$. However, we emphasize that $\tilde{A}_1^{(1)}, \tilde{A}_2^{(1)}, \ldots, \tilde{A}_M^{(1)}$ are nothing but auxiliary matrices and are essentially block tridiagonal matrices in terms of realistic blocks $D_i^{(M)}$, $E_i^{(M)}$, and $F_i^{(M)}$. Furthermore, in the following sections, we should recognize that (8) is a block tridiagonalization and not a block diagonalization of $A^{(M)}$. Figure 2 gives a sketch of a block tridiagonalization of $A^{(M)}$. Noting that the $\mathcal{P}$ is an orthogonal matrix—namely, $\mathcal{P}^\top = \mathcal{P}^{-1}$, we can determine that $\mathrm{diag}(\tilde{A}_1^{(1)}, \tilde{A}_2^{(1)}, \ldots, \tilde{A}_M^{(1)})$ has the same eigenvalues as $A^{(M)}$. To summarize, we can divide a linear system with the block M-tridiagonal coefficient matrix $A^{(M)}$ into M linear systems with the block tridiagonal coefficient matrices $\tilde{A}_1^{(1)}, \tilde{A}_2^{(1)}, \ldots, \tilde{A}_M^{(1)}$ without the loss of the eigenvalues of $A^{(M)}$.

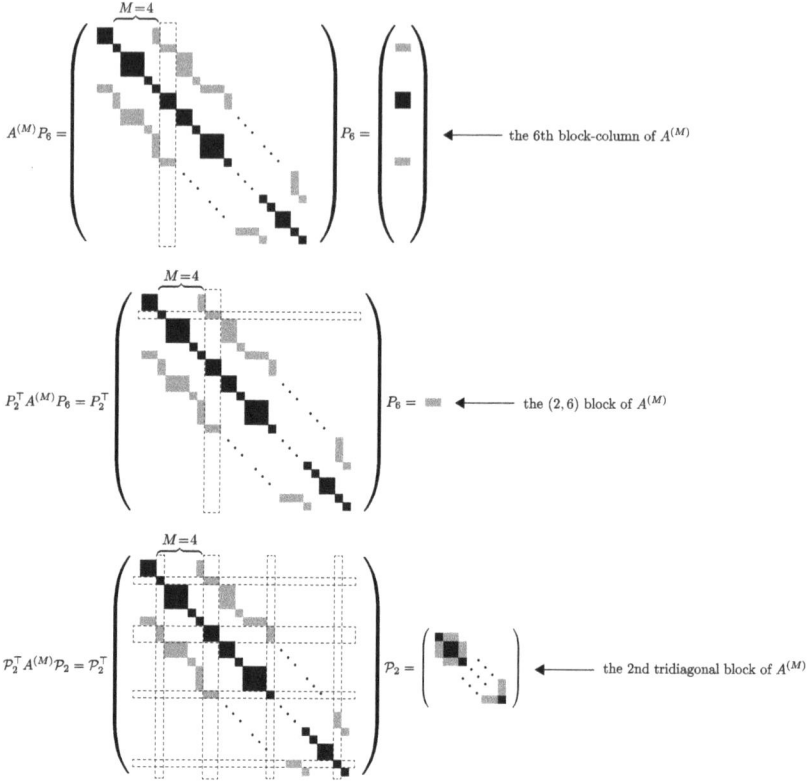

Figure 1. Gathering the block tridiagonal parts of the block M-tridiagonal matrix $A^{(M)}$ with $M = 4$.

Recalling that $A^{(2M)} = T^{(M)}A^{(M)}$, we can decompose $\mathcal{P}^{-1}A^{(2M)}\mathcal{P}$ into:

$$\mathcal{P}^{-1}A^{(2M)}\mathcal{P} = (\mathcal{P}^{-1}T^{(M)}\mathcal{P})(\mathcal{P}^{-1}A^{(M)}\mathcal{P}). \tag{9}$$

Noting that $T^{(M)}$ has the same block structure as $A^{(M)}$, whose block tridiagonalization is shown in Section 3, we can immediately derive:

$$\mathcal{P}^{-1}T^{(M)}\mathcal{P} = \operatorname{diag}(\tilde{T}_1^{(1)}, \tilde{T}_2^{(1)}, \ldots, \tilde{T}_M^{(1)}), \tag{10}$$

where

$$\tilde{T}_j^{(1)} :=$$

$$\begin{pmatrix} I_j & -E_j^{(M)}(D_{j+M}^{(M)})^{-1} & & & \\ -F_j^{(M)}(D_j^{(M)})^{-1} & I_{j+M} & & & \\ & \ddots & \ddots & & -E_{j+(q-1)M}^{(M)}(D_{j+qM}^{(M)})^{-1} \\ & & -F_{j+(q-1)M}^{(M)}(D_{j+(q-1)M}^{(M)})^{-1} & I_{j+(q-1)M} \end{pmatrix},$$

$$j = 1, 2, \ldots, r, \tag{11}$$

$$\tilde{T}_j^{(1)} :=$$

$$\begin{pmatrix} I_j & -E_j^{(M)}(D_{j+M}^{(M)})^{-1} & & & \\ -F_j^{(M)}(D_j^{(M)})^{-1} & I_{j+M} & \ddots & & \\ & \ddots & \ddots & \ddots & \\ & & -F_{j+(q-2)M}^{(M)}(D_{j+(q-2)M}^{(M)})^{-1} & I_{j+(q-2)M} & -E_{j+(q-2)M}^{(M)}(D_{j+(q-1)M}^{(M)})^{-1} \\ & & & -F_{j+(q-2)M}^{(M)}(D_{j+(q-2)M}^{(M)})^{-1} & I_{j+(q-2)M} \end{pmatrix},$$

$j = r+1, r+2, \ldots, M$.

Combining (8) and (10) with (9), we obtain:

$$\mathcal{P}^{-1} A^{(2M)} \mathcal{P} = \mathrm{diag}(\tilde{T}_1^{(1)} \tilde{A}_1^{(1)}, \tilde{T}_2^{(1)} \tilde{A}_2^{(1)}, \ldots, \tilde{T}_M^{(1)} \tilde{A}_M^{(1)}).$$

This implies that the transformation from $A^{(M)}$ to $A^{(2M)}$ can also be completed using three transformations: (1) the block tridiagonalization from $A^{(M)}$ to $\mathcal{P}^{-1} A^{(M)} \mathcal{P}$; (2) the transformations from the block 1-tridiagonal matrices $\tilde{A}_i^{(1)}$ to the block 2-tridiagonal matrices $\tilde{T}_i^{(1)} \tilde{A}_i^{(1)}$; and (3) the block $2M$-tridiagonalization from $\mathcal{P}^{-1} A^{(2M)} \mathcal{P}$ to $A^{(2M)}$. See Figure 3 for the relationships among the block tridiagonal (1-tridiagonal), 2-tridiagonal, M-tridiagonal, and $2M$-tridiagonal matrices.

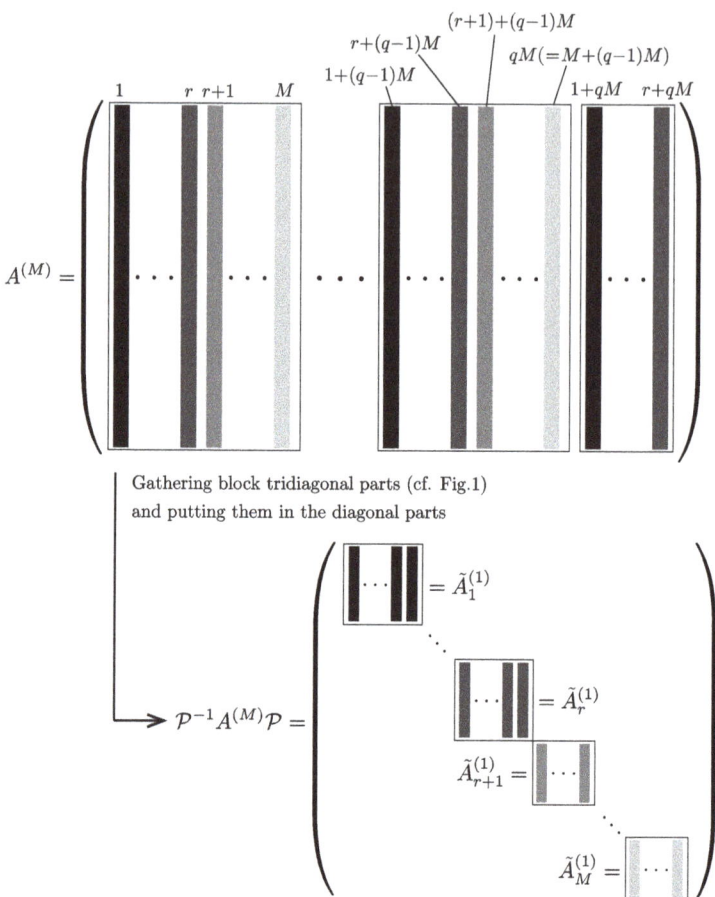

Figure 2. A block tridiagonalization of the block M-tridiagonal matrix $A^{(M)}$.

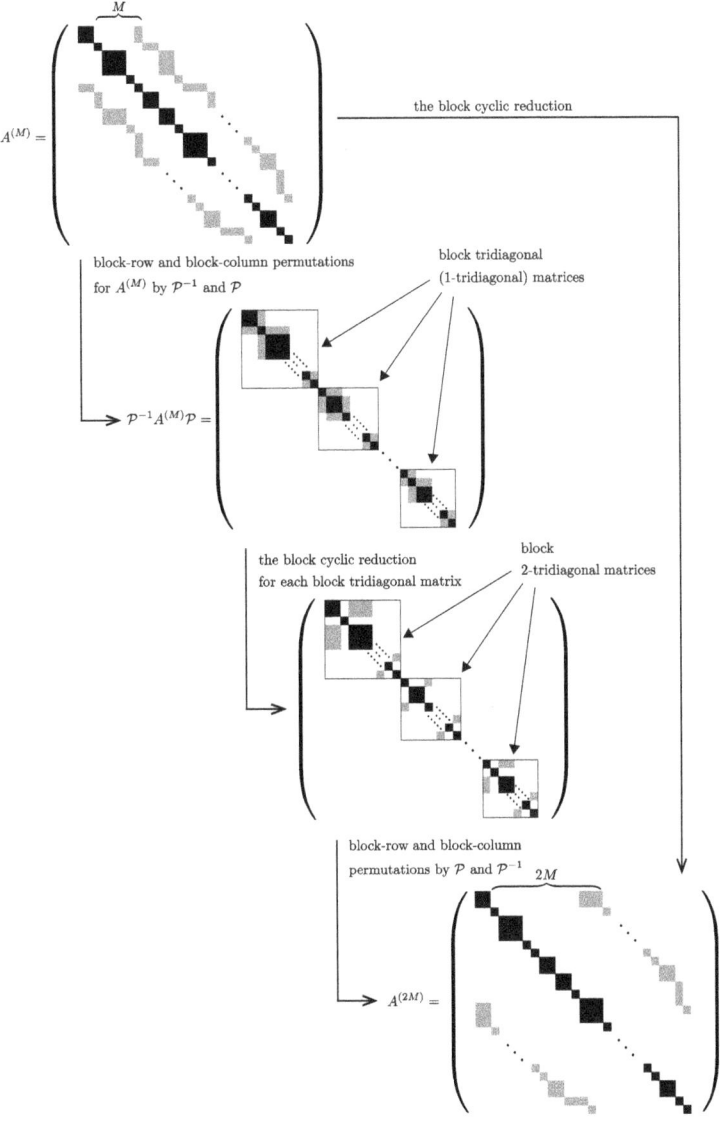

Figure 3. Coefficient matrices in the block cyclic reduction.

4. Inverses of Block 1-Tridiagonal and 2-Tridiagonal Matrices

In this section, we express the inverse of the block 1-tridiagonal matrix $A^{(1)}$ using that of the block 2-tridiagonal matrix $A^{(2)}$. This is useful for comparing the roots of the characteristic polynomials of the block 1-tridiagonal matrix $A^{(1)}$ and the block 2-tridiagonal matrix $A^{(2)}$ in the next section.

We introduce two auxiliary matrices $D := \mathrm{diag}(D_1^{(1)}, D_2^{(1)}, \ldots, D_m^{(1)})$ and $A_R^{(1)} := RA^{(1)}R$, where $R := \mathrm{diag}((-1)I_1, (-1)^2 I_2, \ldots, (-1)^m I_m)$ involving the N_i-dimensional identity matrices I_i. Then, we derive the following lemma for an expression using D and $A_R^{(1)}$ of transformation matrix $T^{(1)}$.

Lemma 1. *The transformation matrix $T^{(1)}$ can be decomposed using D and $A_R^{(1)}$ into:*

$$T^{(1)} = A_R^{(1)} D^{-1}.$$

Proof. It is obvious that $RA^{(1)}$ and $RA^{(1)}R$ are both block 1-tridiagonal matrices. It is easy to check that $(RA^{(1)})_{i,j} = ((-1)^j A^{(1)})_{i,j}$ where $(\cdot)_{i,j}$ denotes the (i,j) blocks of a matrix. Similarly, it turns out that $(RA^{(1)}R)_{i,j} = ((-1)^i R A^{(1)})_{i,j}$. Thus, by noting that $(A_R^{(1)})_{i,j} = ((-1)^{i+j} A^{(1)})_{i,j}$, we can derive:

$$A_R^{(1)} = \begin{pmatrix} D_1^{(1)} & -E_1^{(1)} & & \\ -F_1^{(1)} & D_2^{(1)} & \ddots & \\ & \ddots & \ddots & -E_{m-1}^{(1)} \\ & & -F_{m-1}^{(1)} & D_m^{(1)} \end{pmatrix}.$$

Furthermore, it can easily be observed that $T^{(1)} D = A_R$. Noting that D is nonsingular, we obtain (1). □

Since it is obvious that $R^{-1} = R$, it holds that $A_R^{(1)} = R^{-1} A^{(1)} R$. This implies that the eigenvalues of $A_R^{(1)}$ coincide with those of $A^{(1)}$. Thus, $A_R^{(1)}$ is nonsingular if $A^{(1)}$ is nonsingular. From Lemma 1, it immediately follows that $\det A^{(2)} = (\det A_R^{(1)})(\det D^{-1})(\det A^{(1)})$. Therefore, the inverse of $A^{(2)}$ exists if $A^{(1)}$ is nonsingular. The following proposition gives the relationship of $(A^{(2)})^{-1}$ to $(A^{(1)})^{-1}$ and $(A_R^{(1)})^{-1}$.

Proposition 1. *For the (i,j) blocks $((A^{(1)})^{-1})_{i,j}$ and $((A^{(2)})^{-1})_{i,j}$, it holds that:*

$$((A^{(2)})^{-1})_{i,j} = \begin{cases} ((A^{(1)})^{-1})_{i,j} & \text{if } i+j \text{ is even,} \\ O & \text{if } i+j \text{ is odd,} \end{cases}$$

where O denotes the zero matrix whose entries are all 0 as shown previously. Accordingly,

$$(A^{(2)})^{-1} = \frac{1}{2}((A^{(1)})^{-1} + (A_R^{(1)})^{-1}).$$

Proof. Observing the ith block-row on both sides of the trivial identity $(A^{(1)})^{-1} A^{(1)} = I_N$, we can obtain m matrix equations:

$$\begin{cases} & ((A^{(1)})^{-1})_{i,1} D_1^{(1)} + ((A^{(1)})^{-1})_{i,2} F_1^{(1)} = O, \\ ((A^{(1)})^{-1})_{i,1} E_1^{(1)} + ((A^{(1)})^{-1})_{i,2} D_2^{(1)} + ((A^{(1)})^{-1})_{i,3} F_2^{(1)} = O, \\ \quad \vdots & \quad \vdots \quad\quad \vdots \quad\quad \vdots \\ ((A^{(1)})^{-1})_{i,i-1} E_{i-1}^{(1)} + ((A^{(1)})^{-1})_{i,i} D_i^{(1)} + ((A^{(1)})^{-1})_{i,i+1} F_i^{(1)} = I_i, \\ \quad \vdots & \quad \vdots \quad\quad \vdots \quad\quad \vdots \\ ((A^{(1)})^{-1})_{i,m-2} E_{m-2}^{(1)} + ((A^{(1)})^{-1})_{i,m-1} D_{m-1}^{(1)} + ((A^{(1)})^{-1})_{i,m} F_{m-1}^{(1)} = O, \\ ((A^{(1)})^{-1})_{i,m-1} E_{m-1}^{(1)} + ((A^{(1)})^{-1})_{i,m} D_m^{(1)} = O. \end{cases}$$

Multiplying both sides of the 1st, 2nd, ..., mth equations in (4) from the right by $((A^{(1)})^{-1})_{1,j}, ((A^{(1)})^{-1})_{2,j}, \ldots, ((A^{(1)})^{-1})_{m,j}$, respectively, we can rewrite (4) as:

$$
\begin{cases}
\hat{D}_1^{(1)} + \hat{F}_1^{(1)} &= O, \\
\hat{E}_1^{(1)} + \hat{D}_2^{(1)} + \hat{F}_2^{(1)} &= O, \\
\vdots \quad \vdots \quad \vdots & \vdots \\
\hat{E}_{i-1}^{(1)} + \hat{D}_i^{(1)} + \hat{F}_i^{(1)} &= ((A^{(1)})^{-1})_{i,j}, \\
\vdots \quad \vdots \quad \vdots & \vdots \\
\hat{E}_{m-2}^{(1)} + \hat{D}_{m-1}^{(1)} + \hat{F}_{m-1}^{(1)} &= O, \\
\hat{E}_{m-1}^{(1)} + \hat{D}_m^{(1)} &= O,
\end{cases}
$$

where $\hat{D}_k^{(1)} := ((A^{(1)})^{-1})_{i,k} D_k^{(1)} ((A^{(1)})^{-1})_{k,j}$, $\hat{E}_k^{(1)} := ((A^{(1)})^{-1})_{i,k} E_k^{(1)} ((A^{(1)})^{-1})_{k+1,j}$ and $\hat{F}_k^{(1)} := ((A^{(1)})^{-1})_{i,k+1} F_k^{(1)} ((A^{(1)})^{-1})_{k,j}$. Similarly, by focusing on the jth block column of both sides of $A^{(1)}(A^{(1)})^{-1} = I_N$ and multiplying the 1st, 2nd, ..., mth equations from the left by $((A^{(1)})^{-1})_{i,1}, ((A^{(1)})^{-1})_{i,2}, \ldots, ((A^{(1)})^{-1})_{i,m}$, respectively, we can derive:

$$
\begin{cases}
\hat{D}_1^{(1)} + \hat{E}_1^{(1)} &= O, \\
\hat{F}_1^{(1)} + \hat{D}_2^{(1)} + \hat{E}_2^{(1)} &= O, \\
\vdots \quad \vdots \quad \vdots & \vdots \\
\hat{F}_{j-1}^{(1)} + \hat{D}_j^{(1)} + \hat{E}_j^{(1)} &= ((A^{(1)})^{-1})_{i,j}, \\
\vdots \quad \vdots \quad \vdots & \vdots \\
\hat{F}_{m-2}^{(1)} + \hat{D}_{m-1}^{(1)} + \hat{E}_{m-1}^{(1)} &= O, \\
\hat{F}_{m-1}^{(1)} + \hat{D}_m^{(1)} &= O.
\end{cases}
$$

Adding the kth equation of (4) to that of (4), multiplying this by $(-1)^k$, and letting $G_k^{(1)} := \hat{E}_k^{(1)} + \hat{F}_k^{(1)}$, we can thus obtain:

$$
(-1)^k (G_{k-1}^{(1)} + 2\hat{D}_k^{(1)} + G_k^{(1)}) = \begin{cases} (-1)^i ((A^{(1)})^{-1})_{i,j} & \text{if } k = i, \\ (-1)^j ((A^{(1)})^{-1})_{i,j} & \text{if } k = j, \\ O & \text{otherwise,} \end{cases}
$$

where $G_0^{(1)} := O$ and $G_m^{(1)} := O$. The summation for $k = 1, 2, \ldots, m$ of (4) leads to:

$$
2 \sum_{k=1}^m (-1)^k \hat{D}_k^{(1)} = [(-1)^i + (-1)^j] ((A^{(1)})^{-1})_{i,j}.
$$

From Lemma 1, we can see that: $(A^{(2)})^{-1} = (A_R^{(1)} D^{-1} A^{(1)})^{-1} = (A^{(1)})^{-1} D (A_R^{(1)})^{-1}$. Since it follows from $(A_R^{(1)})^{-1} = (R A^{(1)} R)^{-1} = R(A^{(1)})^{-1} R$ that $((A_R^{(1)})^{-1})_{k,j} = (-1)^{k+j} ((A^{(1)})^{-1})_{k,j}$, we can obtain:

$$
\begin{aligned}
((A^{(2)})^{-1})_{i,j} &= \sum_{k=1}^m (-1)^{k+j} ((A^{(1)})^{-1})_{i,k} D_k^{(1)} ((A^{(1)})^{-1})_{k,j} \\
&= \sum_{k=1}^m (-1)^{k+j} \hat{D}_k^{(1)}.
\end{aligned}
$$

Consequently, by combining (4) with (4), we can derive:

$$((A^{(2)})^{-1})_{i,j} = \frac{1+(-1)^{i+j}}{2}((A^{(1)})^{-1})_{i,j},$$

which implies (1). The matrix identity $(A_R^{(1)})^{-1} = R(A^{(1)})^{-1}R$ also gives the relationship of blocks in $(A^{(1)})^{-1}$ and $(A_R^{(1)})^{-1}$:

$$((A_R^{(1)})^{-1})_{i,j} = \begin{cases} ((A^{(1)})^{-1})_{i,j} & \text{if } i+j \text{ is even,} \\ -((A^{(1)})^{-1})_{i,j} & \text{if } i+j \text{ is odd.} \end{cases}$$

Considering (4) and (4), we then have (1). □

Proposition 1 plays a key role in understanding the change in the roots of characteristic polynomials of coefficient matrices in linear systems after block cyclic reductions.

5. Roots of Characteristic Polynomial Sequence

In this section, we first investigate roots of characteristic polynomials of the block 2-tridiagonal matrix $A^{(2)} = T^{(1)}A^{(1)}$, which is transformed from the block 1-tridiagonal matrix $A^{(1)}$ in the block cyclic reduction under the assumption that $A^{(1)}$ is symmetric positive definite.

With the help of Proposition 1, we present a theorem for the roots of characteristic polynomials of $A^{(1)}$ and $A^{(2)}$.

Theorem 1. *Assume that the block tridiagonal matrix $A^{(1)}$ is symmetric positive definite. Then, for the block 2-tridiagonal matrix $A^{(2)} = T^{(1)}A^{(1)}$, it holds that:*

$$\lambda_N(A^{(1)}) \le \lambda_k(A^{(2)}) \le \lambda_1(A^{(1)}), \quad k = 1, 2, \ldots, N,$$

where $\lambda_k(\cdot)$ denotes the kth largest root of the characteristic polynomial of a matrix—namely, the kth largest eigenvalue of a matrix.

Proof. Let $u_1 \in \mathbb{R}^N$ be a normalized eigenvector corresponding to $\lambda_1((A^{(1)})^{-1}+(A_R^{(1)})^{-1})$. Noting that $(A^{(1)})^{-1}$ and $(A_R^{(1)})^{-1}$ are both symmetric and considering the Rayleigh quotient [10], we can derive:

$$u_1^\top (A^{(1)})^{-1} u_1 \le \lambda_1((A^{(1)})^{-1}),$$
$$u_1^\top (A_R^{(1)})^{-1} u_1 \le \lambda_1((A_R^{(1)})^{-1}) = \lambda_1((A^{(1)})^{-1}).$$

This equality holds in (5) if and only if u_1 is the eigenvector of $(A^{(1)})^{-1}$ corresponding to $\lambda_1((A^{(1)})^{-1})$, while the equality holds in (5) if and only if u_1 is also the eigenvector of $(A_R^{(1)})^{-1}$ corresponding to $\lambda_1((A_R^{(1)})^{-1}) = \lambda_1((A^{(1)})^{-1})$. The inequalities (5) and (5) immediately lead to:

$$u_1^\top ((A^{(1)})^{-1} + (A_R^{(1)})^{-1}) u_1 \le 2\lambda_1((A^{(1)})^{-1}).$$

Using Proposition 1, we can rewrite the Rayleigh quotient $u_1^\top ((A^{(1)})^{-1} + (A_R^{(1)})^{-1}) u_1$ as:

$$u_1^\top ((A^{(1)})^{-1} + (A_R^{(1)})^{-1}) u_1 = 2\lambda_1((A^{(2)})^{-1}).$$

From (5) and (5), we can see that:

Similarly, from a comparison of the Rayleigh quotient $u_1^\top((A^{(1)})^{-1} + (A_R^{(1)})^{-1})u_1$ with the minimal eigenvalue $\lambda_N((A^{(1)})^{-1})$, it follows that:

$$\lambda_k((A^{(2)})^{-1}) \geq \lambda_N((A^{(1)})^{-1}), \quad k = 1, 2, \ldots, N.$$

Thus, by combining (5) with (5), we can obtain:

$$\lambda_N((A^{(1)})^{-1}) \leq \lambda_k((A^{(2)})^{-1}) \leq \lambda_1((A^{(1)})^{-1}), \quad k = 1, 2, \ldots, N.$$

Since the eigenvalues of a matrix are the reciprocals of eigenvalues of its inverse matrix, we therefore have (1). □

The following theorem is a specialization of Theorem 1.

Theorem 2. *Assume that the block tridiagonal matrix $A^{(1)}$ is symmetric positive definite and that its eigenvalues are distinct from each other. Furthermore, let the non-zero blocks all be nonsingular square matrices with the same matrix size. Then, for the block 2-tridiagonal matrix $A^{(2)} = T^{(1)}A^{(1)}$, it holds that:*

$$\lambda_N(A^{(1)}) < \lambda_k(A^{(2)}) < \lambda_1(A^{(1)}), \quad k = 1, 2, \ldots, N.$$

Proof. We begin by reconsidering the proof of Theorem 1. The proof of (2) is completed by proving $\lambda_1(A^{(1)}) > \lambda_1(A^{(2)})$ and $\lambda_N(A^{(1)}) < \lambda_N(A^{(2)})$. The equality in (5) does not hold if the equality in (5) holds. We recall here that the equality in (5) does not hold if u_1 is not the eigenvector of at least either $(A^{(1)})^{-1}$ or $(A_R^{(1)})^{-1}$ corresponding to $\lambda_1((A^{(1)})^{-1}) = \lambda_1((A_R^{(1)})^{-1})$. Noting that $\lambda_N(A^{(1)}) = \lambda_1((A^{(1)})^{-1})$ and $\lambda_N(A^{(2)}) = \lambda_1((A^{(2)})^{-1})$, we can thus see that $\lambda_N(A^{(1)}) < \lambda_N(A^{(2)})$ if the eigenvector of $A^{(1)}$ corresponding to $\lambda_N(A^{(1)})$ is not equal to that of $A_R^{(1)}$ corresponding to $\lambda_N(A_R^{(1)}) = \lambda_N(A^{(1)})$. Similarly, the inequality $\lambda_1(A^{(1)}) > \lambda_1(A^{(2)})$ holds if the eigenvector of $A^{(1)}$ corresponding to $\lambda_1(A^{(1)})$ is not equal to that of $A_R^{(1)}$ corresponding to $\lambda_1(A_R^{(1)}) = \lambda_1(A^{(1)})$.

Let us assume here that v_1 is the eigenvector of both $A^{(1)}$ and $A_R^{(1)}$ corresponding to $\lambda_1(A^{(1)}) = \lambda_1(A_R^{(1)})$—namely, $A^{(1)}v_1 = \lambda_1(A^{(1)})v_1$ and $A_R^{(1)}v_1 = \lambda_1(A^{(1)})v_1$. From $A^{(1)}(Rv_1) = R(A_R^{(1)}v_1)$, we can then derive:

$$A^{(1)}(Rv_1) = \lambda_1(A^{(1)})(Rv_1).$$

This implies that Rv_1 is also the eigenvector of $A^{(1)}$ corresponding to $\lambda_1(A^{(1)})$. Noting that $A^{(1)}$ does not have multiple eigenvalues, we can thus obtain $v_1 = Rv_1$. Let $v_1(i)$ denote the N_i-dimensional vector in the ith block-rows of v_1. Then, by observing that:

$$\begin{pmatrix} v_1(1) \\ v_1(2) \\ \vdots \\ v_1(m) \end{pmatrix} = \begin{pmatrix} -I_1 & & & \\ & I_2 & & \\ & & \ddots & \\ & & & (-1)^m I_m \end{pmatrix} \begin{pmatrix} v_1(1) \\ v_1(2) \\ \vdots \\ v_1(m) \end{pmatrix},$$

we can specify v_1 as:

$$v_1 = \begin{pmatrix} 0 \\ v_1(2) \\ 0 \\ \vdots \\ (-1)^{m-1} v_1(m-1) \\ (-1)^m v_1(m) \end{pmatrix},$$

where o denotes the zero vector whose entries are all 0. Thus, by focusing on the 1st, 3rd, ..., mth block rows on both sides of $A^{(1)}v_1 = \lambda_1(A^{(1)})v_1$ with odd m, we have:

$$\begin{cases} E_1^{(1)} v_1(2) = o, \\ E_2^{(1)\top} v_1(2) + E_3^{(1)} v_1(4) = o, \\ \vdots \\ E_{m-3}^{(1)\top} v_1(m-3) + E_{m-2}^{(1)} v_1(m-1) = o, \\ E_{m-1}^{(1)\top} v_1(m-1) = o. \end{cases}$$

Since $E_1^{(1)}, E_2^{(1)}, \ldots, E_{m-1}^{(1)}$ are all nonsingular, (5) immediately leads to $v_1(2) = o$, $v_1(4) = o, \ldots, v_1(m-1) = o$. Namely, v_1 is the zero vector. This contradicts the assumption that v_1 is the eigenvector of both $A^{(1)}$ and $A_R^{(1)}$ corresponding to $\lambda_1(A^{(1)}) = \lambda_1(A_R^{(1)})$. The contradiction is similarly derived in the case where m is even. Therefore, we conclude that $\lambda_1(A^{(1)}) > \lambda_1(A^{(2)})$. We also have $\lambda_N(A^{(1)}) < \lambda_N(A^{(2)})$ along the same lines as the above proof. □

We recall here that the transformation $A^{(2M)} = T^{(M)} A^{(M)}$ from the block M-tridiagonal matrix $A^{(M)}$ to the block $2M$-tridiagonal matrix $A^{(2M)}$ can be regarded as a composite transformation of the transformations from the block tridiagonal matrices to the block 2-tridiagonal matrices and two similarity transformations. By combining this with Theorems 1 and 2, we can derive the following theorem concerning the roots of the characteristic polynomials of $A^{(M)}$ and $A^{(2M)} = T^{(M)} A^{(M)}$.

Theorem 3. *Assume that the block M-tridiagonal matrix $A^{(M)}$ is symmetric positive definite, where $M = 1, 2, \ldots$. Then, for the block $2M$-tridiagonal matrix $A^{(2M)} = T^{(M)} A^{(M)}$, it holds that:*

$$\lambda_N(A^{(M)}) \leq \lambda_k(A^{(2M)}) \leq \lambda_1(A^{(M)}), \quad k = 1, 2, \ldots, N.$$

Furthermore, let the roots of the characteristic polynomials of $A^{(M)}$ be distinct from each other, the non-zero blocks all be nonsingular square matrices, and their matrix sizes all be the same. Then, it holds that:

$$\lambda_N(A^{(M)}) < \lambda_k(A^{(2M)}) < \lambda_1(A^{(M)}), \quad k = 1, 2, \ldots, N.$$

It is obvious that $A^{(2)} = T^{(1)} A^{(1)}$, $A^{(4)} = T^{(2)} A^{(2)}, \ldots$ are symmetric if the block tridiagonal matrix $A^{(1)} = A$ is also symmetric in the original linear system $Ax = b$. From Theorem 3, we can recursively see that $A^{(2)}, A^{(4)}, \ldots$ are positive definite if the original coefficient matrix $A^{(1)} = A$ is also positive definite. We then conclude that:

$$\cdots \leq \frac{\lambda_1(A^{(2M)})}{\lambda_N(A^{(2M)})} \leq \frac{\lambda_1(A^{(M)})}{\lambda_N(A^{(M)})} \leq \cdots \leq \frac{\lambda_1(A^{(2)})}{\lambda_N(A^{(2)})} \leq \frac{\lambda_1(A^{(1)})}{\lambda_N(A^{(1)})},$$

or

$$\cdots < \frac{\lambda_1(A^{(2M)})}{\lambda_N(A^{(2M)})} < \frac{\lambda_1(A^{(M)})}{\lambda_N(A^{(M)})} < \cdots < \frac{\lambda_1(A^{(2)})}{\lambda_N(A^{(2)})} < \frac{\lambda_1(A^{(1)})}{\lambda_N(A^{(1)})},$$

as long as the block cyclic reductions are repeated. The discussion in this section can easily be changed for the case where the original coefficient matrix $A^{(1)} = A$ is negative definite.

6. Numerical Examples

In this section, we give two examples for observing changes in coefficient matrices in the iterative block cyclic reductions for block tridiagonal linear systems $A^{(1)}x = b$ and

nomials of coefficient matrices. The numerical illustration was carried out on a computer; OS: Mac OS Monterey (ver. 12.0.1), CPU: 2.4 GHz Intel Core i9. For this, we employed the MATLAB software (R2021a). Computed values are given in floating-point arithmetic.

We first consider the case where $A^{(1)}$ is the 9-by-9 symmetric block tridiagonal and positive definite matrix with $\lambda_1(A^{(1)}) \approx 11.3465$, $\lambda_9(A^{(1)}) \approx 0.9931$, and $\lambda_1(A^{(1)})/\lambda_9(A^{(1)}) \approx 11.3465/0.9931 \approx 11.4253$:

$$A^{(1)} = \begin{pmatrix} 2 & 1 & 0 & 0 & 1 & 0 & 0 & 0 & 0 \\ 1 & 3 & 1 & 0 & 0 & 1 & 0 & 0 & 0 \\ 0 & 1 & 4 & 1 & 0 & 0 & 1 & 0 & 0 \\ 0 & 0 & 1 & 5 & 0 & 1 & 0 & 0 & 0 \\ 1 & 0 & 0 & 0 & 6 & 1 & 0 & 1 & 0 \\ 0 & 1 & 0 & 1 & 1 & 7 & 1 & 0 & 1 \\ 0 & 0 & 1 & 0 & 0 & 1 & 8 & 0 & 1 \\ 0 & 0 & 0 & 0 & 1 & 0 & 0 & 9 & 1 \\ 0 & 0 & 0 & 0 & 0 & 1 & 1 & 1 & 10 \end{pmatrix},$$

where the values of $\lambda_1(A^{(1)})$, $\lambda_9(A^{(1)})$ and $\lambda_1(A^{(1)})/\lambda_9(A^{(1)})$ are computed using the MATLAB function eig and rounded to 4 digits after the decimal point. The diagonal blocks are all symmetric and their matrix sizes are distinct from one another. Since the determinants of the $(1,1)$, $(2,2)$, and $(3,3)$ blocks are, respectively, 85, 322, and 89, the diagonal blocks are all nonsingular. The non-zero subdiagonal (and superdiagonal) blocks are not square matrices, but the transposes of the $(1,2)$ and $(2,3)$ blocks coincide with those of the $(2,1)$ and $(3,2)$ blocks, respectively. After the 1st block cyclic reduction, $A^{(1)}$ is transformed to the symmetric block 2-tridiagonal matrix:

$$A^{(2)} = \begin{pmatrix} 1.8292 & 1.0248 & -0.0031 & 0.0248 & 0 & 0 & 0 & -0.1708 & 0.0217 \\ 1.0248 & 2.8509 & 1.0186 & -0.1491 & 0 & 0 & 0 & 0.0248 & -0.1304 \\ -0.0031 & 1.0186 & 3.8727 & 1.0186 & 0 & 0 & 0 & -0.0031 & -0.1087 \\ 0.0248 & -0.1491 & 1.0186 & 4.8509 & 0 & 0 & 0 & 0.0248 & -0.1304 \\ 0 & 0 & 0 & 0 & 5.2759 & 1.2465 & -0.0476 & 0 & 0 \\ 0 & 0 & 0 & 0 & 1.2465 & 6.1930 & 1.0753 & 0 & 0 \\ 0 & 0 & 0 & 0 & -0.0476 & 1.0753 & 7.6048 & 0 & 0 \\ -0.1708 & 0.0248 & -0.0031 & 0.0248 & 0 & 0 & 0 & 8.8292 & 1.0217 \\ 0.0217 & -0.1304 & -0.1087 & -0.1304 & 0 & 0 & 0 & 1.0217 & 9.7609 \end{pmatrix}, \quad (8)$$

where all non-zero entries are rounded to 4 digits after the decimal point. Using the MATLAB function eig, we can see that $\lambda_1(A^{(2)}) \approx 10.4242$ and $\lambda_9(A^{(2)}) \approx 1.0440$. Thus, $\lambda_1(A^{(2)})/\lambda_9(A^{(2)}) \approx 9.9849 < \lambda_1(A^{(1)})/\lambda_9(A^{(1)})$. It is also easy to check that the diagonal blocks of $A^{(2)}$ are all nonsingular. This implies that a block cyclic reduction can again be applied to the linear system with the coefficient matrix $A^{(2)}$. The 2nd block cyclic reduction then simplifies $A^{(2)}$ as the block diagonal matrix:

$$\mathcal{A} = \begin{pmatrix} 1.8257 & 1.0259 & -0.0027 & 0.0259 & 0 & 0 & 0 & 0 & 0 \\ 1.0259 & 2.8490 & 1.0171 & -0.1510 & 0 & 0 & 0 & 0 & 0 \\ -0.0027 & 1.0171 & 3.8715 & 1.0171 & 0 & 0 & 0 & 0 & 0 \\ 0.0259 & -0.1510 & 1.0171 & 4.8490 & 0 & 0 & 0 & 0 & 0 \\ 0 & 0 & 0 & 0 & 5.2759 & 1.2465 & -0.0476 & 0 & 0 \\ 0 & 0 & 0 & 0 & 1.2465 & 6.1930 & 1.0753 & 0 & 0 \\ 0 & 0 & 0 & 0 & -0.0476 & 1.0753 & 7.6048 & 0 & 0 \\ 0 & 0 & 0 & 0 & 0 & 0 & 0 & 8.8052 & 1.0321 \\ 0 & 0 & 0 & 0 & 0 & 0 & 0 & 1.0321 & 9.7475 \end{pmatrix}. \quad (9)$$

The MATLAB function eig immediately returns $\lambda_1(\mathcal{A}) \approx 10.4109$ and $\lambda_9(\mathcal{A}) \approx 1.0445$. Therefore, $\lambda_1(\mathcal{A})/\lambda_9(\mathcal{A}) \approx 9.9674 < \lambda_1(A^{(2)})/\lambda_9(A^{(2)})$.

Next, we deal with the case where $A^{(1)}$ is the 9-by-9 symmetric block tridiagonal and negative definite matrix with $\lambda_1(A^{(1)}) = -1.172$, $\lambda_9(A^{(1)}) = -6.828$ and $\lambda_1(A^{(1)})/\lambda_9(A^{(1)}) \approx 6.828/1.172 \approx 5.826$,

$$A^{(1)} = \begin{pmatrix} -4 & 1 & 0 & 1 & 0 & 0 & 0 & 0 & 0 \\ 1 & -4 & 1 & 0 & 1 & 0 & 0 & 0 & 0 \\ 0 & 1 & -4 & 0 & 0 & 1 & 0 & 0 & 0 \\ 1 & 0 & 0 & -4 & 1 & 0 & 1 & 0 & 0 \\ 0 & 1 & 0 & 1 & -4 & 1 & 0 & 1 & 0 \\ 0 & 0 & 1 & 0 & 1 & -4 & 0 & 0 & 1 \\ 0 & 0 & 0 & 1 & 0 & 0 & -4 & 1 & 0 \\ 0 & 0 & 0 & 0 & 1 & 0 & 1 & -4 & 1 \\ 0 & 0 & 0 & 0 & 0 & 1 & 0 & 1 & -4 \end{pmatrix}. \tag{10}$$

This is an example matrix appearing in the discretization of Poisson's equation [11]. It is different from the 1st example matrix in that all the blocks have the same matrix size. It is obvious that the non-zero blocks are all 3-by-3 nonsingular. A block cyclic reduction then transforms $A^{(1)}$ into the symmetric block 2-tridiagonal matrix:

$$A^{(2)} = \begin{pmatrix} -3.7321 & 1.0714 & 0.0179 & 0 & 0 & 0 & 0.2679 & 0.0714 & 0.0179 \\ 1.0714 & -3.7143 & 1.0714 & 0 & 0 & 0 & 0.0714 & 0.2857 & 0.0714 \\ 0.0179 & 1.0714 & -3.7321 & 0 & 0 & 0 & 0.0179 & 0.0714 & 0.2679 \\ 0 & 0 & 0 & -3.4643 & 1.1429 & 0.0357 & 0 & 0 & 0 \\ 0 & 0 & 0 & 1.1429 & -3.4286 & 1.1429 & 0 & 0 & 0 \\ 0 & 0 & 0 & 0.0357 & 1.1429 & -3.4643 & 0 & 0 & 0 \\ 0.2679 & 0.0714 & 0.0179 & 0 & 0 & 0 & -3.7321 & 1.0714 & 0.0179 \\ 0.0714 & 0.2857 & 0.0714 & 0 & 0 & 0 & 1.0714 & -3.7143 & 1.0714 \\ 0.0179 & 0.0714 & 0.2679 & 0 & 0 & 0 & 0.0179 & 1.0714 & -3.7321 \end{pmatrix}, \tag{11}$$

where $\lambda_1(A^{(2)}) = -1.8123$, $\lambda_9(A^{(2)}) = -5.4142$, and $\lambda_1(A^{(2)})/\lambda_9(A^{(2)}) \approx 2.9875$. Since the non-zero blocks in $A^{(2)}$ are all nonsingular, we can simplify $A^{(2)}$ as the block diagonal matrix:

$$\mathcal{A} = \begin{pmatrix} -3.7052 & 1.0932 & 0.0282 & 0 & 0 & 0 & 0 & 0 & 0 \\ 1.0932 & -3.6770 & 1.0932 & 0 & 0 & 0 & 0 & 0 & 0 \\ 0.0282 & 1.0932 & -3.7052 & 0 & 0 & 0 & 0 & 0 & 0 \\ 0 & 0 & 0 & -3.4643 & 1.1429 & 0.0357 & 0 & 0 & 0 \\ 0 & 0 & 0 & 1.1429 & -3.4286 & 1.1429 & 0 & 0 & 0 \\ 0 & 0 & 0 & 0.0357 & 1.1429 & -3.4643 & 0 & 0 & 0 \\ 0 & 0 & 0 & 0 & 0 & 0 & -3.7052 & 1.0932 & 0.0282 \\ 0 & 0 & 0 & 0 & 0 & 0 & 1.0932 & -3.6770 & 1.0932 \\ 0 & 0 & 0 & 0 & 0 & 0 & 0.0282 & 1.0932 & -3.7052 \end{pmatrix}, \tag{12}$$

with $\lambda_1(\mathcal{A}) = -1.8123$, $\lambda_9(\mathcal{A}) = -5.2230$, and $\lambda_1(\mathcal{A})/\lambda_9(\mathcal{A}) = 2.8820$. Thus, it can numerically be observed that: $\lambda_1(A^{(1)})/\lambda_9(A^{(1)}) > \lambda_1(A^{(2)})/\lambda_9(A^{(2)}) > \lambda_1(\mathcal{A})/\lambda_9(\mathcal{A})$.

7. Concluding Remarks

This paper focused on coefficient matrices in linear systems obtained from block iterative cyclic reductions. We showed that block M-tridiagonal coefficient matrices can be transformed to block tridiagonal matrices without changing the eigenvalues. We interpreted transformations from block M-tridiagonal matrices to block $2M$-tridiagonal matrices as composite transformations of the block tridiagonalizations, with their inverses and transformations from block tridiagonal matrices to block 2-tridiagonal matrices appearing in the first step of the block cyclic reduction method. We then used this interpretation to consider the inverses of block tridiagonal matrices and block 2-tridiagonal matrices in the first step, which helped us to clarify the main results of this paper—i.e., the first step narrows the distribution of roots of characteristic polynomials associated with coefficient matrices, and the other steps also do this if the original coefficient matrices are symmetric positive or negative definite. This property suggests that each block cyclic reduction does not make it difficult to solve a linear system with a symmetric positive or negative definite block tridiagonal matrix, which will be useful for dividing a large-scale linear system into several small-scale ones.

A remarkable point of our approach is, as a result, useful regardless of whether coefficient matrices are tridiagonal or block tridiagonal. However, the coefficient matrices are currently limited to be symmetric positive or negative definite. For example, in the nonsymmetric Toeplitz case [12], our approach cannot grasp root distribution of the characteristic polynomial. Future work thus involves developing our approach so that root distribution can be examined in the cases of various coefficient matrices.

Author Contributions: Conceptualization, M.S., M.I. and Y.N.; Data curation, M.S. and T.W.; Methodology, M.S.; Supervision, Y.N.; Writing—original draft, M.S. and M.I. All the authors contributed equally to this work. All authors have read and agreed to the published version of the manuscript.

Funding: This work was supported by the Grant-in-Aid for Early-Career Scientists No. 21K13844 from the Japan Society for the Promotion of Science.

Institutional Review Board Statement: Not applicable.

Informed Consent Statement: Not applicable.

Data Availability Statement: Not applicable.

Acknowledgments: The authors would like to thank the reviewers for their careful reading and beneficial comments.

Conflicts of Interest: The authors declare no conflicts of interest.

References

1. Gander, W.; Golub, G.H. Cyclic reduction—History and applications. In *Proceedings Workshop Scientific Computing (Hong Kong, 1997)*; Springer: Singapore, 1997; pp. 73–85.
2. Heller, D. Some aspects of the cyclic reduction algorithm for block tridiagonal linear systems. *SIAM J. Numer. Anal.* **1976**, *13*, 484–496. [CrossRef]
3. Amodio, P.; Mazzia, F. Backward Error Analysis of Cyclic Reduction for the Solution of Tridiagonal Systems. *Math. Comput.* **1994**, *62*, 601–617. [CrossRef]
4. Rossi, T.; Toivanen. J. A nonstandard cyclic reduction method, its variants and stability. *SIAM J. Matrix Anal. Appl.* **1999**, *20*, 628–645. [CrossRef]
5. Evans, D.J. Cyclic and stride reduction methods for generalised tridiagonal matrices. *Int. J. Comput. Math.* **2000**, *73*, 487–492. [CrossRef]
6. Nagata, M.; Hada, M.; Iwasaki, M.; Nakamura, Y. Eigenvalue clustering of coefficient matrices in the iterative stride reductions for linear systems. *Comput. Math. Appl.* **2016**, *71*, 349–355. [CrossRef]
7. Wang, T.; Iwasaki, M.; Nakamura, Y. On condition numbers in the cyclic reduction processes of a tridiagonal matrix. *Int. J. Comput. Math.* **2010**, *87*, 3079–3093. [CrossRef]
8. Bini, D.A.; Meini, B. The cyclic reduction algorithm: From Poisson equation to stochastic processes and beyond in memoriam of Gene H. Golub. *Numer. Algor.* **2009**, *51*, 23–60. [CrossRef]
9. Yalamov, P.; Pavlov, V. Stability of the Block Cyclic Reduction. *Linear Algebra Its Appl.* **1996**, *249*, 341–358. [CrossRef]
10. Yanai, H.; Takeuchi, K.; Takane, Y. *Projection Matrices, Generalized Inverse Matrices, and Singular Value Decomposition*; Springer: New York, NY, USA, 2011.
11. Buzbee, B.L.; Golub, G.H.; Nielson, C.W. On direct methods for solving poisson's equations. *SIAM J. Numer. Anal.* **1970**, *7*, 627–656. [CrossRef]
12. Boffi, N.M.; Hill, J.C.; Reuter, M.G. Characterizing the inverses of block tridiagonal, block Toeplitz matrices. *Comput. Sci. Discov.* **2015**, *8*, 015001. [CrossRef]

Article

Approximation Properties of Chebyshev Polynomials in the Legendre Norm

Cuixia Niu [1,2], Huiqing Liao [1], Heping Ma [1,*] and Hua Wu [1]

[1] Department of Mathematics, Shanghai University, Shanghai 200444, China; ncxia@shu.edu.cn (C.N.); liaohuiqing@shu.edu.cn (H.L.); hwu@staff.shu.edu.cn (H.W.)
[2] School of Computer Science and Technology, Shandong Technology and Business University, Yantai 264000, China
* Correspondence: hpma@shu.edu.cn

Abstract: In this paper, we present some important approximation properties of Chebyshev polynomials in the Legendre norm. We mainly discuss the Chebyshev interpolation operator at the Chebyshev–Gauss–Lobatto points. The cases of single domain and multidomain for both one dimension and multi-dimensions are considered, respectively. The approximation results in Legendre norm rather than in the Chebyshev weighted norm are given, which play a fundamental role in numerical analysis of the Legendre–Chebyshev spectral method. These results are also useful in Clenshaw–Curtis quadrature which is based on sampling the integrand at Chebyshev points.

Keywords: Chebyshev polynomials; Chebyshev interpolation operator; the Legendre norm; Legendre–Chebyshev spectral method; Clenshaw–Curtis quadrature; multidomain; multi-dimensions

1. Introduction

Orthogonal polynomials are useful in many areas of numerical analysis and are powerful for function approximation, numerical integration and numerical solution of differential and integral equations [1,2]. The core idea of spectral methods is that any nice enough function can be expanded in a series of orthogonal polynomials so that orthogonal polynomials play a fundamental role in spectral methods [3–6]. Particularly, Chebyshev polynomials and Legendre polynomials are frequently used in spectral methods and are two important sequences in numerical analysis.

The related approximation results of typical Chebyshev and Legendre spectral approximation are discussed in many literatures [3,4,7–10]. These results of Chebyshev spectral approximation are usually in the weighted norm forms. The Legendre–Chebyshev spectral method is a popular numerical method, which enjoys advantages of better stability of the Legendre method and easy implementation of the Chebyshev method. Therefore, it is necessary to develop the approximation properties of Chebyshev polynomials in the Legendre norm. In [11,12], the approximation result of the Chebyshev interpolation operator without the Chebyshev weighted norm was first given. Some other valuable results related to Chebyshev polynomials can be referred to [2,13–19] and references therein.

In addition, Chebyshev polynomials have a special connection with Clenshaw–Curtis quadrature, which uses Chebyshev points instead of optimal nodes. Clenshaw–Curtis quadrature can be implemented in $O(N \log N)$ operations using the fast Fourier transform (FFT) and is used in numerical integration and numerical analysis [20–25]. As we know, Gauss quadrature is a beautiful and powerful idea. Zeros of orthogonal polynomials are chosen as the nodes of Gauss-type quadratures and used to generate computational grids for spectral methods. Yet, the Clenshaw–Curtis formula has essentially the same performance for most integrands and can be implemented effortlessly by the FFT [26]. Thus, the Clenshaw–Curtis and Gauss formulas are employed in the numerical solution of Ordi-

And, Chebyshev polynomials also have an important connection with the mock–Chebyshev subset interpolation exploited to cutdown the Runge phenomenon [29,30], which takes advantages of the optimality of the interpolation processes on Chebyshev–Lobatto nodes.

The purpose of this paper is to present some essential approximation results related to Chebyshev polynomials in the Legendre norm. The first fundamental result of orthogonal polynomials is the Weierstrass Theorem, which is an important element of the classical polynomial approximation theory [31,32]. In numerical analysis of the Legendre–Chebyshev spectral method, we need to consider the stability and approximation properties of the Chebyshev interpolation operator in the L^2-norm rather than in the Chebyshev weighted norm [13]. In the paper, we consider the Chebyshev interpolation operator at the Chebyshev–Gauss–Lobatto (CGL) points. The cases of single domain and multidomain for both one dimension and multi-dimensions are discussed. Some approximation results in the Legendre norm rather than in the Chebyshev weighted norm are given. These results serve as preparations for polynomial-based spectral methods.

The rest of the paper is organized as follows. In Section 2, Chebyshev polynomials are described, and some related notations are introduced. In Section 3, some approximation properties of Chebyshev interpolation operators in one dimension are given. The cases of single domain and multidomain are discussed, respectively. In Section 4, some approximation properties in multi-dimensions are given. The conclusion is given in Section 5.

2. Preliminaries and Notations

In this section, we give a brief description of Chebyshev polynomials and define the Chebyshev interpolation operators. Some notations are also given, which will be used in the following sections.

We consider orthogonal polynomials—Chebyshev polynomials, which are proportional to Jacobi polynomials $\{J_n^{-\frac{1}{2},-\frac{1}{2}}\}$ and are orthogonal with respect to the weight function

$$\omega(x) = (1-x^2)^{-\frac{1}{2}}, \quad x \in [-1,1].$$

The three-term recurrence relation for the Chebyshev polynomials is as follows [6]:

$$\begin{cases} T_0(x) = 1, \\ T_1(x) = x, \\ T_{n+1}(x) = 2xT_n(x) - T_{n-1}(x), \quad n \geq 1, \end{cases}$$

which satisfies

$$\int_{-1}^{1} T_i(x)T_j(x)(1-x^2)^{-\frac{1}{2}}\,dx = \frac{c_i}{2}\delta_{ij},$$

where $c_0 = 2$, $c_i = 1(i \geq 1)$. As we known, there have been many useful properties of Chebyshev polynomials [4,6,28].

Denote $(\cdot,\cdot)_Q$ and $\|\cdot\|_Q$ be the inner product and the norm of the space $L^2(Q)$, respectively. We will drop the subscript Q whenever $Q = I = (-1,1)$. Let $\mathbb{P}_N(I)$ be the space of polynomials with the degree at most N on an interval I. And let $H^\sigma(Q)(\sigma > 0)$ be the classical Sobolev space with norm $\|\cdot\|_{H^\sigma(Q)}$.

Define the Chebyshev interpolation operator at the CGL points by $I_N^C : C(\bar{I}) \to \mathbb{P}_N(I)$ satisfying

$$I_N^C \varphi(x_j) = \varphi(x_j), \quad 0 \leq j \leq N, \tag{1}$$

where $x_j = \cos\frac{\pi j}{N}$.

3. Approximation Properties of Chebyshev Interpolation Operator in One Dimension

In this section, some approximation properties of the Chebyshev interpolation operator in one dimension are derived. The cases of both single domain and multidomain are considered respectively.

3.1. Case of Single Domain in One Dimension

Similar to the approximation results presented in [11] for the Chebyshev interpolation operator I_N^C, we give the following lemma.

Lemma 1 ([11,15]). *If $u \in H^1(I)$, then*

$$N\|I_N^C u - u\| + \|\partial_x I_N^C u\| \leq C\|\partial_x u\|. \tag{2}$$

In addition, if $u \in H^\sigma(I)$ and $\sigma > 1/2$, then

$$\|I_N^C u - u\|_{H^l(I)} \leq C N^{l-\sigma} \|u\|_{H^\sigma(I)}, \quad 0 \leq l \leq 1. \tag{3}$$

We note that the norm in the approximation results (2) and (3) is already without the Chebyshev weighted function and is in Legendre norm. The lemma is important in numerical analysis of Legendre–Chebyshev spectral method.

Next, the applications of the result of interpolation (3) to connect with the Clenshaw-Curtis quadrature are presented as follows. Given

$$I(u) = \int_{-1}^{1} u(x) dx, \quad I_N(u) = \sum_{k=0}^{N} \omega_k u(x_k),$$

where the nodes x_k depend on N. Since the weights ω_k are defined uniquely by the property that I_N is equal to the integral of the degree $\leq N$ polynomial interpolation through the data points. Then we have

$$I_N(u) = \sum_{k=0}^{N} \omega_k u(x_k) = \int_{-1}^{1} I_N^C u(x) dx.$$

For the Clenshaw-Curtis numerical integration in [26], the unique best approximation to u on $[-1,1]$ of degree $\leq N$ with respect to the L^∞-norm.

The following lemma shows that we simply use the L^2-norm estimation result (3) to get the desired error estimate.

Lemma 2. *If $u \in H^\sigma(I)$ and $\sigma > 1/2$, then*

$$|I_N(u) - I(u)| \leq C N^{-\sigma} \|u\|_{H^\sigma(I)}. \tag{4}$$

3.2. Case of Multidomain in One Dimension

For $1 \leq k \leq K$, we denote $-1 = a_0 < a_1 < \cdots < a_K = 1$, and set

$$I_k = (a_{k-1}, a_k], \quad I = \cup_{k=0}^{K} I_k, \quad h_k = a_k - a_{k-1}, \quad v^k \equiv v|_{I_k}.$$

Let $\mathbb{P}_{N_k}(I_k)$ be the space of polynomials with the degree at most N_k on the interval I_k. Denote $\mathcal{N} = (N_1, \cdots, N_K)$.

Define the following space

$$\mathbb{P}_\mathcal{N}(I) = \{u : u|_{I_k} \in \mathbb{P}_{N_k}(I_k), \ 1 \leq k \leq K\}.$$

Set the relationship between I_k and I as follows:

$$v(x) = \hat{v}(\hat{x}), \quad x = \frac{1}{2}(h_k \hat{x} + a_{k-1} + a_k), \quad x \in I_k, \hat{x} \in I.$$

Define the operator $I_\mathcal{N}^C : C(\bar{I}) \to \mathbb{P}_\mathcal{N}$ such that

where $I_{N_k}^C : C(\bar{I}) \to \mathbb{P}_{N_k}(I)$ is the CGL interpolation operator defined as (1).

Lemma 3. *If $v \in H^\sigma(I_k)$ ($\sigma \geq 0$), then*

$$\|\hat{v}\|_{H^\sigma(I)} \leq C h_k^{\sigma-\frac{1}{2}} \|v\|_{H^\sigma(I_k)}, \tag{6}$$

$$\|v\|_{H^\sigma(I_k)} \leq C h_k^{\frac{1}{2}-\sigma} \|\hat{v}\|_{H^\sigma(I)}. \tag{7}$$

Denote $\hbar = \max_{1 \leq k \leq K} \{\frac{h_k}{N_k}\}$. We arrive at the following approximation result.

Theorem 1. *If $u \in H^\sigma(I)$ ($\sigma \geq 1$), then*

$$\|I_N^C u - u\|_{H^l(I)} \leq C \hbar^{\sigma-l} \|u\|_{H^\sigma(I)}, \quad 0 \leq l \leq 1. \tag{8}$$

Proof. Applying Lemma 1 and Lemma 3, we get

$$\|I_N^C u - u\|_{H^l(I)}^2 = \sum_{1 \leq k \leq K} \|(I_N^C u)^k - u^k\|_{H^l(I_k)}^2$$

$$\leq C \sum_{1 \leq k \leq K} h_k^{1-2l} \|I_{N_k}^C \hat{u}^k - \hat{u}^k\|_{H^l(I)}^2$$

$$\leq C \sum_{1 \leq k \leq K} h_k^{1-2l} N_k^{2(l-\sigma)} \|\hat{u}^k\|_{H^\sigma(I)}^2$$

$$\leq C \sum_{1 \leq k \leq K} h_k^{1-2l} N_k^{2(l-\sigma)} h_k^{2\sigma-1} \|u^k\|_{H^\sigma(I_k)}^2$$

$$\leq C \hbar^{2(\sigma-l)} \|u\|_{H^\sigma(I)}^2.$$

Thus, the theorem is proved. □

4. Approximation Properties of Chebyshev Interpolation Operator in Multi-Dimensions

Set $I^i = (-1,1)$ ($i = 1, \cdots, d$), $\Omega_d = I^1 \times I^2 \times \cdots \times I^d$. If $d = 2$, we use $\Omega = I^x \times I^y$ instead of $\Omega_2 = I^1 \times I^2$.

Define the following space

$$\mathbb{P}_\mathbb{N}(\Omega_d) = \mathbb{P}_N(I^1) \otimes \mathbb{P}_N(I^2) \otimes \cdots \otimes \mathbb{P}_N(I^d).$$

Denote $x = (x_1, \cdots, x_d) \in \Omega_d$. With each function v in $C(\bar{\Omega}_d)$, we associate the d-function v_j defined by

$$v_j(x_j)(x_1, \cdots, x_{j-1}, x_{j+1}, \cdots, x_d) = v(x_1, \cdots, x_d), \quad 1 \leq j \leq d.$$

Define the operator $I_\mathbb{N}^C$ by

$$I_\mathbb{N}^C = I_{N,1}^C \circ \cdots \circ I_{N,d}^C, \tag{9}$$

where $I_{N,i}^C$ is the CGL interpolation operator $I_{N,i}^C : C(\bar{I}^i) \to \mathbb{P}_N(I^i)$ defined as (1).

4.1. Case of Single Domain in Multi-Dimensions

According to the one dimensional approximation results, we give some approximation results of the Chebyshev interpolation operators for the case of single domain in multi-dimensions ($d \geq 2$).

Theorem 2. *If $u \in H^\sigma(\Omega_d)$ and $\sigma > \frac{d}{2}$, then*

$$\|I_\mathbb{N}^C u - u\|_{\Omega_d} \leq CN^{-\sigma}\|u\|_{H^\sigma(\Omega_d)}. \tag{10}$$

Proof. Applying (3) in Lemma 1 and noting $L^2(\Omega_d) = L^2(I^j; L^2(\Omega_{d-1}))$, we have

$$\|u - I_\mathbb{N}^C u\|_{\Omega_d} = \|u - I_{N,1}^C \circ \cdots \circ I_{N,d}^C u\|_{\Omega_d}$$
$$\leq \|u - I_{N,1}^C u\|_{L^2(I^1; L^2(\Omega_{d-1}))} + \|u - I_{N,2}^C \circ \cdots \circ I_{N,d}^C u\|_{L^2(I^1; L^2(\Omega_{d-1}))}$$
$$+ \|(I - I_{N,1}^C)(u - I_{N,2}^C \circ \cdots \circ I_{N,d}^C u)\|_{L^2(I^1; L^2(\Omega_{d-1}))}$$
$$\leq CN^{-\sigma}\|u\|_{H^\sigma(I^1; L^2(\Omega_{d-1}))} + \|u - I_{N,2}^C \circ \cdots \circ I_{N,d}^C u\|_{L^2(I^1; L^2(\Omega_{d-1}))}$$
$$+ CN^{-\frac{\sigma}{d}}\|u - I_{N,2}^C \circ \cdots \circ I_{N,d}^C u\|_{H^{\frac{\sigma}{d}}(I^1; L^2(\Omega_{d-1}))}.$$

Repeating the above discussion d times for $\|u - I_{N,2}^C \circ \cdots \circ I_{N,d}^C u\|_{L^2(I^1; L^2(\Omega_{d-1}))}$ and $\|u - I_{N,2}^C \circ \cdots \circ I_{N,d}^C u\|_{H^{\frac{\sigma}{d}}(I^1; L^2(\Omega_{d-1}))}$, and by the following imbedding relationship

$$H^s(\Omega_d) \subset H^k(I^j; H^{s-k}(\Omega_{d-1})), \quad s \geq k,$$

the desired result is obtained. □

Theorem 3. *If $u \in H^\sigma(\Omega_d)$ and $\sigma > \frac{d+1}{2}$, then*

$$\|I_\mathbb{N}^C u - u\|_{H^1(\Omega_d)} \leq CN^{1-\sigma}\|u\|_{H^\sigma(\Omega_d)}. \tag{11}$$

Proof. For $1 \leq j \leq d$, we have

$$\|u - I_\mathbb{N}^C u\|_{H^1(\Omega_d)}^2 \leq \sum_{j=1}^d \|u - I_\mathbb{N}^C u\|_{H^1(I^j; L^2(\Omega_{d-1}))}^2.$$

By (3) in Lemma 1 and Theorem 2, we get

$$\|u - I_\mathbb{N}^C u\|_{H^1(I^j; L^2(\Omega_{d-1}))}$$
$$\leq \|u - I_{N,j}^C u\|_{H^1(I^j; L^2(\Omega_{d-1}))}$$
$$+ \|I_{N,j}^C(u - I_{N,1}^C \circ \cdots \circ I_{N,j-1}^C \circ I_{N,j+1}^C \circ \cdots \circ I_{N,d}^C u)\|_{H^1(I^j; L^2(\Omega_{d-1}))}$$
$$\leq CN^{1-\sigma}\|u\|_{H^\sigma(I^j; L^2(\Omega_{d-1}))}$$
$$+ C\|u - I_{N,1}^C \circ \cdots \circ I_{N,j-1}^C \circ I_{N,j+1}^C \circ \cdots \circ I_{N,d}^C u\|_{H^1(I^j; L^2(\Omega_{d-1}))}$$
$$\leq CN^{1-\sigma}\|u\|_{H^\sigma(I^j; L^2(\Omega_{d-1}))} + CN^{1-\sigma}\|u\|_{H^1(I^j; H^{\sigma-1}(\Omega_{d-1}))}$$
$$\leq CN^{1-\sigma}\|u\|_{H^\sigma(\Omega_d)}.$$

Thus, the theorem is proved. □

4.2. Case of Multidomain in Multi-Dimensions

In this subsection, we give some approximation properties of the CGL interpolation operator for the case of multidomain in multi-dimensions ($d \geq 2$).

For simplicity, we make the same subdivision in each direction of space. Similar to the case of multidomain in one dimension, for $1 \leq k \leq K$, denote $-1 = a_0 < a_1 < \cdots < a_K = 1$, and set

$$I_k^i = (a_{k-1}, a_k], \quad I^i = \cup_{k=0}^K I_k^i, \quad i = 1, \cdots, d.$$

We introduce the space $\mathbb{P}_\mathbb{N}(\Omega_d) = \mathbb{P}_\mathcal{N}(I^1) \otimes \cdots \otimes \mathbb{P}_\mathcal{N}(I^d)$. Define the Chebyshev-Gauss–Lobatto interpolation operator $\mathbf{I}_\mathcal{N}^C$ by

$$\mathbf{I}_\mathcal{N}^C = I_{\mathcal{N},1}^C \circ I_{\mathcal{N},2}^C \circ \cdots \circ I_{\mathcal{N},d}^C, \tag{12}$$

where $I_{\mathcal{N},i}^C : C(\bar{I}^i) \to \mathbb{P}_\mathcal{N}(I^i)$ is the CGL interpolation operator defined as (5).

By the assumption of the same subdivision in each direction of space, we set $\hbar = \max_{1 \leq k \leq K} \{\frac{h_k}{N_k}\}$ and give the following approximation results.

Theorem 4. *Assume that $d = 2$. If $u \in H^\sigma(\Omega)$ and $\sigma > 1$, then*

$$\|\mathbf{I}_\mathcal{N}^C u - u\|_\Omega \leq C\hbar^\sigma \|u\|_{H^\sigma(\Omega)}. \tag{13}$$

Proof. By Theorem 1 and Lemma 1, we get

$$\|u - \mathbf{I}_\mathcal{N}^C u\| = \|u - I_{\mathcal{N},1}^C \circ I_{\mathcal{N},2}^C u\|$$
$$\leq \|u - I_{\mathcal{N},1}^C u\|_{L^2(I^x;L^2(I^y))} + \|u - I_{\mathcal{N},2}^C u\|_{L^2(I^x;L^2(I^y))}$$
$$+ \|(I - I_{\mathcal{N},1}^C)(u - I_{\mathcal{N},2}^C u)\|_{L^2(I^x;L^2(I^y))}$$
$$\leq C\hbar^\sigma \|u\|_{H^\sigma(I^x;L^2(I^y))} + \|u - I_{\mathcal{N},2}^C u\|_{L^2(I^x;L^2(I^y))}$$
$$+ C\hbar\|u - I_{\mathcal{N},2}^C u\|_{H^1(I^x;L^2(I^y))}$$
$$\leq C\hbar^\sigma \|u\|_{H^\sigma(I^x;L^2(I^y))} + C\hbar^\sigma \|u\|_{L^2(I^x;H^\sigma(I^y))} + C\hbar^\sigma \|u\|_{H^1(I^x;H^{\sigma-1}(I^y))}$$
$$\leq C\hbar^\sigma \|u\|_{H^\sigma(\Omega)}.$$

Thus, the proof is completed. □

Theorem 5. *Assume that $d = 2$. If $u \in H^\sigma(\Omega)$ and $\sigma > \frac{d+1}{2} = \frac{3}{2}$, then*

$$\|u - \mathbf{I}_\mathcal{N}^C u\|_{H^1(\Omega)} \leq C\hbar^{\sigma-1} \|u\|_{H^\sigma(\Omega)}. \tag{14}$$

Proof. By Theorem 1 and Lemma 1, we have

$$\|u - \mathbf{I}_\mathcal{N}^C u\|_{H^1(I^x;L^2(I^y))} \leq \|u - I_{\mathcal{N},1}^C u\|_{H^1(I^x;L^2(I^y))} + \|I_{\mathcal{N},1}^C(u - I_{\mathcal{N},2}^C u)\|_{H^1(I^x;L^2(I^y))}$$
$$\leq C\hbar^{\sigma-1} \|u\|_{H^\sigma(I^x;L^2(I^y))} + \|(I - I_{\mathcal{N},1}^C)(u - I_{\mathcal{N},2}^C u)\|_{H^1(I^x;L^2(I^y))}$$
$$+ \|u - I_{\mathcal{N},2}^C u\|_{H^1(I^x;L^2(I^y))}$$
$$\leq C\hbar^{\sigma-1} \|u\|_{H^\sigma(I^x;L^2(I^y))} + C\|u - I_{\mathcal{N},2}^C u\|_{H^1(I^x;L^2(I^y))}$$
$$\leq C\hbar^{\sigma-1} \|u\|_{H^\sigma(I^x;L^2(I^y))} + C\hbar^{\sigma-1}\|u\|_{H^1(I^x;H^{\sigma-1}(I^y))}$$
$$\leq C\hbar^{\sigma-1} \|u\|_{H^\sigma(\Omega)}.$$

Therefore, the desired result is obtained. □

5. Numerical Experiments

In this section, we give some numerical experiments to confirm the theoretical results. The cases of continuous and discontinuous functions are considered, respectively.

The discrete L^2-error used in the following experiments is defined as

$$\mathrm{Err}(u) = \Big(\sum_{i=0}^{n-1}\sum_{j=0}^{n-1} |u(x_i,y_j) - \mathbf{I}_\mathcal{N}^C u(x_i,y_j)|^2 \Delta x \Delta y\Big)^{\frac{1}{2}}, \tag{15}$$

where $x_i = i\Delta x$, $y_j = j\Delta y$, $\Delta x = \Delta y = \frac{1}{n}$, and $n = 100$.

Example 1. We consider the following continuous function in $\tilde{\Omega} = [0,1]^2$:

$$u(x,y) = \frac{k_y}{w}\cos(k_x\pi x)\sin(k_y\pi y), \quad w = (k_x^2 + k_y^2)^{\frac{1}{2}}, \tag{16}$$

which is approximated by the multidomain Chebyshev–Gauss–Lobatto interpolation $\mathbf{I}_{\mathcal{N}}^C u$. We make the same subdivision in x and y directions as follows:

$$\tilde{\Omega} = \{[0,\,0.5] \cup [0.5,\,1]\} \times \{[0,\,0.5] \cup [0.5,\,1]\}.$$

Figure 1 displays the shape of $u(x,y)$ with low frequency $k_x = k_y = 1$ and high frequency $k_x = k_y = 5$, respectively. Table 1 gives the discrete L^2-errors of the Chebyshev-Gauss–Lobatto interpolation for function u. The results show the spectral accuracy of the multidomain interpolation.

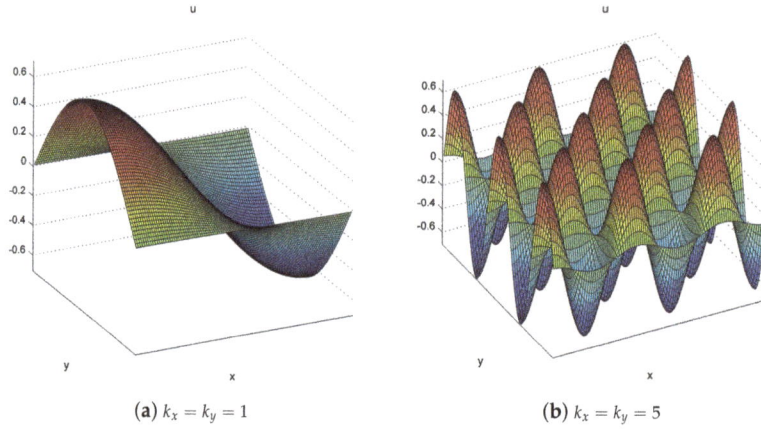

(a) $k_x = k_y = 1$ (b) $k_x = k_y = 5$

Figure 1. The shapes of $u(x,y)$ with low frequency $k_x = k_y = 1$ and high frequency $k_x = k_y = 5$.

Table 1. L^2-errors of Chebyshev-Gauss–Lobatto interpolation for $u(x,y)$.

	$k_x = k_y = 1$			$k_x = k_y = 5$	
$\mathcal{N}_x = \mathcal{N}_y$	Err(u)	Order	$\mathcal{N}_x = \mathcal{N}_y$	Err(u)	Order
(7,7)	2.15×10^{-8}	-	(14,14)	1.76×10^{-8}	-
(10,10)	1.28×10^{-12}	$\hbar^{27.28}$	(18,18)	2.93×10^{-12}	$\hbar^{34.62}$
(13,13)	1.61×10^{-16}	$\hbar^{34.23}$	(22,22)	6.31×10^{-16}	$\hbar^{42.07}$

Example 2. We consider the following discontinuous functions in $\tilde{\Omega} = [0,1]^2$:

$$u_1(x,y) = \frac{k_y}{\epsilon w}\cos(k_x\pi x)\sin(k_y\pi y), \tag{17}$$

$$u_2(x,y) = -\frac{k_y}{\epsilon w}\sin(k_x\pi x)\cos(k_y\pi y), \tag{18}$$

where $w = \left(\dfrac{k_x^2 + k_y^2}{\epsilon}\right)^{\frac{1}{2}}$. The functions are approximated by the multidomain Chebyshev–Gauss–Lobatto interpolation $\mathbf{I}_{\mathcal{N}}^C u$.

Suppose that the parameters ϵ and k_x are piecewise constants:

$$\epsilon = \begin{cases} 1, & 0 \leq x \leq 0.5,\ 0 \leq y \leq 1, \\ 4, & 0.5 \leq x \leq 1,\ 0 \leq y \leq 1, \end{cases} \quad k_x = \begin{cases} 4, & 0 \leq x \leq 0.5,\ 0 \leq y \leq 1, \\ 16, & 0.5 \leq x \leq 1,\ 0 \leq y \leq 1, \end{cases}$$

and $k_y = 8$. The functions are discontinuous at $x = 0.5$. The domain is decomposed as follows:

$$\tilde{\Omega} = \{[0,\,0.5] \cup [0.5,\,1]\} \times \{[0,\,1]\}.$$

Figure 2 displays the shape of $u_1(x,y)$ and $u_2(x,y)$. It is clear that $u_1(x,y)$ is discontinuous and $u_2(x,y)$ is weak discontinuous at $x = 0.5$. Table 2 gives the discrete L^2-errors of the Chebyshev–Gauss–Lobatto interpolation for functions u_1, u_2. The results show the spectral accuracy of the multidomain interpolation for the discontinuous functions.

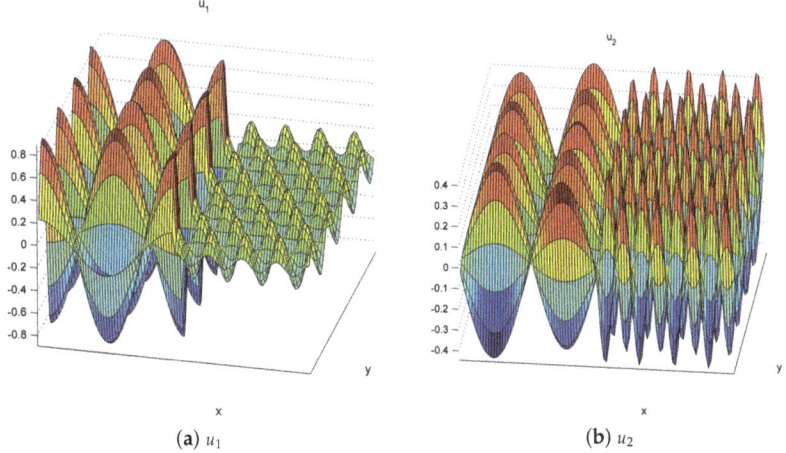

(a) u_1 (b) u_2

Figure 2. The shapes of $u_1(x,y)$ and $u_2(x,y)$.

Table 2. L^2-errors of Chebyshev-Gauss–Lobatto interpolation for $u_1(x,y)$ and $u_2(x,y)$.

$\mathcal{N}_x$	$\mathcal{N}_y$	Err(u_1)	Order	Err(u_2)	Order
(12,26)	26	8.30×10^{-8}	-	4.87×10^{-8}	-
(16,32)	32	8.32×10^{-12}	$\hbar^{32.00}$	4.99×10^{-12}	$\hbar^{31.93}$
(20,38)	38	7.52×10^{-16}	$\hbar^{54.18}$	7.74×10^{-16}	$\hbar^{51.04}$

6. Conclusions

In the paper, we have given some important approximation results of Chebyshev interpolation operators in Legendre norm. The Chebyshev interpolation operators at the Chebyshev–Gauss–Lobatto points is discussed mainly. Moreover, we considered the cases of single domain and multidomain for both one dimension and multi-dimensions, respectively. The approximation results in the Legendre norm are derived. These results play an important role in numerical integration and numerical analysis of the Legendre–Chebyshev spectral method and the Clenshaw–Curtis quadrature.

Author Contributions: Conceptualization, H.M. and C.N.; Data curation, H.M. and H.L.; Formal analysis, H.M. and C.N.; Writing–original draft, C.N., H.L., H.M. and H.W.; Writing–review and editing, C.N., H.M., H.L. and H.W. All authors have read and agreed to the published version of the manuscript.

Funding: This research received no external funding.

Institutional Review Board Statement: Not applicable.

Informed Consent Statement: Not applicable.

Data Availability Statement: Not applicable.

Acknowledgments: The authors sincerely thank the anonymous referees for their very helpful comments and suggestions, which are very helpful for improving the paper.

Conflicts of Interest: The authors declare no conflict of interest.

References

1. Dahlquist, G.; Björck, A.K. *Numerical Methods in Scientific Computing*; Society for Industrial and Applied Mathematics (SIAM): Philadelphia, PA, USA, 2008; Volume I, p. xxviii+717. [CrossRef]
2. Xiang, S.; Chen, X.; Wang, H. Error bounds for approximation in Chebyshev points. *Numer. Math.* **2010**, *116*, 463–491. [CrossRef]
3. Bernardi, C.; Maday, Y. Spectral methods. In *Handbook of Numerical Analysis*; North-Holland: Amsterdam, The Netherlands, 1997; Volume V, pp. 209–485. [CrossRef]
4. Boyd, J.P. *Chebyshev and Fourier Spectral Methods*, 2nd ed.; Dover Publications Inc.: Mineola, NY, USA, 2001; p. xvi+668.
5. Canuto, C.; Hussaini, M.Y.; Quarteroni, A.; Zang, T.A. *Spectral Methods*; Evolution to Complex Geometries and Applications to Fluid Dynamics; Scientific Computation; Springer: Berlin, Germany, 2007; p. xxx+596.
6. Shen, J.; Tang, T.; Wang, L.L. *Spectral Methods*; Springer Series in Computational Mathematics; Algorithms, Analysis and Applications; Springer: Berlin/Heidelberg, Germany, 2011; Volume 41, p. xvi+470. [CrossRef]
7. Maday, Y.; Quarteroni, A. Legendre and Chebyshev spectral approximations of Burgers' equation. *Numer. Math.* **1981**, *37*, 321–332. [CrossRef]
8. Don, W.S.; Gottlieb, D. The Chebyshev-Legendre method: Implementing Legendre methods on Chebyshev points. *SIAM J. Numer. Anal.* **1994**, *31*, 1519–1534. [CrossRef]
9. Shen, J. Efficient Chebyshev-Legendre Galerkin methods for elliptic problems. *Proc. ICOSAHOM95 Houst. J. Math.* **1996**, *95*, 233–239.
10. Wang, H.; Xiang, S. On the convergence rates of Legendre approximation. *Math. Comp.* **2012**, *81*, 861–877. [CrossRef]
11. Ma, H. Chebyshev-Legendre spectral viscosity method for nonlinear conservation laws. *SIAM J. Numer. Anal.* **1998**, *35*, 869–892. [CrossRef]
12. Ma, H. Chebyshev-Legendre super spectral viscosity method for nonlinear conservation laws. *SIAM J. Numer. Anal.* **1998**, *35*, 893–908. [CrossRef]
13. Wu, H.; Ma, H.; Li, H. Optimal error estimates of the Chebyshev-Legendre spectral method for solving the generalized Burgers equation. *SIAM J. Numer. Anal.* **2003**, *41*, 659–672. [CrossRef]
14. Li, H.; Wu, H.; Ma, H. The Legendre Galerkin-Chebyshev collocation method for Burgers-like equations. *IMA J. Numer. Anal.* **2003**, *23*, 109–124. [CrossRef]
15. Wu, H.; Ma, H.; Li, H. Chebyshev-Legendre spectral method for solving the two-dimensional vorticity equations with homogeneous Dirichlet conditions. *Numer. Methods Partial. Differ. Equ.* **2009**, *25*, 740–755. [CrossRef]
16. Zhao, T.; Wu, Y.; Ma, H. Error analysis of Chebyshev-Legendre pseudo-spectral method for a class of nonclassical parabolic equation. *J. Sci. Comput.* **2012**, *52*, 588–602. [CrossRef]
17. Qin, Y.; Li, J.; Ma, H. The Legendre Galerkin Chebyshev collocation least squares for the elliptic problem. *Numer. Methods Partial. Differ. Equ.* **2016**, *32*, 1689–1703. [CrossRef]
18. Xiang, S. On error bounds for orthogonal polynomial expansions and Gauss-type quadrature. *SIAM J. Numer. Anal.* **2012**, *50*, 1240–1263. [CrossRef]
19. Liu, W.; Wang, L.L.; Li, H. Optimal error estimates for Chebyshev approximations of functions with limited regularity in fractional Sobolev-type spaces. *Math. Comp.* **2019**, *88*, 2857–2895. [CrossRef]
20. Davis, P.J.; Rabinowitz, P. *Methods of Numerical Integration*; Computer Science and Applied Mathematics; Academic Press [Harcourt Brace Jovanovich, Publishers]: New York, NY, USA; London, UK, 1975; p. xii+459.
21. Sloan, I.H.; Smith, W.E. Product-integration with the Clenshaw-Curtis and related points. Convergence properties. *Numer. Math.* **1978**, *30*, 415–428. [CrossRef]
22. Johnson, L.W.; Riess, R.D. *Numerical Analysis*, 2nd ed.; Addison-Wesley Publishing Co.: Reading, MA, USA, 1982; p. xii+563.
23. Mason, J.C.; Handscomb, D.C. *Chebyshev Polynomials*; Chapman & Hall/CRC: Boca Raton, FL, USA, 2003; p. xiv+341.
24. Neumaier, A. *Introduction to Numerical Analysis*; Cambridge University Press: Cambridge, UK, 2001; p. viii+356. [CrossRef]
25. Kythe, P.K.; Schäferkotter, M.R. *Handbook of Computational Methods for Integration*; With 1 CD-ROM (Windows, Macintosh and UNIX); Chapman & Hall/CRC: Boca Raton, FL, USA, 2005; p. xxii+598.
26. Trefethen, L.N. Is Gauss quadrature better than Clenshaw-Curtis? *SIAM Rev.* **2008**, *50*, 67–87. [CrossRef]
27. Trefethen, L.N. Spectral Methods in MATLAB. In *Software, Environments, and Tools*; Society for Industrial and Applied Mathematics

28. Canuto, C.; Hussaini, M.Y.; Quarteroni, A.; Zang, T.A. *Spectral Methods*; Fundamentals in Single Domains; Scientific Computation, Springer: Berlin, Germany, 2006; p. xxii+563.
29. De Marchi, S.; Dell'Accio, F.; Mazza, M. On the constrained mock-Chebyshev least-squares. *J. Comput. Appl. Math.* **2015**, *280*, 94–109. [CrossRef]
30. Dell'Accio, F.; Di Tommaso, F.; Nudo, F. Generalizations of the constrained mock-Chebyshev least squares in two variables: Tensor product vs total degree polynomial interpolation. *Appl. Math. Lett.* **2022**, *125*, 107732. [CrossRef]
31. Powell, M.J.D. *Approximation Theory and Methods*; Cambridge University Press: Cambridge, UK; New York, NY, USA, 1981; p. x+339.
32. Trefethen, L.N. *Approximation Theory and Approximation Practice*; Society for Industrial and Applied Mathematics (SIAM): Philadelphia, PA, USA, 2013; p. viii+305.

 *mathematics*

Article
Solution of the Problem $P = L$

Sergey Goncharov *,† and Andrey Nechesov *,†

Sobolev Institute of Mathematics, Academician Koptyug Ave., 4, 630090 Novosibirsk, Russia
* Correspondence: s.s.goncharov@math.nsc.ru (S.G.); nechesov@math.nsc.ru (A.N.)
† These authors contributed equally to this work.

Abstract: The problems associated with the construction of polynomial complexity computer programs require new techniques and approaches from mathematicians. One of such approaches is representing some class of polynomial algorithms as a certain class of special logical programs. Goncharov and Sviridenko described a logical programming language L_0, where programs inductively are obtained from the set of Δ_0-formulas using special terms. In their work, a new idea has been proposed to look at the term as a program. The computational complexity of such programs is polynomial. In the same years, a number of other logical languages with similar properties were created. However, the following question remained: can all polynomial algorithms be described in these languages? It is a long-standing problem, and the method of describing some polynomial algorithm in a not Turing complete logical programming language was not previously clear. In this paper, special types of terms and formulas have been found and added to solve this problem. One of the main contributions is the construction of p-iterative terms that simulate the work of the Turing machine. Using p-iterative terms, the work showed that class P is equal to class L, which extends the programming language L_0 with p-iterative terms. Thus, it is shown that L is quite expressive and has no halting problem, which occurs in high-level programming languages. For these reasons, the logical language L can be used to create fast and reliable programs. The main limitation of the language L is that the implementation of algorithms of complexity is not higher than polynomial.

Keywords: polynomiality; polynomial function; polynomial algorithm; Turing machine; logical programming language; semantic programming; smart contract; blockchain; AI

Citation: Goncharov, S.; Nechesov, A. Solution of the Problem $P = L$. *Mathematics* **2022**, *10*, 113. https://doi.org/10.3390/math10010113

Academic Editors: Francesco Aldo Costabile, Maria I. Gualtieri, Anna Napoli and Radi Romansky

Received: 29 November 2021
Accepted: 28 December 2021
Published: 31 December 2021

Publisher's Note: MDPI stays neutral with regard to jurisdictional claims in published maps and institutional affiliations.

Copyright: © 2021 by the authors. Licensee MDPI, Basel, Switzerland. This article is an open access article distributed under the terms and conditions of the Creative Commons Attribution (CC BY) license (https://

1. Introduction

In the 1980s–1990s, Ershov, Goncharov, and Sviridenko presented the theory of semantic programming [1]. The concepts of Σ-programs and Σ-specifications were introduced in this work. The hereditary finite list superstructure was chosen as a base mathematical model. The universe of this model is the hereditary finite lists generated by elements of the universe of the base model [2], and some LISP-like functions were added. Special logical Σ-formulas with input and output variables were used as Σ-programs [3]. This gave rise to the study of programming language semantics from a mathematical point of view.

Cenzer and Remmel were among the first to study polynomial structures [4]. They investigated the existence of computable isomorphisms between computable and polynomial structures. Then, Lewis and Papadimitriou explored polynomial-time reductions [5]. Then, for a long time, the open problem was to create a logical programming language, which would have polynomial complexity. Mantsivoda developed a logical programming language based on document models. Documents are the main elements of the model universe. Special functions are defined for working with them. Mantsivoda and Ponomaryov formalized this approach in their work [6]. This language is simple and efficient. All operations and relations are polynomial. After that, another type of logical programming language, semantic domain-specific languages, was developed [7]. This language is based on the ideas of semantic programming, where a truth-checking formula on the model replaced computability [1]. All class of polynomial algorithms remained. In the work [8], some interesting results were presented. The authors found that the primitive recursive representation of the algorithm with boundaries of the variables often had a polynomial complexity. Then, Alaev investigated the questions of polynomial representability of various structures in his work [9]. This work gave the key to understanding what polynomiality is. In parallel, Goncharov and Sviridenko developed and presented a new logical programming language in which special terms were used as logical programs [10]. All programs in this language have polynomial computational complexity. However, the main question remains: can all polynomial algorithms be described by this language? The result that will be proved in this work answers this question.

After proving the polynomial analogue of Gandy's fixed point theorem [11], it became clear that the language L_0 is wide enough. This language is used to construct quite complex constructions. In particular, this concerned the inductive construction of new types of data and computer programs in programming.

2. Preliminaries

Let $\mathfrak{B}$ be a p-computable model of the signature σ_0. A p-computable hereditary finite list superstructure $HW(\mathfrak{B})$ [11] was chosen as a mathematical model of the signature σ. The universe of the model $HW(\mathfrak{B})$ consists of elements of the model universe B and hereditarily finite lists $HW(B)$. Signature σ extends σ_0 with the next LISP-like list relations $\in$ (to be an element of a list), $\subseteq$ (to be an initial segment of a list) and the list operations $head$, $tail$, $cons$, $conc$, and constant nil [12]. Define new unary list operations $first$, $cons\_l$, $tail\_l$. The first operation $first$ gets the first list element, the second $cons\_l$ adds the element into the beginning of the list and the last operation $tail\_l$ removes the first element from the list correspondingly. Define new unary operations $strList$, $listStr$. The first operation $strList$ based on the input string of the form $l_1 \ldots l_k$ builds a list of the form $< l_1, \ldots, l_k >$, where $l_i \in \Sigma$, $i \in [1, \ldots, k]$, the second operation $listStr$ based on the input list of the form $< l_1, \ldots, l_k >$ builds a string $l_1 \ldots l_k$, where $l_i \in \Sigma$, $i \in [1, \ldots,]$. The signature σ is an extension of σ_0 with these new operation symbols. The main operations $head$, $tail$, $cons$, $conc$, and relations $\in$, $\subseteq$ have polynomial complexity [12]. It is easy to see that other operations $first$, $cons\_l$, $tail\_l$, $strList$, and $listStr$ have polynomial complexity.

Define Δ_0-formulas as first order formulas of the signature σ in which quantification is of the following two types:

- a restriction onto the list elements $\forall x \in t$ and $\exists x \in t$.
- a restriction onto the initial segments of list $\forall x \subseteq t$ and $\exists x \subseteq t$.

The set of Δ_0-formulas of the signature σ has been extended by induction with several types of terms: conditional terms, b-while terms, bounded recursive terms, and etc. [10] These formulas are denoted as $\Delta_0(\mathfrak{I})$-formulas and new terms are denoted as $\Delta_0(\mathfrak{I})$-terms. Denote the resulting set of $\Delta_0(\mathfrak{I})$-terms as a language L_0.

Definition 1. *Any $\Delta_0(\mathfrak{I})$-term from the language L_0 will be referred to as L_0-program.*

Definition 2. *Any $\Delta_0(\mathfrak{I})$-formula will be referred to as L_0-formula.*

L_0-program property:

- any L_0-program has a polynomial computation complexity on any p-computable enrichment $HW(\mathfrak{B})^*$ of the model $HW(\mathfrak{B})$.

L_0-formula property:

- any L_0-formula has a polynomial truth-checking algorithm on any p-computable enrichment $HW(\mathfrak{B})^*$ of the model $HW(\mathfrak{B})$.

In this work, to construct a suitable logical program for a polynomial function, the concept of a conditional term from the work of Goncharov [13] is used. Let $t_0, t_1, \ldots, t_{n+1}$

is L_0-programs and $\theta_0, \ldots, \theta_n$ is L_0-formulae [10]. Define the concept of a conditional term $t(\bar{v})$ in the next interpretation:

$$
t(\bar{v}) = \begin{cases} t_0(\bar{v}), & \text{if } HW(\mathfrak{B}) \models \theta_0(\bar{v}) \\ t_1(\bar{v}), & \text{if } HW(\mathfrak{B}) \models \theta_1(\bar{v}) \& \neg \theta_0(\bar{v}) \\ \ldots \\ t_n(\bar{v}), & \text{if } HW(\mathfrak{B}) \models \theta_n(\bar{v}) \& \neg \theta_0(\bar{v}) \& \ldots \& \neg \theta_{n-1}(\bar{v}) \\ t_{n+1}(\bar{v}), & \text{otherwise} \end{cases} \quad (1)
$$

where $\bar{v}$ have a form $(v_1, \ldots, v_k)$ for some $k \in N$.

Conditional terms use a construction similar to the operator "if then else" in high-level programming languages. Leave also the other types of terms from [10] for the expressiveness of a new language. However, in the future, to construct a term describing a polynomial function, only conditional terms from work [10] will be used.

3. Polynomial Functions and Turing Machines

Let T_f be a deterministic Turing machine over the alphabet Σ representing polynomial function f. Let S be the set of symbols $\{1, B\}$ and Q be the set of states of the Turing machine, where q_1 is the initial state and q_0 is the final state. Let P_{T_f} be a Turing machine program that implements the function f. Since any program of the Turing machine is implemented through $\sigma : Q \times S \to Q \times S \times \{R, L\}$, then all elements of the program P_{T_f} will be presented in the form of a list $< q_{i_1}, s_{j_1}, q_{i_2}, s_{j_2}, \beta >$. Sequence of the symbols

$$c_i : s_{-m_i} \ldots s_{-2} s_{-1} q_{k_i} s_0 s_1 \ldots s_{n_i} \quad (2)$$

is called the configuration of the Turing machine at the ith step.

Let β be the symbol from the set $\{R, L\}$. Let c_i be some configuration of T_f and there is a element $< q_{i_1}, s_{j_1}, q_{i_2}, s_{j_2}, \beta >$ from the program P_{T_f}. Then, with the help of this element, the configuration c_i will switch to another configuration c_j.

Since the Turing machine T_f represents a polynomial function f over the alphabet Σ, the machine will work on any input $x \in \Sigma^*$ no more than

$$p(|x|) = C_p \cdot |x|^{n_p} \quad (3)$$

steps for some fixed $C_p, n_p \in N$. Let $r(f(x))$ be the computational complexity of the function $f(x)$. From (3), it follows:

$$r(f(x)) \leq p(|x|) \quad (4)$$

If the Turing machine T_f changes configuration c_i on c_{i+1}, then:

$$|c_i| - 1 \leq |c_{i+1}| \leq |c_i| + 1 \quad (5)$$

and from (5) the inequality follows for the final configuration c_{final}:

$$|c_{final}| \leq |c_0| + p(|x|) \leq d(|x|), \text{ for some polynomial } d(|x|) \quad (6)$$

It should be noted that if T_f reached the final configuration $c_{final} = c_j$ for some jth step and $j \leq p(|x|)$; then, all the remaining configurations $c_{j+1}, \ldots, c_{p(|x|)}$ would be equal to c_{final}.

Using the configuration c_i of the form (2) define a machine word w_{c_i} in the next form:

$$w_{c_i} : << s_{-m_i}, \ldots, s_{-1} >, q_{k_i}, < s_0, \ldots, s_{n_i} >> \quad (7)$$

where q_{k_i} is equal to a string $q \ldots q$ of the length $k_i + 1$ and $s_k \in \{B, 1\}, k \in [-m_i, n_i]$.

If configuration c_i has a form $q_{k_i} s_0 \ldots s_{n_i}$, then the machine word w_{c_i} has a form:

$$w_{c_i} :\; <nil, \underline{q_{k_i}}, <s_0, \ldots, s_{n_i}>> \tag{8}$$

Remark 1.
(1) the state $\underline{q_{k_i}}$ is obtained from w_{c_i} and equal $head(tail(w_{c_i}))$
(2) monitored symbol s_0 is obtained from w_{c_i} and equal $first(head(w_{c_i}))$.

Remark 2.
(1) Equality (5) implies that

$$|w_{c_i}| - C \leq |w_{c_{i+1}}| \leq |w_{c_i}| + C, \text{ for some fixed } C \in \mathbb{N} \tag{9}$$

(2) Equalities (6) and (9) imply that

$$|w_{c_{final}}| \leq |w_{c_0}| + p(|x|) \cdot C \leq r'(|x|) \text{ for some polynomial } r'(|x|).$$

Define a new binary operation $\otimes$ using the machine word w_{c_i} and the element $<\underline{q_1}, s_1, \underline{q_2}, s_2, \beta>$ from the program P_{T_f}:

Case 1: element equal $<\underline{q_1}, s_1, \underline{q_2}, s_2, R>$

$$w_{c_i} \otimes <\underline{q_1}, s_1, \underline{q_2}, s_2, R> = \begin{cases} w_{c_j}, & \text{if } head(tail(w_{c_i})) = \underline{q_1} \text{ and } first(head(w_{c_i})) = s_1 \\ nil, & \text{otherwise} \end{cases} \tag{10}$$

and $w_{c_j} = <w_{c_j,1}, w_{c_j,2}, w_{c_j,3}>$, where

$$w_{c_j,1} = cons(first(w_{c_i}), s_2); \; w_{c_j,2} = \underline{q_2};$$
$$w_{c_j,3} = tail\_l(head(w_{c_i}));$$

Case 2: element equal $<\underline{q_1}, s_1, \underline{q_2}, s_2, L>$

$$w_{c_i} \otimes <\underline{q_1}, s_1, \underline{q_2}, s_2, L> = \begin{cases} w_{c_j}, & \text{if } head(tail(w_{c_i})) = \underline{q_1} \text{ and } first(head(w_{c_i})) = s_1 \\ nil, & \text{otherwise} \end{cases} \tag{11}$$

and $w_{c_j} = <w_{c_j,1}, w_{c_j,2}, w_{c_j,3}>$, where

$$w_{c_j,1} = tail(first(w_{c_i})); \; w_{c_j,2} = \underline{q_2};$$
$$w_{c_j,3} = cons\_l(cons\_l(tail\_l(head(w_{c_i})), s_2), head(first(w_{c_i})));$$

Remark 3. Operation $\otimes$ is polynomial.

4. p-Iterative Terms

From the previous section, the length of the final machine word $w_{c_{final}}$ does not exceed the length of the initial machine word w_{c_0} plus the length of some polynomial $r'(|x|)$. The main goal of this section is to construct a p-iterative term so that the length of the final value should not exceed the length of the input value plus the value of some polynomial $v(|x|)$. Furthermore, it will be shown that such extension using p-iterative terms of the language L_0 does not take us beyond the polynomiality.

Let $HW(\mathfrak{B})$ be a p-computable model of the signature σ, $g(x)$ be a L_0-program, $\varphi(x)$ be a L_0-formula. Require $|g(x)| \leq |x| + C_g$ for some $C_g \in \mathbb{N}$. Let $u(|x|)$ be a polynomial such that the complexity of checking the truth of the L_0-formula $\varphi(x)$ on model $HW(\mathfrak{B})$ should not exceed $u(|x|)$. Let computation complexity $r(g(x))$ of L_0-program $g(x)$ be bounded by some polynomial $s(|x|) = C_s \cdot |x|^{n_s}$. Define a p-iterative term $t(x, n)$ using the following iterative construction:

$$g^0(\mathbf{x}) = g(\mathbf{x})$$
$$\ldots$$
$$g^{i+1}(\mathbf{x}) = g(g^i(\mathbf{x})) \qquad (12)$$

The p-iterative term has the form:

$$t(\mathbf{x},n) = \begin{cases} g^i(\mathbf{x}), & \text{if } i \leq n\ HW(\mathfrak{B}) \models \varphi(g^i(\mathbf{x})) \text{ and } \forall j < i\ HW(\mathfrak{B}) \not\models \varphi(g^j(\mathbf{x}))) \\ nil, & \text{otherwise} \end{cases} \qquad (13)$$

Remark 4. $|g^{i+1}(x)| \leq |g^i(x)| + C_g$.

Theorem 1. *Let $HW(\mathfrak{B})$ be a p-computable model, $\varphi(x)$ be a L_0-formula, and $g(x)$ be a L_0-program with the condition $|g(x)| \leq |x| + C_g$, $C_g \in N$. Then, p-iterative term from (13) is a p-computable function.*

Proof. Let $t(\mathbf{x},n)$ be a p-iterative term. If the value of the term $t(\mathbf{a},n_0)$ equal $g^{i+1}(\mathbf{a})$; then, $HW(\mathfrak{B}) \models \varphi(g^{i+1}(\mathbf{a}))$ for some $\mathbf{a} \in HW(B)$, $n_0 \in N$, and $i+1 \leq n_0$. It can be inferred that the length of p-iterative term for $i+1$ iteration:

$$|g^{i+1}(\mathbf{a})| \leq |g^i(\mathbf{a})| + C_g \leq |g^0(\mathbf{a})| + (i+1) \cdot C_g \leq |\mathbf{a}| + (i+2) \cdot C_g$$

and for any $i \leq n_0$:

$$|g^i(\mathbf{a})| \leq |g^0(\mathbf{a})| + n_0 \cdot C_g \leq |\mathbf{a}| + (n_0+1) \cdot C_g \leq (|\mathbf{a}|+n_0) \cdot (C_g+1) + C_g \leq z(|\mathbf{a}|+n_0)$$

where

$$z(|\mathbf{x}|) = (C_g+1) \cdot |\mathbf{x}| + C_g. \qquad (14)$$

The next step is to calculate the computational complexity $r(t(\mathbf{x},n))$ of the p-iterative term. The algorithm is the following for some fixed $\mathbf{a}$ and n_0:

step 0: Calculate $g^0(\mathbf{a})$ (it is necessary to calculate $g(\mathbf{a})$) and check the truth of the L_0-formula $\varphi(g^0(\mathbf{a}))$ on the model $HW(\mathfrak{B})$. If L_0-formula is true, then leave the algorithm running and send value $g^0(\mathbf{a})$; otherwise, go to the next step.

step 1: Calculate $g^1(\mathbf{a})$ (it is necessary to calculate $g(g^0(\mathbf{a}))$), where $g^0(\mathbf{a})$ is known on step 0 and check the truth of the L_0-formula $\varphi(g^1(\mathbf{a}))$ on the model $HW(\mathfrak{B})$. If L_0-formula is true, then leave the algorithm running and send value $g^1(\mathbf{a})$; otherwise, go to the next step.

$\ldots$

step i: Calculate $g^i(\mathbf{a})$ (it is necessary to calculate $g(g^{i-1}(\mathbf{a}))$), where $g^{i-1}(\mathbf{a})$ is known on step $i-1$ and check the truth of the L_0-formula $\varphi(g^i(\mathbf{a}))$ on the model $HW(\mathfrak{B})$. If L_0-formula is true, then leave the algorithm running and send value $g^i(\mathbf{a})$, otherwise go to the next step.

$\ldots$

step n: Calculate $g^{n_0}(\mathbf{a})$ (it is necessary to calculate $g(g^{n_0-1}(\mathbf{a}))$), where $g^{n_0-1}(\mathbf{a})$ is known on step $n-1$ and check the truth of the L_0-formula $\varphi(g^{n_0}(\mathbf{a}))$ on the model $HW(\mathfrak{B})$. If L_0-formula is true, then leave the algorithm running and send value $g^{n_0}(\mathbf{a})$, otherwise send nil.

Let $\mathbf{w}$ be $g^i(\mathbf{a})$ and $|g^i(\mathbf{a})| \leq z(|\mathbf{a}|+n_0)$, as $r(g(\mathbf{w})) \leq s(|\mathbf{w}|)$ it can be inferred that:

$$r(t(\mathbf{a},n_0)) \leq \sum_{i=0}^{n_0}(s(z(|\mathbf{a}|+n_0)) + u(z(|\mathbf{a}|+n_0))) \qquad (15)$$

and get inequality:

$$r(t(\mathbf{a},n_0)) \leq (s(z(|\mathbf{a}|+n_0)) + u(z(|\mathbf{a}|+n_0))) \cdot (n_0+1) \leq d(|\mathbf{a}|+n_0)$$

for some polynomial $d(|x|)$ and polynomial $z(|x|)$ from (14). □

Corollary 1. *Let the conditions of Theorem 1 be satisfied and $f(|x|)$ be some polynomial. Then, any p-iterative term of the form $t(x, f(|x|))$ is a p-computable function relative to variable x.*

Proof. The condition of Theorem 1 implies that there exists a polynomial $z(x)$ from (14)

$$r(t(\mathbf{x}, f(|\mathbf{x}|))) \leq z(|\mathbf{x}| + f(|\mathbf{x}|)) \leq z(w(|\mathbf{x}|)) \leq v(|\mathbf{x}|)$$

where polynomial $w(|\mathbf{x}|)$ has a form $|\mathbf{x}| + f(|\mathbf{x}|)$ and polynomial $v(|\mathbf{x}|)$ has a form $z(w(|\mathbf{x}|))$. □

Definition 3. *Define a new language L. Language L extends L_0 by p-iterative terms. Classes L-formulas and L-programs extend the classes of L_0-formulas and L_0-programs, respectively.*

Theorem 2. *Let $HW(\mathfrak{B})^*$ be a p-computable extension of the p-computable model $HW(\mathfrak{B})$ of the signature σ^*. Then, any L-program has polynomial computational complexity on $HW(\mathfrak{B})^*$.*

Proof. To prove this statement, it is nessesary to use induction on the number of distinct p-iterative terms for some L-program $t(x)$:

Base of induction $n = 0$: $t(x)$ does not contain a p-iterative term. Then computation complexity of the $t(x)$ is polynomial; this follows immediately from the work [10].

Induction step: Let the statement be true for $n = k$; show this for $n = k + 1$. Let $t(x)$ be a L-program with $k + 1$ distinct p-iterative terms. Let $HW(\mathfrak{B})^{**}$ be enrichment of the model $HW(\mathfrak{B})^*$ of the signature $\sigma^{**} = \sigma^* \cup \{t_1\}$, where p-iterative term t_1 is involved in construction $t(x)$. In the new model $HW(\mathfrak{B})^{**}$, L-program $t(x)$ has only k distinct p-iterative terms and by induction step, the L-program $t(x)$ has a polynomial complexity. □

5. Polynomiality via p-Iterative Terms

Let $f(x)$ be a p-computable function, and let $h(|x|)$ be a polynomial, such that $r(f(x)) \leq h(|x|)$.

Let the universe of the model $HW(\mathfrak{B})$ contain the natural numbers N in the main set. Signature σ contains the constants 0 and 1, Σ alphabet, and R and L, contain multiplication $\times$ and addition $+$ operations on N, operation of string concatenation *concat*, and operation of string length $(|\ |)$.

Remark 5. *The new operations $\times$, $+$, concat, and $|\ |$ are polynomial.*

For any polynomial $h(|x|)$, there is a suitable L-program. Let q_{i_1} be a L-program of the form $concat(concat(\ldots concat(q,q)\ldots),q)$, where the function *concat* is used $i_1 + 1$-times. Then, for each element of the form $< q_{i_1}, s_{j_1}, q_{i_2}, s_{j_2}, \beta >$ from the Turing machine program P_{T_f}, there is a suitable L-program $v(q_{i_1}, s_{j_1}, q_{i_2}, s_{j_2}, \beta)$ of the form:

$$v(q_{i_1}, s_{j_1}, q_{i_2}, s_{j_2}, \beta) = cons(cons(cons(cons(cons(nil, q_{i_1}), s_{j_1}), q_{i_2}), s_{j_2}), \beta) \quad (16)$$

Theorem 3. *For any p-computable function, there is an L-program defining this function.*

Proof. Let f be some p-computable function, $h(|x|)$ some polynomial such that:

$$r(f(\mathbf{x})) \leq h(|\mathbf{x}|) \quad (17)$$

Consider the Turing machine T_f over alphabet Σ with program P_{T_f} that realizes the function f. Let us construct a list l_f of terms of the form $v(q_{i_1}, s_{j_1}, q_{i_2}, s_{j_2}, \beta)$ use (16) from the program P_{T_f}, where $\beta \in \{R, L\}$. Then, L-formula $\varphi(x)$ has a form:

$$\varphi(\mathbf{x}) : Final(\mathbf{x}) \quad (18)$$

where predicate $Final(w)$ is true if w is a machine word of the form

$$<< s_{-m}, \ldots, s_{-1} >, \underline{q_0}, < s_1, \ldots, s_k >>$$

It is apparent that the predicate $Final(\mathbf{x})$ has a polynomial complexity.

Define $tail^k(\mathbf{x})$ as applying $tail$ operation k times to $\mathbf{x}$. A conditional term $g(\mathbf{x})$ [10] will be used for constructing a final L-program:

$$g(\mathbf{x}) = \begin{cases} \mathbf{x} \otimes l_1, \text{ where } (l_1 = first(l_f)) \& (\mathbf{x} \otimes l_1 \neq nil) \\ \ldots \\ \mathbf{x} \otimes l_i, \text{ where } (l_i = head(tail^{k-i}(l_f))) \& (\mathbf{x} \otimes l_i \neq nil) \\ \ldots \\ \mathbf{x} \otimes l_k, \text{ where } (l_k = head(l_f)) \& (\mathbf{x} \otimes l_k \neq nil) \\ \mathbf{x}, \text{ otherwise} \end{cases} \quad (19)$$

Define $mw(\mathbf{x})$ as the L-program that transforms a word $\mathbf{w}$ to the machine word of the form $< nil, \underline{q_1}, \mathbf{w} >$. This L-program has a form:

$$mw(\mathbf{x}) = cons(cons\_l(cons(nil, \underline{q_1}), nil), strList(\mathbf{x})) \quad (20)$$

L-program $mw(\mathbf{x})$ transforms the word $\mathbf{x}$ to the machine word for the initial configuration c_0 of the Turing machine T_f.

Define $value(\mathbf{x})$ as the L-program that transforms a machine word w into the word on the tape of the Turing machine T_f. This function is constructed as follows:

$$value(w) = listStr(conc(first(w), head(w))) \quad (21)$$

Define p-iterative term $t(mw(\mathbf{x}), h(|\mathbf{x}|))$ using construction (12) with the L-program $g(x)$ of the form (19), the formula φ from (18), the polynomial $h(|\mathbf{x}|)$ from (17), and L-programs from (20) and (21).

The final L-program representing the function $f(\mathbf{x})$ has the form:

$$value(t(mw(\mathbf{x}), h(|\mathbf{x}|))) \quad (22)$$

Note that the L-program $t(mw(\mathbf{x}), h(|\mathbf{x}|))$ satisfies the conditions of Theorem 1 and, therefore, $value(t(mw(\mathbf{x}), h(|\mathbf{x}|)))$ is a p-computable. □

6. Conclusions

The work shows the equality of classes P and L. The main motivation was to create a not Turing complete logical programming language describing the class of polynomial algorithms. Programs in this language are logical terms and have polynomial complexity. For any polynomial algorithm, there is a program describing it. One of the main contributions of this work is the construction of a new logical language L that is equal to the class P. Another contribution is the construction of a p-iterative term for this. The main limitation is that this language is not Turing complete. Therefore, it is impossible to realize algorithms on it with the complexity being higher than polynomial.

Thus, language L is rich enough to describe any algorithms of polynomial complexity. These results are one more step in the construction of high-level programming languages based on logical language L. Moreover, programs in such languages will remain polynomially computable. It means that programs stop running every time, work quickly, and produce results. It is especially important during the development of blockchain technologies and smart contracts. Since smart contracts are programs in a distributed environment, the correct functioning of the entire blockchain as a whole depends on the result of its execution. Such smart contracts should be executed quickly and should not consume a lot of computing resources.

The work has built a logical language that allows one to create fast and reliable programs. These programs will be used in computer science, robotics, the Internet of things, blockchain

High-quality artificial intelligence requires not only just neural networks and machine learning, but also logical rules and their execution. An effective solution is the hybrid technologies of neural networks and logical rules that will make a breakthrough in the future. To construct such logical rules, the semantic programming theory suits perfectly well.

Author Contributions: Conceptualization, S.G. and A.N.; methodology, S.G. and A.N.; formal analysis, S.G.; validation, S.G.; investigation, S.G. and A.N.; writing—original draft preparation, A.N.; writing—review and editing, A.N.; supervision, S.G.; project administration, S.G.; software, A.N. All authors have read and agreed to the published version of the manuscript.

Funding: Goncharov research was funded by the project of Fundamental Research of the Sobolev institute of mathematics SB RAS number 0314-2019-0002.

Institutional Review Board Statement: Not applicable.

Informed Consent Statement: Not applicable.

Data Availability Statement: Not applicable.

Conflicts of Interest: The authors declare no conflict of interest.

References

1. Ershov, Y.L.; Goncharov, S.S.; Sviridenko, D.I. Semantic programming. In Proceedings of the Information Processing 86: Proceedings of the IFIP 10th World Computer Congress, Dublin, Ireland, 1–5 September 1986; Elsevier Sci.: Dublin, Ireland, 1986; Volume 10, pp. 1113–1120.
2. Goncharov, S.S.; Sviridenko, D.I. Σ-programming. *Transl. II Ser. Am. Math. Soc.* **1989**, *142*, 101–121 .
3. Ershov, Y.L. *Definability and Computability*; Springer: Berlin/Heidelberg, Germany, 1996.
4. Cenzer, D.; Remmel, J. Polynomial-time versus recursive models. *Ann. Pure Appl. Log.* **1991**, *54*, 17–58. [CrossRef]
5. Lewis, H.; Papadimitriou, C. *Elements of the Theory of Computation*; Prentice-Hall: Upper Saddle River, NJ, USA, 1998.
6. Mantsivoda, A.; Ponomaryov, D. *A Formalization of Document Models with Semantic Modelling*; Series Mathematics; The Bulletin of Irkutsk State University: Irkutsk, Russia, 2019; Volume 27, pp. 36–54. [CrossRef]
7. Gumirov, V.; Matyukov, P.; Palchunov, D. Semantic Domain-specific Languages. In Proceedings of the International Multi-Conference on Engineering, Computer and Information Sciences (SIBIRCON), Novosibirsk, Russia, 21–27 October 2019; pp. 955–960. [CrossRef]
8. Kalimullin, I.; Melnikov, A.; Ng, K. Algebraic structures computable without delay. *Theor. Comput. Sci.* **2017**, *674*, 73–98. [CrossRef]
9. Alaev, P.E. Structures Computable in Polynomial Time. I. *Algebra Log.* **2017**, *55*, 421–435. [CrossRef]
10. Goncharov, S.S.; Sviridenko, D.I. Logical language of description of polynomial computing. *Dokl. Math.* **2019**, *99*, 121–124. [CrossRef]
11. Goncharov, S.; Nechesov, A. Polynomial analogue of Gandy's fixed point theorem. *Mathematics* **2021**, *9*, 2102. [CrossRef]
12. Ospichev, S.S.; Ponomaryov, D.K. On the complexity of formulas in semantic programming. *Sib. Electron. Math. Rep.* **2018**, *15*, 987–995. [CrossRef]
13. Goncharov, S.S. Conditional Terms in Semantic Programming. *Sib. Math. J.* **2017**, *58*, 794–800. [CrossRef]

Review

Multivalue Collocation Methods for Ordinary and Fractional Differential Equations

Angelamaria Cardone [1], Dajana Conte [1], Raffaele D'Ambrosio [2,*] and Beatrice Paternoster [1]

[1] Department of Mathematics, University of Salerno, 84084 Fisciano, Italy; ancardone@unisa.it (A.C.); dajconte@unisa.it (D.C.); beapat@unisa.it (B.P.)
[2] Department of Information Engineering and Computer Science and Mathematics, University of L'Aquila, 67100 L'Aquila, Italy
* Correspondence: raffaele.dambrosio@univaq.it

Abstract: The present paper illustrates some classes of multivalue methods for the numerical solution of ordinary and fractional differential equations. In particular, it focuses on two-step and mixed collocation methods, Nordsieck GLM collocation methods for ordinary differential equations, and on two-step spline collocation methods for fractional differential equations. The construction of the methods together with the convergence and stability analysis are reported and some numerical experiments are carried out to show the efficiency of the proposed methods.

Keywords: ordinary differential equations; fractional differential equations; multistep methods; collocation; convergence; stability

MSC: 65L05; 65L20; 26A33

Citation: Cardone, A.; Conte, D.; D'Ambrosio, R.; Paternoster, P. Multivalue Collocation Methods for Ordinary and Fractional Differential Equations. *Mathematics* **2022**, *10*, 185. https://doi.org/10.3390/math10020185

Academic Editors: Francesco Aldo Costabile, Maria I. Gualtieri and Anna Napoli

Received: 29 November 2021
Accepted: 4 January 2022
Published: 7 January 2022

Publisher's Note: MDPI stays neutral with regard to jurisdictional claims in published maps and institutional affiliations.

Copyright: © 2022 by the authors. Licensee MDPI, Basel, Switzerland. This article is an open access article distributed under the terms and conditions of the Creative Commons Attribution (CC BY) license (https://

1. Introduction

Numerical collocation is an effective technique for the approximation of solutions to a given functional equation by means of a continuous approximate belonging to a finite dimensional space spanned by functions chosen in accordance with the qualitative behavior of the exact solution. This idea has successfully been applied in several contexts (a very brief and far from being extensive, list of contributions in the existing literature can be found in [1–36] and references therein).

In this paper, we aim to collect some of our recent results showing the effectiveness of collocation in two selected cases:

- Firstly, the case of stiff differential problems [1–3,37,38], commonly arising from spatially discretized time-dependent partial differential equations. This problem commonly exposes numerical schemes to the order reduction phenomena, typically characterizing low stage-order methods such as Runge–Kutta methods on Gaussian collocation points [1]. It is worth highlighting that improving the numerics for stiff problems has a direct impact on the numerical treatment of a wide class of problems that is interesting in several applications. A relevant case is given, for instance, by multiscale problems: Quoting from [39], "*Stiff equations are multiscale problems*" and this situation typically characterizes coupled physical systems whose components vary on different time-scales. It is the case, for instance, of epidemiological models for influenza or pandemics (see, for instance, refs. [40–42] and references therein), since multiscale models are an ideal framework to simultaneously simulate several processes such as immune response, pharmacokinetics, and interactions between virus and host.

Our proposal to remove order reduction in providing approximate solutions to stiff problems is to employ multivalue numerical methods based on numerical collocation.

These methods are free from order reduction, as it happens for classical collocation methods. This topic is the subject of Sections 2 and 3;

- Secondly, the case of fractional differential problems, representing a fundamental tool to model anomalous diffusion [43], material hereditariness, viscoelastic materials [44], and heat conduction [45]. For these problems, the analytical solution is generally not available and the numerical treatment is not an easy task, due to the lack of smoothness of the analytical solution and general methods for Ordinary Differential Equations (ODEs), applied to Fractional Differential Equations (FDEs), generally exhibit low order of convergence, e.g., predictor-corrector methods [46]. Therefore ad hoc numerical methods should be formulated to obtain a higher degree of accuracy, as for example fractional linear multistep methods [47], a class of product integration methods [48]. In this scenario, an important role is played by collocation methods, as for example B-spline wavelets collocation [28], Chebychev collocation [49], spectral collocation [16,33,50,51], and non-polynomial collocation [25]. In this paper, we focus on spline collocation methods, which were first introduced by Blank [52], however the main contribution to the development and analysis of these methods has been given in [19,29,30,53]. More recently, multivalue spline collocation methods have been proposed [18,20,54]. This topic is the subject of Section 4.

2. Multivalue Collocation Methods

Multivalue methods for the numerical solution of ODEs [1,37,55–57]:

$$\begin{cases} y'(t) = f(y(t)), & t \in [t_0, T], \\ y(t_0) = y_0, \end{cases} \tag{1}$$

with $y : [t_0, T] \to \mathbb{R}^d$ $f : \mathbb{R}^d \to \mathbb{R}^d$, and have the form:

$$\begin{aligned} Y_i^{[n]} &= h \sum_{j=1}^m a_{ij} f\left(Y_j^{[n]}\right) + \sum_{j=1}^r u_{ij} y_j^{[n]}, & i = 1, 2, \ldots, m, \\ y_i^{[n+1]} &= h \sum_{j=1}^m b_{ij} f\left(Y_j^{[n]}\right) + \sum_{j=1}^r v_{ij} y_j^{[n]}, & i = 1, 2, \ldots, r, \end{aligned} \tag{2}$$

where $t_n = t_0 + nh$, $n = 0, 1, \ldots, N$ are the grid points and $h = (T - t_0)/N$ is a fixed stepsize. The matrices:

$$\mathbf{A} = [a_{ij}] \in \mathbb{R}^{m \times m}, \quad \mathbf{U} = [u_{ij}] \in \mathbb{R}^{m \times r}, \quad \mathbf{B} = [b_{ij}] \in \mathbb{R}^{r \times m}, \quad \mathbf{V} = [v_{ij}] \in \mathbb{R}^{r \times r} \tag{3}$$

are the coefficients of the methods and the vector $\mathbf{c} = [c_1, c_2, \ldots, c_m]^T$ is called the abscissa vector. The parameters $c_1, c_2, \ldots, c_m$ are usually included in $[0,1]$, but in some cases can be taken outside this interval in order to obtain A-stability (see for example Figure 1).

The values $Y_i^{[n]} \in \mathbb{R}^d$ are called internal stages and provide an approximation to $y(t_n + c_i h)$, while $y_i^{[n]} \in \mathbb{R}^d$ are called external stages, and each $y_i^{[n]}$ provides an approximation to a linear combination of the derivatives of y at the point t_n. The number of internal stages m and the number of external stages r, influence the order of convergence and the computational cost of the method, as will be shown later for some classes of methods.

As usual, the coefficient matrices of the multivalue numerical method (2) can be gathered in the Butcher tableau:

$$\left[\begin{array}{c|c} \mathbf{A} & \mathbf{U} \\ \hline \mathbf{B} & \mathbf{V} \end{array} \right]. \tag{4}$$

Collocation multivalue numerical methods represent a continuous extension of multivalue numerical methods in the GLM (General Linear Method) form (2), by means of following piecewise collocation polynomial:

$$P_n(t_n + \theta h) = \sum_{i=1}^{r} \alpha_i(\theta) y_i^{[n]} + h \sum_{i=1}^{m} \beta_i(\theta) f(P_n(t_n + c_i h)), \quad \theta \in [0,1], \tag{5}$$

and by interpreting the internal stages in (2) as $Y_i^{[n]} = P_n(t_n + c_i h)$. In (5), the polynomials $\alpha_i(\theta)$ and $\beta_i(\theta)$ have a degree equal to the order p of the method and are usually computed by solving continuous order conditions, as will be described in the following.

Several kind of multivalue collocation methods have been introduced so far, with a different form for the vector of external stages. We will describe in the next two subsections two different choices which lead to two-step collocation methods and Nordsieck GLM collocation methods.

2.1. Two-Step Collocation Methods

Two-step collocation collocation methods have been introduced in [5] and have the form:

$$\begin{aligned} Y_i^{[n]} &= \varphi_0(c_i) y_{n-1} + \varphi_1(c_i) y_n + h \sum_{j=1}^{m} \left(\psi_j(c_i) f\left(Y_j^{[n]}\right) + \chi_j(c_i) f\left(Y_j^{[n-1]}\right) \right) \quad i = 1, 2, \ldots, m, \\ y_{n+1} &= \varphi_0(1) y_{n-1} + \varphi_1(1) y_n + h \sum_{j=1}^{m} \left(\psi_j(1) f\left(Y_j^{[n]}\right) + \chi_j(1) f\left(Y_j^{[n-1]}\right) \right). \end{aligned} \tag{6}$$

with a collocation polynomial defined by:

$$P_n(t_n + \theta h) = \varphi_0(\theta) y_{n-1} + \varphi_1(\theta) y_n + h \sum_{j=1}^{m} \left(\psi_j(\theta) f(P(t_n + c_j h)) + \chi_j(\theta) f(P(t_{n-1} + c_j h)) \right), \tag{7}$$

with $\theta \in [0,1]$ and $Y_j^{[n]} = P(t_n + c_j h)$, $Y_j^{[n-1]} = P(t_{n-1} + c_j h)$.

We observe that such methods can be viewed as multivalue collocation methods (2)–(5), by choosing $r = m + 2$,

$$\alpha_1(\theta) = \varphi_1(\theta), \quad \alpha_2(\theta) = \varphi_0(\theta),$$
$$\alpha_{2+i}(\theta) = \chi_i(\theta), \quad \beta_i(\theta) = \psi_i(\theta) \quad i = 1, \ldots, m$$

and

$$y^{[n]} = \begin{bmatrix} y_n \\ y_{n-1} \\ hF(Y^{[n-1]}) \end{bmatrix} \in \mathbb{R}^{m+2}, \tag{8}$$

where,

$$Y^{[n]} = \begin{bmatrix} Y_1^{[n]} \\ \vdots \\ Y_m^{[n]} \end{bmatrix}, \quad F(Y^{[n]}) = \begin{bmatrix} f(Y_1^{[n]}) \\ \vdots \\ f(Y_m^{[n]}) \end{bmatrix}. \tag{9}$$

With the choice (8) for the external approximation vector, the collocation polynomial (5) is a global smooth extension of the GLM (2) with tableau (4) given by the following matrices:

$$\mathbf{A} = [\beta_j(c_i)]_{i,j=1,\ldots,m} \in \mathbb{R}^{m \times m}, \quad \mathbf{U} = [\alpha_j(c_i)]_{i=1,\ldots,m, j=1,\ldots,r} \in \mathbb{R}^{m \times r},$$
$$\mathbf{w} = [\alpha_j(1)]_{j=1,\ldots,r} \in \mathbb{R}^r, \quad \mathbf{v} = [\beta_j(1)]_{j=1,\ldots,m} \in \mathbb{R}^m$$
$$\mathbf{B} = \begin{bmatrix} \mathbf{v}^T \\ 0 \\ I \end{bmatrix} \in \mathbb{R}^{r \times m}, \quad \mathbf{V} = \begin{bmatrix} \mathbf{w}^T \\ 1 & 0 & 0 \\ 0 & 0 & 0 \end{bmatrix} \in \mathbb{R}^{r \times r},$$

where **I** is the identity matrix of dimension m and **0** is a zero matrix or vector of suitable dimensions.

Order conditions can be formalized by the following theorem [5].

Theorem 1. *A multivalue collocation method (2) with collocation polynomial in (5) and vector of external stages defined by (8) is an approximation of uniform order p to the solution of the well-posed problem approximates in the solution of (1) with uniform order p, if the following conditions are satisfied:*

$$\alpha_1(\theta) + \alpha_2(\theta) = 1$$
$$\frac{\theta^\nu}{\nu!} - \frac{(-1)^\nu}{\nu!}\alpha_2(\theta) - \sum_{i=1}^m \left(\frac{(c_i-1)^{\nu-1}}{(\nu-1)!}\alpha_{2+i}(\theta) + \frac{(c_i)^{\nu-1}}{(\nu-1)!}\beta_i(\theta) \right) = 0, \quad \nu = 1,\ldots,p. \quad (10)$$

The maximum attainable order is $p = m + r - 1$, as in this case of $m + r - 1$ polynomials $\alpha_i(\theta)$ and $\beta_i(\theta)$, which are uniquely derived by solving the continuous order conditions (10), and the corresponding collocation polynomial satisfies the conditions listed in the following corollary [5].

Corollary 1. *The maximum attainable uniform order of convergence for a multivalue collocation method (2) with collocation polynomial in (5) and vector of external stages defined by (8) is $p = 2m + 1 = m + r - 1$. The corresponding collocation polynomial satisfies the following interpolation and collocation conditions:*

$$P_n(t_n) = y_n, \quad P_n(t_{n-1}) = y_{n-1}, \quad (11)$$

$$P'_n(t_n + c_i h) = f(P_n(t_n + c_i h)), \quad P'_n(t_{n-1} + c_i h) = f(P_n(t_{n-1} + c_i h)), \quad i = 1, 2, \ldots, m. \quad (12)$$

2.2. Nordsieck GLM Collocation Methods

Nordsieck GLM collocation methods have been introduced in [4] and rely on the vector of external stages in the so-called Nordsieck form [37]:

$$y^{[n]} = \begin{bmatrix} y_1^{[n]} \\ y_2^{[n]} \\ \vdots \\ y_r^{[n]} \end{bmatrix} \approx \begin{bmatrix} y(t_n) \\ hy'(t_n) \\ \vdots \\ h^{r-1}y^{r-1}(t_n). \end{bmatrix} \quad (13)$$

With this choice for an external approximation vector, the collocation polynomial (5) is a global smooth extension of the GLM (2) with tableau (4) given by the following matrices:

$$\mathbf{A} = [\beta_j(c_i)]_{i,j=1,\ldots,m} \in \mathbb{R}^{m \times m}, \quad \mathbf{U} = [\alpha_j(c_i)]_{i=1,\ldots,m, j=1,\ldots,r} \in \mathbb{R}^{m \times r},$$
$$\mathbf{B} = \left[\beta_j^{(i-1)}(1)\right]_{i=1,\ldots,m, j=1,\ldots,r} \in \mathbb{R}^{r \times m}, \quad \mathbf{V} = \left[\alpha_j^{(i-1)}(1)\right]_{i,j=1,\ldots,r} \in \mathbb{R}^{r \times r},$$

Order conditions have been derived in [4], as stated in the following theorem.

Theorem 2. *A multivalue collocation method (2) with collocation polynomial in (5) and vector of external stages defined by (13) is an approximation of uniform order p to the solution of the well-posed problem approximates of the solution of (1) with uniform order p, if and only if the following conditions are satisfied:*

$$\begin{aligned}&\alpha_1(\theta) = 1\\ &\frac{\theta^\nu}{\nu!} - \alpha_{\nu+1}(\theta) - \sum_{i=1}^{m} \frac{c_i^{\nu-1}}{(\nu-1)!}\beta_i(\theta) = 0, \quad \nu = 1,\ldots,r-1,\\ &\frac{\theta^\nu}{\nu!} - \sum_{i=1}^{m} \frac{c_i^{\nu-1}}{(\nu-1)!}\beta_i(\theta) = 0, \quad \nu = r,\ldots,p.\end{aligned} \qquad (14)$$

Corollary 2. *The maximum attainable uniform order of convergence for a multivalue collocation method (2) with a collocation polynomial in (5) and vector of external stages defined by (13) is $m + r - 1$. The corresponding collocation polynomial satisfies the following interpolation and collocation conditions:*

$$P_n(t_n) = y_1^{[n]}, \quad P_n'(t_n) = y_2^{[n]}, \quad \ldots \quad P_n^{(r-1)}(t_n) = y_{r-1}^{[n]}, \qquad (15)$$

$$P_n'(t_n + c_i h) = f(P_n(t_n + c_i h)), \quad i = 1, 2, \ldots, m. \qquad (16)$$

2.3. Derivation of A-Stable Multivalue Collocation Methods

We describe in this section the existing procedures for the derivation of A-stable uniform order multivalue collocation methods. The advantages of deriving such methods lies in their efficiency in the numerical treatment of stiff problem, as they do not suffer from the order reduction phenomenon [1,2]. We recall that a numerical method is A-stable if its region of absolute stability includes the entire complex half-plane with a negative real part.

As we observe from Corollaries 1 and 2, the maximum attainable uniform order multivalue collocation methods with collocation polynomial in (5) and vector of external stages defined by (8) or (13) is $p = m + r - 1$. With the aim of deriving A-stable methods, according to the Daniel–Moore theorem [1], the order of the method cannot exceed $2m$. Therefore the following Theorem clarifies the restriction, on the number of external stages, necessary for A-stability. The proof can be found in [4].

Theorem 3. *An A-stable multivalue collocation method with collocation polynomial in (5) fulfills the constraint $r \leq m + 1$.*

As a consequence, two-step collocation methods of Section 2.1 cannot be A-stable, as for these methods $r = m + 2$, while A-stable Nordsieck GLM collocation methods of Section 2.2 can be derived with a suitable choice for r.

In regards to two-step collocation methods, in the paper [5], A-stable methods of uniform order $p = m + s$, $s = 1, 2, \ldots, m$ have been derived by imposing not all the order conditions up to $p = 2m + 1$, but just requiring the fulfillment of the first $m + s$ order conditions in (10). This procedure corresponds to relaxing some of the interpolation/collocation conditions in (11) and (12), and the corresponding methods are called two-step almost collocation methods.

In regards to Nordsieck GLM collocation methods, in the paper [4], A-stable methods of uniform order $p = m + r - 1$ with $r = m + 1$ have been provided.

Regarding the computational cost of multivalue collocation methods (2)–(5), it is strongly related to the solution of the nonlinear system for the computation of the vector $Y^{[n]}$ in (2), and depends on the matrix $\mathbf{A} = \left[\beta_j(c_i)\right]_{i,j=1,\ldots,m}$. Two-step almost collocation methods having lower triangular or diagonal coefficient matrix $\mathbf{A}$ that have been derived in [24]. Regarding Nordsieck GLM collocation methods, the requirement for a structured coefficient matrix forces the relaxation of some of the interpolation/collocation conditions (15) and (16), thus leading to Nordsieck GLM almost collocation methods with $r = m + 1$, having order $p = r$ or $p = r - 1$, i.e., obtained by imposing not all the order conditions up to $p = m + r - 1$, but just requiring the fulfillment of the first r or $r - 1$ order conditions in (14).

We now provide examples of A-stable multivalue collocation and almost collocation methods belonging to the class described in Section 2.2. We consider the case of $m = 2$ and $r = m + 1 = 3$. The collocation polynomial assumes the form:

$$P_n(t_n + \vartheta h) = y_1^{[n]} + \alpha_2(\vartheta)y_2^{[n]} + \alpha_3(\vartheta)y_3^{[n]}$$
$$+ h(\beta_1(\vartheta)f(P(t_n + c_1 h)) + \beta_2(\vartheta)f(P(t_n + c_2 h))) \quad (17)$$

and the corresponding Butcher tableau is given by:

$$\left[\begin{array}{c|c} A & U \\ \hline B & V \end{array}\right] = \left[\begin{array}{cc|ccc} \beta_1(c_1) & 0 & 1 & \alpha_2(c_1) & \alpha_3(c_1) \\ \beta_1(c_2) & \beta_2(c_2) & 1 & \alpha_2(c_2) & \alpha_3(c_2) \\ \beta_1(1) & \beta_2(1) & 1 & \alpha_2(1) & \alpha_3(1) \\ \beta_1'(1) & \beta_2'(1) & 0 & \alpha_2'(1) & \alpha_3'(1) \\ \beta_1''(1) & \beta_2''(1) & 0 & \alpha_2''(1) & \alpha_3''(1) \end{array}\right].$$

We consider the following forms for the matrix **A**:

- Full matrix [4] (GLM-F);
- Lower triangular matrix (GLM-T);
- Singly lower triangular matrix (GLM-S);
- Diagonal matrix (GLM-D).

Polynomials $\alpha_j(\theta)$ and $\beta_j(\theta)$ in (17) are constructed by imposing order conditions of Theorem 2 with $p = 4$ in the case of GLM-F and $p = 3$ in the case of GLM-T, GLM-S, and GLM-D. Figure 1 shows the region of A-stability in the (c_1, c_2) plane for all the classes of methods.

Examples of A-stable methods have the following Butcher tableau:

- GLM-F:

$$c = \begin{bmatrix} 3/2 \\ 9/5 \end{bmatrix}, \quad \left[\begin{array}{c|c} A & U \\ \hline B & V \end{array}\right] = \left[\begin{array}{cc|ccc} \dfrac{9}{8} & -\dfrac{125}{288} & 1 & \dfrac{233}{288} & \dfrac{7}{32} \\[6pt] \dfrac{162}{125} & -\dfrac{3}{10} & 1 & \dfrac{201}{250} & \dfrac{27}{125} \\[6pt] \dfrac{14}{27} & -\dfrac{125}{486} & 1 & \dfrac{359}{486} & \dfrac{5}{27} \\[6pt] \dfrac{32}{27} & -\dfrac{125}{243} & 0 & \dfrac{80}{243} & \dfrac{4}{27} \\[6pt] \dfrac{8}{9} & 0 & 0 & -\dfrac{8}{9} & -\dfrac{1}{3} \end{array}\right].$$

- GLM-T:

$$c = \begin{bmatrix} 22/10 \\ 9/10 \end{bmatrix}, \begin{bmatrix} \mathbf{A} & \mathbf{U} \\ \hline \mathbf{B} & \mathbf{V} \end{bmatrix} = \left[\begin{array}{cc|ccc} \dfrac{11}{15} & 0 & 1 & \dfrac{22}{15} & \dfrac{121}{150} \\ -\dfrac{243}{1100} & \dfrac{81}{50} & 1 & -\dfrac{549}{1100} & -\dfrac{567}{1000} \\ \hline -\dfrac{103}{429} & \dfrac{24}{13} & 1 & -\dfrac{20}{33} & -\dfrac{19}{30} \\ -\dfrac{2}{13} & \dfrac{28}{13} & 0 & -1 & -\dfrac{3}{5} \\ \dfrac{118}{143} & -\dfrac{32}{13} & 0 & \dfrac{18}{11} & \dfrac{7}{5} \end{array} \right].$$

- GLM-S:

$$c = \begin{bmatrix} 22/10 \\ 9/10 \end{bmatrix}, \begin{bmatrix} \mathbf{A} & \mathbf{U} \\ \hline \mathbf{B} & \mathbf{V} \end{bmatrix} = \left[\begin{array}{cc|ccc} \dfrac{11}{15} & 0 & 1 & \dfrac{22}{15} & \dfrac{121}{150} \\ -\dfrac{351}{4840} & \dfrac{11}{15} & 1 & \dfrac{3473}{14520} & -\dfrac{21}{220} \\ \hline -\dfrac{335}{4719} & \dfrac{880}{1053} & 1 & \dfrac{2306}{9801} & -\dfrac{19}{198} \\ \dfrac{205}{4719} & \dfrac{3080}{3159} & 0 & -\dfrac{542}{29403} & \dfrac{8}{297} \\ \dfrac{2830}{4719} & -\dfrac{3520}{3159} & 0 & \dfrac{15130}{29403} & \dfrac{203}{297} \end{array} \right].$$

- GLM-D:

$$c = \begin{bmatrix} 3 \\ 29/10 \end{bmatrix}, \begin{bmatrix} \mathbf{A} & \mathbf{U} \\ \hline \mathbf{B} & \mathbf{V} \end{bmatrix} = \left[\begin{array}{cc|ccc} 1 & 0 & 1 & 2 & \dfrac{3}{2} \\ 0 & \dfrac{29}{30} & 1 & \dfrac{29}{15} & \dfrac{841}{600} \\ \hline \dfrac{209}{15} & -\dfrac{37520}{2523} & 1 & \dfrac{24446}{12615} & \dfrac{1589}{870} \\ -\dfrac{62}{5} & \dfrac{11260}{841} & 0 & \dfrac{47}{4205} & -\dfrac{91}{145} \\ -\dfrac{91}{15} & \dfrac{5660}{841} & 0 & -\dfrac{8369}{12165} & -\dfrac{46}{145} \end{array} \right].$$

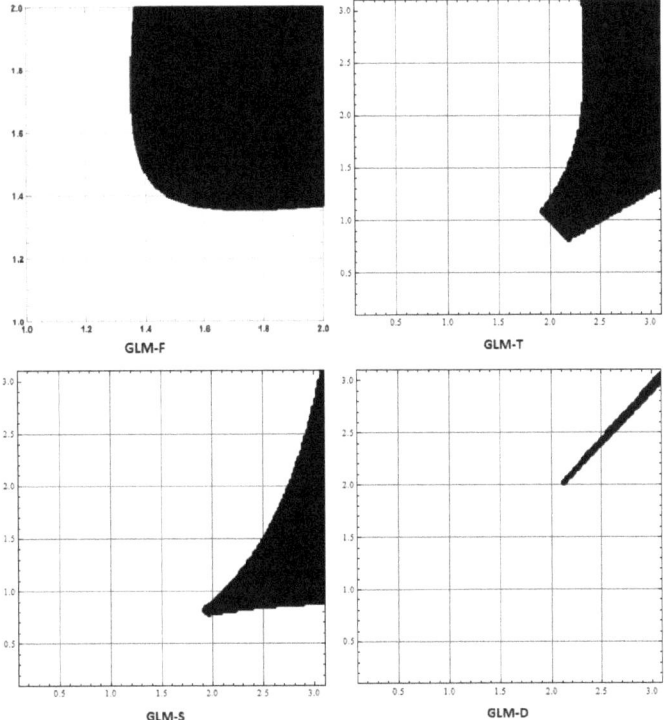

Figure 1. Regions of A-stability in the (c_1, c_2) plane.

2.4. Numerical Illustration

We now show the behavior of the methods listed in the previous section on the Prothero–Robinson problem [1,2]:

$$\begin{cases} y'(t) = \lambda(y(t) - \sin(t)) + \cos(t), & t \in [0, 10], \\ y(0) = 0, \end{cases} \quad (18)$$

which is stiff when $\lambda \ll 0$. We compare the results of the aforementioned methods with those obtained by the two-stage Gaussian Runge–Kutta (RK) method. We report in Table 1 the results obtained for $\lambda = -10^6$ in (18), by applying multivalue collocation and almost collocation methods together with the Runge–Kutta (RK) method of Gauss:

$$\begin{array}{c|cc} \frac{1}{2} - \frac{\sqrt{3}}{6} & \frac{1}{4} & \frac{1}{4} - \frac{\sqrt{3}}{6} \\ \frac{1}{2} + \frac{\sqrt{3}}{6} & \frac{1}{4} + \frac{\sqrt{3}}{6} & \frac{1}{4} \\ \hline & \frac{1}{2} & \frac{1}{2} \end{array} \quad (19)$$

The method (19), which has order 4 and uniform order 2, therefore suffers from order reduction when applied to a stiff problem. Table 1 shows the error in the final step point for different values of the step size and the experimental order of the methods for $\lambda = -10^6$. We observe that the Runge–Kutta method exhibits order reduction, while this is not the case for multivalue collocation and almost collocation methods, having order 4 but uniform order 2, hence it suffers from order reduction on stiff problems, as is visible from

Table 1. Multivalue collocation and almost collocation methods, instead, keep their order of convergence.

Table 1. Absolute errors in the final step point and experimental orders of convergence for problem (18) with $\lambda = -10^6$.

h	GLM-F Error	p	GLM-T Error	p	GLM-S Error	p	GLM-D Error	p	RK Error	p
1/10	2.41×10^{-8}		1.51×10^{-7}		1.51×10^{-7}		4.88×10^{-5}		1.52×10^{-4}	
1/20	7.50×10^{-10}	5.01	9.21×10^{-9}	4.03	9.21×10^{-9}	4.03	3.04×10^{-6}	4.01	3.84×10^{-5}	1.98
1/40	2.21×10^{-11}	5.08	5.69×10^{-10}	4.02	5.70×10^{-10}	4.01	1.89×10^{-7}	4.01	9.99×10^{-6}	1.94
1/80	7.06×10^{-13}	4.97	3.45×10^{-11}	4.04	3.58×10^{-11}	3.99	1.18×10^{-8}	4.00	2.78×10^{-6}	1.85

3. Multivalue Mixed Collocation Methods

In this Section we describe the derivation of Nordsieck GLM mixed collocation methods of the form (2)–(5), with the vector of external stages in Nordsieck form (13). The idea is, instead of considering a basis of polynomials $\{\alpha_i(\theta), \beta_j(\theta), i = 1, \ldots, r, j = 1, \ldots, m\}$, to consider a basis constituted by a combination of trigonometric and polynomial functions. Such methods are useful for problems of the form (1) for which the exact solution is oscillatory with a known frequency of oscillation ω.

As a consequence of Theorem 2, the polynomials $\alpha_i(\theta)$ and $\beta_j(\theta)$, associated to Nordsieck GLM collocation methods of uniform order $p = m + r - 1$, have a degree of at most $m + r - 1$. Therefore, they can be written in the form:

$$\alpha_1(\theta) = 1 \qquad \alpha_{i+1}(\theta) = \sum_{j=1}^{m+r-1} \frac{\overline{\mu}_{i,j-1}}{j} \theta^j, \qquad i = 1, \ldots, r-1, \qquad (20)$$

$$\beta_i(\theta) = \sum_{j=1}^{m+r-1} \frac{\mu_{i,j-1}}{j} \theta^j, \qquad i = 1, \ldots, m. \qquad (21)$$

The idea of Nordsieck GLM mixed collocation methods introduced in [35] relies on considering new basis functions:

$$\{\alpha_i^T(\theta, z), \beta_j^T(\theta, z), i = 1, \ldots, r, j = 1, \ldots, m\},$$

which depend also on the frequency of oscillation of the problem, i.e., depending on $z = \omega h$, of the form:

$$\alpha_1^T(\theta, z) = 1, \qquad (22)$$

$$\alpha_{i+1}^T(\theta, z) = \frac{\overline{a}_i}{z} \sin(z\theta) - \frac{\overline{b}_i}{z} \cos(z\theta) + \frac{\overline{b}_i}{z} + \sum_{j=1}^{m+r-3} \frac{\overline{\gamma}_{i,j-1}}{j} \theta^j \qquad i = 1, \ldots, r-1, \qquad (23)$$

$$\beta_i^T(\theta, z) = \frac{a_i}{z} \sin(z\theta) - \frac{b_i}{z} \cos(z\theta) + \frac{b_i}{z} + \sum_{j=1}^{m+r-3} \frac{\gamma_{i,j-1}}{j} \theta^j \qquad i = 1, \ldots, m. \qquad (24)$$

The next theorem shows the expressions of coefficients $a_i, b_i, \gamma_{i,j}$ in (23) and $\overline{a}_i, \overline{b}_i, \overline{\gamma}_{i,j}$ in (24) in order to obtain the maximum attainable uniform order $p = m + r - 1$. The proof can be found in [35].

Theorem 4. *A multivalue mixed collocation method (2)–(5), with vector of external stages defined by (13) and functional basis $\{\alpha_i(\theta), \beta_j(\theta), i = 1, \ldots, r, j = 1, \ldots, m\}$ defined in (22)–(24), has order $p = m + r - 1$ if:*

$$a_i = \frac{\det M_{i,1}}{\det M}, \qquad b_i = \frac{\det M_{i,2}}{\det M}, \qquad i = 1, \ldots, m, \qquad (25)$$

$$\gamma_{ij} = \begin{cases} (-1)^{\frac{i}{2}+1} a_i \dfrac{z^j}{j!} & j \text{ is even,} \\ & j = 0, \ldots, r-2, \\ (-1)^{\frac{i+1}{2}} b_i \dfrac{z^j}{j!} & j \text{ is odd,} \\ \dfrac{\det M_{i,j-r+4}}{\det M}, & j = r-1, \ldots, m+r-4, \end{cases} \quad, i = 1, \ldots, m, \qquad (26)$$

$$\bar{a}_i = \dfrac{\sum_{k=1}^{m}(-1)^{k+1}\dfrac{c_k^{i-1}}{(i-1)!}\det M_{k,1}}{\det M}, \qquad \bar{b}_i = \dfrac{\sum_{k=1}^{m}(-1)^{k}\dfrac{c_k^{i-1}}{(i-1)!}\det M_{k,2}}{\det M}, \qquad i = 1, \ldots, r-1, \qquad (27)$$

$$\bar{\gamma}_{ij} = \begin{cases} (-1)^{\frac{i}{2}+1}\bar{a}_i \dfrac{z^j + \delta_{i,j+1}}{j!} & j \text{ is even,} \\ & j = 0, \ldots, r-2, \\ (-1)^{\frac{i+1}{2}}\bar{b}_i \dfrac{z^j + \delta_{i,j+1}}{j!} & j \text{ is odd,} \\ \dfrac{\sum_{k=1}^{m}(-1)^{k+j-r+1}\dfrac{c_k^{i-1}}{(i-1)!}\det M_{k,j-r+4}}{\det M}, & j = r-1, \ldots, m+r-4, \end{cases} \quad, i = 1, \ldots, r-1, \qquad (28)$$

where M is a square non singular matrix of order m given by:

$$M = \begin{pmatrix} \cos(zc_1) - \sum_{k=0}^{r_1}(-1)^k\dfrac{(zc_1)^{2k}}{(2k)!} & \sin(zc_1) - \sum_{k=0}^{r_2}(-1)^k\dfrac{(zc_1)^{2k+1}}{(2k+1)!} & c_1^{r-1} & c_1^r & \cdots & c_1^{m+r-4} \\ \cos(zc_2) - \sum_{k=0}^{r_1}(-1)^k\dfrac{(zc_2)^{2k}}{(2k)!} & \sin(zc_2) - \sum_{k=0}^{r_2}(-1)^k\dfrac{(zc_2)^{2k+1}}{(2k+1)!} & c_2^{r-1} & c_2^r & \cdots & c_2^{m+r-4} \\ \vdots & \vdots & \vdots & \vdots & \vdots & \vdots \\ \cos(zc_m) - \sum_{k=0}^{r_1}(-1)^k\dfrac{(zc_m)^{2k}}{(2k)!} & \sin(zc_m) - \sum_{k=0}^{r_2}(-1)^k\dfrac{(zc_m)^{2k+1}}{(2k+1)!} & c_m^{r-1} & c_m^r & \cdots & c_m^{m+r-4} \end{pmatrix},$$

$M_{i,j}$ is the submatrix obtained by deleting the i-th row and j-th column from matrix M, $c_1, \ldots, c_m$ are the collocation points, δ_{ij} is the usual Kronecker delta, and:

$$r_1 = \begin{cases} \dfrac{r-2}{2} & r \text{ is even,} \\ \dfrac{r-3}{2} & r \text{ is odd,} \end{cases} \qquad r_2 = \begin{cases} \dfrac{r-2}{2}-1 & r \text{ is even,} \\ \dfrac{r-3}{2} & r \text{ is odd.} \end{cases}$$

In order to show the performance of Nordsieck GLM mixed collocation methods, we show the results obtained on the following test problems:

- Problem 1:

$$\begin{cases} y'(t) = -(y(t) - \sin(\omega t)) + \omega \cos(\omega t), & t \in [0,10] \\ y(0) = 0, \end{cases} \qquad (29)$$

whose solution is $y(t) = \sin(\omega t)$, so it is a function belonging to the basis.

- Problem 2:

$$\begin{cases} y'(t) = -(y(t) - \sin(\omega t + t)) + (\omega + 1)\cos(\omega t + t), & t \in [0,10] \\ y(0) = 0, \end{cases} \qquad (30)$$

whose solution is $y(t) = \sin(\omega t + t) = \sin \omega t \cos t + \cos \omega t \sin t$, so it is a combination of the basic functions $\sin \omega t$ and $\cos \omega t$.

We put $m = 2$ and $r = 3$ and $c_1 = 3/2, c_2 = 9/5$ and we denote by MGLM-F, the corresponding Nordsieck GLM mixed collocation method. In Table 2, we consider for a comparison, the GLM-F method of Section 2.3. The table clearly shows the advantage of mixed collocation versus polynomial collocation in the case of the oscillatory solution.

Table 2. Absolute errors (in the final step point) and effective orders of convergence. Absolute errors in the final step point and experimental orders of convergence with $\omega = 100$.

h	GLM-F on Problem (29)	MGLM-F on Problem (29)	GLM-F on Problem (30)		MGLM-F on Problem (30)	
	Error	Error	Error	p	Error	p
1/40	0.2764	1.4818×10^{-12}	0.3626		0.0133	
1/80	0.0326	8.4277×10^{-13}	0.0436	3.0560	9.5762×10^{-4}	3.7958
1/160	0.0024	1.2212×10^{-15}	0.0031	3.8140	6.1966×10^{-5}	3.9499
1/320	1.5567×10^{-4}	8.9595×10^{-14}	1.9729×10^{-4}	3.9739	3.9064×10^{-6}	3.9876
1/640	9.8558×10^{-6}	1.4988×10^{-14}	1.2403×10^{-5}	3.9916	2.4468×10^{-7}	3.9969

4. Multivalue Spline Collocation Methods for FDEs

In this section, we review multivalue spline collocation methods [18,20,54], applied to the IVP problem of type:

$$\begin{cases} D^\alpha y(t) = f(t, y(t)), & t \in [0, b], \\ y^{(i)}(0) = \gamma_i, & i = 0, \ldots, n-1, \end{cases} \quad (31)$$

where $n - 1 < \alpha < n$, $n \in \mathbb{N}$, $\gamma_i \in \mathbb{R}$, $f : [0, b] \times \mathbb{R} \to R$. Here we consider the Caputo fractional derivative [58–60]:

$$D^\alpha y(t) = \frac{1}{\Gamma(n-\alpha)} \int_0^t \frac{y^{(n)}(s)}{(t-s)^{\alpha+1-n}} ds.$$

The convergence analysis of spline collocation methods is carried out in the functional space $C^{q,\nu}(0, T]$, defined as follows [15].

Let $q \in \mathbb{N}$ and $\nu \in (-\infty, 1)$, then $y : [0, T] \to \mathbb{R}$ belongs to the space $C^{q,\nu}(0, T]$ if it is q times continuously differentiable in $(0, T]$, and:

$$|y^{(i)}(t)| \leq c \begin{cases} 1 & \text{if } i < 1 - \nu, \\ 1 + |\log t| & \text{if } i = 1 - \nu, \ t \in (0, T], i = 1, \ldots, q. \\ t^{1-\nu-i} & \text{if } i > 1 - \nu, \end{cases}$$

Sufficient conditions for obtaining a solution in the space $C^{q,\nu}(0, T]$ are provided by the following theorem.

Theorem 5 ([30]). *Let $f \in C([0, T] \times \mathbb{R})$, q times continuously differentiable in $(0, T] \times \mathbb{R}$, and $\exists \nu \in [1 - \alpha, 1)$ such that:*

$$\left| \frac{\partial^{i+j}}{\partial t^i \partial y^j} f(t, y) \right| \leq \phi(|y|) \begin{cases} 1 & \text{if } i < 1 - \nu \\ 1 + |\log t| & \text{if } i = 1 - \nu \\ t^{1-\nu-i} & \text{if } i > 1 - \nu \end{cases}, (t, y) \in (0, T] \times \mathbb{R},$$

$\forall i, j \in \mathbb{N}$ with $i + j \leq q$. In addition, for $\alpha \in (0, 1)$ assume that:

$$\left| \frac{\partial^{i+j}}{\partial t^i \partial y^j} [f(t, y_1) - f(t, y_2)] \right| \leq \phi(\max\{|y_1|, |y_2|\}) |y_1 - y_2| \begin{cases} 1 & \text{if } i = 0 \\ t^{1-\nu-i} & \text{if } i > 0 \end{cases},$$

$(t, y_i) \in (0, T] \times \mathbb{R}$, $i = 1, 2$. The function $\phi : [0, \infty) \to \mathbb{R}$ is assumed to be monotonically increasing. Let the fractional IVP (31) have a solution $y \in C[0, T]$ with $D^\alpha y \in C[0, T]$. Then $y \in C^{q,\nu}(0, T]$ and $D^\alpha y \in C^{q,\nu}(0, T]$.

By setting $z = D^\alpha y$, we have:

$$y = J^\alpha z + Q, \quad (32)$$

with,

$$(J^\alpha z)(t) = \frac{1}{\Gamma(\alpha)} \int_0^t (t-s)^{\alpha-1} z(s)\, ds, \quad t > 0, \tag{33}$$

$$Q(t) = \sum_{i=0}^{\lceil \alpha \rceil - 1} \frac{\gamma_i}{i!} t^i, \tag{34}$$

$\lceil \alpha \rceil$ being the smallest integer not less than α. With this position, we may rewrite the IVP (31) as a nonlinear equation:

$$z = f(t, J^\alpha z + Q). \tag{35}$$

Once (35) is solved, y can be computed by (32).

4.1. One-Step Collocation Methods for FDEs

Let us introduce a graded mesh I_N on $[0, T]$ with grading exponent $r \geq 1$:

$$t_j = b \left(\frac{j}{N} \right)^r, \tag{36}$$

and collocation parameters $0 \leq \eta_1 < \cdots < \eta_m \leq 1$. Let,

$$S_k^{(-1)}(I_N) = \{ v : v|_{[t_{j-1}, t_j]} \in \Pi_k, j = 1, \ldots, N \}. \tag{37}$$

The one step collocation method approximates the solution z of (35) by a function $v \in S_{m-1}^{(-1)}(I_N)$. The collocation solution v is computed by imposing these collocation conditions, for $j = 1, \ldots, N$:

$$v_j(t_{jk}) = f(t_{jk}, (J^\alpha v)(t_{jk}) + Q(t_{jk})), \quad k = 1, \ldots, m. \tag{38}$$

where $v_j := v|_{[t_{j-1}, t_j]}$. Then, the approximate solution of (31) is the function y_N, defined as:

$$y_N = J^\alpha v + Q. \tag{39}$$

Collocation conditions (38) give rise to the nonlinear system in the unknowns $z_{jk} := v_j(t_{jk})$:

$$z_{jk} = f\left(t_{jk}, \sum_{\mu=1}^m z_{j\mu} (J^\alpha \varphi_{j,\mu})(t_{jk}) + \sum_{\lambda=1}^{j-1} \sum_{\mu=1}^m z_{\lambda\mu} (J^\alpha \varphi_{\lambda,\mu})(t_{jk}) + Q(t_{jk}) \right), \quad k = 1, \ldots, m,$$

where $\varphi_{\lambda, \mu}$ is equal to the μ-th Lagrange fundamental polynomial corresponding to the nodes $t_{\lambda 1}, \ldots, t_{\lambda m}$ in $[t_{\lambda-1}, t_\lambda]$, and it is null outside this interval.

The error is analyzed in the following theorem, where this quantity is used:

$$E_N(p, \nu, r) = \begin{cases} N^{-r(1-\nu)} & \text{if } 1 \leq r \leq \frac{p}{1-\nu} \\ N^{-p}(1 + \log N) & \text{if } r = \frac{p}{1-\nu} = 1 \\ N^{-p} & \text{if } r = \frac{p}{1-\nu} > 1 \text{ or } r > \frac{p}{1-\nu}. \end{cases} \tag{40}$$

Theorem 6 ([30], [Th. 4.1]). *Let the IVP (31) have a solution $y \in C[0, b]$, with $D^\alpha y \in C[0, b]$ and let $f \in C([0, b] \times \mathbb{R})$ such that its derivatives $\frac{\partial}{\partial t} f(t, y)$ and: $\frac{\partial^2}{\partial t^2} f(t, y)$ are continuous in $(0, b] \times \mathbb{R}$ and*

$$\left| \frac{\partial^j}{\partial y^j} f(t, y) \right| \leq \psi(|y|), \quad (t, x) \in (0, b] \times \mathbb{R}, j = 0, 1, 2.$$

$\psi : [0, \infty) \to \mathbb{R}$ is a monotonically increasing function.

Then there exist $N_0 \in \mathbb{N}$ and $\delta_0 > 0$ such that, for all $N \geq N_0$, the one-step collocation method possesses a unique solution $v \in S_{m-1}^{(-1)}(I_N)$ in the ball $\|u - z\|_\infty \leq \delta_0$, where $z = D^\alpha y \in C[0, b]$. If, in addition, the assumptions of Theorem 5 with $q := m$ and $\nu \in [1-\alpha, 1)$ are fulfilled, then for all $N \geq N_0$, the following error estimate holds:

$$\|y_N - y\|_\infty \leq c E_N(m, \nu, r),$$

with y_N given by Formula (39). Here c is a constant not depending on N, and E_N is defined by (40).

4.2. Two-Step Collocation Methods for FDEs

Given the graded mesh I_N defined in (36) and collocation parameters $0 \leq \eta_1 < \cdots < \eta_m \leq 1$, with $(\eta_1, \eta_m) \neq (0, 1)$, the two-step collocation method approximates the solution z of (35) by a function $v \in S_{2m-1}^{(-1)}(I_N)$. By defining the polynomial $v_j = v|_{[t_{j-1}, t_j]}$, we impose these collocation and interpolation conditions, for $j = 2, \ldots, N$:

$$v_j(t_{jk}) = f(t_{jk}, (J^\alpha v)(t_{jk}) + Q(t_{jk})), \quad k = 1, \ldots, m \quad (41)$$

$$v_j(t_{j-1,k}) = v_{j-1}(t_{j-1,k}), \quad k = 1, \ldots, m \quad (42)$$

The collocation solution $v(t)$ can be expressed as:

$$v(t) = v_1(t) + \sum_{\lambda=2}^{N} \left(\sum_{k=1}^{m} z_{\lambda k} L_{\lambda, m+k}(t) + \sum_{k=1}^{m} z_{\lambda-1, k} L_{\lambda k}(t) \right), \quad t \in [0, T], \quad (43)$$

where v_1 is obtained by a suitable starting procedure (cfr. [20]); $L_{\lambda, \mu} = L_\mu$ in $[t_{\lambda-1}, t_\lambda]$ and it is null outside. L_μ is the μ-th Lagrange fundamental polynomial corresponding to the nodes $\{t_{j-1,k}, t_{j,k} \mid k = 1, \ldots, m\}$. The coefficients $z_{\lambda \mu}$ are the solution of the nonlinear system:

$$z_{jk} = f\left(t_{jk}, (J^\alpha v)(t_{jk}) + Q(t_{jk})\right), \quad k = 1, \ldots, m.$$

A more explicit formulation of the above system is:

$$z_{jk} = f\left(t_{jk}, (J^\alpha v_1)(t_{jk}) + \sum_{\mu=1}^{m} z_{j\mu}(J^\alpha L_{j,m+\mu})(t_{jk}) + \sum_{\lambda=2}^{j-1} \sum_{\mu=1}^{m} z_{\lambda \mu}(J^\alpha L_{\lambda, m+\mu})(t_{jk}) \right.$$
$$\left. + \sum_{\mu=1}^{m} z_{j-1, \mu}(J^\alpha L_{j\mu})(t_{jk}) + \sum_{\lambda=2}^{j-1} \sum_{\mu=1}^{m} z_{\lambda-1, \mu}(J^\alpha L_{\lambda \mu})(t_{jk}) + Q(t_{jk}) \right), \quad (44)$$

$k = 1, \ldots, m$. Although a number of fractional integrals must be computed, they may be analytically evaluated, thus no further approximation is needed.

The main converge result is provided by the following theorem:

Theorem 7 ([20], [Th. 4.5]). *Let hypothesis HP 1 of Theorem 6 hold. Then there exist $N_0 \in \mathbb{N}$ and $\delta_0 > 0$ such that, for all $N \geq N_0$, the two-step collocation method possesses a unique solution $v \in S_{2m-1}^{(-1)}(I_N)$ in the ball $\|u - z\|_\infty \leq \delta_0$, where $z = D^\alpha y \in C[0, T]$. If, in addition, the assumptions of Theorem 5 with $q := 2m$ and $\nu \in [1-\alpha, 1)$ are satisfied, then for all $N \geq N_0$, the error is bounded as follows:*

$$\|y_N - y\|_\infty \leq c E_N(2m, \nu, r),$$

with y_N defined in (39). Here, the value of the constant c does not depend on N, and E_N is defined in (40).

It is evident that a suitable choice of the grading exponent r is the basic step to obtain a high accuracy. The best choice of r grows with m, i.e., with the number of collocation abscissae and also depends on the degree of smoothness of the analytical solution.

By comparing one- and two-step collocation methods, we observe that they have the same computational cost, since they both require the solution of a nonlinear system of dimension m, nevertheless, the error of the two-step method decreases as $O(N^{-2m})$, while the error of the one-step method decreases as $O(N^{-m})$ (for both methods we considered the best case).

We provide a numerical illustration on the following test equation, taken from [61].

$$D^\alpha y(t) = \frac{40320}{\Gamma(9-\alpha)}t^{8-\alpha} - 3\frac{\Gamma(5+\frac{\alpha}{2})}{\Gamma(5-\frac{\alpha}{2})}t^{4-\frac{\alpha}{2}} + \left(\frac{3}{2}t^{\frac{\alpha}{2}} - t^4\right)^3 \quad t \in [0,1],$$
$$+ \frac{9}{4}\Gamma(\alpha+1) - (y(t))^{\frac{3}{2}},$$

$y(0) = 0$,

$\alpha = 1/2$. The exact solution is $y = t^8 - 3t^{4+\alpha/2} + \frac{9}{4}t^\alpha$. The hypotheses of Theorem 5 are satisfied by $\nu = 0.5$ and any $q \in \mathbb{N}$. In Figure 2, we plot the work-precision diagram obtained by one- and two-step collocation methods, with collocation parameters equally spaced in $[0,1]$ with $\eta_0 \neq 0$ and $\eta_m \neq 1$; with $r = \dfrac{m}{1-\nu}$ for the one-step methods and $r = \dfrac{2m}{1-\nu}$ for the two-step methods. We observe that multivalue collocation obtain a definite improvement of one-step collocation methods, except for low accuracy requests.

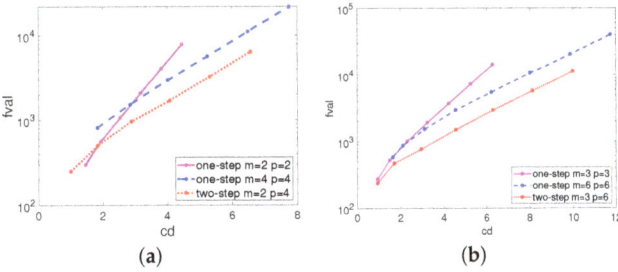

Figure 2. Work-precision diagrams for one- and two-step collocation methods for FDEs, cd is the number of correct digits, and $fval$ is the number of function evaluations. (**a**) One-step methods with $m=2$ and $m=4$, two-step methods with $m=2$; (**b**) one-step methods with $m=3$ and $m=6$, two step methods with $m=3$.

5. Conclusions

We presented a concise selection of our recent results on collocation methods for ODEs and FDE. This technique has exhibited a wide range of benefits in terms of accuracy and efficiency. Moreover, the choice of collocation basis makes the numerics more adapted to the problem, with meaningful improvements when qualitative behaviors of the solution are merged in the numerical scheme. Adapted functional basis are relevant, for instance, in the case of oscillatory problems [62–65]. Further developments of this research will be oriented to the establishment of a theory of collocation methods for stochastic problems (see, for instance, refs. [51,66–71] and references therein).

Author Contributions: All authors A.C., D.C., R.D., B.P. equally contributed to this work. All authors have read and agreed to the published version of the manuscript.

Funding: The authors are members of the INdAM Research group GNCS and are supported by the GNCS-INDAM project. A. Cardone, D. Conte, and R. D'Ambrosio are supported by PRIN2017-MIUR project 2017JYCLSF "Structure preserving approximation of evolutionary problems".

Institutional Review Board Statement: Not applicable.

Informed Consent Statement: Not applicable.

Data Availability Statement: Not applicable.

Conflicts of Interest: The authors declare no conflict of interest.

Abbreviations

The following abbreviations are used in this manuscript:

FDEs	Fractional Differential Equation
GLM	General Linear Method
IVP	Initial Value Problem
ODE	Ordinary Differential Equation
RK	Runge–Kutta

References

1. Butcher, J. *Numerical Methods for Ordinary Differential Equations*, 3rd ed.; John Wiley & Sons, Inc.: Hoboken, NJ, USA, 2016.
2. Hairer, E.; Wanner, G. *Solving Ordinary Differential Equations. II*; Springer Series in Computational Mathematics, Stiff and Differential-Algebraic Problems, Second Revised Edition, Paperback; Springer: Berlin, Germany, 2010; Volume 14, p. xvi+614.
3. Lambert, J. *Numerical Methods for Ordinary Differential Systems: The Initial Value Problem*; John Wiley & Sons, Inc.: Hoboken, NJ, USA, 1991.
4. D'Ambrosio, R.; Paternoster, B. Multivalue collocation methods free from order reduction. *J. Comput. Appl. Math.* **2021**, *387*, 112515. [CrossRef]
5. D'Ambrosio, R.; Ferro, M.; Jackiewicz, Z.; Paternoster, B. Two-step almost collocation methods for ordinary differential equations. *Numer. Algorithms* **2010**, *53*, 195–217. [CrossRef]
6. Costabile, F.; Gualtieri, M.; Napoli, A. Lidstone-based collocation splines for odd-order BVPs. *Math. Comput. Simul.* **2021**, *186*, 124–135. [CrossRef]
7. Costabile, F.; Napoli, A. Collocation for high order differential equations with two-points Hermite boundary conditions. *Appl. Numer. Math.* **2015**, *87*, 157–167. [CrossRef]
8. Costabile, F.; Napoli, A. Collocation for high-order differential equations with Lidstone boundary conditions. *J. Appl. Math.* **2012**, *2012*, 120792. [CrossRef]
9. Costabile, F.; Napoli, A. A class of collocation methods for numerical integration of initial value problems. *J. Appl. Math.* **2011**, *62*, 3221–3235. [CrossRef]
10. Costabile, F.; Napoli, A. Stability of Chebyshev collocation methods. *Comput. Math. Appl.* **2004**, *47*, 659–666. [CrossRef]
11. Lie, I. The stability function for multistep collocation methods. *Numer. Math.* **1990**, *57*, 779–787. [CrossRef]
12. Lie, I.; Nørsett, S. Superconvergence for Multistep Collocation. *Math. Comp.* **1989**, *52*, 65–79. [CrossRef]
13. Blank, L. Stability of collocation for weakly singular Volterra equations. *IMA J. Numer. Anal.* **1995**, *15*, 357–375. [CrossRef]
14. Brunner, H. Cambridge monographs on applied and computational mathematics. In *Collocation Methods for Volterra Integral and Related Functional Differential Equations*; Cambridge University Press: Cambridge, UK, 2004; Volume 15, p. xiv+597.
15. Brunner, H.; Pedas, A.; Vainikko, G. Piecewise polynomial collocation methods for linear Volterra integro-differential equations with weakly singular kernels. *SIAM J. Numer. Anal.* **2001**, *39*, 957–982. [CrossRef]
16. Zayernouri, M.; Karniadakis, G.E. Fractional spectral collocation methods for linear and nonlinear variable order FPDEs. *J. Comput. Phys.* **2015**, *293*, 312–338. [CrossRef]
17. Cardone, A.; Conte, D. Multistep collocation methods for Volterra integro-differential equations. *Appl. Math. Comput.* **2013**, *221*, 770–785. [CrossRef]
18. Cardone, A.; Conte, D.; Paternoster, B. A MATLAB Implementation of Spline Collocation Methods for Fractional Differential Equations. *Lect. Notes Comput. Sci.* **2021**, *12949*, 387–401.
19. Cardone, A.; Conte, D. Stability analysis of spline collocation methods for fractional differential equations. *Math. Comput. Simulat.* **2020**, *178*, 501–514.
20. Cardone, A.; Conte, D.; Paternoster, B. Two-step collocation methods for fractional differential equations. *Discrete Contin. Dyn. Syst. Ser. B* **2018**, *23*, 2709–2725. [CrossRef]
21. Conte, D.; D'Ambrosio, R.; Paternoster, B. Two-step diagonally-implicit collocation based methods for Volterra integral equations. *Appl. Numer. Math.* **2012**, *62*, 1312–1324.
22. Conte, D.; Paternoster, B. Multistep collocation methods for Volterra integral equations. *Appl. Numer. Math.* **2009**, *59*, 1721–1736.
23. Conte, D.; Jackiewicz, Z.; Paternoster, B. Two-step almost collocation methods for Volterra integral equations. *Appl. Math. Comput.* **2008**, *204*, 839–853. [CrossRef]
24. D'Ambrosio, R.; Paternoster, B. Two-step modified collocation methods with structured coefficient matrices. *Appl. Numer. Math.*

25. Ford, N.; Morgado, M.; Rebelo, M. Nonpolynomial collocation approximation of solutions to fractional differential equations. *Fract. Calc. Appl. Anal.* **2013**, *16*, 874–891. [CrossRef]
26. Guo, B.Y.; Yan, J.P. Legendre-Gauss collocation method for initial value problems of second order ordinary differential equations. *Appl. Numer. Math.* **2009**, *59*, 1386–1408.
27. Guo, B.y.; Wang, Z.q. Legendre-Gauss collocation methods for ordinary differential equations. *Adv. Comput. Math.* **2009**, *30*, 249–280. [CrossRef]
28. Li, X. Numerical solution of fractional differential equations using cubic B-spline wavelet collocation method. *Commun. Nonlinear Sci. Numer. Simul.* **2012**, *17*, 3934–3946. [CrossRef]
29. Pedas, A.; Tamme, E. On the convergence of spline collocation methods for fractional differential equations. *J. Comput. Appl. Math.* **2011**, *235*, 3502–3514. [CrossRef]
30. Pedas, A.; Tamme, E. Numerical solution of nonlinear fractional differential equations by spline collocation methods. *J. Comput. Appl. Math.* **2014**, *255*, 216–230. [CrossRef]
31. Pedas, A.; Tamme, E. Spline collocation for nonlinear fractional boundary value problems. *Appl. Math. Comput.* **2014**, *244*, 502–513. [CrossRef]
32. Wang, Z.Q.; Guo, B.Y. Legendre-Gauss-Radau collocation method for solving initial value problems of first order ordinary differential equations. *J. Sci. Comput.* **2012**, *52*, 226–255. [CrossRef]
33. Zayernouri, M.; Karniadakis, G.E. Fractional spectral collocation method. *SIAM J. Sci. Comput.* **2014**, *36*, A40–A62. [CrossRef]
34. Paternoster, B. Phase-fitted collocation-based Runge-Kutta-Nystrom method. *Appl. Numer. Math.* **2000**, *35*, 339–355. [CrossRef]
35. Conte, D.; D'Ambrosio, R.; D'Arienzo, M.P.; Paternoster, B. Multivalue mixed collocation methods. *Appl. Math. Comput.* **2021**, *409*, 126346. [CrossRef]
36. Norsett, S.; Wanner, G. Perturbed collocation and Runge Kutta methods. *Numer. Math.* **1981**, *38*, 193–208. [CrossRef]
37. Jackiewicz, Z. *General Linear Methods for Ordinary Differential Equations*; John Wiley & Sons, Inc.: Hoboken, NJ, USA, 2009; p. xvi+482. [CrossRef]
38. Söderlind, G.; Jay, L.; Calvo, M. Stiffness 1952–2012: Sixty years in search of a definition. *BIT Numer. Math.* **2015**, *55*, 531–558. [CrossRef]
39. Cash, J. Efficient numerical method for the solution of stiff initial-value problems and differential algebraic equations. *R. Soc. Lond. Proc. Ser. A Math. Phys. Eng. Sci.* **2003**, *459*, 797–815. [CrossRef]
40. Bellomo, N.; Bingham, R.; Chaplain, M.A.; Dosi, G.; Forni, G.; Knopoff, D.A.; Lowengrub, J.; Twarock, R.; Virgillito, M.E. A multiscale model of virus pandemic: Heterogeneous interactive entities in a globally connected world. *Math. Models Methods Appl. Sci.* **2020**, *30*, 1591–1651. [CrossRef]
41. Heldt, F.; Frensing, T.; Pflugmacher, A.; Gröpler, R.; Peschel, B.; Reichl, U. Multiscale Modeling of Influenza A Virus Infection Supports the Development of Direct-Acting Antivirals. *PLoS Comp. Biol.* **2013**, *9*, e1003372. [CrossRef]
42. Southern, J.; Pitt-Francis, J.; Whiteley, J.; Stokeley, D.; Kobashi, H.; Nobes, R.; Kadooka, Y.; Gavaghan, D. Multi-scale computational modelling in biology and physiology. *Prog. Biophys. Mol. Biol.* **2008**, *96*, 60–89. [CrossRef] [PubMed]
43. Metzler, R.; Klafter, J. The random walk's guide to anomalous diffusion: A fractional dynamics approach. *Phys. Rep.* **2000**, *339*, 77. [CrossRef]
44. Mainardi, F. *Fractional Calculus and Waves in Linear Viscoelasticity: An Introduction to Mathematical Models*; Imperial College Press: London, UK, 2010; p. xx+347. [CrossRef]
45. Povstenko, Y. Thermoelasticity that uses fractional heat conduction equation. *J. Math. Sci.* **2009**, *162*, 296–305. [CrossRef]
46. Diethelm, K.; Ford, N.J.; Freed, A.D. A predictor-corrector approach for the numerical solution of fractional differential equations. *Nonlinear Dynam.* **2002**, *29*, 3–22. [CrossRef]
47. Lubich, C. Fractional linear multistep methods for Abel-Volterra integral equations of the second kind. *Math. Comp.* **1985**, *45*, 463–469. [CrossRef]
48. Garrappa, R.; Popolizio, M. On accurate product integration rules for linear fractional differential equations. *J. Comput. Appl. Math.* **2011**, *235*, 1085–1097. [CrossRef]
49. Khader, M.M. On the numerical solutions for the fractional diffusion equation. *Commun. Nonlinear Sci. Numer. Simul.* **2011**, *16*, 2535–2542. [CrossRef]
50. Burrage, K.; Cardone, A.; D'Ambrosio, R.; Paternoster, B. Numerical solution of time fractional diffusion systems. *Appl. Numer. Math.* **2017**, *116*, 82–94. [CrossRef]
51. Cardone, A.; D'Ambrosio, R.; Paternoster, B. A spectral method for stochastic fractional differential equations. *Appl. Numer. Math.* **2019**, *139*, 115–119. [CrossRef]
52. Blank, L. *Numerical Treatment of Differential Equations of Fractional Order*; Technical Report, Numerical Analysis Report; Department of Mathematics, University of Manchester: Manchester, UK, 1996.
53. Pedas, A.; Tamme, E. Spline collocation methods for linear multi-term fractional differential equations. *J. Comput. Appl. Math.* **2011**, *236*, 167–176. [CrossRef]
54. Cardone, A.; Conte, D.; Paternoster, B. Stability analysis of two-step spline collocation methods for fractional differential equations. *submitted*.
55. D'Ambrosio, R.; Hairer, E. Long-term stability of multi-value methods for ordinary differential equations. *J. Sci. Comput.* **2014**, *60*, 627–640. [CrossRef]

56. D'Ambrosio, R.; Hairer, E.; Zbinden, C. G-symplecticity implies conjugate-symplecticity of the underlying one-step method. *BIT Numer. Math.* **2013**, *53*, 867–872. [CrossRef]
57. D'Ambrosio, R.; Esposito, E.; Paternoster, B. General linear methods for $y'' = f(y(t))$. *Numer. Algorithms* **2012**, *61*, 331–349. [CrossRef]
58. Diethelm, K. An application-oriented exposition using differential operators of Caputo type. In *The Analysis of Fractional Differential Equations*; Lecture Notes in Mathematics; Springer: Berlin, Germany, 2010; Volume 2004, p. viii+247. [CrossRef]
59. Kilbas, A.A.; Srivastava, H.M.; Trujillo, J.J. *Theory and Applications of Fractional Differential Equations*; North-Holland Mathematics Studies; Elsevier Science B.V.: Amsterdam, The Netherlands, 2006; Volume 204, p. xvi+523.
60. Podlubny, I. *Fractional Differential Equations*; Mathematics in Science and Engineering; Academic Press, Inc.: San Diego, CA, USA, 1999; Volume 198, p. xxiv+340.
61. Diethelm, K.; Ford, N.J.; Freed, A.D. Detailed error analysis for a fractional Adams method. *Numer. Algorithms* **2004**, *36*, 31–52. [CrossRef]
62. Cardone, A.; D'Ambrosio, R.; Paternoster, B. Exponentially fitted IMEX methods for advection–diffusion problems. *J. Comput. Appl. Math.* **2017**, *316*, 100–108. [CrossRef]
63. Cardone, A.; D'Ambrosio, R.; Paternoster, B. High order exponentially fitted methods for Volterra integral equations with periodic solution. *Appl. Numer. Math.* **2017**, *114*, 18–29.
64. Cardone, A.; Ixaru, L.G.; Paternoster, B.; Santomauro, G. Ef-Gaussian direct quadrature methods for Volterra integral equations with periodic solution. *Math. Comput. Simul.* **2015**, *110*, 125–143. [CrossRef]
65. Ixaru, L.G.; Vanden Berghe, G. *Exponential Fitting*; Mathematics and its Applications, with 1 CD-ROM (Windows, Macintosh and UNIX); Kluwer Academic Publishers: Dordrecht, The Netherlands, 2004; Volume 568, p. xiv+308.
66. D'Ambrosio, R.; Giordano, G.; Paternoster, B.; Ventola, A. Perturbative analysis of stochastic Hamiltonian problems under time discretizations. *Appl. Math. Lett.* **2021**, *409*, 107223. [CrossRef]
67. D'Ambrosio, R.; Di Giovacchino, S. Mean-square contractivity of stochastic theta-methods. *Comm. Nonlin. Sci. Numer. Simul.* **2021**, *96*, 105671. [CrossRef]
68. D'Ambrosio, R.; Di Giovacchino, S. Nonlinear stability issues for stochastic Runge-Kutta methods. *Comm. Nonlin. Sci. Numer. Simul.* **2021**, *94*, 105549. [CrossRef]
69. Conte, D.; D'Ambrosio, R.; Paternoster, B. Improved theta-methods for stochastic Volterra integral equations. *Comm. Nonlin. Sci. Numer. Simul.* **2021**, *93*, 105528. [CrossRef]
70. D'Ambrosio, R.; Scalone, C. On the numerical structure preservation of nonlinear damped stochastic oscillators. *Numer. Algorithms* **2021**, *86*, 933–952. [CrossRef]
71. Conte, D.; D'Ambrosio, R.; Giordano, G.; Paternoster, B. Continuous Extension of Euler-Maruyama Method for Stochastic Differential Equations. *Lect. Notes Comput. Sci.* **2021**, *12949*, 135–145.

Article

General Odd and Even Central Factorial Polynomial Sequences

Francesco Aldo Costabile *, Maria Italia Gualtieri and Anna Napoli

Department of Mathematics and Computer Science, University of Calabria, 87036 Rende, CS, Italy;
mariaitalia.gualtieri@unical.it (M.I.G.); anna.napoli@unical.it (A.N.)
* Correspondence: francesco.costabile@unical.it

Abstract: The $\delta^2(\cdot)$ operator, where $\delta(\cdot)$ is the known central difference operator, is considered. The associated odd and even polynomial sequences are determined and their generalizations studied. Particularly, matrix and determinant forms, recurrence formulas, generating functions and an algorithm for effective calculation are provided. An interesting property of biorthogonality is also demonstrated. New examples of odd and even central polynomial sequences are given.

Keywords: polynomial sequences; central factorial polynomials; odd and even polynomials; discrete operators; Hessenberg determinant; recurrence

MSC: 11B83; 11C99

1. Introduction

Polynomials are very useful mathematical tools, as they are defined in a simple way and they can be easily differentiated and integrated. Moreover, they can be quickly calculated on a computer system and are used to form spline functions.

One of the main problems in applied mathematics is the computation of real functions. In general, functions that are given as integro-differential equations cannot be explicitly expressed in terms of the so-called elementary functions. In addition, even elementary functions can take real values that cannot be explicitly given.

For these reasons, we often need to approximate a given function using simpler functions. In 1885, Weierstass [1] proved the approximation theorem according to which any continuous function defined on a closed and bounded interval can be uniformly approximated by a polynomial function. After this theorem, sets or sequences of polynomials were increasingly studied (see, for example, Refs. [2,3]).

Therefore, we find classes of polynomials in different sciences. For example, orthogonal polynomials are frequently used in physics, in the approximation theory [4–6] and also in the solution of differential equations. Hermite polynomials are used in statistics—umbral polynomials in algebra and combinatorics. Particularly, binomial, Appell and Sheffer polynomials are widely used, including more important families as Bernoulli, Euler, Boile, falling factorials, etc. (see [7–12] and the references therein).

In [13], Lidstone generalized an Aitken theorem on interpolation and proposed a two-point expansion of polynomials, in which the polynomial basis, called Lidstone polynomials, is expressed in powers of odd and, respectively, even canonical monomials. After, in [14,15], the authors generalized Lidstone polynomials, introduced odd and even special polynomial sequences and gave some applications to approximation functions, boundary value problems and cubature formulas.

In this paper, we consider other odd and even special polynomial sequences that are connected to the $\delta^2(\cdot)$ operator, with $\delta(\cdot)$ being the central factorial difference operator ([16], p. 7). These polynomials can be the basis for generalized interpolation Everett-type formulas.

The outline of this paper is as follows. In Section 2, we give some preliminary definitions, results and characterizations, and we formalize the problem; in Section 3, we consider

general odd central factorial polynomial sequences and, in Section 4, we consider general even central factorial polynomial sequences. For each kind of sequence (odd and even), we give the matrix form, the conjugate polynomials, recurrence relations and the related determinant forms, the generating function. Finally, we give some examples of new odd and even polynomial sequences. Concluding remarks close the paper.

We will adopt the following abbreviations:

p.s. polynomial sequence
OLPS: odd Lidstone-type p.s.,   ELPS: even Lidstone-type p.s.,
GOCPS: general odd central factorial p.s.,   GECPS: general even central factorial p.s.,
$\widetilde{GOCPS}$: the algebra $(GOCPS, +, \cdot, \circ)$, $\widetilde{GECPS}$: the algebra $(GECPS, +, \cdot, \circ)$.

2. Preliminaries and Problem's Position

In order to make the work as autonomous as possible, we give some preliminary definitions and propositions.

Let $\{p_n\}_{n \in \mathbb{N}}$ be a polynomial sequence (p.s. in the following) [17], such that $p_0(x) = 1$ and, for $n \geq 1$, p_n is a polynomial of degree n on a field $\mathbb{K}$ of characteristic 0 (typically $\mathbb{K} = \mathbb{R}$ or $\mathbb{K} = \mathbb{C}$).

Definition 1. *A polynomial sequence is called symmetric if and only if*

$$\forall n \in \mathbb{N}, \ \forall x \in \mathbb{K}, \qquad p_n(-x) = (-1)^n p_n(x). \tag{1}$$

Proposition 1. *Let $\{p_n\}_{n \in \mathbb{N}}$ be a symmetric p.s. Then, for all $n \in \mathbb{N}$, p_n has the decomposition in classical monomial basis only with powers x^{n-2k}, $k = 0, 1, \ldots, \lfloor \frac{n}{2} \rfloor$.*

Proof. If we set

$$p_n(x) = \sum_{k=0}^{n} t_{n,k} x^k, \qquad t_{n,k} \in \mathbb{K}, \ t_{n,n} \neq 0, \ k = 0, \ldots, n,$$

the result follows from (1). □

This suggests us to give the following definition.

Definition 2. *An odd (resp. even) polynomial sequence is a polynomial sequence whose elements have only odd (resp. even) powers in the canonical decomposition.*

Of course, a symmetric polynomial involves lower computational costs than a polynomial of the same degree. Moreover, every polynomial of an odd (resp. even) p.s. is an odd (resp. even) function.

In [14,15], the authors consider the so-called odd and, respectively, even Lidstone-type polynomial sequences.

We remember that

(a) $\{p_n\}_{n \in \mathbb{N}}$ is an odd Lidstone-type p.s. (OLPS) if and only if

$$\begin{cases} p_n''(x) = 2n(2n+1)p_{n-1}(x) \\ p_n(0) = 0, \quad \deg(p_n) = 2n+1, \ n \geq 0. \end{cases} \tag{2}$$

(b) $\{p_n\}_{n \in \mathbb{N}}$ is an even Lidstone-type p.s. (ELPS) if and only if

$$\begin{cases} p_n''(x) = 2n(2n-1)p_{n-1}(x) \\ p_n'(0) = 0, \quad \deg(p_n) = 2n, \ n \geq 0. \end{cases} \tag{3}$$

In [15], some applications of OLPS and ELPS were proposed.

Now, we observe that the central factorial polynomials ([17], p. 67), ([18], p. 212), Refs. [19,20], ([16], p. 6) are classically denoted by $x^{[n]}$ and are defined as

$$x^{[0]} = 1,$$

$$x^{[n]} = x \prod_{j=1}^{n-1}\left(x + \frac{n}{2} - j\right), \qquad n \geq 1.$$

They satisfy the identity

$$\delta x^{[n]} = n x^{[n-1]}, \qquad n \geq 1,$$

where δ is the central operator ([16], p. 7) defined by

$$\delta f(x) = f\left(x + \frac{1}{2}\right) - f\left(x - \frac{1}{2}\right),$$

with f being a real function of a real variable.

The first of these polynomials are

$$x^{[0]} = 1, \qquad x^{[1]} = x,$$
$$x^{[2]} = x^2, \qquad x^{[3]} = x^3 - \frac{1}{4}x,$$
$$x^{[4]} = x^4 - x^2, \qquad x^{[5]} = x^5 - \frac{5}{2}x^3 + \frac{9}{16}x.$$

Their plots are shown in Figure 1. The figure was made using Matlab/Octave software.

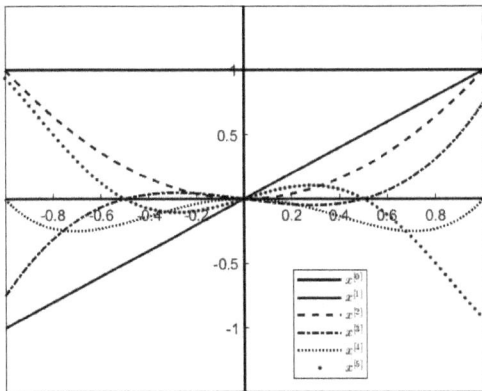

Figure 1. Central factorial polynomials.

In general, it results in ([16], p. 9)

$$x^{[2\nu+1]} = x\left(x^2 - \frac{1}{4}\right)\left(x^2 - \frac{9}{4}\right) \cdots \left(x^2 - \frac{(2\nu - 1)^2}{4}\right), \qquad (4a)$$

$$x^{[2\nu]} = x^2\left(x^2 - 1\right) \cdots \left(x^2 - (\nu - 1)^2\right). \qquad (4b)$$

Remark 1. It is known that $\left\{x^{[\nu]}\right\}_{\nu\in\mathbb{N}}$ is a binomial type sequence ([17], p. 66). It has the following decomposition:

$$x^{[\nu]} = \sum_{k=0}^{\nu} b_{\nu,k} x^k, \qquad \forall \nu \in \mathbb{N},$$

where the $b_{\nu,k}$ are calculated by Algorithm 2.1.1 in ([17], p. 7).

In the literature (see for example [17–19] and references therein), the numbers $b_{\nu,k}$ are denoted by $t(\nu,k)$ and are called *central factorial numbers of the first kind*. There is a wide amount of literature on these numbers (see, for example, [17,21–26] and references therein).

We note that the elements of the subsequence $\left\{x^{[2\nu+1]}\right\}_{\nu\in\mathbb{N}}$ satisfy the following properties:

(1o) $x^{[2\nu+1]}$ contains only odd powers of the variable x and $\deg x^{[2\nu+1]} = 2\nu + 1$;

(2o) $\delta^2 x^{[2\nu+1]} = \delta\left(\delta x^{[2\nu+1]}\right) = 2\nu(2\nu+1)\, x^{[2\nu-1]}$;

(3o) $x^{[2\nu+1]}(0) = 0,\ x^{[2\nu+1]}\left(\dfrac{1}{2}\right) = 0,\quad \nu \geq 1.$

Similarly, the elements of the subsequence $\left\{x^{[2\nu]}\right\}_{\nu\in\mathbb{N}}$ satisfy:

(1e) $x^{[2\nu]}$ contains only even powers of the variable x and $\deg x^{[2\nu]} = 2\nu$;

(2e) $\delta^2 x^{[2\nu]} = \delta\left(\delta x^{[2\nu]}\right) = 2\nu\, \delta x^{[2\nu-1]} = 2\nu(2\nu-1)\, x^{[2\nu-2]}$;

(3e) $x^{[2\nu]}(0) = 0,\ \left(x^{[2\nu]}\right)'(0) = 0,\ x^{[2\nu]}(1) = 0,\quad \nu \geq 1.$

Hence, the subsequences $\left\{x^{[2\nu+1]}\right\}_{\nu\in\mathbb{N}}$ and $\left\{x^{[2\nu]}\right\}_{\nu\in\mathbb{N}}$ are respectively an odd and an even p.s. We call the subsequences $\left\{x^{[2\nu+1]}\right\}_{\nu\in\mathbb{N}}$ and $\left\{x^{[2\nu]}\right\}_{\nu\in\mathbb{N}}$ odd and even central factorial p.s., respectively.

The previous considerations suggest generalizing the problem: we look for, if there exists, the odd p.s. $\{d_n\}_{n\in\mathbb{N}}$ such that

$$\begin{cases} \delta^2 d_n(x) = 2n(2n+1)d_{n-1}(x), & n \geq 1, \\ d_n(0) = 0,\ \deg(d_n) = 2n+1, & n \geq 0. \end{cases} \tag{5}$$

Analogously, we look for, if there exists, the even p.s. $\{e_n\}_{n\in\mathbb{N}}$ such that

$$\begin{cases} \delta^2 e_n(x) = 2n(2n-1)e_{n-1}(x), & n \geq 1, \\ e'_n(0) = 0,\ \deg(e_n) = 2n, & n \geq 0. \end{cases} \tag{6}$$

If these polynomial sequences exist, we call $\{d_n\}_{n\in\mathbb{N}}$ *general odd central factorial p.s.* (GOCPS) and $\{e_n\}_{n\in\mathbb{N}}$ *general even central factorial p.s.* (GECPS).

Remark 2. Note that (5) and (6) differ from (2) and (3) in the operator: in (5) and (6), there is the discrete central finite difference operator δ^2, while, in (2) and (3), there is the differential operator $\dfrac{d^2}{dx^2} \equiv D^2$.

3. General Odd Central Factorial Polynomial Sequences

To study problem (5), proceeding by induction, we note that every term d_n of the sequence $\{d_n\}_{n\in\mathbb{N}}$ is determined by the previous term d_{n-1} and a constant. The following proposition provides an explicit expression for d_n in terms of central factorial polynomials.

Proposition 2. Let $\{d_n\}_{n\in\mathbb{N}}$ be an odd p.s. It is a GOCPS, that is, it satisfies (5) if and only if there exists a numerical sequence $(\alpha_{2n})_{n\in\mathbb{N}}$, with $\alpha_0 \neq 0$, such that

$$d_n(x) = \sum_{k=0}^{n} \binom{2n+1}{2k+1} \frac{\alpha_{2(n-k)}}{2(n-k)+1} x^{[2k+1]}. \tag{7}$$

Proof. If (7) holds, from the linearity of the operator $\delta^2(\cdot)$ and from property (2o), d_n satisfies

$$\delta^2 d_n(x) = 2n(2n+1) d_{n-1}(x).$$

Moreover, it results in $d_n(0) = 0$, $d_0(x) = \alpha_0 x$ and $\deg(d_n)$ is $2n+1$.

Vice versa, we can obtain the result by mathematical induction, taking into account that every odd polynomial can be expressed as a linear combination of $x^{[2i+1]}$, $i \geq 0$. □

Remark 3. From (4a), for $k > 0$,

$$\left(x^{[2k+1]}\right)'(0) = (-1)^k \prod_{i=1}^{k} \frac{(2i-1)^2}{4}.$$

Hence, from (7), for $n > 0$ it results in

$$d'_n(0) = \sum_{k=0}^{n} \binom{2n+1}{2k+1} \frac{\alpha_{2(n-k)}}{2(n-k)+1} (-1)^k \prod_{i=1}^{k} \frac{(2i-1)^2}{4}. \tag{8}$$

Proposition 3. Let $\{d_n\}_{n\in\mathbb{N}}$ be a GOCPS. Then, for $j = 0, \ldots, n$, we obtain

(1) $\delta^{2j} d_n(x) = \dfrac{(2n+1)!}{(2(n-j)+1)!} d_{n-j}(x);$

(2) $\delta^{2j+1} d_n(x) = \dfrac{(2n+1)!}{(2(n-j)+1)!} \delta d_{n-j}(x);$

(3) $\delta^{2j} d_n(0) = 0, \quad \delta^{2j+1} d_n(0) = \dfrac{(2n+1)!}{(2(n-j)+1)!} \delta d_{n-j}(0).$

Proof. The proof follows easily from (5) after some calculations. □

Corollary 1. Let $\{d_n\}_{n\in\mathbb{N}}$ be a GOCPS. Then, $\forall n, j \in \mathbb{N}$ with $j < n$, and we obtain

$$\sum_{k=0}^{2j} \binom{2j}{k} (-1)^k d_n(x+j-k) = \frac{(2n+1)!}{(2(n-j)+1)!} d_{n-j}(x),$$

$$\sum_{k=0}^{2j+1} \binom{2j+1}{k} (-1)^k d_n\left(x+j-k+\frac{1}{2}\right) = \frac{(2n+1)!}{(2(n-j)+1)!} \delta d_{n-j}(x).$$

Proof. The proof follows from Proposition 3 and the known identities on operator δ. □

3.1. Matrix Form

Let $\{d_n\}_{n\in\mathbb{N}}$ be the GOCPS related to the numerical sequence $(\alpha_{2n})_{n\in\mathbb{N}}$, $\alpha_0 \neq 0$, that is, a p.s. as in Proposition 2. The relation (7) suggests to consider the lower infinite triangular matrix $\mathbf{V}_\infty = (v_{i,j})$ with

$$v_{i,j} = \begin{cases} \binom{2i+1}{2j+1} \dfrac{\alpha_{2(i-j)}}{2(i-j)+1}, & i \geq 0, \ j = 0, 1, \ldots, i, \\ 0 & i < j. \end{cases} \tag{9}$$

We note that $\mathbf{V}_\infty$ is a Lidstone-type matrix as defined in [14].

Let $\vec{X}_\infty$ and D_∞ be the infinite vectors

$$\vec{X}_\infty = \left[x^{[1]}, x^{[3]}, \ldots, x^{[2\nu+1]}, \ldots\right]^T, \quad D_\infty = [d_0(x), d_1(x), \ldots, d_\nu(x), \ldots]^T.$$

Then, from (7), we obtain $D_\infty = V_\infty \vec{X}_\infty$, or, for simplicity,

$$D = V\vec{X}, \qquad (10)$$

where, of course, $D = D_\infty$, $V = V_\infty$, $\vec{X} = \vec{X}_\infty$.

If, in (9), we consider $i = 0, \ldots, n$, $n \in \mathbb{N}$, we obtain the principal submatrix of order $n+1$ of V that we denote by V_n. Analogously, $\vec{X}_n$ and D_n are the principal subvectors with $n+1$ components of $\vec{X}_\infty$ and D_∞, respectively.

Then, from (10),

$$D_n = V_n \vec{X}_n. \qquad (11)$$

We call the relation (11) (or (10)) *the first matrix form* of the GOCPS $\{d_n\}_{n\in\mathbb{N}}$.

It is known [14] that the matrix V can be factorized as

$$V = W T_\alpha W^{-1},$$

where $W = \text{diag}\{(2i+1)! \mid i \geq 0\}$ and T_α is the lower triangular Toepliz matrix with elements $t_{i,j}^\alpha = \dfrac{\alpha_{2(i-j)}}{(2(i-j)+1)!}$.

The matrix V is invertible and $V^{-1} = \left(v_{i,j}^{-1}\right)_{i,j\in\mathbb{N}}$, with

$$v_{i,j}^{-1} = \begin{cases} \binom{2i+1}{2j+1} \dfrac{\beta_{2(i-j)}}{2(i-j)+1}, & i \geq 0, \ j = 0, 1, \ldots, i, \\ 0 & i < j, \end{cases}$$

$(\beta_{2n})_{n\in\mathbb{N}}$ being the numerical sequence implicitly defined by [14]

$$\sum_{j=0}^{i} \frac{\beta_{2j}\alpha_{2(i-j)}}{(2j+1)!(2(i-j)+1)!} = \delta_{i0}, \qquad i \geq 0, \qquad (12)$$

and δ_{ij} is the Kronecker symbol.

Remark 4. *The (12) is as an infinite linear system for the calculation of the numerical sequence $(\beta_{2k})_{k\in\mathbb{N}}$. By applying Cramer's rule, the first $n+1$ equations in (12) give*

$$\beta_0 = \frac{1}{\alpha_0}$$

$$\beta_{2i} = \frac{3!\,5!\cdots(2i+1)!}{(-1)^i \alpha_0^{i+1}} \begin{vmatrix} \frac{\alpha_2}{3!} & \frac{\alpha_0}{3!} & 0 & \cdots & \cdots & 0 \\ \frac{\alpha_4}{5!} & \frac{\alpha_2}{3!3!} & \frac{\alpha_0}{5!} & 0 & \cdots & 0 \\ \vdots & \vdots & \vdots & \ddots & & \vdots \\ \vdots & \vdots & \vdots & \ddots & \ddots & \vdots \\ \frac{\alpha_{2(i-1)}}{(2i-1)!} & \frac{\alpha_{2(i-2)}}{(2i-3)!3!} & \frac{\alpha_{2(i-3)}}{(2i-5)!5!} & \cdots & & \frac{\alpha_0}{(2i-1)!} \\ \frac{\alpha_{2i}}{(2i+1)!} & \frac{\alpha_{2(i-1)}}{(2i-1)!3!} & \frac{\alpha_{2(i-2)}}{(2i-3)!5!} & \cdots & \cdots & \frac{\alpha_2}{3!(2i-1)!} \end{vmatrix}, \quad i = 1, \ldots, n. \qquad (13)$$

Furthermore,

where $\mathbf{T}_\beta$ is the lower triangular Toepliz matrix with elements $t_{i,j}^\beta = \dfrac{\beta_{2(i-j)}}{(2(i-j)+1)!}$.

3.2. Conjugate Polynomials

Let $(\alpha_{2n})_{n\in\mathbb{N}}$, $\alpha_0 \neq 0$ be an assigned numerical sequence and $(\beta_{2n})_{n\in\mathbb{N}}$ the sequence related to $(\alpha_{2n})_{n\in\mathbb{N}}$ by (12). Let $\{d_n\}_{n\in\mathbb{N}}$ be the GOCPS related to the sequence $(\alpha_{2n})_{n\in\mathbb{N}}$. For any $k \in \mathbb{N}$, we can consider the polynomial

$$\hat{d}_k(x) = \sum_{j=0}^{k} \binom{2k+1}{2j+1} \frac{\beta_{2j}}{2(k-j)+1} x^{[2(k-j)+1]} = \sum_{j=0}^{k} \binom{2k+1}{2j+1} \frac{\beta_{2(k-j)}}{2(k-j)+1} x^{[2j+1]}. \quad (14)$$

From (14) and Proposition 2, the sequence $\{\hat{d}_k\}_{k\in\mathbb{N}}$ is a GOCPS. We call the sequences $\{d_k\}_{k\in\mathbb{N}}$, $\{\hat{d}_k\}_{k\in\mathbb{N}}$ conjugate odd central polynomial sequences.

By setting $\hat{\mathbf{D}} = \hat{\mathbf{D}}_\infty = \left[\hat{d}_0(x), \hat{d}_1(x), \ldots, \hat{d}_v(x), \ldots\right]^T$ and $\mathbf{A} = \mathbf{V}^{-1} = (a_{i,j})$ with

$$a_{i,j} = \begin{cases} \binom{2i+1}{2j+1} \dfrac{\beta_{2(i-j)}}{2(i-j)+1}, & i \geq 0, \; j = 0, 1, \ldots, i, \\ 0 & i < j, \end{cases}$$

from (14), we have

$$\hat{\mathbf{D}} = \mathbf{A}\vec{\mathbf{X}}$$

and $\hat{\mathbf{D}}_n = \mathbf{A}_n \vec{\mathbf{X}}_n$, $\forall n \in \mathbb{N}$.

If we set $\mathbf{V}^2 = \mathbf{V}\mathbf{V} = \left(v_{i,j}^*\right)$, and $\mathbf{A}^2 = \mathbf{A}\mathbf{A} = \left(a_{i,j}^*\right)$, after easy calculations, we obtain

$$\begin{cases} \mathbf{D} = \mathbf{V}^2 \hat{\mathbf{D}} \\ \hat{\mathbf{D}} = \mathbf{A}^2 \mathbf{D} \end{cases} \text{and, } \forall n \in \mathbb{N}, \quad \begin{cases} \mathbf{D}_n = \mathbf{V}_n^2 \hat{\mathbf{D}}_n \\ \hat{\mathbf{D}}_n = \mathbf{A}_n^2 \mathbf{D}_n. \end{cases}$$

Moreover,

$$d_n(x) = \sum_{j=0}^{n} v_{n,j}^* \hat{d}_j(x), \qquad \hat{d}_n(x) = \sum_{j=0}^{n} a_{n,j}^* d_j(x), \qquad \forall n \in \mathbb{N}.$$

3.3. Recurrence Relation and Related Determinant Form

The elements of a GOCPS satisfy some recurrence relations. In addition, they can be represented as Hessenberg determinants. From the identity (11), being $\mathbf{A}_n = \mathbf{V}_n^{-1}$, we obtain

$$\vec{\mathbf{X}}_n = \mathbf{A}_n \mathbf{D}_n$$

and

$$x^{[2k+1]} = \sum_{j=0}^{k} \binom{2k+1}{2j+1} \frac{\beta_{2(k-j)}}{2(k-j)+1} d_j(x), \qquad k = 0, \ldots, n. \quad (15)$$

Theorem 1 (Recurrence relation). *Let $\{d_n\}_{n\in\mathbb{N}}$ be an odd p.s. It is a GOCPS if and only if there exist numerical sequences $(\alpha_{2n})_{n\in\mathbb{N}}$, $(\beta_{2n})_{n\in\mathbb{N}}$, with $\alpha_0 \neq 0$, $\beta_0 \neq 0$, satisfying the relation (12), such that*

$$d_k(x) = \frac{1}{\beta_0}\left[x^{[2k+1]} - \sum_{j=0}^{k-1} \binom{2k+1}{2j+1} \frac{\beta_{2(k-j)}}{2(k-j)+1} d_j(x)\right], \qquad \forall k \geq 1.$$

Proof. The proof follows from (15). □

Theorem 2 (Determinant form). *Let $\{d_n\}_{n\in\mathbb{N}}$ be a GOCPS as in Theorem 1. Then,*

$$d_0(x) = \frac{1}{\beta_0}x,$$

$$d_k(x) = \frac{(-1)^k}{\beta_0^{k+1}\prod_{i=1}^{k}(2i-1)!} \begin{vmatrix} x^{[1]} & x^{[3]} & \cdots & x^{[2k-1]} & x^{[2k+1]} \\ \beta_0 & \beta_2 & \cdots & \beta_{2(k-1)} & \beta_{2k} \\ 0 & 3!\beta_0 & \cdots & \frac{(2k-1)!}{(2k-3)!}\beta_{2(k-2)} & \frac{(2k+1)!}{(2k-1)!}\beta_{2(k-1)} \\ \vdots & \ddots & \ddots & \vdots & \vdots \\ \vdots & & \ddots & \vdots & \vdots \\ 0 & \cdots & \cdots & (2k-1)!\beta_0 & \frac{(2k+1)!}{3!}\beta_2 \end{vmatrix}, \quad k \geq 1. \quad (16)$$

Proof. The relation (15), for $k = 0,\ldots,n$, can be considered as a linear system in the unknowns $d_j(x)$, $j = 0,\ldots,n$. Solving this system by Cramer's rule provides the result. □

By means of the determinant form (16), we can prove some properties using elementary linear algebra tools. One of these is the following orthogonality conditions.

Proposition 4. *Let X be a linear space of regular real value functions and L be a linear functional on X such that $L[x] \neq 0$ (by normalization $L[x] = 1$). Moreover, let $L\left(\left[x^{[2k+1]}\right]\right) = \beta_{2k}$, $k \geq 0$. If $\{d_k^L\}_{k\in\mathbb{N}}$ is the GOPS defined as in (16), then the following orthogonality conditions hold*

$$L\left(\left[\delta^{(2i)} d_k^L\right]\right) = (2k+1)!\delta_{ik}, \quad i = 0,\ldots,k.$$

Proof. The proof follows from the linearity of the functional L and from Theorem 2. □

Remark 5. *Proposition 4 expresses the biorthogonality of the system $\left(\{d_k^L\}_{k\in\mathbb{N}}, \{L_k\}_{k\in\mathbb{N}}\right)$, where*

$$L_i(\cdot) = L\left(\delta^{2i}(\cdot)\right), \quad \forall i \in \mathbb{N} \cup \{0\}.$$

With the same techniques used to prove Theorems 1 and 2, we can prove the following relations for the conjugate sequence $\{\hat{d}_n\}_{n\in\mathbb{N}}$:

$$\hat{d}_n(x) = \frac{1}{\alpha_0}\left[x^{[2k+1]} - \sum_{j=0}^{k-1}\binom{2k+1}{2j+1}\frac{\alpha_{2(k-j)}}{2(k-j)+1}\hat{d}_j(x)\right]$$

and

$$\hat{d}_0(x) = \frac{1}{\alpha_0}x,$$

$$\hat{d}_k(x) = \frac{(-1)^k}{\alpha_0^{k+1}\prod_{i=1}^{k}(2i-1)!} \begin{vmatrix} x^{[1]} & x^{[3]} & \cdots & x^{[2k-1]} & x^{[2k+1]} \\ \alpha_0 & \alpha_2 & \cdots & \alpha_{2(k-1)} & \alpha_{2k} \\ 0 & 3!\alpha_0 & \cdots & \frac{(2k-1)!}{(2k-3)!}\alpha_{2(k-2)} & \frac{(2k+1)!}{(2k-1)!}\alpha_{2(k-1)} \\ \vdots & \ddots & \ddots & \vdots & \vdots \\ \vdots & & \ddots & \vdots & \vdots \\ 0 & \cdots & \cdots & (2k-1)!\alpha_0 & \frac{(2k+1)!}{3!}\alpha_2 \end{vmatrix}, \quad k \geq 1. \quad (17)$$

Remark 6. *We note that the determinants in (16) and (17) are Hessenberg determinants. It is known [17] that, for their numerical calculation, the Gaussian elimination without pivoting is stable. Furthermore, Proposition 4 shows that (16) is also used for theoretical tools.*

3.4. The Linear Space $\widehat{GOCPS}$

We can extend the classical umbral composition [14,17,19,20] to the set of general odd central factorial polynomial sequences.

Definition 3. *Let $\{d_k\}_{k\in\mathbb{N}}$ and $\{d_k^*\}_{k\in\mathbb{N}}$ be the general central polynomial sequences related to the numerical sequences $(\rho_{2k})_{k\in\mathbb{N}}$ and $(\sigma_{2k})_{k\in\mathbb{N}}$, respectively. That is,*

$$d_k(x) = \sum_{j=0}^{k}\binom{2k+1}{2j+1}\frac{\rho_{2(k-j)}}{2(k-j)+1}x^{[2j+1]}, \qquad \forall k \in \mathbb{N},$$

$$d_k^*(x) = \sum_{j=0}^{k}\binom{2k+1}{2j+1}\frac{\sigma_{2(k-j)}}{2(k-j)+1}x^{[2j+1]}, \qquad \forall k \in \mathbb{N}.$$

The umbral composition of $d_k(x)$ and $d_k^*(x)$ is defined as

$$z_k(x) := (d_k \circ d_k^*)(x) = \sum_{j=0}^{k}\binom{2k+1}{2j+1}\frac{\rho_{2(k-j)}}{2(k-j)+1}d_j^*(x), \qquad \forall k \in \mathbb{N}. \tag{18}$$

Remark 7. *It's easy to verify that*
1. $\{z_k\}_{k\in\mathbb{N}} = \{d_k \circ d_k^*\}_{k\in\mathbb{N}}$ *is a GOCPS;*
2. $\forall k \in \mathbb{N}, \left(d_k \circ \widehat{d_k}\right)(x) = x^{[2k+1]}$.

Theorem 3. *Let "+" and "·" be, respectively, the usual sum and product for a scalar on the set of odd polynomial sequences and "∘" the umbral composition defined in (18). The algebraic structure $\widehat{GOCPS} = (GOCPS, +, \cdot, \circ)$ is an algebra.*

Proof. The sequence $\{i_k\}_{k\in\mathbb{N}}$ with $i_k = x^{[2k+1]}$ is a GOCPS and, for every $\{d_k\}_{k\in\mathbb{N}} \in GOCPS$, we obtain $d_k \circ i_k = d_k$. Moreover, if $\{d_k\}_{k\in\mathbb{N}}$ and $\{\widehat{d_k}\}_{k\in\mathbb{N}}$ are conjugate central factorial polynomial sequences, then $d_k \circ \widehat{d_k} = i_k$. Hence, we can consider the algebraic structure $\widehat{GOCPS}$. It is endowed with the identity $\{i_k\}_{k\in\mathbb{N}}$ and the inverse $\{\widehat{d_k}\}_{k\in\mathbb{N}}$. This concludes the proof. □

3.5. Generating Function

In order to determine a generating function for a GOCPS, we begin by considering the generating function for odd central polynomial sequences.

Let $H(t)$ be the power series

$$H(t) = \sum_{n=0}^{\infty}(-1)^n\left(\prod_{k=1}^{n}\frac{(2k-1)^2}{4}\right)\frac{t^{2n+1}}{(2n+1)!}.$$

Theorem 4. *The following identity is true:*

$$\sinh(xH(t)) = \sum_{v=0}^{\infty}x^{[2v+1]}\frac{t^{2v+1}}{(2v+1)!}.$$

Proof. Taking into account that

$$\sinh(xH(t)) = \sum_{k=0}^{\infty}\frac{(xH(t))^{2k+1}}{(2k+1)!},$$

after some calculations (see also Proposition 2.1 in ([17], p. 8) and ([17], pp. 69–71)), we obtain the polynomials $x^{[2k+1]}$ as expressed in (4a). □

After this theorem, we can say that the function

$$g(x,t) = \sinh(x H(t))$$

is the generating function of the odd central factorial p.s. $\left\{x^{[2\nu+1]}\right\}_{\nu \in \mathbb{N}}$.

In order to determine the generating function of the GOCPS $\{d_k\}_{k \in \mathbb{N}}$ related to the numerical sequence $(\alpha_{2k})_{k \in \mathbb{N}}$, we set

$$l(t) = \sum_{k=0}^{\infty} \alpha_{2k} \frac{t^{2k}}{(2k+1)!}. \tag{19}$$

Theorem 5. *Let $\{d_k\}_{k \in \mathbb{N}}$ be the GOCPS related to $(\alpha_{2k})_{k \in \mathbb{N}}$. Then, the function*

$$F(x,t) = l(t) g(x,t)$$

is its generating function, that is,

$$l(t) \sinh(x H(t)) = \sum_{k=0}^{\infty} d_k(x) \frac{t^{2k+1}}{(2k+1)!}.$$

Proof. Taking into account the previous theorem, relations (19) and (7), the proof follows by standard calculations. □

3.6. Connection to the Basic Monomials x^{2i+1}

In order to write a GOCPS as a linear combination of odd monomials x^{2i+1}, we observe that, from Remark 1,

$$x^{[k]} = \sum_{i=0}^{k} t(k,i) x^i. \tag{20}$$

Then,

$$x^{[2k+1]} = \sum_{i=0}^{k} t(2k+1, i) x^{2i+1}.$$

By setting $\mathbf{W}^t = \left(w_{i,j}^t\right)_{i,j \in \mathbb{N}}$, with

$$w_{i,j}^t = \begin{cases} t(2i+1, j) & i \geq j \\ 0 & i < j, \end{cases}$$

we have

$$\vec{X} = \mathbf{W}^t \widetilde{X}, \tag{21}$$

where $\widetilde{X} = \left[x, x^3, \ldots, x^{2\nu+1}, \ldots\right]^T$.

Let $\{d_k\}_{k \in \mathbb{N}}$ be the GOCPS related to the numerical sequence $(\alpha_{2k})_{k \in \mathbb{N}}$ and $\mathbf{D}$ as in (10). Then, by substituting the relation (21) in (10), we obtain

$$\mathbf{D} = \left(\mathbf{V}\mathbf{W}^t\right)\widetilde{X},$$

that is,

$$d_n(x) = \sum_{j=0}^{n} z_{n,j} x^{2j+1}, \quad \forall n \in \mathbb{N}, \tag{22}$$

with $z_{n,j} = \sum_{k=0}^{n} v_{n,k} w_{k,j}^t$.

For the calculation of the coefficients $z_{n,j}$, $j = 0, \ldots, n$, in (22), a direct algorithm can be applied. It is described in the following theorem.

Theorem 6. *Let* $(z_{n,0})_{n \in \mathbb{N}}$ *be an assigned numerical sequence. Then, the sequence* $\{d_n\}_{n \in \mathbb{N}}$ *with* d_n *as in (22) is a GOCPS if and only if the coefficients* $z_{n,j}$, $j = 0, 1, \ldots, n$ *are the solution of the upper triangular linear system*

$$\sum_{i=j+1}^{n} \binom{2i+1}{2j+1} z_{n,i} = n(2n+1) z_{n-1,j}, \qquad \forall n \geq 1, \quad j = 0, \ldots, n-1. \tag{23}$$

Proof. The polynomial d_n as in (22) satisfies the first of (5) if and only if

$$\sum_{j=0}^{n-1} x^{2j+1} \sum_{i=j+1}^{n} \binom{2i+1}{2j+1} z_{n,i} = n(2n+1) \sum_{j=0}^{n-1} z_{n-1,j} x^{2j+1}.$$

Relation (23) follows by applying the principle of identity of polynomials, observing that $z_{n,n} = z_{n-1,n-1} = \cdots = z_{0,0} = 1$. □

Remark 9. *From Theorem 6, by means of backward substitutions, we have*

$$z_{n,j} = \frac{n(2n+1)}{j(2j+1)} z_{n-1,j-1} - \frac{1}{j(2j+1)} \sum_{i=j+1}^{n} \binom{2i+1}{2j-1} z_{n,i}, \quad j = n-1, \ldots, 1. \tag{24}$$

If $\mathbf{V}\mathbf{W}^t = \mathbf{Z} = (z_{i,j})_{i,j \in \mathbb{N}}$, then, from (22), we obtain the second matrix form for the sequence $\{d_n\}_{n \in \mathbb{N}}$:

$$\mathbf{D} = \mathbf{Z}\tilde{\mathbf{X}}. \tag{25}$$

From (25), Z being invertible,

$$\tilde{\mathbf{X}} = \mathbf{Z}^{-1}\mathbf{D} = (\mathbf{W}^t)^{-1}\mathbf{V}^{-1}\mathbf{D}.$$

If $\mathbf{Z}^{-1} = (z_{i,j}^{-1})_{i,j \in \mathbb{N}}$, then

$$x^{2j+1} = \sum_{i=0}^{j} z_{j,i}^{-1} d_i(x).$$

3.7. Examples

Now, we give some examples of general odd central factorial polynomial sequences.

Given a numerical sequence $(\alpha_{2n})_{n \in \mathbb{N}}$, $\alpha_0 \neq 0$, we determine the related GOCPS $\{d_n\}_{n \in \mathbb{N}}$. From Proposition 2, the elements of $\{d_n\}_{n \in \mathbb{N}}$ are such that

$$d_n(x) = \sum_{k=0}^{n} \binom{2n+1}{2k+1} \frac{\alpha_{2(n-k)}}{2(n-k)+1} x^{[2k+1]}, \qquad \forall n \in \mathbb{N}.$$

In order to write the odd central factorial p.s. in terms of the monomials x^{2j+1}, given a numerical sequence $(z_{n,0})_{n \in \mathbb{N}}$, from Theorem 6, we obtain the sequence $\{d_n\}_{n \in \mathbb{N}}$. For all $n \in \mathbb{N}$, the elements of $\{d_n\}_{n \in \mathbb{N}}$ have the form

$$d_n(x) = \sum_{j=0}^{n} z_{n,j} x^{2j+1}, \tag{26}$$

where the coefficients $z_{n,j}$, $n \geq 1$, $j = 0, \ldots, n-1$ can be calculated by the recurrence relations (24).

Example 1 (Odd Fibonacci-central factorial p.s.). *We will determine the GOCPS $\{d_n\}_{n\in\mathbb{N}}$ such that*

$$d'_n(0) = F_n, \quad \forall n \in \mathbb{N}, \tag{27}$$

where $(F_n)_{n\in\mathbb{N}}$ is the well-known Fibonacci [27,28] numerical sequence given by

$$F_0 = F_1 = 1, \quad F_k = F_{k-1} + F_{k-2}, \quad k \geq 2.$$

Hence, the elements of this p.s. satisfy

$$\begin{cases} \delta^2 d_n(x) = 2n(2n+1)d_{n-1}(x) \\ d_n(0) = 0, \quad d'_n(0) = F_n. \end{cases}$$

We call $\{d_n\}_{n\in\mathbb{N}}$ odd Fibonacci-central factorial p.s., and we denote it by $\{F_n^c\}_{n\in\mathbb{N}}$. The conditions (8) and (27) give

$$\sum_{k=0}^{n} \binom{2n+1}{2k+1} \frac{\alpha_{2(n-k)}}{2(n-k)+1}(-1)^k \prod_{i=1}^{k} \frac{(2i-1)^2}{4} = F_n, \quad n \geq 0.$$

From this, we obtain the coefficients α_{2k}, $k = 0, \ldots, n$. For example, for $n = 4$, we obtain

$$\alpha_0 = 1, \quad \alpha_2 = \frac{5}{4}, \quad \alpha_4 = \frac{119}{48}, \quad \alpha_6 = \frac{1139}{192}, \quad \alpha_8 = -\frac{3427}{1280}.$$

Hence, the first five odd Fibonacci-central factorial polynomials in the basis $x^{[2k+1]}$ are

$$F_0^c(x) = x^{[1]}, \quad F_1^c(x) = x^{[3]} + \frac{5}{4}x^{[1]}, \quad F_2^c(x) = x^{[5]} + \frac{25}{6}x^{[3]} + \frac{119}{48}x^{[1]},$$

$$F_3^c(x) = x^{[7]} + \frac{35}{4}x^{[5]} + \frac{833}{48}x^{[3]} + \frac{1139}{192}x^{[1]},$$

$$F_4^c(x) = x^{[9]} + 15x^{[7]} + \frac{2499}{16}x^{[5]} + \frac{1139}{16}x^{[3]} - \frac{3427}{1280}x^{[1]}.$$

Figure 2 shows the plot of these polynomials.

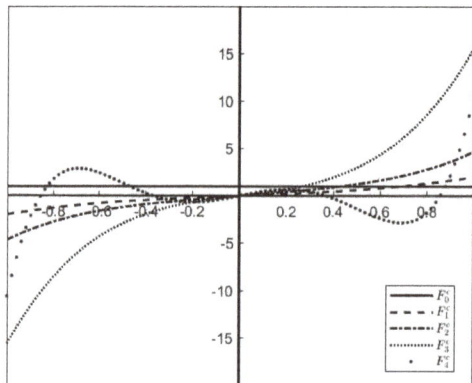

Figure 2. Odd Fibonacci-central factorial polynomials.

The conditions

$$z_{n,0} = F_n, \quad n = 0, 1, \ldots,$$

and the relation (24) allow for obtaining the polynomials written in the monomial basis.
For example, for $n = 0, \ldots, 5$, we have

$$F_0^c(x) = x, \qquad F_1^c(x) = x^3 + x, \qquad F_2^c(x) = x^5 + \frac{5}{3}x^3 + 2x,$$

$$F_3^c(x) = x^7 + \frac{35}{3}x^3 + 3x,$$

$$F_4^c(x) = x^9 - 6x^7 + \frac{273}{5}x^5 - 44x^3 + 5x,$$

$$F_5^c(x) = x^{11} - \frac{55}{3}x^9 + 231x^7 - 913x^5 + \frac{3377}{3}x^3 + 8x.$$

In [27], the Fibonacci p.s. $\{f_n\}_{n \in \mathbb{N}}$ was analyzed. Note that the p.s. $\{f_n\}_{n \in \mathbb{N}}$ has an odd polynomial subsequence $\{f_{2n+1}\}_{n \in \mathbb{N}}$. This subsequence differs from $\{F_n^c\}_{n \in \mathbb{N}}$.

Example 2 (Odd Hermite-central factorial polynomial sequence). Let $\{\mathcal{H}_n\}_{n \in \mathbb{N}}$ be the well-known Hermite p.s. ([17], p. 135), ([29], p. 187). We consider the monic Hermite p.s. $\{H_n\}_{n \in \mathbb{N}}$ and determine the GOCPS $\{d_n\}_{n \in \mathbb{N}}$ such that

$$d_0'(0) = 1, \qquad d_n'(0) = H_n'(0) = \begin{cases} (-1)^n \left(\dfrac{3}{2}\right)_n & \text{for even } n > 0 \\ 0 & \text{for odd } n > 0. \end{cases} \qquad (28)$$

The elements of this p.s. satisfy

$$\begin{cases} \delta^2 d_n(x) = 2n(2n+1)d_{n-1}(x) \\ d_n(0) = 0, \quad d_n'(0) = H_n'(0), \quad n > 0. \end{cases}$$

We call this sequence odd Hermite-central factorial p.s., and we denote it by $\{H_n^c\}_{n \in \mathbb{N}}$. From (8) and (28), for any $n \in \mathbb{N}$, we obtain α_{2k}, $k = 0, \ldots, n$.
For example, for $n = 4$, we have

$$\alpha_0 = 1, \quad \alpha_2 = \frac{5}{4}, \quad \alpha_4 = \frac{23}{48}, \quad \alpha_6 = -\frac{397}{192}, \quad \alpha_8 = -\frac{4259}{1280}.$$

The first five odd Hermite-central factorial polynomials are

$$H_0^c(x) = x^{[1]}, \quad H_1^c(x) = x^{[3]} + \frac{5}{4}x^{[1]}, \quad H_2^c(x) = x^{[5]} + \frac{25}{6}x^{[3]} + \frac{23}{48}x^{[1]},$$

$$H_3^c(x) = x^{[7]} + \frac{35}{4}x^{[5]} + \frac{161}{48}x^{[3]} - \frac{397}{192}x^{[1]},$$

$$H_4^c(x) = x^{[9]} + 15x^{[7]} + \frac{483}{40}x^{[5]} - \frac{397}{16}x^{[3]} - \frac{4259}{1280}x^{[1]}.$$

Figure 3 shows the plot of these polynomials.
By the relations (24) and (26), we obtain the polynomials written in the monomial basis.
For example, for $n = 0, \ldots, 5$, they are

$$H_0^c(x) = x, \qquad H_1^c(x) = x^3 + x, \qquad H_2^c(x) = x^5 + \frac{5}{3}x^3,$$

$$H_3^c(x) = x^7 - \frac{7}{3}x^3 - \frac{3}{2}x,$$

$$H_4^c(x) = x^9 - 6x^7 + \frac{21}{5}x^5 - 14x^3,$$

$$H_5^c(x) = x^{11} - \frac{55}{3}x^9 + 99x^7 - 286x^5 + 297x^3 + \frac{15}{4}x.$$

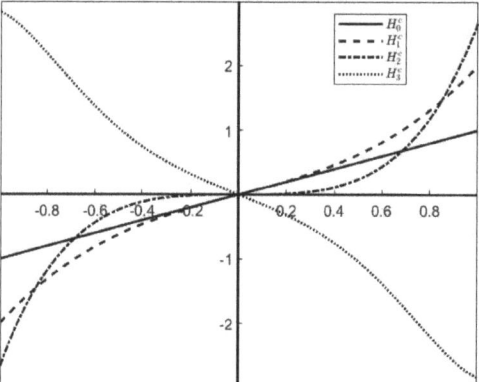

Figure 3. Odd Hermite-central factorial polynomials.

4. General Even Central Factorial Polynomial Sequences

Now, analogous with the odd case, we consider the general even central factorial polynomial sequences, that is, the polynomial sequences $\{e_n\}_{n \in \mathbb{N}}$ whose elements are polynomials of degree $2n$ satisfying

$$\begin{cases} \delta^2 e_n(x) = 2n(2n-1)e_{n-1}(x) \\ e'_n(0) = 0, \quad e_0(x) = 1. \end{cases} \tag{29}$$

Since all the proofs of the results concerning this type of polynomial sequences are similar to those of the odd case, we omit them.

Proposition 5. *Let $\{e_n\}_{n \in \mathbb{N}}$ be an even p.s. It is a GECPS, that is, it satisfies (29) if and only if a numerical sequence $(\gamma_{2n})_{n \in \mathbb{N}}$, with $\gamma_0 \neq 0$, exists such that $\forall n \in \mathbb{N}, \forall x \in \mathbb{K}$,*

$$e_n(x) = \sum_{k=0}^{n} \binom{2n}{2k} \gamma_{2(n-k)} x^{[2k]}.$$

Proposition 6. *Let $\{e_n\}_{n \in \mathbb{N}}$ be a GECPS. Then, for $j = 0, \ldots, n$, we obtain*

(1) $\delta^{2j} e_n(x) = \dfrac{(2n)!}{(2(n-j))!} e_{n-j}(x);$

(2) $\delta^{2j+1} e_n(x) = \dfrac{(2n)!}{(2(n-j))!} \delta e_{n-j}(x);$

(3) $\delta^{2j+1} e_n(0) = 0, \quad \delta^{2j} e_n(0) = \dfrac{(2n)!}{(2(n-j))!} \delta e_{n-j}(0).$

Corollary 2. *For a GECPS $\{e_n\}_{n \in \mathbb{N}}, \forall n, j \in \mathbb{N}$ with $j < n$, the following identities hold:*

$$\sum_{k=0}^{2j} \binom{2j}{k} (-1)^k e_n(x+j-k) = \frac{(2n)!}{(2(n-j))!} e_{n-j}(x);$$

$$\sum_{k=0}^{2j+1} \binom{2j+1}{k} (-1)^k e_n\left(x+j-k+\frac{1}{2}\right) = \frac{(2n)!}{(2(n-j))!} \delta e_{n-j}(x).$$

4.1. Matrix Form

Given a numerical sequence $(\gamma_{2k})_{k\in\mathbb{N}}$, $\gamma_0 \neq 0$, let us consider the lower infinite triangular matrix $U_\infty = (u_{i,j})$ with

$$u_{i,j} = \begin{cases} \binom{2i}{2j} \gamma_{2(i-j)}, & i \geq 0, \ j = 0, 1, \ldots, i \\ 0 & i < j \end{cases}$$

The first matrix form of a GECPS is:

$$\mathbf{E}_\infty = \mathbf{U}_\infty \overline{\mathbf{X}}_\infty, \quad \text{or} \quad \mathbf{E} = \mathbf{U}\overline{\mathbf{X}}, \tag{30}$$

where $\mathbf{U} = \mathbf{U}_\infty$,

$$\overline{\mathbf{X}} = \overline{\mathbf{X}}_\infty = \left[1, x^{[2]}, \ldots, x^{[2\nu]}, \ldots\right]^T, \quad \mathbf{E} = \mathbf{E}_\infty = [e_0(x), e_1(x), \ldots, e_\nu(x), \ldots]^T.$$

The matrix $\mathbf{U}$ can be factorized [14] as $\mathbf{U} = \mathbf{G}\mathbf{T}_\mathbf{\gamma}\mathbf{G}^{-1}$, where $\mathbf{G} = diag\{(2i)! \mid i \geq 0\}$ and $\mathbf{T}_\gamma$ is a lower triangular Toepliz matrix with elements $t_{i,j}^\gamma = \dfrac{\gamma_{2(i-j)}}{(2(i-j))!}$.

$\mathbf{U}$ is invertible and $\mathbf{U}^{-1} = \mathbf{G}\mathbf{T}_1\mathbf{G}^{-1}$, where $\mathbf{T}_1$ is a lower triangular Toepliz matrix with elements $t_{i,j}^\beta = \dfrac{\zeta_{2(i-j)}}{(2(i-j))!}$, $(\zeta_{2k})_{k\in\mathbb{N}}$ being the numerical sequence defined by

$$\sum_{j=0}^{i} \frac{\gamma_{2j} \zeta_{2(i-j)}}{(2j)!(2(i-j))!} = \delta_{i0}, \quad i \geq 0. \tag{31}$$

Let $\mathbf{U_n}$ be the principal submatrix of order $n+1$ of $\mathbf{U}$ and let $\overline{\mathbf{X}}_n$ and $\mathbf{E}_n$ be the principal subvectors with $n+1$ components of $\overline{\mathbf{X}}_\infty$ and $\mathbf{E}_\infty$, respectively. Then, from (30),

$$\mathbf{E_n} = \mathbf{U_n}\overline{\mathbf{X}_n}. \tag{32}$$

4.2. Conjugate Even Polynomials

Let $(\gamma_{2k})_{k\in\mathbb{N}}$, $\gamma_0 \neq 0$, be a given numerical sequence and $(\zeta_{2k})_{k\in\mathbb{N}}$ the related sequence defined as in (31). For any $k \in \mathbb{N}$, we can consider the polynomial

$$\widehat{e}_k(x) = \sum_{j=0}^{k} \binom{2k}{2j} \zeta_{2j} x^{[2(k-j)]} = \sum_{j=0}^{k} \binom{2k}{2j} \zeta_{2(k-j)} x^{[2j]}. \tag{33}$$

From this identity and Proposition 5, the sequence $\{\widehat{e}_k\}_{k\in\mathbb{N}}$ is a GECPS. We call the sequences $\{e_k\}_{k\in\mathbb{N}}$, $\{\widehat{e}_k\}_{k\in\mathbb{N}}$ *conjugate even central polynomial sequences*.

By setting $\mathbf{B} = (b_{i,j})$, with

$$b_{i,j} = \begin{cases} \binom{2i}{2j} \zeta_{2(i-j)}, & i \geq 0, \ j = 0, 1, \ldots, i \\ 0 & i < j, \end{cases}$$

and $\widehat{\mathbf{E}} = \widehat{\mathbf{E}}_\infty = [\widehat{e}_0(x), \widehat{e}_1(x), \ldots, \widehat{e}_\nu(x), \ldots]$, from (33), we have

$$\widehat{\mathbf{E}} = \mathbf{B}\overline{\mathbf{X}} \quad \text{and} \quad \widehat{\mathbf{E}}_n = \mathbf{B_n}\overline{\mathbf{X}}_n, \quad \forall n \in \mathbb{N}.$$

Moreover,

$$\begin{cases} \mathbf{E} = \mathbf{U}^2 \, \widehat{\mathbf{E}} \\ \widehat{\mathbf{E}} = \mathbf{B}^2 \, \mathbf{E} \end{cases} \text{ and } \begin{cases} \mathbf{E}_n = \mathbf{U}_n^2 \, \widehat{\mathbf{E}}_n \\ \widehat{\mathbf{E}}_n = \mathbf{B}_n^2 \, \mathbf{E}_n, \end{cases} \forall n \in \mathbb{N},$$

where $\mathbf{U}^2 = \mathbf{U}\,\mathbf{U} = \left(u^*_{i,j}\right)$, and $\mathbf{B}^2 = \mathbf{B}\,\mathbf{B} = \left(b^*_{i,j}\right)$. Finally, $\forall n \in \mathbb{N}$,

$$e_n(x) = \sum_{j=0}^n u^*_{n,j} \widehat{e}_j(x), \qquad \widehat{e}_n(x) = \sum_{j=0}^n b^*_{n,j} e_j(x).$$

4.3. Recurrence Relation and Related Determinant Form

From the identity (32), we have

$$\overline{\mathbf{X}}_n = \mathbf{U}_n^{-1} \, \mathbf{E}_n,$$

and, for $k = 0, \ldots, n$,

$$x^{[2k]} = \sum_{j=0}^k \binom{2k}{2j} \zeta_{2(k-j)} e_j(x).$$

Theorem 7 (Recurrence relation). *Let $\{e_n\}_{n \in \mathbb{N}}$ be an even p.s. It is a GECPS if and only if there exist numerical sequences $(\gamma_{2k})_{k \in \mathbb{N}}$, $(\zeta_{2k})_{k \in \mathbb{N}}$, with $\gamma_0 \neq 0$, $\zeta_0 \neq 0$, satisfying the relation (31), such that, $\forall k \geq 1$,*

$$e_k(x) = \frac{1}{\zeta_0} \left[x^{[2k]} - \sum_{j=0}^{k-1} \binom{2k}{2j} \zeta_{2(k-j)} e_j(x) \right].$$

Remark 10. *For the elements of the conjugate sequence $\{\widehat{e}_n\}_{n \in \mathbb{N}}$, the first recurrence relation is*

$$\widehat{e}_n(x) = \frac{1}{\gamma_0} \left[x^{[2k]} - \sum_{j=0}^{k-1} \binom{2k}{2j} \gamma_{2(k-j)} \widehat{e}_j(x) \right].$$

Theorem 8 (Determinant form). *Let $\{e_n\}_{n \in \mathbb{N}}$ be a GECPS as in Theorem 7. Then,*

$$e_0(x) = \frac{1}{\zeta_0},$$

$$e_k(x) = \frac{(-1)^k}{\zeta_0^{k+1}} \begin{vmatrix} 1 & x^{[2]} & x^{[4]} & \cdots & x^{[2k-2]} & x^{[2k]} \\ \zeta_0 & \zeta_2 & \zeta_4 & \cdots & \zeta_{2(k-1)} & \zeta_{2k} \\ 0 & \zeta_0 & \binom{4}{2}\zeta_2 & \cdots & \binom{2k-2}{2}\zeta_{2(k-2)} & \binom{2k}{2}\zeta_{2(k-1)} \\ \vdots & & \ddots & & \vdots & \vdots \\ \vdots & & & \ddots & \vdots & \vdots \\ 0 & \cdots & \cdots & & \zeta_0 & \binom{2k}{2(k-1)}\zeta_2 \end{vmatrix}, \quad k \geq 1.$$

The elements of the conjugate sequence $\{\hat{e}_n\}_{n\in\mathbb{N}}$ are such that

$$\hat{e}_0(x) = \frac{1}{\gamma_0},$$

$$\hat{e}_k(x) = \frac{(-1)^k}{\gamma_0^{k+1}} \begin{vmatrix} 1 & x^{[2]} & x^{[4]} & \cdots & x^{[2k-2]} & x^{[2k]} \\ \gamma_0 & \gamma_2 & \gamma_4 & \cdots & \gamma_{2(k-1)} & \gamma_{2k} \\ 0 & \gamma_0 & \binom{4}{2}\gamma_2 & \cdots & \binom{2k-2}{2}\gamma_{2(k-2)} & \binom{2k}{2}\gamma_{2(k-1)} \\ \vdots & \ddots & \ddots & & \vdots & \vdots \\ \vdots & & \ddots & & \vdots & \vdots \\ 0 & \cdots & \cdots & & \gamma_0 & \binom{2k}{2(k-1)}\gamma_2 \end{vmatrix}, \quad k \geq 1.$$

4.4. The Linear Space $\widetilde{GECPS}$

Definition 4. *Let $\{e_k\}_{k\in\mathbb{N}}$ and $\{e_k^*\}_{k\in\mathbb{N}}$ be the general central polynomial sequences related to the numerical sequences $(\eta_{2k})_{k\in\mathbb{N}}$ and $(v_{2k})_{k\in\mathbb{N}}$, respectively. That is, $\forall k \in \mathbb{N}$,*

$$e_k(x) = \sum_{j=0}^{k} \binom{2k}{2j} \eta_{2(k-j)} x^{[2j]}, \qquad e_k^*(x) = \sum_{j=0}^{k} \binom{2k}{2j} v_{2(k-j)} x^{[2j]}.$$

For all $k \in \mathbb{N}$, the umbral composition of $e_k(x)$ and $e_k^*(x)$ is

$$w_k(x) := (e_k \circ e_k^*)(x) = \sum_{j=0}^{k} \binom{2k}{2j} \eta_{2(k-j)} e_j^*(x).$$

It is easy to verify that

1. $\{w_k\}_{k\in\mathbb{N}} = \{e_k \circ e_k^*\}_{k\in\mathbb{N}}$ is a GECPS;
2. $\forall k \in \mathbb{N}, (e_k \circ \hat{e}_k)(x) = x^{[2k]}$.

Moreover, if "+" and "·" are, respectively, the usual sum and product for a scalar on the set of even polynomial sequences, then $\widetilde{GECPS} = (GECPS, +, \cdot, \circ)$ is an algebra.

4.5. Generating Function

Let $G(t)$ be the power series

$$G(t) = t + \sum_{n=1}^{\infty} (-1)^n \left(\prod_{k=1}^{n} \frac{(2k-1)^2}{4} \right) \frac{t^{2n+1}}{(2n+1)!}.$$

Then, taking into account that

$$\cosh x(xG(t)) = \sum_{k=0}^{\infty} \frac{(xG(t))^{2k}}{(2k)!},$$

we have

$$\cosh(xG(t)) = \sum_{\nu=0}^{\infty} x^{[2\nu]} \frac{t^{2\nu}}{(2\nu)!}.$$

Hence, the function

$$g(x,t) = \cosh(xG(t))$$

is the generating function of even central factorial polynomials $x^{[2\nu]}$.

Theorem 9. *The generating function of a GECPS related to the numerical sequence $(\gamma_{2k})_{k \in \mathbb{N}}$ is*

$$F(x,t) = l(t)\, g(x,t),$$

with

$$l(t) = \sum_{k=0}^{\infty} \gamma_{2k} \frac{t^{2k}}{(2k)!}.$$

4.6. Connection to the Basic Monomials x^{2i}

From (20),

$$x^{[2k]} = \sum_{i=0}^{k} t(2k,i) x^{2i}.$$

If $\Omega^t = (\omega^t_{i,j})_{i,j \in \mathbb{N}}$, with

$$\omega^t_{i,j} = \begin{cases} t(2i,j) & i \geq j \\ 0 & i < j, \end{cases}$$

then

$$\overset{\frown}{X} = \Omega^t \widetilde{X}, \qquad (34)$$

where $\widetilde{X} = [1, x^2, \ldots, x^{2\nu}, \ldots]^T$.

Let $\{e_k\}_{k \in \mathbb{N}}$ be the GECPS related to the numerical sequence $(\gamma_{2k})_{k \in \mathbb{N}}$. Let E be as in (30). Then, by substituting (34) in (30), we obtain

$$E = (U W^t) \widetilde{X},$$

that is,

$$e_n(x) = \sum_{j=0}^{i} s_{n,j} x^{2j} \quad \text{with} \quad s_{n,j} = \sum_{k=0}^{n} u_{n,k} w^t_{k,j}. \qquad (35)$$

Remark 11. *The following identity holds*

$$e_n(0) = s_{n,0}, \qquad n \geq 0. \qquad (36)$$

Theorem 10. *Let $(s_{n,0})_{n \in \mathbb{N}}$ be an assigned numerical sequence. Then, the sequence $\{e_n\}_{n \in \mathbb{N}}$ with e_n as (35) is a GECPS if and only if the coefficients, $s_{n,j}$, $j = 0, 1, \ldots, n$, are the solution of the system*

$$\sum_{i=j+1}^{n} \binom{2i}{2j} s_{n,i} = n(2n-1) s_{n-1,j}, \qquad j = 0, \ldots, n-1.$$

Remark 12. *From backward substitutions,*

$$s_{n,j} = \frac{n(2n-1)}{j(2j-1)} s_{n-1,j-1} - \frac{1}{j(2j-1)} \sum_{i=j+1}^{n} \binom{2i}{2j-2} s_{n,i}, \qquad j = n-1, \ldots, 1. \qquad (37)$$

4.7. Examples

Now, we give some examples of general even central factorial polynomial sequences.

Firstly, from Proposition 5, if $(\gamma_{2k})_{k \in \mathbb{N}}$, $\gamma_0 \neq 0$, is an assigned numerical sequence, we determine the related GECPS, that is, the p.s. $\{e_n\}_{n \in \mathbb{N}}$ such that

$$e_n(x) = \sum_{k=0}^{n} \binom{2n}{2k} \gamma_{2(n-k)} x^{[2k]}, \qquad \forall n \in \mathbb{N},\ \forall x \in \mathbb{K}.$$

Then, we write e_n in the monomial basis x^{2i}, according to (35). It satisfies (36).

Example 3 (Even Fibonacci-central factorial p.s.). *We will determine the GECPS $\{e_n\}_{n \in \mathbb{N}}$ such that*
$$e_n(0) = F_n, \quad \forall n \in \mathbb{N}, \tag{38}$$
where $(F_n)_{n \in \mathbb{N}}$ is the Fibonacci numerical sequence.
The elements of this p.s. satisfy
$$\begin{cases} \delta^2 e_n(x) = 2n(2n-1)e_{n-1}(x) \\ e'_n(0) = 0, \quad e_n(0) = F_n. \end{cases}$$

In this case, we call $\{e_n\}_{n \in \mathbb{N}}$ even Fibonacci-central factorial p.s. and we denote it by $\{F_n^e\}_{n \in \mathbb{N}}$.
For every $n \in \mathbb{N}$, the conditions (38) give the coefficients $\gamma_{2k} = F_k$, $k = 0, \ldots, n$.
For example, for $n = 0, \ldots, 4$, we obtain the polynomials

$$F_0^e(x) = x^{[0]}, \quad F_1^e(x) = x^{[2]} + x^{[0]}, \quad F_2^e(x) = x^{[4]} + 6x^{[2]} + 2x^{[0]},$$
$$F_3^e(x) = x^{[6]} + 15x^{[4]} + 30x^{[2]} + 3x^{[0]},$$
$$F_4^e(x) = x^{[8]} + 28x^{[6]} + 140x^{[4]} + 84x^{[2]} + 5x^{[0]}.$$

Figure 4 shows the plot of these polynomials.

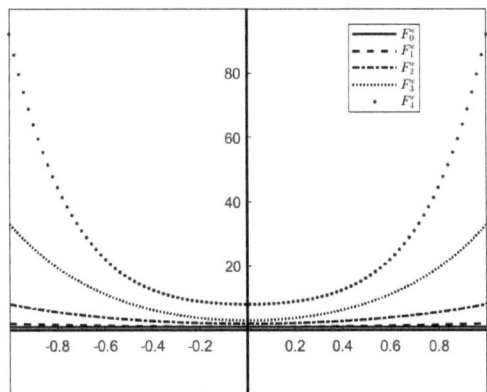

Figure 4. Even Fibonacci-central factorial polynomials.

From the relations (36) and the conditions
$$F_n^e(0) = s_{n,0} = F_n, \quad n = 0, 1, \ldots,$$
we obtain the polynomials F_n^e written into the even monomial basis.
For example, for $n = 5$, we have

$$F_0^e(x) = 1, \quad e_1(x) = x^2 + 1, \quad F_2^e(x) = x^4 + 5x^2 + 2,$$
$$F_3^e(x) = x^6 + 10x^4 + 19x^2 + 3,$$
$$F_4^e(x) = x^8 + 14x^6 + 49x^4 + 20x^2 + 5,$$
$$F_5^e(x) = x^{10} + 15x^8 + 63x^6 - 85x^4 + 231x^2 + 8.$$

Example 4 (Even Hermite-central factorial p.s.)**.** *Now, we determine the GECPS* $\{e_n\}_{n\in\mathbb{N}}$ *such that*

$$e_0(0) = 1, \qquad e_n(0) = H_n(0) = \begin{cases} (-1)^n \left(\dfrac{1}{2}\right)_n & \text{for even } n > 0 \\ 0 & \text{for odd } n > 0, \end{cases} \qquad (39)$$

$\{H_n\}_{n\in\mathbb{N}}$ *being the monic Hermite p.s. ([17], p. 135).*
The elements of $\{e_n\}_{n\in\mathbb{N}}$ *satisfy*

$$\begin{cases} \delta^2 e_n(x) = 2n(2n+1) e_{n-1}(x) \\ e_n(0) = 0, \quad e_n(0) = H_n(0). \end{cases}$$

We call $\{e_n\}_{n\in\mathbb{N}}$ *even Hermite-central factorial p.s., and we denote it by* $\{H_n^e\}_{n\in\mathbb{N}}$.
From (39), *for any* $n \in \mathbb{N}$, *we obtain* $\gamma_{2n} = H_n(0)$.
The first five odd Hermite-central factorial polynomials are

$$H_0^e(x) = x^{[0]}, \qquad H_1^e(x) = x^{[2]}, \qquad H_2^e(x) = x^{[4]} - \frac{1}{2} x^{[0]},$$

$$H_3^e(x) = x^{[6]} - \frac{15}{2} x^{[2]},$$

$$H_4^e(x) = x^{[8]} - 35 x^{[4]} + \frac{3}{4} x^{[0]}.$$

Figure 5 shows the plot of these polynomials.

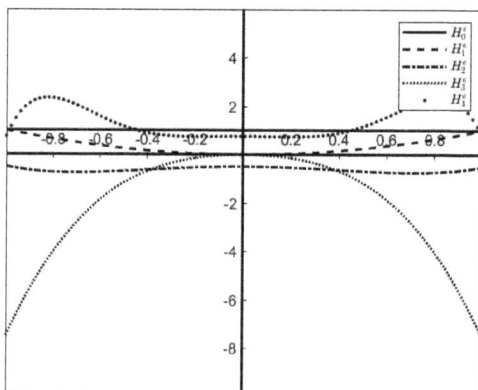

Figure 5. Even Hermite-central factorial polynomials.

Written in the monomial basis, they become

$$H_0^e(x) = 1, \qquad H_1^e(x) = x^2, \qquad H_2^e(x) = x^4 - x^2 - \frac{1}{2},$$

$$H_3^e(x) = x^6 - 5x^4 - \frac{7}{2} x^2,$$

$$H_4^e(x) = x^8 - 14 x^6 + 14 x^4 - x^2 + \frac{3}{4}.$$

5. Conclusions

In this paper, we considered the operator $\delta^2(\cdot)$, where $\delta(\cdot)$ is the known central difference operator. The general polynomial solutions of the following two problems

$$\begin{cases} \delta^2 d_n(x) = 2n(2n+1)d_{n-1}(x), & n \geq 1 \\ d_n(0) = 0, \quad \deg(d_n) = 2n+1, & n \geq 0 \end{cases}$$

and

$$\begin{cases} \delta^2 e_n(x) = 2n(2n-1)e_{n-1}(x), & n \geq 1 \\ e'_n(0) = 0, \quad \deg(e_n) = 2n, & n \geq 0, \end{cases}$$

have been studied.

These solutions were called *general odd* (respectively, *even*) *central factorial* polynomial sequences and denoted by GOCPS and GECPS, respectively. Each polynomial has been written both in the basis $x^{[2i+1]}$ (resp. $x^{[2i]}$) and in the basis x^{2i+1} (resp. x^{2i}). The matrix and determinant forms and a recurrence formula have been provided. The generating functions for the two kinds of polynomial sequences have also been obtained. An interesting property of biorthogonality has been demonstrated. Finally, two new general odd (even) central factorial p.s., called Fibonacci central factorial and Hermite central factorial p.s., have been given.

Future research in this direction, both theoretical and computational, is possible. For example, the general operator of the type $Qy = \sum_{k=1}^{\infty} c_k y^{(2k)}$, $c_1 \neq 0$ can be considered and the associated odd and even polynomial sequences can be determined. Computational applications, such as linear interpolation, quadrature formulas and approximation functions, can be studied. Boundary and initial value problems for difference equations can also be considered.

Author Contributions: Conceptualization, F.A.C., M.I.G. and A.N.; methodology, F.A.C., M.I.G. and A.N.; software, M.I.G. and A.N. All authors have read and agreed to the published version of the manuscript.

Funding: This research received no external funding.

Institutional Review Board Statement: Not applicable.

Informed Consent Statement: Not applicable.

Data Availability Statement: Not applicable.

Conflicts of Interest: The authors declare no conflict of interest.

References

1. Weierstrass, K. Über die analytische Darstellbarkeit sogenannter willkürlicher Funktionen einer reellen Veränderlichen. *Sitzungsberichte der Königlich Preussischen Akademie der Wissenschaften zu Berlin* **1885**, 633–639, 789–805.
2. Chen, X.; Tan, J.; Liu, Z.; Xie, J. Approximation of functions by a new family of generalized Bernstein operators. *J. Math. Anal. Appl.* **2017**, *450*, 244–261.
3. Srivastava, H.M.; Ansari, K.J.; Özger, F.; Özger, Z.Ö. A link between approximation theory and summability methods via four-dimensional infinite matrices. *Mathematics* **2021**, *9*, 1895.
4. Steffens, K. *The History of Approximation Theory: From Euler to BErnstein*; Springer Science Business Media: Berlin, Germany, 2007.
5. Szegô, G. *Orthogonal Polynomials*; American Mathematical Society: Providence, RI, USA, 1939; Volume 23.
6. Whittaker, J.M. *Interpolatory Function Theory*; The University Press: Cambridge/London, UK, 1935; Volume 33.
7. Costabile, F.A.; Gualtieri, M.I.; Napoli, A. Recurrence relations and determinant forms for general polynomial sequences. Application to Genocchi polynomials. *Integral Transform. Spec. Funct.* **2019**, *30*, 112–127.
8. Costabile, F.A.; Longo, E. A determinantal approach to Appell polynomials. *J. Comput. Appl. Math.* **2010**, *234*, 1528–1542.
9. Costabile, F.A.; Longo, E. The Appell interpolation problem. *J. Comput. Appl. Math.* **2011**, *236*, 1024–1032.
10. Costabile, F.A.; Longo, E. δ_h–Appell sequences and related interpolation problem. *Numer. Algorithms* **2013**, *63*, 165–186.
11. Costabile, F.A.; Longo, E. An algebraic approach to Sheffer polynomial sequences. *Integral Transform. Spec. Funct.* **2014**, *25*, 295–311.

12. Costabile, F.A.; Longo, E. An algebraic exposition of umbral calculus with application to general linear interpolation problem: A survey. *Publ. L'Inst. Math.* **2014**, *96*, 67–83.
13. Lidstone, G.J. Notes on the Extension of Aitken's Theorem (for Polynomial Interpolation) to the Everett Types. *Proc. Edinb. Math. Soc.* **1930**, *2*, 16–19.
14. Costabile, F.A.; Gualtieri, M.I.; Napoli, A. Odd and even Lidstone-type polynomial sequences. Part 1: Basic topics. *Adv. Differ. Equation* **2018**, *2018*, 299.
15. Costabile, F.A.; Gualtieri, M.I.; Napoli, A. Odd and even Lidstone-type polynomial sequences. Part 2: Applications. *Calcolo* **2020**, *57*, 1–35.
16. Steffensen, J.F. *Interpolation*; Courier Corporation: Chelmsford, MA, USA, 2006.
17. Costabile, F.A. *Modern Umbral Calculus. An Elementary Introduction with Applications to Linear Interpolation and Operator Approximation Theory*; Walter de Gruyter GmbH & Co. KG: Berlin, Germany, 2019; Volume 72.
18. Riordan, J. *Combinatorial Identities*; Wiley: Hoboken, NJ, USA, 1968.
19. Roman, S. *The Umbral Calculus*; Academic Press: New York, NY, USA, 1984.
20. Roman, S.M.; Rota, G.C. The umbral calculus. *Adv. Math.* **1978**, *27*, 95–188.
21. Butzer, P.L.; Schmidt, K.; Stark, E.L.; Vogt, L. Central factorial numbers; their main properties and some applications. *Numer. Funct. Anal. Optim.* **1989**, *10*, 419–488.
22. Butzer, P.L.; Schmidt, M. Central factorial numbers and their role in finite difference calculus and approximation. *Colloq. Math. Soc.* **1990**, *58*, 127–150.
23. Gelineau, Y.; Zeng, J. Combinatorial interpretations of the Jacobi-Stirling numbers. *arXiv* **2009**, arXiv:0905.2899.
24. Kang, J.Y.; Ryoo, C.S. A research on a certain family of numbers and polynomials related to Stirling numbers, central factorial numbers, and Euler numbers. *J. Appl. Math.* **2013**, *2013*, 158130.
25. Merca, M. Connections between central factorial numbers and Bernoulli polynomials. *Period. Math. Hungar.* **2016**, *73*, 259–264.
26. Zaid, Y.H.; Shiha, F.A.; El-Desouky, B.S. Generalized central factorial numbers with odd arguments. *Open J. Model. Simul.* **2020**, *8*, 61–72.
27. Costabile, F.A.; Gualtieri, M.I.; Napoli, A. Polynomial sequences: Elementary basic methods and application hints. A survey. *Rev. Real Acad. Cienc. Exactas, FíSicas Nat. Ser. MatemáTicas* **2019**, *113*, 3829–3862.
28. Vorobiev, N.N. *Fibonacci Numbers*; Springer Science & Business Media: Berlin, Germany, 2002.
29. Rainville, E.D. *Special Functions*; Chelsea Publishing Company: New York, NY, USA, 1960; Volume 5.

Article

Rate of Weighted Statistical Convergence for Generalized Blending-Type Bernstein-Kantorovich Operators

Faruk Özger [1], Ekrem Aljimi [2,*] and Merve Temizer Ersoy [3]

[1] Department of Engineering Sciences, İzmir Katip Çelebi University, İzmir 35620, Turkey; farukozger@gmail.com
[2] Faculty of Applied Sciences, Public University "Kadri Zeka", 60000 Gjilan, Kosovo
[3] Faculty of Engineering and Architecture, Department of Software Engineering, Nisantasi University, Istanbul 34398, Turkey; merve.temizerersoy@nisantasi.edu.tr
* Correspondence: ekrem.halimi@uni-gjilan.net

Abstract: An alternative approach, known today as the Bernstein polynomials, to the Weierstrass uniform approximation theorem was provided by Bernstein. These basis polynomials have attained increasing momentum, especially in operator theory, integral equations and computer-aided geometric design. Motivated by the improvements of Bernstein polynomials in computational disciplines, we propose a new generalization of Bernstein–Kantorovich operators involving shape parameters λ, α and a positive integer as an original extension of Bernstein–Kantorovich operators. The statistical approximation properties and the statistical rate of convergence are also obtained by means of a regular summability matrix. Using the Lipschitz-type maximal function, the modulus of continuity and modulus of smoothness, certain local approximation results are presented. Some approximation results in a weighted space are also studied. Finally, illustrative graphics that demonstrate the approximation behavior and consistency of the proposed operators are provided by a computer program.

Keywords: weighted $\mathcal{B}$-statistical convergence; shape parameter α; shape parameter λ; blending-type operators; computer graphics

MSC: 41A10; 41A25; 41A36; 26A16; 40C05

1. Introduction

The Weierstrass approximation theorem asserts that there exists a sequence of polynomials $r_p(u)$ that converges uniformly to $r(u)$ for any continuous function $r(u)$ on the closed interval $[a, b]$ [1]. Bernstein provided an alternative proof of the well-known Weierstrass approximation theorem, nowadays called Bernstein polynomials. The following Bernstein operators

$$\mathcal{B}_p(r;u) = \sum_{i=0}^{p} b_{p,i}(u) r\left(\frac{i}{p}\right),$$

where,

$$b_{p,i}(u) = \binom{p}{i} u^i (1-u)^{p-i}, u \in \mathcal{I}$$

were given in [2] to approximate a given continuous function $r(u)$ on $[0,1] = \mathcal{I}$.

In this sense, an approximation process for Lebesgue integrable real-valued functions defined on $\mathcal{I}$ was presented by replacing sample values $r(\frac{i}{p})$ with the mean values of r in the interval $\left[\frac{i}{p}, \frac{i+1}{p}\right]$ (see [3]). It is well known that these operators involving Lebesgue integrable functions on $\mathcal{I}$ can be expressed by means of the Bernstein basis function $b_{p,i}(u)$,

$$\mathcal{K}_p(r;u) = (p+1) \sum_{i=0}^{p} b_{p,i}(u) \int_{\frac{i}{p+1}}^{\frac{i+1}{p+1}} r(t)\, dt.$$

There are several generalizations and different modifications of the Kantorovich operators $\mathcal{K}_p$ in the literature (see e.g., [4–8]).

Approximation methods by Bernstein-type operators have been used both in pure and applied mathematics, as well as in certain computer-aided geometric design and engineering problems. For instance, a numerical scheme for the computational solution of certain classes of Volterra integral equations of the third kind and an algorithm for the approximate solution of singularly perturbed Volterra integral equations were provided with the help of Bernstein-type operators [9,10].

A new class of Bernstein operators for the continuous function $r(u)$ on $\mathcal{I}$, which includes the shape parameter α and named hereafter as α-Bernstein operators, were constructed in [11]. Many modifications of α-Bernstein operators have been studied (see [4,5,12]). A new basis with shape parameter $\lambda \in [-1,1]$ was introduced in [13], and a new type λ-Bernstein operators were constructed by shape parameter λ in [14]. Shape parameters α and λ were used to modify Bernstein operators to α-Bernstein-type (see [4,11,12,15,16]) and λ-Bernstein-type operators (see [6,13,17–25]) in order to have better approximation results.

Quite recently, Cai et al. estimated rates convergence of univariate and bivariate blending-type operators, which were introduced in [26], by a weighted A-statistical summability method [27].

The motivation of the paper is to extend Bernstein-type operators and introduce a novel generalization of blending-type Bernstein–Kantorovich operators that include many known sequences of linear operators in the literature.

The outline of the paper is as follows: In Section 2, we provide the needed background that includes definitions of α-Bernstein and λ-Bernstein-type operators. In Section 3, we introduce a novel generalization of Bernstein–Kantorovich operators with the help of a new class of basis polynomials involving two shape parameters and a positive integer. We also obtain moments and central moments and provide a classical Korovkin-type theorem. In Section 4, we focus on the convergence properties and a Voronovskaja-type approximation result of the operators through the notion of weighted $\mathcal{B}$-statistical convergence. Further, we estimate the rate of the weighted $\mathcal{B}$-statistical convergence of the proposed operators. In Section 5, we obtain some pointwise and weighted approximation results. In Section 6, we provide certain computer graphics for different kinds of functions to see the approximation of the defined operators. In Section 7, we provide a conclusion to summarize the obtained results.

2. Preliminaries

In this part, we provide the needed background that includes definitions of α-Bernstein, λ-Bernstein and blending (α, λ, s)-Bernstein basis functions; also, the definitions of α-Bernstein, λ-Bernstein and blending (α, λ, s)-Bernstein operators are provided.

Throughout the paper, let the binomial coefficients be given by the formula

$$\binom{p}{i} = \begin{cases} \frac{p!}{i!(p-i)!}, & 0 \leq i \leq p, \\ 0, & \text{otherwise.} \end{cases}$$

The known α-Bernstein operators (see [11]) were introduced as

$$T_{p,\alpha}(r;u) = \sum_{i=0}^{p} w_{p,i}^{(\alpha)}(u) r\left(\frac{i}{p}\right),$$

where $w_{1,0}^{(\alpha)}(u) = 1 - u$, $w_{1,1}^{(\alpha)}(u) = u$, and α-Bernstein basis is given as

$$w_{p,i}^{(\alpha)}(u) = \left[(1-\alpha)\binom{p-2}{i}u + (1-\alpha)\binom{p-2}{i-2}(1-u) + \alpha\binom{p}{i}u(1-u)\right]u^{i-1}(1-u)^{p-i-1},$$

for $\alpha, u \in \mathcal{I}, p \geq 2, r(u) \in C[0,1]$.

The λ-Bernstein operators were given as (see [14])

$$B_{p,\lambda}(r;u) = \sum_{i=0}^{p} \tilde{b}_{p,i}(u) r\left(\frac{i}{p}\right),$$

where λ-Bernstein basis is given as

$$\tilde{b}_{p,i}(\lambda;u) = \begin{cases} b_{p,0}(u) - \frac{\lambda}{p+1} b_{p+1,1}(u), & \text{if } i=0, \\[4pt] b_{p,i}(u) + \lambda\left(\frac{p-2i+1}{p^2-1} b_{p+1,i}(u)\right) \\ \quad -\lambda\left(\frac{p-2k-1}{p^2-1} b_{p+1,i+1}(u)\right), & \text{if } 1 \leq i \leq p-1, \\[4pt] b_{p,p}(u) - \frac{\lambda}{p+1} b_{p+1,p}(u), & \text{if } i=p. \end{cases} \quad (1)$$

Generalized blending-type α-Bernstein operators with a positive integer s were introduced in [15] as

$$\mathcal{L}_p^{\alpha,s}(r;u) = \sum_{i=0}^{p} \left\{ (1-\alpha)\binom{p-s}{i-s} u^{i-s+1}(1-u)^{p-i} + (1-\alpha)\binom{p-s}{i} u^i(1-u)^{p-s-i+1} \right.$$
$$\left. + \alpha \binom{p}{i} u^i(1-u)^{p-i} \right\} r\left(\frac{i}{p}\right), \quad \text{for } p \geq s$$

and

$$\mathcal{L}_p^{\alpha,s}(r;u) = \sum_{i=0}^{p} \binom{p}{i} u^i(1-u)^{p-i} r\left(\frac{i}{p}\right), \quad \text{for } p < s$$

which depend on shape parameter α, where $u, \alpha \in \mathcal{I}, r(u) \in C[0,1]$.

Finally, blending-type (α, λ, s)-Bernstein operators were constructed in [26] as follows:

$$\mathcal{L}_{p,\lambda}^{(\alpha,s)}(r;u) = \sum_{i=0}^{p} \tilde{b}_{p,i}^{\alpha,s}(\lambda;u) r\left(\frac{i}{p}\right),$$

where $0 \leq \alpha \leq 1$, $-1 \leq \lambda \leq 1$ and s is a positive integer and the blending-type (α, λ, s) basis is given as

$$\tilde{b}_{p,i}^{\alpha,s}(\lambda;u) = \begin{cases} \tilde{b}_{p,i}(\lambda;u), & \text{if } p < s \\ (1-\alpha)\left[u \tilde{b}_{p-s,i-s}(\lambda;u) + (1-u)\tilde{b}_{p-s,i}(\lambda;u)\right] \\ \quad + \alpha \tilde{b}_{p,i}(\lambda;u), & \text{if } p \geq s \end{cases}$$

and $\tilde{b}_{p,i}(\lambda;u)$ is defined in Equation (1).

Lemma 1 ([26],Theorem 2). *If $p \geq s$, for any $0 \leq \alpha \leq 1$ and $-1 \leq \lambda \leq 1$ we have*

$$\mathcal{L}_{p,\lambda}^{(\alpha,s)}(1;u) = 1;$$

$$\mathcal{L}_{p,\lambda}^{(\alpha,s)}(t;u) = u + (1-\alpha)\lambda \left[\frac{1 - 2u + u^{p-s+1} - (1-u)^{p-s+1}}{p(p-s-1)} \right]$$
$$+ \alpha\lambda \left[\frac{1 - 2u + u^{p+1} - (1-u)^{p+1}}{p(p-1)} \right];$$

$$\mathcal{L}_{p,\lambda}^{(\alpha,s)}(t^2;u) = u^2 + \frac{[p + (1-\alpha)s(s-1)]u(1-u)}{p^2} + \frac{\alpha\lambda}{p}\left[\frac{2u - 4u^2 + 2u^{p+1}}{(p-1)}\right];$$
$$+ \frac{(1-\alpha)\lambda}{p}\left[\frac{2u - 4u^2 + 2u^{p-s+1}}{(p-s-1)}\right] + \frac{\alpha\lambda}{p^2}\left[\frac{u^{p+1} + (1-u)^{p+1} - 1}{(p-1)}\right]$$
$$+ \frac{(1-\alpha)\lambda}{p^2}\left[\frac{u^{p-s+1} + (1-u)^{p-s+1} - 1}{(p-s-1)}\right] + \left[\frac{2su(u^{p-s+1} - (1-u)^{p-s+1})}{(p-s-1)}\right].$$

3. Blending (α, λ, s)-Bernstein–Kantorovich Operators

Let $L_1[0,1]$ denote the space of all Lebesgue integrable functions on the interval $\mathcal{I}$. We introduce the following sequence of operators involving shape parameters λ and α, and a positive integer s:

$$\mathcal{K}_{p,\lambda}^{(\alpha,s)}(r;u) = (p+1) \sum_{i=0}^{p} \tilde{b}_{p,i}^{\alpha,s}(\lambda;u) \int_{\frac{i}{p+1}}^{\frac{i+1}{p+1}} r(t)dt \qquad (2)$$

and call it blending (α, λ, s)-Bernstein–Kantorovich operators.

Lemma 2. *Let s be a positive integer, $\lambda \in [-1,1]$ and α be a non-negative integer, then the moments of blending (α, λ, s)-Bernstein–Kantorovich operators are as follows:*

$$\mathcal{K}_{p,\lambda}^{(\alpha,s)}(1;u) = 1;$$

$$\mathcal{K}_{p,\lambda}^{(\alpha,s)}(t;u) = \frac{1+2pu}{2(p+1)} + \frac{\alpha\lambda}{(p+1)(p-1)}\left[1 - 2u + u^{p+1} - (1-u)^{p+1}\right]$$
$$+ \frac{(1-\alpha)\lambda}{(p+1)(p-s-1)}\left[1 - 2u + u^{p-s+1} - (1-u)^{p-s+1}\right];$$

$$\mathcal{K}_{p,\lambda}^{(\alpha,s)}(t^2;u) = \frac{1+3pu(1+pu)}{3(p+1)^2} + \frac{2(1-\alpha)\lambda u}{(p-s-1)(p+1)^2}\left[(p+1)u^{p-s} + p(1-2u) - 1\right]$$
$$+ \frac{2p^2 su^2}{(p-s-1)(p+1)^2}\left[u^{p-s} - (1-u)^{p-s}\right] + \frac{(p + (1-\alpha)s(s-1))u(1-u)}{(p-1)(p+1)^2}$$
$$+ \frac{2\alpha\lambda u}{(p-1)(p+1)^2}\left[(p+1)u^p + p(1-2u) - 1\right].$$

Proof. Since it is easy to prove the first part of the theorem we skip it. Bearing in mind the definition of operators (2) and Lemma 1, we have

$$\mathcal{K}_{p,\lambda}^{(\alpha,s)}(t;u) = (p+1)\sum_{i=0}^{p} \tilde{b}_{p,i}^{\alpha,s}(\lambda;u) \int_{\frac{i}{p+1}}^{\frac{i+1}{p+1}} t\, dt = \sum_{i=0}^{p} \tilde{b}_{p,i}^{\alpha,s}(\lambda;u) \frac{2i+1}{2(p+1)}$$

$$= \frac{p}{p+1}\mathcal{L}_{p,\lambda}^{(\alpha,s)}(t;u) + \frac{1}{2(p+1)}\mathcal{L}_{p,\lambda}^{(\alpha,s)}(1;u)$$

$$= \frac{1+2pu}{2(p+1)} + \alpha\lambda\left[\frac{1-2u+u^{p+1}-(1-u)^{p+1}}{(p+1)(p-1)}\right]$$

$$+ (1-\alpha)\lambda\left[\frac{1-2u+u^{p-s+1}-(1-u)^{p-s+1}}{(p+1)(p-s-1)}\right],$$

which completes the proof of second part. Now, we prove the third part:

$$\mathcal{K}_{p,\lambda}^{(\alpha,s)}(t^2;u) = (p+1)\sum_{i=0}^{p} \tilde{b}_{p,i}^{\alpha,s}(\lambda;u) \int_{\frac{i}{p+1}}^{\frac{i+1}{p+1}} t^2\, dt = \sum_{i=0}^{p} \tilde{b}_{p,i}^{\alpha,s}(\lambda;u) \frac{3i^2+3i+1}{3(p+1)^2}$$

$$= \frac{p^2}{(p+1)^2}\mathcal{L}_{p,\lambda}^{(\alpha,s)}(t^2;u) + \frac{p}{(p+1)^2}\mathcal{L}_{p,\lambda}^{(\alpha,s)}(t;u) + \frac{1}{3(p+1)^2}\mathcal{L}_{p,\lambda}^{(\alpha,s)}(1;u)$$

$$= \frac{1+3pu(1+pu)}{3(p+1)^2} + \frac{2(1-\alpha)\lambda u}{(p-s-1)(p+1)^2}\left[(p+1)u^{p-s}+p(1-2u)-1\right]$$

$$+ \frac{2p^2su^2}{(p-s-1)(p+1)^2}\left[u^{p-s}-(1-u)^{p-s}\right] + \frac{(p+(1-\alpha)s(s-1))u(1-u)}{(p-1)(p+1)^2}$$

$$+ \frac{2\alpha\lambda u}{(p-1)(p+1)^2}\left[(p+1)u^p+p(1-2u)-1\right].$$

□

Corollary 1. *The following relationships are satisfied:*

$$\mathcal{K}_{p,\lambda}^{(\alpha,s)}(t-u;u) = (p+1)\left[\sum_{i=0}^{p} \tilde{b}_{p,i}^{\alpha,s}(\lambda;u) \int_{\frac{i}{p+1}}^{\frac{i+1}{p+1}} t\, dt - u\sum_{i=0}^{p} \tilde{b}_{p,i}^{\alpha,s}(\lambda;u) \int_{\frac{i}{p+1}}^{\frac{i+1}{p+1}} dt\right]$$

$$= \frac{1-2u}{2(p+1)} + \frac{\alpha\lambda}{(p+1)(p-1)}\left[1-2u+u^{p+1}-(1-u)^{p+1}\right]$$

$$+ \frac{(1-\alpha)\lambda}{(p+1)(p-s-1)}\left[1-2u+u^{p-s+1}-(1-u)^{p-s+1}\right];$$

$$\mathcal{K}_{p,\lambda}^{(\alpha,s)}((t-u)^2;u) = (p+1)\left[\sum_{i=0}^{p} \tilde{b}_{p,i}^{\alpha,s}(\lambda;u) \int_{\frac{i}{p+1}}^{\frac{i+1}{p+1}} t^2\, dt - 2u\sum_{i=0}^{p} \tilde{b}_{p,i}^{\alpha,s}(\lambda;u) \int_{\frac{i}{p+1}}^{\frac{i+1}{p+1}} t\, dt\right]$$

$$+ (p+1)u^2\sum_{i=0}^{p} \tilde{b}_{p,i}^{\alpha,s}(\lambda;u) \int_{\frac{i}{p+1}}^{\frac{i+1}{p+1}} dt$$

$$= \frac{2(1-\alpha)\lambda u}{(p-s-1)(p+1)^2}\left[(p+1)(1-u)^{p-s+1}+(1-u)u^{p-s}-1+2u\right]$$

$$+ \frac{2p^2su^2}{(p-s-1)(p+1)^2}\left[u^{p-s}-(1-u)^{p-s}\right] + \frac{(p+(1-\alpha)s(s-1))u(1-u)}{(p-1)(p+1)^2}$$

$$+ \frac{2\alpha\lambda u}{(p-1)(p+1)^2}\left[(p+1)(u^p-u^{p+1}-(1-u)u^{p-s})-1+2u\right] + \frac{3u^2-3u+1}{3(p+1)^2}.$$

Theorem 1. *Let* $r \in L_1[0,1]$, *then we have*

$$\lim_{p \to \infty} \mathcal{K}_{p,\lambda}^{(a,s)}(r;u) = r(u)$$

uniformly on $[0,1]$.

Proof. Using the commonly stated Bohman–Korovkin theorem [28,29], our aim is to prove the following uniform convergence condition:

$$\lim_{p \to \infty} \mathcal{K}_{p,\lambda}^{(a,s)}(e_k;u) = u^k \qquad (k=0,1,2)$$

where $e_k(u) = u^k$, $u \in \mathcal{I}$. Clearly, from the first and second parts of Lemma 2, we obtain

$$\lim_{p \to \infty} \mathcal{K}_{p,\lambda}^{(a,s)}(e_0;u) = 1 \quad \text{and} \quad \lim_{p \to \infty} \mathcal{K}_{p,\lambda}^{(a,s)}(e_1;u) = u.$$

By the third part of Lemma 2, the following relationship is satisfied

$$\mathcal{K}_{p,\lambda}^{(a,s)}(e_2;u) \to u^2 \qquad (p \to \infty).$$

□

4. Convergence Properties

In this part, we focus on the convergence properties and a Voronovskaja-type approximation result of operators $\mathcal{K}_{p,\lambda}^{(a,s)}$ through the notion of weighted $\mathcal{B}$-statistical convergence. Further, we estimate the rate of the weighted $\mathcal{B}$-statistical convergence of the proposed operators. We refer to [30,31] and the references therein for further information about statistical convergence and its weighted forms, including the regular summability matrix.

Let $K \subseteq \mathbb{N}_0 := \mathbb{N} \cup \{0\}$ and $K_p = \{k \leq p : k \in K\}$. Then $\delta(K) = \lim_{p \to \infty} \frac{1}{p}|K_p|$ is called the *natural density* of K, if the limit exists. A sequence $u = (u_p)$ is called statistically convergent to a number L if, for each $\epsilon > 0$, $\delta\{p : |u_p - L| \geq \epsilon\} = 0$. The notion of weighted statistical convergence is given as:

Let $q = (q_p)$ be a sequence of non-negative numbers with $q_0 > 0$ and $Q_p = \sum_{k=0}^{p} q_k \to \infty$ as $p \to \infty$, then $u = (u_p)$ is weighted statistically convergent to a number L if, for every $\varepsilon > 0$,

$$\frac{1}{Q_p}|\{k \leq Q_p : q_k|u_k - L| \geq \varepsilon\}| \to 0 \quad \text{as } p \to \infty.$$

In [32], a new matrix method, which is known as $\mathcal{B}$-summability, was defined. Let $\mathcal{B} = (\mathcal{B}_i)$ be a sequence of infinite matrices with $\mathcal{B}_i = (b_{pk}(i))$. Then $u \in \ell_\infty$ is said to be $\mathcal{B}$-summable to the value $\mathcal{B}\text{-}\lim u$, if $\lim_{p \to \infty}(\mathcal{B}_i u)_p = \mathcal{B}-\lim u$ uniformly for $i = 0, 1, 2, \cdots$.

The method $\mathcal{B} = (\mathcal{B}_i)$ is regular if and only if the following conditions hold true (see [33,34]):

$\|\mathcal{B}\| = \sup_{p,i} \sum_k |b_{pk}(i)| < \infty$;
$\lim_{p \to \infty} b_{pk}(i) = 0$ uniformly in i for each $k \in \mathbb{N}$;
$\lim_{p \to \infty} \sum_k b_{pk}(i) = 1$ uniformly in i, $\forall k$.

By $\mathcal{R}^+$ we denote the set of each regular method $\mathcal{B}$ with $b_{pk}(i) \geq 0$ for each p, k and i. Given a regular non-negative summability matrix $\mathcal{B} \in \mathcal{R}^+$, $u = (u_k)$ is said to be $\mathcal{B}$-statistically convergent to the number ℓ if, for every $\epsilon > 0$,

$$\sum_{k:|u_k - \ell| \geq \epsilon} b_{pk}(i) \to 0$$

uniformly in i, $(p \to \infty)$.

Definition 1 ([35]). *Let $\mathcal{B} = (\mathcal{B}_i)_{i \in \mathbb{N}} \in \mathcal{R}^+$. Further, let $q = (q_k)$ be a sequence of nonnegative numbers with $p_0 > 0$ and $Q_p = \sum_{k=0}^{p} q_k \to \infty$ as $p \to \infty$. A sequence $u = (u_k)$ is said to be weighted $\mathcal{B}$-statistically convergent to the number ℓ if, for every $\epsilon > 0$,*

$$\lim_{m \to \infty} \frac{1}{Q_m} \sum_{p=0}^{m} q_p \sum_{k: |u_k - \ell| \geq \epsilon} b_{pk}(i) = 0 \quad \text{uniformly in } i, \forall k.$$

In this case, we denote it by writing $[\text{stat}_\mathcal{B}, q_p] - \lim u = \ell$.

Theorem 2. *Let $\mathcal{B} \in \mathcal{R}^+$ and $r \in C[0,1]$. Then*

$$[\text{stat}_\mathcal{B}, q_p] - \lim_{p \to \infty} \|\mathcal{K}_{p,\lambda}^{(\alpha,s)}(r; u) - r\|_{C[0,1]} = 0.$$

Proof. Let $r \in C[0,1]$ and $u \in \mathcal{I}$ be fixed. In view of the Korovkin theorem, it is sufficient to show that

$$[\text{stat}_\mathcal{B}, q_p] - \lim_{p \to \infty} \|\mathcal{K}_{p,\lambda}^{(\alpha,s)}(e_j; u) - e_j\|_{C[0,1]} = 0,$$

where $e_j(u) = u^j$, $u \in \mathcal{I}$ and $j = 0, 1, 2$. By Lemma 2 and Corollary 1 we deduce that

$$[\text{stat}_\mathcal{B}, q_p] - \lim_{p \to \infty} \|\mathcal{K}_{p,\lambda}^{(\alpha,s)}(e_0; u) - e_0\|_{C[0,1]} = 0. \tag{3}$$

Using the definition of proposed operators and Corollary 1, for $j = 1$ one has

$$\sup_{u \in \mathcal{I}} \left| \mathcal{K}_{p,\lambda}^{(\alpha,s)}(e_1; u) - e_1(u) \right| = \sup_{u \in \mathcal{I}} \left| \frac{1 + 2pu}{2(p+1)} + \frac{\alpha \lambda}{(p+1)(p-1)} \left[1 - 2u + u^{p+1} - (1-u)^{p+1}\right] \right.$$

$$\left. + \frac{(1-\alpha)\lambda}{(p+1)(p-s-1)} \left[1 - 2u + u^{p-s+1} - (1-u)^{p-s+1}\right] - u \right|$$

$$\leq \frac{5}{p+1}.$$

Now, for a given $\epsilon' > 0$, choosing a number $\epsilon > 0$ such that $\epsilon < \epsilon'$. Then setting

$$\mathcal{J} := \left\{ p \in \mathbb{N} : \|\mathcal{K}_{p,\lambda}^{(\alpha,s)}(e_1; u) - e_1\| \geq \epsilon' \right\}, \quad \mathcal{J}_1 := \left\{ p \in \mathbb{N} : \frac{5}{p+1} \geq \epsilon' - \epsilon \right\}.$$

Thus we find that

$$\frac{1}{Q_m} \sum_{p=0}^{m} q_p \sum_{k \in \mathcal{J}} b_{pk}(i) \leq \frac{1}{Q_m} \sum_{p=0}^{m} q_p \sum_{k \in \mathcal{J}_1} b_{pk}(i).$$

Letting $m \to \infty$ in the last inequality we obtain

$$[\text{stat}_\mathcal{B}, q_p] - \lim_{p \to \infty} \|\mathcal{K}_{p,\lambda}^{(\alpha,s)}(e_1; u) - e_1\|_{C[0,1]} = 0. \tag{4}$$

By definition of the proposed operators and Lemma 2, we have the following relationships:

$$\sup_{u\in I} |\mathcal{K}_{p,\lambda}^{(\alpha,s)}(e_2;u) - e_2(u)| = \sup_{u\in I} \left| \frac{2(1-\alpha)\lambda u}{(p-s-1)(p+1)^2}\left[(p+1)u^{p-s} + p(1-2u) - 1\right] \right.$$
$$+ \frac{2p^2 s u^2}{(p-s-1)(p+1)^2}\left[u^{p-s} - (1-u)^{p-s}\right]$$
$$\frac{1+3pu(1+pu)}{3(p+1)^2} + \frac{(p+(1-\alpha)s(s-1))u(1-u)}{(p-1)(p+1)^2}$$
$$\left. + \frac{2\alpha\lambda u}{(p-1)(p+1)^2}\left[(p+1)u^p + p(1-2u) - 1\right] - u^2 \right|$$
$$\leq \frac{10}{(p-1)(p+1)^2}.$$

In conclusion, using the same technique as above, we have the following result:

$$[\mathrm{stat}_\mathcal{B}, q_p] - \lim_{p\to\infty} \|\mathcal{K}_{p,\lambda}^{(\alpha,s)}(e_2;u) - e_2\|_{C[0,1]} = 0. \tag{5}$$

Therefore, we conclude the proof by combining (3), (4) and (5). □

Definition 2 ([30]). *Let $\mathcal{B} \in \mathcal{R}^+$. A sequence $u = (u_p)$ is statistically weighted $\mathcal{B}$-summable to L if, for each $\epsilon > 0$,*

$$\lim_j \frac{1}{j}\left|\left\{m \leq j : \left|\frac{1}{Q_m}\sum_{n=0}^m q_p \sum_{k=1}^\infty u_p b_{pk}(i) - L\right| \geq \epsilon\right\}\right| = 0 \quad \text{uniformly in } i.$$

In this case, we denote it by $\overline{N}_\mathcal{B}(\mathrm{stat}) - \lim u = L$.

Theorem 3 ([30]). *Let $u = (u_p)$ be a bounded sequence. If u is weighted $\mathcal{B}$-statistically convergent to L then it is statistically weighted $\mathcal{B}$-summable to the same limit L, but not conversely.*

Corollary 2. *Let $\mathcal{B} \in \mathcal{R}^+$ and $r \in C[0,1]$. Then*

$$\overline{N}_\mathcal{B}(\mathrm{stat}) - \lim \|\mathcal{K}_{p,\lambda}^{(\alpha,s)}(r,u) - r\|_{C[0,1]} = 0.$$

Proof. The proof is a direct consequence of Theorems 2 and 3. Hence the details are omitted. □

Next, we estimate the rate of weighted $\mathcal{B}$-statistical convergence of $\mathcal{K}_{p,\lambda}^{(\alpha,s)}$ to $r \in C[0,1]$ with the help of modulus of continuity of first order.

Definition 3 ([30]). *Let $\mathcal{B} \in \mathcal{R}^+$. Suppose that (w_k) is a positive non-decreasing sequence. A sequence $u = (u_k)$ is said to be weighted $\mathcal{B}$-statistically convergent to ℓ with the rate $o(w_k)$ if, for any $\epsilon > 0$,*

$$\lim_{m\to\infty} \frac{1}{w_m Q_m} \sum_{p=0}^m q_p \sum_{k:|u_k-\ell|\geq\epsilon} b_{pk}(i) = 0 \quad \text{uniformly in } i. \tag{6}$$

In this case, we denote it by $u_k - \ell = [\mathrm{stat}_\mathcal{B}, q_p] - o(w_k)$.

Theorem 4. *Let $(c_p)_{p\in\mathbb{N}}$ and $(d_p)_{p\in\mathbb{N}}$ be two positive non-decreasing sequences and let $\mathcal{B} \in \mathcal{R}^+$. Assume that the following conditions hold true:*

(i) $\|\mathcal{K}_{p,\lambda}^{(\alpha,s)}(e_0;u) - e_0\|_{C[0,1]} = [\mathrm{stat}_\mathcal{B}, q_p] - o(c_p),$

(ii) $\omega(r; \delta_p) = [\text{stat}_\mathcal{B}, q_p] - o(d_p)$ on $\mathcal{I}$, where $\delta_p := \|\mathcal{K}_{p,\lambda}^{(\alpha,s)}(\mu; u; \lambda)\|_{C[0,1]}^{1/2}$ with $\mu(u) = (t-u)^2, t \in \mathcal{I}$. Then

$$\|\mathcal{K}_{p,\lambda}^{(\alpha,s)} - r\|_{C[0,1]} = [\text{stat}_\mathcal{B}, q_p] - o(e_p) \qquad (r \in C[0,1]),$$

where ω is the usual modulus of continuity and $e_p = \max\{c_p, d_p\}$.

Proof. Let $r \in C[0,1]$ and $u \in [0,1]$ be fixed. Since $\mathcal{K}_{p,\lambda}^{(\alpha,s)}$ is linear and monotone, we may write that

$$|\mathcal{K}_{p,\lambda}^{(\alpha,s)}(r(t); u) - r(u)| \leq \mathcal{K}_{p,\lambda}^{(\alpha,s)}(|r(t) - r(u)|; u) + |r(u)| |\mathcal{K}_{p,\lambda}^{(\alpha,s)}(e_0; u) - e_0|$$

$$\leq \omega(r,s) \mathcal{K}_{p,\lambda}^{(\alpha,s)}\left(\frac{|t-u|}{s} + 1; u\right) + |r(u)| |\mathcal{K}_{p,\lambda}^{(\alpha,s)}(e_0; u) - e_0|$$

$$= \omega(r,s) \left\{ \mathcal{K}_{p,\lambda}^{(\alpha,s)}(e_0; u) + \frac{1}{s^2} \mathcal{K}_{p,\lambda}^{(\alpha,s)}(\mu; u) \right\} + |r(u)| |\mathcal{K}_{p,\lambda}^{(\alpha,s)}(e_0; u) - e_0|. \qquad (7)$$

Taking the supremum over $u \in [0,1]$ on both sides of (7), we observe that

$$\|\mathcal{K}_{p,\lambda}^{(\alpha,s)} - r\|_{C[0,1]} \leq \omega(r,s) \left\{ \frac{1}{s^2} \|\mathcal{K}_{p,\lambda}^{(\alpha,s)}(\mu; u)\|_{C[0,1]} + \|\mathcal{K}_{p,\lambda}^{(\alpha,s)}(e_0; u) - e_0\|_{C[0,1]} + 1 \right\}$$
$$+ D\|\mathcal{K}_{p,\lambda}^{(\alpha,s)}(e_0; u) - e_0\|_{C[0,1]},$$

where $D = \|r\|_{C[0,1]}$. Now, if we take $\delta_p = \|\mathcal{K}_{p,\lambda}^{(\alpha,s)}(\mu; u)\|_{C[0,1]}^{1/2}$ in the last relation, we obtain

$$\|\mathcal{K}_{p,\lambda}^{(\alpha,s)} - r\|_{C[0,1]} \leq \omega(r, \delta_p) \|\mathcal{K}_{p,\lambda}^{(\alpha,s)}(e_0; u) - e_0\|_{C[0,1]} + 2\omega(r, \delta_p) + D\|\mathcal{K}_{p,\lambda}^{(\alpha,s)}(e_0; u) - e_0\|_{C[0,1]}$$

$$\leq N\{\omega(r, \delta_p) \|\mathcal{K}_{p,\lambda}^{(\alpha,s)}(e_0; u) - e_0\|_{C[0,1]} + \omega(r, \delta_p) + \|\mathcal{K}_{p,\lambda}^{(\alpha,s)}(e_0; u) - e_0\|_{C[0,1]}\},$$

where $N = \max\{2, D\}$. For a given $\epsilon > 0$, we define the sets:

$$\mathcal{U} = \left\{ p : \|\mathcal{K}_{p,\lambda}^{(\alpha,s)} - r(u)\|_{C[0,1]} \geq \epsilon \right\},$$
$$\mathcal{U}_1 = \left\{ p : \omega(r, \delta_p) \|\mathcal{K}_{p,\lambda}^{(\alpha,s)}(e_0; u) - e_0\|_{C[0,1]} \geq \frac{\epsilon}{3N} \right\},$$
$$\mathcal{U}_2 = \left\{ p : \omega(r, \delta_p) \geq \frac{\epsilon}{3N} \right\},$$
$$\mathcal{U}_3 = \left\{ p : \|\mathcal{K}_{p,\lambda}^{(\alpha,s)}(e_0; u) - e_0\|_{C[0,1]} \geq \frac{\epsilon}{3N} \right\}.$$

Then the inclusion $\mathcal{U} \subset \cup_{j=1}^3 \mathcal{U}_j$ holds and

$$\frac{1}{e_m Q_m} \sum_{p=0}^m q_p \sum_{k \in \mathcal{U}} b_{pk}(i) \leq \frac{1}{e_m Q_m} \sum_{p=0}^m q_p \sum_{k \in \mathcal{U}_1} b_{pk}(i) + \frac{1}{d_m Q_m} \sum_{p=0}^m q_p \sum_{k \in \mathcal{U}_2} b_{pk}(i)$$
$$+ \frac{1}{c_m Q_m} \sum_{p=0}^m q_p \sum_{k \in \mathcal{U}_3} b_{pk}(i).$$

By hypotheses (i) and (ii), we have

$$\|\mathcal{K}_{p,\lambda}^{(\alpha,s)} - r\|_{C[0,1]} = [\text{stat}_\mathcal{B}, q_p] - o(e_p), \qquad e_p = \max\{c_p, d_p\}.$$

This completes the proof of Theorem 4. □

Let $C^2[0,1]$ be the space of all functions $r \in C[0,1]$ such that $r', r'' \in C[0,1]$.

Theorem 5. Let $\mathcal{B} = (\mathcal{B}_i)_{i\in\mathbb{N}} \in \mathcal{R}^+$. Let $r \in C[0,1]$ and let u be a point of $\mathcal{I}$ at which $r''(u)$ exists. Then

$$[\text{stat}_\mathcal{B}, q_p] - \lim_{p\to\infty} \{p[\mathcal{K}^{(\alpha,s)}_{p,\lambda}(r,u) - r(u)]\} = (\frac{1}{2} - u)r'(u) \quad \text{(uniformly in } i\text{)}.$$

If $r \in C^2[0,1]$, the convergence is also uniform in $u \in \mathcal{I}$.

Proof. Let $r \in C^2[0,1]$ and $u \in [0,1]$ be fixed. By taking into account Taylor's expansion with Peano's form of reminder we conclude that

$$r(t) - r(u) = (t-u)r'(u) + \frac{1}{2}(t-u)^2 r''(u) + (t-u)^2 r_u(t), \tag{8}$$

where $r_u(t)$ is the remainder term such that $r_u(t) \in C[0,1]$ and $r_u(t) \to 0$ as $t \to x$. Applying $\mathcal{K}^{(\alpha,s)}_{p,\lambda}$ to identity (8), we get

$$\mathcal{K}^{(\alpha,s)}_{p,\lambda}(r,u) - r(u) = r'(u)\mathcal{K}^{(\alpha,s)}_{p,\lambda}(t-u;u) + \frac{r''(u)}{2}\mathcal{K}^{(\alpha,s)}_{p,\lambda}((t-u)^2;u) + \mathcal{K}^{(\alpha,s)}_{p,\lambda}((t-u)^2 r_u(t);u). \tag{9}$$

By multiplying both sides of (9) by p and using the Cauchy–Schwarz inequality, we have

$$p\mathcal{K}^{(\alpha,s)}_{p,\lambda}((t-u)^2 r_u(t);u) \leq \sqrt{p^2\mathcal{K}^{(\alpha,s)}_{p,\lambda}((t-u)^4;u)}\sqrt{\mathcal{K}^{(\alpha,s)}_{p,\lambda}(r_u(t);u)}.$$

Hence, in view of Lemma 2 and boundedness of the expression $[\text{stat}_\mathcal{B}, q_p] - \lim p^2\mathcal{K}^{(\alpha,s)}_{p,\lambda}((t-u)^4;u)$, we have

$$[\text{stat}_\mathcal{B}, q_p] - \lim_{p\to\infty} p[\mathcal{K}^{(\alpha,s)}_{p,\lambda}((t-u)^2 r_u(t);u)] = 0,$$

which completes the proof. □

5. Some Approximation Theorems Including Pointwise and Weighted Approximation

In this part, we provide some pointwise and weighted approximation results for operators $\mathcal{K}^{(\alpha,s)}_{p,\lambda}$. Moreover, we establish two local approximation theorems for $\mathcal{K}^{(\alpha,s)}_{p,\lambda}$ by the second-order modulus of smoothness and the usual modulus of continuity.

Lipschitz class is defined as follows: Let $0 < \rho \leq 1$, $T \subset \mathbb{R}_+ = [0,\infty)$ and $C(\mathbb{R}_+)$ denote the space of all continuous functions r on $\mathbb{R}_+$. Then, a function r in $C_B(\mathbb{R}_+)$ belongs to $Lip(\rho)$ if the condition

$$|r(t) - r(u)| \leq S_{r,\rho}|t-u|^\rho \quad (t \in T, u \in \mathbb{R}_+)$$

holds, where the constant $S_{r,\rho}$ depends on r and ρ.

Theorem 6. Let $r \in C_B(\mathbb{R}_+)$, $0 < \rho \leq 1$ and $T \subset \mathbb{R}_+$ then, for each $u \in \mathbb{R}_+$,

$$|\mathcal{K}^{(\alpha,s)}_{p,\lambda}(r,u) - r(u)| \leq S_{r,\rho}\Bigg\{\bigg(\frac{2(1-\alpha)\lambda u}{(p-s-1)(p+1)^2}\Big[(p+1)(1-u)^{p-s+1}\Big]$$

$$\times((1-u)u^{p-s} - 1 + 2u) + \frac{2p^2 s u^2}{(p-s-1)(p+1)^2}\Big[u^{p-s} - (1-u)^{p-s}\Big]$$

$$+ \frac{3u^2 - 3u + 1}{3(p+1)^2} + \frac{2\alpha\lambda u}{(p-1)(p+1)^2}\Big[(p+1)(u^p - u^{p+1} - (1-u)u^{p-s}) - 1 + 2u\Big]$$

$$+ \frac{(p + (1-\alpha)s(s-1))u(1-u)}{(p-1)(p+1)^2}\bigg)^{\rho/2} + 2d^\rho(u,T)\Bigg\},$$

where $d(u, T)$ is the distance between u and T, defined by

$$d(u, T) = \inf\{|t - u| : t \in T\}.$$

Proof. Let $v \in \bar{T}$ so that $|u - v| = d(u, T)$, where $\bar{T}$ is a closure of T, then one has

$$|r(t) - r(u)| \leq |r(u) - r(v)| + |r(t) - r(v)| \quad (u \in \mathbb{R}_+).$$

By the help of relation

$$|\mathcal{K}_{p,\lambda}^{(\alpha,s)}(r,u) - r(u)| \leq \mathcal{K}_{p,\lambda}^{(\alpha,s)}(|r(u) - r(v)|; u) + \mathcal{K}_{p,\lambda}^{(\alpha,s)}(|r(t) - r(v)|; u)$$

we have

$$\begin{aligned}
|\mathcal{K}_{p,\lambda}^{(\alpha,s)}(r,u) - r(u)| &\leq S_{r,\rho}\left\{|x - v|^\rho + \mathcal{K}_{p,\lambda}^{(\alpha,s)}(|t - v|^\rho; u)\right\} \\
&\leq S_{r,\rho}\left\{|x - v|^\rho + \mathcal{K}_{p,\lambda}^{(\alpha,s)}(|t - u|^\rho + |x - v|^\rho; u)\right\} \\
&= S_{r,\rho}\left\{2|x - v|^\rho + \mathcal{K}_{p,\lambda}^{(\alpha,s)}(|t - u|^\rho; u)\right\}.
\end{aligned}$$

We obtain the following relationships applying Hölder inequality to the above inequality for $A = 2/\rho$ and $B = 2/(2 - \rho)$:

$$\begin{aligned}
|\mathcal{K}_{p,\lambda}^{(\alpha,s)}(r,u) - r(u)| &\leq S_{r,\rho}\left\{2d^\rho(u,T) + \mathcal{K}_{p,\lambda}^{(\alpha,s)\frac{1}{A}}(|t - u|^{A\rho}; u)\mathcal{K}_{p,\lambda}^{(\alpha,s)\frac{1}{B}}(1^B; u)\right\} \\
&= S_{r,\rho}\left\{2d^\rho(u,T) + \mathcal{K}_{p,\lambda}^{(\alpha,s)\frac{\rho}{2}}(|t - u|^2; u)\right\}.
\end{aligned}$$

We complete the proof by Lemma 2. □

Let $u \in \mathbb{R}_+$ and $0 < \rho \leq 1$, then Lipschitz-type maximal function of order ρ [36] is expressed as

$$\omega_\rho(r; u) = \sup_{v \in \mathbb{R}_+, v \neq u} \frac{|r(v) - r(u)|}{|v - u|^\rho}. \tag{10}$$

We provide a local direct estimate for $\mathcal{K}_{p,\lambda}^{(\alpha,s)}$ by the next theorem.

Theorem 7. *Let $r \in C_B(\mathbb{R}_+)$ and $0 < \rho \leq 1$, then, we have*

$$\begin{aligned}
|\mathcal{K}_{p,\lambda}^{(\alpha,s)}(r,u) - r(u)| \leq \omega_\rho(r;u) &\left\{\frac{3u^2 - 3u + 1}{3(p+1)^2} + \frac{(p + (1-\alpha)s(s-1))u(1-u)}{(p-1)(p+1)^2}\right. \\
&+ \frac{2p^2su^2}{(p-s-1)(p+1)^2}\left[u^{p-s} - (1-u)^{p-s}\right] \\
&+ \frac{2(1-\alpha)\lambda u}{(p-s-1)(p+1)^2}\left[(p+1)(1-u)^{p-s+1} + (1-u)u^{p-s} - 1 + 2u\right] \\
&\left.+ \frac{2\alpha\lambda u}{(p-1)(p+1)^2}\left[(p+1)(u^p - u^{p+1} - (1-u)u^{p-s}) - 1 + 2u\right]\right\}^{\frac{\rho}{2}}
\end{aligned}$$

for all $u \in \mathbb{R}_+$.

Proof. We have the following relations

$$|\mathcal{K}_{p,\lambda}^{(\alpha,s)}(r,u) - r(u)| = |\mathcal{K}_{p,\lambda}^{(\alpha,s)}(r,u) - r(u)\mathcal{K}_{p,\lambda}^{(\alpha,s)}(1;u)|$$
$$\leq \mathcal{K}_{p,\lambda}^{(\alpha,s)}(|r(t) - r(u)|;u)$$
$$\leq \omega_\rho(r;u)\mathcal{K}_{p,\lambda}^{(\alpha,s)}(|t-u|^\rho;u)$$

by the help of (10). Further, applying Hölder inequality to the last inequality for

$$A = 2/\rho \quad \text{and} \quad B = 2/(2-\rho)$$

we observe that

$$|\mathcal{K}_{p,\lambda}^{(\alpha,s)}(r,u) - r(u)| \leq \omega_\rho(r;u)\mathcal{K}_{p,\lambda}^{(\alpha,s)}{}^{\frac{B}{2}}(|t-u|^2;u).$$

The last inequality, together with Lemma 2 and the relation in (10) concludes the proof. □

Let $\psi(u) = 1 + u^2$ be a weight function then, the weighted space $B_\psi(\mathbb{R}_+)$ denotes the set of all functions r on $\mathbb{R}_+$ having the property

$$|r(u)| \leq \psi(u)S_r,$$

where a constant $S_r > 0$ depending on r. It is known that $B_\psi(\mathbb{R}_+)$ is a Banach space equipped with the norm

$$\|r\|_\psi = \sup_{u \in \mathbb{R}_+} \frac{|r(u)|}{\psi(u)}.$$

Moreover, $C_\psi(\mathbb{R}_+)$ denotes the subspace of all continuous functions in $B_\psi(\mathbb{R}_+)$ and

$$C_\psi^*(\mathbb{R}_+) = \left\{ r \in C_\psi(\mathbb{R}_+) : \lim_{u \to \infty} \frac{|r(u)|}{\psi(u)} < \infty \right\}.$$

Theorem 8. Let $\psi(u) = 1 + u^2$ then, for all $r \in C_\psi^*(\mathbb{R}_+)$, we have

$$\lim_{p \to \infty} \|\mathcal{K}_{p,\lambda}^{(\alpha,s)}(r,u) - r\|_\psi = 0.$$

Proof. In view of the weighted Korovkin theorem, Definition 1 and Corollary 1, it is easy to see that

$$\lim_{p \to \infty} \|\mathcal{K}_{p,\lambda}^{(\alpha,s)}(e_i;u) - e_i\|_\psi = 0$$

holds for $i = 0, 1, 2$. This completes the proof. □

Theorem 9. Let $\psi(u) = 1 + u^2$ and $r \in C_\psi^*(\mathbb{R}_+)$ then, one has

$$\lim_{p \to \infty} \sup_{u \in \mathbb{R}_+} \frac{|\mathcal{K}_{p,\lambda}^{(\alpha,s)}(r,u) - r(u)|}{\psi^{1+\theta}(u)} = 0. \tag{11}$$

Proof. We have the following relationshops for any fixed $\gamma > 0$:

$$\sup_{u\in\mathbb{R}_+}\frac{|\mathcal{K}_{p,\lambda}^{(\alpha,s)}(r,u)-r(u)|}{\psi^{1+\theta}(u)} \leq \sup_{u\leq\gamma}\frac{|\mathcal{K}_{p,\lambda}^{(\alpha,s)}(r,u)-r(u)|}{\psi^{1+\theta}(u)}+\sup_{u\geq\gamma}\frac{|\mathcal{K}_{p,\lambda}^{(\alpha,s)}(r,u)-r(u)|}{\psi^{1+\theta}(u)}$$

$$\leq \|\mathcal{K}_{p,\lambda}^{(\alpha,s)}(r,u)-r\|_{C[0,\gamma]}+\|r\|_\psi \sup_{u\geq\gamma}\frac{|\mathcal{K}_{p,\lambda}^{(\alpha,s)}(1+t^2;u)|}{\psi^{1+\theta}(u)}$$

$$+\sup_{u\geq\gamma}\frac{|r(u)|}{\psi^{1+\theta}(u)}. \tag{12}$$

Using the fact $|r(u)|\leq \psi(u)N$ we have

$$\sup_{u\geq\gamma}\frac{|r(u)|}{\psi^{1+\theta}(u)} \leq \frac{\|r(u)\|_\psi}{(1+\gamma^2)^{1+\theta}}.$$

Let $\epsilon>0$ be given. We can choose γ to be so large that the following inequality holds:

$$\frac{\|r(u)\|_\psi}{(1+\gamma^2)^{1+\theta}}<\epsilon/3. \tag{13}$$

By the help of Corollary 1, we obtain

$$\|r\|_\psi \frac{|\mathcal{K}_{p,\lambda}^{(\alpha,s)}(1+t^2;u)|}{\psi^{1+\theta}(u)} \to 0\ (p\to\infty).$$

Further, for the choice of γ as large enough, we have

$$\|r\|_\psi \sup_{u\geq\gamma}\frac{|\mathcal{K}_{p,\lambda}^{(\alpha,s)}(1+t^2;u)|}{\psi^{1+\theta}(u)}<\epsilon/3. \tag{14}$$

Moreover, bearing in mind the Korovkin theorem, the first term on the right-hand side of inequality (12) becomes

$$\|\mathcal{K}_{p,\lambda}^{(\alpha,s)}(r;u)-r\|_{C[0,\gamma]}<\epsilon/3. \tag{15}$$

Combining the results in (13)–(15), we obtain the desired result. □

In order to give a local approximation theorem, we need to remember certain notions regarding the modulus of continuity, modulus of smoothness and Peetre's K-functional. The modulus of continuity $w(r,\delta)$ of $r\in C[a,b]$ is defined by

$$w(r,\delta):=\sup\{|r(u)-r(v)|:u,v\in[a,b],|u-v|\leq\delta\},$$

where $\delta>0$. The following inequality is satisfied for any $\delta>0$ and each $u\in[a,b]$:

$$|r(u)-r(v)|\leq w(r,\delta)\left(\frac{|u-v|}{\delta}+1\right).$$

The second-order modulus of smoothness of $r\in C[0,1]$ is defined as follows:

$$w_2(r,\sqrt{\delta}):=\sup_{0<h\leq\sqrt{\delta}}\sup_{u,u+2h\in\mathcal{I}}\{|r(u+2h)-2r(u+h)+r(u)|\},$$

and the related K-functional is defined by

$$K_2(r,\delta)=\inf\{\|r-g\|_{C[0,1]}+\delta\|g''\|_{C[0,1]}:g\in W^2[0,1]\},$$

where $\delta > 0$ and $W^2[0,1] = \{g \in C[0,1] : g', g'' \in C[0,1]\}$. It is also known that the inequality

$$K_2(r, \delta) \leq C w_2(r, \sqrt{\delta}) \tag{16}$$

holds for all $\delta > 0$, in which the absolute constant $C > 0$ is independent of δ and r (see [37]).

Now, we establish a direct local approximation theorem for operators $\mathcal{K}_{p,\lambda}^{(\alpha,s)}$.

Theorem 10. *The following inequality is satisfied for the operators $\mathcal{K}_{p,\lambda}^{(\alpha,s)}$:*

$$|\mathcal{K}_{p,\lambda}^{(\alpha,s)}(r,u) - r(u)| \leq C w_2\left(r, \frac{\psi_n(u)}{2}\right) + w(r, \alpha_p(u)),$$

where C is an absolute positive constant, $\psi_p(u) = \frac{1}{2}\sqrt{\beta_p(u) + \alpha_p^2(u)}$ and

$$\alpha_p(u) = \mathcal{K}_{p,\lambda}^{(\alpha,s)}((t-u); u), \quad \beta_p(u) = \mathcal{K}_{p,\lambda}^{(\alpha,s)}((t-u)^2; u)$$

such that both terms $\alpha_p(u)$ and $\beta_p(u)$ converge to zero when $p \to \infty$.

Proof. We construct the operators $\mathbf{K}_{p,\lambda}^{(\alpha,s)}$, which preserves constants and linear functions for $u \in [0,1]$:

$$\mathbf{K}_{p,\lambda}^{(\alpha,s)}(r;u) = \mathcal{K}_{p,\lambda}^{(\alpha,s)}(r,u) + r(u) - r\left[\frac{1+2pu}{2(p+1)} + \frac{\alpha\lambda}{(p+1)(p-1)}\left(1 - 2u + u^{p+1} - (1-u)^{p+1}\right)\right.$$
$$\left. + \frac{(1-\alpha)\lambda}{(p+1)(p-s-1)}\left(1 - 2u + u^{p-s+1} - (1-u)^{p-s+1}\right)\right]. \tag{17}$$

Let $t, u \in [0,1]$, then Taylor's expansion formula for $g \in W^2[0,1]$ is

$$g(t) = g(u) + (t-u)g'(u) + \int_u^t (t-s)g''(s)ds. \tag{18}$$

Applying $\mathbf{K}_{p,\lambda}^{(\alpha,s)}$ to both sides of (18), we get

$$\mathbf{K}_{p,\lambda}^{(\alpha,s)}(g;u) - g(u) = g'(u)\mathbf{K}_{p,\lambda}^{(\alpha,s)}(t-u;u) + \mathbf{K}_{p,\lambda}^{(\alpha,s)}\left(\int_u^t (t-s)g''(s)ds; u\right)$$
$$= \mathcal{K}_{p,\lambda}^{(\alpha,s)}\left(\int_u^t (t-s)g''(s)ds; u\right) - \int_u^{\alpha_p(u)+u} (\alpha_p(u) + u - s)g''(s)ds.$$

So

$$|\mathbf{K}_{p,\lambda}^{(\alpha,s)}(g;u) - g(u)| \leq \mathcal{K}_{p,\lambda}^{(\alpha,s)}\left(\left|\int_u^t |t-s| \, |g''(s)|ds\right|; u\right) - \int_u^{\alpha_p(u)+u} |\alpha_p(u) + u - s| \, |g''(s)| \, ds$$
$$\leq \|g''\|_{C[0,1]}(\mathcal{K}_{p,\lambda}^{(\alpha,s)}((t-u)^2; u) + \mathcal{K}_{p,\lambda}^{(\alpha,s)^2}(t-u; u)).$$

We get the following relationships taking (17) into account:

$$\|\mathbf{K}_{p,\lambda}^{(\alpha,s)}(g;u)\|_{C[0,1]} \leq \|\mathcal{K}_{p,\lambda}^{(\alpha,s)}(g;u)\|_{C[0,1]} + \|g(u)\|_{C[0,1]} + \|g(\alpha_p(u)+u)\|_{C[0,1]} \leq \|3g\|_{C[0,1]}. \tag{19}$$

By (17) and (19) we get

$$|\mathcal{K}_{p,\lambda}^{(\alpha,s)}(r,u) - r(u)| \leq |\mathbf{K}_{p,\lambda}^{(\alpha,s)}(f-g;u)| + |\mathbf{K}_{p,\lambda}^{(\alpha,s)}(g;u) - g(u)|$$
$$+ |g(u) - r(u)| + |r(\alpha_p + u) - r(u)|$$
$$\leq 4\|r-g\|_{C[0,1]} + \psi_p^2(u)\|g''\|_{C[0,1]} + w(r,\alpha_n(u)),$$

where $g \in W^2[0,1]$ and $r \in C[0,1]$. By inequality (16) and taking infimum on the right-hand side of the above inequality over all $g \in W^2[0,1]$, we get

$$|\mathcal{K}_{p,\lambda}^{(\alpha,s)}(r,u) - r(u)| \leq 4K_2(r,\psi_p^2(u)/4) + w(r,\alpha_p(u)) \leq C\, w_2\left(r, \frac{\psi_p(u)}{2}\right) + w(r,\alpha_p(u)),$$

which completes the proof. □

Theorem 11. Let $r \in C^1[0,1]$. For any $u \in [0,1]$, the following inequality holds:

$$|\mathcal{K}_{p,\lambda}^{(\alpha,s)}(r,u) - r(u)| \leq |\alpha_p(u)|\,|r'(u)| + 2\sqrt{\beta_p(u)}w(r',\sqrt{\beta_p(u)}\,).$$

Proof. We have the following relationship

$$r(t) - r(u) = (t-u)r'(u) + \int_u^t (r'(s) - r'(u))ds$$

for any $t,\ u \in [0,1]$. Applying $\mathcal{K}_{p,\lambda}^{(\alpha,s)}$ to the sides of the above relationship, we obtain

$$\mathcal{K}_{p,\lambda}^{(\alpha,s)}(r(t) - r(u); u) = r'(u)\mathcal{K}_{p,\lambda}^{(\alpha,s)}(t-u;u) + \mathcal{K}_{p,\lambda}^{(\alpha,s)}\left(\int_u^t (r'(s) - r'(u))ds; u\right).$$

It is well known that for any $\zeta > 0$ and each $s \in [0,1]$,

$$|r(s) - r(u)| \leq w(r,\zeta)\left(\frac{|s-u|}{\zeta} + 1\right), \quad r \in C[0,1].$$

By the above inequality we have

$$\left|\int_u^t (r'(s) - r'(u))ds\right| \leq w(r',\zeta)\left(\frac{(t-u)^2}{\zeta} + |t-u|\right).$$

Hence, we have

$$|\mathcal{K}_{p,\lambda}^{(\alpha,s)}(r,u) - r(u)| \leq |r'(u)|\,|\mathcal{K}_{p,\lambda}^{(\alpha,s)}(t-u;u)| + w(r',\zeta)\left\{\frac{1}{\zeta}\mathcal{K}_{p,\lambda}^{(\alpha,s)}((t-u)^2;u) + \mathcal{K}_{p,\lambda}^{(\alpha,s)}(t-u;u)\right\}. \quad (20)$$

We get the following inequality if we apply the Cauchy–Schwarz inequality on the right hand side of (20):

$$|\mathcal{K}_{p,\lambda}^{(\alpha,s)}(r,u) - r(u)| \leq |r'(u)||\alpha_p(u)| + w(r',\zeta)\left(\frac{1}{\zeta}\mathcal{K}_{p,\lambda}^{(\alpha,s)^{1/2}}((t-u)^2;u) + 1\right)\mathcal{K}_{p,\lambda}^{(\alpha,s)^{1/2}}((t-u)^2;u).$$

We prove the theorem if we choose ζ as $\zeta = \beta_p^{1/2}(u)$. □

6. Convergence by Graphics

In this section, we provide some graphics that demonstrate the consistency, accuracy and convergence of the proposed blending operators for different kinds of functions.

Example 1. Consider the trigonometric function

$$r_1(u) = \frac{1}{5}\left(0.5u^2 + 4\right)\sin(3\pi u)$$

on the closed interval $\mathcal{I}$. In Figures 1 and 2, we demonstrate approximation and maximum error of approximation of the proposed operators with the values $s = 3$, $\alpha = 0.9$ and $\lambda = 1$.

Example 2. Consider the piece-wise function

$$r_2(u) = \begin{cases} 8u & 0 \leq u \leq \frac{1}{5} \\ \frac{4(1+u)}{3} & \frac{1}{5} < u \leq \frac{1}{2} \\ \frac{4(2-u)}{3} & \frac{1}{2} < u \leq \frac{4}{5} \\ 8(1-u) & \frac{4}{5} < u \leq 1 \end{cases}$$

on the interval $\mathcal{I}$ (see [38]). In Figures 3 and 4, we fix the values $s = 3$, $\alpha = 0.9$ and $\lambda = 1$, and change the values of p to see the approximation behavior and maximum error of approximation of the proposed operators.

Example 3. Consider the trigonometric function

$$r_3(u) = \frac{\cos(7\pi u)}{2.5u^2 - 10}$$

on the closed interval $\mathcal{I}$. In Figures 5 and 6, we demonstrate approximation and maximum error of approximation of the proposed operators with certain different values of s, α and λ, and the fixed value of $p = 20$.

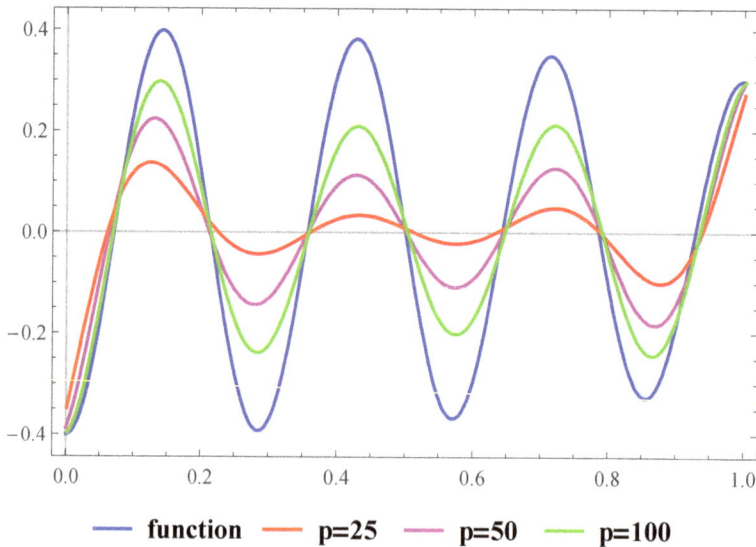

Figure 1. Approximations by $\mathcal{K}_{p,\lambda}^{(\alpha,s)}$ for function $r_1(u)$.

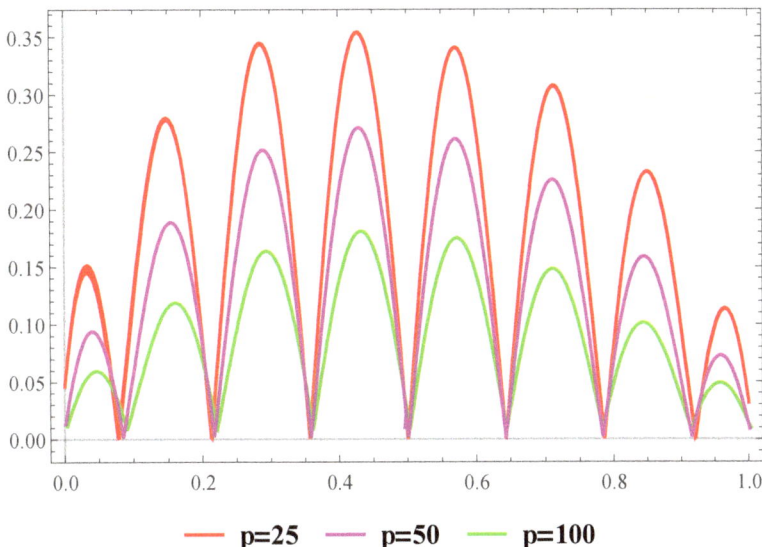

Figure 2. Maximum error of approximation for function $r_1(u)$.

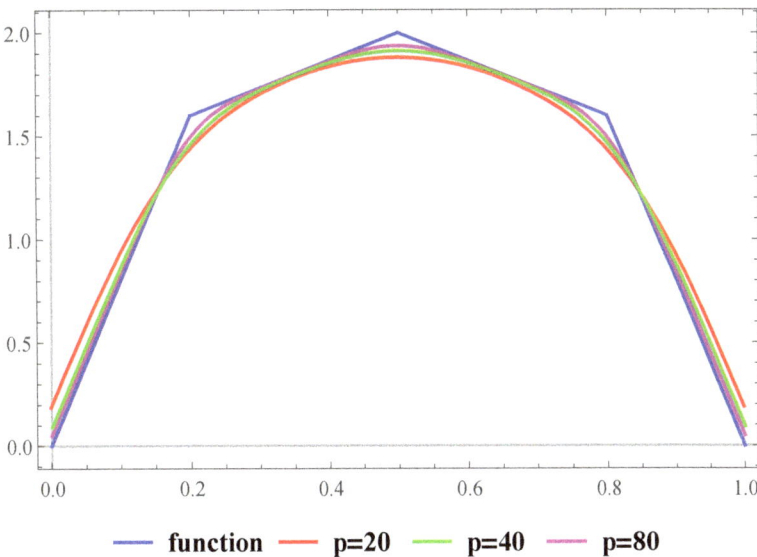

Figure 3. Approximations by $\mathcal{K}_{p,\lambda}^{(\alpha,s)}$ for function $r_2(u)$.

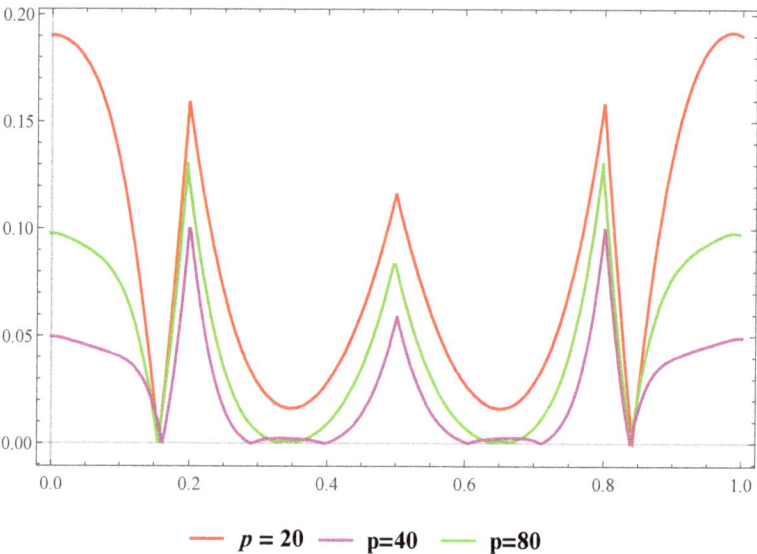

Figure 4. Maximum error of approximation for function $r_2(u)$.

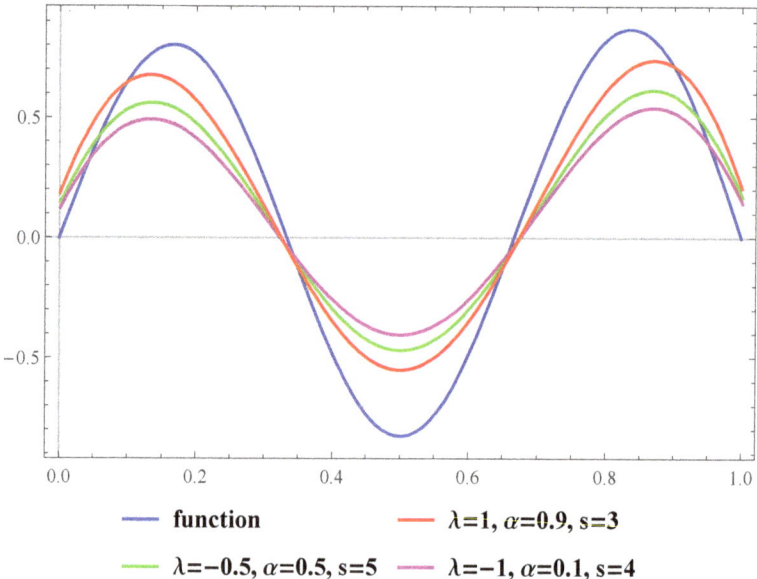

Figure 5. Approximations by $\mathcal{K}_{p,\lambda}^{(\alpha,s)}$ for function $r_3(u)$.

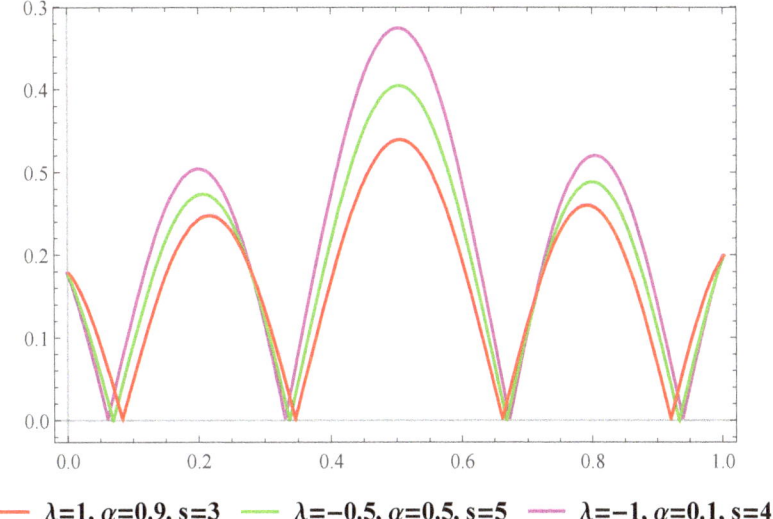

— λ=1, α=0.9, s=3   — λ=−0.5, α=0.5, s=5   — λ=−1, α=0.1, s=4

Figure 6. Maximum error of approximation for function $r_3(u)$.

Therefore, we demonstrate the consistency and accuracy of convergence behavior for the proposed blending-type operators via certain computer graphics. The graphics show that the proposed operators approximate different kinds of functions for different values of parameters λ, α and s.

7. Conclusions

Many convergence results, including weighted $\mathcal{B}$-statistical, pointwise and weighted convergences, are obtained for the following introduced blending (α, λ, s)-Bernstein–Kantorovich operators:

$$\mathcal{K}^{(\alpha,s)}_{p,\lambda}(r;u) = (p+1)\sum_{i=0}^{p}\tilde{b}^{\alpha,s}_{p,i}(\lambda;u)\int_{\frac{i}{p+1}}^{\frac{i+1}{p+1}} r(t)dt$$

The proposed operators extend the current literature for certain values of λ, α and the positive integer s:

(i) If we take $\alpha = 1$, $\lambda = 0$ and $s = 2$, $\mathcal{K}^{(\alpha,s)}_{p,\lambda}$ becomes the classical Kantorovich operators defined in [3].

(ii) If we take $\alpha = 1$ and $s = 2$, $\mathcal{K}^{(\alpha,s)}_{p,\lambda}$ becomes the λ–Kantorovich operators defined in [6,39].

(iii) If we take $\lambda = 0$ and $s = 2$, $\mathcal{K}^{(\alpha,s)}_{p,\lambda}$ becomes the α–Kantorovich operators defined in [4].

As a continuation of this study, we will focus on a bivariate version of the proposed operators defined in this paper.

Author Contributions: Methodology, M.T.E. and E.A.; Visualization, F.Ö.; Supervision, F.Ö. and E.A.; Validation, E.A.; Writing (original draft), F.Ö.; Writing (review and editing), F.Ö., E.A. and M.T.E. All authors have read and agreed to the published version of the manuscript.

Funding: This research is in the process of getting support from the Ministry of Education and Science of Kosovo.

Institutional Review Board Statement: Not applicable.

Informed Consent Statement: Not applicable.

Data Availability Statement: Not applicable.

Acknowledgments: The authors extend their appreciation to the Ministry of Education and Science of Kosovo for funding this work.

Conflicts of Interest: The authors declare no conflict of interest.

References

1. Weierstrass, V.K. *Über die Analytische Darstellbarkeit Sogennanter Willkürlicher Functionen Einer Reellen Veränderlichen*; Koniglich Preussischen Akademie der Wissenschcaften zu Berlin: Berlin, Germany, 1885; pp. 633–639, 789–805.
2. Bernstein, S. Dámonstration du tháorème de weirstrass. Foundeá sur le calcul des probabilitás. *Commun. Soc. Math. Kharkow* **1912**, *13*, 1–2.
3. Kantorovich, L.V. Sur certains developements suivant les polynomes de la forme de S. Bernstein I, II. *Dokl. Akad. Nauk SSSR* **1930**, *568*, 595–600.
4. Mohiuddine, S.A.; Özger, F. Approximation of functions by Stancu variant of Bernstein-Kantorovich operators based on shape parameter α. *RACSAM* **2020**, *114*, 70. [CrossRef]
5. Mohiuddine, S.A.; Ahmad, N.; Özger, F.; Alotaibi, A.; Hazarika, B. Approximation by the parametric generalization of Baskakov-Kantorovich operators linking with Stancu operators. *Iran. J. Sci. Technol. Trans. Sci.* **2021**, *45*, 593–605. [CrossRef]
6. Özger, F. Weighted statistical approximation properties of univariate and bivariate λ-Kantorovich operators. *Filomat* **2019**, *33*, 11. [CrossRef]
7. Kanat, K.; Sofyalıoğlu, M. On Stancu type generalization of (p,q)-Baskakov-Kantorovich operators. *Commun. Fac. Sci. Univ. Ank. Ser. A1 Math. Stat.* **2019**, *68*, 1995–2013. [CrossRef]
8. Kadak, U.; Özger, F. A numerical comparative study of generalized Bernstein-Kantorovich operators. *Math. Found. Comput.* **2021**, *4*, 311. [CrossRef]
9. Usta, F.; Akyiğit, M.; Say, F.; Ansari, K.J. Bernstein operator method for approximate solution of singularly perturbed Volterra integral equations. *J. Math. Anal. Appl.* **2022**, *507*, 125828. [CrossRef]
10. Usta, F. Bernstein approximation technique for numerical solution of Volterra integral equations of the third kind. *Comput. Appl. Math.* **2021**, *40*, 161. [CrossRef]
11. Chen, X.; Tan, J.; Liu, Z.; Xie, J. Approximation of functions by a new family of generalized Bernstein operators. *J. Math. Anal. Appl.* **2017**, *450*, 244–261. [CrossRef]
12. Özger, F.; Srivastava, H.M.; Mohiuddine, S.A. Approximation of functions by a new class of generalized Bernstein–Schurer operators. *RACSAM* **2020**, *114*, 173. [CrossRef]
13. Ye, Z.; Long, X.; Zeng, X.M. Adjustment algorithms for Bézier curve and surface. In Proceedings of the 2010 5th International Conference on Computer Science & Education, Hefei, China, 24–27 August 2010.
14. Cai, Q.B.; Lian, B.-Y.; Zhou, G. Approximation properties of λ-Bernstein operators. *J. Inequal. Appl.* **2018**, *2018*, 61. [CrossRef] [PubMed]
15. Aktuğlu, H.; Yashar, Z.S. Approximation of functions by generalized parametric blending-type Bernstein operators. *Iran. J. Sci. Technol. Trans. Sci.* **2020**, *44*, 1495–1504. [CrossRef]
16. Mohiuddine, S.A.; Kajla, A.; Mursaleen, M.; Alghamdi, M.A. Blending type approximation by τ-Baskakov-Durrmeyer type hybrid operators. *Adv. Differ. Equ.* **2020**, *2020*, 467. [CrossRef]
17. Özger, F. On new Bezier bases with Schurer polnomials and corresponding results in approximation theory. *Commun. Fac. Sci. Univ. Ank. Ser. A1 Math. Stat.* **2020**, *69*, 376–393.
18. Srivastava, H.M.; Özger, F.; Mohiuddine, S.A. Construction of Stancu-type Bernstein operators based on Bézier bases with shape parameter λ. *Symmetry* **2019**, *11*, 316. [CrossRef]
19. Aslan, R. Some approximation results on λ−Szász-Mirakjan-Kantorovich operators. *Fundam. J. Math. Appl.* **2021**, *4*, 150–158.
20. Cai, Q.B.; Aslan, R. On a New construction of generalized q−Bernstein Polynomials Based on Shape Parameter λ. *Symmetry* **2021**, *13*, 1919. [CrossRef]
21. Cai, Q.B.; Aslan, R. Note on a new construction of Kantorovich form q−Bernstein operators related to shape parameter λ. *Comput. Model. Eng. Sci.* **2022**, *130*, 1479–1493. [CrossRef]
22. Ansari, K.J.; Özger, F.; Ödemiş Özger, Z. Numerical and theoretical approximation results for Schurer–Stancu operators with shape parameter λ. *Comput. Appl. Math.* **2022**, *41*, 1–18. [CrossRef]
23. Srivastava, H.M.; Ansari, K.J.; Özger, F.; Ödemiş Özger, Z. A link between approximation theory and summability methods via four-dimensional infinite matrices. *Mathematics* **2021**, *9*, 1895. [CrossRef]
24. Özger, F.; Ansari, K.J. Statistical convergence of bivariate generalized Bernstein operators via four-dimensional infinite matrices. *Filomat* **2022**, *36*, 507–525. [CrossRef]
25. Özger, F.; Demirci, K.; Yıldız, S. Approximation by Kantorovich variant of λ-Schurer operators and related numerical results. In *Topics in Contemporary Mathematical Analysis and Applications*; CRC Press: Boca Raton, FL, USA, 2021; pp. 77–94. ISBN 9780367532666.

26. Gezer, H.; Aktuğlu, H.; Baytunç, E.; Atamert, M.S. Generalized blending type Bernstein operators based on the shape parameter λ. *J. Inequal. Appl.* **2022**, *2022*, 1–21.
27. Cai, Q.B.; Ansari, K.J.; Temizer Ersoy, M.; Özger, F. Statistical blending-type approximation by a class of operators that includes shape parameters λ and α. *Mathematics* **2022**, *10*, 1149. [CrossRef]
28. Korovkin, P.P. *Linear Operators and Approximation Theory*; Hindustan Publishing Corporation: Delhi, India, 1960.
29. Bohman, H. On approximation of continuous and of analytic functions. *Ark. Math.* **1952**, *2*, 43–56. [CrossRef]
30. Kadak, U.; Braha, N.L.; Srivastava, H.M. Statistical weighted B-summability and its applications to approximation theorems. *Appl. Math. Comput.* **2017**, *302*, 80–96.
31. Kadak, U. Statistical Summability of double sequences by the weighted mean and associated approximation results. In *Applied Mathematical Analysis: Theory, Methods, and Applications*; Springer: Cham, Switzerland, 2020; pp. 61–85.
32. Kolk, E. Matrix summability of statistically convergent sequences. *Analysis* **1993**, *13*, 77–84. [CrossRef]
33. Stieglitz, M. Eine verallgemeinerung des begriffs der fastkonvergenz. *Math. Japon* **1973**, *18*, 53–70.
34. Bell, H.T. Order summability and almost convergence. *Proc. Am. Math. Soc.* **1973**, *38*, 548–552. [CrossRef]
35. Mursaleen, M.; Nasiruzzaman, M.; Srivastava, H.M. Approximation by bicomplex beta operators in compact-disks. *Math. Methods Appl. Sci.* **2016**, *39*, 2916–2929. [CrossRef]
36. Lenze, B. On Lipschitz-type maximal functions and their smoothness spaces. *Indag. Math.* **1988**, *91*, 53–63. [CrossRef]
37. DeVore, R.A.; Lorentz, G.G. *Constructive Approximation*; Springer: Berlin, Germany, 1993.
38. Khosravian-Arab, H.; Dehghan, M.; Eslahchi, M.R. A new approach to improve the order of approximation of the Bernstein operators: Theory and applications. *Numer. Algorithms* **2018**, *77*, 111–150. [CrossRef]
39. Özger, F. Applications of generalized weighted statistical convergence to approximation theorems for functions of one and two variables. *Numer. Funct. Anal. Optim.* **2020**, *41*, 1990–2006. [CrossRef]

Article

A Matlab Toolbox for Extended Dynamic Mode Decomposition Based on Orthogonal Polynomials and p-q Quasi-Norm Order Reduction

Camilo Garcia-Tenorio and Alain Vande Wouwer *

Systems, Estimation, Control and Optimization (SECO), Université de Mons, 7000 Mons, Belgium
* Correspondence: alain.vandewouwer@umons.ac.be

Abstract: Extended Dynamic Mode Decomposition (EDMD) allows an approximation of the Koopman operator to be derived in the form of a truncated (finite dimensional) linear operator in a lifted space of (nonlinear) observable functions. EDMD can operate in a purely data-driven way using either data generated by a numerical simulator of arbitrary complexity or actual experimental data. An important question at this stage is the selection of basis functions to construct the observable functions, which in turn is determinant of the sparsity and efficiency of the approximation. In this study, attention is focused on orthogonal polynomial expansions and an order-reduction procedure called p-q quasi-norm reduction. The objective of this article is to present a Matlab library to automate the computation of the EDMD based on the above-mentioned tools and to illustrate the performance of this library with a few representative examples.

Keywords: extended dynamic mode decomposition; Koopman operator; orthogonal polynomials; mathematical modeling; dynamic systems

MSC: 37-04

1. Introduction

In contrast to traditional modeling approaches, in which it is necessary to formulate a general nonlinear model that depends on a set of parameters to replicate the dynamics of a system under consideration, the EDMD [1] builds upon numerical data (simulation or actual experiments) to provide a finite-dimensional (truncated) linear representation of the system dynamics in a lifted space of nonlinear observable functions, making it akin to a black box modeling paradigm, e.g., transfer functions or autoregressive models [2–4]. While the approximation provided by EDMD therefore remains nonlinear in the original state variables, it is linear in a transformed space, which is called the observable space, function space, or vector-valued function of observables (VVFO), among others (for the remainder of this article, we use *observables* when referring to this space, while the example codes use the VVFO terminology). In other words, The EDMD formulation does not represent the system by a linearized representation of the form $x(k+1) = Ax(k)$ (where A is a Jacobian); rather, it describes the evolution of observables $f(x(k))$ through a linear operator U, i.e.,

$$f(x(k+1)) = Uf(x(k)). \qquad (1)$$

EDMD is closely related to other decompositions such as Karhunen–Loeve decomposition (KLD) [5], singular value decomposition (SVD) [6], proper orthogonal decomposition (POD) [7], and its direct precursor, dynamic mode decomposition (DMD) [8]. These decompositions all produce linear approximations of the behavior of the system near a fixed point, offering the possibility of using linear system analysis tools. EDMD extends this possibility to a region of the state space which is larger than the neighborhood of the fixed

point. Indeed, EDMD describes the nonlinear dynamics while being linear in the function space, and therefore provides more than local information while preserving the linear characteristics of the above-mentioned decompositions (KLD, SVD, POD, DMD). As such, it is sometimes called a *linearization in the large*.

Koopman mode decomposition (KMD) [9–11] emerges from the linearity of decompositions that use their spectrum (eigenvalues and eigenvectors) to obtain an approximation of the Koopman operator [12]. From an approximation of the Koopman operator, it is possible to analyze nonlinear systems in terms of their stability and regions of attraction [9,13–15]. Additionally, EDMD (or the approximate Koopman operator) can be used in the context of optimal control and model predictive control [16–19]. These developments show the importance of having accurate EDMD approximations for analysis and control.

There are several variants of the EDMD algorithm, which use norm-based expansions, radial-basis functions, kernel-based representations [20], orthogonal polynomials, and their variations [21,22]. These representations provide tools for analyzing nonlinear systems via spectral decomposition, and represent the fundamentals for developing synthesis algorithms such as EDMD for control [23].

In this paper, attention is focused on the use of orthogonal polynomials for the expression of the observable functions and an order reduction method based on p-q quasi norm [24,25]. Several application examples are described together with Matlab codes which constitute a practical library for users interested in applying EDMD to engineering and scientific problems.

The library provides several Matlab functions to compute a pq-EDMD approximation of a dynamical system based on one of three possible algorithms. The first algorithm is the original least squares solution, which is suitable for data with a high signal-to-noise ratio. For data with higher levels of noise, a maximum likelihood approximation is proposed, which is valid for unimodal Gaussian distributions (i.e., Gaussian noise for a system with a unique stable equilibrium point). Finally, a solution based on regularized least squares is provided, which promotes sparsity in the regression matrix.

2. Extended Dynamic Mode Decomposition

This section starts with an introduction to the traditional EDMD formulation to identify nonlinear models of dynamical systems. The procedure is exemplified by the Duffing equation, a benchmark problem in the literature for testing the reliability of the algorithm.

The core idea of the EDMD algorithm is to transform a nonlinear system into an augmented linear system. The first proponent of this idea was Takata [26], who describes the method as a formal linearization. Much later, the method emerged in its current form after the development of the dynamic mode decomposition algorithm [8] and its several extensions. In the following, the original EDMD algorithm [1] is first presented, followed by pq-EDMD, which makes use of orthogonal polynomials and order reduction based on p-q quasi-norm. This later version is particularly interesting as it yields increased numerical accuracy and systematic application.

2.1. The Basic EDMD Formulation

Consider as an example the unforced Duffing oscillator, which is a nonlinear spring that has different behaviors depending on the parameterization. The set of differential equations that govern this system is

$$\dot{x}_1 = x_2 \qquad (2)$$
$$\dot{x}_2 = -\delta x_2 - x_1(\alpha + \beta x_1^2). \qquad (3)$$

where state x_1 is the displacement, state x_2 is the velocity, α is the stiffness of the spring, which is related to the linear force of the spring according to Hooke's law, δ is the amount of damping in the system, and β is the proportion of nonlinearity present in the stiffness of the spring.

Figure 1 shows the phase plane of the system for three different sets of parameters and six random initial conditions (i.e., six initial conditions are generated randomly within the range ics $\in [-2, 2]^2$ starting from a known seed rng(1)). This choice of initial conditions produces an appropriate set of trajectories for calculating the approximation and testing its accuracy. The system of Equations (2) and (3) is integrated with a Matlab ODE solver, e.g., ode23s, and the results are collected at a constant sample period $\Delta t = 0.1$ s for a total of 20 s. The result of this numerical integration is a set of six trajectories of two state variables with 201 points per variable. Each of these trajectories is an element of a structure array in Matlab with the fields "Time" and "SV". The choice of a structure array instead of a tensor comes from the possibility of having trajectories of different lengths, e.g., experimental data of different lengths, a feature that becomes important in systems where having redundant data near the asymptotically stable attractors has a negative impact on the approximation.

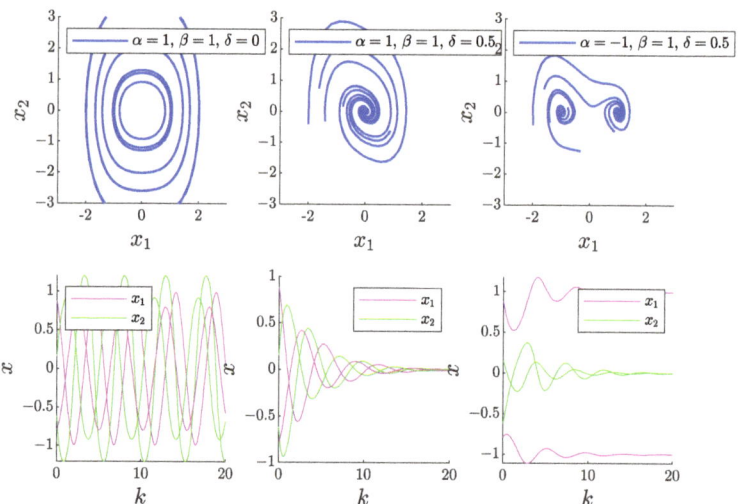

Figure 1. Orbits of the Duffing equation for different parameterizations. (**Left**): undamped, (**Center**): hard spring, (**Right**): soft spring, (**Top row**): phase plane, (**Bottom**): states versus time of two trajectories.

As the EDMD is a data-driven algorithm, certain trajectories serve as a training set while others serve as a testing set. The amount of data necessary to obtain an accurate approximation depends on the system under consideration as well as its information content (large data sets can bear little information content if experiments are not properly designed). The EDMD algorithm captures the dynamic of the system on the portion of the state space covered by the trajectories in the training set. Therefore, designing experiments that maximize the coverage of the state space can reduce the amount of data while having a positive effect on accuracy.

Each trajectory of the training set is in discrete-time, i.e., $x(k+1) = T(x(k))$, where $x \in \mathbb{R}^n$ are the states of the system, $k \in \mathbb{Z}_0^+$ is the non-negative discrete time, and $T: \mathbb{R}^n \to \mathbb{R}^n$ is an unknown nonlinear mapping that provides the evolution of the discrete-time trajectories. To construct the database, the training trajectories are organized in so-called snapshot pairs $\{(x_i, y_i)\}_{i=1}^N$, where $y_i = T(x_i)$. The snapshots function presented in Listing 1 handles the available trajectories, dividing them into training and testing sets of the appropriate type; the training set consists of matrices containing the x and y data, while the testing set is a cell array containing one orbit per index of the cell. The choice of cell arrays instead of a tensor is to offer the possibility of testing trajectories of different lengths. The tr_ts argument is a Matlab structure containing the indexes of the original set of orbits, which serve as the training and testing sets. The fields of this structure must be tr_index and ts_index, respectively. In addition, there is a normalization flag to use when necessary, e.g., when the order of magnitude of different states is dissimilar.

Listing 1. Function *snapshots* used to create the data pairs for training and testing.

```matlab
function [xtr, ytr, xts, yts, center, scale] = snapshots(
    system, tr_ts, normalization)
% Number of trajectories from the system to populate the
% snapshots
training_number = numel(tr_ts.tr_index);
% First, store the snapshots in a cell
[xtr_cell, ytr_cell] = deal(cell(training_number,1));
for trj = 1 : training_number
    % Extract the appropriate data points for x and y
    xtr_cell{trj} = system(tr_ts.tr_index(trj)).SV(1:end
        -2,:);
    ytr_cell{trj} = system(tr_ts.tr_index(trj)).SV(2:end
        -1,:);
end
% Turn cells into a matrix
xtr = cell2mat(xtr_cell);
ytr = cell2mat(ytr_cell);
% Normalize if necessary
if normalization
    [xtr,center,scale] = normalize(xtr,``zscore'');
    ytr = normalize(ytr,'center',center,'scale',scale);
else
    center = zeros(1, size(xtr,2));
    scale = ones(1, size(xtr,2));
end
% For the test trajectories, we need each of them in a
% differerent cell because we want to compare the whole
% trajectory based on the initial condition
testing_number = numel(tr_ts.ts_index);
[xts, yts] = deal(cell(testing_number,1));
for trj = 1 : testing_number
    xts{trj} = normalize(system(tr_ts.ts_index(trj)).SV(1:
        end-2,:), ...
        'center',center(1:size(system(tr_ts.ts_index(trj)).
        SV,2)), ...
        'scale',scale(1:size(system(tr_ts.ts_index(trj)).SV
        ,2)));
    yts{trj} = normalize(system(tr_ts.ts_index(trj)).SV(2:
        end-1,:), ...
        'center',center(1:size(system(tr_ts.ts_index(trj)).
        SV,2)), ...
        'scale',scale(1:size(system(tr_ts.ts_index(trj)).SV
        ,2)));
end
end
```

Notice that the generation of the snapshots avoids the last element in each trajectory, SV(1:end-2) for x and SV(2:end-1) for y. As stated before, avoiding redundant data at the asymptotically stable attractors improves the performance of the algorithm. In Matlab, stopping the simulation early, e.g., as convergence towards the attractor has been achieved, causes the last output interval $\Delta t \neq 0.1$. This small difference can increase the error in the construction of the approximation. Conversely, if the numerical integration of the system is not stopped near the steady state, it is not necessary to eliminate the last element in the trajectories.

The next step in the development of the EDMD is the definition of the observable space as a set of functions $f_i(x)\colon \mathbb{R}^n \to \mathbb{C}$ for $i = 1, \ldots, d$, which represent a transformation from the state space into an arbitrary function space. This transformation of the state is equivalent to a change of variables $z = f(x)$, where $z \in \mathbb{C}^d$. In the Matlab library, the observables are described by orthogonal polynomials, where each element of the set of observables is the tensor product of n univariate polynomials up to order $p \in \mathbb{N}_+$. For example, in the Duffing oscillator, a set of observables with $p = 2$ and a Hermite basis of orthogonal polynomials is provided by

$$f(x) = \begin{bmatrix} 1 & 2x_1 & 4x_1^2 - 2 \\ 2x_2 & 4x_1 x_2 & 2x_2(4x_1^2 - 2) \\ 4x_2^2 - 2 & 2x_1(4x_2^2 - 2) & (4x_1^2 - 2)(4x_2^2 - 2) \end{bmatrix}^\top. \quad (4)$$

Note that the first entry is the product of a zero-order polynomial in both of the state variables; the orders of the polynomial basis in the two state variables can be summarized by

$$\begin{array}{l} x_1\colon\ 0\ 1\ 2\ 0\ 1\ 2\ 0\ 1\ 2 \\ x_2\colon\ 0\ 0\ 0\ 1\ 1\ 1\ 2\ 2\ 2 \end{array} \quad (5)$$

making the generation of observables a problem of accurately handling indexes. Notice that the full basis of indexes (5) is equivalent to counting numbers on a $p+1$ basis with n significant figures. From such a set of indexes, a method to generate a set of observables with a Hermite base is proposed in Listing 2.

Listing 2. Generation of a set of observables with a Hermite basis.

```
% Generate the matrix p of indexes
hpm = flip(dec2base(0:(p+1)^n - 1, p+1) - '0',2)'
% Create an array of symbolic variables for the state
xsym = sym('x',[1 n],'real');
% Preallocate the matrix of symbolic variables
sym_univariate = sym(ones(size(hpm)));
% Loop over the state variables to assign the polynomial
% according to the order and variable
for state_variable = 1 : n
  sym_univariate(state_variable,1:end) = hermiteH(hpm(
      state_variable,1:end), xsym(state_variable));
end
base = prod(sym_univariate,1);
% The function omits the intercept (first element).
% Otherwise, the evaluation of the whole training matrix
% is not possible at once, and the calculation should be
% achieved in a loop.
f = matlabFunction(base(2:end),'var',{xsym})
```

The function f can evaluate the complete set of training trajectories at once with the omission of the first observable that corresponds to the intercept or constant value (the consideration of this observable would require another programming strategy involving loops, resulting in higher computational time and memory allocation). Notice the versatility of using orthogonal polynomials, as the whole realm of available orthogonal polynomials in Matlab is a valid choice, e.g., Laguerre, Legendre, Jacobi, etc. Note that the code snippet defines the function of observables as a row vector, instead of the column vector notation in the theoretical descriptions.

After the observables have been defined, their time evolution can be computed according to

$$f(x(k+1)) = Uf(x(k)) + r(x), \qquad (6)$$

where $U \in \mathbb{R}^{d \times d}$ is the matrix that provides the linear evolution of the observables and $r(x)$ is the error in the approximation. One of the main advantages of the EDMD algorithm resides in the fact that the system description is linear in the function space. The solution to (6) is the matrix U that minimizes the residual term $r(x)$, which can be expressed as a least-squares criterion:

$$l(x,y) = \frac{1}{N} \sum_{i=1}^{N} \frac{1}{2} \| f(y_i) - Uf(x_i) \|_2^2, \qquad (7)$$

where N is the total number of samples in the training set. The ordinary least-squares (OLS) solution is provided by

$$U = A/G, \qquad (8)$$

where the A/G notation replaces the inverse of the design matrix G, as even when using a basis formed by the products of orthogonal polynomials, the design matrix can be close to ill-conditioned (i.e., close to singular). This notation, particularly in Matlab, specifies that a more robust algorithm compared to the inverse or pseudo-inverse is necessary to obtain the approximation.

For the solution of (8), the matrices $G, A \in \mathbb{R}^{d \times d}$ are defined by

$$G = \frac{1}{N} f(x) f(x)^\top \qquad (9)$$

$$A = \frac{1}{N} f(x) f(y)^\top. \qquad (10)$$

Setting the observables as products of univariate orthogonal polynomials is an improvement, as it generally avoids the need to use a pseudo-inverse approach. Even though the sequence of polynomials in the set of observables is no longer orthogonal, it is less likely to have co-linear columns in the design matrix, improving the numerical stability of the solution. With the training set and the observables, the method for calculating the regression matrix U is shown in Listing 3. Notice that this code defines and uses all the arrays as their transpose. This change is related to the approximation of the Koopman operator, where it is necessary to calculate the right and left eigenvectors of U. The eigenfunctions of the Koopman operator are determined from the left eigenvectors of the spectral decomposition. In Matlab, the left eigenvectors result from additional algebraic manipulations of the right eigenvectors and the diagonal matrix of eigenvalues, thereby decreasing the numerical precision of the eigenfunctions. This problem is alleviated by computing $U^\top$ and its spectral decomposition so that the left eigenvectors are immediately available. In general, if U is a normal matrix (diagonalizable), the additional steps involve the inverse of the right eigenvectors to obtain the left eigenvectors and the calculation of this inverse, considering again that the problem is close to being ill-conditioned, which reduces the accuracy of the eigenfunctions.

Listing 3. Computation of the approximate Koopman operator for an OLS problem.

```
function u = getU(f, X, Y)
%GETU produces the U matrix of the decomposition

% Evaluate the snapshots with the f functions of the
% observables
x_eval = [ones(size(X,1),1), f(X)];
y_eval = [ones(size(Y,1),1), f(Y)];
% Calculates the G and A matrices
g = (x_eval'*x_eval)*(1/size(X,1));
a = (x_eval'*y_eval)*(1/size(Y,1));
% Notice that this returns the transpose
% of u
u = g\a;
end
```

Numerical Results with EDMD

Here, the EDMD algorithm is tested with the second case scenario for the Duffing oscillator with hard damping. The EDMD algorithm can capture the dynamics of the portion of the state space covered by the training set, which is therefore selected as the outermost trajectory in Figure 2. The five remaining trajectories are used for testing. Table 1 provides the parameters of the original EDMD algorithm.

Table 1. Approximation parameters for the hard spring Duffing oscillator.

Parameter	Value
α	1
β	1
δ	0.5
ics	4*rand(6,2)-2;
final_time	20
n_points	201
solver	ode23s
tr_idex	3
ts_index	[1 2 4 5 6]
polynomial	laguerreL
N	199
p	4
observables	25
testing error	6.1370×10^{-05}

In Figure 2, the graph on the left displays the phase plane of the system and shows the training trajectory and testing trajectories along with their approximation by the EDMD algorithm with the Laguerre polynomial basis. EDMD achieves a good approximation while using only a small amount of data. However, notice that the discrete-time approximation of a system of order 2 is of dimension twenty-five. In view of this dimensionality explosion with regard to the original dimension of the state and the complexity of the system, it is necessary to introduce reduction techniques that decrease the necessary number of observables to increase the accuracy of the algorithm [24].

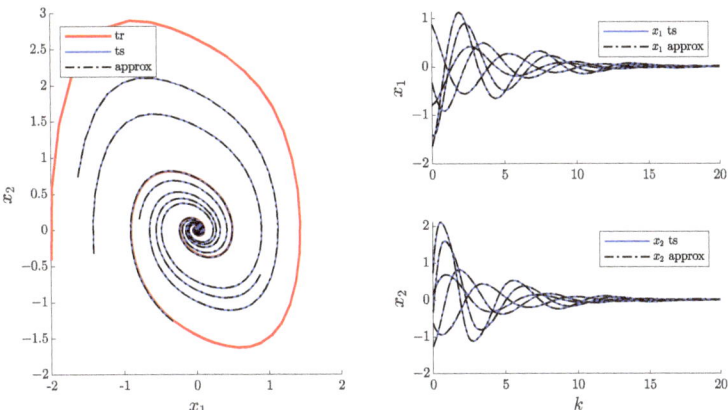

Figure 2. EDMD approximation of the hard damping Duffing oscillator.

2.2. pqEDMD Algorithm

The extension of the EDMD algorithm is a result of speculation on the good performance of the original algorithm when coupled with a set of observables based on products of univariate-orthogonal polynomials. The idea is to introduce a reduction method, based on p-q quasi-norms, first introduced by Konakli and Sudret [27] for fault detection in polynomial chaos problems. The reduction proceeds in the following way: if the q-quasi-norm of the indexes that provide the order of the univariate-orthogonal polynomials is less than the maximum order p of a particular observer, then this observer is eliminated from the set. To implement this procedure, the orders of an observer are defined as α_i, and the q-quasi norm of these orders as

$$\|\alpha\|_q = \left(\sum_{i=1}^{n} \alpha_i^q\right)^{\frac{1}{q}}, \tag{11}$$

where $q \in \mathbb{R}_+$ and Equation (11) represent a norm only when q is an integer. When p is redefined as the maximum order of a particular multivariate polynomial instead of the maximum order of the univariate elements, the sets of polynomial orders that remain in the basis are those that satisfy

$$\alpha_i = \{\alpha \in \mathbb{N}^n \colon \|\alpha\|_q \leq p\}. \tag{12}$$

The code snippet used to generate a set of observables based on Laguerre polynomials with a maximum multivariate order $p = 4$ and a q-quasi-norm $q = 0.7$ is provided in Listing 4.

The reduction of the basis is not only dimensional, as the p-q quasi-norm reduction reduces the maximum order of the observables as well. As a rule of thumb (considering various application examples), the higher-order observables usually have a negative contribution to the accuracy of the solution.

Listing 4. Generation of a p-q-reduced set of observables with a Laguerre basis.

```
1  p=4;
2  n=2;
3  q=0.7;
4  % Generate the matrix p of indexes
5  hpm = flip(dec2base(0:(p+1)^n - 1, p+1) - '0',2)';
6  % Reduce the basis
7  orders = hpm(:,vecnorm(hpm,q)<=p);
8  % Create an array of symbolic variables for the state
9  xsym = sym('x',[1 n],'real');
10 % Preallocate the matrix of symbolic variables
11 xPsi = sym(ones(size(orders)));
12 % Loop over the state variables to assign the polynomial
13 % according to the order and variable
14 for state_variable = 1 : n
15     xPsi(state_variable,1:end) = laguerreL(orders(
           state_variable,1:end), xsym(state_variable));
16 end
17 base = prod(xPsi,1);
18 f = matlabFunction(base(2:end),'var',{xsym});
```

Numerical Results with the pqEDMD

The algorithm is now applied to the Duffing oscillator with soft damping. The pqEDMD algorithm can capture the dynamics of the two attractors provided that the training set has at least one trajectory that converges to each of them. Additionally, as is the case for the hard damping, each of these trajectories should be the outermost (see Figure 3). Table 2 lists the parameters of the pqEDMD algorithm.

Table 2. Approximation parameters for the soft spring Duffing oscillator.

Parameter	Value
α	−1
β	1
δ	0.5
ics	equal to hard spring
final_time	20
n_points	201
solver	ode23s
tr_idex	[1 3]
ts_index	[2 4 5 6]
polynomial	laguerreL
N	398
p	5
q	$\infty \to 1$
observables	$36 \to 21$
testing error	$2.3770 \times 10^{-4} \to 1.1464 \times 10^{-6}$

Even though the full basis achieves a low approximation error of 2.3770×10^{-4}, the reduction of the observables order reduces the empirical error by two orders of magnitude. Comparing the dimension of the full basis to the reduced one does not represent a large improvement. However, this result is due to the comparison between the best result after performing a sweep over several p-q values. Imposing lower p-q values on the approximation has the potential to provide smaller sets of observables while sacrificing accuracy.

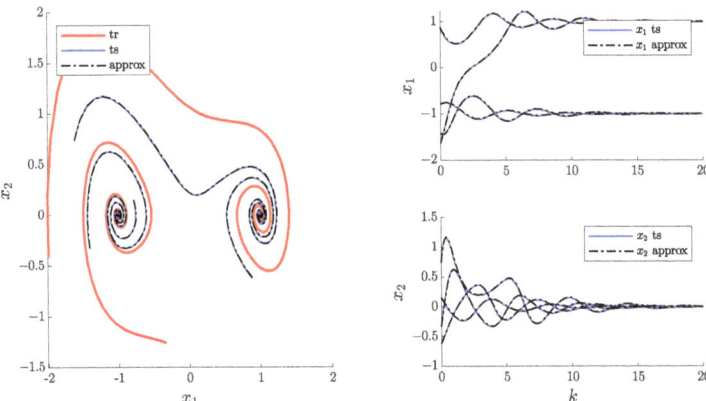

Figure 3. pqEDMD approximation for the soft damping Duffing oscillator.

Next, the first case scenario is considered; here, the damping parameter is zero and the system oscillates around the fixed point at the origin. The pqEDMD algorithm can capture the dynamics of the system if the innermost and outermost limit cycles compose the training set; otherwise, the algorithm cannot capture the dynamics. Table 3 shows a summary of the simulations along with the results; it is apparent that even though the empirical error is higher than in the other two case scenarios, the approximation is accurate (see Figure 4).

Table 3. Approximation parameters for the undamped Duffing oscillator.

Parameter	Value
α	1
β	1
δ	0
ics	same as hard spring
final_time	20
n_points	201
solver	ode23s
tr_idex	[3 4]
ts_index	[1 2 5 6]
polynomial	hermiteH
N	398
p	4
q	$\infty \to 1.1$
observables	$25 \to 15$
testing error	$0.1209 \to 0.0023$

The sweep over different p-q values provides a reduced basis with lower error than with the full basis.

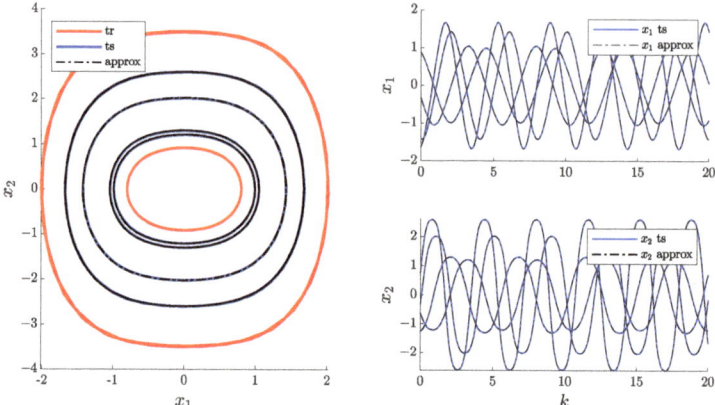

Figure 4. pqEDMD approximation for the undamped Duffing oscillator.

Even though p-q quasi-norm reduction produces more accurate and tractable solutions, having products of orthogonal univariate polynomials does not necessarily produce an orthogonal basis. In certain scenarios, the evaluation of the observables produces an ill-conditioned design matrix G. Therefore, the next section proposes a way to eliminate even more observables from the basis, improving the numerical stability of the solution.

2.3. Improving Numerical Stability via QR Decomposition

QR decomposition [28] can be used to improve the numerical stability and reduce the number of observables even further. If we assume that the design matrix $G \in \mathbb{R}^{d \times d}$ in Equation (9) is obtained based on the products of orthogonal polynomials and that there are no co-linear columns, or, in other words, that $\text{rank}(G) = d$ holds, then it is possible to decompose this matrix into the product

$$G = QR, \qquad (13)$$

where $Q \in \mathbb{R}^{d \times d}$ is orthogonal, i.e., $Q^\top Q = I_d$ and $R \in \mathbb{R}^{d \times d}$ is upper triangular. Column pivoting methods for QR decomposition rely on exchanging the rows of G such that in every step of the diagonalization of R and the subsequent calculation of the orthogonal columns of Q the procedure starts with a column that is as independent as possible from the columns of G already processed. This method yields a permutation matrix $P \in \mathbb{R}^{d \times d}$ such that

$$GP = QR, \qquad (14)$$

where the permutation of columns makes the absolute value of the diagonal elements in R non-increasing, i.e., $|r_{1,1}| \geq |r_{2,2}| \geq \cdots \geq |r_{d,d}|$. Furthermore, considering that the permutation process selects the most linearly independent column of G in every step of the process, the last columns in the analysis are the ones that are close to being co-linear. Therefore, eliminating the observable related to the last column improves the residual condition number of G. The modified function for the calculation of the regression matrix U is provided in Listing 5.

Listing 5. Computation of the regression matrix based on QR decomposition.

```matlab
function u = getU(obj, X, Y)
%GETU produces the U matrix of the decomposition

% Evaluate the snapshots with the f function of the
% observables (called psi in the following)
Psi = obj.VVFO.Psi;
x_eval = [ones(size(X,1),1), Psi(X)];
y_eval = [ones(size(Y,1),1), Psi(Y)];
% Calculates the G matrix
g = (x_eval'*x_eval)*(1/size(X,1));
% qr decomposition and elimination
% of near-co-linear observables
while rcond(g) <= eps
    [~,~,E] = qr(g,0);
    % Check that the last element is not an
    % order one polynomial, if it is,
    % shift the array
    while any(E(end)==find(sum(obj.VVFO.polynomials_order)==1))
        E = circshift(E,1);
    end
    % Eliminate the observable correspondint to the last
        element
    % of E
    obj.VVFO.polynomials_order = obj.VVFO.polynomials_order(:,sort(E(1:end-1)));
    % Get the observables matlabFunction updated
    Psi = obj.VVFO.Psi;
    % Evaluate again
    if all(~logical(obj.VVFO.polynomials_order(:,1)))
        x_eval = [ones(size(X,1),1), Psi(X)];
        y_eval = [ones(size(Y,1),1), Psi(Y)];
    else
        x_eval = Psi(X);
        y_eval = Psi(Y);
    end
    g = (x_eval'*x_eval)*(1/size(X,1));
end
a = (x_eval'*y_eval)*(1/size(Y,1));

% This returns the transpose of U because it avoids
% numerical errors if it is considered as a Koopman
    operator
% and the espectral decomposition is necessary
u = g\a;
end
```

In addition, the code snippet shows particular aspects of the overall solution. First, an object containing the observables, i.e., the matlabFunction obj.VVFO.Psi, replaces the original matlabFunction f for the evaluation of the snapshots. Second, note that the exclusion of observables avoids the elimination of the first order univariate polynomials in the basis, as they are used to recover the state. Finally, the method checks for the existence of the constant observable or the intercept, as it could be eliminated due to being close to co-linear with another observable, which we obviously do not want to happen.

2.4. Matlab Package

pqEDMD() is the main class of the Matlab package that provides an array of decompositions based on the pqEDMD algorithm pqEDMD_array. The cardinality of the array of solutions may be less than the product of the cardinality of p and q, as certain p-q pairs produce the same set of indices, i.e., the algorithm would compute the same decomposition more than once. In addition, it calculates the empirical error of the approximations based on the test set and returns the best-performing approximation from the array as a separate attribute best_pqEDMD. The code provides the complete set of solutions, as a user may opt to use a compact solution that is not as accurate as the best one for tractability reasons, e.g., an MPC controller, where a smaller basis guarantees feasibility for longer horizons and has a lower computational cost.

The only required input for pqEDMD() is the system argument, where it is necessary to provide a structure array with the Time and SV fields with at least two trajectories in the array, one for training and one for testing. The remaining arguments are optional, e.g., the array of positive-integer values p, the array of positive values q, the structure of training and testing trajectories with the fields tr_index and ts_index, the string specifying the type of polynomial, the array of polynomial parameters (if the polynomial type is either "Jacobi" or "Gegenbauer"), the boolean flag of normalization, and the string indicating the decomposition method. For example, Listing 6 shows a call to the algorithm with a complete set of arguments.

Listing 6. Complete call to the pqEDMD algorithm.

```
pqEDMD(system, [3 4 5], [0.2 0.5 0.7 inf],...
    'polynomial','Jacobi','polyParam',[2 3],'method','OLS
    ',...
    'tr_ts',struct('tr_index',tr_index,'ts_index',
    ts_index),...
    'normalization',false);
```

To provide the different approximations in the main class, pqVVFO() handles the observables for different values of p, q, and the polynomial type. Its output is the matrix of polynomial indexes, a symbolic vector of observable functions, and a matlabFunction Psi to evaluate the observables arithmetically and efficiently; it accepts a matrix of values, avoiding evaluation with loops.

The remaining classes are the implementations of different decompositions based on different algorithms. The ExtendedDecomposition() is the traditional least-squares method described in this article. In addition, there are two additional available decompositions. MaxLikeDecomposition() is used for data with noise, where the maximum likelihood algorithm assumes that the transformation of the states in the function space preserves a unimodal Gaussian distribution of the noise in the state space (this is a work in progress; preliminary results can be found in [29]). These properties of the distribution of noise in the function space are a strong assumption; nonetheless, it is sometimes possible to identify dynamical systems corrupted with noise. The last decomposition leverages the advantages of regularized lasso regression to produce sparse solutions, i.e., RegularizedDecomposition(). Even though the solutions are more tractable, the regularized method sacrifices accuracy.

Figure 5 shows the architecture of the solution with the relationship between classes. The current functionality requires the user to call pqEDMD() with the appropriate inputs and options in order to obtain an array of decompositions. This class handles the creation of the necessary pqVVFO() objects to feed into the required decomposition. It is possible to use and extend the observable class to use in other types of decompositions without the use of the main class. The code is available for download in the Supplementary Materials section of this paper.

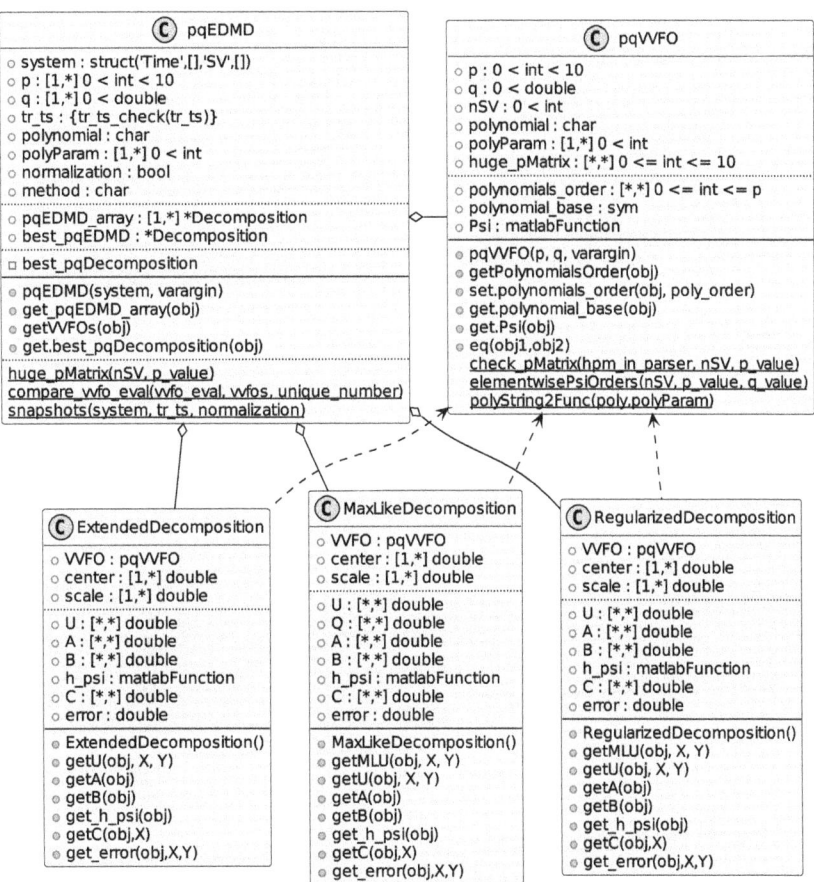

Figure 5. Package architecture.

3. An Additional Application Example

To conclude this article, an additional case study is discussed involving a set of reactions occurring in a continuously stirred tank reactor, described by

$$s_1 + 2s_3 \xrightarrow{r_1} s_2 + 3s_3$$
$$s_2 + 2s_4 \xrightarrow{r_2} 3s_4 \quad (15)$$
$$s_3 \xrightarrow{r_3} s_5$$
$$s_4 \xrightarrow{r_4} s_5$$

where there are two types of substrate, s_1 and s_2. The first substrate is the only component in the inflow, and is the only component necessary for the replication of the first species s_3 according to the replication rate constant r_1. In addition to the replication of s_3, the product of the first reaction is the second substrate s_2, which in turn is necessary for the replication of the second species s_4 according to the replication rate constant r_2. The remaining variable s_5 is the combination of the dead species from the two groups, where each group dies according to the reaction rates r_3 and r_4, respectively. The ordinary differential equations that describe the dynamics of network (15) according to the polynomial formulation of mass action kinetics [30] and the material exchange with the environment are provided by

$$\begin{aligned}
\dot{x}_1 &= -r_1 x_1 x_3^2 + d - dx_1 \\
\dot{x}_2 &= +r_1 x_1 x_3^2 - r_2 x_2 x_4^2 - dx_2 \\
\dot{x}_3 &= +r_1 x_1 x_3^2 - r_3 x_3 - dx_3 \\
\dot{x}_4 &= +r_2 x_2 x_4^2 - r_4 x_4 - dx_4 \\
\dot{x}_5 &= +r_3 x_3 + r_4 x_4 - dx_5,
\end{aligned} \qquad (16)$$

where $d = 0.5$ is the in/out-flow (dilution rate) of the system and the values for the reaction rates are $r = [7\ 5\ 0.3\ 0.05]^\top$. With these rate constants, the system has three asymptotically stable points: the working point, where the two species s_3 and s_4 coexist, a point where species s_3 thrives and species s_4 washes out, and a wash-out point, where the concentration of both species vanishes. To construct the database, the strategy is to generate a set of orbits with an even distribution of initial conditions converging to each of the equilibrium points. Certain trajectories converging to each point are used as the training set to produce a linear expanded approximation of the system.

The set of orbits is taken from the numerical integration of the ODE (16) via the ode23s method with an output sampling $\Delta t = 0.1$ for an arbitrary number of initial conditions until the full set of orbits has a total of 20 trajectories that converge to each point, resulting in 60 trajectories in total for the execution of the algorithm.

From each of the sets of orbits that converge to the fixed points, 50% are used for the approximation and the remaining for testing the solution. It is important to have a training set with sufficient information about the trajectories of the system, and in a similar way as for the second and third scenarios of the Duffing equation, to select the trajectories that are far away from the equilibrium point. For system (16), the choice of trajectories for the training set are the ten trajectories that at any given time are furthest away from the equilibrium point to which they converge. Figure 6 shows a selection of training and testing trajectories.

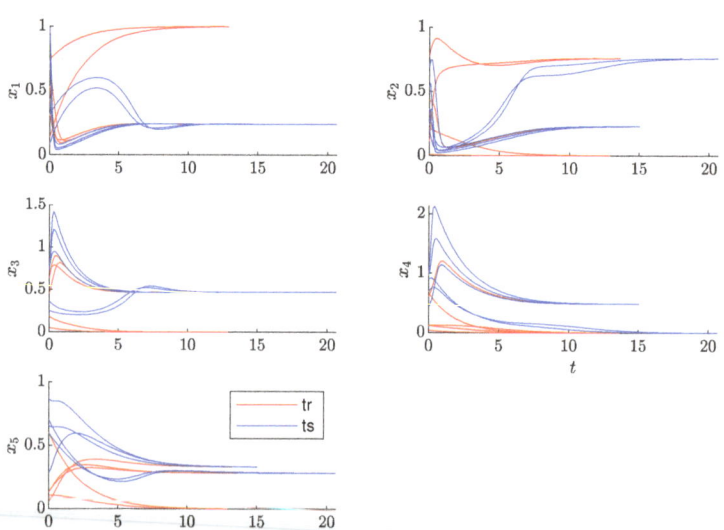

Figure 6. Training and testing trajectories of the biochemical reaction system.

Assuming that the orbits of the system are in a structure array with the appropriate fields named system and that the training and testing indexes for the approximation have been carefully selected and placed in a structure named tr_ts, the call to the pqEDMD() class that provides an accurate approximation is shown in Listing 7, where the solution is obtained through the default decomposition method (ordinary least squares), the default polynomial type (Legendre), and without normalization.

Listing 7. Class call to approximate the reaction network dynamics.

```
% the pqEDMD!!!
p = [3 4 5];
q = [0.5 0.7 0.9];
mak_net_approx = pqEDMD(system,p,q,'tr_ts',tr_ts);
```

Table 4 shows a summary of the simulation parameters used to generate the orbits and to obtain the approximation. The clear advantage of using the reduction method lies in the comparison between the full basis of polynomials, i.e., from 3125 observables for $p = 4$ and a system of five state variables to a basis of 51 polynomials for $q = 0.7$. Although the computation with a full basis is computationally intensive, it leads to a solution that is not satisfactory, as the state matrix is not Hurwitz and the trajectories diverge, leading to a result with an infinite error metric.

Figure 7 depicts the comparison of several testing trajectories with their corresponding approximations. It is clear that certain trajectories converge to a different fixed point than the one they are supposed to. This phenomenon causes the empirical error grow while remaining bounded. The reason for this behavior is the lack of training trajectories near the boundary of the attraction regions of the asymptotically stable equilibrium points. For better performance of the algorithm in terms of the number of orbits necessary for the approximation, and possibly the dimension of the observable basis, an experimental design procedure is required.

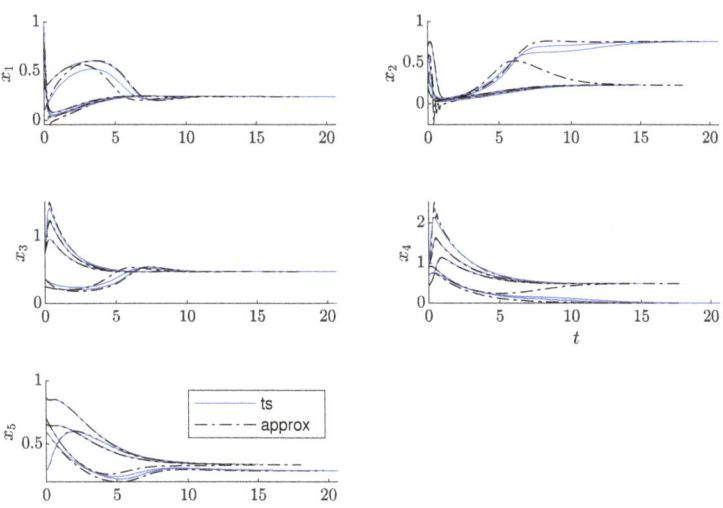

Figure 7. Comparison between the testing and approximation trajectories of the biochemical reaction system.

Table 4. Approximation parameters for the reaction network.

Parameter	Value
r_1	7
r_2	5
r_3	0.3
r_4	0.05
ics	20 per x^*
final_time	stoped when converges
delta_t	0.1
solver	ode15s
tr_idex	max(vecnorm(SV-x_ast))
ts_index	~tr_index
polynomial	Laguerre
N	3874
p	4
q	$\infty \to 0.7$
observables	$3125 \to 51$
testing error	$\infty \to 12.94$

4. Conclusions

This paper presents a methodology to derive discrete-time approximations of nonlinear dynamical systems via the pqEDMD algorithm and proposes a Matlab library that can hopefully help popularize the use of the method by non-expert users. The discussion of the methodology and codes is illustrated with several case studies related to the Duffing oscillator and by an example involving a biochemical reaction network.

Supplementary Materials: The following supporting information can be downloaded at: https://www.mdpi.com/article/10.3390/math10203859/s1. A Matlab library is readily available in the Supplementary Materials.

Author Contributions: Conceptualization, C.G.-T. and A.V.W.; methodology, C.G.-T. and A.V.W.; software, C.G.-T.; writing—review and editing, C.G.-T. and A.V.W. All authors have read and agreed to the published version of the manuscript.

Funding: This research received no external funding.

Data Availability Statement: Not applicable.

Conflicts of Interest: The authors declare no conflict of interest.

References

1. Williams, M.O.; Kevrekidis, I.G.; Rowley, C.W. A Data-Driven Approximation of the Koopman Operator: Extending Dynamic Mode Decomposition. *J. Nonlinear Sci.* **2015**, *25*, 1307–1346. [CrossRef]
2. Ljung, L. *System Identification: Theory for the User*, 2nd ed.; Prentice Hall: Hoboken, NJ, USA, 1999.
3. John, L.; Crassidis, J.L.J. *Optimal Estimation of Dynamic Systems*, 1st ed.; Chapman & Hall/CRC Applied Mathematics & Nonlinear Science; Chapman and Hall/CRC: Boca Raton, FL, USA, 2004.
4. Penny, W.; Harrison, L. CHAPTER 40—Multivariate autoregressive models. In *Statistical Parametric Mapping*; Friston, K., Ashburner, J., Kiebel, S., Nichols, T., Penny, W., Eds.; Academic Press: London, UK, 2007; pp. 534–540.
5. Roger, G.; Ghanem, P.D.S. *Stochastic Finite Elements: A Spectral Approach*, Revised ed.; Dover Publications: Mineola, NY, USA, 2003.
6. Stewart, G.W. On the Early History of the Singular Value Decomposition. *SIAM Rev.* **1993**, *35*, 551–566. [CrossRef]
7. Chatterjee, A. An introduction to the proper orthogonal decomposition. *Curr. Sci.* **2000**, *78*, 808–817.
8. Schmid, P.J. Dynamic mode decomposition of numerical and experimental data. *J. Fluid Mech.* **2010**, *656*, 5–28. [CrossRef]
9. Mezić, I. Spectral Properties of Dynamical Systems, Model Reduction and Decompositions. *Nonlinear Dyn.* **2005**, *41*, 309–325. [CrossRef]
10. Mezić, I.; Mezi, I. On applications of the spectral theory of the Koopman operator in dynamical systems and control theory. In Proceedings of the 2015 54th IEEE Conference on Decision and Control (CDC), Osaka, Japan, 16–18 December 2015; pp. 7034–7041.
11. Mezic, I.; Surana, A. Koopman Mode Decomposition for Periodic/Quasi-periodic Time Dependence—The funding provided by UTRC is greatly appreciated. *IFAC-PapersOnLine* **2016**, *49*, 690–697. [CrossRef]

12. Koopman, B.O. Hamiltonian Systems and Transformation in Hilbert Space. *Proc. Natl. Acad. Sci. USA* **1931**, *17*, 315–318. [CrossRef]
13. Mauroy, A.; Mezić, I. A spectral operator-theoretic framework for global stability. In Proceedings of the 52nd IEEE Conference on Decision and Control, Firenze, Italy, 10–13 December 2013; pp. 5234–5239.
14. Mauroy, A.; Mezic, I. Global Stability Analysis Using the Eigenfunctions of the Koopman Operator. *IEEE Trans. Autom. Control* **2016**, *61*, 3356–3369. [CrossRef]
15. Garcia-Tenorio, C.; Tellez-Castro, D.; Mojica-Nava, E.; Vande Wouwer, A. Evaluation of the Region of Attractions of Higher Dimensional Hyperbolic Systems using the Extended Dynamic Mode Decomposition. *arXiv* **2022**, arXiv:2209.02028.
16. Brunton, S.L.; Brunton, B.W.; Proctor, J.L.; Kutz, J.N. Koopman invariant subspaces and finite linear representations of nonlinear dynamical systems for control. *PLoS ONE* **2016**, *11*, e0150171. [CrossRef]
17. Korda, M.; Mezić, I. Linear predictors for nonlinear dynamical systems: Koopman operator meets model predictive control. *Automatica* **2018**, *93*, 149–160. [CrossRef]
18. Tellez-Castro, D.; Garcia-Tenorio, C.; Mojica-Nava, E.; Sofrony, J.; Vande Wouwer, A. Data-Driven Predictive Control of Interconnected Systems Using the Koopman Operator. *Actuators* **2022**, *11*, 151. [CrossRef]
19. Garcia-Tenorio, C.; Vande Wouwer, A. Extended Predictive Control of Interconnected Oscillators. In Proceedings of the 2022 8th International Conference on Control, Decision and Information Technologies (CoDIT), Istanbul, Turkey, 17–20 May 2022; Volume 1, pp. 15–20.
20. Williams, M.O.; Rowley, C.W.; Kevrekidis, I.G. A kernel-based method for data-driven koopman spectral analysis. *J. Comput. Dyn.* **2016**, *2*, 247–265. [CrossRef]
21. Kaiser, E.; Kutz, J.N.; Brunton, S.L. Sparse identification of nonlinear dynamics for model predictive control in the low-data limit. *Proc. R. Soc. A Math. Phys. Eng. Sci.* **2018**, *474*, 20180335. [CrossRef] [PubMed]
22. Li, Q.; Dietrich, F.; Bollt, E.M.; Kevrekidis, I.G. Extended dynamic mode decomposition with dictionary learning: A data-driven adaptive spectral decomposition of the Koopman operator. *Chaos Interdiscip. J. Nonlinear Sci.* **2017**, *27*, 103111. [CrossRef]
23. Proctor, J.L.; Brunton, S.L.; Kutz, J.N. Dynamic Mode Decomposition with Control. *SIAM J. Appl. Dyn. Syst.* **2016**, *15*, 142–161. [CrossRef]
24. Garcia-Tenorio, C.; Delansnay, G.; Mojica-Nava, E.; Vande Wouwer, A. Trigonometric Embeddings in Polynomial Extended Mode Decomposition—Experimental Application to an Inverted Pendulum. *Mathematics* **2021**, *9*, 1119. [CrossRef]
25. Garcia-Tenorio, C.; Mojica-Nava, E.; Sbarciog, M.; Vande Wouwer, A. Analysis of the ROA of an anaerobic digestion process via data-driven Koopman operator. *Nonlinear Eng.* **2021**, *10*, 109–131. [CrossRef]
26. Takata, H. Transformation of a nonlinear system into an augmented linear system. *IEEE Trans. Autom. Control* **1979**, *24*, 736–741. [CrossRef]
27. Konakli, K.; Sudret, B. Polynomial meta-models with canonical low-rank approximations: Numerical insights and comparison to sparse polynomial chaos expansions. *J. Comput. Phys.* **2016**, *321*, 1144–1169. [CrossRef]
28. Gander, W. Algorithms for the QR decomposition. *Res. Rep* **1980**, *80*, 1251–1268.
29. Garcia-Tenorio, C.; Vande Wouwer, A. Maximum Likelihood pqEDMD Identification. In Proceedings of the 26th International Conference on System Theory, Control and Computing 2022 (ICSTCC), Sinaia, Romania, 19–21 October 2022.
30. Chellaboina, V.; Bhat, S.P.; Haddad, W.M.; Bernstein, D.S. Modeling and analysis of mass-action kinetics. *IEEE Control Syst. Mag.* **2009**, *29*, 60–78.

Review

Towards the Centenary of Sheffer Polynomial Sequences: Old and Recent Results

Francesco Aldo Costabile, Maria Italia Gualtieri * and Anna Napoli

Department of Mathematics and Computer Science, University of Calabria, 87036 Rende, CS, Italy
* Correspondence: mariaitalia.gualtieri@unical.it

Abstract: Sheffer's work is about to turn 100 years after its publication. In reporting this important event, we recall some interesting old and recent results, aware of the incompleteness of the wide existing literature. Particularly, we recall Sheffer's approach, the theory of Rota and his collaborators, the isomorphism between the group of Sheffer polynomial sequences and the so-called Riordan matrices group. This inspired the most recent approaches based on elementary matrix calculus. The interesting problem of orthogonality in the context of Sheffer sequences is also reported, recalling the results of Sheffer, Meixner, Shohat, and the very recent one of Galiffa et al., and of Costabile et al.

Keywords: sheffer sequence; recurrence relation; polynomial sequences; generating functions; umbral calculus

MSC: 11B37; 11B83; 05A40; 05E35

Citation: Costabile, F.A.; Gualtieri, M.I.; Napoli, A. Towards the Centenary of Sheffer Polynomial Sequences: Old and Recent Results. *Mathematics* 2022, *10*, 4435. https://doi.org/10.3390/math10234435

Academic Editor: Valery Karachik

Received: 6 October 2022
Accepted: 21 November 2022
Published: 24 November 2022

Publisher's Note: MDPI stays neutral with regard to jurisdictional claims in published maps and institutional affiliations.

Copyright: © 2022 by the authors. Licensee MDPI, Basel, Switzerland. This article is an open access article distributed under the terms and conditions of the Creative Commons Attribution (CC BY) license (https://creativecommons.org/licenses/by/4.0/).

1. Introduction

I.M. Sheffer's 1939 seminal work [1] was inspired by Pincherle's paper [2] on the study of the difference equation

$$\sum_{n=1}^{k} c_n \phi(x + h_n) = f(x). \tag{1}$$

For the solution of this equation, Pincherle considered a set of Appell [3] polynomials, and wrote the solutions as an infinite series of them.

Previously, in 1936, Sheffer [4] had studied the solution of the same equation by means of a different Appell set. In [5] he treated the more general equation

$$L[y(x)] := a_0 y(x) + a_1 y'(x) + \cdots = f(x),$$

and found a solution, under suitable conditions on L and f. As a tribute to Sheffer, we reproduce part of his introduction in full.

"Here, too, it was possible to relate the equation to a corresponding problem of expanding functions in series of Appell polynomials.

As is well known, Appell sets $\{P_n\}_{n \in \mathbb{N}}$ are characterized by one of the equivalent conditions

$$P'_n(x) = P_{n-1}(x), \quad (P_n \text{ a polynomial of degree } n); \tag{2}$$

$$A(t)e^{xt} = \sum_{n=0}^{\infty} P_n(x)t^n, \tag{3}$$

where $A(t) = \sum_{n=0}^{\infty} a_n t^n$ is a formal power series, and where the product on the left of (3) is formally extended in a power series in accordance with the Cauchy rule. We shall say that the series $A(t)$ is the *determining series* for the set $\{P_n\}_{n \in \mathbb{N}}$.

For the particular equation

$$y(x+1) - y(x) = f(x),$$

Pincherle used the Appell set with $A(t) = \frac{1}{e^t-1}$, getting essentially the Bernoulli polynomials.

We used $A(t) = e^t - 1$, so that $n! P_n(x) = (x+1)^n - x^n$.

Now this equation is also associated with the important set of Newton polynomials

$$N_0(x) = 1, \quad N_n(x) = \frac{x(x-1)\cdots(x-n+1)}{n!}, \quad n \geq 1,$$

which is not an Appell set. Yet, it has properties analogous to those ((2) and (3)) of Appell polynomials. In fact,

$$\Delta N_n(x) := N_n(x+1) - N_n(x) = N_{n-1}(x),$$

$$(1+t)^x = 1 \cdot e^{x \log(1+t)} = \sum_{n=0}^{\infty} N_n(x) t^n.$$

It is thus suggested that we define a class of difference polynomial sets, of which $\{N_n\}_{n \in \mathbb{N}}$ is a particular set, by means of the relations

$$\Delta P_n(x) = P_{n-1}(x), \quad n \geq 0.$$

And more generally, we can use other operators than $\frac{d}{dx}$ and Δ, to define further sets. We thus obtain all polynomial sets of *type zero* (as we denote them). The definition of sets of type zero generalizes readily to give sets of type one, two, ... and of infinite type" [1].

After the publicaton of Sheffer's paper [1], a wide class of related works have been written, many of which are quite recent. Some of these works also develope a basic-type of characterization and relationship by modern umbral calculus (see for example [6–16]).

Other papers contains applications in various disciplines. For example:

- probability theory [17–22];
- number theory [23,24];
- linear recurrence [7,25];
- general linear interpolation [26–29];
- operators approximation theory [29–34];
- specific A-type zero orthogonal polynomial sequences [35–47];
- extension of Sheffer sequences also in the multidimensional case [48,49].

Moreover we point out that a sufficiently comprehensive bibliography up to 1995 is in [50].

According to Galiffa et al. [51] "Indeed, research on the Sheffer sequence is an active area and important in its own right".

The present paper is structured in two parts and in six main Sections, some of which contain subsections:

- Part 1: 1939–2000
  - Section 2: Sheffer's approach
  - Section 3: Rota's et al. contributions
- Part 2: 2001–2022
  - Section 4: The Riordan group and the Sheffer group
  - Section 5: Elementary matrix calculus approach to umbral calculus
  - Section 6: Sheffer A-type zero orthogonal polynomial sequences
  - Section 7: Relationship between Sheffer A-type zero sequences and monomiality principle.

We will use the following notations, unless otherwise specified:

- $\mathcal{P}$ is the set of polynomials in the variable $x \in \mathbb{K}$ (usually $\mathbb{R}$ or $\mathbb{C}$); for any $n \in \mathbb{N}$, $\mathcal{P}_n$ is the set of polynomials of degree $\leq n$;
- $\{p_n\}_{n \in \mathbb{N}}$ is a polynomial sequence (p.s.), that is, for any $n \in \mathbb{N}$, p_n is a polynomial of degree exactly n;
- $(a_i)_{i \in \mathbb{N}}$ is a numerical sequence with elements a_i;
- $A = (a_{i,j})_{i,j \in \mathbb{N}}$ is an infinite lower triangular matrix with entries $a_{i,j}$; A_n is the leading submatrix of order n.

Every time we insert a bibliographical citation we also intend to refer to the references therein.

PART 1.

2. Sheffer'S Approach

"... and more generally, we can use other operators than $\frac{d}{dx}$ and Δ, to define further sets. We thus obtain all polynomial sets of type zero (as we denote them)." [1].

Hence, in his paper, I.M. Sheffer had the goal of determining more general polynomial sequences then those of P. Appell [3] and of binomial type [6,8,9,52]. However, preliminarily, he introduced a classification of polynomial sequences into different types.

2.1. Sheffer Classification

Let $\phi = \{\phi_n\}_{n \in \mathbb{N}}$ be a p.s., that is, for any $n \in \mathbb{N}$, ϕ_n is a polynomial of degree exactly n. We define the set of polynomials (not necessarily a p.s.) v_n, $n \geq 0$, by recurrence

$$\begin{cases} v_0(x) D \phi_1(x) = \phi_0(x) \\ v_n(x) D^{n+1} \phi_{n+1}(x) = \phi_n(x) - \sum_{k=0}^{n-1} v_k(x) D^{k+1} \phi_{n+1}(x), & n > 0. \end{cases} \quad (4)$$

Remark 1. *We note that, being ϕ_n of degree exactly n, for any $n \in \mathbb{N}$, it follows that v_n is uniquely defined and has degree $\leq n$.*

Let us define $V_\phi = \{v_n \mid \forall n \in \mathbb{N}, v_n \text{ is polynomial as in (4)}\}$.

Theorem 1 ([53]). *For the p.s. $\{\phi_n\}_{n \in \mathbb{N}}$ there exists a unique differential operator of the form*

$$J := J_\phi(x, D) = \sum_{k=0}^{\infty} v_k(x) D^{k+1}, \qquad v_k \in V_\phi, \quad \forall k \in \mathbb{N}, \quad (5)$$

such that

$$J[\phi_0] = 0, \qquad J[\phi_n] = \phi_{n-1}, \quad n \geq 1. \quad (6)$$

It is said that the p.s. $\{\phi_n\}_{n \in \mathbb{N}}$ belongs to the operator J and that J is the operator associated with the p.s. $\{\phi_n\}_{n \in \mathbb{N}}$.

Remark 2 ([53]). *Not every operator of the form (5) is associated with a p.s. in the sense previously defined. An operator J of the form (5) is associated with a p.s. if and only if J maps x^n into $n x^{n-1}$. Hence it maps each polynomial of degree exactly n into a polynomial of degree exactly $n - 1$.*

There is only one operator associated with a given p.s., but there are infinitely many polynomial sequences belonging to the same operator.

Theorem 2 ([1]). *To each operator J of the form (5) correspond infinitely many polynomial sequences for which (6) holds. In particular, one and only one of these polynomial sequences, which we call the basic sequence and denote by $\{b_n\}_{n \in \mathbb{N}}$, is such that*

$$b_0(x) = 1, \qquad b_n(0) = 0, \quad n \geq 1.$$

Corollary 1 ([1]). *Necessary and sufficient condition for $\{\psi_n\}_{n\in\mathbb{N}}$ to be a p.s. belonging to J is that there exists a numerical sequence $(a_n)_{n\in\mathbb{N}}$ such that*

$$\psi_n(x) = \sum_{i=0}^{n} a_i\, b_{n-i}(x), \qquad a_0 \neq 0, \qquad \forall n \in \mathbb{N}, \tag{7}$$

where $\{b_n\}_{n\in\mathbb{N}}$ is the basic sequence for J.

Definition 1 ([1]). *If no polynomial v_k in the set V_ϕ is of degree greater than m, but at least one is of degree m, the p.s. $\{\phi_n\}_{n\in\mathbb{N}}$ is of A-type m. If the degrees of the polynomials v_k are unbounded, then $\{\phi_n\}_{n\in\mathbb{N}}$ is of infinite type.*

From Theorem 1 the following corollary holds.

Corollary 2 ([1]). *There are infinitely many polynomial sequences for every A-type (finite or infinite).*

Example 1 ([1,54]). *Any Appell p.s. is of A-type zero. In fact, in this case, $J = D$.*

Example 2 ([54]). *Let $(a_i)_{i\in\mathbb{N}}$ be a numerical sequence with $a_0 \neq 0$. It is proved [54] that the p.s. $\{a_k\}_{k\in\mathbb{N}}$ defined as*

$$a_k(x) = \sum_{i=0}^{k} \binom{k}{i} a_{k-i} \frac{x^i}{i!}$$

is of A-type 1 and the corresponding operator is

$$J_\phi(x, D) = D + xD^2.$$

In order to characterize the polynomial sequences of A-type m, $m > 0$, we remember the result of Huff and Rainville [55]. They showed, among other things, that a p.s. with generating function

$$\phi(t)f(xt) = \phi(t)\,_0F_m(-;\beta_1,\beta_2,\ldots,\beta_m;\sigma xt) = \sum_{n=0}^{\infty} y_n(x)t^n,$$

with σ constant and ϕ analytic and not zero at $t = 0$, is of A-type m.

The Sheffer paper [1] contains a study on polynomial sequences of any A-type, but the most satisfying results are those related to polynomial sequences of A-type zero.

2.2. Polynomial Sequences of A-Type Zero

Sheffer found several characterizations of polynomial sequences of A-type zero. It will be convenient to restate the conditions for a p.s. to be of A-type zero as follows: $\{\phi_n\}_{n\in\mathbb{N}}$ is a p.s. of A-type zero if

$$J[\phi_n] = \phi_{n-1}, \quad n > 0,$$

where J is the operator

$$J[y] = \sum_{k=1}^{\infty} c_k\, y^{(k)}, \qquad c_1 \neq 0,\ c_k \in \mathbb{K},\ \forall k \in \mathbb{N}. \tag{8}$$

With the operator (8) Sheffer associated the formal power series

$$J(t) = \sum_{k=1}^{\infty} c_k\, t^k, \tag{9}$$

called the *generating function* of the operator (8).

The formal power series (9), being $c_1 \neq 0$, is invertible. Following Roman and Rota [8] we call it a δ-series and we call its inverse *compositional inverse*. It is denoted by

$$H(t) = \sum_{k=1}^{\infty} s_k t^k, \qquad s_1 \neq 0, \ s_k \in \mathbb{K}, \ \forall k \in \mathbb{N}, \tag{10}$$

and verifies

$$J(H(t)) = H(J(t)) = t. \tag{11}$$

Remark 3. *Sheffer's paper [1] (p. 596) in a footnote describes a recurrence procedure for the calculation of the coefficients $s_i = s_i(c_j)$, $i \geq 1$. Indeed they can be numerically generated by means of a formal algorithm [6] (pp. 6–8).*

Then Sheffer gave the first characterization for polynomial sequences of A-type zero.

Theorem 3. *A necessary and sufficient condition for $\{\phi_n\}_{n\in\mathbb{N}}$ to be of A-type zero corresponding to the operator J as in (8) is that a numerical sequence $(a_i)_{i\in\mathbb{N}}$, $a_0 \neq 0$, exists such that, setting*

$$A(t) = \sum_{i=0}^{\infty} a_i t^i,$$

we get

$$A(t) e^{xH(t)} = \sum_{n=0}^{\infty} \phi_n(x) t^n, \tag{12}$$

with $H(t)$ as in (10).

Proof. The proof follows after observing that

$$e^{xH(t)} = \sum_{n=0}^{\infty} b_n(x) t^n,$$

where $\{b_n\}_{n\in\mathbb{N}}$ is the basic p.s. for J. Hence both the necessary and sufficient parts follow by (7) in Corollary 1. □

The formal power series

$$A(t) = \sum_{i=0}^{\infty} a_i t^i.$$

is called by Sheffer [1] *determining series* of the p.s. $\{\phi_n\}_{n\in\mathbb{N}}$.

It is observed, also, that every p.s. satisfies infinitely many linear functional equations. One of the simplest equations for polynomial sequences of A-type zero is given in the following theorem.

Theorem 4 ([1]). *Let $\{\phi_n\}_{n\in\mathbb{N}}$ be a p.s. of A-type zero corresponding to operator J, and let $A(t)$ be its determining series. Then $\{\phi_n\}_{n\in\mathbb{N}}$ satisfies the equation*

$$L[y(x)] := \sum_{k=1}^{\infty} (q_{k,0} + x\, q_{k,1}) J^k[y] = \lambda y, \tag{13}$$

where $\lambda = n$, for $y = \phi_n$. The coefficients q are defined by

$$\frac{A'(t)}{A(t)} = \sum_{k=0}^{\infty} q_{k+1,0}\, t^n, \tag{14}$$

$$H'(t) = \sum_{k=0}^{\infty} q_{k+1,1} t^k. \tag{15}$$

Proof. The proof is based on (12). □

From (13) in Theorem 4 a further characterization of polynomial sequences of A-type zero, expressed only in terms of the elements of the p.s. itself, follows.

Theorem 5 ([1]). *A necessary and sufficient condition for a p.s. $\{\phi_n\}_{n \in \mathbb{N}}$ to be of A-type zero is that constants $q_{k,0}$, $q_{k,1}$ exist so that*

$$\sum_{k=1}^{\infty} (q_{k,0} + x q_{k,1}) \phi_{n-k}(x) = n \phi_n(x), \qquad \phi_{n-k}(x) = 0 \text{ for } k > n. \tag{16}$$

The operator J and the determining series A for $\{\phi_n\}_{n \in \mathbb{N}}$ are related to the coefficients q by (14)–(15).

By differentiating both sides of (12) with respect to x, by equating coefficients of the same powers of t, we obtain

$$\phi_n'(x) = s_1 \phi_{n-1}(x) + s_2 \phi_{n-2}(x) + \ldots + s_n \phi_0(x), \qquad n \geq 1. \tag{17}$$

This identity generates a further characterization.

Theorem 6 ([1]). *A necessary and suffient condition for a p.s. $\{\phi_n\}_{n \in \mathbb{N}}$ to be of A-type zero is that a numerical sequence $(s_n)_{n \in \mathbb{N}}$ exists for which (17) holds. In this case the operator J corresponding to $\{\phi_n\}_{n \in \mathbb{N}}$ is determined through $(s_n)_{n \in \mathbb{N}}$ by means of (10) and (11).*

Another important topic in Sheffer's paper concerns the orthogonality of the polynomial sequences of A-type zero. It is described in the following Subsection.

2.3. A-Type Zero Polynomial Sequences That Are Orthogonal Polynomials

J. Shohat [56] proved that Hermite polynomials [6] (p. 134) are an Appell p.s., hence of A-type zero, but are also orthogonal polynomials [57,58]. Another orthogonal p.s. of A-type zero is Laguerre p.s. [6] (p. 184). This suggests the problem of determining all A-type zero polynomial sequences that are, also, orthogonal. J. Meixner [59] treated this problem by using Laplace transformation and taking

$$A(t) e^{xH(t)} = \sum_{n=0}^{\infty} \phi_n(x) t^n \tag{18}$$

as definition of A-type zero.

Sheffer in [1] gave a quite different treatment by means of the known properties of A-type zero polynomial sequences and the three-term recurrence relation for monic orthogonal polynomial sequences [57,58]

$$\phi_n(x) = (x + \lambda_n) \phi_{n-1}(x) - \mu_n \phi_{n-2}(x), \qquad n \geq 1, \tag{19}$$

with λ_n, μ_n real constants, $\mu_n > 0$, $n > 1$.

Combining (16) and (19), the basic result of Sheffer is the following theorem.

Theorem 7 ([1]). *A necessary and sufficient condition for an A-type zero p.s. $\{\phi_n\}_{n \in \mathbb{N}}$ to satisfy (19) is that*

$$\lambda_n = \alpha + bn, \quad \text{and} \quad \mu_n = (n-1)(c + dn), \qquad \alpha, b, c, d \in \mathbb{K},$$

with $c + dn \neq 0$ for $n > 1$.

With further analysis Sheffer characterized the A-type zero polynomial sequences that are, also, orthogonal, by the following result.

Theorem 8 ([1]). *A p.s.* $\{\phi_n\}_{n\in\mathbb{N}}$ *is of A-type zero and orthogonal if and only if the generating function (18) is expressed in one of the following forms*

$$A(t)e^{xH(t)} = \mu(1-bt)^c e^{\frac{d+atx}{1-bt}}, \qquad a, b, c, \mu \neq 0; \tag{20}$$

$$A(t)e^{xH(t)} = \mu e^{t(b+ax)+ct^2}, \qquad a, c, \mu \neq 0; \tag{21}$$

$$A(t)e^{xH(t)} = \mu e^{ct}(1-bt)^{d+ax}, \qquad a, b, c, \mu \neq 0; \tag{22}$$

$$A(t)e^{xH(t)} = \mu\left(1-\frac{t}{c}\right)^{d_1+\frac{x}{a}}\left(1-\frac{t}{b}\right)^{d_2-\frac{x}{a}}, \qquad a, b, c, \mu \neq 0, \; b \neq c. \tag{23}$$

By properly choosing each of the parameters in (20)–(23) we can obtain all the Sheffer A-type zero orthogonal polynomial sequences (see [60]).

3. Rota's et al. Contributions

In 1970 G.C. Rota and his pupils [10,11,22,52] began to construct a completely rigorous theory of the "classical modern" umbral calculus. Classical umbral calculus, as it was from 1850 to 1970, consists of a symbolic technique for the manipulation of the sequences, whose mathematical rigor leaves much to be desidered. Just remember Eric Temple Bell's failed attempt, in 1940, to persuade the mathematical community to accept umbral calculus as a legitimate mathematical tool. The theory of Rota et al. is based on the ideas of linear functional, linear operator and adjuint. In 1977 the authors was lucky enough to join in on formal theory, that can be called modern umbral calculus. A full exposition of this theory can be found in Roman's book [9]. The second chapter of this book contains definitions and general properties of the Sheffer sequences (i.e., A-type zero polynomial sequences) that are the main object of the study.

Sheffer Polynomial Sequences

Let $\mathcal{P}$ be the algebra of polynomials in the single variable x over the field $\mathbb{K}$ of characteristic zero. Let $\mathcal{P}^*$ be the vector space of all linear functionals on $\mathcal{P}$. The authors use the notation

$$\langle L \mid p \rangle$$

to denote the action of a linear functional L on a polynomial p. The formal power series

$$f(t) = \sum_{k=0}^{\infty} a_k \frac{t^k}{k!} \tag{24}$$

defines a linear functional on $\mathcal{P}$ by setting

$$\langle f \mid x^n \rangle = a_n.$$

If the notation t^k is used for the k-th derivative operator on $\mathcal{P}$, that is,

$$t^k x^n = \begin{cases} (n)_k x^{n-k} & k \leq n \\ 0 & k > n, \end{cases}$$

where $(n)_k = n(n-1)\cdots(n-k+1)$, then any power series (24) is a liner operator on $\mathcal{P}$. It is defined as

$$f(t)x^n = \sum_{k=0}^{n} \binom{n}{k} a_k x^{n-k}.$$

So $f(t)p(x)$ denotes the action of the operator $f(t)$ on the polynomial $p(x)$. Thus a formal power series plays three roles in the umbral calculus theory of Rota et al.: a formal power series, a linear functional and a linear operator. S. Roman seems to encourage the young reader: "A little familiarity should remove any discomfort that may be felt by the use of this trinity" [9] (p. 12).

Let g be an invertible power series, that is,

$$g(t) = \sum_{k=0}^{\infty} a_k \frac{t^k}{k!}, \qquad a_0 \neq 0,$$

and lef f be a δ-power series, that is

$$f(t) = \sum_{k=1}^{\infty} b_k \frac{t^k}{k!}, \qquad b_1 \neq 0.$$

Theorem 9 ([9] (p. 17)). *There exists a unique p.s. $\{s_n\}_{n \in \mathbb{N}}$ satisfying the orthogonality conditions*

$$\left\langle g(t)f(t)^k \mid s_n(x) \right\rangle = n! \, \delta_{n,k}, \tag{25}$$

for all $n, k \geq 0$.

Proof. The uniqueness is based on the order of the power series $g(t)f(t)^k$, that is, $o\!\left(g(t)f(t)^k\right) = k$, for any $k > 0$. The existence of the solution s_n, for any $n \in \mathbb{N}$, is obtained from the solution of a nonsingular triangular system. $\square$

Following Roman's book [9], we say that the p.s. $\{s_n\}_{n \in \mathbb{N}}$ in (25) is the Sheffer sequence for the pair $(g(t), f(t))$, or that $\{s_n\}_{n \in \mathbb{N}}$ is Sheffer for $(g(t), f(t))$.

There are two important special cases of Sheffer sequences:

(a) the Sheffer sequence for $(1, f(t))$ is the associated sequence for $f(t)$ (or the binomial p.s. [6] (p. 24) or the basic p.s. for the operator $f(t)$ [1]);
(b) the Sheffer sequence for $(g(t), t)$ is the Appell p.s. [3] for $g(t)$.

The term *Appell sequence* in other sources [1] can differs for the factor $n!$.

Roman gave some characterization of Sheffer sequences.

Theorem 10 ([9] (p.18)). *The p.s. $\{s_n\}_{n \in \mathbb{N}}$ is Sheffer for $(g(t), f(t))$ if and only if*

$$\frac{1}{g(\overline{f}(t))} e^{y\overline{f}(t)} = \sum_{k=0}^{\infty} s_k(y) \frac{t^k}{k!} \tag{26}$$

for all $y \in \mathbb{K}$, where $\overline{f}$ is the compositional inverse of f.

Remark 4. *If we use for a formal power series the two variables x and t, we could write (26) as*

$$\frac{1}{g(\overline{f}(t))} e^{x\overline{f}(t)} = \sum_{k=0}^{\infty} s_k(x) \frac{t^k}{k!}. \tag{27}$$

It is the usual form for an exponential generating function.

Remark 5. *Sheffer [1] characterized A-type zero polynomial sequences by the generating function*

$$A(t) e^{xH(t)} = \sum_{k=0}^{\infty} u_k(x) \, t^k,$$

where $A(t)$ is an invertible power series and $H(t)$ is a δ-series.

From the comparison with (27) it follows that $\{s_n\}_{n\in\mathbb{N}}$ is a Sheffer sequence in the sense of Roman if and only if $\{\frac{1}{n!}s_n\}_{n\in\mathbb{N}}$ is a sequence of Sheffer A-type zero.

Remark 6. *Just for historical record, polynomial sequences of Sheffer A-type zero are called poweroids by Steffensen [61] and sequences of generalized Appell-type by Erdelyi [62]. Although in Boas and Buck [63] the latter term is used for a more general set of polynomial sequences.*

The generating function (27) provides a representation of Sheffer sequences in classical monomials.

Theorem 11 ([9] (p.19)). *The p.s $\{s_n\}_{n\in\mathbb{N}}$ is Sheffer for $(g(t), f(t))$ if and only if*

$$s_n(x) = \sum_{k=0}^{n} \frac{1}{k!} \left\langle g(\bar{f}(t))^{-1} f(t)^k \mid x^n \right\rangle x^k, \qquad \forall n \in \mathbb{N}. \tag{28}$$

Proof. The thesis follows by applying both sides of (26) to x^n. □

Remark 7. *For an explicit calculation of the coefficients in (28) see [6] (pp. 11–13).*

Theorem 12 ([9] (p.20)). *A p.s $\{s_n\}_{n\in\mathbb{N}}$ is Sheffer for $(g(t), f(t))$ if and only if*

$$f(t)s_n(x) = n\, s_{n-1}(x).$$

Interesting is the characterization of Sheffer polynomial sequences that generalizes the binomial formula.

Theorem 13 ([9] (p.21)). *A p.s $\{s_n\}_{n\in\mathbb{N}}$ is Sheffer for $(g(t), f(t))$ if and only if*

$$s_n(x+y) = \sum_{k=0}^{n} \binom{n}{k} p_k(y) s_{n-k}(x), \qquad \forall n \in \mathbb{N}, y \in \mathbb{K}, \tag{29}$$

where $\{p_n\}_{n\in\mathbb{N}}$ is the (binomial) p.s. associated (basic) with the linear operator f.

Corollary 3. *By interchanging x and y in (29) and setting $y = 0$, we get*

$$s_n(x) = \sum_{k=0}^{n} \binom{n}{k} p_k(x) s_{n-k}(0), \qquad \forall n \in \mathbb{N}.$$

Thus, given a p.s. $\{p_n\}_{n\in\mathbb{N}}$ associated (basic) with f, each Sheffer p.s. $\{s_n\}_{n\in\mathbb{N}}$ that uses f as its δ-power series is uniquely determined by the numerical sequence $(s_n(0))_{n\in\mathbb{N}}$.

Another important topic introduced by Rota at al. is the *umbral composition*.

Theorem 14 ([9] (p.44)). *The set of Sheffer sequences is a group under umbral composition. In particular, if $\{s_n\}_{n\in\mathbb{N}}$ is Sheffer for $(g(t), f(t))$ and $\{r_n\}_{n\in\mathbb{N}}$ is Sheffer for $(h(t), l(t))$, then $\{r_n \circ s_n\}_{n\in\mathbb{N}}$ is Sheffer for $(g(t)h(f(t)), l(f(t)))$. The identity under umbral composition is the Sheffer p.s. $\{x^n\}_{n\in\mathbb{N}}$ and the inverse of $\{s_n\}_{n\in\mathbb{N}}$ is the Sheffer sequence for $\left(g(t) \left(\bar{f}(t)\right)^{-1}, \bar{f}(t) \right)$.*

Remark 8. *In Roman's book [9] the problem of orthogonal polynomial sequences which are also Sheffer is mentioned [9] (p.156–159), but in a more general way.*

PART 2.

In the following Sections we want to discuss some of the more interesting results that have appeared in the last thirty years or so.

4. The Riordan Group and the Sheffer Group

L. Shapiro et al. in 1991 [64] found a new group of infinite lower triangular matrices. They called this group *Riordan group*. This name seems appropriate because due to J. Riordan's then recent death. Later the concept of Riordan matrices was generalized to exponential Riordan matrices by many authors [65,66]. An exponential Riordan matrix is an infinite lower triangular matrix whose j-th column (being the first indexed with 0) has the generating function

$$\frac{1}{j!}g(t)f(t)^j,$$

where $g(t)$ is an invertible power series and $f(t)$ is a δ-series, that is,

$$g(t) = \sum_{i=0}^{\infty} a_i \frac{t^i}{i!}, \quad a_0 \neq 0, \qquad f(t) = \sum_{i=1}^{\infty} b_i \frac{t^i}{i!}, \quad b_1 \neq 0.$$

The exponential Riordan matrix generated by the formal power series $g(t), f(t)$ is denoted by $[g(t), f(t)]$.

Remark 9. *As mensioned in [67], "the concept of representing columns of an infinite matrix by formal power series is not new and goes back to Shur's paper and Faber polynomials in 1945".*

In the set of exponential Riordan matrices, given $A = [g(t), f(t)]$ and $B = [h(t), l(t)]$, the matrix multiplication can be defined:

$$A \cdot B = [g(t), f(t)] \cdot [h(t), l(t)] = [g(t)h(f(t)), l(f(t))]. \tag{30}$$

The reader will have no difficulty in proving by himself that
- the identity is $I = [1, t]$;
- the inverse matrix is

$$[g(t), f(t)]^{-1} = \left[\frac{1}{g\left(\bar{f}(t)\right)}, \bar{f}(t)\right],$$

where $\bar{f}(t)$ is the compositional inverse, hence is such that $f\left(\bar{f}(t)\right) = \bar{f}(f(t)) = t$.

Theorem 15. [64] *The set of exponential Riordan matrices is a group with respect to the operation of matrix multiplication as defined in (30), called* Riordan group.

In 2007 T.X. He et al. [68] considered the Sheffer group and proved that it is isomorphic to the Riordan group.

Using the notation of He, a Sheffer p.s. $\{p_n\}_{n \in \mathbb{N}}$ is defined as

$$g(t)e^{xf(t)} = \sum_{n=0}^{\infty} p_n(t)t^n. \tag{31}$$

This definition differs from Roman definition [9] by a constant $n!$, but it coincides with that in [1].

In the set of Sheffer polynomial sequences, if $\{p_n\}_{n \in \mathbb{N}}$ and $\{q_n\}_{n \in \mathbb{N}}$ are Sheffer polynomial sequences, He [68] defined the umbral composition "#" in this way:

$$p_n \# q_n = r_n, \qquad \forall n \in \mathbb{N}, \tag{32}$$

where, if $p_n(x) = \sum_{k=0}^{n} p_{n,k} x^k$ and $q_n(x) = \sum_{k=0}^{n} q_{n,k} x^k$, then

$$r_n(x) = \sum_{k=0}^{n} r_{n,k} x^k,$$

with

$$r_{n,k} = \sum_{j=k}^{n} j! p_{n,j} q_{j,k}, \qquad n \geq j \geq k.$$

Theorem 16 ([68]). *The set of all Sheffer polynomial sequences defined as in (31) with the operation "#" defined as in (32) is a group called the Sheffer group and denoted by $\left(\{p_n\}_{n \in \mathbb{N}}, \# \right)$. The identity of the group is $\left\{ \frac{x^n}{n!} \right\}_{n \in \mathbb{N}}$. The inverse of $\{p_n\}_{n \in \mathbb{N}}$ generated by $g(t) e^{xf(t)}$ is the Sheffer p.s. generated by*

$$\frac{1}{g(\bar{f}(t))} e^{x \bar{f}(t)},$$

being $\bar{f}$ the compositional inverse of f.

Remark 10. *The result in the previous theorem, up to the factor $n!$, is conceptually identical to Roman's one [9] (p. 44).*

Finally, the isomorphism between the groups is given by mapping

$$\{p_n\}_{n \in \mathbb{N}} \longrightarrow [g(t), f(t)],$$

that is, by associating with the Sheffer p.s. the exponential Riordan matrix whose rows are the coefficients of the polynomial p_n for any n.

For details we refer to [68], where there are also many examples and some applications.

5. Elementary Matrix Calculus Approach to Umbral Calculus

After isomorphism between Sheffer polynomials and exponential Riordan matrices in [6,26–28,69–73], there is an attempt to construct the modern umbral calculus trought elementary matrix calculus. This is in contrast with the previous approaches considered very formal [74]. Furthermore S. Khan et al. wrote "The simplicity of the algebraic approach to the Appell and Sheffer sequences established in [69,72], allows several applications" [49].

Let $\{p_n\}_{n \in \mathbb{N}}$ be a p.s. with

$$p_n(x) = \sum_{k=0}^{n} t_{n,k} x^k, \qquad t_{n,k} \in \mathbb{K}, \ t_{n,n} \neq 0 \ \forall n \in \mathbb{N}. \tag{33}$$

Setting

$$T_n = (t_{i,k})_{i,k \in \mathbb{N}}, \qquad k \leq i, \ i = 0, \ldots, n, \ \forall n \in \mathbb{N},$$

$$X_n = \left[1, x, x^2, \ldots, x^n \right]^T,$$

we have

$$P_n = T_n X_n, \tag{34}$$

where

$$P_n = [p_0(x), p_1(x), \ldots, p_n(x)]^T.$$

For $n \to \infty$, with obvious meaning of the symbols, we can write

$$P = T X, \tag{35}$$

where $T = (t_{ik})_{ik \in \mathbb{N}}$ is an infinite, nonsingular, lower triangular matrix [75] and T_n is the leader submatrix of order n, for any $n \in \mathbb{N}$. Formulas (34) and (35) are called *matrix forms* of the p.s. $\{p_n\}_{n \in \mathbb{N}}$.

The concept of representing polynomial sequences by lower triangular matrices is not new and goes back to G. Polya [76] and I. Shur [77]. In fact, Polya gave a solution of the Cauchy-Bellman functional equation for matrices

$$M(x)M(y) = M(x+y) \qquad (36)$$

in the form

$$\begin{bmatrix} 1 & 0 & 0 & \cdots & \cdots & 0 \\ x & 1 & & \ddots & & \\ x^2 & 2x & 1 & \ddots & & \\ x^3 & 3x^2 & 3x & 1 & & \\ \vdots & & & & \ddots & 0 \\ x^n & \binom{n}{n-1}x^{n-1} & \binom{n}{n-2}x^{n-2} & \cdots & \cdots & 1 \end{bmatrix}$$

Then Vein [12] observed that the $(n+1)$-th row of the matrix contains the terms of the polynomial expansion of $(1+x)^n$, and the elements in the $(n+1)$-th column are the terms of the infinite series expansion of $(1-x)^{-(n+1)}$.

Moreover, for the solution of (36), Vein in [13] proved the relation

$$M(x) = e^{xQ}, \qquad (37)$$

where Q is an infinite triangular matrix with constant elements, and observed that

$$Q = M'(0). \qquad (38)$$

From this relation Vein proved some identities among triangular matrices and inverse relations. Thereafter, he determined two sets of triangular matrices. The elements of one set are related to the terms of Laguerre, Hermite, Bernoulli, Euler and Bessel polynomials, whereas the elements of the other set consist of Stirling numbers of both kinds, the two-parameter Eulerian numbers and a the numbers introduced by Touchard [78]. Hence it has been shown that these matrices are related by a number of identities. Some known and lesser known pairs of inverse scalar relations that arise in combinatorial analysis have been shown to be derivable from simple and obviously inverse pairs of matrix relations. Vein in [13] wrote "The referee has pointed out that this work is an explicit matrix version of the umbral calculus as presented by Rota et al. [9–11]".

In [6] the author aims to find well-known results on the umbral calculus and also new identities and properties of Sheffer sequences, by means of elementary matrix calculus. The approach is very different from Vein's. In fact, the starting point are the relations (33)–(35) and not (36)–(38), which indeed will be never considered.

Now we make a mention of the methods used in [6], through an historical and constructive path.

5.1. Appell Polynomial Sequences

Let $(a_i)_{i \in \mathbb{N}}$ be a numerical sequence with $a_0 \neq 0$. The infinite lower triangular matrix $A = (a_{i,j})_{i,j \in \mathbb{N}}$ with

$$a_{i,j} = \binom{i}{j} a_{i-j}$$

is called *Appell-type matrix* [6] (pp. 9–10). Then we consider the p.s. $\{a_n\}_{n \in \mathbb{N}}$ with

$$a_n(x) = \sum_{j=0}^{n} a_{n,j} x^j = \sum_{j=0}^{n} \binom{n}{j} a_{n-j} x^j, \quad \forall n \in \mathbb{N}, \tag{39}$$

called *Appell p.s.*

It's easy to verify that the matrix form

$$A X = \mathfrak{A}, \quad \text{and} \quad A_n X_n = \mathfrak{A}_n, \quad \forall n \in \mathbb{N}, \tag{40}$$

holds, where

$$\mathfrak{A} = [a_0(x), a_1(x), \ldots, a_n(x), \ldots]^T, \quad X = \left[1, x, x^2, \ldots, x^n, \ldots\right]^T$$

and

$$\mathfrak{A}_n = [a_0(x), a_1(x), \ldots, a_n(x)]^T, \quad X_n = \left[1, x, x^2, \ldots, x^n\right]^T.$$

The Appell-type matrix is nonsingular and its inverse is also an Appell-type matrix [6]. Moreover, if we set

$$g(t) = \sum_{i=0}^{\infty} a_i \frac{t^i}{i!}, \quad a_0 \neq 0,$$

$g(t)$ is an invertible power series and its inverse is

$$\frac{1}{g(t)} = \sum_{i=0}^{\infty} \bar{a}_i \frac{t^i}{i!},$$

where

$$\sum_{k=0}^{n} \binom{n}{k} a_k \bar{a}_{n-k} = \delta_{n,0}, \quad \forall n \in \mathbb{N}.$$

Then, if we set $A^{-1} = \overline{A} = (\bar{a}_{i,j})_{i,j \in \mathbb{N}}$, we have

$$\bar{a}_{i,j} = \binom{i}{j} \bar{a}_{i-j}. \tag{41}$$

The matrix $\overline{A}$ generates the p.s. $\{\bar{a}_n\}_{n \in \mathbb{N}}$ such that

$$\bar{a}_n(x) = \sum_{j=0}^{n} \binom{n}{j} \bar{a}_{n-j} x^j.$$

Moreover

$$\overline{A} X = \overline{\mathfrak{A}}, \quad \text{and} \quad \overline{A}_n X_n = \overline{\mathfrak{A}}_n, \quad \forall n \in \mathbb{N}.$$

For details we refer to [6] (p. 14).

The p.s. $\{\bar{a}_n\}_{n \in \mathbb{N}}$ is hence an Appell p.s., called *conjugate* of the p.s. $\{a_n\}_{n \in \mathbb{N}}$. The reader will have no difficulty in proving by himself the known identities

$$a'_n(x) = n \, a_{n-1}(x), \quad n \geq 1 \tag{42}$$

$$g(t) e^{xt} = \sum_{n=0}^{\infty} a_n(x) \frac{t^n}{n!}$$

that characterize an Appell p.s. [3].

From the matrix form (40) we get

$$X_n = \overline{A}_n \mathfrak{A}_n \tag{43}$$

and
$$x^n = \sum_{j=0}^{n} \bar{a}_{n,j} a_j(x), \quad \forall n \in \mathbb{N}. \tag{44}$$

From the latest formula we can derive a recurrence formula and a determinant form.

Theorem 17 ([6]). *For the Appell p.s.* $\{a_n\}_{n\in\mathbb{N}}$ *defined as in (39) the following identities hold:* $a_0(x) = \dfrac{1}{\bar{a}_0}$ *and, for any* $n \geq 1$,

$$a_n(x) = \frac{1}{\bar{a}_0}\left[x^n - \sum_{k=0}^{n-1}\binom{n}{k}\bar{a}_{n,k}a_k(x)\right]; \tag{45}$$

$$a_n(x) = \frac{(-1)^n}{\bar{a}_0^{n+1}}\begin{vmatrix} 1 & x & \cdots & x^{n-1} & x^n \\ \bar{a}_0 & \bar{a}_1 & \cdots & \bar{a}_{n-1} & \bar{a}_n \\ \vdots & & \ddots & & \vdots \\ \vdots & & & \ddots & \vdots \\ 0 & \cdots & \cdots & \bar{a}_0 & \binom{n}{n-1}a_1 \end{vmatrix}. \tag{46}$$

Proof. Relation (45) follows from (43). The (46) follows by Cramer's rule applied to the linear system (44), with $n = 0, \ldots, M$, for any $M \in \mathbb{N}$.

The details can be found in [6] (pp. 83–84). □

Remark 11. *We note that the determinant form (46) is in [69]. Almost in the same period a similar form has been given by Yang et al. [79], but with very different and more sophisticated techniques.*

An analogous result as in Theorem 17 holds for the conjugate sequence $\{\bar{p}_n\}_{n\in\mathbb{N}}$.

For an Appell p.s. a second recurrence relation and determinant form hold.

Theorem 18 ([6]). *With the previous hypothesis and relations, for an Appell p.s. the following relations hold*

$$a_{n+1}(x) = (x + b_0)a_n(x) + \sum_{k=0}^{n-1}\binom{n}{k}b_{n-k}a_k(x), \tag{47}$$

where $(b_i)_{i\in\mathbb{N}}$ *is the numerical sequence given by*

$$\frac{g'(t)}{g(t)} = \sum_{i=0}^{\infty} b_i \frac{t^i}{i!}; \tag{48}$$

and
$$a_0(x) = 1,$$
$$a_{n+1}(x) = \begin{vmatrix} x+b_0 & -1 & 0 & \cdots & \cdots & 0 \\ b_1 & x+b_0 & -1 & 0 & \cdots & 0 \\ b_2 & \binom{2}{1}b_1 & x+b_0 & -1 & \cdots & 0 \\ \vdots & & & \ddots & \ddots & \vdots \\ \vdots & & & & \ddots & \vdots \\ b_n & \binom{n}{1}b_{n-1} & \cdots & \cdots & \binom{n}{n-1}b_1 & x+b_0 \end{vmatrix} \tag{49}$$

with b_i *as in (48).*

Proof. Cfr. [6] (pp. 83–86). □

Remark 12. For the numerical sequence $(b_i)_{i\in\mathbb{N}}$ as in (48) we have the representation

$$b_n = \sum_{k=0}^{n} \binom{n}{k} a_{k+1} \bar{a}_{n-k}, \qquad \forall n \in \mathbb{N}.$$

Remark 13. We observe that if

$$\sum_{k=0}^{n-2} \binom{n}{k} b_{n-k} a_k(x) = 0, \qquad \forall x \in \mathbb{R}, \ \forall n \geq 2,$$

then the recurrence relation (47) becomes a three-term relation and, consequently, in suitable hypothesis, the sequence $\{a_n\}_{n\in\mathbb{N}}$ is also orthogonal [57,80]. It is known [56] that among classical orthogonal polynomials, only the Hermite sequence is, also, an Appell p.s. We will consider this topic afterwards.

Remark 14. The second recurrence relation and the second determinant form for Appell polynomial sequences are, also, in [81], but they are determined by a more general and complicate procedure.

The previous recurrence relations generate some differential equations for Appell polynomial sequences. For this, firstly we observe that from (42) we have

$$a_{n-k}(x) = \frac{a_n^{(k)}(x)}{n(n-1)\cdots(n-k+1)}, \qquad \forall k = 0, \ldots, n. \tag{50}$$

Then, using this relation we can prove the following theorem.

Theorem 19 ([6]). *Let $\{a_n\}_{n\in\mathbb{N}}$ be the A.p.s. associated with matrix $A = (a_{i,j})_{i,j\in\mathbb{N}}$. Then $\{a_n\}_{n\in\mathbb{N}}$ satisfies the following differential equation*

$$\frac{\bar{a}_n}{n!} y^{(n)}(x) + \frac{\bar{a}_{n-1}}{(n-1)!} y^{(n-1)}(x) + \cdots + \bar{a}_0 y(x) = x^n.$$

Proof. The proof is obtained by putting (50) in the first recurrence relation. □

Combining (50) and (47), a second differential equation for Appell polynomial sequences can be obtained.

The first determinant form (46) allows to calculate the numerical value of $a_n(x)$ for every fixed value of the variable x. In fact, it is knows that Gauss elimination without pivoting for an Hessenberg matrix is stable [82]. Moreover, it allows to prove the following orthogonality property.

Let L be a linear functional on $\mathcal{P}$. If we set

$$L(x^i) = \bar{a}_i, \qquad i \geq 0,$$

the relation (46) allows to define the Appell p.s. denoted by $\{a_n^L\}_{n\in\mathbb{N}}$. Then we consider the $n+1$ linear functionals $L_i, \ i = 0, \ldots, n$ such that

$$L_0(x^i) = L(x^i), \qquad L_j(x^i) = L(D^j x^i), \quad j \leq i, \ i = 0, \ldots, n. \tag{51}$$

Theorem 20 ([26,27]). *For the Appell p.s. $\{a_n\}_{n\in\mathbb{N}}$ the following relations hold*

$$L_i(a_n^L) = n! \delta_{i,n}, \qquad i = 0, \cdots, n.$$

Proof. The proof follows from (46). □

Corollary 4. *The Appell p.s.* $\{a_n^L\}_{n \in \mathbb{N}}$ *is the solution of the general linear interpolation problem*

$$L_i(a_n(x)) = n!\delta_{i,n}, \qquad i = 0, \cdots, n, \tag{52}$$

Remark 15. *We note that* (52) *is equivalent to Theorem 2.3.1 in* [8] *for Appell polynomial sequences.*

Theorem 21 ([28]). *(**Representation theorem**) With the previous hypothesis and notations, for any* $P_n(x) \in \mathcal{P}_n$ *we have*

$$P_n(x) = \sum_{k=0}^{n} \frac{L\left(P_n^{(k)}\right)}{k!} a_k^L(x). \tag{53}$$

Relation (53) is a natural generalization of the classic Taylor polynomials.

The previous theorem is extensible to the linear space X of real continuous functions defined in the interval $[a, b]$, with continuous derivatives of all necessary orders.

Theorem 22 ([28]). *For any* $f \in X$ *the polynomial*

$$P_n[f](x) = \sum_{i=0}^{n} \frac{L\left(f^{(i)}\right)}{i!} a_i^L(x) \tag{54}$$

is the unique polynomial of degree $\leq n$ *such that*

$$L\left(P_n[f]^{(i)}\right) = L\left(f^{(i)}\right), \qquad i = 0, \ldots, n. \tag{55}$$

The polynomial (54) is called *Appell* or *umbral interpolant* for the function f.
In [28] the estimation of the remainder

$$R_n[f](x) = f(x) - P_n[f](x)$$

can be found.

The second determinant form (49) allows to say that any Appell polynomial is the characteristic polynomial of a suitable Hessenberg matrix. In fact it has been proved [6] (p. 86) that if $\{a_n\}_{n \in \mathbb{N}}$ is the Appell p.s. with matrix A and related conjugate matrix $\overline{A}$, then every $a_n(x)$ is the characteristic polynomial of the production matrix [6] (p. 18) of $\overline{A}$, that is,

$$R_n = \overline{A}_n \hat{A}_n,$$

where $\hat{A}_n$ is the matrix A_n with its first row and last column removed. Hence the roots of an Appell polynomial $a_n(x)$ are the eingenvalues of matrix R_n.

For other properties we refer to a wide literature (see [6]).

5.2. Binomial-Type Polynomial Sequences

Roman and Rota [8] observed: "It remains a mystery why so many polynomial sequences occurring in various mathematical circumstances turn out to be of binomial-type". They said, also, that "the notion of polynomial sequences of binomial-type goes back to E.T. Bell" [83,84], and we add to Aitken [85], "Steffens was the first to observe that the sequence associated with delta operators in the way as D is to x^n are of the binomial-type, but failed to notice the converse of this fact, which was first stated and proved by Mullin and Rota [52]". In 1970 Mullin and Rota gave the first systematic theory, using operators methods instead of the less efficient generating functions methods [1], that had been exclusively used until then.

Garsia [74] observed: "Unfortunately, the notions and the proofs in that very original paper ([52], A/N) in some instances leave something to be desidered, and even tend to obscure the remarkable simplicity and beauty of the results".

An algebraic approach to Rota-Mullin theory has been considered in [14].

In the following we will use a matrix-calculus based approach.

Let $(b_i)_{i\in\mathbb{N}}$, $b_0 = 0$, $b_1 \neq 0$, $b_i \in \mathbb{K}$, $i \geq 0$, be a numerical sequence. We define the matrix $P = (p_{n,k})_{n,k\in\mathbb{N}}$ [6] (pp. 7–8) such that

$$\begin{cases} p_{n,0} = \delta_{n,0} & n \geq 0 \\ p_{n,1} = b_n & n \geq 1 \\ p_{n,k} = \dfrac{1}{k}\sum_{i=1}^{n-k+1} \binom{n}{i} p_{i,1} p_{n-i,k-1} & n \geq 2; k = 2,\ldots,n \\ p_{n,k} = 0 & k > n. \end{cases} \tag{56}$$

P is called *binomial-type matrix* [6]. It is a non singular, infinite lower triangular matrix. Then we can consider the polynomial sequence

$$\begin{cases} p_0(x) = 1 \\ p_1(x) = p_{1,0} + p_{1,1}(x) \\ \ldots \\ p_n(x) = p_{n,0} + p_{n,1}(x) + \cdots + p_{n,n}x^n \\ \ldots \end{cases}$$

It will be called *binomial-type polynomial sequence* (b.p.s. in the following).

The following carachterization explains the construction of a binomial-type matrix P as in (56).

Theorem 23 ([6] (pp. 24,26)). *Let $\{p_n\}_{n\in\mathbb{N}}$ be a polynomial sequence. It is a b.p.s. if and only if there exists a numerical sequence $(b_i)_{i\in\mathbb{N}}$, with $b_0 = 0$, $b_1 \neq 0$, such that, for any $n \in \mathbb{N}$,*

$$\begin{cases} p'_n(x) = \sum_{i=1}^{n} \binom{n}{i} b_i p_{n-i}(x) = \sum_{i=0}^{n-1} \binom{n}{i} b_{n-i} p_i(x) \\ p_n(0) = 0, \; p_0(x) = 1 \end{cases}$$

and

$$e^{xf(t)} = \sum_{n=0}^{\infty} p_n(x) \frac{t^n}{n!}, \tag{57}$$

where $f(t) = \sum_{i=0}^{\infty} b_i \dfrac{t^i}{i!}$.

Proof. Let $\{p_n\}_{n\in\mathbb{N}}$ be a b.p.s.. Hence there exists a numerical sequence $(b_i)_{i\in\mathbb{N}}$ with $b_0 = 0$, $b_1 \neq 0$ such that $p_n(x) = \sum_{k=0}^{n} p_{n,k} x^k$, where $p_{n,k}$ are defined as in (56). Then we have

$$p'_n(x) = \sum_{k=1}^{n} p_{n,k} k\, x^{k-1} = \sum_{k=1}^{n} \left(\sum_{i=1}^{n-k+1} \binom{n}{i} b_i p_{n-i,k-1} \right) x^{k-1} = \sum_{k=1}^{n} \binom{n}{k} b_k p_{n-k}(x). \tag{58}$$

With the reverse procedure, after integration, the opposite implication follows.

Property (57) follows by easy manipulations [6] (pp. 26–27). □

Proposition 1 ([6] (pp. 6–9)). *With the previous notations and hypothesis we get*

$$f\left(\overline{f}(t)\right) = \overline{f}(f(t)) = t$$

if and only if

$$\overline{f}(t) = \sum_{i=0}^{\infty} \overline{b}_i \frac{t^i}{i!},$$

where $(\overline{b}_i)_{i \in \mathbb{N}}$ *is defined by*

$$\sum_{k=1}^{n} p_{n,k} \overline{b}_k = \delta_{n,1}, \quad n \geq 1,$$

being $p_{n,k}$ as in (56).

Power series $f(t)$ and $\overline{f}(t)$ are the compositional inverse of each other. From the numerical sequence $(\overline{b}_k)_{k \in \mathbb{N}}$ we can construct the matrix $\overline{P} = (\overline{p}_{n,k})_{n,k \in \mathbb{N}}$, called the *conjugate binomial matrix* of P. It is proved [6] (p. 14) that $\overline{P} = P^{-1}$. The matrix $\overline{P}$ allows considering the p.s. $\{\overline{p}_n\}_{n \in \mathbb{N}}$, called the *conjugate* p.s. of $\{p_n\}_{n \in \mathbb{N}}$, with elements

$$\begin{cases} \overline{p}_0(x) = 1 \\ \overline{p}_1(x) = \overline{p}_{1,0} + \overline{p}_{1,1}(x) \\ \cdots \\ \overline{p}_n(x) = \overline{p}_{n,0} + \overline{p}_{n,1}(x) + \cdots + \overline{p}_{n,n} x^n \\ \cdots \end{cases}$$

Proposition 2. *If $\{\overline{p}_n\}_{n \in \mathbb{N}}$ and $\{p_n\}_{n \in \mathbb{N}}$ are conjugate b.p.s., we have*

$$(p_n \circ \overline{p}_n)(x) = p_n(\overline{p}_n(x)) = \overline{p}_n(p_n(x)) = x^n. \tag{59}$$

Theorem 24. *Let $\mathcal{B}$ be the set of binomial polynomial sequences and "$\circ$" the umbral composition [86] defined in $\mathcal{B}$. Then the algebraic structure $(\mathcal{B}, \circ)$ is a group.*

Remark 16. *An analogous result holds for the set $\mathcal{A}$ of Appell polynomial sequences. That is, the algebraic structure $(\mathcal{A}, \circ)$ is a group.*

For the conjugate b.p.s. $\{\overline{p}_n\}_{n \in \mathbb{N}}$ and $\{p_n\}_{n \in \mathbb{N}}$, if we set

$$\widehat{P}(x) = [p_0(x), \ldots, p_n(x), \ldots], \quad \widehat{\overline{P}}(x) = [\overline{p}_0(x), \ldots, \overline{p}_n(x), \ldots],$$

we get the matrix forms

$$\widehat{P} = P X, \quad \text{and} \quad \widehat{P}_n = P_n X_n, \quad \forall n \in \mathbb{N},$$
$$\widehat{\overline{P}} = \overline{P} X, \quad \text{and} \quad \widehat{\overline{P}}_n = \overline{P}_n X_n, \quad \forall n \in \mathbb{N}.$$

Theorem 25 ([6]). *For the conjugate b.p.s. $\{\overline{p}_n\}_{n \in \mathbb{N}}$ and $\{p_n\}_{n \in \mathbb{N}}$ the following identities hold*

- $p_n(x) = \dfrac{1}{\overline{p}_{n,n}} \left[x^n - \displaystyle\sum_{k=0}^{n-1} \overline{p}_{n,k} p_k(x) \right];$

- $\overline{p}_n(x) = \dfrac{1}{p_{n,n}} \left[x^n - \displaystyle\sum_{k=0}^{n-1} p_{n,k} \overline{p}_k(x) \right];$

- $\hat{c}_0 p_{n+1}(x) = -(n\hat{c}_1 - x)p_n(x) - \sum_{k=2}^{n} \hat{c}_k p_{n-k+1}(x)$, where

$$\sum_{k=0}^{n} \binom{n}{k} \hat{c}_k b_{n-k+1} = \delta_{n,0}, \quad \forall n \in \mathbb{N},$$

with initial conditions $\hat{c}_0 = 1$, $b_1 = 1$, $p_0(x) = x$;

- $p_n(x) = \dfrac{(-1)^{n+1}}{\prod_{k=0}^{n} \overline{p}_{k,k}} \begin{vmatrix} x & x^2 & \cdots & x^{n-1} & x^n \\ \overline{p}_{1,1} & \overline{p}_{2,1} & \cdots & \overline{p}_{n-1,1} & \overline{p}_{n,1} \\ 0 & \overline{p}_{2,2} & \cdots & \overline{p}_{n-1,2} & \overline{p}_{n,2} \\ \vdots & & \ddots & \vdots & \vdots \\ 0 & \cdots & & \overline{p}_{n-1,n-1} & \overline{p}_{n,n-1} \end{vmatrix}, \quad n \geq 1$

and

- $\overline{p}_n(x) = \dfrac{(-1)^{n+1}}{\prod_{k=0}^{n} p_{k,k}} \begin{vmatrix} x & x^2 & \cdots & x^{n-1} & x^n \\ p_{1,1} & p_{2,1} & \cdots & p_{n-1,1} & p_{n,1} \\ 0 & p_{2,2} & \cdots & p_{n-1,2} & p_{n,2} \\ \vdots & & \ddots & \vdots & \vdots \\ 0 & \cdots & & p_{n-1,n-1} & p_{n,n-1} \end{vmatrix}, \quad n \geq 1;$

- referring to Sheffer's approach, the operator $J := J(x, D) = \sum_{i=1}^{\infty} \overline{b}_i D^{(i)}$, is the corresponding operator to the b.p.s. $\{p_n\}_{n \in \mathbb{N}}$ and this is the basic sequence for J, that is, $J[p_n] = n\, p_{n-1}$ [6] (p. 36).

For further details and properties we refer to [6] (pp. 24–45).

5.3. Sheffer Polynomial Sequences

In order to give an appropriate matrix-calculus based approach of Sheffer A-type zero polynomial sequences we consider

- two numerical sequences

$$(a_n)_{n \in \mathbb{N}}, \text{ with } a_0 \neq 0, \ a_i \in \mathbb{K}, \ i \in \mathbb{N},$$

$$(b_n)_{n \in \mathbb{N}} \text{ with } b_0 = 0, \ b_1 \neq 0, \ b_i \in \mathbb{K}, \ i \in \mathbb{N};$$

- the Appell-type matrix $A = (a_{i,j})_{i,j \in \mathbb{N}}$, with $a_{i,j} = \binom{i}{j} a_{i-j}$;
- the binomial-type matrix $P = (p_{i,j})_{i,j \in \mathbb{N}}$, with $p_{i,j}$ defined as in (56);
- the Appell p.s. $\{a_n\}_{n \in \mathbb{N}}$ with

$$a_n(x) = \sum_{k=0}^{n} \binom{n}{k} a_{n-k} x^k, \quad \forall n \in \mathbb{N};$$

- the binomial p.s. $\{p_n\}_{n \in \mathbb{N}}$ with

$$p_n(x) = \sum_{k=0}^{n} p_{n,k} x^k, \quad \forall n \in \mathbb{N};$$

- the formal power series

$$g(t) = \sum_{i=0}^{\infty} a_i \frac{t^i}{i!}, \qquad f(t) = \sum_{i=0}^{\infty} b_i \frac{t^i}{i!}$$

and the related inverse and compositional inverse

$$\frac{1}{g(t)} = \sum_{i=0}^{\infty} \bar{a}_i \frac{t^i}{i!}, \quad \bar{f}(t) = \sum_{i=0}^{\infty} \bar{b}_i \frac{t^i}{i!};$$

- the linear operator

$$J[y] = \sum_{i=1}^{\infty} \bar{b}_i \frac{y^{(i)}}{i!},$$

where $(\bar{b}_i)_{i \in \mathbb{N}}$ is defined as in Proposition 1.

Then we consider the umbral composition of the polynomial sequences $\{a_n\}_{n \in \mathbb{N}}$ and $\{p_n\}_{n \in \mathbb{N}}$, denoted by $\{s_n\}_{n \in \mathbb{N}}$, that is [86],

$$s_n(x) = \sum_{i=0}^{n} \binom{n}{i} a_{n-i} p_i(x), \quad \forall n \in \mathbb{N}. \tag{60}$$

We call *Sheffer* p.s. the sequence $\{s_n\}_{n \in \mathbb{N}}$ related to the numerical sequences $(a_i)_{i \in \mathbb{N}}$, $(b_i)_{i \in \mathbb{N}}$ as defined above [72].

We denote by $S = (s_{i,j})_{i,j \in \mathbb{N}}$ the infinite lower triangular matrix associated with the p.s. $\{s_n\}_{n \in \mathbb{N}}$, that is,

$$s_n(x) = \sum_{k=0}^{n} s_{n,k} x^k, \quad \forall n \in \mathbb{N}. \tag{61}$$

Proposition 3. *With the previous notations and hypothesis we get*

$$S = AP. \tag{62}$$

Proof. See [6,72]. □

As for Appell and binomial-type polynomial sequences, we will define the conjugate sequence of a Sheffer p.s. $\{s_n\}_{n \in \mathbb{N}}$, that is, the p.s. with matrix S^{-1} (see [6] (p. 14, pp. 150–151)).

For that, we consider the p.s. $\{\bar{s}_n\}_{n \in \mathbb{N}}$ such that

$$\bar{s}_n(x) = \sum_{i=0}^{n} \bar{s}_{n,j} x^j, \quad \forall n \in \mathbb{N},$$

where

$$\bar{s}_{n,j} = \sum_{k=0}^{n} \binom{n}{k} \hat{g}_k \bar{p}_{n-k,j}, \quad j = 0, \ldots, n, \ n \in \mathbb{N}$$

being $(g_i)_{i \in \mathbb{N}}$ defined by

$$\sum_{i=0}^{k} \binom{k}{i} \hat{g}_i g_{k-i} = \delta_{k,0}, \quad \text{with} \quad \hat{s}_k = \sum_{j=1}^{k} a_j \bar{p}_{k,j}.$$

Let $\bar{S} = (\bar{s}_{i,j})_{i,j \in \mathbb{N}}$ be the infinite lower triangular matrix associated with the p.s. $\{\bar{s}_n\}_{n \in \mathbb{N}}$.

Proposition 4 ([6] (p. 14)). *With the previous notations and hypothesis we get*

$$\bar{S} = S^{-1}. \tag{63}$$

Remark 17. By construction the matrix $\overline{S}$ is the product of an Appell matrix and a binomial-type matrix. This is not evident from (62).

Hence the p.s. $\{\overline{s}_n\}_{n\in\mathbb{N}}$, being the umbral composition of an Appell and a binomial-type p.s., is a Sheffer p.s., called conjugate of the p.s. $\{s_n\}_{n\in\mathbb{N}}$.

Now we give the matrix form of a Sheffer p.s. We set

$$S(x) = [s_0(x), \ldots, s_n(x), \ldots], \quad \text{and} \quad S_n(x) = [s_0(x), \ldots, s_n(x)], \quad \forall n \in \mathbb{N},$$
$$\overline{S}(x) = [\overline{s}_0(x), \ldots, \overline{s}_n(x), \ldots], \quad \text{and} \quad \overline{S}_n(x) = [\overline{s}_0(x), \ldots, \overline{s}_n(x)], \quad \forall n \in \mathbb{N},$$
$$P(x) = [p_0(x), \ldots, p_n(x), \ldots], \quad \text{and} \quad P_n(x) = [p_0(x), \ldots, p_n(x)], \quad \forall n \in \mathbb{N}.$$

Therefore we have

$$S(x) = S X = (A P) X = A (P X) \tag{64}$$

and

$$S_n(x) = S_n X_n = (A_n P_n) X_n = A_n (P_n X_n).$$

From these matrix forms we can derive recurrence relations, determinant forms and differential equations. For details we refer to [6] (pp. 149–165).

Theorem 26 ([6] (pp. 158–159)). *For the Sheffer p.s.* $\{s_n\}_{n\in\mathbb{N}}$ *the following identities hold*

$$\frac{1}{k!} s_n^{(k)}(x) = \sum_{i=k}^{n} \binom{n}{i} p_{i,k} s_{n-i}(x), \quad \forall n \in \mathbb{N}, \ k = 0, \ldots, n.$$

Particularly, for $k = 1$,

$$s_n'(x) = \sum_{i=0}^{n-1} \binom{n}{i} b_{n-i} s_i(x).$$

Proof. The proof follows by differentiation of (60), taking into account (64) and (56). □

Proposition 5 ([6] (p. 159)). *The following recurrence relation for the columns of the matrix S holds*

$$s_{n,k+1} = \frac{1}{k+1} \sum_{i=k}^{n} \binom{n}{i} b_{n-i} s_{i,k} = \frac{1}{k+1} \sum_{i=1}^{n-k} \binom{n}{i} b_i s_{n-i,k}, \quad k = 0, \ldots, n-1,$$

with boundary conditions

$$s_{n,0} = a_n, \quad s_{n,n} = a_0 b_1^n, \quad n \geq 0.$$

In order to determine the relationship with Sheffer A-type zero polynomial sequences we get the following theorem.

Theorem 27 ([6] (p. 153)). *For a Sheffer p.s.* $\{s_n\}_{n\in\mathbb{N}}$ *defined as in (60) or (61) we have*

$$g(t) e^{xf(t)} = \sum_{n=0}^{\infty} s_n(x) \frac{t^n}{n!},$$

$$J s_n = n s_{n-1}.$$

Now we can say that the p.s. $\{s_n\}_{n\in\mathbb{N}}$, defined above, is a Sheffer A-type zero p.s. For other properties we refer to a wide existing literature (see, for example [6]).

Finally we can observe that the previous construction allows us to write an explicit algorithm (Algorithm 1) for the numerical generation of a Sheffer p.s.

Algorithm 1 Appell, binomial-type, Sheffer polynomial sequences.

1: Inizialization: N, a_i, b_i, $i = 0, \ldots, N$;
2: Appell-type matrix:
$$A = (a_{i,j})_{i,j=0,\ldots,N}, \qquad a_{i,j} = \binom{i}{j} a_{i-j}, \quad i = 0, \ldots, N, \quad j = 0, \ldots, i;$$
3: binomial-type matrix:
$$P = (p_{n,k})_{n,k=0,\ldots,N},$$
$p_{n,k}$ as in (56);
4: Appell p.s.:
$$a_n(x) = \sum_{k=0}^{n} \binom{n}{k} a_{n-k} x^k, \quad n = 0, \ldots, N;$$
plot a_n;
5: binomial-type p.s.:
$$p_n(x) = \sum_{k=0}^{n} p_{n,k} x^k, \quad n = 0, \ldots, N;$$
plot p_n;
6: Sheffer-type matrix:
$$S = (s_{i,j})_{i,j=0,\ldots,N}, \qquad s_{i,j} = \sum_{k=0}^{j} \binom{i}{k} a_{i-k} p_{k,j}, \quad i = 0, \ldots, N, \quad j = 0, \ldots, i;$$
7: Sheffer p.s.:
$$s_n(x) = \sum_{k=0}^{n} \binom{n}{k} a_{n-k} p_k(x), \quad n = 0, \ldots, N;$$
plot s_n;
8: end.

6. Sheffer A-Type Zero Orthogonal Polynomial Sequences

We have observed that I.M. Sheffer in his work [1] characterized the A-type zero polynomial sequences which satisfy, also, an orthogonal condition.

This problem has been considered before by Meixner [59], Sholat [56], but with a different analysis. Recently, D.J. Galiffa et al. [51] showed that all Sheffer A-type zero orthogonal polynomial sequences can be characterisized by using only the generating function that defines this class and a monic three-term recurrence relation. They, therefore, simplified Sheffer's analysis.

6.1. Galiffa et al. Analysis

It is suitable to use the same definitions and notations as in [51].

Definition 2. *A p.s. $\{P_n\}_{n \in \mathbb{N}}$ is classified as A-type zero if there exist two numerical sequences $(a_i)_{i \in \mathbb{N}}$ and $(h_i)_{i \in \mathbb{N}}$ such that*
$$A(t) e^{xH(t)} = \sum_{n=0}^{\infty} P_n(x) t^n, \qquad (65)$$
with
$$A(t) = \sum_{i=0}^{\infty} a_i t^i, \qquad a_0 = 1,$$
$$H(t) = \sum_{i=1}^{\infty} h_i t^i, \qquad h_1 = 1.$$

To determine which orthogonal set satisfy (65), Sheffer used a monic three-term recurrence relation of the form [57,58]

$$P_{n+1}(x) = (x + \lambda_{n+1})P_n(x) - \mu_{n+1}P_{n-1}(x), \quad n \geq 0, \tag{66}$$

with $\mu_n > 0$, for any $n \in \mathbb{N}$ and $P_{-1} = 0$.

The idea of Galiffa et al. [51] consists in obtaining some coefficients of P_n by (65). They observed that

$$\sum_{n=0}^{\infty} a_n t^n e^{x(t+h_2 t^2 + h_3 t^3 + \cdots)} = \sum_{n=0}^{\infty} a_n t^n e^{xt} e^{h_2 x t^2} e^{h_3 x t^3} \cdots$$

$$= \sum_{k_0=0}^{\infty} a_{k_0} t^{k_0} \sum_{k_1=0}^{\infty} \frac{(xt)^{k_1}}{k_1!} \sum_{k_2=0}^{\infty} \frac{(h_2 x t^2)^{k_2}}{k_2!} \sum_{k_3=0}^{\infty} \frac{(h_3 x t^3)^{k_3}}{k_3!} \cdots.$$

The general term in each of the products above is

$$a_{k_0} t^{k_0} \frac{x^{k_1} t^{k_1}}{k_1!} \frac{h_2^{k_2} x^{k_2} t^{2k_2}}{k_2!} \frac{h_3^{k_3} x^{k_3} t^{3k_3}}{k_3!} \cdots$$

Thus, discovering the coefficient of $x^r t^r$ is equivalent to determining all of the nonnegative integer solutions $\{k_0, k_1, k_2, \ldots\}$ of the linear Diophantine equations

$$k_1 + k_2 + k_3 + \cdots = r \tag{67}$$

$$k_0 + k_1 + 2k_2 + 3k_3 + \cdots = s, \tag{68}$$

where (67) represents the x-exponents and (68) the t-exponents.

In order to satisfy (66) we have to observe the coefficients $x^n t^n$, $x^{n-1} t^{n-1}$ and $x^{n-2} t^{n-2}$. We omit the calculation, for which we refer to [51].

Lemma 1. *For the Sheffer A-type zero polynomial $P_n(x) = c_{n,0} x^n + c_{n,1} x^{n-1} + c_{n,2} x^{n-2} + O(x^{n-3})$ as in (66) we have*

$$c_{n,0} = \frac{1}{n!}, \quad c_{n,1} = \frac{a_1}{(n-1)!} + \frac{h_2}{(n-2)!}$$

$$c_{n,2} = \frac{a_2}{(n-2)!} + \frac{a_1 h_2 + h_3}{(n-3)!} + \frac{h_2^2}{2!(n-4)!}.$$

Interestingly enough, the coefficients $c_{n,0}, c_{n,1}, c_{n,2}$ above are expressed in terms of only the first two nonunitary coefficients of t in $A(t)$ as $H(t)$, that is a_1, a_2, h_2, h_3.

Then the authors in [51] showed that Sheffer A-type zero polynomial sequences satisfy a monic three-term recurrence relation if and only if

$$\lambda_{n+1} = a_1 + 2h_2 n$$

$$\mu_{n+1} = (a_1^2 - 2a_2 + 2a_1 h_2 - 4h_2^2 + 3h_3)n + (4h_2^2 - 3h_3)n^2.$$

Hence the following orthogonal polynomial sequences all necessarily belong to the Sheffer A-type zero classes

$$\{(-1)^n n! L_n^{(\alpha)}(x)\}, \quad \{2^{-n} H_n(x)\}, \quad \{(-a)^n C_n(x;a)\},$$

$$\left\{\frac{c^n(\beta)_n}{(c-1)^n} M_n(x;\beta,c)\right\}, \quad \{(2\sin\phi)^{-n} n! P_n^{(\lambda)}(x;\phi)\}, \quad \{(-N)_n p^n K_n(x;p,N)\}.$$

These are respectively the monic forms of the Laguerre, Hermite, Charlier, Meixner, Meixner–Pollaczek and Krawtchouk polynomials, as defined in [51,60].

6.2. A Further Note on the Orthogonality of Sheffer A-Type Zero Polynomial Sequences

The analysis of Galiffa et al. in [51] can be further improved, by using an equivalent definition of Sheffer A-type zero polynomial sequences. In fact, assuming as definition a differential relation by using Theorem 26 and Proposition 5, we get

Theorem 28 ([54]). *For monic Sheffer A-type zero polynomial sequences we have*

$$s_{n,n} = 1, \quad s_{n,n-1} = na_1 + \frac{n(n-1)}{2}b_2,$$

$$s_{n,n-2} = \frac{n(n-1)}{2}a_2 + \frac{n(n-1)(n-2)}{2}a_1 b_2 + \frac{n(n-1)(n-2)}{6}b_3$$

$$+ \frac{n(n-1)(n-2)(n-3)}{8}b_2^2.$$

Proof. Cfr. [54]. □

Theorem 29 ([54]). *A monic Sheffer p.s. satisfies the three-term recurrence relation if and only if*

$$\lambda_{n+1} = -(a_1 + n\, b_2)$$

$$\mu_{n+1} = n\left(a_1^2 - a_2 + a_1 b_2 - b_2^2 + \frac{1}{2}b_3\right) + n^2\left(b_2^2 - \frac{1}{2}b_3\right).$$

Proof. From the comparison between (66) and (61) we have

$$\lambda_{n+1} = s_{n,n-1} - s_{n+1,n}$$

$$\mu_{n+1} = -\lambda_{n+1}s_{n,n-1} + s_{n,n-2} - s_{n+1,n-1}.$$

From Theorem 28 we get the result. □

We observe that these results coincide with the ones in [51].

Remark 18. *In the set of the Appell polynomial sequences we have the family of the monic orthogonal polynomials with*

$$\lambda_{n+1} = -a_1, \quad \mu_{n+1} = \left(a_1^2 - a_2\right)n, \quad a_1^2 - a_2 > 0.$$

In particular, among the classic orgonal polynomials only Hermite polynomial sequences [6] (p. 134) are also Appell polynomial sequences.

7. Relationship between Sheffer A-Type Zero Sequences and Monomiality Principle

The idea of monomiality goes back to J. Steffenson [61] but only in the last thirty years this idea has been systematically used by other authors (see [87–89]).

Definition 3. *A polynomial sequence $\{p_n\}_{n \in \mathbb{N}}$ is quasi monomial if and only if there exist two linear operators $\widehat{P}$, $\widehat{M}$, independent on n, called derivative and multiplicative operators, respectively, verifying the identities*

$$\widehat{P}(p_n(x)) = n\, p_{n-1}(x), \quad n \geq 1, \tag{69}$$

$$\widehat{M}(p_n(x)) = p_{n+1}(x), \quad n \geq 0. \tag{70}$$

Hence $\widehat{P}$ and $\widehat{M}$ play an analogous role to that of derivative and multiplicative operators, respectively, on classic monomials.

The operators $\widehat{P}$ and $\widehat{M}$ satisfy the following commutative property

$$\left[\widehat{P}, \widehat{M}\right] = \widehat{P}\,\widehat{M} - \widehat{M}\,\widehat{P} = \widehat{1},$$

so they display a Veyl group structure.

Let the p.s. $\{p_n\}_{n\in\mathbb{N}}$ be quasi monomial with respect to the operators $\hat{P}, \hat{M}$. Then some of its properties can be easily derived from those of the operators themselves:

1. if $\hat{P}, \hat{M}$ have a differential representation, that is, $\hat{P} = \hat{P}(D_x)$, $\hat{M} = \hat{M}(x, D_x)$, then for any $n \in \mathbb{N}$ the polynomial p_n satisfies the differential equations

$$\hat{M}\hat{P}(p_n(x)) = n\, p_n(x),$$
$$\hat{P}\hat{M}(p_n(x)) = (n+1)p_n(x);$$

2. assuming $p_0(x) = 1$, p_n can be explicitely constructed as

$$p_n(x) = \hat{M}^n(1);$$

3. from the above identity it follows that the exponential generating function of $\{p_n\}_{n\in\mathbb{N}}$ is given by

$$e^{t\hat{M}}(1) = \sum_{n=0}^{\infty} \frac{(t\hat{M})^n}{n!}(1),$$

and therefore

$$e^{t\hat{M}}(1) = \sum_{n=0}^{\infty} p_n(x)\frac{t^n}{n!}.$$

Let $\{s_n\}_{n\in\mathbb{N}}$ be a Sheffer A-type zero p.s. with exponential generating function [6] (p. 153)

$$g(t)e^{xf(t)} = \sum_{n=0}^{\infty} s_n(x)\frac{t^n}{n!},$$

where

$$g(t) = \sum_{i=0}^{\infty} a_i \frac{t^i}{i!}, \quad a_0 \neq 0, \quad a_i \in \mathbb{K},$$

$$f(t) = \sum_{i=1}^{\infty} b_i \frac{t^i}{i!}, \quad b_1 \neq 0, \quad b_i \in \mathbb{K}.$$

It has been showed [90,91] that a Sheffer A-type zero p.s. is quasi monomial with respect to the differential operators

$$\hat{P} = \bar{f}(D_x)$$
$$\hat{M} = x f'\left(\bar{f}(D_x)\right) + \frac{g'\left(\bar{f}(D_x)\right)}{g\left(\bar{f}(D_x)\right)}.$$

Conversely, if $\{s_n\}_{n\in\mathbb{N}}$ is a p.s. satisfying (69), (70), with $\hat{M} = \hat{M}(x, D_x)$, $\hat{P} = \hat{P}(x, D_x)$, then necessarily it is of Sheffer A-type zero.

8. Conclusions

As the centenary of the publication of I.M. Sheffer's famous paper approaches, we wanted to honor his memory by recalling some old and recent results. In particular we recalled the idea of the classification of polynomials by means of suitable linear differential operators and Sheffer's method for the study of A-type zero polynomials.

Later Rota et al., in 1970, framed the study of A-type zero polynomials with the umbral calculus. Indeed, after the theory of Rota et al., modern umbral calculus was essentially confused with the study of polynomials of A type zero. Another relevant idea was the isomorphism between the group of A-type zero polynomials and the Riordan group of exponential-type matrices introduced at the end of the last century. This gave a different vision to the subject and allowed the development of algebraic methods. For example, the attempt to set modern umbral calculus on elementary matrix calculus. The simplicity of this result has allowed numerous theoretical and computational applications.

The constant proliferation of new ideas, theoretical and applicative, involving polynomial sets, make us believe that the Sheffer sequences are an active and important research area in its own right.

Author Contributions: Conceptualization, F.A.C. and M.I.G. and A.N.; Validation, F.A.C. and M.I.G. and A.N.; Investigation, M.I.G. and A.N.; Writing—review & editing, M.I.G. and A.N.; Supervision, F.A.C. All authors have read and agreed to the published version of the manuscript.

Funding: This research received no external funding.

Institutional Review Board Statement: Not applicable.

Informed Consent Statement: Not applicable.

Data Availability Statement: Not applicable.

Conflicts of Interest: The authors declare no conflict of interest.

References

1. Sheffer, I. Some properties of polynomial sets of type zero. *Duke Math. J.* **1939**, *5*, 590–622. [CrossRef]
2. Pincherle, S. Sur la résolution de l'équation fonctionnell $\sum h_v \phi(x + a_v) = f(x)$ à cofficients constants. *Acta Math.* **1926**, *48*, 279–304. [CrossRef]
3. Appell, P. Sur une classe de polynômes. *Ann. Sci. Éc. Norm. Supéer.* **1880**, *9*, 119–144. [CrossRef]
4. Sheffer, I. A local solution of the difference equation $\Delta y(x) = F(x)$ and of related equations. *Trans. Amer. Math. Soc.* **1936**, *39*, 345–379. [CrossRef]
5. Sheffer, I. Concerning Appell sets and associated linear functional equations. *Duke Math. J.* **1937**, *3*, 593–609. [CrossRef]
6. Costabile, F. *Modern Umbral Calculus. An Elementary Introduction with Applications to Linear Interpolation and Operator Approximation Theory*; Walter de Gruyter GmbH & Co KG: Berlin, Germany, 2019; Volume 72.
7. Niederhausen, H. *Finite Operator Calculus with Applications to Linear Recursions*; Florida Atlantic University: Boca Roton, FL, USA, 2010.
8. Roman, S.; Rota, G. The umbral calculus. *Adv. Math.* **1978**, *27*, 95–188. [CrossRef]
9. Roman, S. *The Umbral Calculus*; Academic Press: New York, NY, USA, 1984.
10. Rota, G.; Kahaner, D.; Odlyzko, A. On the foundations of combinatorial theory VIII. Finite operator calculus. *J. Math. Anal. Appl.* **1973**, *42*, 684–760. [CrossRef]
11. Rota, G.; Taylor, B. The classical umbral calculus. *SIAM J. Math. Anal.* **1994**, *25*, 694–711. [CrossRef]
12. Vein, P. Matrices which generate families of polynomials and associated infinite series. *J. Math. Anal. Appl.* **1977**, *59*, 278–287. [CrossRef]
13. Vein, P. Identities among certain triangular matrices. *Linear Algebra Its Appl.* **1986**, *82*, 27–79. [CrossRef]
14. Fillmore, J.; Williamson, S. A linear algebra setting for the Rota-Mullin theory of polynomials of binomial type. *Linear Multilinear Algebra* **1973**, *1*, 67–80. [CrossRef]
15. Di Bucchianico, A. Representations of Sheffer polynomials. *Stud. Appl. Math.* **1994**, *93*, 1–14. [CrossRef]
16. Di Nardo, E.; Niederhausen, H.; Senato, D. A symbolic handling of Sheffer polynomials. *Ann. Mat. Pura Appl.* **2011**, *190*, 489–506. [CrossRef]
17. Cheng, S. Characterization for binomial sequences among renewal sequences. *Appl. Math.* **1992**, *7*, 114–128.
18. Crăciun, M.; Di Bucchianico, A. Sheffer sequences, probability distributions and approximation operators. *SPOR Rep.* **2005**, *4*, 1–25.
19. Di Bucchianico, A. Probabilistic and analytical aspects of the umbral calculus. *CWI/TRACT* **1996**.
20. Di Nardo, E.; Senato, D. Umbral nature of the Poisson random variables. In *Algebraic Combinatorics and Computer Science*; Springer: Berlin/Heidelberg, Germany, 2001; pp. 245–266.
21. Di Nardo, E.; Senato, D. An umbral setting for cumulants and factorial moments. *European J. Combin.* **2006**, *27*, 394–413. [CrossRef]
22. Rota, G.; Shen, J. On the combinatorics of cumulants. *J. Combin. Theory Ser. A* **2000**, *91*, 283–304. [CrossRef]
23. Dong Quan, N. The classical umbral calculus and the flow of a Drinfeld module. *Trans. Amer. Math. Soc.* **2017**, *369*, 1265–1289. [CrossRef]
24. Gessel, I. Applications of the classical umbral calculus. *Algebra Universalis* **2003**, *49*, 397–434. [CrossRef]
25. Curtis, R. Handbook of discrete and combinatorial mathematics. *Math. Gaz.* **2000**, *84*, 364–365. [CrossRef]
26. Costabile, F.; Longo, E. The Appell interpolation problem. *J. Comput. Appl. Math.* **2011**, *236*, 1024–1032. [CrossRef]
27. Costabile, F.; Longo, E. Algebraic theory of Appell polynomials with application to general linear interpolation problem. In *Linear Algebra-Theorems and Applications*; InTech: Rijeka, Croatia, 2012; pp. 21–46.
28. Costabile, F.; Longo, E. Umbral interpolation. *Publ. Inst. Math.* **2016**, *99*, 165–175. [CrossRef]

29. Sucu, S.; Büyükyazici, I. Integral operators containing Sheffer polynomials. *Bull. Math. Anal. Appl.* **2012**, *4*, 56–66.
30. Agratini, O. *Binomial Polynomials and Their Applications in Approximation Theory*; Aracne: Rome, Italy, 2001.
31. Jakimovski, A.; Leviatan, D. Generalized Szász operators for the approximation in the infinite interval. *Mathematica* **1969**, *11*, 97–103.
32. Popa, E. Sheffer polynomials and approximation operators. *Tamkang J. Math.* **2003**, *34*, 117–128. [CrossRef]
33. Sucu, S.; Ibikli, E. Rate of convergence for Szász type operators including Sheffer polynomials. *Stud. Univ. Babes-Bolyai Math* **2013**, *1*, 55–63.
34. Costabile, F.; Gualtieri, M.; Napoli, A. Some results on generalized Szász operators involving Sheffer polynomials. *J. Comput. Appl. Math.* **2018**, *337*, 244–255. [CrossRef]
35. Akleylek, S.; Cenk, M.; Özbudak, F. Polynomial multiplication over binary fields using Charlier polynomial representation with low space complexity. In *Progress in Cryptology—INDOCRYPT 2010. Lecture Notes in Computer Science*; Gong, G., Gupta, K.C., Eds.; Springer: Berlin/Heidelberg, Germany, 2010; Volume 6498, pp. 227–237.
36. Chen, X.; Chen, Z.; Yu, Y.; Su, D. An unconditionally stable radial point interpolation meshless method with Laguerre polynomials. *IEEE Trans. Antennas Propag.* **2011**, *59*, 3756–3763. [CrossRef]
37. Coffey, M. On finite sums of Laguerre polynomials. *Rocky Mountain J. Math.* **2011**, *41*, 79–93. [CrossRef]
38. Khan, M.; Khan, A.; Singh, M. Integral representations for the product of Krawtchouk, Meixner, Charlier and Gottlieb polynomials. *Int. J. Math. Anal., Ruse* **2011**, *5*, 199–206.
39. Kuznetsov, A. Expansion of the Riemann Ξ function in Meixner–Pollaczek polynomials. *Canad. Math. Bull.* **2008**, *51*, 561–569. [CrossRef]
40. Miki, H.; Vinet, L.; Zhedanov, A. Non-Hermitian oscillator Hamiltonians and multiple Charlier polynomials. *Phys. Lett. A* **2011**, *376*, 65–69. [CrossRef]
41. Ferreira, C.; López, J.; Pagola, P. Asymptotic approximations between the Hahn-type polynomials and Hermite, Laguerre and Charlier polynomials. *Acta Appl. Math.* **2008**, *103*, 235–252. [CrossRef]
42. Mouayn, Z. A new class of coherent states with Meixner–Pollaczek polynomials for the Goldman–Krivchenkov Hamiltonian. *J. Phys. A* **2010**, *43*, 295201. [CrossRef]
43. Sheffer, I. Some applications of certain polynomial classes. *Bull. Amer. Math. Soc.* **1941**, *47*, 885–898. [CrossRef]
44. Vignat, C. Old and new results about relativistic Hermite polynomials. *J. Math. Phys.* **2011**, *52*, 093503. [CrossRef]
45. Wang, J.; Qiu, W.; Wong, R. Uniform asymptotics for Meixner–Pollaczek polynomials with varying parameters. *C. R. Math.* **2011**, *349*, 1031–1035. [CrossRef]
46. Wang, X.; Wong, R. Global asymptotics of the Meixner polynomials. *Asymptot. Anal.* **2011**, *75*, 211–231. [CrossRef]
47. Yalçinbaş, S.; Aynigül, M.; Sezer, M. A collocation method using Hermite polynomials for approximate solution of pantograph equations. *J. Franklin Inst.* **2011**, *348*, 1128–1139. [CrossRef]
48. Shukla, A.; Rapeli, S. An extension of Sheffer polynomials. *Proyecciones J. Math.* **2011**, *30*, 265–275. [CrossRef]
49. Khan, S.; Riyasat, M. A determinantal approach to Sheffer–Appell polynomials via monomiality principle. *J. Math. Anal. Appl.* **2015**, *421*, 806–829. [CrossRef]
50. Di Bucchianico, A.; Loeb, D. A selected survey of umbral calculus. *Electron. J. Combin* **1995**, *2*, 28.
51. Galiffa, D.; Riston, T. An elementary approach to characterizing Sheffer A-type 0 orthogonal polynomial sequences. *Involv. J. Math.* **2014**, *8*, 39–61. [CrossRef]
52. Mullin, R.; Rota, G.C. *On the Foundations of Combinatorial Theory III. Theory of Binomial Enumeration*; Graph Theory and Its Applications; North Carolina State University. Dept. of Statistic: Raleigh, NC, USA, 1970; pp. 167–213.
53. Rainville, E. *Special Functions*; Chelsea Publishing Company: New York, NY, USA, 1960; Volume 5.
54. Costabile, F.; Gualtieri, M.; Napoli, A. *Polynomial Sequences: Basic Methods, Special Classes and Computational Applications*; Walter de Gruyter GmbH & Co KG: Berlin, Germany, 2019.
55. Huff, W.; Rainville, E. On the Sheffer A-type of polynomials generated by $\varphi(t)f(xt)$. *Proc. Am. Math. Soc.* **1952**, *3*, 296–299. [CrossRef]
56. Shohat, J. The relation of the classical orthogonal polynomials to the polynomials of Appell. *Amer. J. Math.* **1936**, *58*, 453–464. [CrossRef]
57. Chihara, T. *An Introduction to Orthogonal Polynomials*; Gordon and Beach: New York, NY, USA, 1978.
58. Gautschi, W. Orthogonal polynomials. Constructive theory and applications. *J. Comput. Appl. Math.* **1985**, *12*, 61–76. [CrossRef]
59. Meixner, J. Orthogonale Polynom systeme mit einer besonderen Gestalt der erzeugenden Funktion. *Lond. Math. Soc.* **1934**, *1*, 6–13. [CrossRef]
60. Koekoek, R.; Swarttouw, R. The Askey-Scheme of Hypergeometric Orthogonal Polynomials and Its q-Analogue. Report 98-17. Delft University of Technology. 1998. Available online: https://homepage.tudelft.nl/11r49/documents/as98.pdf (accessed on 5 October 2022).
61. Steffensen, J. The poweroid, an extension of the mathematical notion of power. *Acta Math.* **1941**, *73*, 333–366. [CrossRef]
62. Bateman, H. *Higher Transcendental Functions*; McGraw-Hill: New York, NY, USA, 1953; Volume I–III.
63. Boas, R.; Buck, R. *Polynomial Expansions of Analytic Functions*; Springer: Berlin, Germany, 1958.
64. Shapiro, L.; Getu, S.; Woan, W.J.; Woodson, L. The Riordan group. *Discrete Appl. Math.* **1991**, *34*, 229–239. [CrossRef]
65. Barry, P. On a family of generalized Pascal triangles defined by exponential Riordan arrays. *J. Integer Seq.* **2007**, *10*, 2–3.

66. Cheon, G.S.; Kim, H.; Shapiro, L. Riordan group involutions. *Linear Algebra Appl.* **2008**, *428*, 941–952. [CrossRef]
67. Nkwanta, A. A Riordan matrix approach to unifying a selected class of combinatorial arrays. *Congr. Numer.* **2003**, *160*, 33–45.
68. He, T.X.; Hsu, L.; Shiue, P.S. The Sheffer group and the Riordan group. *Discrete Appl. Math.* **2007**, *155*, 1895–1909. [CrossRef]
69. Costabile, F.; Longo, E. A determinantal approach to Appell polynomials. *J. Comput. Appl. Math.* **2010**, *234*, 1528–1542. [CrossRef]
70. Costabile, F.; Longo, E. Δ h-Appell sequences and related interpolation problem. *Numer. Algorithms* **2013**, *63*, 165–186. [CrossRef]
71. Costabile, F.; Longo, E. An algebraic exposition of umbral calculus with application to general linear interpolation problem. A survey. *Publ. Inst. Math.* **2014**, *96*, 67–83. [CrossRef]
72. Costabile, F.; Longo, E. An algebraic approach to Sheffer polynomial sequences. *Integral Transforms Spec. Funct.* **2014**, *25*, 295–311. [CrossRef]
73. Costabile, F.; Longo, E. A new recurrence relation and related determinantal form for binomial type polynomial sequences. *Mediterr. J. Math.* **2016**, *13*, 4001–4017. [CrossRef]
74. Garsia, A. An exposá of the Mullin-Rota theory of polynomials of binomial type. *Linear Multilinear Algebra* **1973**, *1*, 47–65. [CrossRef]
75. Verde-Star, L. Infinite triangular matrices, q-Pascal matrices, and determinantal representations. *Linear Algebra Appl.* **2011**, *434*, 307–318. [CrossRef]
76. Polya, G. Über die funktionalgleichung der exponentialfunktion im matrixkalkul. *Sitzber. Preuss. Akad. Wiss* **1928**, 96–99.
77. Schur, I. On Faber polynomials. *Amer. J. Math.* **1945**, *67*, 33–41. [CrossRef]
78. Touchard, J. Sur la théorie des différences. *Proc. Int. Cong. Math. Toronto* **1924**, *1*, 623–629.
79. Yang, Y.; Youn, H. Appell polynomial sequences: A linear algebra approach. *J. Algebr. Number Theory Appl.* **2009**, *13*, 65–98.
80. Szegö, G. *Orthogonal Polynomials*; American Mathematical Soc.: Providence, RI, USA, 1939; Volume 23.
81. Yang, S. Recurrence relations for the Sheffer sequences. *Linear Algebra Appl.* **2012**, *437*, 2986–2996. [CrossRef]
82. Higham, N. *Accuracy and Stability of Numerical Algorithms*; SIAM: Philadelphia, PA, USA, 2002.
83. Bell, E. Invariant sequences. *Proc. Natl. Acad. Sci. USA* **1928**, *14*, 901–904. [CrossRef]
84. Bell, E. Exponential polynomials. *Ann. Math.* **1934**, *35*, 258–277. [CrossRef]
85. Aitken, A. A general formula of polynomial interpolation. *Proc. Edinb. Math. Soc.* **1929**, *1*, 199–203. [CrossRef]
86. Costabile, F.; Gualtieri, M.; Napoli, A. Polynomial sequences: Elementary basic methods and application hints. A survey. *RACSAM* **2019**, *113*, 3829–3862. [CrossRef]
87. Cação, I.; Ricci, P. Monomiality principle and eigenfunctions of Differential Operators. *Int. J. Math. Math. Sci.* **2011**, *2011*, 856327. [CrossRef]
88. Dattoli, G.; Germano, B.; Martinelli, M.; Ricci, P. Monomiality and partial differential equations. *Math. Comput. Model.* **2009**, *50*, 1332–1337. [CrossRef]
89. Dattoli, G. Hermite-Bessel, Laguerre-Bessel functions: A by-product of the monomiality principle. In *Advanced Special Functions and Applications, Proceedings of the Melfi School on Advanced Topics in Mathematics and Physics; Melfi, Italy, 9–12 May 1999*; Cocolicchio, D., Dattoli, G., Srivastava, H.M., Eds.; Aracne Editrice: Roma, Italy, 2000; pp. 147–164.
90. Blasiak, P.; Dattoli, G.; Horzela, A.; Penson, K. Representations of monomiality principle with Sheffer-type polynomials and boson normal ordering. *Phys. Lett. A* **2006**, *352*, 7–12. [CrossRef]
91. Dattoli, G.; Migliorati, M.; Srivastava, H. Sheffer polynomials, monomiality principle, algebraic methods and the theory of classical polynomials. *Math. Comput. Model.* **2007**, *45*, 1033–1041. [CrossRef]

MDPI
St. Alban-Anlage 66
4052 Basel
Switzerland
www.mdpi.com

Mathematics Editorial Office
E-mail: mathematics@mdpi.com
www.mdpi.com/journal/mathematics

Disclaimer/Publisher's Note: The statements, opinions and data contained in all publications are solely those of the individual author(s) and contributor(s) and not of MDPI and/or the editor(s). MDPI and/or the editor(s) disclaim responsibility for any injury to people or property resulting from any ideas, methods, instructions or products referred to in the content.